THE WARS OF LOUIS XIV

MODERN WARS IN PERSPECTIVE

General Editors: *H. M. Scott and B. W. Collins*

This ambitious new series offers wide-ranging studies of specific wars, and distinct phases of warfare, from the close of the Middle Ages to the present day. It aims to advance the current integration of military history into the academic mainstream. To that end, the books are not merely traditional campaign narratives, but examine the causes, course and consequences of major conflicts, in their full international political, diplomatic, social and ideological contexts.

ALREADY PUBLISHED

Mexico and the Spanish Conquest
Ross Hassig

The Anglo-Dutch Wars of the Seventeenth Century
J. R. Jones

The Wars of Louis XIV, 1667–1714
John A. Lynn

The War of the Austrian Succession, 1740–1748
M. S. Anderson

The Wars of Frederick the Great
Dennis Showalter

The Wars of Napoleon
Charles J. Esdaile

The Spanish–American War: Conflict in the Caribbean and the Pacific 1895–1902
Joseph Smith

The Wars of French Decolonization
Anthony Clayton

China at War, 1901–1949
Edward L. Dreyer

THE WARS OF LOUIS XIV
1667–1714

John A. Lynn

An imprint of Pearson Education

Harlow, England · London · New York · Reading, Massachusetts · San Francisco
Toronto · Don Mills, Ontario · Sydney · Tokyo · Singapore · Hong Kong · Seoul
Taipei · Cape Town · Madrid · Mexico City · Amsterdam · Munich · Paris · Milan

Pearson Education Limited
Edinburgh Gate,
Harlow, Essex CM20 2JE,
United Kingdom

and Associated Companies throughout the world

Visit us on the World Wide Web at:
www.pearsoned.co.uk

© Addison Wesley Longman 1999

The right of John A. Lynn to be identified
as author of this Work has been asserted by him
in accordance with the Copyright, Designs and
Patents Act 1988.

All rights reserved; no part of the publication may be
reproduced, stored in a retrieval system, or transmitted
in any form or by any means, electronic, mechanical,
photocopying, recording, or otherwise, without either the
prior written permission of the Publishers or a licence
permitting restricted copying issued by the Copyright Licensing Agency Ltd.,
90 Tottenham Court Road, London W1T 4LP

First published 1999

ISBN 978-0-582-05629-9

British Library Cataloguing in Publication Data
A catalogue record for this book is available from the British Library

Library of Congress Cataloging-in-Publication Data
Lynn, John A, (John Albert), 1943–
    The wars of Louis XIV, 1664–1714 / John A. Lynn.
        p.   cm. — (Modern wars in perspective)
    Includes bibliographical references and index.
    ISBN 0–582–05629–2 (ppr)
    1. Louis XIV, King of France, 1638–1715—Military leadership.
2. Military art and science. 3. France—History, Military—17th
century. I. Title. II. Series.
DC127.6.L86   1999
355'.00944'09032—dc21   98–52972
                                                              CIP

18 17 16
11 10

Set by 35 in 10/12 pt Sabon
Printed in Malaysia, VP

To my sons,
Daniel Morgan Lynn
Nathanael Greene Lynn

CONTENTS

List of Maps, Tables, and Figures	viii
Abbreviations	ix
Acknowledgements	x
Introduction	1
1 Prologue: International and Internal Conflict, 1495–1661	6
2 Louis XIV, *Gloire*, and Strategy	17
3 The Army, the Navy, and the Art of War	47
4 Wars of *Gloire*: The War of Devolution and the Dutch War	105
5 Violence and State Policy: Reunions, Mediterranean Expeditions, and Internal Struggles	160
6 The Great Miscalculation: The Nine Years War	191
7 The Final Contest: The War of the Spanish Succession	266
8 The Wars of Louis XIV in the Context of the History of War	361
Chronology	377
Glossary	385
Bibliographical Essay	388
Index	395

LIST OF MAPS, TABLES, AND FIGURES

MAPS

Europe in the era of Louis XIV   xii–xiii

4.1	The battleground of Europe: the Spanish Low Countries	107
4.2	The Rhine from the North Sea to Switzerland	116
4.3	Turenne's campaigns in 1674–75	134
6.1	Battle of Fleurus, 1 July 1690	208
6.2	Provence, Dauphiné, Savoy, and north Italy	212
6.3	Siege of Namur, 25 May–1 July 1692	224
7.1	Battle of Blenheim, 13 August 1704	292
7.2	Battle of Ramillies, 23 May 1706	305
7.3	Battle of Malplaquet, 11 September 1709	333

TABLES

3.1	A sample of battalion and squadron sizes in the French army	61
3.2	Comparative sizes of Dutch and French battle fleets, 1670–80	98
3.3	Comparative sizes of allied and French battle fleets, 1690–1700	98
8.1	France at war, 1495–1815	364

FIGURES

3.1	The artillery fortress	74
3.2	Siege operations	77

ABBREVIATIONS

AG	Service Historique de l'Armée de Terre, Archives de guerre
Lossky, *Louis XIV*	Andrew Lossky, *Louis XIV and the French Monarchy* (New Brunswick, NJ, 1994)
Quincy, *Histoire militaire*	Charles Sévin, marquis de Quincy, *Histoire militaire de Louis le Grand roi de France* (7 vols; Paris, 1726)
Rousset, *Histoire de Louvois*	Camille Rousset, *Histoire de Louvois* (4 vols; Paris, 1862–64)
Wolf, *Louis XIV*	John B. Wolf, *Louis XIV* (New York, 1968)

ACKNOWLEDGEMENTS

As it has been throughout the twenty years I have been teaching at my Alma Mater, the Research Board of the University of Illinois at Urbana-Champaign was generous in supporting my work. In particular, I must thank it for providing me with a research assistant, William Reger. In addition, I am indebted to Martha Friedman of the History and Philosophy Library who kindly arranged for the purchase of a microfilm copy of Quincy, *Histoire militaire de Louis le Grand roi de France*, an absolutely essential source for this volume.

Chapter 2 of this book is based on my chapter 'A Quest for Glory: The Formation of Strategy under Louis XIV, 1661–1715', in *The Making of Strategy: Rulers, States, and War*, Williamson Murray, MacGregor Knox, and Alvin Bernstein, eds (Cambridge: Cambridge University Press, 1994). Chapters 3 and 8 rely heavily on parts of my *Giant of the Grand Siècle: The French Army, 1610–1715* (New York: Cambridge University Press, 1997). I would like to thank Cambridge University Press for its permission to use parts of these publications.

I must express my tremendous gratitude to two wonderful scholars and extremely nice individuals who read this work in earlier drafts. John Rule, now emeritus at my other university home, the Ohio State University, went through the text page by page and called upon his great knowledge of international affairs during the reign of Louis XIV to save me from my own ignorance. Hamish Scott of St Andrews is an editor's editor, whose command of the subject and generous suggestions made this a far better volume than it might otherwise have been.

In addition, thanks also go to Andrew MacLennan of Addison Wesley Longman for his support and patience.

Lastly, I am always in debt to my wife, Andrea E. Lynn, my best friend, lifelong love, and demanding editor, who never tires of things French, but is wearying of Louis Quatorze at this point.

J. A. L.

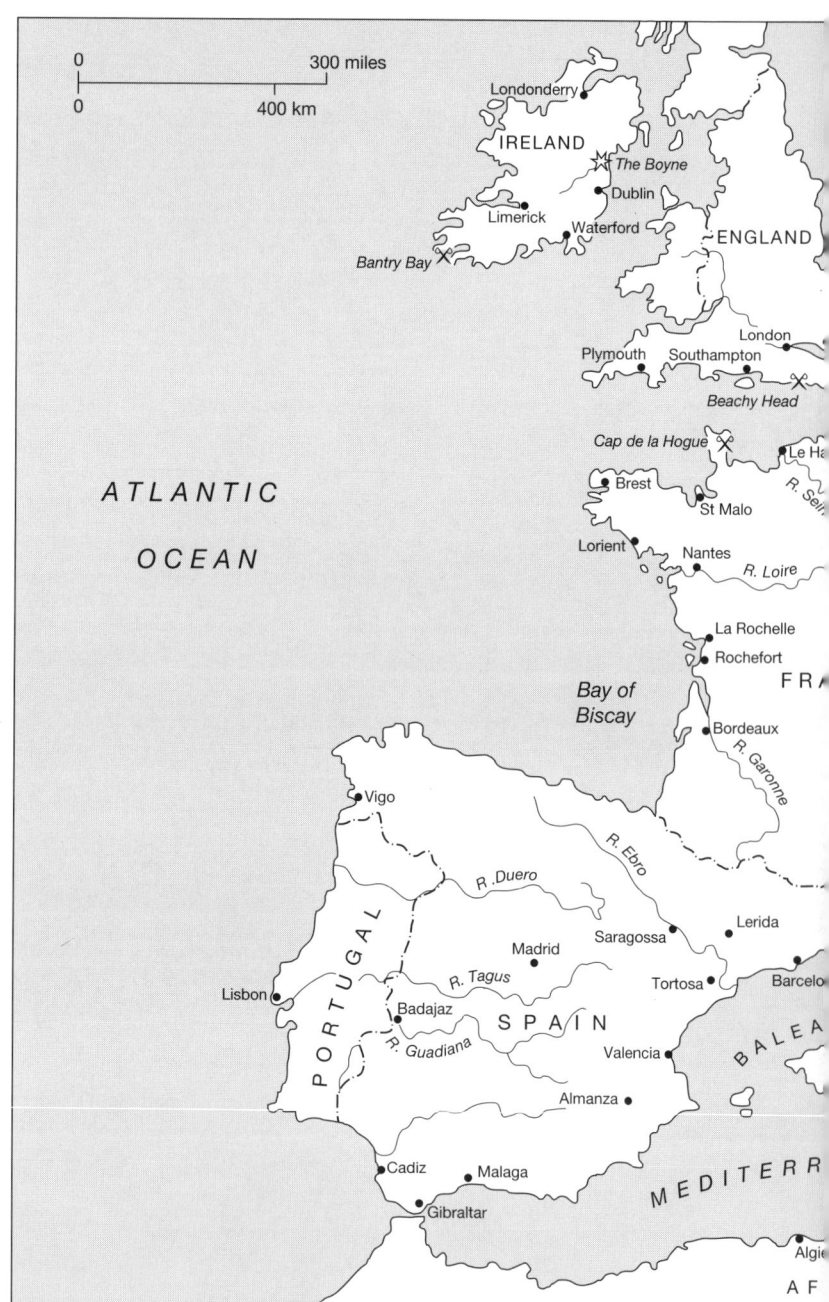

Europe in the era of Louis XIV

INTRODUCTION

Late in his reign, Louis XIV, the Sun King, sat for two state portraits by the court artist, Hyacinthe Rigaud. Standing in identical poses, the two images differ only in their attire. The first is the justly renowned portrait of the king as absolute monarch, wearing formal state robes, embroidered with *fleurs de lis* and lined with ermine. Crowned by a great wig, the regal head exhibits pride and power. In the second and relatively little-known painting, Louis addresses the onlooker with the same gaze, but now he is clad in armour. The right hand that rests upon a sceptre in the first portrait grasps a marshal's baton to symbolize military command in the second. Countless reproductions, including plates in many textbooks, have familiarized generations with the icon of Louis as monarch, but few have seen the image of Louis as general. This volume about the wars of Louis XIV chronicles the Sun King in armour.

It is a story worth the telling, but, surprisingly, it has been left largely untold. Look through any library catalogue or any bibliography of historical works in search of a book describing the wars of Louis XIV in their entirety. You will be disappointed. The only work to deal with them as a whole was published over two and a half centuries ago, and it can be found today only in the rare book collections of a handful of research libraries.[1] Within the modern literature of military history, the sole war fought by Louis XIV that has received considerable attention as a military phenomenon is the War of the Spanish Succession, but then it is mainly the duke of Marlborough and Prince Eugene who dominate the narrative, which comes to the reader as an account of allied brilliance.

Some might argue that the wars of the great monarch have received adequate discussion in biographies of Louis XIV, and there

---

1 This volume, Charles Sévin, marquis de Quincy, *Histoire militaire de Louis le Grand roi de France* (7 vols; Paris, 1726), is a marvellous piece of work, carefully researched, highly detailed, and surprisingly well balanced most of the time. In fact, it served me as the single most useful source while writing this volume.

certainly have been plenty of these. Valuable studies by John B. Wolf, François Bluche, and Andrew Lossky are available today at good bookstores. While these historians deal with the wars as episodes in the king's life and as problems in foreign policy, they do not examine the campaigns as military enterprises. The authors are hardly to blame; there is so much to do just to recount the life of a monarch who reigned as boy and then man for over seventy years. While it is hard to imagine adding something of value here beyond what has already been written about the diplomacy of the wars, there is still much to be discovered concerning the clash of arms in the field and at sea.

Recognizing what yet needs to be said, this volume provides a military narrative and analysis of Louis's wars, with the conviction that this ultimately mattered quite a lot. War may be a continuation of politics by other means, but once these means are taken they become cardinal to the formation and implementation of policy and to the existence of those caught up in the maelstrom of violence. This military treatment will necessarily concentrate on the operational and strategic level, because the difficulty of covering fifty years of warfare in only 375 pages of text rules out presenting much tactical detail. Thus, campaigns show up reasonably well here, while few battles and sieges are described in anything other than cursory form.

There is a temptation in narrating the course of a war to move quickly from high point to high point in order to hold the reader's interest. However, if such a dramatic style were used in describing the wars of Louis XIV, the prose would distort the reality of what were all too often lethargic and inconclusive campaigns. When presenting these conflicts it is vital to tell the stories that did not happen, the battles not fought and the fronts where little was accomplished. To describe only the great confrontations would give an impression of action and energy that simply was not typical most of the time.

A central thesis of this work is that warfare during the seventeenth and eighteenth centuries differed fundamentally from warfare as exemplified by Napoleon. The form of conflict fought by Louis XIV is defined here as 'war-as-process'. Five characteristics define war-as-process: the indecisive character of battle and siege, the slow tempo of operations, the strong resolve to make war feed war, the powerful influence of attrition, and the considerable emphasis given to ongoing diplomatic negotiations. I have chosen not to lay out this thesis in detail until the conclusion, when I can draw upon the evidence presented in the previous chapters to make my case, but it shapes the approach to this entire volume.

One intriguing aspect of adopting a military focus here is the prospect of exploring the ways in which contemporary military institutions and military culture set the parameters of warfare. Along with the approach of war-as-process, this is the most original aspect of these pages. It would appear, for example, that Louis's preference for siege warfare is best understood not simply in terms of some taste for details and rational order, but also by reference to the problems of contemporary logistics and his personal desire to make warfare predictable and limit its human costs.

Modern sensitivities often condemn war as a meaningless misfortune, and there is nothing particularly new about this view. Still, the wars of Louis XIV mattered. Of course, even if only their negative results are put in the balance, a tally of casualties is a tally of consequences, at least for those who have suffered directly. And some of the brutalities of war lived beyond the deaths of their victims. French excesses in devastating the Palatinate, 1688–89, created animosities that continued to torment Europe into the world wars of the twentieth century.

The wars of Louis XIV also had immense importance beyond the fate of the fallen and abused. For one thing, conflict changed the borders of Europe, and France in particular. Louis added significant parts of Flanders, Artois, and Hainault to France, as well as Franche-Comté and Alsace. His occupation of Lorraine laid the foundation for the absorption of that province in the eighteenth century. His conquests brought hundreds of thousands of individuals and millions of their descendants into France.

Perhaps the greatest impact of the wars upon France was not in augmenting its population but in augmenting the powers of central government and in creating a French nation. The wars of Louis XIV changed the government of France, as the monarchy struggled to feed the growing appetite of Mars. Meeting the needs of war required the state bureaucracy to expand in personnel and authority. While the process was certainly not as thorough as once imagined, local privileges and institutions diminished as those at the centre increased. Not all of Louis's government and financial innovations endured; some became casualties of war when Louis overturned reforms in order to find *ad hoc* sources of revenue. However, the overall change was very substantial, even if it was not revolutionary. In both substance and style, Louis's more bureaucratic and centralized monarchy served as a model for Europe. To the extent that war provided the rationale for government growth, it became an important force in the state formation.

More basically, but also more difficult to document, the wars of Louis XIV probably contributed to the growth of national consciousness in France. The unprecedented size of Louis's armed forces spread the experience of defending king and country throughout a large percentage of the population. As it struggled on the borders to keep the enemy from invading and exploiting France, the army became a protector of a country and a people. Moreover, men who never would have seen much of France in civilian life now marched its length and breadth. It is reasonable to infer that those who survived to be demobilized, and there were tens of thousands of such veterans, brought back and spread an idea of France and of being French. To be sure, historians who want to see widespread patriotic sentiment in 1709 put the cart before the horse. Military life did not express patriotism under Louis XIV; rather, it laid the foundation for nationalism in generations to come. The nationalism that inspired the defence of 1792 is best explained with some reference to the long wars of the Sun King. In the words of Fernand Braudel, 'Along with the monarchy, the army thus became the most active tool in *la formation unitaire* of France.'[2]

The immense consequences for France of the wars of Louis XIV, plus the lack of a unified treatment of those wars from a French perspective, justify a decidedly French approach here. Against the objection that it would be better to deal with these international conflicts from a thoroughly international perspective, one could respond that the need to fit the page limit and character of this series prohibits an exhaustive coverage from all points of view. In such a brief treatment, one could not adequately detail the politics of London, The Hague, and Vienna or the actions of their armies during their half-century struggle with France. It is more than enough to sketch decision-making at the French court in so slim a volume. All this would be a reasonable argument, yet the fact remains that even if this volume were twice as long, I would still choose to treat the subject as I have.

This volume is, in fact, one of a trilogy. The first, my *Giant of the Grand Siècle: The French Army, 1610–1715* (New York: Cambridge University Press, 1997), describes the seventeenth-century army as an institution, complete with its tools and techniques of warfare. This present volume, the second instalment, details the wars fought by that army during the reign of the Sun King. The third, and yet

---

2 Fernand Braudel, *L'Identité de la France, I: Éspace et histoire* (Paris, 1986), p. 338.

unwritten, work will examine how that army and those wars shaped the state and government of France. Ultimately, those two portraits of Louis confront me with the greatest challenges – first, to demonstrate that Louis the supreme general is as important as Louis the absolute monarch, and, second, to demonstrate that the one could not have existed without the other.

1 PROLOGUE: INTERNATIONAL AND INTERNAL CONFLICT, 1495–1661

War dominated the days of the Sun King, and throughout his long life the great king knew war like a malevolent brother. When, as a young boy of four, Louis came to the throne in 1643, France had been at war for eight years; it would continue so until 1659. Both physically and spiritually, Louis was conceived in war. Even though this was the longest conflict of Louis's reign, historians do not include it among the 'wars of Louis XIV', for it was initiated by his father, Louis XIII, and directed by the two great first ministers, Cardinal Richelieu and Cardinal Mazarin. Louis only served his apprenticeship during this earlier conflict, and would not come into his own until after the death of Mazarin. Then as an adult, Louis engaged in five declared wars, two of them minor affairs – the War of Devolution (1667–68) and the War of the Reunions (1683–84) – and three of them major struggles – the Dutch War (1672–78), the Nine Years War (1688–97), and the War of the Spanish Succession (1701–14) – but his use of military force extended even beyond these conflicts.

Our drama begins when Louis personally took control of the French state, but to understand the challenges that faced him and his measures of triumph and tragedy in meeting them, we must first turn to the history of Europe and France itself long before Louis seized the reins of power. The past was, indeed, prologue for the great monarch.

EVENTS AND STRUGGLES, 1495–1661

The preceding hundred and sixty years bequeathed to Louis international and internal realities that provided context and cause for his use of armed force, for his wars. Great power conflict, religious turmoil, local revolt, and aristocratic independence all threatened the monarchy before the personal reign of Louis XIV, and he would have to confront every one of them himself, although not in the same manner as did his predecessors.

Prologue

The long series of wars that pitted the French against the Habsburgs, a traditional conflict that continued through the reign of Louis XIV, can be traced back to the French invasion of Italy in 1495. After the insertion of French armies there, the Spanish sought to deny the peninsula to the Valois. Spain posed the greatest international threat to France throughout this period. Spain dominated the sixteenth century and continued to wield unmatched power well into the seventeenth. In contrast, Germany, loosely united as the Holy Roman Empire, but split religiously and politically, provided the French with allies as well as enemies. The Habsburg Holy Roman Emperor exercised more or less power as time passed, but by the mid-seventeenth century the empire was too weakened by the Thirty Years War to endanger France. This would not be a permanent situation, because the Austrian Habsburgs would grow in power considerably by the end of the century as they drove back the Ottoman Turks in the Balkans. Although the English fought against the French during the first half of the sixteenth century, the growing power of Spain eventually focused their energies on this common enemy. The Dutch Netherlands, or more properly the United Provinces, emerged as an important maritime power in the late sixteenth and seventeenth centuries, fought first the Spanish and then the English, but remained allies of the French well into the 1660s, for the French repeatedly aided them as a way of undermining the Spanish.

With seemingly invincible armies and formidable fleets Spain conquered and held an empire that encompassed continents, as the riches of the New World poured into its coffers. Even if Philip II (1556–98) knew frustration – his armadas failed in their goals, and he was unable to bring the rebellious Dutch to heel – he remained a world monarch of unequalled power and wealth. His successors continued to pose such a threat to France that Spanish power preoccupied Bourbon monarchs until the Treaty of the Pyrenees recognized French victory over their long-time rivals.

The French–Spanish confrontation began in Italy, where the French Valois monarchs tried to extend their control during a long series of wars, 1495–1559. Through most of this long struggle, the Spanish throne and that of the Holy Roman Empire in Germany were united in one monarch titled Carlos I as a Spanish king and Charles V as an emperor. Charles ruled an extensive domain unparalleled since the Roman empire. It was, in fact, too much for one man, so in 1556 he stepped down and split his vast holdings, giving Spain and its dependencies to his son Philip II, and the imperial title to his brother, Ferdinand I. The Spanish and German Habsburg lines

7

would never again reunite, but their policies were often in accord, and the French saw them, and often fought them, as a single foe.

Of the two Habsburg branches, the Spanish was unquestionably the more powerful, and its holdings literally surrounded France on its land borders. The Pyrenees separated France and Spain to the south, while Spanish territory and influence in northern Italy made that a hostile border for the French as well. On the northeast the Spanish held the Low Countries, from Flanders on the French frontier to what would become the Dutch Netherlands in the north. Linking the Low Countries to Spanish supply bases in Italy ran the 'Spanish Road', a string of territories such as the free country of Burgundy, or Franche-Comté, that belonged to Spain, certain small German principalities under Spanish influence, and obliging or overawed provinces, including certain Swiss cantons. The Spanish Road would become crucial when troubles broke out in the north.

The greatest sixteenth-century challenge to Spanish power came not from France or England but from dissatisfied elements in the Low Countries. The revolt they launched began both in the southern and northern Netherlands, but for a variety of reasons flourished best in the north, in what would become the United Provinces. The fighting, which went on from 1568 to 1648, goes by several names: the Revolt of the Netherlands, the Eighty Years War, and the Dutch Revolt. Feeling threatened by Spain, the French acted in accord with the Dutch; while, wishing to paralyse France, the Spanish intervened in domestic French quarrels.

And it was a time of troubles in France, because the French tore at each other in a series of religious civil wars, 1562–98. These civil wars were, indeed, fought between Catholic and Protestant parties, but they also involved other dimensions. The monarchy and its forces played a difficult middle game in an attempt to keep from being overwhelmed by either extreme. With different factions mustering contending forces, this was an era of private armies created and led by great nobles, *les grands*, who wished to assert their own power in opposition to that of the monarch. So the Wars of Religion brought not only sectarian strife, but also an assertion of aristocratic independence. The Spanish were quick to fish in these troubled waters. For a long time their meddling was restricted to aiding the extreme Catholic faction against both the Protestants and, from time to time, the monarchy. More than anything else, Philip II wanted simply to neutralize France and so leave himself a free hand in his other struggles. However, when the Bourbon head of the Protestant cause, Henri of Navarre, came into line to succeed to the French throne with the death of Henri III (1574–89), the Catholic party refused to recognize him and the Spanish sent troops to defeat the Bourbon.

Henri IV (1589–1610) won over the Catholic majority by converting to Catholicism in 1593 and guaranteed toleration, security, and political power to the Protestant minority with the Edict of Nantes in 1598. That same year he concluded the Treaty of Vervins with Spain, ending a war that pitted Spain and the Catholic League against Henri for over decade. Thus, he brought peace to a France that had suffered nearly forty years of civil war. Henri IV did much to bind up France's wounds, even if they did not completely heal. Henri's victory was an additional setback to the Spanish, but they were still a force to be reckoned with. In 1610, as he was preparing to launch a new war against the Habsburgs, a Catholic fanatic assassinated the French king, and, thus, put an end to his work.

Henri's nine-year-old son became Louis XIII (1610–43), but while Louis remained a boy, real power passed into the hands of Henri's wife, Marie de Medici. Contentious great French lords troubled much of Louis's reign. They reasserted themselves while Marie served as regent by challenging her authority in petty rebellions and in threats of revolt that she quieted with bribes. In 1617, the young Louis XIII assumed power himself, but it did not end all turmoil. The armed risings, known as princes' wars, continued for some years. Armed resistance broke out sporadically into the 1630s. Gaston of Orléans, the brother of Louis XIII, played a conspicuous role fronting certain of these rebellious ventures, even heading a mercenary army invading France in 1632.

Louis appointed Armand du Plessis, Cardinal Richelieu, as his first minister in 1624, a post he held until his death in 1642. With Louis's constant support, Richelieu pursued a series of strong policies. Above all he wished to break the Habsburg encirclement of France, but first he had to deal with a resurgence of religious civil war in 1625. The height of this struggle was the siege of the Protestant seaport La Rochelle, 1627–28. A new peace settlement with the Protestants in 1629 preserved their religious rights but ended the political and military privileges granted them by the Edict of Nantes – privileges that had constituted the Protestant community as a state within the greater state of France. In his efforts to quell opposition to the crown, Richelieu also concluded that he must labour to humble *les grands*, but here his success was more limited, as aristocratic conspiracy and revolt continued to shake the monarchy.

Meanwhile, the Thirty Years War (1618–48) dominated the international arena, as the Germanies were submerged in turmoil that pitted the Catholic League and the emperor against their Protestant opponents. In 1621 fighting also broke out again in the Low Countries between Spain and the Dutch, and this struggle merged into the Thirty Years War. Richelieu wanted to aid the Dutch and the German Protestants, but did not believe France was ready to enter the war directly. After some efforts to block the Spanish Road, the French opted to back a proxy. King Gustavus Adolphus of Sweden stood ready to commit himself to the Protestant cause in Germany, but lacked the resources. In 1630 the French supplied a subsidy to Gustavus, and he landed in northern Germany. His victories over imperial forces helped stall a Catholic and Habsburg juggernaut, but Gustavus was mortally wounded at the Battle of Lutzen in 1632. His lieutenants, however, continued to command Swedish forces ably until they suffered a terrible defeat at Nördlingen in 1634.

Richelieu then recognized that the French must enter the war directly in 1635, but neither he nor his king realized as they committed armies to battle that this war would last for twenty-five years. The war see-sawed back and forth. The French gained victories in 1635, but suffered a frightening invasion by Spanish forces in 1636. Then, in 1643, the young duke of Enghien won a crushing victory at Rocroi, where the French literally destroyed the Spanish forces that stood against them. This battle did not end the power of Spain, but it certainly put the lie to the reputation of Spanish infantry as invincible and demonstrated French military prowess. Soon Enghien assumed his father's title as Louis II, prince of Condé (1621–86), and became known as the Great Condé.

By Rocroi, however, much had changed. Richelieu died in 1642 and was succeeded as first minister by his protégé, the Italian-born cardinal Giulio Mazarini, better known as Jules Mazarin. Cardinal Mazarin held his new post until his own death in 1661. Three days before Rocroi, the sickly king also succumbed, and his young son, born in 1638, became Louis XIV. Just as in the case of his father some thirty years before, real power passed into the hands of the boy-king's mother, the regent Anne of Austria. Anne formed a political and personal attachment to Mazarin, who also served as the boy's protector, tutor, and surrogate father. Louis would learn the art of diplomacy from Mazarin, who skilfully guided French policy, although he endured continual challenges to his authority.

The need to raise more money to fight in the Thirty Years War drove the French monarchy to increase taxes dramatically. Claude Bullion, *surintendant des finances*, expected to levy 22,600,000 livres of direct taxes for 1634, but in 1635 this amount climbed to 36,200,000, and by 1643, direct levies had risen to 72,600,000 livres.[1] Such tax hikes precipitated a series of municipal and regional tax revolts. The most important of these was the rising of the Nu-Pied rebels in Normandy in 1639, but this was simply one of many insurgencies that caused the monarchy to make war on French rebels as well as foreign enemies.

The Thirty Years War came to an end in 1648 with the Treaty of Westphalia, but while this brought peace to the Germanies, independence from Spain to the Dutch Netherlands, and independence from the German empire to the Swiss Confederation, it did not end the war between France and Spain, which continued for another eleven years. If anything, things got worse for the French monarchy, for while it was no longer necessary to maintain an army in Germany, a civil war known as the Fronde now shattered the internal peace of France from 1648 to 1653. In a sense the Fronde was the greatest of the tax revolts of the seventeenth century, because malcontents regarded payments imposed upon office-holders as one of their initial grievances; however, more was at stake. Expanded powers wielded by the monarchy and its provincial agents, *intendants*, came under attack; so the Fronde was also an assault on the growing authority of the monarchy at the expense of traditional institutions. In addition, the Fronde provided a new theatre for resistance by *les grands*, particularly the grandest of all – the *ducs et pairs* and others with particular power who enjoyed the highest standing at court. Actual fighting between royal and rebel forces ravaged much of France, the Parisian area being particularly hard hit.

The Spanish supplied aid and applied military pressure in conjunction with Frondeur rebels. Henri de la Tour d'Auvergne, viscount Turenne (1611–75), probably Louis's greatest marshal, at first joined the Frondeurs, but then came over to the king. The Great Condé, the other dominant soldier of his age, travelled just the opposite course, first defending the monarchy and then leading a rebel army. When the teenaged Louis, with the aid and guidance of Mazarin, finally reestablished the authority of his government in 1653, Condé offered his sword to the Spanish against Louis. Eventually, in 1658 at the Battle of the Dunes, Marshal Turenne at the head of a royal army defeated Condé, who led Spanish forces that day. The Treaty of the Pyrenees signed the next year finally brought an end to the horrendous war between France and Spain.

[1] Richard Bonney, *The King's Debts: Finance and Politics in France, 1589–61* (Oxford, 1981), pp. 177, 198n.

The Treaty of the Pyrenees recognized the new reality of Continental power: Spain had declined to second-rate status, while France now stood as Christian Europe's preeminent land power. Mazarin skilfully designed the treaty to recognize France's grandeur and to increase Bourbon claims to Spanish lands in the future. The Spanish king, Philip IV, handed over his daughter Marie Thérèse to be wife of the young Louis XIV. Although she renounced her claims to any claims on Spanish territory, contingent upon the paying of a considerable dowry, the French would eventually claim that her renunciation was void because the dowry went unpaid.

France poised at unquestioned greatness. Two years after this triumph, Mazarin died, and Louis, now twenty-two years old, believed himself capable of directing the state without a first minister. He proved himself correct and refused to vest any minister with such great power again. Louis's assertion of his own authority immediately after the death of Mazarin marked the start of the period known as the personal reign. The age of Louis XIV, and his wars, had begun.

THE STRATEGIC LEGACY OF MAZARIN

Twenty-five years of war, intensified by internal revolt, had sapped France, and it would be nearly a decade before the French embarked on war again. However, French victory over Spain and the consequent decline of that once great power left the way clear for Louis XIV to establish that Bourbon France stood alone in the first rank of European states.

Working from the premise that France required friends, the wise Mazarin created a network of alliances among German Protestant states and other principalities, such as Bavaria, that feared the Austrian Habsburgs. This put his Most Christian King, the king of France, in league with heretics, but French policy had to be guided by reason of state, not confessional bias, at least outside of France. Because smaller German states regarded the greater threat as a too-powerful emperor who might try to dominate Germany, France could pose as a defender of the liberties of the lesser states. During the negotiations that ended the Thirty Years War, Mazarin carefully respected his commitments to weaker allies, protecting their interests even when this prolonged the war.[2] While fighting still continued between France

---

2 Charles Derek Croxton, 'Peacemaking in Early Modern Europe: Cardinal Mazarin and the Congress of Westphalia, 1643–1648', Ph.D. dissertation, University of Illinois at Urbana-Champaign, 1995.

and Spain, Mazarin formed an alliance between neutral German states that became the League of the Rhine in 1658, thus breaking Habsburg encirclement. France viewed the League as a way of keeping Emperor Leopold from aiding the Spanish in the Netherlands, while the German states saw it as a way of keeping the emperor's troops from marching through their lands. In any case, it served the interests of all parties and also helped to shelter the French frontier. Mazarin was so clever in forging peace in 1659 that the historian Andrew Lossky claims, 'It can be said that never did France enjoy such near-perfect security on its frontiers as in the last years of Mazarin's life' – a security it had not experienced in the preceding three and a half centuries.[3]

Mazarin may have been so accommodating, and ultimately successful, in diplomacy and statecraft because he dealt from a position of weakness. His own situation as first minister was not really secure until the defeat of the Fronde. As an Italian, he was always seen as foreign, and even though nationalism was not a force at this time, a foreigner was still under suspicion. Mazarin suffered attacks during a scurrilous pamphlet war in which authors fired broadside after broadside at the cardinal. He was forced to leave court more than once, although Anne, the queen mother, continued to accept his counsel. In this difficult position he employed a finesse never practised by Richelieu before him, and, unfortunately, not typical of Louis XIV either. Mazarin also came to office when Spain was still strong, and France could not dictate. He saw Europe as a system with many players, and he regarded that French interests would best be served if it worked in concert with others.

Louis learned the art of diplomacy under Mazarin, but he eventually took a very different course. His plans to seize parts of the Spanish inheritance with the War of Devolution cost him the League of the Rhine, as members declined to renew their association in 1666 and 1667. Initially, Louis succeeded in isolating his foes, first in 1667 and again in 1672, but by the mid-1670s, France enjoyed the support of only a few friends while standing against large alliances. Mazarin's legacy was forgotten; or perhaps it would be better to say that Louis eventually came to see France as powerful enough to fight alone if it had to, and he was unwilling to accommodate the interests and outlooks of others.

---

[3] Andrew Lossky, *Louis XIV and the French Monarchy* (New Brunswick, NJ, 1994), p. 60.

THE DICTATES OF GEOGRAPHY

France as defined by the Treaty of the Pyrenees had four essentially different land borders, and these drew Louis's primary concern. As was the case with his predecessors, Louis gave much less thought to his considerable coastline. Geography made France a Continental power whose survival depended on defence of its frontiers. So while France also had hundreds of miles of coast on the Atlantic and the Mediterranean, strength at sea was much less essential than was strength on land. Given this, it is most impressive how Louis's finance minister, Colbert, was able to build a powerful navy by the 1680s, but it was sacrificed in order to concentrate resources upon the army after the first years of the Nine Years War. France had much to lose or gain on land, while a naval presence would be at best a luxury.

The greatest threat to Bourbon security came from the Spanish Netherlands to the northeast. Not only was it occupied by a rival power, but the rivers there flowed southward like the fingers of a hand grasping at France and threatening Paris. An extensive series of fortresses guarded this frontier, because no formidable natural barriers impeded an enemy driving south from that border to strike the French capital. Before 1659 the Spanish had sent armies into France along this route more than once. Both because of its key strategic value and because Louis hoped to gain territory there, he thought primarily of this frontier, and before advancing age prohibited him from campaigning with his armies, he would usually command in person in the Netherlands rather than elsewhere.

After 1659, the second major border area, the valleys of the Moselle and the Rhine, did not pose a threat to Paris as great as that to the north, but it still troubled Louis. The Treaty of Westphalia awarded France considerable lands in Alsace, along the Rhine. Alsace experienced a number of invasions during the Dutch War, and Louis became preoccupied with protecting his new province. In particular, Louis sought to make the Rhine a firm natural frontier, and so based his defence on it rather than depend upon a thick band of fortifications such as girded the Netherlands.

The third and fourth frontiers, those on the Pyrenees and the Alps, shared common characteristics. Both were buttressed by mountainous terrain. Both were Mediterranean fronts, as fighting in the Pyrenees inevitably concerned the western part of that range between Roussillon and Catalonia. Both were far from the heart of France, and thus remained subordinate fronts. And both were essentially stable, with little to be lost or won. The only major exception to this rule was the allied invasion of Provence in 1707, but this threatened only Toulon, and was repulsed by the French.

LEGACIES OF INTERNAL DISCORD

Mazarin's international diplomacy was not the only strategic inheritance bequeathed to Louis. Various forms of internal discord had struck France and called forth military responses before 1659, and the wars of Louis XIV would encompass these intrastate struggles as well as the interstate clashes that pitted the French against foreign foes.

As explained above, religious turmoil stretched back at least a century before Louis came into his own in 1661. The resolution with French Protestants, or Huguenots, reached in 1629 promised to become a permanent settlement, combining Bourbon political unity with Protestant religious rights. But the preservation of religious diversity did not accord with Louis's sense of rational order nor with his self-serving belief that the Huguenots had become weak in conviction and few in number. In the 1680s, he tried to impose confessional unity on France with a combination of administrative action and military force. As will be seen, he then committed French troops to the virtual genocide of a Protestant community in the Alps, an act which remains the greatest stain on his reputation. During the War of the Spanish Succession, a final major Protestant rising challenged Louis in the Cévennes. Louis finally sent his greatest general at the time, Marshal Claude Villars, to put an end to this armed rebellion, which he did with a mixture of force and compromise. Thus, the history of religious discord continued throughout Louis's personal reign, although not with the intensity of earlier times.

Louis hoped to avoid the tax revolts that plagued France during the long war with Spain, 1635–59. He would, in fact, suffer far less from such risings than had Richelieu and Mazarin, but part of the price for internal peace would be heavy reliance on expensive, short-term credit instead of even higher levels of taxation. None the less, Louis's first great conflict, the Dutch War, brought local tax revolt, so he was unable to escape this fate entirely. Another form of armed unrest that so vexed his father and challenged Mazarin's regime, revolt by *les grands*, was very fresh in political memory when Louis took full authority in 1661. Louis adopted such successful measures against this sort of uprising that it would be the one kind of war that, while a major factor in the past, would not trouble him.

The history of French international and internal conflict provides essential background for understanding the wars of Louis XIV, both because it explains many of the problems inherited by Louis and because it allows us to appreciate what was novel about his reign. On the one hand, for example, the religious turmoil that had disturbed France for so long would threaten the monarchy again as it had before. On the other, Louis was able to assert his own unprecedented Continental preeminence because Mazarin had completed the defeat of Spain before Louis took the reins of power. Louis did not write on a blank slate, but neither was he bound by an iron rule of destiny. His actions would display both continuity and contrast with the past, making the story of the wars of Louis XIV all the more interesting, and all the more important.

Beyond the restraints imposed by the past and the possibilities it also presented, Louis worked within other parameters as well. He ruled within the context of 'absolute' monarchy, guided by his own aristocratic values. In addition, he commanded a much improved and refined army that shaped the operational and strategic character of his wars. Consequently, before this volume turns to Louis's wars themselves, the next two chapters will explore his regime and his armed forces.

2 LOUIS XIV, *GLOIRE*, AND STRATEGY

To speak of the conflicts fought in Western Europe from 1667 to 1714 as the wars of Louis XIV is more than a convenience, more than a shorthand manner of referring to a series of clashes simply because they all occurred during the reign of a single monarch. No, Louis so defined the causation and character of these contests that they did not simply take place while he was on the French throne; they were in very important ways *his* wars. Therefore, to label them as the wars of Louis XIV is to say a great deal about them.

To understand these wars, then, you must begin by understanding the king. This proud monarch, who accepted the sun as his emblem, stood at the centre of his universe; he chose his advisers and set his policies as he saw fit. During his unusually long reign, the strategic challenges that confronted him changed, and he met them with different responses, sometimes products of careful reflection and sometimes bursts of ill-considered arrogance. He grew up in a Europe overshadowed by Spanish power. As a young adult, the splendid Sun King, he led a France that had itself become the preeminent power on the Continent. In old age he grappled with coalitions that overmatched even the resources of mighty France, and death found him chastened. The history of the wars of Louis XIV is a story of a larger-than-life monarch and of his quest for glory – *gloire* – a quest that spanned more than half a century.

ABSOLUTISM UNDER LOUIS XIV

The France of Louis XIV lay somewhere between medieval and modern. Scholars continue to debate exactly where it was along that spectrum. In times past, historians were too willing to credit Louis with wrenching France from chaos to control, with imposing a rational, statist, and essentially modern stamp on society and government; they characterized Louis as an absolute monarch. Recently, historians have turned about to stress the continuities in French society and conclude that France remained essentially feudal, thus medieval, under

Louis.[1] They argue that Louis maintained his authority not by challenging traditional élites and institutions but by accommodating them; to such historians Louis was not essentially modern, hardly an absolutist. This volume takes a middle course, by accepting present-day scholarship concerning élites, provincial institutions, and state finance, but arguing none the less that Louis strengthened and rationalized royal authority in the central government and the military, and that he brooked no interference in matters of foreign policy and war. The change he wrought was great enough to merit a title, and 'absolutism' construed in this more limited sense still seems an appropriate label.[2]

In substance and style, Louis XIV defined the pattern of absolutism. An absolute monarch in Louis's mould was not a dictator; to cast him as such would be anachronistic. His authority knew limits set by tradition and necessity, and he exercised it while considering the privilege and power of existing élites. However, in those matters over which he claimed authority, most notably in matters dealing with the conduct of foreign policy and war and with military institutions, all highly relevant to this volume, he tolerated no interference from traditional power brokers. Here he set and managed policy on a daily basis within limits set by social, political, and financial necessity. He achieved his goals by both overwhelming and conciliating competitors for central authority during his lifetime. France's medieval representative assembly, the Estates General, had last met in 1614, and it would not assemble again until 1789. The great sovereign law courts of France, known as *parlements*, had attempted to assert their authority during the Fronde, but failed, and under Louis XIV they remained relatively docile. Louis also rendered his own government servants more obedient, both those at the centre and those in the provinces.

Louis designed his government to ensure his authority. True enough, the mechanisms of authority were becoming increasingly

---

1 See William Beik, *Absolutism and Society in Seventeenth-Century France* (Cambridge, 1985) for a thorough presentation of the 'feudal' Louis.

2 In a review of my *Giant of the Grand Siècle* posted on H-France in April 1998, Paul Sonnino argued that my restricted definition of absolutism should not be called 'absolutism' at all. He insists, 'Relative absolutism is a contradiction in terms.' Yet it seems to me that he says much the same thing in his *Louis XIV and the Origins of the Dutch War* (Cambridge, 1988), p. 7. Roger Mettam, in his review of *Giant of the Grand Siècle* in the *Times Literary Supplement*, 19 June 1998, p. 10, uses the arguments and data presented in my book to attack absolutism, even though I continue to use the term. Again, I have no quarrel with Mettam's point; it comes down to a definition. In attacking older, all-encompassing concepts of absolutism we are in accord. I am simply willing to confine the term to the areas I examine most, military institutions and the conduct of war, where there was real change. This change was hardly total, but it was substantial enough to warrant a label.

bureaucratic, yet the monarch dominated. While Louis XIV sought to rule in a rational manner, he crafted his bureaucracy not to govern in his stead, but to ensure that he alone ruled. The fact that French bureaucracy later developed into a perpetual motion machine, as bureaucracies tend to do, is beside the point.

To a considerable degree, Louis limited or suppressed independent action among the agents of his authority, particularly in the case of his military commanders. More authority concentrated at court, under the direct supervision of the king. This made the roles of the king and those ministers and secretaries of state immediately around him all the more important, for at the top of the power structure stood very few individuals.

DECISION-MAKING AND THE FORMATION OF STRATEGY UNDER LOUIS

Louis XIV sat in the centre of the web; he insisted on debating issues, making decisions, and monitoring execution. Freed from the influence of traditional rivals, he exercised complete authority and responsibility for the formation of foreign policy and the drafting of strategy. He shared it only with those rare trusted advisers he called to aid him.

Louis could not expect to master every detail of government; rather he saw his role as making decisions based on common sense. This put him in need of experts. Five major administrative offices stood directly below Louis at the apex of the power pyramid. These numbered four secretaries of state – foreign affairs, war, navy, and royal household – and one controller-general of finances. While the bureaucratic departments of state, particularly war and foreign affairs, were expanded and rationalized during his regime, this did not threaten Louis's control.

The authority wielded by the small knot of advisers and administrative heads around Louis derived not from their own birth and wealth, but from the fact that Louis called upon them to serve. He scrupulously kept powerful nobles from old families, scions of the mighty military families, and the peers of France out of high bureaucratic posts and the councils. He once explained that 'it was not in my interest to seek men of a more eminent birth because having need above all to establish my own reputation, it was important that the public know by the rank of those whom I choose to serve me, that I had no intention of sharing my authority with them'.[3] Men he placed in power possessed legal and administrative backgrounds and came from families only recently ennobled. There were only rare exceptions:

---

3 Louis in André Corvisier, *Louvois* (Paris, 1983), p. 278.

Marshal Turenne, for example, enjoyed great influence over military policy in the 1660s. Since the secretaries of state and the controller-general commanded considerable patronage, they accumulated networks of clients, men who depended on their good will and who in turn acted as their supporters. This gave Louis's major servants something of an independent power base. However, while such a network might aid a secretary in rising to power, maintaining himself in office, or in fending off his rivals, it was not a tool to assert independence against the will of the king. By ferociously pursuing and punishing his finance minister Fouquet in 1661, Louis gave notice to his premier advisers and administrators that he would not tolerate even the slightest threat to his authority.

Louis regularized the decision-making process in a series of councils. By chairing meetings of the most prominent councils, he kept his finger on the pulse of government affairs. Paramount among these councils was the *Conseil d'en haut*, or Council of State, which dealt with the most important matters, including war and peace issues. Those who sat on it could call themselves 'ministers' of state. Louis refused to set the membership of this council by ordinance, leaving himself free to choose the three, four, or five who regularly attended its meetings. He kept its size small to ensure secrecy. The most common members included the secretaries of state for foreign affairs and for war, as well as the controller-general of finances. Often the same man held more than one high office; thus Jean-Baptiste Colbert (1619–83) served as secretary of state for the navy and for the royal household, plus being controller-general of finances from 1669 to 1683. The post of secretary of state did not necessarily carry with it automatic *entrée* into the *Conseil*. One secretary of state for war, the marquis of Barbezieux (1668–1701), did not receive an invitation to the *Conseil d'en haut*, owing to his youth and profligate lifestyle, to the fact that the king was consciously trying to reduce the authority of his secretary of state for war, and to the king's preference for the opinions of the marquis of Chamlay (1650–1719), his personal military adviser. Louis kept control over this council in other ways as well. He expressly forbade his ministers to meet if he were not present.[4]

The members of the *Conseil* vied for influence amongst themselves. In fact, Louis encouraged dissension among his advisers so as to give

---

4 John C. Rule, 'Colbert de Torcy, an Emergent Bureaucracy, and the Formulation of French Foreign Policy, 1698–1715', in Ragnhild Hatton, ed., *Louis XIV and Europe* (Columbus, OH, 1976), p. 281.

himself leverage and leeway. Such conflicts most commonly pitted the two major ministerial families – the Le Telliers and the Colberts – against one another in battles over policy, patronage, and power. Ministers differed at critical times. For example, as the Dutch War approached, the core of the *Conseil* was composed of Colbert plus the old secretary of state for war, Michel Le Tellier (1603–85), and the secretary of state for foreign affairs, Hugues de Lionne (1611–71). Understandably, Le Tellier regarded the approach of armed conflict without much misgiving, since it would place more power in his hands and in those of his son, the marquis of Louvois (1641–91), who also lobbied for war. In contrast, Colbert argued for winning the struggle with the Dutch by means short of a war on the Continent.[5] Although he believed that commerce was war, it was 'perpetual and peaceable war of wit and hard work', not an affair of battalions and cannon.[6] Only through continued peace could he continue his financial reforms and better the economic position of the monarchy. Lionne had his own priorities, hoping that Louis could avoid a war that would put in jeopardy the very favourable secret treaty contracted with the emperor in 1668 that partitioned the possessions of the Spanish king, Carlos II (1665–1700), much to Louis's advantage. Neither Colbert nor Lionne could moderate Louis's drive to war in this case. When the king's mind was firm, ministers eventually fell in behind their monarch, to further his will and to protect their own positions.

The *Conseil d'en haut* usually met on Sundays and Wednesdays, although when the need arose it convened on other days at the king's pleasure. Louis used his *Conseil* as he saw fit; however, at times he seems to have viewed it as an annoyance, since his elevated civil servants might try to temper or oppose his designs. Inside the council, members discarded the formalities of court. Discussions were extremely open and kept strictly confidential. There, ministers criticized the king's positions, though in public they dared not. After an issue was discussed and the ministers made their opinions known, Louis usually decided with the majority on the merits of the case.

Members of the *Conseil* were privy to information shared by them and the king alone. Louis often played his diplomatic games through secret treaties and covert payments, and only the ministers

---

[5] This is the argument of Sonnino, *Louis XIV and the Origins of the Dutch War*, p. 7. 'Colbert, contrary to the scholarly consensus, was completely opposed to any war, but insisted on burying his head in the sand until it was too late....'
[6] Colbert in Pierre Clément, ed., *Lettres instructions et mémoires de Colbert*, vol. vi (1869), pp. 269–70, in Andrew Lossky, *Louis XIV and the French Monarchy* (New Brunswick, NJ, 1994), p. 99.

of the *Conseil* knew the full range of these arrangements. Even high-placed diplomats remained in the dark as to the treaties and agreements that were not their direct concern.

Beyond his bureaucratic chiefs and the *Conseil*, Louis had need of military advisers. He turned to his leading generals, such as Turenne, Condé, Vauban, Luxembourg, and Villars, for specialized advice. In addition to such personal evaluations, Louis also appealed to periodic councils of war, which involved leading generals and the minister of war sitting as a group. In the case of the Dutch War, for example, Louis's first actual war plans evolved in consultation with the *Conseil d'en haut*. He then requested the Great Condé to examine its details. Condé sent out his own supporter, Chamilly, on an extended voyage of reconnaissance. After this intelligence gathering, Condé suggested major alterations in the campaign plan. Later, Condé charged his own fortifications expert, Descombes, to scout enemy fortresses. While Sébastien le Prestre de Vauban (1633–1707) was the most able military engineer of the day, he was Louvois's protégé, and Condé wanted to set his own man to the task.

For this system to function under the monarch's real, as well as theoretical, control, the king had to possess a great appetite for work – and Louis XIV did. He remained attentive and active during endless royal council meetings, only dozing off twice throughout his long reign, it was said. He wrote, 'I imposed upon myself the rule of working regularly twice a day two or three hours each time with divers persons of government, not counting the hours I spend myself or the time required for extraordinary affairs.'[7] Beyond time spent in council, he discussed matters of foreign policy, strategy, and operations with his secretaries of state and other experts, one on one. Even lesser officials conferred directly with the king on a regular basis.

The Dutch War witnessed an important change in the level and style of command Louis and the *Conseil d'en haut* asserted over operations and strategy. Circumstance and effort placed more immediate authority in the *Conseil d'en haut* and the secretary of state for war. Traditionally, major French commanders had enjoyed considerable independence in the field. Le Tellier described such independence in 1650: 'The army was a veritable republic and . . . the lieutenant generals considered their brigades like so many cantons.'[8]

In a sense, the two great commanders whom Louis inherited in 1661, Turenne and Condé, symbolized that independent style of

---

[7] Louis in John B. Wolf, *Louis XIV* (New York, 1968), p. 168.
[8] Le Tellier in Corvisier, *Louvois*, p. 80.

command. As unusually powerful nobles – the former held courtly rank as a sovereign prince, and the second bore the elevated status of a prince of the blood – they resented directives from the kind of bureaucrats who advised and served the king. These one-time rebels from the Fronde expected a high degree of autonomy and opposed the kind of bureaucratic absolutism that Louis sought to impose. Chafing under orders from the minister of war, Turenne complained that he saw 'the direction of armies in the hands of those who better merit the title of valet than that of captain, that the king had resolved to gather for himself alone the *gloire* of all the victories and that there would remain to the generals only the disgrace of their defeats'.[9]

A single year, 1675, removed both these key players: Turenne by death and Condé by retirement. From that point on Louis practised '*guerre de cabinet*', in which he and his civilian advisers, in consultation with military commanders, drafted strategic and operational policy from the seat of government. Generals might well lobby for their own plans, but they did not dictate actions. Louis was often with his main forces until age prohibited him from going into the field, but even when he was not there to take direct command on campaign, he commanded his armies from afar.

Louis's system demanded reasonable competence and dependable regularity, not outstanding genius. Louis and his minister of war, the marquis of Louvois, seemed more interested in exacting obedience from their officers than in creating or encouraging brilliance. In a revealing passage written in 1688, Chamlay, confidant of Louvois and later military adviser to Louis, boasted:

> The difference that exists between the present situation of the king's affairs and that of [the Dutch War] is that in those previous times, the fortune of His Majesty and of his kingdom was in the hands of men who, by being killed or by making a bad decision, could lose it in a moment, or at least compromise it in some way by the loss of a battle [from] which it had been difficult to reestablish. Whereas, presently, because of the great conquests that have been made, and because of the advantageous situation of the places that have been fortified, the king finds himself able to grant command of his armies to whomever it pleases him, without having anything to fear from the mediocre capacity of those to whom he confides it.[10]

---

9 Remarks of Turenne to Primi Visconti, in Jean-Baptiste Primi Visconti, *Mémoires sur la cour de Louis XIV, 1673–81*, ed. Jean-François Solnon (Paris, 1988), p. 63.
10 Chamlay, 27 October 1688, in Corvisier, *Louvois*, p. 459.

Chamlay believed that Louis enjoyed an optimal situation, in which advantageous frontiers and superior military institutions rendered excellence on the part of field commanders unnecessary. War could be controlled and rationalized by bureaucrats. The years 1675 and 1676 also marked a shift in French goals and strategy which accompanied the change in the style of command, but there will be more to say about this later.

THE LIMITS OF ABSOLUTISM: LOUIS'S INABILITY TO PAY FOR HIS WARS

Although Louis shaped French foreign policy and commanded his military forces, he never overcame the constant and crippling obstacles that kept him from efficiently mobilizing the wealth of France to support his wars. Money was truly the sinews of war, and the lack of it could lead to frustration and defeat. The financial weakness of the state demonstrated the limitations of absolutism, a form of government based on accommodation as well as authority. To get what he needed he had to secure the support of the nobility and powerful traditional bodies, such as the provincial estates. Heavy-handed compulsion risked sparking revolt, as it had during his childhood, so Louis avoided resistance by seeking compromise and by simply not trying to move some immovable objects. He found it was easier in the short run to borrow than to tax, but borrowing would eventually bankrupt the state.

Crisis came not because France was a poor region unable to match the wealth of its opponents. Quite to the contrary, seventeenth-century France was the richest and most populous state in Christian Europe, possessing resources adequate to great tasks. During the last few years of the century French authorities carried out the first official count of the population; from it Vauban concluded that France totalled 19,000,000 souls.[11] Agriculturally, France was rich; only the great famines of 1693–94 and 1709–10 reduced it to such material extremes that the feeding of great armies may have exceeded its means, but even then armies kept the field.

Louis's problem lay not in poverty, but in his inability to mobilize the very considerable wealth of France. The Sun King failed to cut the Gordian knot of war finance.[12] Mobilizing adequate funds to

---

[11] Ernest Labrousse, Pierre Léon, Pierre Goubert, Jean Bouvier, Charles Carrière, and Paul Harsin, *Histoire économique et sociale de la France*, vol. ii (Paris, 1970), p. 12.

[12] On war finance in the seventeenth century, see Daniel Dessert, *Argent, pouvoir et société au Grand Siècle* (Paris, 1984) and Françoise Bayard, *Le Monde des financiers*

sustain a major war without exhausting the state proved to be an administrative, political, and social problem too great even for Louis. Long war meant ruin, and Louis regularly backed himself into long wars.

Military success so often came down to a question of money; a state with cash to pay could buy men and material. French government finances lay in shambles by the late 1650s. Given time and peace, however, some reform was possible. While it used to be fashionable to credit Colbert with a transformation of monarchical finances, it is now agreed that though he accomplished significant reforms, he was unable to revamp Bourbon finances in a revolutionary manner. Without taking anything away from him, it is fair to say that whoever occupied the office of controller-general of finances after 1661 would have been able to carry out a modest reform.[13] The *sine qua non* for such reform was not Colbert's genius but the return of peace. Colbert enjoyed the good fortune of serving during more than a decade of peace, interrupted only by the relatively minor crisis of the War of Devolution. The Dutch War cut short much of the progress he made.

Reform required the ability to tax by regular and rational means and to live within those means; however, warfare quickly outstripped the level of moneys produced by taxation. Driving up tax rates during wartime could at best only cover part of the increased demands of warfare, and at worst higher taxes could bring resistance and rebellion. Consequently, Louis handled the increased expenses primarily through borrowing. But since Colbert made no fundamental change in French methods of securing credit, as soon as the regular flow of tax revenues proved insufficient, the state resorted to familiar and destructive expedients. These expedients came primarily as short-term credit measures.

'By 1661, the royal finances had been almost entirely subverted by the search for short-term credit,' writes historian Julian Dent.[14] To win over new creditors, government financiers awarded creditors

---

au XVIIe siècle (Paris, 1988). For the period before 1661 see as well Julian Dent, *Crisis in Finance* (New York, 1973), Richard Bonney, *The King's Debts* (Oxford, 1981), and David Parrott, 'The Administration of the French Army During the Ministry of Cardinal Richelieu', Ph.D. dissertation, Oxford University, 1985.

13 Peter Jonathan Berger, 'Military and Financial Government in France, 1648–1661,' Ph.D. dissertation, University of Chicago, 1979, argues that no real reform occurred before 1659, but that a certain amount of reform was virtually inevitable with the return of peace

14 Dent, *Crisis in Finance*, p. 232.

illegally high interest and slipped them illicit payments. At least from the time of Cardinal Richelieu, much had been sacrificed to officeholders to gain short-term funds at long-term costs. Before 1661, when things were at their worst, official accounts had to hide where the money was really going rather than render an exact report of transactions.

Certainly Colbert had the power, energy, and talent to put back some sense in French financial practices. Yet even he could not and did not clear up all the confusion in a system that, in his own words, 'the cleverest men in the realm, concerned in it for forty years, had so complicated in order to make themselves needed [since] they alone understood it'.[15] Financial improvements modified the system so that it could function at levels of moderate intensity. But in order to handle wartime crisis, the state had to return to traditional abuses – the sale of offices, short-term bills of credit, alienation of future revenues, etc.

No one could rebuild the foundations of French finance so long as French society operated as a strict social hierarchy with great privileges, including tax exemptions, for those at the top. The tax privileges that so favoured the Church and the nobility insulated much of their wealth from the state. Colbert could not end them; nor could he abolish the purchase of titles of nobility and offices that extended them to greater numbers of the well-to-do.

Louis's style of monarchy may itself have made impossible the creation of a national bank, the kind of institution that rewarded the Dutch and the English with such great advantages. In contrast to the French, the Dutch set up the Bank of Amsterdam in 1609, and the English established the Bank of England in 1694, which buttressed the credit of the state by raising funds with long-term, low-interest loans. The English Parliament that controlled government finances represented the very classes of men made wealthy by land and commerce who financed the state and its wars. Parliament would not go bad on its debts and defraud its own. But French kings were notorious for reneging on their debts; this flowed from political necessity as well as from financial want. State finance under the Bourbon monarchy remained complex and tortured, and Louis found it necessary to delegate the collection of revenues to tax farmers all too often. However, Louis tried to retain what leverage he had over taxation and the budget, and he certainly did not want to place the power of the purse in the hands of a representative assembly; such would have been

---

15 Colbert in P. G. M. Dickson and John Sperling, 'War Finance, 1689–1714', in *New Cambridge Modern History*, vol. iv (Cambridge, 1970), p. 298.

antithetical to his brand of absolutism. Therefore the absolutist state never effectively mobilized credit through a state bank; the first attempt at a French national bank, under Law in 1716, failed. The French would not really have a national bank until 1800, and it required a revolution to make such an institution possible.

The problems of taxation and credit not only undermined the monarchy, they also cramped the strategic options open to Louis. The expense of maintaining an army in the field made it desirable to support troops by levying demands on the enemy's population, thus the strategic advisability of sending your armies to fight on enemy territory. This, as we shall see, was a major strategic technique for the French.

Financial weakness also forced the delay or elimination of offensives. In 1695, though Louis would have liked to undertake a major attack in Italy, he had to tell his Marshal Nicolas de Catinat 'the only difficulty that presents itself for pursuing offensive war is the considerable sum of money that it requires... and after having examined the state of my finances... I have, despite myself, been obliged to resolve to pursue only defensive war during the coming year'.[16] In Louis's last war, money problems also crippled strategic options, since 'it was clear that French financial weakness precluded any large-scale offensive after 1709'.[17]

VALUES THAT GUIDED DECISION-MAKING: WAR AND *GLOIRE*

Within the parameters of power set by absolutism, Louis, aided by a handful of top advisers, directed the state. Today, it is common to emphasize institutions and to show how individuals are imprisoned by them. To be sure, in the realm of finance Louis was not omnipotent, but in international affairs and warfare he ruled and imposed his own will on policy.

The personality and values of Louis XIV as an individual did much to guide French strategy; with Louis, it is nearly impossible to separate the monarch from the man. From birth he was groomed to rule France. Louis's well-known dictum, 'I am the state,' is probably apocryphal, but his person and the state were still inseparably linked. For modern readers prone to interpret Louis in twentieth-century terms, it is important to recognize that Louis belonged to the seventeenth century. And as the first gentleman of France, the Sun King's

16 Louis to Catinat, AG, A^{1}1326, no. 1.
17 Dickson and Sperling, 'War Finance', p. 305.

value system was fundamentally aristocratic, guided by baroque concepts of war, dynasty, and *gloire*.

While not great in size, the nobility dominated French society. *Circa* 1700, when the French population numbered roughly 19,000,000 souls, the nobility included about 260,000, no more than 1.4 per cent of the population, yet nobles controlled vast wealth and property.[18] Monarchy and a nobility were compatible; to the political philosopher Montesquieu, in fact, monarchy necessarily implied a nobility.

The nobility set the values of society, and formed those of the king. To the degree that he lived an isolated life spent within a court populated by nobles, that court served as a lens through which he viewed and measured his goals and policies. While the interests of Louis as absolute monarch ran counter to the desire of the nobility to become a centre of independent authority and influence, his opinions on other matters of importance coincided with the well-born minority who surrounded him. In the language of modern historiography, he shared the *mentalité* of the nobility.

This is in no case more central than in the king's attitude towards war. For the nobleman, combat tested his manhood, and for the king, warfare tested his reign. His young courtiers were sure to push for vigorous military action, for they needed an arena in which to win fame. When contemporaries remarked about the king, 'He shows the greatest passion for war, and is in despair when he is prevented from going [to the front],' it was to award him highest praise.[19] The thirst for military renown afflicted women as well as men. Noble young ladies were said to give their favours only to soldiers; war, it would seem, was an aphrodisiac.[20] War, 'the most important of all the professions',[21] was to be sought, as a good in itself. Christian virtue fell victim to Roman *virtù* – at least until Louis had proved himself.

War was the true *métier du roi* – the proper business of the king. This required that Louis be trained to become a soldier-king. When a boy he practised the manual of arms with musket and pike and drilled his companions; he learned about fortification in a play fort constructed in the gardens of the Palais Royal. As a youth he visited his armies in the field, where Mazarin reported to Queen Anne that

18 Roger Mettam, 'The French Nobility, 1610–1715', in Hamish Scott, ed., *The European Nobilities*, (2 vols; London, 1995), vol. i, p. 114.
19 Contemporary description in Wolf, *Louis XIV*, p. 78.
20 Primi Visconti, *Mémoires*, p. 146.
21 Paul Hay de Chastenet, *Traité de la guerre* (Paris, 1668), p. 1.

Louis was 'indefatigable; he goes the entire day with the army, and on arriving here he makes a tour of the advance guards' posts . . . he has just returned . . . not worn out by fifteen hours on horseback'.[22] Louis would become renowned for his hearty constitution and his willingness to endure the fatigues of campaign life.

Deep-seated values compelled him to war; they explain why he attended eighteen of the forty-two sieges directed by Vauban. However, he also realized that he must demonstrate his interest and ability in war in order to command the respect of the social and political élite and, thus, govern effectively. Joël Cornette argues convincingly that war was more than just an essential activity; it was a fundamental attribute of Louis's sovereignty.[23] War justified regal authority and defined kingship and the élite's relationship to the monarch, so to be a complete ruler, Louis must represent himself as a warrior-king. In such a political culture, war was an activity with merit quite beyond its utility in international politics.

Such a view of war runs at odds with modern interpretations of it as a struggle over pragmatic economic concerns. Louis cared little for the commercial calculations of merchants, although he would gain trade advantages if they presented themselves. The proper prize of war was territory, land being a supreme good in the aristocratic value system. Even the Dutch War, often ascribed to economic competition, was fundamentally territorial from the Sun King's point of view; Colbert's arguments lost to those of Le Tellier and Louvois.[24]

Louis also shared the aristocratic concern with family, with the noble 'house'. It would be anachronistic to see Louis's vision of Europe as 'national'. He acted for the French state and for the good of his dynasty, the Bourbons. Ruling was a family affair, or at least it was an affair of families. A monarch was both a ruler and a head of a house, and he was expected to use his power in the first role when exercising his responsibilities in the second. Without giving due consideration to his strong dynastic orientation, his policies leading up to and during the War of the Spanish Succession become incomprehensible. He ventured French fortune and lives to secure the Spanish throne for his grandson, knowing full well that the crowns of France and Spain would probably never be united. It was enough that a Bourbon ruled Spain.

---

22 Mazarin in Wolf, *Louis XIV*, p. 78.
23 Joël Cornette, *Le Roi de guerre: Essai sur la souveraineté dans la France du Grande Siècle* (Paris, 1993).
24 See Sonnino, *Louis XIV and the Origins of the Dutch War*.

More than any other, the term *'gloire'* encompasses Louis's aristocratic *mentalité. Gloire* translates best as renown, reputation, or prestige. Pursuit of this ultimate quality did not only derive from the desire to enjoy great repute in one's lifetime, but also from the resolution to create an enduring aura that would win the praise of posterity. Concern for *gloire* guided the king's actions in a wide range of ventures. It inspired Louis's creation of the Academy of Sciences and his sponsorship of the composer Lully, as well as his wars. Policies that benefited the people and the state added to *gloire*. In linking the monarch with the state, Louis wrote, 'The good of the one gives rise to the *gloire* of the other.'[25]

Louis was by no means exceptional in his desire for *gloire*; it was an age in which the powerful and privileged cared much for this intangible. Madame de Sévigné saw the pursuit of *gloire* as a critical and worthwhile element in the education of French nobles: 'Since one constantly tells men that they are only worthy of esteem to the extent that they love *gloire*, they devote all their thoughts to it.'[26] The Frondeur Cardinal de Retz defined humanity itself in terms of *gloire*: 'That which makes men truly great and raises them above the rest of the world is the love of *la belle gloire*....'[27] Louis was literally a child of his time. Instructions drafted for his upbringing spoke of *gloire*. He was not to be taught methods of hunting that involved deception and trickery, since such practices were unworthy of a prince and did not add to his glory.[28] Mazarin, in his role of tutor and adviser to the young Louis, directed him, 'It is up to you to become the most glorious king that has ever been.'[29]

Essential to a prince's *gloire* was his success in the international arena, and this meant victory in war. *Gloire* predisposed a monarch to desire war, especially a young monarch in need of establishing his own reputation. Louis admitted that it pulled at him. Accounting for his attack on the Dutch in 1672, he wrote, 'I shall not attempt to justify myself. Ambition and [the pursuit of] glory are always

25 Louis in William F. Church, 'Louis XIV and Reason of State', in John C. Rule, ed., *Louis XIV and the Craft of Kingship* (Columbus, OH, 1969), p. 371.
26 Letter from Mme de Sévigné to the count of Bussy, 23 October 1683, *Lettres de madame de Sévigné*, ed. Gault-de-Saint-Germain (12 vols; Paris, 1822–23), vol. vii, p. 394.
27 Cardinal de Retz in Gaston Zeller, 'French Diplomacy and Foreign Policy in Their European Setting', *New Cambridge Modern History*, vol. v (Cambridge, 1961), p. 207.
28 Ruth Kleinman, *Anne of Austria* (Columbus, OH, 1985), p. 122.
29 Letter from Mazarin to Louis, in Wolf, *Louis XIV*, p. 89.

pardonable in a prince, and especially in a young prince so well treated by fortune as I was....'[30] When the young man came into his own with the death of Mazarin, he was bound to try his hand at war. The Dutch statesman John de Witt foresaw the inevitable in a 1664 memoir presented to the States, or assembly, of Holland. France had 'a twenty-six year-old king, vigorous of body and spirit, who knows his mind and who acts on his own authority, who possesses a kingdom populated by an extremely bellicose people and with very considerable wealth'. Such a king would have to 'have an extraordinary and almost miraculous moderation, if he stripped himself of the ambition which is so natural to all princes ... to extend his frontiers'.[31]

Should Louis be condemned for such frivolous, though deadly, concerns? And were they really frivolous? For one thing, the love of *gloire* cannot be dismissed as an exclusively 'French disease'; the concern was a European, not a national, obsession. Other rulers also spoke of *gloire*.[32] For another thing, Louis employed the term much as a modern statesmen speaks of national prestige or national interest. And these are regarded as reasonable motivations today. Louis defended *gloire* with convincing authority when he wrote, 'A king need never be ashamed of seeking fame, for it is a good that must be ceaselessly and avidly desired, and which alone is better able to secure success of our aims than any other thing. Reputation is often more effective than the most powerful armies. All conquerors have gained more by reputation than by the sword....'[33] *Gloire* was a potent weapon of intimidation and a vital deterrent. Louis was no fool; *gloire* was no mere fluff.

The pursuit of *gloire*, of his personal grandeur, did not compel Louis to act in ways that ran counter to the more immediate interests of his dynasty and his state – at least not obviously so. His *gloire* depended on actual achievement. As Vauban once stated, 'True *gloire* does not flit like a butterfly; it is only acquired by real and solid actions.'[34]

30 Louis in ibid., p. 217.
31 De Witt in Ernest Lavisse, *Histoire de la France*, vol. vii, pt 2 (Paris, 1906), p. 281.
32 For example, Leopold I, Charles XII, and even William III did so. Ragnhild Hatton, 'Louis XIV and his Fellow Monarchs', in Rule, *Louis XIV and the Craft of Kingship*.
33 Louis in Wolf, *Louis XIV*, p. 185. In a similar manner, Vauban, who was little interested in conquest, wrote, 'states maintain themselves more by reputation than by force'. Vauban in Michel Parent and Jacques Verroust, *Vauban* (Paris, 1971), p. 78.
34 Vauban, 'Pensées diverses', in Albert Rochas d'Aiglun, ed., *Vauban, sa famille et ses écrits* (2 vols; Paris, 1910), vol. i, p. 627.

Therefore, the precise role played by a concern for *gloire* in determining royal actions cannot be easily isolated, since that achievement required reasonable and rewarding policies. But it was not so much reason and reward, but reputation that ruled. Historians have long tried to unearth a single principle behind the foreign policy and strategy of Louis XIV. To François Mignet it was the pursuit of the Spanish throne, while to Albert Sorel it was a drive for natural frontiers; both theories have weathered the storms of debate poorly. Gaston Zeller represents the majority view today, a view he helped to define. 'The quest for glory, then, took the place of a programme for Louis XIV.'[35] The erudite and wise Andrew Lossky expresses much the same opinion in somewhat more charitable terms: 'His aim was quite simple: to increase the grandeur of his State and of his House, so that his own pre-eminence as "the greatest king in Christendom" would be beyond dispute.'[36]

THE EVOLUTION OF LOUIS'S STRATEGY

The personalities, structures, and policies discussed thus far need to considered over the course of Louis's reign, because both international circumstances and the great monarch himself evolved over the fifty-four years that he personally wielded power. That evolution can be divided usefully, if not neatly, into three eras. In the first, 1661–75, Louis aggressively sought to advance his *gloire* by conquering new territory for France. In the second, 1676–97, French strategy was far more defensive in its goals, though often aggressive in its means. Louis sought to establish defensible frontiers for France, along which French forces would seize the strategic high ground and dig in, literally. While Louis gained territory, he added it in the name of strengthening the wall on his northern and eastern borders. In the last phase, 1697–1714, the struggle over the Spanish succession dominated. At first Louis sought peace by bargaining for rather little of the Spanish inheritance; however, the will of Carlos II gave him little choice but to accept it all for his grandson Philippe of Anjou, knowing that this would lead to war with Emperor Leopold I (1658–1705). In the conflict that followed, the French strategic situation differed from any Louis had faced before. Now he could establish his armies on friendly land outside French boundaries and fight a holding action.

---

35 Zeller, 'French Diplomacy and Foreign Policy', p. 207.
36 Andrew Lossky, 'International Relations in Europe', *New Cambridge Modern History*, vol. vi (Cambridge, 1970), p. 189.

The first era, 1661–75

During the early 1660s, the young Sun King burned to prove himself in a great war, one which would add land to his domains and brilliance to his *gloire*. He might reasonably have hoped to pick up some of the territory belonging to once-mighty Spain. The enmity between Bourbon France and Habsburg Spain was well established by the time Louis came of age. So long as Spain remained strong, France was besieged. But Spain had declined, losing its long struggle with France. Now Louis stood in an excellent position to seize booty Spain could no longer protect, and the Spanish Netherlands tempted his appetite most; the first period was devoted to trying to satisfy this hunger.

The young noblemen surrounding Louis at court encouraged him in this venture, and his primary military advisers did nothing to dissuade him. At this time, in the mid-1660s, Marshal Turenne tutored Louis on military affairs, even attending some meetings of the *Conseil d'en haut*. Turenne never agreed with Mazarin's decision to end the war with Spain in 1659, when the French could have conquered the Spanish Netherlands with one more campaign. Now armed force could make amends for diplomatic weakness. For a time Turenne eclipsed the more conservative Le Tellier and Louvois. Louis could learn from the great Turenne what he could not from his bureau chiefs, since the marshal was a great field commander.

The death of Philip IV, king of Spain (1621–65), set Louis to constructing a claim to Flanders, as the French generally called the Spanish-held parts of three provinces: Flanders, Hainault, and Brabant. (This volume will adopt this practice when it is useful to distinguish this area from the broader holdings of the Spanish Netherlands.) The Spanish had never paid Louis the large dowry promised in the Treaty of the Pyrenees. Because Marie Thérèse had forfeited her claim to any Spanish inheritance contingent upon payment of that dowry, her renunciation was null and void, and Louis felt justified in disputing her father's will. He did so by appealing to a law that pertained in several provinces of the Spanish Netherlands, a law which held that a daughter from a first marriage could claim a share of her father's possessions, even though there was a son from a second marriage. Louis insisted on applying this law by claiming that lands within the Spanish Netherlands should go to – should 'devolve' upon – his wife.

Counting on the Dutch to let their old allies, the French, have their way with the Spanish, Louis led his armies across the border, beginning the War of Devolution. However, Louis's success frightened the Dutch, who patched together a Triple Alliance with England and

Sweden to forestall further French advances. Not prepared to meet this unexpected challenge, Louis grudgingly accepted peace with the gain of only twelve fortified towns on the border. He would be back. He still wanted to seize the Spanish Netherlands in part or in whole, but to gain this prize he had to drive the Dutch out of the picture. The attempt to consume Flanders alarmed the Dutch, who recognized that a descending Spain was now a safer neighbour than an ascending France. Geographical proximity took precedence over traditional animosity. In the past, the French and the Dutch had allied against the Spanish in the sixteenth and early seventeenth centuries, their common enemy making friends of them. But the United Provinces secured their hard-won independence from Spain in 1648, by which point the Dutch wielded great commercial and naval power. That independence, no longer threatened by Spain, could suffer if the French advanced to their border. In addition, the Dutch and French had become commercial rivals, and while that fact may not have been a prime mover of French aggression, it weighed heavily in Dutch policy.

To neutralize the Dutch, and thus allow French grabs in Flanders, Louis plotted the Dutch War. In addition, he was infuriated by the Dutch. From his point of view, he had faithfully stood by them, and they had repaid him with treachery. Louis isolated the Dutch by skilful diplomacy, aided by judicious payments. And in 1672 he 'commanded' the army that advanced through the Bishopric of Liège and crossed the Rhine, with Turenne and Condé to direct the troops and Vauban to conduct the sieges. This war began with great successes.

But the obstinate Dutch, now led by the young William III of Orange, stadholder from 1672 to 1702, refused to surrender, even though the French occupied many of their southern towns. Instead, the Dutch inundated their land, thus preserving Amsterdam. French aggression soon won allies for the Dutch, when the elector of Brandenburg, the emperor, and the king of Spain joined them. In 1674 Louis withdrew his forces from Dutch soil. His withdrawal was the beginning of the end to Louis's youthful lust for armed conquest as a route to *gloire*. The death of the bellicose Turenne in 1675 aided this change of focus and tone, as did Condé's retirement the same year.

The second era, 1676–97

Louis's campaigns of 1676 and 1677 showed that Louis had switched policies in mid-war, as he now identified his personal *gloire* with defending his lands rather than with seizing more territory. The return to peace in 1678 further established this second era in French foreign policy and military strategy. Louis was now 'Louis le Grand'. He had proved his power and won his *gloire* by the Treaty of Nijmegen that ended the Dutch War. France was greater on the map, since Louis added important cities and an entire province, Franche-Comté. Although Louis offered to return Lorraine, which he had seized in 1670, he did so on terms so unacceptable to its duke that he refused, so Louis retained possession of this province for an additional twenty years. Louis also realized that he could never gain the entire Spanish Netherlands without the acquiescence of the Dutch, and that he would not be able to compel their agreement through military action. The most he might accomplish was to chip away at the Spanish border of Flanders and Hainault, so Louis put aside grander goals.

With Turenne and Condé gone, direction of French strategy fell even more to the secretaries of state, in particular to Louvois, who gave the generals less leeway. As military adviser, Vauban, now the brilliant protégé of Louvois, had the king's ear. Louis saw his strategic problem as predominantly defensive, and Vauban was the unequalled master of that *sine qua non* of defence, fortifications.

Louis and his advisers came to view France as a beleaguered monarchy, surrounded by all the other great powers of the seventeenth century. In the words of Vauban, 'Almost in the middle of the most considerable powers of Christendom, she is equally in range of blows from Spain, Italy, Germany, the Low Countries, and England.' A victorious France threatened to become a lightning rod, drawing to it assaults from all quarters. Vauban believed that 'France has today attained a high degree of elevation that renders her formidable to her neighbours, in a manner that they all interest themselves in her ruin, or at least in the diminution of her power.'[37] To be sure, Vauban was by nature a worrier, but so was Louis XIV.

While France possessed a long sea coast, both on the Atlantic and on the Mediterranean, the pressures of its extensive land boundaries demanded the first priority and thus ultimately denied France the maritime predominance that Colbert worked to attain. In seventy-seven years Louis only saw ships three times: once as a boy of nine at Dieppe, once in a mock galley battle at Marseilles in 1660, and once at Dunkirk in 1680. This last occasion was the only in which Louis actually embarked on one of his vessels, the *Entreprenant*. Louis was impressed at the moment, and he certainly supported the development of a powerful battle fleet under Colbert; however, it is to be

---

37 Vauban in Alfred Rebelliau, *Vauban* (Paris, 1962), pp. 141–2.

doubted that he understood the use of sea power, and he certainly did not identify with his navy in the way he did with his army. Circumstances encouraged, if they did not compel, Louis to sacrifice his navy in order to support and expand his army. Along his northern and western coastlines, Louis eventually turned to militia and regular forces to protect his land from sea-borne invasion. From 1695 the Sun King eschewed fleet warfare, *guerre d'escadre*, and relied primarily upon commerce raiding, *guerre de course*, to wear down his enemies at sea. Privateers prowled the seas from such ports as Dunkirk and St Malo, as well as Brest. In the Mediterranean, Louis's naval forces were limited, although they proved adequate to assist land-based campaigns and one serious amphibious operation during the Dutch War.

Crucial to French policy in the second era was the important Continental struggle between the Habsburgs and the Ottomans. The end of the Thirty Years War left the Austrian Habsburgs exhausted, but they rebuilt. They possessed extensive lands in their own right and still reigned as Holy Roman Emperors, a rump authority perhaps, but still an advantage. Peace in Germany did not mean that the Austrian Habsburgs were unmolested, for to their southeast, a resurgent Ottoman Empire threatened. A brief go at war, 1663–64, was followed twenty years later by the Ottoman siege of Vienna, the most dramatic episode in a war which lasted from 1682 to 1699. In defeating the Turks, Emperor Leopold I gained resources and created armies to challenge those of Louis XIV. The Sun King and his advisers recognized this and believed that time was working against France.

It would not be too far from the truth to say that the era of French dominance was a brief span between the decline of two empires. Spanish decline allowed the French to assert their preeminence, and Ottoman decline freed the emperor and his forces to challenge the French and punish their transgressions along the Rhine.

Not surprisingly, during the second half of his personal reign, Louis regarded the Germans as his major enemies. In a 1684 letter to Vauban, Louvois warned against 'the Germans, who from now on ought to be considered as our true enemies and the only from whom we can receive injury if they have an emperor who wants to mount a horse'.[38] So Louis adopted a policy designed to block any invasion attempt from the east. This defensive strategy was the

---

38 Letter from Louvois to Vauban, 28 June 1684, AG, A^{1}714, no. 807. The full text of this quotation explains more fully that it is Alsace and the defensive line that made the Germans the enemy.

creation of Louis and Louvois, with Vauban as both adviser and technical expert. For all his obsession with *gloire*, Louis harboured in his heart more fear of invasion than lust for conquest. Clausewitz concluded that 'It had become almost a question of honour for Louis XIV to defend the frontiers of the kingdom from all insult, as insignificant as it might be.'[39] According to Vauban, a system of defensible frontiers for France required both rationalizing French borders and buttressing them with fortifications. There are two ways to straighten a jagged and confused frontier: sacrifice advanced positions, falling back to a defensible line; or add new pieces of territory to form a defensible line forward. The king, who insisted that not a foot of his territory should be violated, had only one choice – fill out his territory to defensible contours by addition, by conquest. This creates the paradox that while Louis's ultimate goals were essentially defensive, he pursued them by aggressive means, or '*la défense aggressive*'.

Louis's attention shifted to the defence of Alsace, which had suffered invasion and occupation during the Dutch War. To cover his eastern frontier with German states, he believed that he needed Strasbourg, Luxembourg, and certain other positions. He grabbed them through the 'Reunions', a strange mixture of legality and force. Treaty language often defined acquisitions in ambiguous terms – one gained a town or area 'and its dependencies'. The question was, what were its dependencies? Louis established Chambers of Reunion to determine if such and such a plum really had historically been a dependency of territory conceded to France. When, to no surprise, the French court found in his favour, he then might choose to enforce his claim. There were precedents to such legal procedures, and Louis's claims were at times fairly strong.[40] However, his seizure of Strasbourg in 1681 had little to do with legal niceties. The issue was not justice but security. By taking Strasbourg, Louis controlled two of the three critical bridgeheads over the Rhine that might be used by an invading enemy. (The others were Breisach, already in French hands, and Philippsburg, which the French lost by the Treaty of Nijmegen.)

While Louis may have viewed his land grabs as essentially defensive in nature, Europe read them otherwise. The reasons are not hard to find. The lesser part of the answer was style; while Louis desired security, the overbearing monarch acted as if he wanted to conquer

---

39 Karl von Clausewitz in Jean Bérenger, *Turenne* (Paris, 1987), p. 514.
40 Church, 'Louis XIV and Reason of State', p. 389, defends the relative validity of Louis's claims.

or emasculate. But the greater part of the answer was substance, for the image of Louis with an infinite appetite for conquest was well founded in his first two wars. His rationale for both did not go much beyond desire for *gloire* and lust for the Spanish Netherlands. The Dutch War cast a brazen image of Louis the relentless, voracious conqueror, and he never succeeded in erecting another to take its place. The Dutch War convinced contemporary statesmen of the reality of Louis's aggressive intent, and that conviction was subsequently reinforced by the brutal seizures of land along French borders after 1678. In seeking to deter his enemies by constructing 'impregnable' borders during the 1680s, he so alarmed his foes that he made virtually inevitable the very war he sought to avoid. Paradoxically, in demanding ever more guarantees of his security he appeared the insatiable aggressor. Louis never appreciated how his quest for absolute security threatened his neighbours. Thus, bridgeheads he held on the Rhine in order to deny the enemy the opportunity to attack him provided him with the avenues to attack them. His fortresses not only covered his frontiers, they projected French power.[41] His security must by nature compromise theirs. It was thus reasonable for those suspicious of the French to read Louis's intentions as offensive.

The Spanish became so furious over Louis's attack on the fortress of Luxembourg that Carlos II declared war in October 1683, starting the War of the Reunions. Receiving only minimal Dutch support, Carlos II appealed in vain to the emperor for aid. Alarmed as he might be, the emperor was too busy fighting off the Turks to resist the French challenge in the Spanish Netherlands and along the Rhine. Carlos II admitted defeat and Emperor Leopold acquiesced to the Truce of Ratisbon in 1684, which agreed to twenty years of peace between France and the Empire, giving Louis at least a long-term lease on the territories he had seized.

However, even the truce failed to calm Louis's insecurity. When the emperor's forces advanced against the Turks, Louis feared that the emperor would attack France once he had defeated the Ottomans. Louis responded by issuing an ultimatum that the Truce of Ratisbon be converted into a permanent peace by 1 April 1687. This was an act of Louis on the defensive to be sure, but it was carried out in the blustering manner so typical of the 1680s. Finally, in 1688 Louis brought on a general war when he succumbed to what Paul Sonnino

---

41 It was my graduate student, George Satterfield, who first attached the modern strategic term 'power projection' to Louis's fortresses.

has labelled his 'fatal predilection for the preemptive strike' by seizing Philippsburg.[42] In purely military terms this attack made sense, since it closed off the Rhine frontier of Alsace, but in political terms it both alienated the Germans and went a long way to convince the Dutch to support William's expedition to England, with all the drastic implications this had for Louis and France.

Louis believed that the Nine Years War was imposed upon him.[43] He saw his opening moves as essentially defensive – the seizure of Philippsburg in order to close off the Rhine and the devastation of the Palatinate in order that it could not be used by the Germans to launch an offensive. It was beyond Louis's intentions, and perhaps beyond his control, that the short defensive war he wanted turned out to be a long war of attrition that exhausted France.

The third era, 1697–1714

The return of peace in 1697 seemed to bring a change. The Nine Years War had driven the state to bankruptcy, exhausted the French people, and chastised their proud monarch. A once haughty Louis seemed contrite; clearly, he pursued a policy of peace at nearly any price.

The primary concern of French diplomacy, and eventually strategy, was the fate of the Spanish monarchy. Early modern rulers often based policy on dynastic considerations, and the late seventeenth century presented Europe with a dynastic crisis of the first magnitude, the Spanish succession. The plain fact that the sickly and deformed Carlos II would die childless dictated that those with a claim to the throne jockey for position in this crucial race. While the succession was never far from Louis's mind throughout his reign, with the return of peace it dominated his thought and policy.

With good reason, Louis argued that his progeny had the strongest claim deriving from the fact that both his mother and his wife were Spanish infantas. However, Leopold I promoted his second son, Archduke Charles, as a rival for the Spanish crown. With Louis and Leopold headed for confrontation, a third candidate, the child Joseph Ferdinand, electoral prince of Bavaria, seemed to provide a way out of the impasse. The contending parties agreed to a partition treaty in 1698 that awarded almost all the Spanish inheritance to Joseph

---

42 Paul Sonnino, 'The Origins of Louis XIV's Wars', in Jeremy Black, ed., *The Origins of War in Early Modern Europe* (Edinburgh, 1987), p. 122.

43 The Nine Years War goes by other names, notably the War of the League of Augsburg or the War of the Grand Alliance. My mentor, Andrew Lossky, always insisted on the 'Nine Years War', and in respect for him, I employ this title.

Ferdinand, leaving only Milan to Archduke Charles and Naples, Sicily, and parts of Tuscany to the dauphin. But Joseph Ferdinand died the next year, throwing everything into turmoil again. Hastily Louis agreed to a new treaty with William III in 1700; it awarded Spain, the Spanish Netherlands, and the Indies to Charles, while the dauphin would receive the Italian territories promised in the 1698 treaty plus Milan, with the proviso that the dauphin would offer these Italian lands to the duke of Lorraine or the duke of Savoy in exchange for their ancestral holdings.[44] These two partition treaties certainly demonstrate the moderation of Louis, who was willing to give up a great deal to secure peace. However, Leopold refused to even consider the second treaty, for by this point he insisted on everything for Charles.

Despite Louis's good intentions, the long-awaited death of Carlos II unglued all prior arrangements, because his will offered everything to Louis's grandson, Philippe of Anjou, with the proviso that if Philippe or his brother, the duke of Berry, would not accept the Spanish inheritance as a whole, it was to be given to Archduke Charles. At this point, Louis had little choice but to accept the generous offer in the name of Philippe of Anjou. To be sure, this meant war with Leopold, but the only way to avoid a conflict with Leopold was to hand everything to the archduke, and Louis could not conscience that.

But if Louis was reasonable to accept the will of Carlos II over the partition treaties, he now acted in a manner that the rest of Europe interpreted as aggressive and threatening. By refusing to remove Philippe from the French succession, Louis appeared to want to unify the two thrones. When he occupied the barrier fortresses that were so dear to William's concept of Dutch security, William became furious. Then Louis alarmed English merchants by securing the *asiento*, the right to supply slaves to the Spanish colonies, for French traders. Lastly, he insisted on recognizing the son of James II as the rightful king of England when the father died. Louis believed that by divine right he had no choice, but his minister of foreign affairs, the marquis of Torcy (1665–1746), urged him at least not to announce his recognition, but to no avail. Louis is at least guilty of being foolishly oblivious to the way in which his actions would be interpreted. The English and the Dutch now sided with the emperor, ensuring another general European war.

[44] These were complicated arrangements, and each historical account describes the settlement differently; see Lossky, *Louis XIV*, pp. 258–9, and Wolf, *Louis XIV*, pp. 498–9.

The strategic challenge of the War of the Spanish Succession differed from that of Louis's earlier wars. At the start of this struggle Louis boasted alliances with the new king of Spain, the duke of Savoy, the elector of Bavaria, and the archbishop of Cologne. Instead of being aggressors in the Spanish Netherlands or northern Italy, his armies now came as defenders, and his forces could even be welcomed in the heart of Germany. Although some historians have presented Louis as bent on European domination in this conflict, it was his most profoundly defensive effort. To claim victory, all he had to do was maintain the positions he held at the start of the conflict. Ironically, with the most modest of goals, the assistance of allies, and the advantage of holding important territorial buffers protecting French frontiers, Louis suffered his worst rebuff. Not only was he driven out of Flanders and the Po Valley, but enemy armies occupied portions of northern France and nearly broke through the fortress barrier that armoured the French frontier. The Allies came very close to imposing a humiliating defeat on Louis, but by outlasting the will of his enemies Louis finally acheived his dynastic purpose and established Philippe on the Spanish throne, although at great cost to the French people.

CONTRADICTIONS BETWEEN POLICY AND PRIDE

Louis's policies must be comprehended on at least three levels: (1) Louis's rational and usually reasonable policies; (2) Louis's periodic bouts of insolent assertion and bad judgement; and (3) the perceptions of both by his foes. Louis's pursuit of *gloire* by conquest was a phenomenon of his early reign through to 1675. In actions not unexpected by his rivals, his aggressive impulses led to two wars for which he prepared carefully, both diplomatically and militarily. These first two wars also added substantially to French territory. However, their relative success does not imply that they were the product of his most modest or reasonable policies. In fact, his later, costlier, and nearly disastrous wars broke out as a result of more 'sensible' defensive policies. After 1675, Louis came to see his *gloire* as founded upon his ability to hold and protect nearly every foot of his terrain. Under the guidance of Louvois and Vauban, the Sun King sought defensible frontiers, which he then delineated and buttressed with fortifications. In a striking metaphor, the historian Georges Livet wrote of Louis: 'He marked France [with fortresses] like a peasant sets out boundary stones on his land.'[45] Even his most aggressive seizures, such as those

---

[45] Georges Livet, *L'Équilibre européen de la fin du XVᵉ à la fin du XVIIIᵉ siècle* (Paris, 1976), p. 94.

Luxembourg and Strasbourg, were conceived of as defensive moves, and there is little evidence that they were simply steps along a much longer journey of conquest. But if a reasonable desire to protect his lands guided Louis, he also gave way to unreasonable bouts of arrogance, or at the very least he demonstrated a thick-skinned insensitivity to the way in which his acts would be interpreted by contemporary statesmen. Time and again, success tempted him to make ill-considered and excessive demands while fear goaded him into acts of unnecessary brutality. The outrageous terms he tried to impose upon the Dutch in the summer of 1672, his rapacious assault on the Palatinate in 1688–89, and the series of acts he committed immediately after accepting the will of Carlos II in 1700 worked against his primary policy goals and drove other European states into coalitions that brought France to the edge of ruin.

Louis was hardly stupid, but he muddled acceptable strategy by foolish acts. The explanation for such mistakes are best sought in the psychology of the man, which is by nature a mystery that we can only know in part. His arrogance may be as simple as an exaggerated idea of personal *gloire*. On the one hand, Louis's exalted sense of self led him to regard success as a sign of superiority, even of divine favour, that, in turn, justified more extreme actions or demands. On the other hand, so prickly was he toward perceived slights or threats that he reacted with extreme retribution in defence of his interests and his *gloire*. Andrew Lossky provides a more complex picture of Louis's intellectual and emotional life over the course of his reign.[46] While Louis remained grounded in assumptions about the natural order of things, he subtly but importantly shifted his beliefs over the course of his long reign, although he continually expressed reverence for the fundamental laws of the state and the principle of legitimacy. But beyond these nuanced changes, the great king experienced a decade of confusion in both his personal and public lives during the 1680s. In what might be ascribed to a mid-life crisis, he gave up casual dalliances in the bedchamber but became overly aggressive, with a penchant for brutality, in the theatre of Europe.

Part of this resulted from the fact that Louis was a man of principle; however, his principles were rigid and self-serving, and they justified imperious statements and actions. His insistence on supporting James II, on eradicating Protestantism in France, and on insisting on the right of Philippe of Anjou to succeed to the French throne

---

[46] Andrew Lossky, 'Some Problems of Tracing the Intellectual Development of Louis XIV', in Rule, *Louis XIV and the Craft of Kingship*, pp. 317–44.

were all declarations of principle. Had Louis been more pragmatic and opportunistic, in other words had he been less principled, he might have been more effective in the international arena. Not surprisingly, European statesmen interpreted Louis's displays of hubris as designs for hegemony. As early as the 1670s the anti-French polemicist and diplomat Lisola warned that Louis wanted to establish a 'universal monarchy' to rule all of Europe. As explained above, European statesmen regarded Louis's efforts to establish defensible frontiers for France by driving forward between the Meuse and the Rhine as a prelude to further advances that he, in fact, never intended. Louis so mishandled things in 1700–1 that his most 'blameless' war, a conflict he did not want and had tried to avoid, could be interpreted as a renewed scheme to dominate Europe. The European reading, or misreading, of Louis's strategic goals derived both from his aggressive tactics and from his imperious style. Had Louis been more perceptive, he might have seen that his long-term goals required him to moderate his actions and that his manner contradicted his intentions, but typically his political vision blurred at critical moments.

LOUIS AND THE DEFENSIVE: INSIGHTS FROM PROSPECT THEORY

Prospect theory, borrowed from political science, offers another and valuable insight into the Sun King's international behaviour, behaviour that some see as irrational or power-hungry.[47] Despite the work of revisionists who argue that Louis's actions were basically reasonable after 1675, the more common interpretation established by generations of historians describes his aggressive assertion, his willingness to take offensive action and accept high risks, as evidence of a desire to achieve hegemony. At the least, his behaviour is condemned as a series of poorly conceived and awkward attempts to extend French domination. However, prospect theory suggests that it is possible to regard Louis's most extreme behaviour as evidence of intensely defensive intentions rather than as proof of boundless ambition.

Cut to essentials, prospect theory argues that individuals choose actions or objects not simply by rationally weighing their intrinsic value or 'utility', but by considering important factors beyond intrinsic utility. The theory states this by arguing that people measure utility

---

47 For a short course in prospect theory, see articles by Jack Levy, 'An Introduction to Prospect Theory', *Political Psychology* 13 (1992), and 'Prospect Theory, Rational Choice, and International Relations', *International Studies Quarterly* 41 (1997), pp. 87–112.

by some variable reference point, not by some immutable scale. Psychological experiments and observations of consumer, investment, and insurance behaviour demonstrate that individuals are more sensitive to changes in the levels of their assets, or possessions, than to the total amount of those assets, and that people are particularly concerned not to lose what they have. Tests show that people place higher value on things that they already regard as their own than on comparable things that they do not possess. Also, individuals will accept more risk to keep something than to gain something; the theoretical language here is risk-acceptant and risk-averse behaviour. Thus, the same individual would be risk-acceptant in order to avoid losing something, but risk-averse when it was a matter of gaining something else of the same intrinsic utility. This also means that people more easily accommodate gains than they accept losses. There is also an interesting corollary, that the way in which the reference point is defined, or 'framed', can strongly influence behaviour, because the same intended result can often be described as either a loss or a gain. In some way, this is a variant on the old glass-is-half-full or glass-is-half-empty dichotomy, but with more interesting implications.

It is very difficult to establish the validity of prospect theory in the complex international arena, but at the very least the theory provides an intriguing interpretation of the conduct of statesmen and states. In the case of Louis XIV, it promises to explain a good deal. According to prospect theory, it would be entirely reasonable for Louis to invest great effort and accept high risk in the name of defending his old territories and new acquisitions. Here extreme behaviour would be the natural product of a defensive mentality and not of an acquisitive drive. Of course, if this explains the Nine Years War and the War of the Spanish Succession (once Louis had accepted the will of Carlos II and, therefore, regarded Spain as the rightful possession of his dynasty), it does not account for the War of Devolution and the Dutch War. In those earlier conflicts, the demand to establish his *gloire* outweighed every other consideration. There was no other course of action that promised equal utility. But the interesting thing is how quickly he turned to a defensive mind-set after establishing his *gloire* as a warrior-king in the 1670s. From that point on, he redefined *gloire* in terms of protecting his people and guarding every foot of his territory; in other words, he framed his reference point differently after his initial gains, for the greatest insult to his *gloire* would be the inability to maintain what he had won. At first glance, prospect theory may seem counter-intuitive, but it fits the reality of Louis XIV with uncanny accuracy.

LOUIS AND THE FALLACY OF THE SHORT WAR

As it was, the Sun King fell victim to his own miscalculations, persistently failing to predict the magnitude and length of the conflicts that he precipitated. Time and again he naïvely accepted the promise of the short war, but none of his three great wars went as he had expected. The Dutch War, supposed to last but a single campaign, dragged on for six years. Louvois believed that the war in 1688 would be over in only four months, since his goals were modest. However, the four months' 'blitz' he expected turned into the Nine Years War. The War of the Spanish Succession was even worse; what might have been only a brief contest between Louis and Leopold ravaged western Europe for fourteen years. Why did it go wrong so often?

The way to answer this question is to reply that Louis and his ministers expected to fight wars against isolated enemies, or at most small and weak coalitions, but by 1674 France was always opposed by powerful alliances. Louis had studied international relations under Cardinal Mazarin; he could hardly have had a better teacher. Mazarin relied on supple alliances to aid French security. Louis, however, conceived of France as a hegemon capable of asserting and maintaining international preeminence by its wealth and arms alone. Despite his diplomatic preparations for the Dutch War, Louis was soon isolated, facing William of Orange, the elector of Brandenburg, the emperor, and the king of Spain. In 1688 Louis prepared to meet only Germans on the field of honour, a duel he believed he could win with a single shot. Yet by May 1689 he faced the Dutch Netherlands, England, Spain, and Savoy, in addition to the emperor and his German allies. In 1700 Louis knew that in accepting the will of Carlos II, he must at least fight the emperor, but he need not have faced a renewal of the Grand Alliance. Yet in September 1701 the Maritime Powers joined with the emperor.

Another tack would be to argue that Louis's hopes for a short decisive conflict ran counter to the very nature of war in the seventeenth and eighteenth centuries. Interestingly enough, Louis's three great conflicts were surprisingly similar in nature, taking a form that will be discussed under the label 'war-as-process' in chapter 8, two of the characteristics of which were the indecisive character of military campaigns and the slow tempo of operations. Louis's army and the style of war it fought were not tailored to isolating single foes and imposing a rapid decision upon them. He came closest to accomplishing his goal in 1672 against the Dutch, but even here he failed. The structures and practices of war and diplomacy dictated that short war gambits had little chance of succeeding, and once they had failed, the only other alternative was war-as-process. By relying upon a quick and powerful military stroke to achieve his international goal he was mounting a tightrope, and it would have required a level of talent and finesse greater than he possessed to keep from falling off. Once he lost his footing, which he repeatedly did, the only alternative was to fall into a long and costly conflict. The ease with which Louis accepted the seemingly inevitable but unintended long war may indicate that he appreciated the danger implicit in letting slip the dogs of war, but he still accepted the risk.

When short wars turned into long ones, the impact of this unwanted metamorphosis was immense, because they drained France. Playing what he thought would be a winning hand at first, Louis could afford the initial ante, but when the stakes rose far beyond his expectations, he stayed, unwilling to fold his cards, even when the odds turned against him. Instead, he matched the raises that the alliances were willing and able to put on the table.

As the French pursued these struggles with military establishments of unprecedented size year after year, sheer exhaustion set in. The strain on French government, finances, and society was monumental. To meet the unexpectedly high demands of warfare, Louis pushed the bureaucratization of absolutism even further. In order to collect and disperse the necessary resources, government bureaus expanded at the centre and the authority of the king's representatives in the provinces grew. Faced with the demands of seemingly endless war, the inequitable and inefficient tax system and poor fiscal management eventually weakened the monarchy. The government sought resources with rapacious energy but still had to engage in expedients that ruined any neat plans to put the financial practices of the monarchy on an efficiently rational basis.

In retrospect, Louis's wars were not military defeats. His armies were clearly victorious in the War of Devolution, the Dutch War, the War of the Reunions, and the Nine Years War; and while his generals suffered at the hands of Marlborough and Eugene during the War of the Spanish Succession, Louis won a series of victories during the last two years of the fighting. Louis also did well at the peace table; he gained territory in his first two wars, secured recognition of his frontiers in 1697, and, as bad as things looked at times from 1704 to 1711, compelled Europe to accept a Bourbon king on the Spanish throne by 1714. Louis had won, but at an unacceptable cost to France and its people.

3 THE ARMY, THE NAVY, AND THE ART OF WAR

Wars are not games played by dilettantes who rest in arm-chair comfort across a table and achieve victory simply by intelligently moving their ivory pieces. Difficult, dirty, and deadly, wars require special abilities and great effort. To try to think of war as a board game is foolish, but historians who assume that they can explain the character and result of a conflict simply by considering the directives of diplomats and strategists come close to committing such folly. On the contrary, to comprehend a war we must understand the complexities of its campaigns, and to do this we must consider a number of factors, from the limitations imposed by military institutions to the power wielded by contemporary weaponry. Therefore, as a necessary preliminary, this chapter presents the fundamental parameters and practices of warfare on land and at sea.

THE ARMY

The state commission army: officers and men

The French army of the second half of the seventeenth century had evolved into a style of armed force new to Europe, a form called here the 'state commission army'. It stood in sharp contrast to the forces employed by the French monarchy in the previous century.[1] To appreciate its important innovations, this style of force must be compared to that which preceded it, a form that can be called the 'aggregate contract army'.

The aggregate contract army, whose heyday ran from the fifteenth century through the mid-seventeenth century, was assembled from diverse sources, including a small nucleus of the king's own troops, local traditional forces, hired mercenary units, and private armies

---

1 For a discussion of changing army styles, see John A. Lynn, 'The Evolution of Army Style in the Modern West, 800–2000', *International History Review* 18, no. 3 (August 1996), pp. 505–45.

raised by powerful nobles. These last two, in particular, gave the aggregate contract army its character in France. Foreign mercenaries constituted a large and important percentage of the wartime army, particularly of the infantry. The Valois kings signed on entire bands of soldiers through their captains, using a kind of business contract. The most notable mercenary units, Swiss pikemen and German Landsknechts, provided a ready supply on demand. Once parties agreed on the terms, these units would quickly arrive armed, trained, organized, and ready to fight. When François I faced invasion from Henry VIII to the north and Charles V to the east in 1544, he contracted in July for 16,000 Swiss, who reached France in time to form the heart of his main army at the camp of Jalons in late August.[2] Such mercenary bands could be purchased 'off the shelf' for a particular campaign and then dismissed as soon as no longer needed, so there was little reason to maintain armies from year to year, or even over the winter, when weather prohibited campaigning.

French monarchs of the sixteenth and early seventeenth centuries, including Louis XIII, the father of the Sun King, also relied upon forces raised personally by great nobles in the king's name. The age of the aggregate-contract army provided a magnificent theatre for the private army, both in the service of and in opposition to the monarch. During the Wars of Religion, the dukes of Guise alternately aided and challenged the king of France. Two generations later, Louis XIII both employed private forces raised by the duke of Epernon and found them arrayed against him in revolt. Because an aggregate-contract army was composed in large part of mercenary bands and private forces, troops felt little allegiance to the ruler they fought for beyond the obligation to give service for pay. Given the right circumstances, captains and major nobles turned on their employers; troops were as ready to mutiny as to fight, and unpaid soldiers pillaged the subjects of the monarchs for whom they fought.

After his problems with the older forms of troops, Louis XIII refused to accept large privately raised French contingents in 1635. He had not entirely rejected aggregate-contract practices, however, because he hired a German mercenary army led by Bernard of Saxe Weimar, and many fortress governors commanded troops they raised and maintained independently until the end of the war with Spain. None the less, Louis XIII took a major step toward the new state commission style of army, and Louis XIV embraced it completely.

[2] See Ferdinand Lot, *Recherches sur les effectifs des armées françaises des Guerres d'Italie aux Guerres de Religion, 1494–1562* (Paris, 1962), pp. 87–114.

Although the state commission army that emerged by mid-century at first bore the same weapons and fought in the same way as the aggregate contract army, it was quite different. Now, the great bulk of the king's army was raised from his own subjects, although foreign regiments still supplemented native troops. Both French and foreign regiments in French service were organized and commanded on a standard pattern, not according to the whims of mercenary captains. Soldiers enlisted as individuals in particular companies and regiments. Such enlistment was in principle voluntary, as the poverty and limited options of civilian life usually convinced enough men to enter the service willingly. When recruits could not be found easily, recruiters turned to fraud and violence, even though prohibited by law to do so. After joining their regiments, recruits received clothing, equipment, and arms and commenced training.

In his last two wars, Louis supplemented voluntary enlistment with compulsory service in a new militia. Under the direction of the marquis of Louvois, the French conscripted royal provincial militia units in 1688 at the start of the Nine Years War. During that conflict, militia fought in their own battalions alongside the regular regiments, but during the War of the Spanish Succession, the royal militia conscripts simply provided recruits to be distributed to existing regular regiments. Creating and expanding a state commission army in this manner through individual voluntary enlistment and limited conscription took much longer than hiring the old 'off the shelf' mercenary units or the private forces of great nobles, but the resultant army was more reliable, obedient, and, ultimately, more competent.

A hallmark of the state commission army was the relationship between the king and an officer corps that was now directly responsible to the monarch. No longer mercenary military entrepreneurs or leaders empowered by some great noble, officers now received their commissions to raise and command troops directly from the king. With this authorization came supervision. Through administrators and inspectors, the king regulated the raising, training, and supplying of his troops. Louis and his war ministers, particularly Louvois, enforced more professional standards of expertise and obedience upon his officers. When Louis came to power in 1661, his generals still feuded among themselves and refused to obey men they felt to be their social inferiors. Commanders disobeyed direct orders when they believed that their personal honour or professional judgement justified resistance. Despite royal efforts, this problem persisted at least into the Dutch War. Even the great Turenne refused to obey directives sent by Louvois, whom Turenne dismissed as unfit to command him.

Turenne was such a talented commander that the king could tolerate his independence, but not so that of others. After the death of Turenne in 1675, Louis promulgated the *ordre de tableau* that established a hierarchy based on seniority among the marshals, the highest-ranking officers of the army. Just as the king established a strict order of command at the top, he did so throughout the army, and the chain of command from ensigns and *sous-lieutenants* (second lieutenants) up through lieutenants, captains, colonels, and general officers took its modern form. An interchange on the grounds of the king's palace at Versailles illustrates the new standards of obedience and hierarchy. Louvois, a man of great authority but of relatively humble origins, confronted Nogaret, a high-born captain, who was enjoying the pleasures of court rather than caring for his men at the front.

Louvois: Monsieur, your company is in very bad condition.
Nogaret: Monsieur, I did not know that.
Louvois: It is your business to know. Have you seen it?
Nogaret: Monsieur, I will give the order.
Louvois: You ought to have given it already. You must make up your mind, Monsieur, either declare yourself to be a courtier, or do your duty as an officer.[3]

One can only imagine the fury felt by the arrogant young noble when he was upbraided in public, but he obeyed.

Under Louis XIV the French army also grew to unprecedented proportions.[4] Army size during the late sixteenth and early seventeenth centuries remained about what it had been since the late Middle Ages. Peacetime forces rarely exceeded 10,000 men, and often were smaller; wartime strength does not seem to have exceeded 70,000. Louis XIII probably mustered a maximum of around 125,000 men after the French entered the Thirty Years War, so the size of the wartime army nearly doubled by the mid-seventeenth century. Then, during the Dutch War, Louis XIV commanded a force that on paper numbered 279,000 men, and this increased to 420,000 troops at the height of the Nine Years War. This latter official tally should be discounted to roughly

---

3 Letter from Mme de Sévigné to Mme de Grignan, 4 February 1689, *Lettres de madame de Sévigné*, ed. Gault-de-Saint-Germain (12 vols; Paris, 1822–23), vol. ix, pp. 144–5.
4 John A. Lynn, 'Recalculating French Army Growth During the *Grand siècle*, 1610–1715', *French Historical Studies*, 18, no. 4 (Fall 1994), pp. 881–906, reprinted in Cliff Rogers, ed., *The Military Revolution Debate: Readings on the Military Transformation of Early Modern Europe* (Boulder, CO, 1995), pp. 117–47.

340,000 men actually present under arms, but this is still many-fold larger than was the army in the previous century. By the late seventeenth century, the standing, or peacetime, army grew to an official figure of about 150,000 men, an even more impressive percentage increase than that of wartime forces. Created in the first instance for defence, this standing army also provided an instrument of state coercion against the civilian population. The force levels attained by Louis XIV would not be surpassed until the French Revolution.

What stake had these ever greater numbers of soldiers in the wars they fought; what motivated their deeds and sacrifices? Increased army size under Louis XIV did not reflect popular devotion to the causes of the monarch. Patriotism did not stir the heart of the common soldier; rather, law and discipline bound him to the army. And with soldiers relatively unconnected to the territorial and dynastic rationale for wars, desertion continually ate away at Louis's army. The political reliability of the state commission army style resulted from an obedient officer corps dependent upon and dedicated to the Bourbon king, not upon a devoted rank and file. This is not to say that the common soldier had no motivation except fear of the lash. He usually bore loyalty to his regiment and his comrades, and perhaps to his officers as well, if they had earned it. A successful general inspired confidence and even affection among his troops, and many a lesser man felt a reverence for the exalted person of the king. Still, a great many soldiers expected little more than meals and wages in the army, and hoped only to survive.

If common soldiers were loosely bound to the king's army, their officers greatly desired military service and lusted for combat. Nobles pursued commissions in the overwhelmingly noble officer corps for reasons that were quite specific to their class. Military service made up a very important element in the identity of the nobility, specifically for the 'sword' nobility, which claimed its origins in armed service to the crown, as opposed to the 'robe' nobles, who gained noble status from judicial and administrative posts. For individuals with the money to afford them, commissions as colonels and captains allowed nobles to build networks of patronage among the officers who served below them. For poor but proud nobles, military service in the lower echelons offered a meagre but honourable income. Above all, a commission gave a noble the chance to demonstrate his status and his adherence to aristocratic values.

The aristocratic code of values demanded that a man, to reap his own glory, must display courage in combat. It was not enough to be brave; bravery had to be displayed and proven to gain masculine *gloire*. The noble officer's search for personal *gloire* echoed Louis's quest, though on a more modest stage. For the young blade ready to make his mark, military service provided very much the same opportunity to test his courage as did duelling. A compelling either–or logic linked war and the duel, as in the 1645 *Catéchisme royal*, which put the following question in the mouth of the young Louis XIV: 'If one forbids duels, how is it that the Nobility can give evidence of their courage?' This inquiry elicited the response, 'In your armies, Sire.'[5] The monarchy repeatedly tried to outlaw the duel during the seventeenth century, but failed to eradicate this aristocratic blood sport because it was so deeply embedded in the aristocratic psyche. Young noblemen yearned to try their swords against another, so they were quick to make or accept a challenge from a rival and they were quick to seek military command, even though the latter was costly in both blood and money, as we shall see.

Military administration and the expenses of war

The growing army required better military administration, that is, better provision of food, pay, equipment, and services; in turn, more effective military administration allowed the army to continue to expand. The first half of the seventeenth century gave ample evidence that when soldiers did not receive pay and food, they pillaged to get what they needed and what they wanted. Rampaging soldiers who stole, raped, and murdered plagued France throughout the long war with Spain that ended only in 1659. Louis's troops victimized his own subjects, and with the return of peace Louis vowed to protect his people. Early in his reign, he wrote that 'Any prince who cherishes his reputation ... will not doubt that it is founded as much upon defending the goods of his subjects from pillage by his own troops as upon defending against pillage by his enemies.'[6] Part of the answer lay in greater discipline of both officers and men, but this would not have worked if Louis had not succeeded in providing his troops with food, pay, and other necessities.

To match the needs of the growing army, the personnel of the military administration multiplied. At the peak of this pyramid was the secretary of state for war, and beneath him were various secretaries and clerks who made up the central bureaucracy of the department

---

5 *Catéchisme royal* by Pierre Fortin de la Hoguette in Micheline Cuénin, *Le Duel sous l'ancien régime* (Paris, 1882), p. 140.

6 Louis XIV, *Oeuvres de Louis XIV*, eds Philippe Grimoard and Philippe-Grouvelle (6 vols; Paris, 1806), vol ii, p. 92.

of war housed in Paris and Versailles.[7] The archives that contain their correspondence today provide a measure of the mounting flood of paperwork handled by the department. Compare the yearly average of 830 letters for the administration of Able Servien, 1630–35, and the 1,100 each year under François Sublet de Noyers, 1635–43, with the annual peak of 10,000 pieces of correspondence during the Louvois administration at the start of the Nine Years War or the equally high totals during the War of the Spanish Succession.[8] The key administrative personnel in the provinces and with the armies on campaigns were the *intendants*, who answered directly to the secretaries of state. Provincial and army *intendants*, assisted by their own staffs, exercised considerable authority to supply and regulate the military in their jurisdictions. The French army developed a form of dual command in which an army's general handled tactical and operational decisions, while the *intendant* with the army handled supply, pay, military justice, and other administrative matters.

Even the greater numbers of administrators were not able to handle all the work required to maintain the army, so the task of supplying troops was left to private entrepreneurs and to regimental officers. Whereas a modern government will supply its troops directly with food, Louis's troops received their bread on campaign from private war contractors, or *munitionnaires*, who agreed to provide bread for a given number of troops at a fixed price. The king's officials simply regulated and inspected the process to make sure that the *munitionnaires* did as they were supposed to. Most of the clothing supplied to soldiers was provided to them by the captains commanding their companies. Officers received allowances from the government or deducted a prescribed amount from soldiers' pay to buy clothing for their men. However, this left the door open to fraud, because an officer could pocket some or all of the money for himself if he shortchanged his soldiers by giving them cheap shoddy goods or by simply providing them with nothing at all. A greedy captain might also claim to have soldiers he did not have in order to gain allowances for these phantom men. Inspections by representatives of the military administration were designed to ferret out such practices.

---

7 There was no formal title of department of war, but officials spoke of their jurisdictions as '*départements*', and in this sense the documents of the time speak of a department of war as the personnel responsible to the secretary of state for war and that secretary's powers and responsibilities.

8 André Corvisier has tallied the amount of correspondence produced by the various secretaries of war as a rough measure of the amount of work they performed. Philippe Contamine, ed., *Histoire militaire de la France*, vol. i (Paris, 1992), pp. 391–2.

Although excesses continued, the administrative agents of Louis XIV were apparently quite successful in abolishing the majority of abuses. The most important necessities for armies on campaign were not weapons or ammunition, but food and fodder. To march and fight, armies required bread supplied by *munitionnaires*, who bought and stored grain, provided ovens and bakers, and furnished the teamsters and wagons to transport bread from ovens to troops – all under the watchful eyes of *intendants*. While soldiers might forage for food in the field, rarely could they maintain themselves for long without a regular supply of food; consequently, a formal system of baking and transportation, including convoys, was essential. Better regular supply allowed an army to be far larger, but it also meant that an army could not outmarch its provisions without running great risks.

If bread had to be brought to the men through a regular system, the grass that their horses ate could only be secured locally. It was a matter of weight. A French soldier required only a pound and a half of bread to sustain him each day, but his horse consumed twenty pounds of dried fodder or fifty pounds of fresh green grass cut from the fields in addition to oats. A field force of 60,000 men could contain 40,000 horses, who would consume 1,000 tons of green fodder daily. Such weights could not be hauled over long distances. Therefore, armies had to send out huge foraging parties numbering hundreds or thousands of men to cut fodder for their horses and bring it back to camp. When an army had exhausted the fodder close to camp, it would have to move to a new camp simply to feed its horses. For example, in 1696 Louis urged Villeroi to set up a camp at Malhelem and stay there until 'the lack of forage obliges you to change it'.[9] The lack of sufficient grass in the fields could force an army to abandon a siege or alter its campaign plans. In 1684, the French wanted to besiege Mons, but gave up on the idea owing to lack of forage in the area and chose less desirable targets instead.[10] Likewise, it was very difficult to campaign in the late autumn, winter, and early spring, because the horses would starve. This dictated that in general, the year was divided into the campaign season from May through October, and the winter, from November through April, when armies rested and refitted in quarters. Winter campaigns were rare. The modern reader may be

9 AG, A¹888, #68, 22 July 1696, Louis to Villeroi.
10 Louvois to Chamlay, 12 June 1684, in Jacques Hardré, ed., *Letters of Louvois, University of North Carolina Studies in the Romance Languages and Literatures*, no. 10 (Chapel Hill, NC, 1949), pp. 366–7. See, as well, the similar problem at Luxembourg. Siege instructions to Créqui, 1 April 1684, in ibid., pp. 408–14; see also p. 425.

amazed at just how much logistics determined the rhythms of campaigns and the details of military life in the early modern era.

By storing food and dried fodder in magazines established in towns and fortresses along the frontier, the French gained considerable advantages over their enemies, particularly in the Spanish Netherlands. Louvois gets the credit for having set up an extensive and permanent system of magazines that allowed the French to supply their armies better with food and fodder and take to the field earlier than could their foes. While the Dutch had to wait for the grass to grow, the French could assemble forces weeks earlier by sustaining the horses for a time on dried fodder. The Dutch council of war bemoaned, 'The French habitually made considerable progress in the Spanish Netherlands in the winter and early spring, before we could subsist in the open field. This advantage is not just a question of superior forces, but proceeds from the practice of making magazines on the borders.... On our side, in that season,... we lack the fodder.'[11]

Just as the provision of pay, food, and fodder were improved, so was the supply of clothing to troops. In earlier centuries, troops wore clothing they had brought with them into service or purchased individually while they were in the ranks; there was little uniformity. However, during the seventeenth century, the French monarchy made greater efforts to ensure that its troops received adequate clothing from their captains. By the end of the century the French instituted the wearing of standardized military uniforms. Uniformity guaranteed adequate quality to maintain the health of the men and improved the appearance and bearing of the troops.

The Sun King also concerned himself with providing services to French troops, as he improved the lot of sick, wounded, and invalided soldiers. Medical service improved during his reign. Each regiment brought to the field its own surgeon; each army on campaign was to have its own field hospital, and permanent hospitals were established for the troops in the rear. Louis accepted as his responsibility soldiers too maimed or infirm to serve him any longer. In the first half of the century, the fate of a soldier past useful service was to be pitied, and the discharged and broken veteran reduced to begging became something of a stereotype. Louis attempted to give such men security and honour. In 1674 he opened the Hôtel des Invalides in Paris, an old soldiers' home of grand proportions. His motives flowed both from a

---

11 Christopher Duffy, *The Fortress in the Age of Vauban and Frederick the Great, 1660–1789, Siege Warfare*, vol. ii (London, 1985), p. 11.

moral sense that he ought to care for those who had served him and from a practical recognition that the existence of such care would encourage men to enlist. As the bishop of Nantes stated in 1691: 'I know that the establishment of the Invalides in Paris has brought many men into the service who would never have entered out of apprehension that had they been crippled and unable to make a living, they would have found themselves reduced to demanding alms in order to live.'[12] The growing size of his armies and the intensity of his wars soon created more disabled veterans than could be cared for in Paris, but Louis awarded pensions to those who could not be admitted to the Invalides.

Larger numbers of troops and higher standards of supply and administration produced a powerful new army, but at greatly increased cost, and, as explained in chapter 2, Louis never really solved the monarchy's financial problems. The state commission army became both a necessity and a luxury for Louis – he needed it for a strong combination of international and domestic reasons, but it was more than he could afford.

Making war feed war

As heavy as was the strain on state finances, war also consumed funds beyond those that came out of the king's purse. The practice of the day demanded that war feed war; therefore, armies on campaign were supposed to collect some of the money and goods they needed themselves. They could do this in several ways. Earlier in the century pillage had been a common, though undisciplined and unregulated, way for war to feed war. Louis's troops continued to pillage at times when they campaigned on enemy land and suffered from poor supply. Sometimes French soldiers were ordered to be rapacious for strategic reasons, as when they tried to make the Dutch capitulate in 1672 and 1673 by making war horribly costly. In 1674 and 1688–89 French severity in the Palatinate had the goal of collecting all manner of things that would be of use to Louis's army and destroying everything else to deny it to their foes. Since armies drew supplies from local sources, a conscious scorched-earth policy against a particular area could make it difficult or impossible for an enemy to maintain an army there.

In general, however, Louis viewed pillage with disdain and tried to suppress it. Pillage disorganized an army, undermining discipline

---

12 Letter #990, September 1691, in *Correspondance des contrôleur généraux des finances*, ed. A. M. Boislisle, vol. i (Paris, 1874), p. 261.

and unit cohesion. Rapacious conduct also hurt an army's chances of being able to supply itself in the long run. If an army drove off the local population, who took with them their stores, livestock, and labour, troops would not be able to find what they needed. As Marshal Villars confided to his king in 1703, 'where there are no peasants there are no supplies'.[13] The marshal repeated this conviction dramatically in an address to his troops at the opening of his successful 1707 German campaign: 'My friends. . . . If you burn, if you make the people run away, you will die of hunger.'[14]

The most regular and lucrative way to make war feed war was to impose contributions upon hostile, or even neutral, populations. Contributions were essentially a kind of protection money paid by populations to avoid being ravaged by an occupying or passing army. A town or village that failed to pay the contributions demanded ran the risk of 'execution', which meant destruction by fire of the resisting town. Armies had long extorted payments and goods from towns and districts unlucky enough to lie in their paths, but they had done so in a hit or miss fashion. In the 1620s the imperial general Albrecht von Wallenstein perfected past practices when he demanded money payments made in regular instalments according to a contractual agreement with the victims. The practice became quite regular to the point that it approximated normal taxation, and, in fact, contributions were often set in the Spanish Netherlands based upon a town's or village's usual tax burden.

The hunt for contributions drove strategy in a way that seems odd to the modern mind. Occupying enemy territory became a way of financing a war effort, so it was quite reasonable for Louis to try to seize an area during a war that he fully intended to return when peace returned. Fortresses were also valued for their ability either to protect friendly regions from enemy contributions or to impose contributions on surrounding areas. Some campaigns were undertaken with contributions as an important or even a primary goal. The proud Sun King stipulated that enforcing contributions ranked as a major objective for Villars's 1703 and 1707 campaigns in Germany. It is impossible to say exactly how much the French garnered from contributions, but it is reasonable to estimate that they supplied about 25 per cent of French military expenses in wartime.

13 AG, A¹1676, #118, 17 June 1703, in Ronald Thomas Ferguson, 'Blood and Fire: Contribution Policy of the French Armies in Germany (1668–1715)', Ph.D. dissertation, University of Minnesota, 1970, p. 211.
14 Claude Louis Hector Villars, *Mémoires du maréchal de Villars*, ed. marquis de Vogüé (5 vols; Paris, 1884–95), vol. ii, pp. 229–30.

Beyond royal funds and the income from contributions, French officers were also expected to contribute their own wealth and credit toward the maintenance of their units. This obligation fell predominantly upon colonels and captains. Contrary to popular belief, it would seem that the average French officer did not become rich through command; there were handsome rewards for successful generals, but not for those further down the ladder. Captains and colonels were required to supply men with everything from clothing to weapons, with the expectation that they would be reimbursed by the state, but payments usually came late and were often less than officers had laid out. As a consequence, officers needed private resources if they wished to command a company or a regiment, and poor officers remained marooned in the lower ranks. In a letter of 1675, Vauban complained of this problem to Louvois: 'I have a poor devil of a cousin, a lieutenant in the cavalry Regiment of Nonan, a good and old officer who would have been a captain a long time ago if he had the secret of turning bad companies into good ones without ruining himself.'[15] 'Turning bad companies into good ones' required a personal fortune. The wonder is that men vied so eagerly to gain military commissions that would cost them so much. However, the need to win personal *gloire* and honour through military command led wealthy officers to compete intensely for companies and regiments.

Weapons and tactics

At the height of its success in the final third of the seventeenth century, the French state commission army won an impressive string of victories over its enemies during the Dutch War and the Nine Years War. Louis's army had become a paradigm for the rest of Europe, and while it may have lost some of its tactical edge by the War of the Spanish Succession, it remained the single most potent army on the Continent. Infantry weaponry and tactics continually evolved during the reign of Louis XIV, while cavalry displayed greater continuity. Artillery enjoyed a formidable reputation, but remained devoted to heavy pieces more suited to siege warfare than to the open field.

Infantry

Early in the seventeenth century, infantry carried matchlock firearms and pikes, but it would discard these for flintlocks and bayonets by the War of the Spanish Succession. The favoured matchlock weapon,

---

15 Letter of 19 September 1675 in Albert Rochas d'Aiglun, *Vauban, sa famille et ses écrits* (2 vols; Paris, 1910), vol. ii, p. 130.

the musket, was the basic firearm of the infantry throughout most of the century, although the French also employed its lighter cousin, the arquebus. The term 'musket' has become something of a generic term for any muzzle-loading weapon, but the word must be used with greater precision here. A musket was a smooth-bore, muzzle-loading, shoulder arm; it fired by means of a matchlock, which ignited the powder with a lighted 'match', a cord of flax or hemp soaked in a nitrate solution so that it would smoulder, much like a modern cigarette. The glowing match was clamped to the end of a short pivoting arm, or cock, that snapped down when the soldier pulled the trigger and ignited the powder charge that propelled the lead ball toward its target. Although the musket ball could carry 250 yards or further, aimed fire was effective only to about 80 yards. The complicated loading procedure limited the rate of fire to one shot per minute, and even then, the rate of misfire could be as high as 50 per cent.[16] In addition, loading was dangerous because the musketeer had to handle a lighted match in the presence of gunpowder, and on occasion a clumsy musketeer could blow up himself and his comrades while loading.

Companion to the musket, the pike, a formidable spear about fourteen feet long, bristled with an iron point and was girded with metal strips for a yard or so from the point to prevent swordsmen from hacking off its lethal tip. The French employed the pike primarily as a defensive weapon to keep attacking cavalry at bay. Its great length allowed the weapons of men in rear ranks to protrude well in front of the formation, so that a solid block of infantry with pikes lowered threatened its enemy with a hedgehog of steel points. Such a wall was necessary because the time-consuming loading process left musketeers defenceless much of the time, since an unloaded musket was no better than a club in a fight. When challenged by a swift cavalry charge, musketeers had to shelter behind the pikes of their comrades to keep from being ridden down by the horsemen.

The fusil slowly supplanted the musket during the second half of the seventeenth century until an ordinance of 1699 entirely eliminated the earlier weapon. Fusils were lighter and handier than their predecessors, but their greatest advantage lay in their flintlock firing mechanism. Instead of using a lighted, and therefore dangerous, match, a fusil relied upon flint striking steel to generate the spark needed to ignite the powder. When the soldier pulled the trigger, the flintlock

---

16 David Chandler, *The Art of Warfare in the Age of Marlborough* (New York, 1976), pp. 76–7.

mechanism snapped forward the cock that held a piece of flint, which then struck a vertical iron plate, called a frizzen, and the spark ignited the charge. There was no awkward match to handle, and once loaded, the weapon could be stacked or slung, leaving the hands free for other tasks. Fusils loaded in less time and suffered fewer misfires, but their more complicated mechanism made them more expensive than muskets, a factor which slowed their adoption.

As the fusil won universal adoption at the end of the century, it became an even more potent weapon because of the invention of the socket bayonet. The desire to give the musket value in close combat by turning it into a short but stout spear produced the plug bayonet about 1640.[17] This crude bayonet consisted a knife blade about a foot long attached to a tapered wooden handle that could be jammed down the barrel of a musket if needed. Of course, when a plug bayonet was in place the musket could not be fired. But even this crude bayonet proved its value, and the Dutch War witnessed the first French bayonet charges.[18] Then in the late 1680s Vauban developed a bayonet attached to a socket that fitted around, not in, the barrel of a fusil and allowed a soldier to load and fire with bayonet in place. Vauban claimed that now 'a soldier, with a single arm, would have two of the best weapons in the world, a spontoon and a good fusil, with which he could fire and load quickly without removing the bayonet'.[19] An order of 1692 prescribed that socket bayonets should be provided to each fusilier or musketeer.[20] The bayonet rendered the pike unnecessary, since now men armed with firearms could present their own hedgehog of sharp points to discourage an enemy onrush at close range, so in 1703 pikes disappeared just as had muskets a few years before.

Infantry were organized as regiments, but the tactical unit was the battalion. An infantry regiment could contain one or more battalions. The number of men in a battalion varied, but regulations usually set the size of a French battalion during the great wars of Louis XIV at about 800 men grouped into from 12 to 16 companies. Of course, during wartime the number of men in a battalion almost always fell

---

17 Louis André, *Michel Le Tellier et l'organisation de l'armée monarchique* (Paris, 1906), p. 344.
18 AG, A¹531, 18 March 1677, Louvois to Courtin, in Camille Rousset, *Histoire de Louvois* (4 vols; Paris, 1862–64), vol. ii, p. 288.
19 Vauban letter to Louvois, dated 21 December 1687 in Rochas d'Aiglun, *Vauban*, vol. ii, pp. 287–8.
20 Victor Belhomme, *Histoire de l'infanterie en France* (5 vols; Paris, 1893–1902), vol. ii, p. 213.

Table 3.1 A sample of battalion and squadron sizes in the French army

Period	Official battalion size	Actual battalion size	Official squadron size	Actual squadron size
1676–77	800	712	150	144
1689–92	800	664	160	139
1695–96	715	572	160	140
1702–4	585	421	140	135
1710–11	650	422	140	121

Source: Figures derived from John A. Lynn, *Giant of the Grand Siècle: The French Army, 1610–1715* (New York, 1997), pp. 51–5, 465–8, and 492–5. Numbers of men given for actual unit size are only approximations.

short of regulations. With actual unit size varying in the field, contemporary records usually list the size of an army on campaign as a certain number of infantry battalions and cavalry squadrons, and this usage will often be employed in this volume. Table 3.1 can be used as a guide to estimating the number of troops in a French army when only figures on battalions and squadrons are given.

The fundamental tactical problem inherited from the sixteenth century was the proper mating of firearms, or 'shot', and pikes within the battalion to create the most effective military force. Only the triumph of fusil and bayonet eliminated this complication at the start of the War of the Spanish Succession. Early in the 1600s, some military handbooks recommended a ratio of three pikes to two muskets, but ordinances of the 1650s required a one to two mix, as commanders rated shot as more valuable than pikes. The great imperial general Montecuccoli might still consider the pike the 'queen of the infantry',[21] but it continued to decline in French units. In the 1670s the ratio fell to one pike for every three muskets or fusils, and during the Nine Years War it declined further to one to four and a half.

In general, pikemen massed in the centre of the battalion with musketeers and fusiliers marshalled at the wings. Battalions stood ten ranks deep at the start of the century in accord with the fashionable Dutch practice, but became thinner and wider with the decades. The depth of the formation reflected the length of time it took to load a musket, step forward, fire it, and then retreat into the battalion to

---

21 Montecuccoli in Brent Nosworthy, *The Anatomy of Victory: Battle Tactics, 1689–1763* (New York, 1990), p. 29.

reload. For example, if men required a minute to load, and if the commander wanted to fire a volley every six seconds, he would have to stack his musketeers ten deep.[22] From the 1630s the French adopted the Swedish practice of standing only six ranks deep and continued to do so through the Dutch War, although French formations could be even thinner in practice. According to the military authority Puységur, during the Dutch War battalions stood six deep at the beginning of the campaign season, when they had a full complement, but as losses diminished the number of men 'towards the end of the campaigns the ranks were reduced to five'.[23] The Nine Years War regulations cut the depth to five, although they often reduced to only four when casualties brought down the size of battalions. With the War of the Spanish Succession, regulation depth decreased to four, which, once again, was further thinned in practice to three.[24]

Cavalry
Cavalry underwent little change in weaponry and tactics compared with the constant evolution of infantry. The heavily armoured cavalry of earlier ages was a thing of the past by the personal reign of Louis XIV; only the regiment of Royal Cuirassiers still wore a breastplate, or *cuirasse*.[25] The basic and most important weapon of the French cavalry was the sword, which remained a heavy straight-bladed weapon through the Dutch War, after which Louvois replaced the straight blade with a curved one better suited to slashing from horseback. Cavalrymen also carried pistols of one type or another, and some special units carried short rifled shoulder arms known as carbines.

As early as the War of Devolution, Louis added dragoon regiments to his army, and these increased in number continually during his reign. Dragoons were mounted troops trained to fight on foot; in a sense, they were mounted infantry who employed their horses more for mobility than for combat. Thus, strictly speaking, dragoons were not cavalry, although they too fought from horseback when required. In the 1690s the French added some light cavalrymen, hussars, who fought in Hungarian style, but they were never very numerous.

By the Dutch War, French cavalry were organized into regiments, as was the infantry. Each regiment contained two or three squadrons

---

22 Nosworthy, ibid., p. 14, posits a fire rate of one volley each six seconds.
23 Jacques-François de Chastenet de Puységur, *Art de la guerre par principes et par règles* (2 vols; Paris, 1748), vol. i, p. 56.
24 Ibid., p. 57.
25 Louis Susane, *Histoire de la cavalerie française* (3 vols; Paris, 1874), vol. i, p. 136.

at first, but included four squadrons by the 1690s. Like battalions in the infantry, squadrons constituted the tactical unit for the cavalry. Squadrons usually included three companies, which numbered fifty men each during the Dutch War, but only thirty or thirty-five during the Nine Years War and the War of the Spanish Succession. Thus a cavalry regiment with four squadrons, each of three companies containing thirty-five men, numbered 420 men if it was at full strength.

Throughout the reign of Louis XIV, native French cavalry squadrons stood in three ranks for battle, as the Swedes had done before them. However, as was the case for infantry, when casualties cut the number of men actually present in a squadron, it thinned its formation. Puységur comments concerning the War of the Spanish Succession that 'on entering the campaign, they were not all in three ranks, because all were not complete, towards the middle many were in two ranks, and towards the end, few were in three ranks.'[26] Generally the best men rode in the front rank and on the flanks of the squadron.[27]

The ultimate cavalry tactic was, of course, the charge, which was not simply a hell-for-leather dash at the enemy. In general, cavalry had to balance order with momentum; the slower the pace, the better the squadron could maintain its formation, but the faster the pace, the greater the shock of the charge. The French compromised by advancing at the trot in order to maintain cohesion and to avoid exhausting the horses; then they spurred into a gallop for no more than the last fifty yards. Once they accelerated, there could be little chance to maintain exact order and distances.

Artillery
Artillery increased in importance over the course of the *grand siècle* due to its value on the battlefield and its prominence in siege warfare, which certainly became the more common form of conflict during this period. While the French exploited the destructive potential of the mortar in siege warfare, the primary artillery piece was the cannon. These guns fired solid round shot and various packaged rounds. These latter, anti-personnel, rounds included grapeshot, composed of a cluster of smaller balls, and canister, containers of musket balls that gave a cannon the destructive potential of a huge shotgun at short ranges. Solid shot was, however, the primary projectile of the cannon, and calibres were rated by the weight of shot that they could fire.

---

[26] Puységur, *Art de la guerre*, vol. i, pp. 52, 58.
[27] AG, Archives historiques 78, fol. 71–2. 'Disposition de la cavalerie reglée par Sa Majesté pour un jour de combat'.

By mid-century the French had settled essentially on a system of six calibres – 33-, 24-, 16-, 12-, 8-, and 4-pounders – but this apparently rational system encompassed much more variety, and much less uniformity, than might at first be obvious. Cannon throwing the same weight of ball could be made with varying thicknesses of chambers to accommodate greater or lesser powder charges, and the variety did not end here, as barrels supposed to be of the same calibre were, in fact, of somewhat different-sized bores depending on where they were manufactured.

Standard artillery barrels were extremely heavy, because they were cast to deal with large powder charges, and because all guns were designed for use in siege warfare. Even light calibres were cast long, so that barrels for the entire range of calibres varied only from 10 feet 7 inches to 11 feet 1 inch. This length resulted from a self-conscious decision to make every cannon long enough to protrude through gun embrasures on fortress walls or in siege works. A barrel that was too short could damage an embrasure with its muzzle blast. Casting every piece long meant that fortress pieces were interchangeable with field pieces; only their carriages differed. There was some attempt to introduce shorter, lighter models for use in field warfare, the cannon *de nouvelle invention*, but conservative, siege-minded artillerists rejected this attempt at an artillery 'revolution'.

Contemporary authorities differed somewhat on the range of artillery. Many authorities believed that on the field of battle, effective artillery range did not exceed 500 yards. Vauban, who studied such matters with scientific rigour, credited heavy artillery with a maximum range of about 2,500 yards in siege warfare.[28] This range was neither aimed nor effective but was simply the greatest distance that a cannonball might fly through the air in the best of conditions and then skip or roll along the ground with the potential of hitting anything. To do real damage to fortress walls, he too would bring his heavy siege artillery closer, to about 600 yards.

By contrast to the cannon, which was a weapon of field battle and siege, the mortar was a weapon of the siege alone. It launched a hollow iron bomb filled with powder and fired by a fuse that either the gunner lit or that lit automatically when the mortar fired. French siege mortars ran from six to eighteen inches in bore.[29] The mortar itself looked rather like an inverted pot and sat on a wheel-less

28 Rochas d'Aiglun, *Vauban*, vol. i, p. 181.
29 Contamine, *Histoire militaire*, vol. i, pp. 410–11. Saint-Rémy listed four main calibres of mortars in the late seventeenth century: 18, 12$\frac{1}{2}$, 8$\frac{1}{3}$, and 6$\frac{1}{4}$ inches. Chandler, *The Art of Warfare*, p. 252.

carriage set upon the ground. It threw its deadly package at a very high trajectory to sail over walls and other obstacles. When its shell exploded, it spewed shrapnel about and set fire to buildings. Bombardment via mortars enjoyed a deadly vogue during the 1680s. Louvois and Louis became fascinated with mortars as terror weapons. Bombardment could bully or punish an adversary without risking loss to French troops, who would not have to storm a city to destroy it. At Mons in 1683, Louvois wanted 2,500 to 3,000 bombs thrown into the city by mortars, and the bombardment of Genoa the next year further revealed the brutality of Louvois.[30] The taste for bombardment became something of a blood lust for Louvois and Louis, but it did not go unopposed. Both Marshals Luxembourg and Vauban argued against it on a number of grounds.

Throughout the early modern era, French field armies dragged along an impressive number of cannon, but the number of guns per thousand troops remained surprisingly stable. The wars of Louis XIV generally saw artillery ratios of one gun per thousand men. In 1674, at Ensheim, Turenne had thirty guns for 25,000 troops; at Neerwinden in 1693, Luxembourg brought seventy-one guns to the field for an army of 80,000; and Villars counted eighty guns for a force of 75,000 at Malplaquet in 1709.

The pieces with an army were organized in its artillery train. These were temporary entities tailored to the particular size and mission of the force. Saint-Rémy suggested an ideal train for a French army of 50,000, which was subdivided into five brigades. It included four 24-pounders, six 12-pounders, twenty 8-pounders, twenty 4-pounders, a pontoon train of twenty boats, 220 wagons, 1,225 horses, and about 1,000 men.[31]

When an army undertook a siege, the royal siege park joined it. In 1690, Louis XIV's siege train included ten 33-pounders, thirty-six 24-pounders, four 16-pounders, and eight 12-pounders, along with two 18-inch mortars, twenty-four 12-inch mortars, twelve 8-inch mortars, and eight perriers, stone-throwing artillery.[32] It and its considerable supply of ammunition, including a million pounds of gunpowder, were assembled at Douai, Valenciennes, and Tournai. It would eventually see service before Mons in the spring of 1691. So massive was a siege train both in the size of the guns and in their sheer number that it was advantageous to move it by water if possible.

[30] 20 October 1683 in Hardré, *Letters of Louvois*, p. 277; and Rousset, *Histoire de Louvois*, vol. iii, pp. 274–6.
[31] Chandler, *The Art of Warfare*, pp. 170–1.
[32] Victor Belhomme, *L'Armée française en 1690* (Paris, 1895), p. 136.

Learning and practising the art of field warfare

Louis commented, 'Good order makes us look assured, and it seems enough to look brave, because most often our enemies do not wait for us to approach near enough for us to have to show if we are in fact brave.'[33] The secret was to appear unshakeable. For generals and military thinkers, battle, particularly infantry combat, had become a test of wills, and the victory would go not to the force that inflicted the greatest physical casualties on the other side, but to the force that could maintain its order while absorbing the worst its enemy could inflict. This may be related to early modern ideals of military self-sacrifice, to a model of conduct that Joël Cornette refers to as 'the perfect stoic soldier'.[34] Marshal Catinat, a practical soldier, in describing an assault, insisted that 'One prepares the soldier to not fire and to realize that it is necessary to suffer the enemy's fire, expecting that the enemy who fires is assuredly beaten when one receives his entire fire.'[35] The surprising truth is that seventeenth-century Europe developed a battle culture based less upon fury than upon forbearance.

This battle culture of forbearance underlay Louis's attitude toward combat in the field, where heavy casualties were inevitable. The triumph of firepower brought the triumph of suffering. Cannon could destroy at great range, and little could be done about it, save to cross the valley of death to seize the guns. In addition, losses could be staggering when two opposing infantry formations stood at close range pouring volley after volley into each other.

The ability to perform with forbearance in the face of such danger and chaos was far from natural; it had to be learned. Some of this had to do with weapons handling, but much had to do with attitude. Training was based on obedience and restraint. It was not enough to master the tools of war; the soldier himself must be mastered. In later ages, officers would come to trust in the initiative of their troops, but during the wars of Louis XIV such confidence was forestalled by an attitude among officers that assumed a low level of honour and motivation among the rank and file. So self-control had to give way to control by officers. Actions must be automatic and obedience complete, and both must be drilled into recruits. Drill was the key, and

---

33 Louis XIV, *Mémoires de Louis XIV pour l'instruction du dauphin*, ed. Charles Dreyss (2 vols; Paris, 1860), vol. ii, pp. 112–13.
34 Joël Cornette, *Le Roi de guerre* (Paris, 1993), p. 50.
35 Catinat in Jean Colin, *L'Infanterie au XVIIIe siècle: La Tactique* (Paris, 1907), p. 25.

it was an invention of the century – what Michael Roberts terms 'the revolution in drill'.[36] It was not enough simply to practise the practical, mechanical movements of musket loading or pike handling; these actions had to become so automatic and obedience so complete that troops performed their duties regardless of danger, that they suffered and endured without losing their effectiveness or resolution. Drill, which imparted necessary skills of weapons handling and marching to troops, thus did much more.

No monarch surpassed Louis XIV's intense interest in drill. He was convinced that 'many more battles are won by good march order and by good bearing [*contenance*] than by sword blows and musketry.... This habit of marching well and of keeping order can only be acquired by drill.'[37] Here again, he repeated the theme that the maintenance of disciplined order, rather than bloody combat, wins battles. As a child, he practised the manual of arms for the pike as one of his physical exercises and never lost his interest in drill. Louis attended exercises and personally commanded when possible. He devoted particular attention to model military units, the most important of which was his cherished Régiment du Roi, created in 1663 for display, experiment, and training.

Louis desired that his troops devote considerable time to drill and that they train in larger units when possible. Soldiers in garrison were to drill at least twice a week. Winter quarters figured large in training, because during this period, soldiers in temporary garrisons had the time and energy to devote to drill. In addition, recruits arrived in the months between campaigns and had to be taught their craft. The French also occupied peacetime summers with training camps and great military reviews, which allowed large bodies of troops to manoeuvre together. At a camp near Bouquenon on the Sarre, established in the summer of 1683, Louis visited his troops. The infantry drilled within their companies from 5 to 10 a.m. and then manoeuvred by battalion or brigade from 4 to 7 p.m.; once a week the entire assemblage of twenty-four battalions of infantry manoeuvred as a whole.[38] In wartime and peacetime, the inspectors-general played a vital role in training French troops, for they provided a mechanism to ensure standard and uniform drill. In 1667, the office of inspector-general for infantry was created and filled by Jean Martinet, whose name has become a byword for rigorous discipline and drill.

---

36 Michael Roberts, *The Military Revolution, 1560–1660* (Belfast, 1956), p. 10.
37 Louis XIV, *Mémoires*, vol. ii, pp. 112–13.
38 Belhomme, *Histoire de l'infanterie*, vol. ii, pp. 236–8.

By allowing greater control over large armies, better training and discipline facilitated an increase in the number of troops actually mustered to fight together on battlefields during Louis's reign, at least until the War of the Spanish Succession.[39] During the long war with Spain, 1635–59, the average French field army mustered 14,700 men. With the Dutch War, the average size of armies in battle rose to 24,500, while the Great Condé commanded the largest French force committed to battle – the 50,000 who fought at Seneffe in August 1674. The Nine Years War witnessed field forces that swelled again to reach an average strength of 39,000. At Neerwinden in 1693, Marshal Luxembourg led 80,000 men in victory over William III. By then, the maximum size of field armies in battle probably exceeded levels that a single general could effectively control. Turenne argued, 'An army larger than 50,000 men is awkward to the general who commands it, to the soldiers who compose it, and to the *munitionnaires* who supply it.'[40] The War of the Spanish Succession did not bring a further growth in battlefield forces.

As a general rule, cavalry made up about one-third of field armies. French armies had about 30 per cent horsemen during the Nine Years War, and this figure only shrank slightly to 27 per cent during the War of the Spanish Succession, when the French were pressed to exhaustion. Cavalry possessed great importance as a decisive force in battle, for its mobility allowed it to exploit circumstances that arose only in the course of fighting. A glance at the great battles of the era demonstrates that they often ended in a cavalry charge. Louis believed that cavalry combat was by nature less costly and more decisive than infantry fighting within the context of the battle culture of forbearance. So adamant was Louis that he instructed Marshal Luxembourg: '[M]ake use of my cavalry rather than engaging yourself in an infantry battle, which causes the loss of a lot of men but which never decides anything.'[41] In addition to its role on the battlefield, cavalry proved its value on campaign in reconnaissance and in garnering supplies on campaign. French armies fighting along the Rhine during the Dutch War included a larger percentage of horsemen than did those campaigning in the Spanish Netherlands largely because in Germany

---

39 Battle size data from Gaston Bodart, *Militär-historisches Kriegs-Lexikon* (1618–1905) (Vienna and Leipzig, 1908).
40 Turenne in Xavier Audouin, *Histoire de l'administration de la guerre* (4 vols; Paris, 1811), vol. ii, p. 244.
41 Louis XIV to Luxembourg, 5, 10, 12 August 1691, in Rousset, *Histoire de Louvois*, vol. iv, p. 510.

mounted detachments performed the important task of foraging for supplies to maintain an army in the field.

Throughout the wars of Louis XIV, armies arrayed for battle according to a single basic plan. The bulk of the battalions and squadrons stood in two main lines, one behind the other. A reserve stationed itself to the rear of both lines. Early in the seventeenth century, large gaps separated battalions in the infantry lines, but as the decades passed, the intervals shrank, although they never entirely disappeared.[42] With these as the basic themes, a number of variations fitted the changing circumstances and styles. By the late seventeenth century, French field armies organized in brigades, temporary units formed for a particular campaign. *Circa* 1690, infantry brigades contained four to six battalions and cavalry brigades eight to twelve squadrons. These brigades then became the building blocks of the lines of battle.

The number and position of artillery batteries varied according to the situation. In general, commanders prized high ground from which artillery could command a large part of the battlefield. Battery size generally varied between four and twenty guns; Sainte-Hilaire at Ensheim put thirty-two cannon in four batteries, and the battery on the right side of the French line at Malplaquet mounted twenty guns.[43]

Combat often began with an artillery exchange or cavalry action. The logic of opening with a barrage is obvious, since cannon could usually hit the enemy before any other weapons could be brought to bear. Cannon fire practically became the formal announcement of battle. Still, many fights, such as those at Rocroi and Seneffe, began with a clash of cavalry, because the mobility of horsemen usually allowed them to close before the infantry could. Yet at some point, most combats became battles of attrition between rival infantry who approached to within firing range and blasted away at each other, producing great carnage. After infantry was either decimated or badly shaken by fire, it was vulnerable to an advance by opposing infantry or to a cavalry charge.

Discussion of battle should not lead a reader to believe that fighting on campaign was restricted to great clashes; on the contrary, the most common and continual combat was on a smaller scale in what the contemporaries called '*petite guerre*' or 'little war', but

---

42 Nosworthy, *Anatomy of Victory*, pp. 25, 83, emphasizes this difference between the gapped line and what he calls a *truly linear order*, a line without major intervals between units, which was common after 1715.

43 Chandler, *The Art of Warfare*, p. 205.

which will be termed here 'partisan warfare', meaning the actions of war parties. These performed a variety of functions vital to seventeenth-century warfare; some applied directly to the daily operations of an army in the field, while others had more to do with fuelling the war effort by procuring supplies and money through contributions and raids, which were known at the time as 'courses'. Parties foraged for fodder, protected friendly convoys and attacked enemy convoys, gathered intelligence, provided security from enemy parties, and sealed roads leading to besieged fortresses. Stealth and ambush were their stock in trade. Parties also performed most of the nasty duties associated with contributions. They imposed demands, took hostages, gathered in the take, and executed villages that refused to pay. Parties also raided for livestock, particularly cattle, and penetrated deep into enemy territory on courses, to seize whatever they could lay their hands on. Lastly, when a scorched-earth strategy ruled, they ravaged the countryside to deny its resources to the enemy.

Partisan warfare demanded a high level of skill from its practitioners, who could be regular troops or specialists at irregular warfare. A successful leader must be master of the tactics and tricks of the trade, know the country, and command the local language. Partisan warfare involved a considerable variety of fighting forces. Regular line regiments detached parties. The mobility of cavalry gave them an advantage; but infantry also marched off on courses or rode double with cavalry.[44] Handbooks intended for cavalry officers made a point of discussing the conduct of partisan warfare. Regular troops from a field army often undertook 'little war' tasks that maintained that army on campaign, such as foraging and convoy escort, or attacks on enemy forage parties and convoys. Beyond the intermittent use of regular troops for this irregular warfare, certain specialists did little else; they earned the title 'partisan'. Because professional partisans claimed a percentage of what they brought in, there was something of the buccaneer about them. The king put bodies of partisans in frontier fortresses, paying and feeding them as if they were regulars.

It is not surprising that because forbearance emphasized the horrendous costs of combat in the open field, Louis generally sought to avoid it. Early in his personal reign, Turenne and Condé were battle generals above all, but after their departure from the scene, Louis

[44] Feuquières wrote of one raid: 'I made good speed with 800 cavalry and 500 infantry on their cruppers.' Feuquières in ibid., p. 52.

demonstrated a marked preference for siege warfare, a less costly and far more predictable form of combat. Thus, perhaps the most important consequence of the battle culture of forbearance for Louis was the predominance of sieges. But it should be noted that this was not just the case for the French. Even Marlborough, a commander who proclaimed that he desired to fight in the field, engaged in only five major battles, while he conducted twenty-six sieges during the War of the Spanish Succession.

Positional warfare

Positional warfare, as defined here, encompasses the construction, defence, and attack of fortifications, be they fortresses or entrenched lines. Through most of Louis's personal reign, sieges were the most common form of military operation. Fortresses controlled territory, and given the territorial definition of war under the Sun King, it is not surprising that Louis persevered on positional warfare; it fitted his strategic goals. Positional warfare appealed to Louis on other levels as well. He seems to have enjoyed the meticulous detail of sieges. In addition, positional warfare fitted into his passion for control and his desire to run things from afar in *guerre de cabinet*. And, of course, Louis XIV's emphasis on sieges grew not only out of his personality and policy but out of his sombre expectations of field battle. Behr exemplified the trend favouring positional warfare when he wrote: 'Field battles are in comparison scarcely a topic of conversation.... Indeed at the present time the whole art of war seems to come down to shrewd attacks and artful fortifications.'[45]

During the *grand siècle*, positional warfare played a wider variety of roles in war than might at first be apparent. Most obviously, fortresses stood like stone-faced sentinels guarding the land of their master and denying it to his enemies. Implied in a fortress's ability to bar a path to the enemy was its promise to open that path to friendly forces, and fortresses provided bridgeheads across rivers or controlled passes that the French could employ as invasion routes. By dominating major routes, fortresses also made logistics easier for friends and more difficult for foes. Fortresses not only guarded supply routes, they also served as the storehouses; here were found Louis's magazines. Fortifications also served as bases from which to impose contributions on the enemy and from which to launch raids against his territory. Conversely, fortresses and fortified lines were designed to shield areas

45 Behr in Duffy, *The Fortress in the Age of Vauban*, pp. 13–14.

from enemy raids. During the War of the Spanish Succession, the French constructed several complete systems of lines to cover the Spanish Netherlands from the Meuse to the sea. Lastly, citadels dominated cities and proved useful in controlling potentially rebellious subjects, inhabitants of newly acquired lands, and populations of territories occupied in war.

European positional warfare reached its apogee during the reign of Louis XIV and is most associated with the work of his great engineer, Vauban, whose career spanned nearly the entire personal reign of the Sun King. Vauban was but the son of a minor and recently ennobled Burgundian family, yet even the diarist Saint-Simon, a snob of the highest order, praised him as 'the most honest man, and the most virtuous, perhaps, of his century'.[46] While his family arose in a milieu of law and commerce, Vauban's father, Urbain, took up the sword. Vauban's skills won him the post of *commissaire général des fortifications* in 1678, and while no engineer officer before him had risen beyond the rank of captain, he became a brigadier in 1674, and in 1703 he acheived the highest French military rank, marshal, albeit in the twilight of his life. Vauban's military career was extraordinarily busy. He drafted plans for about 160 forts, in whole or in part, and directed 48 sieges. He also took to the road continually on tours of inspection, for, as he quipped, troops might be brought to an inspector, but fortifications demanded that he visit them: 'there is not a single watch-tower in all the king's fortresses which will move so much as an inch at my command'.[47] His able pen bore witness to his inexhaustible curiosity. His most important military works were two treatises on siegecraft, but he also wrote manuscripts on a wide range of subjects, including pig breeding. Although a reformer at heart, he was a discreet reformer who wished to operate from the top down, so his memoranda circulated privately. However, one of his final proposals, a plan for an egalitarian tax that would hit nobles as well as commoners, was so revolutionary that it caused him to lose favour during the last years of his life. He loved neither war nor conquest, but represented Louis's desire to defend his frontiers. With unvarnished realism, Vauban condemned war: 'War has interest for its father, ambition for its mother, and for close relatives all the passions that lead us to evil.'[48]

---

[46] Saint-Simon, Louis de Rouvroy, duc de, *Mémoires*, ed. A. de Boislisle (42 vols; Paris, 1879–1930), vol. xi, p. 27.

[47] Letter of 10 May 1696 from Vauban to Le Peletier de Souzy in Rochas d'Aiglun, *Vauban*, vol. ii, pp. 442–3.

[48] Vauban in Pierre Lazard, *Vauban, 1633–1707* (Paris, 1934), p. 486.

The design of fortresses and fortress systems
Vauban perfected the design of what can be called the 'artillery fortress'. This type of fortification mastered the problem of how to resist artillery.[49] Medieval castles had relied on tall, relatively thin, walls to keep out enemy infantry and to resist contemporary siege engines, but in the fifteenth and sixteenth centuries, cannon battered down such walls. The Italians solved this problem by building low, thick-walled fortifications surrounded by a deep and broad ditch. Its walls both resisted the destructive force of round shot and provided a fine platform on which to site defensive artillery to keep attackers at a distance. The success of the Italian artillery fortress won it acceptance across Europe.

This new style also incorporated pointed bastions at the corners and various outworks detached from the main fortress which gave the design the appearance of a star. The angles of bastions and outworks allowed defenders to sweep the ditch in front of any wall with musket and cannon fire and to deny attackers any shelter. Older square or round towers had allowed 'dead zones' where defending fire could not reach attackers, but angled bastions eliminated these. In making additional improvements to the outlines of walls and bastions Vauban raised this style of fortification to its highest level.

The final characteristic of the artillery fortress was the contouring of the surrounding terrain to expose attackers to the fire of defenders. The sloping ground leading up to the ditch was known as the glacis. This ended at the chemin couvert, or covered way, a sunken firing position for infantry on the outside edge of the ditch. (It was 'covered' because its sunken position entirely protected, or covered, soldiers there.) As we shall see, the only safe way an attacker could cross the glacis in the face of musketry from the chemin couvert and artillery fire from the walls was to dig approach trenches to shelter his own troops. In a sense, a fortress was an engineered battlefield, which employed geometry and architecture to ensure all the possible advantages that nature only rarely provided. Exploiting these advantages a smaller force could hold a far larger one at bay.

Not only individual fortresses or citadels took the new pattern, but entire cities were fortified in this style. However, the size of Paris, the largest Christian city on the European continent, and the great cost of updating and expanding its fortifications to meet current

---

49 See John A. Lynn, 'The *trace italienne* and the Growth of Armies: the French Case', *Journal of Military History*, July 1991, for a definition and description of the 'artillery fortress'.

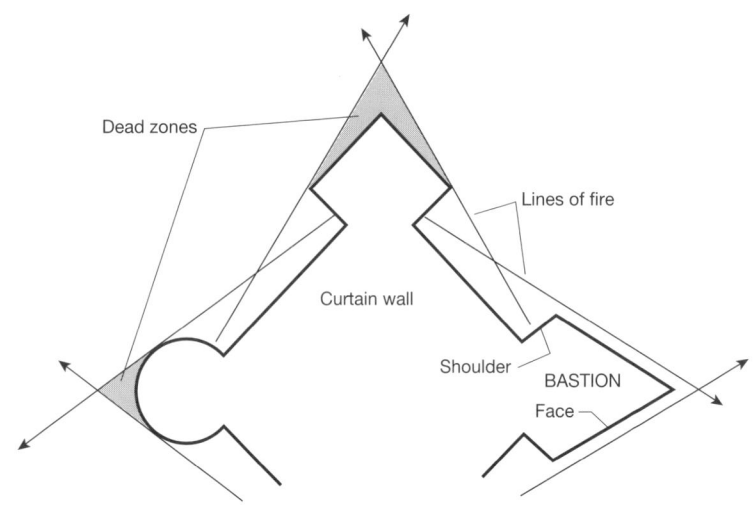

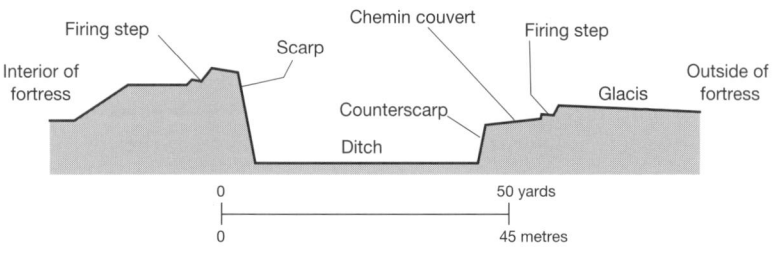

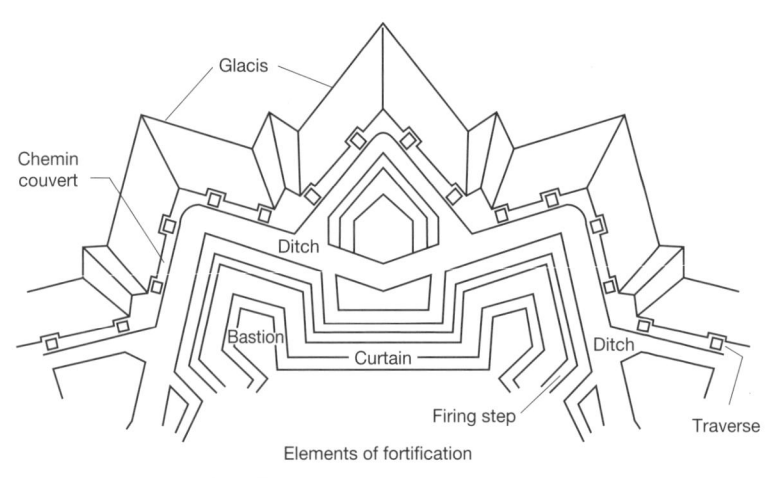

Figure 3.1 **The artillery fortress**

standards convinced Louis XIV to eliminate its existing outdated fortifications and leave it without walls in the 1670s; Paris would be defended at the frontier.

Vauban not only invented sophisticated improvements for individual fortresses, he also conceived of a rationally designed barrier of fortresses to shield French borders. He saw France as an assailed giant, standing alone amidst a hostile Europe, an image that demanded that France receive an impregnable shield. Therefore, he advocated a fortified frontier that he labelled a *pré carré*, a term susceptible to two interpretations. On the one hand, the term meant a duelling field; on the other hand, it implied that the frontiers would be straightened out, or squared off, to make them more defensible. In a famous letter of January 1673, Vauban proposed that 'The king must think some about creating a *pré carré*. I do not like this pell-mell confusion of our's and the enemy's fortresses. . . . That is why, be it by treaties, or by a good war, if you believe what I say, Monseigneur, always preach squaring things off, not the circle, but the *pré*.'[50]

His most elaborate plan dealt with the highly vulnerable frontier with the Spanish Netherlands, the border most dependent on masonry to establish a defensible line in depth. There he achieved a defensive zone, which he described as 'two lines of fortresses' formed 'in imitation of an army's order of battle'.[51] Major forces in the first line included Dunkirk, Ypres, Lille, Tournai, Valenciennes, Maubeuge, and Dinant, while important bastions in the second were Gravelines, St Omer, Aire, Arras, Douai, Cambrai, Landrecies, Rocroi, and Carleville.[52] Not meant for flexible defence, he intended this barrier as an enemy-tight seal designed to preserve the sacred land of France. In pursuit of his goal, Vauban proposed to Louvois and Louis which fortresses ought to be taken in war to rationalize the frontier, and which could be regarded as expendable. Thus, the *pré carré* became a goal of warfare, a direction for strategy.

Practice of siege warfare
The conduct of sieges had become a specialized form of warfare in which the spade triumphed over the sword, as fortifications were taken not so much by impetuous storm as by methodical digging. The siege began as attacking troops, usually cavalry, 'invested' the fortress – that is, they surrounded it to cut it off from reinforcement

50 AG A¹337, #111, 20 January 1673, Vauban to Louvois.
51 Vauban, 'Mémoire des places frontières de Flandres', November 1678 in Rochas d'Aiglun, *Vauban*, vol. i, p. 189.
52 See the excellent map in Duffy, *The Fortress in the Age of Vauban*, p. 9.

and resupply. Investments were often carried out at night to heighten surprise and limit losses. Besieging forces then surrounded their prey with complete rings of entrenchments: one facing inward toward the besieged works, the lines of contravallation; and the other facing outward to protect the attackers from attack by a relief army, the lines of circumvallation. Lines encircled a fortress beyond the absolute maximum range of the cannon mounted on its walls – a range that Vauban estimated as over a mile and a half. Such lines could be quite long; at the siege of Lille in 1667 they ran for fifteen miles. Because these lines were constructed out of enemy range, they were not only the work of soldiers, but also of thousands of peasant labourers, called pioneers, commandeered for duty from the surrounding countryside. For example, at Mons in 1691, 20,000 pioneers laboured on the lines of circumvallation.[53]

Approach trenches drove from lines of contravallation toward the enemy fortress, into the range of its guns, and were, consequently, the work of soldiers, who were known as 'sappers' when they were engaged in digging trenches, or 'saps'. Owing to the danger, beginning work on the approach trenches, called 'opening of the trenches', took place at night to give the sappers as much cover as possible. This was a key moment of the siege. Approach trenches zigzagged a course toward the fortress and across the glacis. Their angular paths denied the enemy a clean shot up the trenches, and to guarantee their protection, they took on sharper and sharper angles as they inched forward. Digging these trenches was a dangerous business because, by nature, sappers laboured on incomplete works. Engineers suffered as well; so many were killed or wounded in the trenches that Vauban pronounced them the 'martyrs of the infantry'.[54]

With Vauban, the practice of besieging a fortress became more sophisticated, rational, and predictable. Vauban changed the traditional technique of assault in ways that strengthened, rather than challenged, the methodical nature of siegecraft. His most important innovation was the use of 'parallels'. At the important siege of Maastricht in 1673, he first introduced his system of parallels, which were trenches dug parallel to the walls of the besieged fortress that allowed attacking parties to assemble and coordinate much better than in the old practice of simply having them jump off from the heads of approach trenches.[55] Parallels also provided excellent defensive positions to

---

53 Charles Sévin, marquis de Quincy, *Histoire militaire de Louis le Grand roi de France* (7 vols; Paris, 1726), vol. ii, p. 347.
54 AG, A^{1}832, #5, 2 November 1688, letter from Vauban to Louvois.
55 Rousset, *Histoire de Louvois*, vol. i, p. 460.

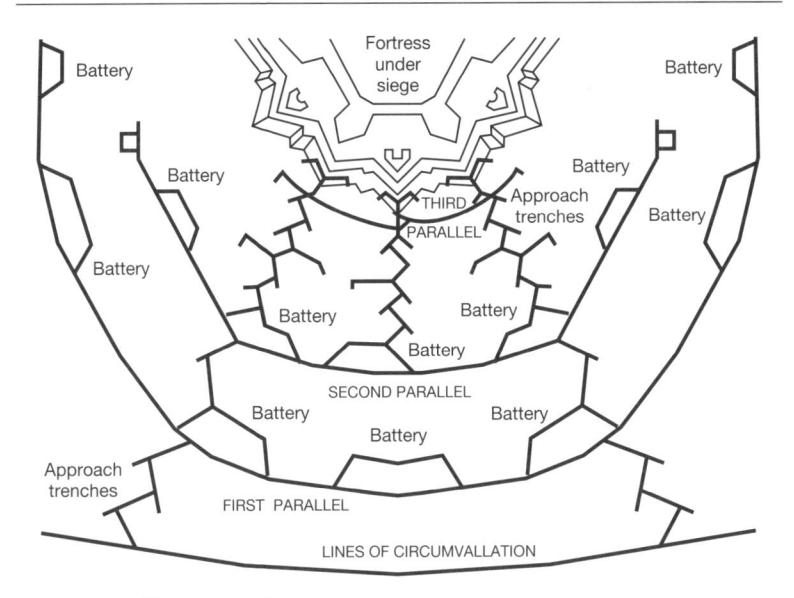

Figure 3.2 Siege operations

counter enemy sorties designed to ruin siege works or drive back the attackers. Vauban set his first parallel and its batteries at about 600 yards, from where the heavy cannon could do considerable damage to the enemy walls.[56] From there, sappers drove forward toward the enemy and dug a second parallel, again complete with artillery batteries, at about 250 yards. The third parallel, with breaching batteries, was sited at the chemin couvert, only 30 to 60 yards from the wall. Parallels also economized on labour because they could replace lines of contravallation.

Vauban's methodical techniques contrasted sharply with the chaotic carnage of battle. If Vauban's methods were applied intelligently, a fortress was almost always doomed from the moment the first spade broke the ground. He was so bold as to promise in one treatise: 'I guarantee an infallible success without a day's extra delay if you will defer to my opinion and follow faithfully the rules I lay down.'[57] His techniques spared lives as well; he took the fortress of Ath in only two weeks with a loss of but 53 dead and 106 wounded against a garrison of 3,850.

[56] Vauban, *De l'attaque et de la défense des places*, pp. 51, 53; Sébastien le Prestre de Vauban, *Oeuvres de M. de Vauban* (3 vols; Amsterdam and Leipzig, 1771).

[57] Sébastien le Prestre de Vauban, *A Manual of Siegecraft and Fortification*, trans. G. A. Rothrock (Ann Arbor, MI, 1968), p. 65.

But while his techniques were economical in blood, they were expensive in money. The amount of stores necessary for a major siege was staggering.[58] Saint-Rémy calculated that an army involved in a major siege would require 3,300,000 rations for the troops involved and 730,000 forage rations for the horses in a forty-day period. Such a theoretical force would also require 40,000 24-pound shot and an equal number of grenades, in addition to 944,000 pounds of gunpowder.[59] This says nothing of the mountains of other supplies necessary for the work. Sieges conducted by Vauban's principles required so many troops and were so expensive that the French rarely conducted more than one at a time.

Posts and lines

In addition to fortresses and fortified cities, positional warfare also encompassed the digging of fortified lines of great length and complexity. Such lines defended different locales, but the greatest ones crossed the Spanish Netherlands from the Meuse to the sea, covering distances that could exceed a hundred miles. They descended from earlier strings of outposts designed for much the same reason, to protect French-held resource areas from exploitation by the enemy. Vauban proposed lines 'in order to deny entry into our territories [*pays*] to the enemy and limit him from putting them under contribution'.[60] Praising the effect of entrenched lines in the 1690s, the engineer Caligny wrote 'the inhabitants have not been bothered at all by enemy raids during the war'.[61]

French defensive lines appeared first in the Dutch War, became more prevalent during the Nine Years War, and rose to paramount importance in the War of the Spanish Succession. Such lines used rivers and canals as wet-ditch barriers whenever possible, buttressing these barriers with redoubts and where necessary running overland with entrenchments embodying state-of-the-art defensive architecture. In form, such lines were not simple trenches, but earthen walls. Pioneers began by excavating a ditch and using the dirt to erect a wall on the near side of the ditch, giving this earthwork a cross-section resembling that of a fortress. At intervals, these entrenchments also employed

---

58 AG, A¹209, #49, 21 June 1667. Carlier lists the amount of supplies necessary for the expedition to Limbourg.
59 Chandler, *The Art of Warfare*, p. 241.
60 Vauban in Rochas d'Aiglun, *Vauban*, vol. i, p. 165.
61 Caligny memoire from 1697–98, Bibliothèque National, fonds français 22220, fol. 53. This document is one of many presented in André Corvisier, *Les Français et l'armée sous Louis XIV* (Vincennes, 1975).

angles like those of bastions. Defenders occupied firing steps on the wall rather than sheltering in the ditch.

For the French, the defensive ruled supreme during the War of the Spanish Succession, so it is little wonder that entrenched lines played such a great role in this conflict. At the start of the war, French and Spanish constructed the lines of Brabant beginning at Antwerp and stretching for 130 miles past Diest to the Meuse, just below Namur.[62] These first lines continued the tradition of halting enemy raids, but the French used such fortifications more and more to hinder the movements of enemy armies as well as to bar hostile courses. French field armies now occupied lines or stood behind them, employing them as prepared defensive positions. As the French lost ground in the Spanish Netherlands, lines became more substantial because they served as a barrier to guard France itself. Villars constructed the last and most imposing lines in 1711, christening them the Ne Plus Ultra lines. It is not inappropriate to compare the defensive lines built during the War of the Spanish Succession with the trench lines of World War I, although the actual construction of the two was quite different.[63]

The military parameters of indecisive warfare on land

The military institutions and fighting styles described above provided the parameters of warfare during the personal reign of Louis XIV and determined that combat, both battles and sieges, would be relatively indecisive. Logistical pressures required that armies move slowly and consider the needs for food and fodder above all else. Independent of the territorial desires of a state, armies occupied land for no other reason than to exploit its resources during the struggle. The predominance of siege warfare played into this need and also limited the impact of battle. Time consumed in creating slow-mobilizing state commission armies allowed wars to grow into great affairs on multiple fronts, which tended to complicate operations and put limits on the harm that any defeat might do.

The need to supply an army in the field greatly influenced the conduct of operations. Louis's generals and *intendants* had to feed both men and horses. The complicated process of carting grain, grinding flour, baking bread, and then convoying the bread to the troops limited the speed and distance that armies could move, hobbling manoeuvres. Because armies depended on horses for mobility and

---

62 Duffy, *The Fortress in the Age of Vauban*, p. 35.
63 Duffy, ibid., p. 36, certainly thinks this is reasonable.

carting, fodder played an inordinately large role in shaping campaigns. Armies had to forage for fodder in the surrounding area. The abundance or lack of grass could determine the goal of a campaign. Rather than responding to some pressing operational need, armies continually marched from position to position, from camp to camp, for no other reason than finding new pastures.

Constrained by the need to find sufficient fodder for horses, armies could only campaign seasonally, although fodder stored in magazines could allow the French to take to the fields earlier than their foes on occasion. With rare exceptions, cold weather and the end of the growing season forced armies into winter quarters. This meant that every year would see a six months' hiatus in operations, a pause that stopped the progress of successful armies and allowed defeated forces to restore themselves. As such, logistics and weather made it difficult to maintain a momentum of victory and drive a foe to surrender.[64]

Supply in the broad sense of making war feed war also drove campaigns. The need for contributions required that armies launch raids and undertake entire campaigns, such as Villars's German campaign of 1707, with little other reason than imposing payments on enemy populations. Most importantly, Louis made great efforts to take and hold areas during a war that he had no intention of retaining in the peace settlement. The Spanish Netherlands repeatedly fell victim to this kind of occupation for the purpose of exploitation. Instead of exploiting an advantage to attack a foe, armies were more likely to secure and exploit territory to sustain the war effort.

The essential role of supply and the way in which it depended upon territorial control contributed to the dominance of positional warfare under Louis XIV. Fortresses, fortified towns, and entrenched lines performed a varied list of functions but none more critical than their roles in denying, opening, or exploiting territory for resource mobilization. The preeminence of positional warfare also grew out of the power of fortresses to close frontiers to enemy invasion – so vital considering Louis's obsession for defensible frontiers. The value of sieges became even more apparent because they promised predictable results and moderate casualties, in contrast to the threat of loss without result posed by the battle culture of forbearance.

The predominance of positional warfare tended to limit decisive operations. Fortresses hampered a victorious army's ability to follow

---

[64] This idea concerning the influence of winter quarters was suggested to me by my graduate student Maj. John Katz.

up success on the battlefield. Forces bested on the battlefield could flee to friendly fortifications, making it harder to bag up defeated units with a vigorous pursuit. In fact, after battle, victors faced the frustrating possibility of simply running up against the walls of enemy fortresses which stood as barriers to continued advance. Armies that suffered serious casualties in battle could not only shelter behind fortifications but rebuild their numbers quickly by siphoning off troops from less vital garrisons, as William III did after the Battle of Seneffe. By obstructing a foe's advance, fortresses also could buy time while reinforcements arrived from a less threatened front to buttress the one in greater danger.

In fact, Louis characteristically fought his wars on multiple fronts, which further hampered decisive operations. In contrast to Louis's campaigns, Napoleon's later success in his great campaigns of 1805–9 required the ability to concentrate the vast majority of his army against a single foe on a single front along a single line of operations. Such concentration produced decisive results – that is, the destruction of enemy armies and the quick elimination of a foe. However, Louis was unable to achieve such single-minded operational focus, except perhaps during the opening drive of the Dutch War, the most dramatic French advance of his reign.

At the start of each of his major wars, Louis assumed that he could defeat an isolated enemy in little time, but then became mired in a situation that forced him to mobilize much greater forces than he had originally intended. The state commission army could only expand slowly; it lacked the convenience of earlier 'off the shelf' mercenary bands or the later efficient conscription of Napoleon's *grande armée*. Beyond this, the tenets of the battle culture of forbearance demanded that troops be mechanically drilled and thoroughly trained in a lengthy process. As a consequence of military institutions and practices, then, Louis consumed a long time in fleshing out his existing regiments and creating new ones; meanwhile, his foes used this time to form great alliances that increased the threat to France. Louis inevitably ended up with a much larger and more diverse challenge than he had originally anticipated. Unable to dispose quickly of his original adversary on a single front, Louis faced an assortment of enemies on several fronts. The Dutch War expanded beyond the United Provinces to encompass the Moselle basin, much of the Rhineland, the eastern Pyrenees, and Sicily. The Nine Years War spread from the Palatinate to the Netherlands, Italy, and Roussillon/Catalonia.

The need to defend multiple fronts kept Louis from marshalling the full military might of his kingdom on any single one of them.

81

This made it unlikely that Louis would have the forces needed to destroy an opponent by offensive operations in any particular theatre. While multiple fronts hobbled his offensive capacity, they also shored up the defence, because the armies stationed on different fronts could function as reserves for each other. That is, a French army in a more secure situation could send reinforcements to bolster one that had fared badly. So, when Turenne was killed in 1675 and his army retreated back across the Rhine into Alsace, it received additional troops and the Great Condé himself from the army fighting in the Netherlands, and this infusion stopped the enemy advance. In fact, one of the common characteristics of the wars of Louis XIV was the continual shifting of French forces from one front to another. Here the fact that fortresses could buy time by delaying an enemy on one front worked into a grander pattern, because it aided the transfer of forces between fronts.

Logistical parameters, slow mobilization, predominant positional warfare, and multi-front operations all conspired to hamper decisive action. As a result, the wars of Louis XIV were long struggles, rather than brief conflicts resolved by combat in the field, the hallmark of Napoleonic warfare. Without doubt, Louis's strategic conceptions and the diplomatic environment of the era also pushed warfare in this direction, but the factors discussed in this chapter deserve primary consideration. War became something of a perpetual motion machine, best designed to compel a settlement only when it was impossible for the parties to continue the vicious cycle any longer. This partially defined a style of warfare that will become evident in the following pages and that will be defined in this volume as 'war-as-process', but much more will be said on that topic in chapter 8.

THE NAVY

The French fought their long wars not only on land, but at sea as well. Even more than the army, the navy was a creation of Louis XIV. To be sure, the army expanded many-fold under the aegis of the Sun King, but the navy went from but a mere handful of vessels at the start of his personal reign to a mighty battle fleet within a decade. Yet if the proportion and pace of naval expansion dramatically exceeded that of the army, it followed a parabolic course, suffering decline after its apogee in the Nine Years War. French sea and land forces existed in a special symbiosis that employed the navy as a handmaiden to the army. For the paramount 'naval' task as defined by Louis XIV, coastal defence, the two were essentially interchangeable, and the army was always more important to the prosecution of French strategy as a whole. Therefore, when financial crisis forced the government to decide that it could not adequately support both services, the navy was doomed to suffer. At the Battle of Beachy Head in 1690, the French navy won the greatest tactical victory it ever gained over its English and Dutch foes, but within a few years the French had abandoned major fleet actions, *guerre d'escadre*, and turned to *guerre de course*, commerce raiding. The active forces of France at sea metamorphosed from the king's naval vessels to privateers, ships financed by private entrepreneurs holding a royal commission who hoped to reap a hefty profit by capturing enemy merchant vessels. In the wars of attrition that consumed the second half of Louis's personal reign, *guerre de course* matched the king's purposes and his pocket book.[65]

Naval administration

Louis's navy was created and directed by two administrative dynasties, the Colberts and the Pontchartrains. Jean-Baptiste Colbert built an almost non-existent navy into a formidable instrument with a system and permanence it never had enjoyed before. As controller-general of finance in function from 1661 and in title from 1665, Colbert busied himself not only with collecting revenues, but with fostering the economy as well. The wealth of the Dutch taught him that finance, commerce, and naval power were interdependent, so Colbert gained *de facto* authority over the navy at the start of the personal reign and officially became secretary of state for the navy in 1669.

The navy had enjoyed only occasional support before Colbert, and it had not developed the permanent institutions that would sustain it in the future. The sailing fleet concerned Colbert above all. Galleys, those rowed vessels inherited from a previous age, no longer had much value in the Atlantic, and while they could still usefully supplement the sailing fleet in the Mediterranean, even there galleys had conceded dominance to the great ships of the line. Henri IV had

---

[65] Very useful recent accounts of the navy have been supplied by Daniel Dessert, *La Royale: Vaisseaux et marins du Roi-Soleil* (Paris, 1996); Jan Glete, *Navies and Nations: Warships and State Building in Europe and America, 1500–1760* (2 vols; Stockholm, 1993), vol. i; and by Jean Meyer in his chapter 19 in Contamine, *Histoire militaire*, vol. i. In addition, Geoffrey Symcox, *The Crisis of French Sea Power 1688–1697: From the guerre d'escadre to the guerre de course* (The Hague, 1974) is an excellent study. The account presented here derives primarily from Dessert and Symcox. When other sources elaborate or differ, they are noted.

83

been the first to build a specialized war fleet, but it vanished after his death. Richelieu rebuilt the navy to a force of 60 sailing vessels and 25 galleys in 1642. Traditionally, historians have often claimed that this incarnation of the navy rotted away under Mazarin; however, Jan Glete argues that this is a misconception, and that the navy, while remaining quite small compared with that of England or the Dutch Republic, had not suffered a dramatic decline in the 1650s.[66] In any case, the navy expanded phenomenally under Colbert. In 1670 it surpassed both the English and the Dutch in the number of war vessels.[67] By 1672 Colbert had moved heaven and earth to create a French sailing navy of 120 major vessels, of which 33 were of the largest size, first and second raters. This fleet was essentially complete; it would increase a bit further to 137 large war vessels in 1695–97, after which it would fall in numbers. Financial collapse during the War of the Spanish Succession brought down the number of ships dramatically, so the navy only boasted 80 major ships by 1715.[68]

The difficulty, and thus the magnitude, of Colbert's accomplishment should not be underestimated. Creating a navy meant much more than simply building ships. Colbert had to enlarge and improve port facilities, build arsenals, warehouses, and docks. These had to be administered efficiently and staffed by thousands of skilled personnel. Forests had to be managed and harvested to produce the necessary timber. Top to bottom, it was a mighty effort much to the credit of the great Colbert.

The process of expansion can be split into two periods and the creation of what some have called two navies. The first grew rapidly but without a great deal of regularity and rationalization. Ordinances and regulations promulgated from the late 1660s on established a system with more uniform and improved standards and procedures. When in the mid-1680s it came time to refit or replace vessels from the first burst of naval growth, a second and better fleet took shape

---

66 Glete, *Navies and Nations*, vol. i, pp. 186–7. He argues that in 1660 the English contained vessels totalling 88,000 tons displacement, the Dutch 62,000 tons, and the French only 20,000 tons. In comparison, the French navy under Richelieu in the 1630 did not exceed 30,000 tons displacement. Daniel Dessert, *La Royale*, pp. 301–2, states that by 1661 Louis had at his command only nine ships of the line, and this included nothing larger than a third rater.

67 Glete, *Navies and Nations*, p. 192, presents figures for 1670 that demonstrate the French navy had 114 vessels, more than either the English (84 vessels) or the Dutch (102 vessels).

68 The figures here for 1695 and 1715 come from Dessert, *La Royale*, p. 302. Comparable figures from Glete for 'battle fleets' are 119 in 1695 and 62 in 1715. Glete, *Navies and Nations*, vol. i, p. 226.

under the direction of Colbert's son, the marquis of Seignelay (1651–90), who succeeded his father. Seignelay, while brought up in government service and finance like his father, showed greater personal knowledge of the navy; he has even been called a 'sailor minister'. If he loved pomp and displayed an arrogant streak, he was a hard worker none the less. After purchasing the right to succeed his father in 1669, Seignelay took on steadily increasing responsibilities, finally assuming the office outright when Colbert died in 1683. Seignelay's naval ordinance of 1689 achieved much that his father had worked for, but an early death a year later removed Seignelay, a staunch advocate of *guerre d'escadre*, from office. Now the office came into the hands of Louis Phélypeaux, count of Pontchartrain (1643–1727), another controller-general of finance who learned quickly in naval office and who, like Colbert, was succeeded by his son, Jérôme (1674–1747) in 1699. The Pontchartrains have received blame for instituting the change from *guerre d'escadre* to *guerre de course* and, thus, dismantling the great navy of the Colberts. However, this charge is unfair because such compelling circumstances argued for this switch in strategy that it is hard to imagine that even Seignelay could have continued to send a large battle fleet to sea had he lived.

Just as the secretary of state for war relied on *intendants* and private entrepreneurs to administer and maintain, so too did the secretary of state for the navy. Key to the operation of the navy, the *intendants* of port towns supervised construction, refitting, arming, provisioning, and manning of naval vessels. These were peacetime as well as wartime duties, so unlike the army *intendants*, naval *intendants* in the ports were permanent officials, rather than being commissioned only for specific campaigns. Pierre Arnoul, a particularly important naval *intendant*, served in Marseilles (1673–74), then went on to Toulon (1674–79), Le Havre (1683–88), and Rochefort (1683–88). *Intendants* delegated much of their work to *commissaires*, and the selection of naval *intendants* and their *commissaires* had much to do with patronage, just as it did in the army. The work of supplying the essentials, from wood, to foodstuffs, to gunpowder, fell to private *munitionnaires* and *fournisseurs*. Such men belonged primarily to the world of finance, not manufacturing, for the key to supply was nearly always money. Often contractors joined the naval administration, blurring the line between the two. As is also true of the institutions of warfare on land, it is accurate to speak of a military-financial complex, or, in this case, a naval-financial complex, as the twentieth century would discuss a military-industrial complex.

Ports and problems
Because of the need to concentrate docks, shipyards, naval storehouses, dock facilities, and the skilled labour force to work in them at only a few ports, those ports became far more central to the operation of the navy than did any garrison town to the welfare of the army. When he first came to power, Colbert fixated on Rochefort as his major Atlantic port, but after 1674 Brest gradually eclipsed Rochefort, which was not well suited to serve as a major naval base. Experience revealed that only Brest really could harbour a war fleet along the Atlantic and Channel coasts, other ports being too shallow or too small. The lack of adequate ports on the Channel put Louis's navy at great disadvantage in a struggle with the English. The French had no acceptable naval port from Brest to Dunkirk, and even Dunkirk, while well placed to harbour privateers, was inadequate for ships of the line. On the Mediterranean, Marseilles remained the primary galley port, but Toulon came into its own as the main sailing port during the Dutch War.

Yet even as Brest and Toulon emerged as the great French naval bases, they suffered from real shortcomings. Neither could accommodate the entire fleet; Brest, for example, could only handle about sixty ships. Since a voyage of 1,500 miles separated the two ports, massing the fleet proved very difficult for the French. As it turned out, a delay in gathering the fleet proved deadly to the French navy in 1692, as would the problem of communicating with Paris, because an essential order arrived too late. French ports were so distant from the capital and court that it took days or weeks for messages to pass between Louis and his fleet.

Maintaining a fleet required an immense amount of materiel and labour. The construction of a fleet demanded forests of timber; about 3,000 oaks went into the building of a single first-rate ship of the line. The French would never manage an easy supply of necessary wood, and, in any case, harvesting the trees and transporting the wood to shipyards took a great deal of time and, thus, slowed construction.[69] Once it reached the yards, timber could be transformed into ships only by the hands of highly skilled labour. Toulon counted only about 500 naval workers in 1665, but as the number of ships increased it employed between 1,500 and 2,000 during peak periods of the Dutch War. But even with their expansion, French navy yards

---

69 See Dessert, *La Royale*, appendix 4, p. 298, for the trees required for different rates of ships according to the 1689 ordinance; see Paul W. Bamford, *Forests and Sea Power, 1660–1789* (Toronto, 1956).

were never large enough to deal in a timely manner with the tasks demanded of them.

In addition to construction, repairs, and refitting, 'armament' demanded a great deal of muscle. The need for armament resulted from the seasonal nature of naval warfare. Navies campaigned from the late spring to the early autumn, after which ships returned to port to avoid cold weather and storms. Except for a few ships maintained as a winter guard, the fleet 'disarmed' in the autumn; provisions, ammunition, cannon, and other tackle were removed from war vessels, because it was found that this preserved both ships and equipment. Should repairs be necessary, the decks were now literally clear to perform them. In February or March orders would come to prepare a given number of ships for the next campaign season, and one by one they would be brought into dock and laboriously rearmed and provisioned. Usually only part of the fleet would be armed, so that there could be quite a difference between the total tally of ships in the French navy and the actual number of vessels under sail any particular year. Disarming and arming ships employed many men even if no new ships were under construction.

The ships
The first rush to create a great fleet did not allow for much study and standardization, but with the years French builders and administrators mastered and coordinated the design of French vessels until they were equal or superior to anything afloat. This process took time, so that only after the first fleet of Colbert was essentially intact did the regulations and practices come on line that would shape the re-creation of the fleet in the 1680s.

French naval historian Daniel Dessert criticizes French shipyards for building ships that were not particularly well suited to French needs. Although few French harbours could berth ships with a deep draft, Louis's shipwrights eschewed the more stable Dutch flat-bottomed design and embraced more tapered, or *coupée*, hulls with deeper keels. Colbert also favoured extremely heavy construction using a massive bulk of oak and iron that resulted in heavier and slower vessels than the Dutch, who employed lighter materials. French vessels resembled English ships more than their Dutch contemporaries, but France was not blessed with the harbour facilities enjoyed by the English. By the 1680s, however, Dessert concedes that the French had mastered the problems of construction and were not behind any other European power. Even as the French drew abreast of and surpassed others in ship design, it is worth noting that when the French won their most

87

impressive tactical victory at Beachy Head they were closer in time to the Spanish débâcle of the Armada in 1588 than to Nelson's triumph at Trafalgar in 1805, and ships still lacked many of the refinements they would boast a century later.

The Colbertian navy eventually applied the rationalism and centralization once believed to have typified Louis's reign in all its aspects. At first, design and construction were left in the hands of master shipwrights, but with time, Louis's ministers imposed royal control. In 1671, Colbert founded two *conseils de construction* at Rochefort and Toulon, and soon a third appeared at Brest, these councils uniting shipwrights, naval officers, and royal administrators to determine the navy's needs. Colbert followed these councils in 1680 with *écoles de construction*, and in 1683 the master carpenter Coulumb wrote the first manual of ship construction in France. Soon after, Louis created an inspector-general of naval construction in 1684, an office that went to Langeron.

Ordinances of 1674 and 1689 defined a rate system to classify French war ships. A first rater by the 1674 ordinance boasted about 80 guns (the heaviest being a 24-pounder) and drew 1,400–1,500 tons, but the 1689 ordinance shifted the standard upward. By it, a first rater mounted about 100 guns (with the heaviest being a 36-pounder) and drew 1,600 to 2,200 tons.[70] Second, third, fourth, and fifth raters were successively smaller, with a fifth rater carrying 36 cannon. Frigates were even smaller vessels carrying fewer guns. Fleets at this time were usually described in terms of how many vessels (meaning first to fifth raters) they included and in addition how many frigates, fireships, and flutes (supply ships that accompanied the fleet). Sometimes authors refer to all the first to fifth raters as 'ships of the line'. In these pages the distinction will be made simply between rated vessels and other types.

The largest ships built during the personal reign were the *Soleil Royal* and the *Royal Louis*, both rated at 120 guns and 2,400 tons, but which never carried their full complement of cannon. These monsters were too large for practical purposes, and the first, built in 1669–71 at Brest, only sailed on campaign in 1690–92 and was a casualty at La Hogue, while the second was only armed for a single campaign in 1677, after which it languished in port until put up for sale in 1694.

Construction of ships of the line consumed vast quantities of wood. According to the 1689 ordinance, a first rater required 3,100

---

[70] Symcox, *Crisis of French Sea Power*, p. 36.

oak trees and a third rater 2,400. Colbert's forest ordinance of 1669 was primarily concerned with guaranteeing future supplies of wood. Assuming the supplies had been gathered, a ship could be built in relatively little time; an average ship of the line could be fashioned in a matter of months. Once, using prefab construction, dock workers assembled a 30-gun frigate in a day, but that was a unique occasion.[71]

Crews

Finding enough sailors to man the fleet in wartime posed a problem the French never really solved by a rational system. Fleets during the Nine Years Wars required as many men as a field army. In 1690, 26,000 men manned Tourville's victorious fleet, and three years later his massive fleet of ninety-three rated vessels and thirty-eight frigates carried 45,000 men on board. While not all these were skilled seamen, the numbers of experienced sailors was still impressive, considering that at that point the seafaring population of France numbered only about 55,000.

Before Colbert, the French, like the English, relied on a form of impressment that was casual, sporadic, and often violent to bully sailors into service, but Colbert established a far more rational system. Following precedents from earlier in the century, he ordered a census of the French seafaring population in 1668. In 1670, sailors were divided into three classes, and annually one of these was to serve in the navy. The law barred merchant vessels from signing on sailors from that class. The work of census and administration of this new form of naval conscription fell to *commissaires aux classes*. Sailors were to carry books that listed their class and services. It is worth noting that twenty years before Louvois instituted the royal provincial militia, Colbert brought systematic conscription to the navy.

As always in the *ancien régime*, a chasm separated regulation from reality. Flight and resistance hampered maritime conscription so that while it succeeded in supplying enough sailors for the new navy during peacetime, the class system came up short in wartime.[72] Over the years, the number of sailors inscribed fell; in 1686, the rolls listed 59,494, but by 1696 that number had decreased to 50,569, a decline of 16 per cent. A memoir of 1690 called the sailor 'a species of bird from all countries without belonging to a single one and who stays only where he finds it best'.[73] Such birds would fly when the

---

71 Dessert, *La Royale*, p. 157.
72 Eugene L. Asher, *Resistance to the Maritime Classes: The Survival of Feudalism in the France of Colbert* (Berkeley, 1960).
73 Mémoire in Dessert, *La Royale*, p. 210.

situation became difficult and unrewarding. Desertion plagued the class system; in 1686 the administrative district of La Tremblade, with a census of 2,076 sailors, suffered 1,000 desertions, and probably 9,000 sailors fled the kingdom.[74] Merchant vessels and privateers paid more, and the temptation proved irresistible for many. Sailors who avoided service were supposed to suffer awful punishment, but in fact the normal penalty was simply a year in the king's service without pay. Simple flight was not the only unwanted response to maritime conscription. In 1675 the *Entendu* was burned by its crew as an act of resistance to unwanted service. Brittany and Provence both suffered minor rebellions from seamen who had no desire to man the king's ships. Resistance to naval conscription seemed to be a reasonable reaction to the prospect of being forced into a life typified by hard working conditions and great danger from disease and malnutrition.

Authorities resorted to expedients to fill the shortfall left by the class system during wartime. In 1690 when Tourville's fleet required 26,000 men, the class system was supposed to supply only 13,811 sailors that year.[75] Crews had to be found by other means, so the navy took on vagabonds and others forced to join the fleet, and, as in times past, ports were closed and men pressed into service until the quota was filled. The needs of the navy to man its ships during the summer could effectively eliminate commercial traffic for want of sailors.

Officers

Staffing the navy with qualified officers posed a more difficult problem than finding cadres for the army, but this was not because the navy demanded huge numbers of officers. The officer corps that commanded the king's ships was not particularly large. In 1673, a time when the navy numbered 120 rated ships, it included 80 captains, 100 lieutenants, 620 ensigns, 20 captains of frigates, and 12 captains of flutes, whereas the army at its greatest wartime strength under Louis XIV was led by over 20,000 officers.[76] Staffing problems in the navy derived from problems concerning professional skill and social class. Naval service simply demanded a greater level of skill and experience than was required by the army, for the consequences of incapacity at sea were more disastrous.

Undoubtedly, Louis would have preferred a navy commanded by the social élite of France, his beloved nobility. However, French nobles did not dominate naval command to the same degree that they did

---

74 Ibid., p. 214.
75 'État abrégé de la marine du roi, 1690', in ibid., p. 348.
76 See for example, AG, MR1701 on the size of the French army in 1710.

the army's officer corps, and the navy welcomed a greater percentage of *roturiers*, or non-nobles, into its commissioned ranks. French aristocratic traditions put a premium on service in the army rather than the navy, so service at sea was less attractive. *Roturiers*, however, benefited from the value placed upon practical service at sea, even in the merchant trade. Even among captains, a fairly elevated rank, old families did not dominate, as they did among army colonels. From 1669 to 1715, 30 per cent of his captains were *roturiers* and another 24 per cent were recently ennobled (*anoblis*) or the sons of *anoblis*.[77] To be sure, over the course of the personal reign, the proportion of captains from the oldest families increased from 18 to 31 per cent, while that of *roturiers* fell from 39 to 31 per cent, so the corps was becoming increasingly composed of nobles, but it still presented many possibilities to *roturiers* and *anoblis*. This is not to deny that noble birth mattered in the navy; there was but a single *roturier* among the *chefs d'escadre* who served the Sun King during his personal reign. Not surprisingly, the coastal provinces of France supplied the lion's share of officers.

The personal wealth of officers was also an issue, although it was not as important as it was in the army. Money became particularly important for privateer captains, who were investors as well as commanders. And individuals might serve alternately as naval officers and as privateers. Some sailed as privateers when the fleet was in for the winter; others went over to privateering when the navy eschewed *guerre d'escadre*.

Aspirants to commissioned rank could learn their trade in several ways. They might have served in the merchant service or as privateers, or they might enter the king's service as ensigns, essentially to apprentice. Shortly before his death, Colbert established the Gardes marines to train young officers. Three companies of Gardes marines, each commanded by a naval captain, taught seamanship, hydrography, navigation, mathematics, and astronomy. They produced as many as 2,000 new officers during the 1680s, but their output fell off after that. Another route for nobles intent on entering the navy was via service on the galleys of the Knights of Malta. These individuals generally joined the king's galleys, but others, among them Tourville, commanded sail.

At the official head of naval command stood the admiral of France. This once powerful post had lapsed, was re-created by Louis in 1669 and filled first by one and then another of his illegitimate sons. In its

---

77 Dessert, *La Royale*, pp. 223–4.

new form, the post of admiral carried honour but not much authority, although it still was lucrative. The count of Toulouse (1678–1737), the natural child of Louis and the marquise of Montespan, gained the office as a small boy after the death of his half-brother, the duke of Vermandois (1667–83). Beneath the admiral were two officers of ability and authority, the vice-admirals of the Ponant, headquartered in Brest, and of the Levant, headquartered in Toulon. D'Estrées held the first post from 1669 until his death in 1707, when he was succeeded by his son; Tourville rose to vice-admiral of the Levant in 1689 and held the rank until his death in 1701. Ranking below the vice-admirals were the lieutenants-general of the naval armies, of which twenty-two served Louis during the personal reign; next came the *chefs d'escadre*, or commodores, of which there were seventy.[78]

The most famous naval commanders of the day, Duquesne, d'Estrées, Tourville, Bart, and Duguay-Trouin were very different sorts. Abraham Duquesne (*ca.* 1610–88), known as an able old sea dog, saw his great days during the French expedition to Sicily during the Dutch War, when the admiral was in his late sixties or early seventies. This salty old Protestant, who refused to abjure in 1685, lusted after honours and preferments, and to achieve them became a self-promoter of the first order. Historians have generally praised Duquesne, but the prominent naval scholar Dessert recently criticized him as a fine sailor but an indifferent fleet commander. Seignelay dismissed Duquesne's requests for still more honours by saying, 'I believe that to merit the distinctions he has requested he must perform services of another nature than those he has rendered up to the present moment.'[79] Jean d'Estrées (1624–1707), whom some have dismissed as a court amateur, was, in fact, a well-born but none the less able commander with a strong interest in the West Indies. After rising to vice-admiral in 1669, his campaigns in the Dutch War brought notable victories. Anne-Hilarion de Costentin de Tourville (1642–1701) stands out as the greatest French admiral of the entire *ancien régime* and as the only French sailor of Louis's reign who bears comparison with the great Dutch and English admirals. Tourville teamed his ability at sea with the talents of a savvy courtier. The Nine Years War marked the apogee both of the navy and of his career.

[78] Ibid., pp. 229, 353. Dessert is a bit confusing in that he calls the *chefs d'escadre* 'admirals' at times.
[79] Seignelay, AN, Mar., B2 51, fol. 187v, 6/4/1684 in Dessert, *La Royale*, p. 248. Dessert concludes derisively that 'All the so-called glory of Duquesne comes down to two days' (p. 245), and that in neither case did Duquesne show great talent when commanding a fleet.

Jean Bart (1650–1702) represents the strong and important French privateering tradition. Sailing from Dunkirk, the best sited of French privateering ports, he won both military and commercial success. He also exemplifies the blurred line between service in the king's navy and sailing as a privateer, for he crossed that line, spending most of the Nine Years War commanding squadrons of the king's vessels. Réné Duguay-Trouin (1673–1736), the youngest of the lot, ranks as the king of the privateers. This hard-living sailor came of a good family who set him up with his own ship as a privateer at age eighteen when his taste for women made it clear that the family's initial intention that he enter the church would not do. He sailed from Brest and St Malo during the War of the Spanish Succession to great success, carrying out the most audacious and lucrative raid of that war at Rio de Janeiro.

Guerre d'escadre

Guerre d'escadre, the clash of fleets, presents the classic picture of warfare at sea in the age of fighting sail. Adversaries arrayed in line ahead across from each other closed to less than a hundred yards as they thundered volley after volley. This style of warfare, though dramatic and deadly, was, all too often, disappointing. *Guerre d'escadre* was still in its infancy, and ultimately success depended not on tactical brilliance but on sheer numbers. And in this competition, the French were doomed to fail in the long run.

Tactics of guerre d'escadre

Combat between fleets at sea came down to cannon duels; the other tactical alternatives simply did not work very well. Fireships, which almost always accompanied a fleet on campaign, were intended to set enemy ships alight. Smaller expendable vessels filled with combustibles and explosives, fireships would be sailed ablaze at the foe, but it was not difficult to turn these vessels aside by sending longboats to grapple them. In fact, fireships were most useful against anchored ships which could not manoeuvre to avoid them. In line of battle they were of little or no value. Boarding, a venerable tactic at sea, retained its value for privateers who wished to seize a ship and cargo. However, to succeed, the vessel attempting to board had to concentrate its crew on deck to overwhelm the opponent while skilfully manoeuvring to come along side; all this called not only for fine seamanship and luck but it also left the exposed boarders particularly vulnerable to a heavily gunned opponent. In addition, boarding tactics would force an aggressive squadron to break apart and attack an enemy ship by ship, something late seventeenth-century admirals were loath to do. The only other major tactic of sailing fleets was to fire mortar shells from the new bomb ketches, an innovation of the 1680s, but this destructive technique was valuable only against stationary targets – essentially bomb ketches were a tool for shore bombardment.

Thus, mighty fleets fought in line ahead, with one ship following another, as they hurled cannonballs at the foe. Opposing lines had to come very close, often to pistol range or less, because the natural inaccuracy of smoothbore cannon, multiplied by inadequate aiming practices and the unavoidable pitching of a ship, rendered gunfire nearly random at greater distances. Line ahead tactics allowed fleets to coordinate vessels which were of different sizes, speeds, and manoeuvrability in a united and simple formation. Line ahead also did not ask too much of captains and crews of varying abilities. Simplicity was a real advantage, as the seventeenth-century French naval commentator Hoste wrote, 'Moreover, naval evolutions are very simple and assume no knowledge of geometry. A little application with the experience of two or three campaigns will suffice to give the least able all the use of evolutions.'[80]

Gunfights at sea did not allow commanders many tactical choices. Fleets could strive to take the weather or lee gauge. Seventeenth-century ships of the line were square-rigged vessels that relied on the wind to push them through the waves; therefore, they could only make headway if the wind was coming from a direction relatively behind them. In the language of the sea, they could not sail close to the wind. Wind obviously strongly influenced battle tactics, and one of the key decisions a naval commander made was to strive to be windward or leeward of his enemy. (For landlubbers, windward is the direction from which the wind is blowing, and leeward is the direction or side opposite from that.) Fighting on a windward gauge a ship would be better able to close with its opponent, since the wind would push it toward its foe. This made it superior for an aggressive commander. However, it also had disadvantages. The force of the wind keeled a ship over a bit, and if sufficiently strong might force a ship to windward to close its lower gun ports to keep the sea from pouring in. Thus, a strong wind could effectively rob a ship to windward of its largest armament, since the heaviest cannon were carried on the lowest deck to increase stability. The leeward gauge suited

---

80 Hoste in Dessert, *La Royale*, pp. 266–7.

more cautious tactics, because it made it easier to sail away from the enemy and because a damaged ship which could no longer manoeuvre well would naturally drift behind the cover of its own fleet instead of drifting into the dangerous area between the contending fleets, as it would tend to do if it was windward of its enemies.

Captains could also direct their crews to fire at their opponents' hulls or rigging. Firing at the hull attempted to damage the ship's structure, dismount its cannon, and kill its crew. Perhaps in the mayhem below decks fires would start, consuming the ship and exploding its gunpowder. Firing at the rigging tore sails and brought down spars and masts, hindering the use of cannon on the open deck and making the ship unmanoeuvrable or dead in the water. Such a ship would impede its own fleet and become an easier and safer target for its foes, who could capture or attack it later. Firing at the rigging seemed to suit the leeward gauge, because there the force of the wind elevated a ship's guns, making it easier to strike at an enemy's rigging. Moreover, the same caution that advised assuming the leeward gauge also advised hamstringing a foe by damaging his rigging rather than closing to attack his hull. In general, the French favoured the leeward gauge and fired at rigging, while the English preferred the windward gauge and fired at hulls.

The number of cannon that major fleets mounted was staggering by contemporary standards. As previously noted, Saint-Rémy theorized that the ideal artillery train for a field army of 50,000 men should include 50 cannon, 40 of which were light 8- and 4-pounders. At the Battle of Neerwinden in 1693, Marshal Luxembourg, in command of as large a field army as Louis XIV ever committed to a single battle, brought with him 71 cannon. A single ship of the line could carry as many guns, and all of them would be heavy pieces. At Beachy Head in 1690, Tourville's fleet boasted 4,600 cannon against the 4,153 guns in the allied fleet, and at the Battle of Velez-Málaga in 1704, the French fleet alone fire 102,886 cannonballs from 3,522 cannon.

Yet despite the thousands of guns brought to bear in a fleet action, cannon fire was not especially deadly to wooden vessels. Cannonballs punched holes through hulls, but these could be patched without much difficulty; simply stuffing a sailor's hammock into the hole could effectively seal it to the sea. Moreover, shots rarely damaged a ship below the waterline, because the water killed or deflected the balls. The best chance to sink an enemy ship was not holing it, but setting it afire with a fortunate shot, for fire was the worst enemy of a wooden warship.

Decisive battles and decisive numbers

Seventeenth-century sea battles were not particularly decisive. It was next to impossible to inflict losses of ships or men on such a level that they would reduce an enemy to impotence for long. The number of ships sunk would not in itself be catastrophic, even in a major defeat at sea. At Beachy Head the English and Dutch fleets lost only ten ships, and at the disaster of La Hogue two years later, Tourville lost no ships during the actual fighting, but fifteen after his fleet disengaged and withdrew toward Brest. And since ships were not that difficult to replace, the French soon made good their losses. Similarly, the loss of life in battle was relatively modest. Victory at Beachy Head cost the French navy only 344 men killed and 811 wounded, while success at Fleurus the same year cost the French army about 3,000 killed and 3,000 wounded. In addition, because fleet battles were slugging matches which wore down victor as well as vanquished, exploitation of tactical success was limited. As the English admiral Shovell explained in the year of Beachy Head, 'at sea, if the fleets be near equal, there must be great success to win a great victory, for by the time one is beaten the other generally is weary'.[81]

Awed by the victories won by Horatio Lord Nelson and influenced by the naval theories of Alfred Thayer Mahan, which post-dated the career of Tourville by a century and more, historians have condemned Louis's navy for its ultimate failure to gain command of the sea by *guerre d'escadre*. However, more recent considerations of the French situation have led to a better understanding of the structural limitations that made it unlikely or impossible for Bourbon France to carry off lasting victory against the Maritime Powers at sea. France suffered serious and unavoidable disadvantages in comparison with its maritime enemies, particularly England. The most oppressive would be Louis's paramount need to maintain a large army; there will be more to say about that below. But there were other problems as well. And even the limited resources that the French could devote to the navy had to be split between two seas, making it difficult to concentrate the Brest and Toulon fleets against a single foe. The lack of good ports between Brest and Dunkirk also put the French at a great disadvantage when confronting the English in the Channel. If the French were defeated, their ships could not find safe harbour; this explains the loss of ships after the initial sea fight at La Hogue. In contrast, a

---

81 Sir Clowdesley Shovell in 1690, Symcox, *Crisis of French Sea Power*, p. 56, from Herbert Richmond, *The Navy as an Instrument of Policy, 1558–1727* (Cambridge, 1953), p. 202.

defeated English fleet could find ready shelter, limiting the impact of any French victory. However, an emphasis on sea battle may miss the point altogether, for, given the characteristics of ships and tactics, sea battles may have not had the potential to yield decisive results, at least in the long run. Numerous inconclusive fights suggest that the most effective use of fleets may have been in simply positioning a force correctly to bar trade or drive a foe's naval vessels back to port, as did the English and Dutch fleet in 1694–95, when by shifting to the Mediterranean it made a French siege of Barcelona impossible.

Decision did not come down to battle but to numbers, and once the Allies enjoyed a clear superiority, the French found it wise not to contest them in fleet actions. In a particularly perceptive analysis, the historian Geoffrey Symcox writes, 'Ascendancy could only be attained as the result of a long, cumulative process in which one side built up a crushing numerical superiority; in the end victory became a matter of aggregate numbers.'[82] This was a competition the French could not win from the 1690s on. It had been one thing for the French to take on the Dutch alone at sea during the 1670s, but in Louis's last two wars the combined English and Dutch fleets were simply too much for the French to handle. Against the Dutch, the French enjoyed a considerable numerical advantage by the midst of the Dutch War, as Table 3.2 makes clear. However, owing to the need to maintain a huge army during a long war of attrition exacerbated by famine and financial crisis, the French fell behind the Allies in ship construction during the Nine Years War. At the start of that conflict, the French fleet had 118 rated vessels and a total of 295 ships of all types; by the end Louis could claim 137 rated vessels, which amounted to only a small increase. In contrast, the English fleet started the war with 173 ships and ended it with 323.[83] From 1694 to 1697 the French built 19 first to fifth rate ships, totalling 15,410 tons, while the English constructed 58 such ships, totalling 41,844 tons and the Dutch added another 22.[84] Thus, the Allies outbuilt the French four to one. Table 3.3 demonstrates just how dramatically the allied fleets came to outnumber and outclass the French, until by 1700 they enjoyed a

[82] Symcox, *Crisis of French Sea Power*, p. 57.
[83] Ibid., pp. 42, 77; Dessert, *La Royale*, annex 7, pp. 301–2.
[84] French totals include some warships financed by private funds. Symcox, *Crisis of French Sea Power*, appendix 2, pp. 235–7, from J. C. de Jonge, *Geschiedenis van het Nederlandsche zeewezen* (5 vols; 1st edn, Amsterdam, 1833–48, 2nd edn, Haarlem, 1858–62), vol. iii, pp. 730–4; R. C. Anderson, *English Ships 1649–1702* (London, 1966); and Pierre Le Conte, *French Ships, 1648–1700* (Cambridge, 1935).

Table 3.2 Comparative sizes of Dutch and French battle fleets, 1670–80

Year	Dutch battle fleet Warships	Displacement in tons	French battle fleet Warships	Displacement in tons
1670	129	102,000	120	114,000
1675	111	89,000	134	138,000
1680	93	66,000	135	135,000

Source: Figures from Jan Glete, *Navies and Nations: Warships and State Building in Europe and America, 1500–1860* (2 vols; Stockholm, 1993), vol. i, p. 199.

Table 3.3 Comparative sizes of allied and French battle fleets, 1690–1700

Year	English and Dutch battle fleets Warships	Displacement in tons	French battle fleet Warships	Displacement in tons
1690	135	171,000	89	122,000
1695	189	236,000	119	190,000
1700	210	271,000	108	176,000

Source: Figures from Jan Glete, *Navies and Nations: Warships and State Building in Europe and America, 1500–1860* (2 vols; Stockholm, 1993), vol. i, pp. 220, 226.

two to one advantage. Victory lay not in destruction of enemy vessels but in construction of your own.

Just like warfare on land, conflict at sea became attrition above all, a match in which the goal was to outlast rather than to destroy one's opponent. Little wonder, then, that both the English and the French adopted theories of a 'fleet in being' at this time. Both believed that the very existence of a fleet was key, perhaps more important than risking it on campaign.[85] Seventeenth-century naval war had its own logic; sea battle was not particularly decisive, and fleets may have lacked the technology and knowledge to alter the character of combat. Nelson would fight with different ships and captains a century later.

[85] Symcox, *Crisis of French Sea Power*, p. 68.

Guerre de course

War against enemy maritime commerce, in contrast to war against the enemy fleet, had a long history as a secondary option for French naval strategy, but the crisis of the Nine Years War convinced the French to embrace *guerre de course* as their primary naval strategy and to abandon *guerre d'escadre*. *Guerre de course* may not have been considered as honourable as *guerre d'escadre*, but it was a reasonable and even wise choice. In a war of attrition, it made perfect sense to try to undermine the sea-borne trade of the Maritime Powers, particularly when a direct assault on the larger allied fleet threatened to lead only to frustration or defeat.

Even when the French still attempted to challenge English and Dutch main forces at sea, commerce was always seen as a valid target both for the fleet and for privateers. In 1693, Louis instructed Tourville to employ his fleet to attack the great allied commercial convoy headed for the Mediterranean. Privateers reaped considerable profits before the emphasis on *guerre de course*. In fact, in 1689, the prize courts, those judicial and administrative bodies charged with handling the prizes in port, were so swamped with captured enemy vessels, or prizes, that they authorized French privateers to ransom ships back to their owners at sea rather than to sail them back to France.

The logic behind guerre de course

Only in 1694–95 did the French question the validity of continuing *guerre d'escadre*, and they did so for compelling reasons. It would be tempting to see the defeat at La Hogue in 1692 as a deciding factor, but this would be misleading. In fact, the next year Louis armed a far larger fleet and sent it to sea. The true precipitating factor was the crop failure of 1693–94 and the subsequent famine, economic catastrophe, and fiscal crisis. This was one of the two major ecological disasters of Louis's reign, and it came in the midst of a costly war. With state revenues sure to plummet, hard choices had to be made. This forced Louis to consider the iron law of French naval strategy – although France possessed a long coastline and benefited from maritime commerce, armies, not navies, were paramount to the country's survival. In the words of one important French administrator, Chamillart, who downplayed the need for a battle fleet in 1694, 'I am convinced that there is nothing more important than to have a force of troops sufficient to prevent the enterprises that the enemy may try on land, those at sea being far more uncertain and less dangerous.' He concluded that royal funds 'are insufficient to support both land and sea forces at the same rate as hitherto'.[86] Armies that had expanded to unprecedented size demanded unprecedented resources, and the navy would suffer. This is why the French did not return to *guerre d'escadre* even when the economy took an upturn after 1695.

No less a figure than Vauban devoted his very considerable talent and authority to the question of *guerre de course* in a 'Mémoire concernant la caprerie' in 1695.[87] This was not the first time he considered this question, since he had addressed a letter to Louvois on the subject in 1675, when he suggested that with more support from the navy, French privateers 'would do much more harm to the Dutch by their piracy than all our land armies'.[88] Vauban's memoir argued that 'one will find that all the great fleets have been very expensive, and that all have turned to pure loss', so other means had to be employed. Because of its potential to hamstring allied commerce and because it was 'the easiest, the least expensive, the least hazardous . . . to the state', *guerre de course* should become the preferred naval strategy for France.

While the French could ill afford even to maintain their navy at its current levels, they definitely could not pay the bill to add to the size of their fleet so as to keep pace with allied naval increases. The budget for the sailing ship navy declined from a peak in 1692 of 29,007,000 livres to 13,728,000 livres in 1695, a decrease of 52.7 per cent. During these same years, the army budget fell from 109,890,000 livres to 100,005,000 livres, only a 9.0 per cent decline during the same financial crisis.[89] In other words, budgetary restraint hit the navy nearly six times as hard.

So the French navy eschewed *guerre d'escadre* from 1695, at least in northern waters; it would only mount a battle fleet in the Mediterranean where it could fight with advantage. However, the change away from *guerre d'escadre* to *guerre de course* involved more than leaving the Brest battle fleet in port; it meant adopting policies and practices to aid privateers. Procedures for adjudicating prizes were streamlined and tilted to the benefit of the entrepreneurs

---

86 Budget plan prepared by Michel Chamillart for Mme de Maintenon, 14 July 1694, in ibid., p. 149.
87 'Mémoire concernant la caprerie', 30 November 1695, in Rochas d'Aiglun, *Vauban*, vol. i, pp. 454–61. 'Caprerie' was another word for commerce raiding.
88 Letter of 31 August 1675 from Vauban to Louvois, in ibid., vol. ii, p. 124.
89 These budgetary figures come from AN, KK 355, 'État par abrégé des recettes et dépenses, 1662–1700'. The army budget is calculated here as the sum of the following accounts: *extraordinaire* and *ordinaire des guerres*, *garnisons*, *étapes*, *pain de munition*, *artillerie*, *fortifications*, *gratifications aux troupes*, and *gratifications aux marechaux*.

who fitted out vessels for *guerre de course*. Vauban suggested just such reform to make this warlike commerce more attractive to *armateurs*, as these privateering entrepreneurs were known. In addition, the king offered to lease royal war vessels to private contractors at very favourable terms. There was actually provision to do this in 1688 as well, but that ordinance demanded that two-thirds of the profit from such a venture go to the king.[90] An October 1694 regulation changed the terms: *armateurs* received ships from the king fully equipped and provisioned; they would not be responsible for damage or loss of the ships, nor would they have to pay for provisions or ammunition consumed in cruising against enemy commerce; and the state would receive only 20 per cent of the net profit from the voyage.[91] The state might even raise the crew by naval conscription in some cases, although the *armateurs* had to pay them. If *armateurs* wanted fine new war vessels, the king would supply the building materials from royal ship yards, and the *armateurs* would simply hire the labour. The ships thus built would revert to the navy only after the *armateurs* had recouped their costs. Such a privatization of the navy shocks modern sensibilities, but as Chamillart commented, 'it seems to me that it would be better to put the ships to some use, rather than let them sit idle on the pretext of some conception of honour which is purely imaginary'.[92] Considering that the army depended on tapping the private wealth and credit of its officer corps, it must have seemed reasonable that the navy could mobilize private sources to continue its maritime war.

The tactics and take of guerre de course
Privateers cruised as individuals and also sailed as squadrons. The great majority of *armateurs* sent out small cruisers mounting only a few cannon. A regulation of 1681 stipulated that privateers carry at least six cannon, but this order was not always obeyed. Since they preferred to take their targets by boarding if it came to a fight and because they might have to supply men to sail a prize back to port, privateering vessels tended to have large crews relative to the size of the ships. As a rule, privateers preferred not to fight, but would rather take their prizes simply by threat, because fighting caused damage that cut into profits. Of the 2,000 or so prizes registered at the prize court of St Malo during the Nine Years War, only about fifty

---

90 Symcox, *Crisis of French Sea Power*, p. 77.
91 Ibid., pp. 174–5.
92 Budget plan prepared by Michel Chamillart for Mme de Maintenon, 14 July 1694, in ibid., p. 149.

were taken by fighting.[93] Some *armateurs* created whole squadrons complete with ships of the line, but such expensive ventures were uncommon; there were only about fifteen such French privateering squadrons during the Nine Years War. These squadrons could engage in major combat at sea or even engage in amphibious operations. While too small to accommodate the fleet, French Channel ports were well placed for privateers, lying as they did on the flanks of allied trade routes. St Malo and Dunkirk served the privateers particularly well. Dunkirk posed such a threat that the English devoted as many as thirty ships to blockading the port.

The most impressive acts of the *armateurs* were associated with the privateer squadrons.[94] The marquis of Nesmond mounted a venture with seven ships of the line and several frigates in 1695. In addition to other prizes, he captured ships of the English East India Company, richly laden with goods from the east; these ships alone are said to have yielded 10,000,000 livres, and gave his investors a handsome profit. In 1697 Pointis led another privateer squadron of seven ships of the line, three frigates, and one bomb ketch to attack Cartagena in modern-day Colombia. This colonial raid landed and seized the town, taking another 10,000,000 livres of booty from it. Duguay-Trouin's raid on Rio de Janeiro in 1711 exacted a ransom of 2,200,000 livres from that colonial town. There was little effective difference between squadrons of privateers and squadrons of the king's vessels. In May 1696 the famous Jean Bart slipped the allied blockade of Dunkirk in command of a royal squadron and raided into the North Sea. Bart as a king's officer still carried out *guerre de course*, striking a Dutch convoy and burning forty-five of its ships. He was so effective that he tied down about fifty enemy vessels.

The symbiosis of naval and land warfare

Much has been written condemning Louis's eventual reliance upon *guerre de course*, including the classic *Influence of Sea Power upon History, 1660–1783* by Mahan.[95] Mahan argued that the proper goal of a great navy was to maintain overseas commerce, and deny it to the enemy, by achieving 'command of the sea' through fleet actions.

93 Ibid., p. 69.
94 For more information on privateers, see John S. Bromley, *Corsairs and Navies, 1660–1760* (London, 1986).
95 Alfred Thayer Mahan first published his *The Influence of Sea Power upon History, 1660–1783* in 1890. This book and his other voluminous publications defined naval strategy from the late nineteenth through most of the twentieth century.

He saw sea power as the deciding factor in the seventeenth century and failed to recognize that the wars of Louis XIV were primarily land wars of attrition. In Mahan's opinion, the Sun King committed a fatal error in abandoning *guerre d'escadre*. However, close examination leads one to question if *guerre d'escadre* as practised by the French ever matched Mahan's criteria in the first place and, thus, if the abandonment of this strategy really meant what Mahan thought it did.

Louis did not use his fleets in a Mahanian fashion to achieve command of the sea; rather, French fleet operations were usually related to land campaigns. Louis charged his navy with amphibious operations against Sicily and Ireland and with attempts to land troops in England. These operations were all designed primarily as diversions to draw enemy attention and resources elsewhere and thus aid French land campaigns on the Continent. In more obvious support of the army, the navy took part in sieges of Mediterranean coastal towns in order to cork the bottle formed by French siege lines on land. The French navy also carried out its own assaults on coastal targets without the aid of the army when it bombarded towns from the sea, as in the case of Genoa. Fleet actions directed precisely to control the sea lanes and cut off the flow of commerce were comparatively rare, although Tourville's campaigns of 1691 and 1693 qualify.

As different as the navy was from the army – and they were very different – the two existed and developed within a unique symbiosis. It is difficult to avoid the conclusion that Louis regarded his navy as an extension of his army. During wartime, Louis defined the most important role of his navy as protecting the coast of France from enemy sea-borne invasion. Fear of hostile descents upon land of France repeatedly obsessed Louis, who regarded any violation of his territory as anathema. In this, the ultimate task, the Sun King viewed the army and the navy as alternative solutions to the same problem. Ultimately, Louis's advisers determined that it was equally effective and far less costly to respond to the coastal threat with fortifications and land forces rather than with an expensive war fleet. This either/ or logic made the fleet vulnerable, even expendable, when the king faced the difficult necessity of allocating limited resources during long wars of attrition. The change from *guerre d'escadre* to *guerre de course* recognized that a battle fleet was a luxury beyond Louis's means, while the army was essential to French success.

This switch also recognized, however, that the French could carry out one of the essential tasks of a naval war of attrition, damaging enemy commerce, without putting a battle fleet to sea. Paradoxically, because *guerre d'escadre* had so often been linked with land operations, by turning to *guerre de course* directed against sea-borne commerce and colonial wealth, the French adopted a more thoroughly naval strategy, one independent of dictates imposed by land campaigns. It may have fallen short of Nelsonian, or Mahanian, ideals, but it suited French purposes and possibilities during the wars of Louis XIV.

During the personal reign of the Sun King, his army and navy developed in certain fundamentally similar ways. Both expanded to unprecedented size; both underwent major reform; both became far more professional and capable. However, both were also ill suited to produce decisive results. And, to the navy's detriment, both were very expensive and drew from the same pool of resources, a fact that compelled the king to choose between the two when that pool threatened to run dry. His choice was no choice, for it was clear that Louis had to maintain the army first and foremost. Ultimately it was obvious to all: Louis's wars were always at their core European land wars.

4 WARS OF *GLOIRE*: THE WAR OF DEVOLUTION AND THE DUTCH WAR

Louis's first two wars were fought for glory and the inheritance of Philip IV of Spain. In a number of ways the two wars are best seen as one, broken by a four years' truce. Given the *mentalité* of the young Louis XIV, the War of Devolution and the Dutch War were all but inevitable. The king had to establish his greatness through military action, and he believed, or wanted to believe, that he could legitimately claim Spanish lands through his wife. So unlike his last two wars, Louis sought these conflicts with eyes wide open; he did not back into them. Unfortunately for Louis, he so established an image of the ambitious conqueror in these conflicts that he never overcame it, even though it can be argued he had already moderated his goals and perceptions before these wars were over.

LOGIC OF THE WAR OF DEVOLUTION

The Treaty of the Pyrenees that ended France's long war with Spain in 1659 presented Louis with a Spanish wife, the infanta Marie Thérèse, daughter of Philip IV by his first marriage. While she explicitly renounced her claims to any Spanish inheritance, she did so contingent upon the payment of a dowry of 500,000 escudos, a figure so high that it was never paid. Thus from an entirely legalistic point of view, Marie Thérèse retained any claims she had. But such a narrowly construed argument misses the point that Louis would probably never have accepted that any treaty could alter the divinely sanctioned rules of inheritance.

When Philip IV died in September 1665, he was succeeded by his son by a second marriage, the sickly boy of five, Carlos II. Louis did not dispute that the crown belonged to Carlos, but he claimed that, according to the law of Spanish Netherlands, the daughter from a first marriage retained rights to inherit goods and property over a son of a second marriage – that property 'devolved' upon the earlier children. On this fairly flimsy legal reed of devolution, Louis rested claims on parts of the Spanish Netherlands for his wife. Marie Thérèse's more legitimate rights would ultimately spark the War of the Spanish Succession, but that was over thirty years in the future. At this point, the young Louis was asserting his own claims to be a grand monarch through the device of protecting his wife's rights.

Louis prepared for this War of Devolution by beefing up his military and by preparing the diplomatic ground. The French army shrank to a force of perhaps 50,000 men in the years immediately following the Treaty of the Pyrenees, but Louis began to build up troop strength in 1665 so that by 1667 it had climbed to 80,000. Louis expected the Dutch to accede to his wishes in the Netherlands because of long-standing French support for the Dutch in past conflicts with Spain. In addition, after the Treaty of the Pyrenees, Louis concluded a defensive alliance with the Dutch, and lived up to its terms; when the bishop of Münster occupied Dutch territory in 1665–66, French intervention forced him to withdraw his forces. France also stood by the Dutch in their war with the English that broke out in 1666. With Spain weak, particularly in the Southern Netherlands, with England tied up in a war with the United Provinces, and with the Dutch friendly to France, Louis saw a clear path to conquest.

CONDUCT OF THE WAR OF DEVOLUTION

The war began in grand style as the French attack, spearheaded by the main army led by Marshal Turenne, advanced into Spanish territory on 24 May 1667. 'The King left ... with the most handsome and pretentious suites that anyone could ever see. There were eight in his carriage; the king, the queen, Monsieur, the duchess of Orléans, the duchess of Monpensier, the duchess de la Vallière, the countess of Bethume, and the marquise of Montespan.'[1] The image of the king riding to war in the company of his wife and two of his mistresses – la Vallière and Montespan – seems all too fitting in this struggle designed to prove the masculine glory of the young monarch. Throughout his first wars, he would go to the front accompanied by members of the court, including ladies.

This brief conflict was essentially a walkover by mighty France against feeble Spain. It saw some skirmishes but no great field battle;

---

1 Saint Maucice in John B. Wolf, *Louis XIV* (New York, 1968), p. 201. Monsieur was the king's brother, Philippe, duke of Orléans; the duchess of Monpensier was the king's cousin. I have altered this quotation somewhat to be consistent with the forms of names employed in this volume.

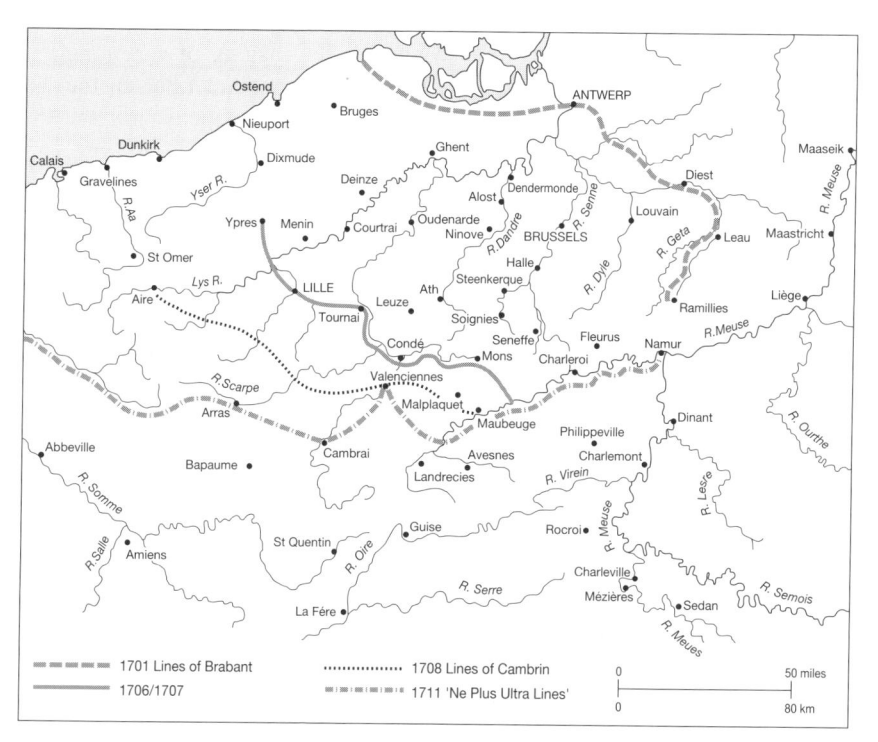

Map 4.1 The battleground of Europe: the Spanish Low Countries
Adapted from: Gabriel Hanoteau, ed., *Histoire de la nation française*,
vol. vii, *Histoire militaire et navale*, pt i (Paris, 1925); John A. Lynn,
Giant of the Grand Siècle: The French Army, 1610–1715 (New York,
1997); and Christopher Duffy, *The Fortress in the Age of Vauban and
Frederick the Great, 1660–1789, Siege Warfare*, vol. ii (London, 1985)

instead it was a war of seizures and sieges. Bergues, Ath, Charleroi, Tournai, Douai, Oudenarde, and Alost fell immediately or after only very brief sieges. Only Lille held out for long. Louis attended this siege; Marshal Turenne exercised effective command over the army of 30,000, while the engineers Clerville and Vauban directed the siege. French cavalry invested the fortress – on 28 August. The king arrived on 10 September in time to witness the digging of very long lines of circumvallation, which ran fifteen miles around Lille. In the next stage of the siege, the approach trenches were opened on the night of 18–19 September.

The garrison sortied out to attack the French on the morning of 19 September, but to no effect. The first French batteries opened fire at daybreak two days later. Troops from the Gardes françaises and the Regiments of Picardy and Orléans assaulted the chemin couvert at midnight on 25 September, and the next night attacked *demi-lunes*, or fortress outworks in the ditch. Finally the governor, or commander, of the fortress ordered his troops to the beat the chamade, a drum call signalling a willingness to parley, and he surrendered the fortress and town. By his timely surrender, the governor won for his troops the honours of war, and the surviving garrison of 2,500 troops marched out the next day and headed down the road to the Spanish fortress of Ypres.

Meanwhile French success worried the Dutch. They had been fighting a naval war with the English since 1665 and had humiliated their foe by burning the English fleet at the Medway in June 1667. However, because a tired and inactive Spain promised to be a better neighbour than a powerful and aggressive France, the Dutch felt some urgency in turning their attentions south, so they signed a treaty with the English at Breda on 21 July to free their hands. By the end of January 1668, the United Provinces, England, and Sweden concluded the Triple Alliance, which declared that Spain must accede to demands of Louis XIV for certain towns, but that if Louis increased his demands or continued his conquests, the Allies would fight to reestablish the borders of 1659. Louis regarded this as a betrayal, a Dutch betrayal.

Despite the declaration of the Triple Alliance, some fighting continued to the south. The prince of Condé, who had remained in Burgundy in semi-disgrace since his return to France, now received command of the troops who invaded and took Franche-Comté in February, having met no substantial resistance. Louis accompanied the successful troops.

THE TREATY OF AIX-LA-CHAPELLE AND PREPARATION FOR THE DUTCH WAR

Unprepared to resist the Triple Alliance, the French concluded the Treaty of Aix-la-Chapelle with Spain on 2 May 1668. Turenne opposed the peace, since he believed that he could have conquered the Spanish Netherlands in that year. While the French returned Franche-Comté (but only after dismantling its defences), they received several important towns, including Oudenarde, Tournai, and, especially, Lille. Louis celebrated a success, but harboured deep resentment of the Dutch. He had been stopped short of his goal and prepared to gain what he was convinced should be his. Even Vauban counselled, 'There is no judge more equitable than cannons. They go directly to the goal and they are not corruptible. See to it that the king takes them as arbiters if he wishes to have good and quick justice for his rightful claims.'[2] Fittingly, French cannon at this time were emblazoned with the motto 'Ultima Ratio Regis', the final argument of the king.

Louis clearly felt betrayed by an ally the French had supported for generations, and not too long after signing the Treaty of Aix-la-Chapelle he began to set the stage for a new war. He certainly regarded Dutch behaviour as treachery and was offended by what he saw as Dutch pride. An indignant Louis accused them of 'ingratitude, bad faith, and insupportable vanity'.[3] Louis, whose emblem was the sun, broiled at a medal struck honouring the anti-French diplomat Coenraad van Beuningen, showing him as Joshua stopping the sun in the sky. The Dutch must be taught to never again block the path and policy of France. Louis carefully prepared for this war over several years; it would not be a last-minute affair.

Before he could settle the score with the Dutch, Louis had to dismantle the Triple Alliance. Skilful diplomacy and the judicious use of money accomplished the task. Payments to the regency government in Sweden convinced it to abandon the alliance. Louis also drove a wedge between the Dutch and English by buying the support of King Charles II, who chafed under Parliament's power. In the secret Treaty of Dover, 1 June 1670, he agreed to declare himself a Catholic when it would be expedient and to break with the Dutch; in exchange, Louis promised him a fat subsidy of 2,000,000 livres and up to 6,000 troops to put down civil disturbance in England. Beyond

---

2 AG, A^{1}228, 13 October 1668, Vauban to Louvois in ibid., p. 211.
3 Louis in a memoir printed in Camille Rousset, *Histoire de Louvois* (4 vols; Paris, 1862–64), vol. i, p. 517.

this, Charles could expect yearly subsidies of 3,000,000 livres if he joined a war against the Dutch. Louis successfully misled John de Witt, who as the Grand Pensionary of Holland was the most powerful Dutch political figure at this time. Charles assisted in the deception, repeatedly assuring the Dutch of his friendship. De Witt, who was also talking with the French at this time, made what was to be a fatal mistake by believing, in the words of his biographer, 'that if worse came to worse a settlement could always be made with France'.[4] By late summer 1670, rumour spread of the Treaty of Dover. Still, during 1671, when war seemed likely and increasingly inevitable, De Witt hoped to avert a French attack by convincing the Spanish to pacify the French with a limited surrender of territory.

Louis also worked to neutralize Germany as best he could before undertaking his next war. Bavaria and Saxony would join the French camp, while Brandenburg switched back and forth. Frederick William, the Great Elector of Brandenburg, was caught diplomatically, if not physically, between Leopold I and Louis XIV, and feared each.[5] Frederick William had married a daughter of the Dutch house of Orange, and his Calvinist faith also drew him to the Dutch. However, state interest was more ambiguous. He stayed aloof from the Triple Alliance, and Louis rewarded him with a subsidy and supported his candidate for the crown of Poland, a prime concern of Frederick William. In 1669, Louis began negotiations which led to a secret treaty with the Great Elector in January 1670, although this was not directed against the Dutch. However, at this time Louis's more aggressive policies alienated many German states that then let their membership in the Rhine League lapse in 1666–67. When a French army seized Lorraine in August 1670, this further threatened the Germans. Lorraine lay across the path from Paris to Louis's new possessions in Alsace. Lorraine also bordered on Champagne and gave an enemy a quick invasion route threatening the French capital. Lorraine had sided against France in the Thirty Years War, and Louis wanted to remove the anxiety of having a potential enemy so close to the heart of France. But driving Duke Charles IV of Lorraine from his lands in peacetime struck Europeans as an extreme action.

---

4 Hobert H. Rowen, *John de Witt, Grand Pensionary of Holland, 1625–1672* (Princeton, NJ, 1978), p. 737.

5 See Derek McKay, 'Small-Power Diplomacy in the Age of Louis XIV: The Foreign Policy of the Great Elector during the 1660s and 1670s', in Robert Oresko, G. C. Gibbs, and Hamish Scott, eds, *Royal and Republican Sovereignty in Early Modern Europe* (Cambridge, 1997), pp. 118–215.

Understandably, Charles would lead allied troops against Louis in the Dutch War. Louis had originally wanted to attack in 1671, but developments in Germany caused him to postpone the conflict for a year. As war approached in 1672, Brandenburg moved closer to the Dutch and finally concluded a treaty to aid them with 20,000 troops against France, but the Great Elector's army did not enter the war soon enough to oppose the initial French invasion of the United Provinces. While Emperor Leopold I encouraged Brandenburg's aid to the Dutch, he avoided a commitment. In 1668, Louis and Leopold concluded a treaty to partition Spanish lands at a time when it was expected that Carlos II would die soon. This evidence of *rapprochement* was followed in November 1671 by another treaty that promised Leopold's neutrality in case of a Franco-Dutch War. By this treaty Leopold sought to limit the extent of the war, and he made his agreement conditional upon the preservation of the settlements reached in the treaties of Münster and Aix-la-Chapelle concerning Germany and the Spanish Netherlands.

Preparation for the war was far more than simply diplomatic. After the War of Devolution, the army, which had expanded to a paper strength of 134,000 during the war, returned to a peacetime force of about 70,000, but Louis added 20,000 new men in 1670 and continued to flesh out the army in 1671 so that it reached a strength of 120,000 in February 1672; and before he declared war, Louis issued orders to expand the army by a further 26,000.[6]

The logistic arrangements made for the coming conflict demonstated the great abilities of Louis's great minister of war, Louvois. This tireless and highly capable administrator literally inherited his post as secretary of state for war from his father, Michel Le Tellier. Louvois began learning the ropes and sharing responsibility with his father from 1662; after 1670 he was essentially in charge, although his father resigned officially only in 1677. The well-born nobles of court looked down on his meagre pedigree – he came from a recently ennobled robe family – his fat appearance, and his domineering personality. Saint-Simon described Louvois as 'haughty, brutal, coarse', while to Primi Visconti he had a 'hard and violent character'.[7] During a procession of the knights of the Order of the Holy Spirit, an order

---

[6] Paul Sonnino, *Louis XIV and the Origins of the Dutch War* (Cambridge, 1988), pp. 127–8, 155, 162, 177; Rousset, *Histoire de Louvois*, vol. i, pp. 346–7; AG, Bibliothèque du ministère de guerre, Tiroirs de Louis XIV, pp. 46–8, 50–64, 76–7.

[7] Saint-Simon and Primi Visconti in André Corvisier, *Louvois* (Paris, 1983), pp. 151–2.

to which Louvois belonged, the wife of Philippe of Orléans yelled 'See how Louvois has the air of a bourgeois! . . . No Order can hide his condition.'[8] In defence of Louvois, it can be argued that Louis could not have brought his officer corps to heel without an agent so thick-skinned and aggressive; in the words of his biographer, Camille Rousset, 'The genius of Louvois was will.'[9] During Louis's reign, the vast majority of his generals were of elevated birth and status, the social superiors of Louvois; almost two-thirds of the lieutenant-generals were titled nobility, and only one in fifteen were non-nobles.[10] Louvois could hardly be deferential and make himself obeyed. However, in the 1680s Louvois's tendency to favour force over finesse in the international arena encouraged Louis to bully his adversaries in ways that were both unnecessary and unwise.

Louvois demonstrated the potential of his magazine system by stocking necessary foodstuffs and materiel for the considerable forces that would march north. At the outset of the 1672 advance, he had accumulated enough grain for 200,000 rations a day for a full six months in magazines at Kaiserwerth, Dorsten, Liège, Charleroi, Ath, and Mézières.[11] In the same magazines he had collected extensive stores of other war material: cannon, cannonballs, lead, powder, grenades, entrenching tools, and a bridge train of thirty boats.

From a purely administrative perspective, the Dutch War stands as Louvois's *chef d'oeuvre* and Louis's most successful martial effort. After thirteen years of peace, interrupted only by the brief War of Devolution, the French enjoyed the benefit of Le Tellier's and Louvois's military reforms as well as cashing in on Colbert's fiscal and economic efforts. Through financial reform, the very able Colbert, aided by the return of peace, was able to build up a budgetary surplus year by year after 1662, except during the War of Devolution.[12] To be sure, the pressures of war would buckle and break much of Colbert's reform and bring back inefficient expedients, but the war began from a much more secure footing than did Louis's later conflicts.

---

8 Jean-Baptiste Primi Visconti, *Mémoires sur la cour de Louis XIV, 1673–81*, ed. Jean-François Solnon (Paris, 1988), p. 27.

9 Rousset, *Histoire de Louvois*, vol. i, p. 176.

10 See Corvisier's figures in Philippe Contamine, ed., *Histoire militaire de la France*, vol. i (Paris, 1992), pp. 542–3, and his article 'Les Généraux de Louis XIV et leur origine sociale', *XVIIe siècle* 42–3 (1959), pp. 23–53.

11 Louis XIV, *Oeuvres de Louis XIV*, eds Philippe Grimoard and Grouvelle (6 vols; Paris, 1806), vol. iii, pp. 116–17.

12 Pierre Goubert, *Louis XIV and Twenty Million Frenchmen*, trans. Anne Carter (New York, 1970), pp. 123–4.

THE OPENING PHASE OF THE DUTCH WAR, 1672-73

The Dutch War began with what seemed like an irresistible French juggernaut; however, by the end of the war's second year, Dutch resistance and the formation of an anti-French alliance compelled Louis to withdraw from the United Provinces and face a multi-front war. The actual fighting began in the spring of 1672 not with a French advance but with an English naval attack against a Dutch convoy in the Channel on 23 March 1672. Two weeks later, Louis eschewed the tradition of dispatching a herald to declare war and instead issued a manifesto announcing his motives on 6 April.

1672

The well-laid French plans directed three invading armies towards the Dutch Netherlands. Marshal Turenne with the main army of about 50,000 troops from Charleroi proceeded up the Sambre to the Meuse and then north along the left bank of that river. The Great Condé led another force from Sedan up the right bank of the Meuse, while in Westphalia, Lieutenant-General Luxembourg assembled an army composed mainly of France's German allies. Louis arrived at Charleroi to advance with Turenne's army on 5 May, while the marshal had already left Liège with half this force, heading for Maastricht. The rest of the army marched out of Charleroi on 11 May. Turenne and Condé met up finally at Visé, between Liège and Maastricht. After a council of war, Turenne's forces crossed the Meuse on a pontoon bridge, putting all the major forces on the right bank of the Meuse. The French bypassed Maastricht, but stormed the smaller nearby fortress of Maaseik to gain a base from which to contain the garrison of Maastricht. Because the French had stashed supplies at Liège and Kaiserwerth, they were moving toward their magazines, not away from them, when they left France.

After the fall of Maaseik, Louvois rushed north to Kaiserwerth to make ready for the king's arrival and to direct the preparation and supply of the allied German troops from Cologne and Münster. By late May the main French armies had reached Cleves, where Dutch garrisons had held several fortresses on the lower Rhine since the end of the Thirty Years War. In quick order Turenne's troops invested Orsoy and Rheinberg on 24 May and then surrounded Burick as well. Condé marched past to invest Wesel on 1 June. Louis boasted, 'I considered it more advantageous to my designs and less common for my *gloire* to attack four fortresses on the Rhine and to command in person all the sieges at the same time. I chose to that end Rheinberg, Wesel, Burick, and Orsoy.... I hope no one complains that I disappointed public expectations.'[13] With small garrisons, little hope of relief, and an adamant French attack, these four fortresses held out for a matter of days only. The fact is that throughout the wars of Louis XIV, most towns and fortresses fell in much less time than one would expect, and only a minority of cases required the full process of a lengthy formal siege.

With the lower Rhine secure from Cleves back down through Cologne, Louis could turn west against the United Provinces, which at first offered little defence. The Dutch army was small and ill prepared for war, with its 40,000 men mainly dispersed in garrisons. The Dutch appointed young William III, prince of Orange, as their captain-general in February, and he commanded a field force of only about 14,000.[14] As bad turned to worse, and riots rocked the Netherlands in early July, William took executive authority as stadholder, displacing from power the De Witt brothers, who were then lynched by an Orangist mob that held them responsible for the disasters suffered that year.

On 12 June French troops led by the Great Condé crossed the Rhine at Tolhuis. Louis would celebrate this crossing of the Rhine as one of his greatest military accomplishments, commemorating it allegorically in the great plaster medallion decorating the wall of the Salle de guerre at Versailles. In it, Louis, dressed as a Roman commander on horseback, hurdles fallen Germanic foes, symbolizing the Rhine. Actually, the Rhine splits into two arms as it crosses the Dutch border. The main flow is known as the Waal, and the lesser retains the name Rhine. It was this lesser Rhine that the French crossed. The original plan had been to build a bridge of much prized copper pontoons, but when this went too slowly, Condé impatiently decided to ford the river after finding a crossing where his horses would only have to swim about 200 paces. Batteries were established on the French side to drive defenders to cover, and French cavalry made their crossing under the eyes of their king, who was, in fact, angry at Condé for his ill-considered impetuosity. Condé, meanwhile, was wounded in the hand during the action. Once the bridgehead

13 *Oeuvres de Louis XIV*, vol. iii, p. 183, 31 May 1672, in Rousset, *Histoire de Louvois*, vol. i, p. 356.
14 Andrew Lossky, *Louis XIV and the French Monarchy* (New Brunswick, NJ, 1994), p. 143. Charles Sévin, marquis de Quincy, *Histoire militaire de Louis le Grand roi de France* (7 vols; Paris, 1726), vol. i, p. 326, states the size of William's field army as only about 13,000 after the French crossed the Rhine.

was secure, the French completed the pontoon bridge, and troops poured across. The crossing compromised Dutch defences along the Issel to the north, where Luxembourg's German troops had captured a number of towns, including Deventer. Now William dropped back after putting more troops in Nijmegen. Luxembourg's army would finally be rebuffed at Groningen, but only after ravaging much of the northern United Provinces.

William had little chance now of defending the province of Utrecht, even though his meagre forces had been supplemented with a few Spanish regiments supplied in accord with treaty obligations by the governor of the Spanish Netherlands, the count of Monterey. William fell back to the city of Utrecht, but the townspeople sent representatives to Louis to surrender the town to avoid a destructive siege. Louis made a grand entrance into Utrecht on 30 June.

Back toward the border with Cleves, Turenne's army invested Nijmegen, which boasted a garrison of 4,000 infantry and 400 cavalry, on 3 July. The French opened the trenches on the night of 4–5 July, and on 9 July the fortress capitulated since there was little hope of relief. The garrison marched out with the honours of war on 10 July as a reward for its speedy surrender. From Nijmegen, Turenne moved to Crève-Coeur, which fell in only two days.

At sea the Dutch had been much more effective than they had been on land, because their navy was in far better shape than their army. Admiral Michiel de Ruyter with seventy-five ships surprised a combined English and French fleet at Sole Bay on 7 June. When the French vessels under Count Jean d'Estrées withdrew, De Ruyter was able to mass against the English and deal out heavy punishment before De Ruyter retired when English reinforcements arrived. The day counted as a Dutch victory, but this was the last major naval action for over a year.

Faced with a seemingly irresistible invasion, the Dutch sued for peace, offering Louis generous terms in late June. Louis could take the Generality Lands, a band of territory on the south of the United Provinces which the Dutch had taken from the Spanish in Brabant and Flanders. In addition, the French could add Maastricht, as yet still in Dutch hands, plus an indemnity of 10,000,000 livres. The French foreign minister who succeeded Lionne after his death in 1671, Simon Arnauld, marquis of Pomponne (1618–99), favoured accepting the Dutch offer, but Louvois, now in the ascendant, opposed him. Louis, a lifelong victim of recurrent bouts of arrogance, overplayed his hand through July and asked for rapacious terms, including the secession of Gelderland, Overijssel, and Utrecht. Such terms

The Wars of Louis XIV

Map 4.2 The Rhine from the North Sea to Switzerland

would have left the United Provinces dependent on France. While negotiators haggled, the situation improved for the Dutch, and they finally broke off negotiations.

In this crisis, the Dutch called upon their old enemy and friend, the sea. As the French threatened Amsterdam, the Dutch opened the sluices at Muiden. On 20 June, some French cavalry under the marquis of Rochefort had ranged so far as to enter Muiden and become masters of the town for a time, but they were too few to hold it and probably unaware of its importance. Dutch commanded by Prince Maurice retook the town and prepared it to withstand an assault. On 22 June they opened the sluices to bar the French advance on Amsterdam by inundating the land around the city and, thus, robbing the French of possible triumph.

Unprepared to carry out an amphibious campaign over the flooded fields of Holland, the French offensive bogged down. The prospects for immediate victory seemed so slim then that Louis left and returned to St-Germain in France on 1 August. The situation began to tip somewhat in Dutch favour. Louis released 20,000 prisoners to William on the payment of scant ransom. This ill-considered act and further efforts by William and his new military adviser, Waldeck, allowed the prince to expand and improve his army. Also, the weather did not favour the French, who hoped winter would freeze the water that blocked their path to Amsterdam. During the cold-weather months, Condé tried to take Amsterdam and the duke of Luxembourg attempted to march on Leiden and The Hague, but all efforts were stymied by a sudden thaw.

Meanwhile, Brandenburg honoured its commitment to come to the aid of the Dutch, and Habsburg and imperial forces took the field even though Emperor Leopold refrained from declaring war on France. Spain also did not enter the war outright, frustrating Louis's hopes to expose the Spanish Netherlands to attack and conquest. Charles II's alliance with Louis met mounting Parliamentary resistance in England. None the less, the French possessed strong advantages by occupying Dutch territory. There they not only lived off enemy territory but tried to force Dutch accession to their demands by ravaging the countryside.

When Louis returned to France in mid-summer of 1672, he ordered Turenne to Germany to hold back forces of the emperor and the elector of Brandenburg, so from August 1672 to May 1673, Turenne campaigned along the Rhine. With this move of a major army to a second front, the French lost the concentration of forces and purpose that they enjoyed in the initial assault; they would never regain it. Turenne had as many as 25,000 infantry and 18,000 cavalry.[15] At the approach of the Brandenburgers, he moved into the

---

15 The Venetian ambassador gave the total as 43,000. Jean Bérenger, *Turenne* (Paris, 1987), p. 394. Quincy, *Histoire militaire*, vol. i, p. 344, says that he assembled only 12,000 in his camp between Cologne and Bonn.

country around Trier, where he put his men in quarters. Turenne repeatedly disputed directives from Louvois at this time, unlike the more compliant Condé. In November Turenne rejected an order from Louvois because he believed that Versailles had a poor conception of the situation at the front, 'If you were here,' he chided the war minister, 'you would laugh at that idea.'[16] Condé wrote to Louvois succinctly, 'I strongly doubt that he will do what he has been ordered to do.'[17] And when Turenne wanted to carry out an autumn campaign, Louvois vetoed it. At this point William attempted a counterstroke while the French forces were dispersed from Alsace to Holland, and he descended upon Charleroi, but his attack was unsuccessful.

During the winter, Turenne took the field and drove the Brandenburg army back. Learning in late January that imperials under Montecuccoli had effected a juncture with the elector of Brandenburg and that they intended to cross the Rhine at Koblenz with an army of 25,000 men, Turenne decided to march against them. By skilful manoeuvre, Turenne succeeded in driving the elector back across northern Germany and finally out of the war. Turenne's troops had set up in quarters in Mark for only a few days when he reassembled part of his army, marched across Westphalia to Hoester, seized it, and crossed the Weser. The elector of Brandenburg had already retired to the east side of Westphalia, but on Turenne's approach he retreated further, into his own lands, and Turenne pursued. Turenne's army entered the elector's lands and so desolated them that the elector agreed to peace, solemnized in the Treaty of Vassem, 6 June. Here Turenne's rapacious troops both supplied themselves by their exactions and used living off the country as a way of driving an enemy out of the war.

1673

For the campaign season of 1673, Louis divided his forces into three main field armies. He led the first along the Meuse with his brother Philippe as generalissimo. It numbered 40,000 troops and included lieutenant-generals la Feuillade, de Lorge, Rochefort, Monmouth, Estrades, and Fourille. The Great Condé led a second army around Utrecht to observe the Dutch and maintain the pressure on them.

---

16 AG, A^{1}280, 14 November 1672, Turenne to Louvois, in Rousset, *Histoire de Louvois*, vol. i, p. 401.
17 AG, A^{1}280, 16 November 1672, Condé to Louvois, in Rousset, *Histoire de Louvois*, vol. i, p. 400.

Turenne commanded a third army to cover the upper Rhine and the Moselle, as he had done over the winter and into the spring.

The most notable achievement of French arms in 1673 was the taking of Maastricht by the king's army. In order to speed their advance to the United Provinces, the French bypassed Maastricht and its Dutch garrison in 1672, but it was an obvious impediment to operations along the Meuse, so with operations stalled on Dutch territory, Louis turned to the task of taking this powerful fortress. Maastricht commanded a bridge on the Meuse with the town itself on the left bank and a fortified suburb, Wick, guarding the bridgehead on the right bank. To effectively surround the fortress, a besieging army must establish itself on both sides of the Meuse; thus, the river would dissect the attacking force. To maintain communications between troops on opposite banks, the French would have to construct bridges both upstream and downstream from Maastricht.

Louis began by feigning an assault on Brussels to attract the attention of the Spanish governor, Monterey, in that direction. But as Monterey cobbled together a force to resist this threat, Louis dispatched Montal to pull garrisons out of Tongres and Maaseik and invest Maastricht, which he did on 6 June. The next day de Lorge, with troops detached from Turenne's army, closed in from the east and blockaded Wick. On 8 June, 7,000 commandeered peasant pioneers began to dig the extensive lines of circumvallation and contravallation surrounding the town.[18] Despite the overwhelming force that clamped down on Maastricht, it promised to be a long and costly siege, because the garrison numbered 5,000 infantry and 1,000 cavalry under a skilled commander, Fariaux, an officer of French origin who had prepared the town for siege. Fariaux's resolution was stiffened by the belief that William must attempt to relieve the fortress.

On 10 June Louis joined the army of 45,000 troops and 58 cannon that assembled around Maastricht and Wick. Louvois accumulated enough food and ammunition in the camp's magazine to

18 Quincy, *Histoire militaire*, vol. i, p. 350, states that 7,000 peasant pioneers dug the siege lines; M. S. Anderson, *War and Society in Europe of the Old Regime, 1618–1789* (New York, 1988), p. 140, states that 20,000 pioneers were employed. Christopher Duffy, *The Fortress in the Age of Vauban and Frederick the Great, 1660–1789, Siege Warfare*, vol. ii (London, 1985), p. 10, also gives the figure as 20,000. The painting by Jean-Paul de Marly shows no lines of contravallation (Vezio Melegari, *The Great Military Sieges* [New York, 1972], pp. 156–7), but the detailed map in Quincy, *Histoire militaire*, vol. i, between pp. 350 and 351, does. Rousset, *Histoire de Louvois*, vol. i, p. 458, explicitly mentions lines of circumvallation and contravallation.

support this sizeable force for six weeks.[19] Whereas in the past, generals had commanded sieges at their whim with engineers simply as technical experts, Louis gave Vauban direct authority over the conduct of siege operations.[20] After the siege lines were completed on 14 June, the French opened the attack trenches on the night of 17–18 June. Vauban justified Louis's confidence, for as the count of Aligny wrote: 'The first days of open trench did not cost much; Monsieur Vauban, in this siege as in so many others, saved many men by his knowledge.'[21]

Vauban drove the French trenches toward the Tongres gate, the focus of the assault. The first French batteries opened fire on 18 June, and over the next thirty hours, these 26 cannon fired over 5,000 rounds. The great engineer displayed his genius by employing parallels for the first time at Maastricht.

The fighting to seize the outworks of the fortification was particularly heavy, with positions changing hands; the list of the slain included the famed d'Artagnan, who commanded the king's musketeers in one of the assaults. Still the French drove forward. The pace of the French attack quickened when Louis learned that William III was assembling all his forces to relieve Maastricht. After the French had placed mines and directed artillery to breach the main wall of the fortress, Fariaux succumbed to pressures from the garrison and the inhabitants and beat the chamade on 30 June. After parleying, the articles of surrender were signed the next day. The entire siege had lasted only twenty-five days since the investment, or less than two weeks from the opening of the trenches.

Louis's attentions now turned elsewhere. There was little else to do on this front, because the inundations of Dutch territory prohibited the French from undertaking other major sieges then. But new dangers threatened from other quarters. As a coalition against him formed, Louis's most immediate worry centred on Germany and his lands bordering on it. Louis first dispatched part of his army to reinforce Condé, exemplifying again what would become his common practice of shifting troops from one front to another in mid-campaign to respond to changing circumstances. The Great Condé left Luxembourg in command around Utrecht and moved south towards Flanders with part of his army to observe the Spanish, who could enter the war at any moment. Louis sent another large body of 18,000 troops under

19 AG, A¹315, 24 June 1673, Louvois to Le Tellier, in Rousset, *Histoire de Louvois*, vol. i, p. 459.
20 Rousset, *Histoire de Louvois*, vol. i, p. 459.
21 *Mémoires inédits du comte d'Aligny*, in ibid., p. 461.

the marquis of Rochefort to Trier, because its elector had broken his neutrality. Rochefort seized small towns and chateaux and put all the elector's lands under contribution, that is, he demanded contribution payments from the inhabitants. While Rochefort ravaged, the king went to Lorraine, which appeared restive when word reached it that the emperor had sided against France. During a stay of three weeks, Louis fortified Nancy to better hold the province; he then marched into Alsace to guarantee the submission of towns there. The king returned to France towards the end of September, after reinforcing Turenne with additional troops.

Turenne's task for the campaign season of 1673 turned out to be a particularly thankless one of trying to keep an imperial army under the extremely talented general Raimondo Montecuccoli from linking up with the Dutch.[22] Turenne with an army of 20,000 men received instructions that he protested were contradictory – to bar Montecuccoli's army of 25,000 men from reaching the Dutch Netherlands, while guarding Alsace and avoiding harm to neutral German states that might drive them into the enemy camp.[23] Turenne's first intention was to establish his army in Franconia to put pressure on Bavaria, which, though Francophile, was vacillating. Once in Franconia, he could threaten the heartland of Germany and Bohemia, hopefully diverting Montecuccoli to the defensive. From August through November, Turenne and Montecuccoli manoeuvred against one another in a game of march and countermarch eventually won by Montecuccoli. His forces were better supplied, while the French, who lacked bread, resorted to pillage. Montecuccoli finally joined William III at Bonn, where both armies besieged the city, and the French garrison capitulated on 12 November. Turenne put his troops into winter quarters in Alsace and Germany.

In late August 1673, Madrid and Vienna entered a formal alliance and then signed separate alliances with the United Provinces. The treaty between the Spanish and the Dutch stated that France would be reduced to its borders of 1659.[24] At the same time, with the prospects growing that the Dutch would survive the French onslaught, Louis moderated his demands, and reduced them further by late September, but the Dutch were now too strong. The alliance further grew in strength when Charles of Lorraine joined in October.

---

22 See C. J. Ekberg, 'The "Great Captain's Greatest Mistake": Turenne's German Campaign of 1673', *Military Affairs* 41, no. 3 (1980), pp. 114–18.
23 Bérenger, *Turenne*, p. 398 for size of Turenne's forces.
24 Lossky, *Louis XIV*, pp. 147–8.

As late as the first weeks of September, Louis still hoped to goad the Spanish into attacking, but he finally despaired of this and on 24 September commanded that his officials prepare a declaration of war against Spain. However, emboldened by the mounting success of the imperials and the Dutch, including their taking of Naarden on 13 September, and encouraged by their new offensive alliance commitments, the Spanish finally declared war outright on 16 October. The French then followed with a declaration on 19 October. Louis had his open war with Spain finally, but not at all on the conditions that he had desired. At this time, the elector of Brandenburg reentered the war as well, and Louis's situation again worsened when the English concluded a separate peace with his enemies through the Treaty of Westminster on 19 February 1674, although English regiments that had fought alongside the French on land continued to do so. On 28 May that year the Imperial Diet declared war against France, although not all German states joined the struggle. Louis now faced the kind of broad alliance and, consequently, long war that he would repeatedly face throughout the rest of his reign.

THE SECOND PHASE OF THE WAR, 1674-75

With Spain now fully in the war and supported by an extensive alliance, the occupation of the still defiant United Provinces became an unnecessary diversion of men and resources away from the real field of battle, the Spanish Netherlands. The next two years would see the French withdraw from Dutch territory and engage in an offensive on Spanish lands. At the same time the French repeatedly had to defend Alsace and parry German moves along the Rhine. In addition, the war expanded to Mediterranean fronts. Spanish and French forces duelled in Catalonia and Roussillon, and when revolt in Messina threatened the Spanish hold over Sicily, the French came to the rebels' aid. The campaign of 1675 brought the end of an era when a cannonball killed Turenne in July. The passing of the old guard, completed with the retirement of Condé and Montecuccoli later that year, resulted not simply in a change of command but brought a fundamental shift in Louis's strategic goals as well. The second phase of the war still retained the offensive, but the final phase became fundamentally defensive.

1674

Louis concentrated his forces for the 1674 campaign in the Spanish Netherlands, where he hoped to take several fortresses that year.[25] Late in 1673, Luxembourg began to withdraw his troops from the United Provinces. The withdrawal continued through the spring, as Louis intended to evacuate all his troops from Dutch lands, except for the fortress of Grave on the Meuse. Louvois sent orders detailing that by 20 April all the occupied fortresses were to be disarmed and abandoned, and their cannon and ammunition shipped to Grave, which became an over-stuffed arsenal. Certain fortresses were to be handed over to French allies. At the end of the month, all French troops were to march out and concentrate on the Meuse, between Maaseik and Maastricht.[26] Marshal Bellefonds, showing the kind of independence exemplified by Turenne and once typical of high-placed officers, opposed the withdrawal, and was replaced by de Lorge, better attuned to the new subordination expected of field commanders. In fact, the evacuation took only a bit more time than expected, and the French garrisons assembled in a body of 15,000 men around Rheinberg. A force of 4,000 men under Nicholas, count of Chamilly, remained to hold Grave.

Forced to expand the army to meet the challenge of a wider war, Louis concluded that he could not also afford a large navy, so he demobilized a number of naval units. With English withdrawal from the war, Louis opted to keep his Atlantic fleet in port. This was not, in the words of Quincy, for lack of captains for ships, but because the navy 'demanded an excessive expense, and because one was obliged to do so much on the land, it was decided to disarm at sea'.[27] In order to provide security against attacks on the Atlantic and Channel coasts, authorities in Normandy, Brittany, and Aunis raised the traditional levy of regional nobility, the *arrière ban*, and militia forces to deal with potential landing parties once they had come ashore rather than trying to keep enemy ships at bay with naval forces. The French did not mount a major challenge to Dutch naval forces in the Atlantic and let the initiative pass to the Dutch. In 1674 De Ruyter tried to take Martinique, but the Dutch lost so many men in the ground assault that they reembarked the same day they landed and sailed back to Holland. Admiral Cornelis Tromp, with an invasion force of 10,000 troops and siege equipment, descended upon Belle Île off Brittany in June. They landed on 27 June, but after two fruitless months returned to their ships. The Dutch threatened landings around

---

25 Louis hoped to take Namur, Mons, Condé, Cambrai, and Bouchain during 1674, although this was not to happen. AG, A¹398, 8 June 1674, Louvois to Condé.

26 AG, A¹379, 24 and 30 March 1673, Louvois to Robert, army *intendant* at Nijmegen, in Rousset, *Histoire de Louvois*, vol. ii, p. 12.

27 Quincy, *Histoire militaire*, vol. i, p. 373.

Poitou, at Dieppe, and near Bayonne. This was enough to concern Louis and divert French troops to guard against a descent on the French coasts. A scheme to deliver Harfleur was discovered, and the chief plotter beheaded at the Bastille. Reduction of the Atlantic fleet, however, did not bring with it destruction of the fleet in the Mediterranean, where the French would intervene in the Sicilian revolt.

As French troops pulled out of the United Provinces they invaded Franche-Comté, which Louis viewed as a part of the Spanish inheritance that he might justly claim. Louis had hoped to grab Franche-Comté before the end of 1673, but his troops were needed elsewhere. Now the duke of Navailles laid siege to Gray early in 1674, opening the trenches on 28 February. After the first assault on the chemin convert, an attack made all the more difficult by the fact that inundations forced the French soldiers to advance through waist-deep water, the Spanish capitulated. The garrison commander was allowed to leave with part of his goods and forced to swear that he would not serve the king of Spain for six months.[28] From Gray, Navailles marched to Vesoul, which surrendered at the first French demand; meanwhile, the duke of Enghien, son of the Great Condé, marched against Besançon, which he invested on 25 April. At this time the king journeyed to the front to be with his conquering troops; again bringing his queen and court, he reached the army just as it invested Besançon, where the full siege began on 2 May. With great effort, Swiss troops seized a neighbouring mountain that dominated the rocky citadel perched above the city. The trench was opened to assault the town on the night of 7–8 May, while a continual downpour soaked the troops. The French drove forward despite the weather and enemy sorties, and on 14 May the fortress governor asked to surrender the town, although the citadel held out for a few days more. On 27 May, Louis left Besançon for Dole, which a detachment under Enghien had already invested. After the French succeeded in seizing a section of the chemin couvert on the night of 29–30 May, they established a battery to breach the fortress walls and also dug mines. The governor beat the chamade on 6 June. After the fall of Dole, Louis and the court returned to Paris. When Salins fell too, the French had secured the entire province in a campaign of only six weeks. This was as Louis desired, because he wanted to seize Franche-Comté before the campaign began in the Spanish Netherlands.

There, the Dutch would besiege Grave and Maastricht, while the Spanish attacked Charleroi. The emperor favoured vigorous action

28 Ibid., p. 375.

in the Netherlands, where Condé commanded, because this would tie down French troops so that he could not reinforce Turenne along the Rhine, the theatre in which imperial forces would make their major effort. The Allies disputed their best course of action, but in late July a force of 10,000 to 12,000 under General Rabenhaut besieged Grave. William, with forces totalling 65,000 Dutch, imperial, and Spanish troops, chose to cover the siege actively by threatening an invasion of French Flanders and Hainault that would compel Condé to react to allied moves. Condé, who had been uncharacteristically indecisive, commanded an army of about 45,000 entrenched near Seneffe. William approached Condé's position on 9 August; then the Allies decamped on 11 August, fully expecting the French to follow them. William's forces moved off in three columns, with a rear guard of 6,000. Seeing an opportunity to defeat the enemy in detail, Condé reverted to his aggressive, even rash, self of old. He dispatched the able partisan Saint Clar to harass the vanguard. Saint Clar led his small force of 400 cavalry down between the enemy columns without being observed, and then attacked the van. Meanwhile, Condé jumped the enemy rear guard with a mobile French force composed primarily of cavalry and devoid of artillery. During the morning, Condé enjoyed the advantage. Although so crippled by gout that he could not wear his boots, Condé still rode at the head of his squadrons in charge after charge. When Condé drew his sword to lead a cavalry charge, a young and exuberant Villars cried out, 'Now I have seen what I most longed to see! – the Great Condé, sword in hand!'[29] As the hours passed, William rallied his forces, and the rest of the French army joined Condé. Had Condé pulled back after his initial victory over the allied rear guard, the Battle of Seneffe could have been regarded as a definite, though modest, victory, but now that Condé's blood was up, he continued to persevere after the battle degenerated into a slugging match. Firing lines formed at close range and blasted into each other in particularly confused and bloody fighting which lasted well into the night. Only after the moon set did both armies retire from the battlefield.

The butcher's bill for this fighting exceeded any that Louis would have to pay before the War of the Spanish Succession. Voltaire would write of Seneffe, 'it was only carnage'.[30] French casualties may have

---

29 Villars in Eveline Godley, *The Great Condé: A Life of Louis II de Bourbon, Prince of Condé* (London, 1915), p. 564.
30 Voltaire, *Le Siècle de Louis XIV*, vol. i (Paris, 1929), p. 149.

mounted to as many as 10,000 killed, wounded, and captured, while the Allies lost a total of 15,000 on the field of battle with thousands of additional wounded.[31] When the casualty lists arrived in Paris, the sorrow was great; Mme de Sévigné wrote, 'We have lost so much by this victory that without the Te Deum and some [captured] flags brought to Notre Dame, we would believe we had lost the battle.'[32] This Pyrrhic victory epitomized the costs and limited value of combat in a battle culture of forbearance, and, coming so early in his personal reign, the losses suffered there can only have strengthened Louis's penchant for the more predictable and profitable results of positional warfare. Compare the carnage at Seneffe with the minimal costs at the siege of Maastricht the preceding year. The day after Seneffe, Vauban wrote to Louvois, 'I believe that the enemies ought to seek a battle and we to avoid one, since to avoid fighting is the sure means to beat them.'[33]

Seneffe would be the only major battle that Condé commanded during the personal reign of Louis XIV.[34] Condé's costly resolve can be defended by arguing that it forestalled any allied threat against French territory for a long time, but the immediate effect seemed inconclusive. William withdrew garrisons from a number of towns, added these to his field army, and rebuilt his army rapidly. After Seneffe, Condé and William sparred with one another, but no battle resulted. In September, William besieged Oudenarde, but when Condé marched to its relief, the Allies withdrew. Condé could have had a battle there had he wished, but Seneffe had chastened him.

To the north, Grave held out against the allied siege. Grave was too far distant to relieve; all that could be expected was a tenacious defence that would occupy enemy forces for a long time. As it was, Chamilly conducted an active and effective defence of the town. Before the siege began, Louvois worried that the town was so stuffed with ammunition gathered from other fortresses that it might blow

---

31 Casualty estimates for Seneffe vary considerably. Gaston Bodart, *Militärhistorisches Kriegs-Lexikon, 1618–1905* (Vienna and Leipzig, 1908), p. 95, puts them at 10,000 for the French and 14,000 for the Allies; R. Ernest Dupuy and Trevor N. Dupuy, *The Encyclopedia of Military History* (New York, 1970), p. 565, agree with the figure for the French but put allied dead at 10,000, captured at 5,000, with as many as an additional 15,000 wounded.

32 Letter from Mme de Sévigné to the count of Bussy, 5 September 1674, *Lettres de Madame de Sévigné*, ed. Gault-de-Saint-Germain (12 vols; Paris, 1822–23), vol. iii, p. 353.

33 AG, A¹371, 12 August 1674, Vauban to Louvois, in Rousset, *Histoire de Louvois*, vol. ii, p. 55.

34 This fact leads Wolf, *Louis XIV*, p. 241, to wonder why historians place such emphasis on Condé's importance during Louis's personal reign.

up, and, in a move incomprehensible in terms of modern warfare, authorized Chamilly to sell half the gunpowder, at a good price, to the Dutch, a suggestion welcomed and acted upon by the fortress commander![35] The French not only gathered powder at Grave, but they assembled all the hostages seized to guarantee the payment of contributions by the Dutch. The hope of liberating these individuals, and thus ending contribution payments, made Grave an even more attractive target to the Allies. Because the hostages were considered particularly valuable, the French hustled them out of Grave and send them to Maastricht under the very noses of the enemy.

After abandoning the siege of Oudenarde, William III brought his Dutch troops to join the siege of Grave, as did the duke of Lorraine by late October. The long course of the siege, which began in late July and was to last over three months, destroyed the town. Louis appreciated the heroism and resolve of Chamilly and the garrison, but finally commanded Chamilly to capitulate. Only after receiving this royal permission did Chamilly surrender on 26 October, having tied up an allied army for most of the summer and into the autumn. Chamilly received great honour from the enemy; he marched out with his garrison, horses to haul twenty-six cannon, and an entire pontoon train of copper boats. The Dutch provided river transport to take all to Maastricht. Nevertheless, Chamilly's determined defence, valiant as it was, could not hide the fact that the French had surrendered their last conquest from the invasion of the United Provinces.

Along the Rhine, Turenne fought what can only be called a great campaign from the summer of 1674 through the following winter. More than any other campaign fought during the wars of Louis XIV, this demonstrated the possibilities of manoeuvre as a means of defence. However, it also revealed the limitations of manoeuvre to achieve decision.

Turenne was Louis's most talented general. In 1674, the Great Condé, only in his early fifties, was an old man, soon to be forced by infirmities to stop campaigning, but Turenne, a full ten years Condé's senior, was at the height of his powers – a French vintage that only improved with the years. Born into the family La Tour d'Auvergne, a very prestigious Protestant house that claimed the status of foreign princes within France, Turenne was very proud and jealous of his position. The austere Turenne, while no fanatic, was very serious about religion, and as an act of conscience he converted to Catholicism in

[35] Rousset, *Histoire de Louvois* vol. ii, p. 64.

1668. He began his military career when hardly more than a boy, and raised his first regiment at the age of nineteen. During the initial stage of the Fronde, his pride led him to join the rebels, although he soon reverted to the king's service, where he became Louis's most trusted and able commander. Turenne's pride, and confidence in his own judgement, led him to disobey orders from the minister of war, Louvois, but Louis did not call him to task for it. While Turenne lacked the reckless dash of the Great Condé, he was a smarter campaigner. Turenne learned from experience, and fought his finest campaign now, in the last months of his life. A true soldier of the Thirty Years War, the marshal demonstrated concern for his soldiers' welfare but callous indifference to the abuse of the civilian population by his troops.

Turenne had wintered troops in Alsace and in the Palatinate, an act that drove the elector Palatine into the emperor's camp. When the elector agreed to hand over Germersheim to the emperor, Louis ordered that it be seized, and Vaubrun marched to take it on 26 February; it yielded immediately when the French summoned the commander to surrender. Turenne began the campaign in earnest by summoning his troops to Saverne under the pretext of holding a review, but then on 12 June he marched rapidly with about 6,000 cavalry, 2,000 infantry, and 6 cannon toward Philippsburg, where they crossed the Rhine two days later on a bridge of boats that had been constructed for this purpose.[36] He hoped to strike General Enea Caprara and the duke of Lorraine before they could be reinforced by Bournonville. On 16 June, this cavalry-heavy force confronted similarly composed imperial forces of 7,000 cavalry and 2,000 infantry, who had taken up a strong position across the French line of advance. The French met the imperials on high ground just across the Elsanx stream near the town of Sinzheim. After Turenne's infantry took the town and its bridge, his cavalry fought through defiles and uphill against the large mounted force of the enemy. Much in the style of Condé, Turenne led cavalry charges himself, sword in hand. Turenne would comment, 'I have never seen such a dogged battle.'[37] In the first enemy charge, all the general officers of the French army were either wounded or

---

36 Authorities disagree on the composition of Turenne's army at Sinzheim. Rousset, ibid., p. 72, states his figures at 1,500 infantry, plus some troops taken from local garrisons, and 6,000 cavalry. Napoleon in his précis of the campaign credits Turenne with 9,000 troops, 5,000 of which were cavalry. Turenne, *Mémoires de Turenne* (Paris, 1872), p. 448. Quincy, *Histoire militaire*, vol. i, p. 394, claims Turenne had 12,000 men against 15,000.

37 Turenne in Rousset, *Histoire de Louvois*, vol. ii, p. 73.

struck blows with their own weapons; two brigadiers died. Turenne won a complete victory at a cost of 1,500 casualties against 2,500 losses for the enemy. After marching up to the gates of Heidelberg, Turenne soon returned to the west bank of the Rhine to rest his army around Neustadt; there the troops he had left in Alsace joined him. Within two weeks, Turenne took the offensive again, crossing the Rhine at Philippsburg on 3 July and marching directly for the imperial headquarters near Heidelberg. The imperials too had rallied and received reinforcements, with the arrival of General Bournonville with 5,000 fresh troops. When the imperials saw the French approach the Neckar and make ready to cross it, they retreated rapidly north and crossed to the right, or north, bank of the Main. Turenne commented, 'There was in their troops a terror not to be believed.'[38] The memory of Sinzheim was worth many battalions. This precipitous withdrawal exposed the now defenceless Palatinate to the French army.

Turenne's success encouraged the king to reinforce him. Rochefort was dispatched from the Netherlands to station his troops between the Meuse and the Moselle to support either Condé or Turenne as circumstances demanded. However, the king feared for Lorraine and Alsace and he believed that French occupation of the Palatinate would only drive more German princes into the imperial camp. Turenne resisted the king's cautious orders to withdraw to the Moselle. Although Turenne returned to the left bank of the Rhine on 28 July, he only went as far as Landau, ready to go back to the Palatinate should circumstances require. To the king's proposal that it might be best to draw troops out of Alsace to stiffen defences further to the west, Turenne replied that 'it would be better for your service if I would lose a battle than if I would cross the [Vosges] mountains and leave Alsace'.[39] During this pause in active operations, both Bournonville and Turenne received reinforcements, although Turenne got only part of Rochefort's army when the bulk of it was ordered to rejoin Condé.

Throughout the summer of 1674, the Palatinate suffered, for Turenne supplied his army by exploiting its resources. Making war feed war by living off enemy or neutral resources was a goal of seventeenth-century commanders, and in his long years of campaigning in Germany, Turenne had become expert. When he argued that fully half of an army in Germany should be cavalry, he spoke to the necessity

---

[38] AG, A¹413, 8 July 1674, Turenne to Louvois in ibid., p. 76.
[39] AG, A¹414, 8 August 1674, Turenne to Louis, in ibid., p. 78 from *Lettres et Mémoires de Turenne*, vol. ii, p. 548.

for mobile mounted forces to seize the wherewithal to keep an army in the field.[40] Before July, the French had placed areas of the Palatinate under contribution; during July, Turenne's troops occupied the Palatinate on the far side of the Rhine, while August found his troops similarly demanding contributions from the Palatinate on the left bank. As explained before, 'execution', that is burning, was the common fate of villages which failed to pay what was demanded of them, and the Palatinate burned. When the French occupied the right bank of the Rhine, they also adopted the policy of destroying as much fodder as possible so that the enemy could not operate from the Neckar to Philippsburg, thus helping to protect that fortress from enemy operations. As Turenne explained, 'nothing in the world is so key to hindering a siege of Philippsburg than to have foraged all the places where the enemy could assemble to sustain himself'. Louis worried that Turenne's actions would so infuriate German princes that new allies would join the emperor. But to Turenne, 'the ruin of the country of the elector Palatine will chill [the Allies] more than inspire [*échauffe*] them'.[41]

This was all made worse by the fact that in addition to the normal, though brutal, policy of extracting funds and goods from the villages and destroying the fodder necessary to sustain an enemy advance, French troops also simply marauded, adding to the suffering, in response to which the local peasantry fought back. Armed peasants, called *schnapphahns* – literally, 'highwaymen', but who would be called guerrillas in today's vocabulary – attacked isolated French bands of soldiers and sniped at troops on the road. This infuriated French troops, who, after seeing their often horribly mutilated comrades, carried out their own reprisals by fire and sword.

While impromptu devastation drew strong condemnation, even the elector of the Palatinate, in complaining to Turenne, had to accept the rigours of executions: 'It seems to me that every effort should be made to put to the torch only those places that refused to pay contributions.'[42] Louvois considered that villages who refused to pay were mocking the French, and he demanded stronger measures.[43]

---

40 Louis Susane, *Histoire de la cavalerie française* (3 vols; Paris, 1874), vol. i, p. 106. As much as half of his army of 10,000 men in Germany during the 1640s was composed of cavalry. Charles Derek Croxton, 'Peacemaking in Early Modern Europe: Cardinal Mazarin and the Congress of Westphalia, 1643–1648', Ph.D. dissertation, University of Illinois at Urbana-Champaign, 1995, p. 101.
41 AG, A¹380, 27 July 1674, Turenne to Louis, in Rousset, *Histoire de Louvois*, vol. ii, pp. 81–2.
42 Elector Palatine to Turenne in ibid., p. 79.
43 AG, A¹380, 11 June 1674, Louvois to La Grange, in Rousset, *Histoire de Louvois*, vol. ii, p. 80.

As late as September, Dufay, the governor of Philippsburg, reported, 'In the last two weeks I have burned thirteen towns and villages,' but he said 'there was not a soul left in any of them'.[44] The devastation of the Palatinate in 1674 would not be as severe as that in 1688–89, but it provided a precedent.

By the end of August imperial forces had grown and expected more reinforcements, so at a council of war held in Frankfurt, they resolved to march against Turenne. By crossing the Rhine at Mainz with about 30,000 troops, the imperials under Bournonville threatened a descent on Alsace or Lorraine. The Allies thought they greatly outnumbered Turenne, but he had also increased his force to about 25,000 troops. While Louvois wanted Turenne to withdraw, the marshal stood firm, arguing that the imperials would have nothing to eat. Turenne concentrated between Landau and Wissembourg, blocking the imperial army and forcing them to subsist on the devastated Palatinate. After less than a month, the imperials abandoned this venture and returned to the right bank of the Rhine on 20 September.

Bournonville now marched south to seize the neutral city of Strasbourg and its vital bridge. Imperial emissaries were already negotiating with the magistrates of Strasbourg to abandon their neutrality, and the approach of Bournonville's army made their case altogether convincing. The fall of Strasbourg into imperial hands was a bloodless victory on the scale of a major battle. Now imperial forces could cross into the heart of Alsace, realizing Louis's fears.

Learning of the imperial coup, and now aware that the elector of Brandenburg was advancing with an army of 20,000 to link up with Bournonville, Turenne resolved to attack Bournonville before the elector arrived to boost imperial forces to 50,000. In response to the enemy seizure of Strasbourg, Turenne had shifted his army to Wantzenau, just north of Strasbourg. He now he decided to put his army between Strasbourg and the main enemy forces encamped around Ensheim. Marching his troops all night on 2–3 October and through the next day, he arrived at Molsheim threatening enemy communications with Strasbourg.

On the morning of 4 October, Turenne left his army's baggage at Molsheim and advanced against the enemy. The French deployed into two lines with a cavalry reserve immediately behind the first and an additional reserve stationed behind the second. The imperials rested the left of their line on a wood that Turenne recognized as the key to

---

44 AG, A¹414, 9 September 1674, Dufay to Louvois, in Rousset, *Histoire de Louvois*, vol. ii, p. 80.

the position, and it would see the majority of the fighting. The young brigadier, Louis-François, marquis of Boufflers, led dragoons into the wood, where they were supported by detachments of musketeers. In response, Bournonville threw in most of the infantry from his second line and his reserve. French and English battalions under Turenne, including one led by the future duke of Marlborough, had very nearly succeeded in driving the Germans from the woods when Bournonville redoubled his efforts. A constant rain made it difficult for Turenne to bring up artillery to support the battle on this flank. Bournonville committed more units from his centre, while, with great reluctance, Turenne dispatched three battalions from his first line along with the cavalry of his right wing. With these reinforcements the French drove their foes from the wood, but imperial field fortifications kept Turenne's troops from advancing any further.

The removal of three battalions from the first line and the shift of the French right into the battle for the woods left a hole in the French centre that Bournonville now exploited with his cavalry. One body of horsemen charged the French squadrons of the left and another bore down on the remaining seven battalions in the first line. The French battalions formed 'in order to face to all sides, with a unequalled silence', and resisted the enemy cavalry.[45] Although the imperial horsemen drove back the first French squadrons they encountered, the cavalry of the second line and the reserve charged, sending the imperials back to their lines. The imperials withdrew that night, but the French who had marched and fought in the mud for two days were too exhausted to pursue. Tactically the Battle of Ensheim was little better than a draw; the French lost about 3,500 casualties and the imperials about 3,000.

Turenne had been unable to prevent the juncture of Bournonville's army with that of the elector of Brandenburg, so the marshal was compelled by this superior force to fall back to Deittweiler, where his entrenched camp protected both Saverne and Haguenau. After some dispute over the goals of the next campaign, Louis ordered Condé to send twenty battalions and twenty-four squadrons to Turenne, as again one French army was used as a reserve for another. Louis had also summoned the *arrière ban*, from an area within 100 leagues of Alsace, to augment Turenne's forces at this critical juncture.[46] Between

---

45 Battle report in Rousset, *Histoire de Louvois*, vol. ii, p. 89.
46 On the *ban* in 1674, see ibid., pp. 96–101. In 1674, nobles of the *arriére ban* were called up elsewhere than along the German frontier. When in June 1674 the Spanish menaced Bayonne, 10,000 militia and 500 of the *arrière ban* were summoned.

5,000 and 6,000 assembled at Nancy, where Marshal François-Joseph, marquis of Créqui, took command of them. When they appeared in Turenne's camp in October, he could tolerate them for only a week, after which he sent them to Lorraine. There Marshal Créqui gratefully received permission to disband them in November. 'I ardently hope that the king will never again have any need to assemble his nobles,' the frustrated marshal complained, 'because it is a corps incapable of action and more proper to provoke disorders than to remedy accidents.'[47]

Turenne now waited for the enemy to go into winter quarters before making his move to free Alsace of foreign occupation. The month of November passed without any major movement or combat. Then the troops under Bournonville and the elector of Brandenburg swung a little south to take up quarters in the rich area around Colmar and Sélestat. In early December, with snow already on the ground, Turenne made ready to begin his brief but famous winter campaign. Owing to the almost inevitable lack of food and forage, as well as the rigours of the cold, winter campaigns could ruin an army, so commanders avoided them. However, Louvois added his considerable administrative skills to the task, commanding *intendants* of neighbouring provinces to gather oats and dry forage to feed the army's horses, while *munitionnaires* of considerable skill, Jacquier and Berthelot, prepared stores of flour for bread. Turenne feigned going into winter quarters himself by leaving small garrisons in Saverne and Haguenau and crossing the Vosges to Lorraine, where he joined up with the reinforcements dispatched from Condé's army. After selecting only the men and horses who were in good condition for such a demanding campaign, he put these troops on the roads in mid-December. Using the Vosges to cover their movements, they slipped far to the south and then crossed the mountains by different routes to reassemble at Belfort during the last days of December.

The enemy scrambled to reassemble their troops, but confusion reigned. On 29 December Turenne surprised and shattered the enemy cavalry near Mulhouse, after which he marched on Colmar, where the elector of Brandenburg laboured to rally the allied troops. He succeeded in bringing 30,000 to 40,000 men to the field between Colmar and Turkheim, but they had not really gelled into an army

---

Foucault, *Mémoires*, pp. 24–8, in Jacques Gébelin, *Histoire des milices provinciales (1688–1791): Le Tirage au sort sous l'ancien régime* (Paris, 1882), p. 22n.

47 AG, A^{1}414, 22 November 1674, Créqui to Le Tellier, in Rousset, *Histoire de Louvois*, vol. ii, p. 101.

The Wars of Louis XIV

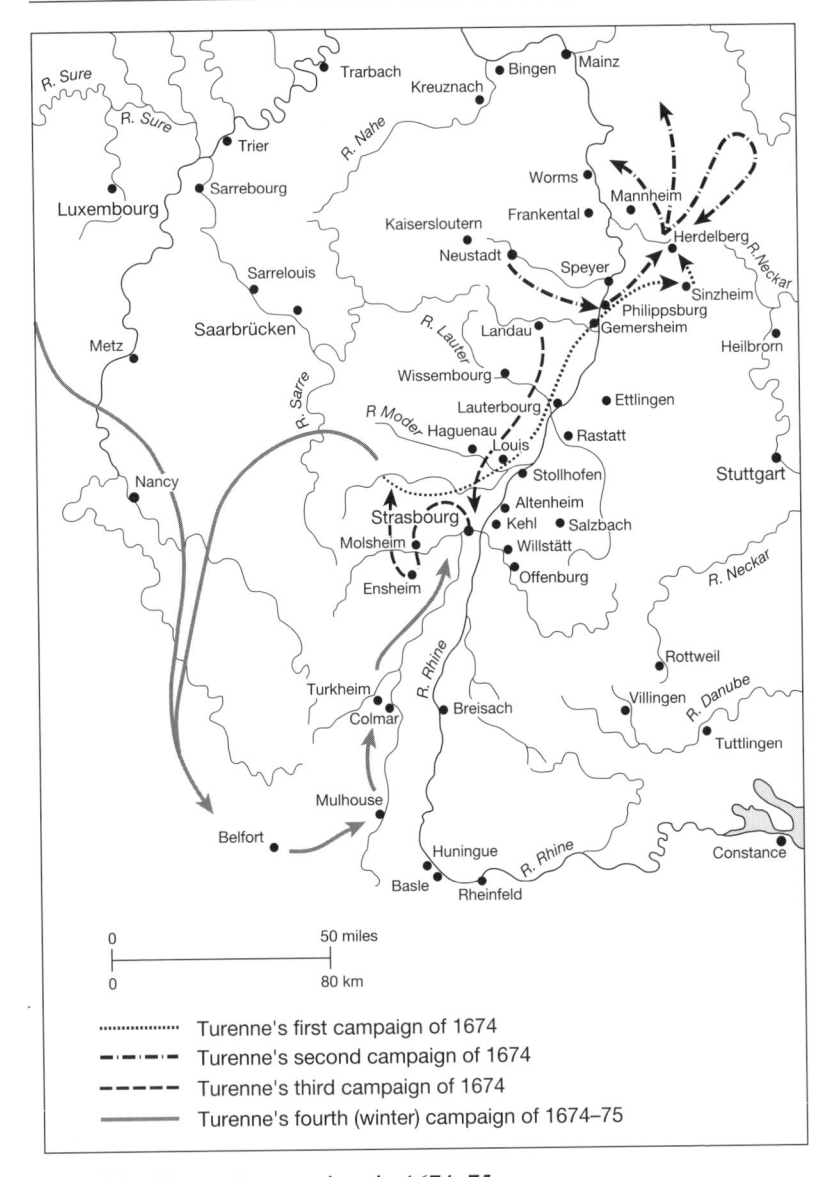

.... Turenne's first campaign of 1674
—·—·— Turenne's second campaign of 1674
— — — Turenne's third campaign of 1674
———— Turenne's fourth (winter) campaign of 1674–75

Map 4.3 **Turenne's campaigns in 1674–75**
Adapted from: Gabriel Hanoteau, ed., *Histoire de la nation française*, vol. vii, *Histoire militaire et navale*, pt 1 (Paris, 1925)

when, on 5 January, Turenne attacked with 30,000 troops. Turenne rivetted his foe's attention by feinting toward the centre and right, while he hurried infantry off to the left to outflank the German position by taking Turkheim. The terrain hid their flanking movement until, after hard fighting, the French secured Turkheim. When the Germans attempted to retake it, they met heavy fire and then reeled back before an infantry charge. The Germans fled, leaving 3,000 casualties, and sought the safety of Strasbourg, crossing its bridge to return to the right bank of the Rhine. Turenne did not pursue in strength after the Battle of Turkheim, but was happy enough to watch the Germans abandon Alsace. After putting his own troops into well-deserved winter quarters, Turenne left for the interior on 22 January to enjoy the praise won by this, his greatest campaign.

The year 1674 saw fighting not only on the northeast and Rhine frontiers, but along the Pyrenees as well. In Roussillon, Friedrich Hermann von Schomberg led a small French army against the Spanish.[48] Schomberg was in such need of manpower that Louis called up about 10,000 local militia from Languedoc, who made up nearly all of Schomberg's infantry.[49] With so few regulars, Schomberg felt himself to be at a disadvantage *vis-à-vis* the Spanish. Early in the campaign season, the Spanish took Bellegarde on the spine of the Pyrenees; Schomberg ordered the commander at Bellegarde to be arrested for having offered too feeble a defence. The loss of this post forced Schomberg to moderate his plans. On 19 June the French suffered another setback at Maureillas, where inexperienced cavalry lost the day and cost the French 800 killed and 1,500 captured.

The Mediterranean provided a final front for the war when the Messenians erupted against their Spanish masters in reaction to new tax demands. This revolt against Spanish authority in Sicily now balanced the situation along the Pyrenees, because the Spanish commander, Saint-Germain, had to hold his troops ready to be shipped to that island to reinforce the Spanish presence there. When Saint-Germain retired with most of his forces into Catalonia, Schomberg could become more aggressive, although the inexperience of his troops still limited him. After a spoiled attempt on Collioure, Schomberg drew

---

[48] On Roussillon during the Wars of Louis XIV, see David Stewart, *Assimilation and Acculturation in Seventeenth-Century Europe: Roussillon and France, 1659–1715* (Westport, CT, 1997).
[49] Foucault in Gébelin, *Histoire des milices*, p. 22n. For other levies of *miliciens* in the Dutch War, see ibid., pp. 22n–3n. See also ibid., pp. 21–7, and Léon Hennet, *Les Milices et les troupes provinciales* (Paris, 1884), pp. 275–96.

back to Elne, which he fortified. From there he contented himself by raiding into the Cerdanya, a mountainous region of Catalonia on the Spanish slope of the Pyrenees, which had failed to pay contributions to the French. Saint-Germain finally dispatched troops from his forces in Catalonia to beef up Spanish forces on Sicily, and the French sent supplies aid to the rebels in September 1674. The French found it necessary to take part militarily as well, when soldiers from the Toulon fleet, under Louis-Victor de Rochechouart, duke of Vivonne, had to assist the Messenians in retaking a small fort that hampered entrance into the harbour. From this point on, the war in Roussillon and Catalonia would be affected by the fighting in Sicily.

1675

To meet the large forces of the coalition, Louis filled the gaps in his ranks and expanded his forces again for the campaign of 1675. The pressures of the war, notably the creation of a new stamp tax to fund it, would precipitate internal revolts in France during 1675. Although these would not seriously threaten the monarchy, they did divert some troops to the west. (More will be said concerning this revolt in chapter 5.) The two major fronts of the war remained the Spanish Netherlands and the Rhineland, with the two Mediterranean fronts, Catalonia/Roussillon and Sicily, demanding a modest military and a major naval commitment.

In the Spanish Netherlands, the primary effort of the French came along the Meuse valley, where success erected a defensive barrier that isolated Spanish and Dutch forces to the west from their German allies to the east.[50] Liège provided the first battle ground of the new campaign. Maastricht, the only major fortress on the Meuse that the French still held by the end of 1674, anchored the French barrier, but its supply depended on the neutral city of Liège, which had to be secured in some fashion or another. The Spanish increased their hold around that city by taking Huy and Dinant in 1674 and soon they made a grab for Liège itself. Spanish plots against it date at least back to January 1674, when Lisola, the virulently anti-French imperial emissary, tried to win over the burghers of Liège. By early 1675 an anti-French coup, encouraged with imperial gold, seemed imminent; however, the French won over the commander of the Liège

---

50 I must thank my student George Satterfield for his research paper on the 1675 Meuse valley campaign, which I have employed for this section.

citadel with skilful propaganda and a healthy bribe. On 31 March a French garrison of 1,500 men marched into the citadel of Liège to guarantee the continued neutrality of the city. Citadels, after all, were designed to control the population of a city, not simply to defend it from external attack; their guns faced both ways. In response the Spanish brought troops into the neighbourhood, as anti-French riots broke out in the city. Yet when Louvois ordered Marshal Créqui to march on Liège with enough troops to put down any resistance, the Liègeois backed down and accepted their now involuntary neutrality in April.

To secure the valley, Louis planned to lead an army of 40,000 under his personal command north down the Sambre and then along the Meuse. As he advanced, Louis would gather forces and be joined by Condé, whose infirmities now forced him to ride about in a carriage, as adviser and commander in the king's absence. Under shelter of this army, two separate forces under the marquis of Rochefort and Marshal Créqui would isolate Charlemont and then take Dinant, Huy, and Limbourg. It was hoped that after the fall of Dinant and Huy, both Namur and Charlemont would also capitulate for lack of water-borne supplies. Limbourg, which lay to the east of Liège and Maastricht, would help to cover those key fortifications.

Once again, the able and efficient Louvois prepared magazines to support the king's armies. He ordered a total of 327,000 bushels of grain to be collected and stored at Maastricht and Liège, enough for seventy-five days at the stipulated rate of 80,000 rations per day.[51] With such supplies, the French could get the jump on their foes once again by taking to the field in mid-April and early May. Interestingly, the grain in Liège was to be stored under the name of a merchant in order to prevent the Allies from learning that it was intended for military use.

Louis left St Germain on 11 May to join his army. His personal route and the supply preparations were designed to mislead the enemy that he intended to strike Brussels. By the time Louis reached Cateau, he knew that the Spanish and Dutch forces were not yet assembled. In addition, the Dutch were hampered by the illness of William III. At this time, while Louis's army assembled, it drew from supplies suitably collected at other lesser fortresses, such as Tournai.

51 AG, A¹433, 5 April 1675, Louvois to Morceau. The records give the amount stored in septiers. According to Marcel Marion, *Dictionnaire des institutions de la France aux XVIIe et XVIIIe siècles* (Paris, 1923; reprint Paris, 1972), p. 375, a septier equalled 288 litres, or 8.17 US bushels, since a US bushel contains 35.24 litres.

Créqui, at the head of 10,000 men, left Charleville on 19 May, and his forces attacked Givet the next day with the intention of burning it and ravaging the surrounding area to deprive the Spanish garrison in neighbouring Charlemont of supplies. Créqui next moved north to invest Dinant on 21 May, where forces under Rochefort had already bridged the river with pontoons to ensure French supply. Dinant was well fortified by nature and protected by a small castle located on difficult high ground. The town held an imperial garrison of no more than 250 men, but they proved to be very resolute. Créqui opened the trenches to attack the castle on the night of 22–3 May, and after the firing of two mines beneath the castle's walls on 29 May, the garrison capitulated the next day. Following the fall of Dinant, Créqui marched southeast with 8,000 troops to observe the duke of Lorraine at Metz.

While Dinant lay under siege, Louis's main army arrived at Charleroi, where it was reinforced to a total of 50,000 men. Again, Charleroi had been stocked to support this army; in fact, so extensive were the stores that they even had to be stashed in the cathedral. On 24 May, the army marched toward the Meuse. That same day, with Condé as guide, the King visited the battlefield of Seneffe, where remains exhumed from shallow graves by animals poisoned the air with the smell of death.[52] A week later, Louis's forces were at Taviers, just north of Namur.

Rochefort, who had been with Créqui, split off after Dinant and marched for Huy, the next target of the French campaign. Louis moved the large supporting army to a camp about ten miles from Huy on the Méhaigne River. Rochefort invested Huy on the night of 31 May–1 June. The next day, the French constructed a pontoon bridge just north of Huy to ensure communications between French forces. The 550-man garrison of Huy commanded by Negrelli and Pinelli was well supplied. The main defence was a castle perched atop a formidable rock mass that made the usual technique of assault by trenches impossible. It was decided to storm positions up the hill and then to lodge batteries there. The assault began on 2 June, and the next day a battery of six 24-pounders opened fire, but more guns were required. The French set off a mine on 3 June that was ineffective, but the 24-pounders, now increased to twelve, continued to do their work. The threat of another mine on 6 June convinced Negrelli and Pinelli to beat the chamade, and the garrison was allowed to

---

[52] Paul Pellisson-Fontainier, *Lettres historiques de monsieur Pellisson*, vol. ii (3 vols; Paris, 1729), pp. 258–61.

leave with flags waving and to march to Bonn. Despite Negrelli's original boast that he could repose in his room in slippers for two weeks before having to worry about the French attack, the castle had fallen in only five days.

Only the conquest of Limbourg remained to complete the campaign. After a few days' respite at Huy, Rochefort's troops headed for Limbourg and invested that fortress on 10 June. Louis, with the main army, made his way to Visé to screen the besiegers from the allied army, which had finally assembled 19,000 Dutch and 10,000 Spanish troops around Louvain. William was now ready to move as French parties reconnoitred his army. In the meantime, Louis had ordered Créqui, now on the Moselle, to bring all his cavalry to Limbourg immediately, while his infantry joined the garrison at Trier. Créqui's horsemen reached Rochefort's camp by 16 June. With all French efforts focused on this siege, Limbourg would still prove to be the greatest challenge of the campaign.

Limbourg was guarded by an aged castle and encircled by concentric rings of medieval walls, buttressed by several bastions of modern designs. Like Dinant and Huy, Limbourg too perched on rocky high ground that would limit an attacker's options. The count of Nassau commanded a garrison of 1,000 troops with adequate supplies.[53] On 13 June Condé and Enghien, who had taken leave of Louis at Visé, arrived at Limbourg, where Enghien took command of the siege. Lines of circumvallation were already dug at this point. After positioning cannon to fire on strongpoints within the town, the French opened their assault trenches on the night of 13–14 June. The next day, a rash French attempt to cross the ditch and establish a position near the citadel met a bloody repulse. The siege returned to more doctrinaire methods, and the French reached the chemin couvert on 16 June.

William's army, now numbering 40,000 troops, moved steadily on Roermond to block any repeat of the French advance in 1672. This decided Louis to break camp at Visé on 18 June, cross the Meuse, and position his army to the east of the Meuse between Roermond and Limbourg.

On 20 June the French exploded three mines against the bastions, and followed with an assault. Soldiers of the Regiment du Roi scored a signal triumph, not only taking the bastion but capturing seventy or eighty of the defenders. The loss of the bastion and its

---

[53] Quincy, *Histoire militaire*, vol. i, p. 433, argued that the garrison of Limbourg numbered 2,500 with about 5,000 local forces.

defenders was so great that the remaining troops in the castle beat the chamade and asked for terms. Terms agreed to on 21 June permitted the garrison of 700 survivors to march out and join William's army at Roermond. The French occupied Limbourg the next day. Louis had achieved all his objectives and could consider the campaign a great success. He traversed the Meuse once again and marched by Tongres, St Trond, and Tirlemont, threatening Brussels. At this, William abandoned Roermond and hurried to Diest on the flank of the French advance. But although this French advance spread terror through Brabant, it resulted in no attack. Instead Louis now detached six battalions and twelve squadrons to reinforce Turenne, as he had in previous years after the main fighting in the Spanish Netherlands had subsided. Then the monarch left for St Germain on 17 July, and on his departure cautioned Condé, the 'victor' of Seneffe, not to hazard a battle. Before the end of the month, Louis learned of the death of Turenne and sent Condé south with additional troops to defend Alsace.

The campaign of 1675 began in Germany at about the same time that it got underway in Flanders. The emperor put Montecuccoli in command of troops once again to square off against his old foe Turenne. Montecuccoli hoped to cross the Rhine at Strasbourg to invade Alsace. Turenne, who had reassembled his army of some 25,000 around Sélestat, approached Strasbourg to compel its burghers to deny their bridge to Montecuccoli, who commanded an army of similar size. The Great Elector had marched off to defend his own lands against the Swedes, so Montecuccoli did not have Brandenburg's troops.

In a game of move and counter-move, Montecuccoli marched down the Rhine to Philippsburg and crossed there on 31 May, but Turenne correctly saw this as a ruse to draw him north so that German troops left at Offenburg could seize Kehl, Strasbourg's bridgehead on the right bank of the Rhine. In fact, Montecuccoli returned to the right bank of the Rhine and dismantled his bridge five days later. On 7–8 June, Turenne, who remained in Alsace up to this point, crossed pontoon bridges established at Ottenheim and took up a position at Willstätt between Offenburg and Kehl in order to deny the latter to the Germans. Montecuccoli marched back to Offenburg and then advanced one flank to the Schutter River, as if to threaten the French bridges, although in fact this was simply another attempt to draw the French away from Kehl. Turenne simply broke up the bridges at Ottenheim and shifted them north to Altenheim. After a week, lack of forage compelled Montecuccoli to withdraw his troops to Offenburg, and then in the first days of July he retired to Urloffen and finally to the juncture of the Rench River with the Rhine, about ten miles down river from Strasbourg. Imperial agents in Strasbourg had arranged to float a bridge train and supplies down to Montecuccoli at his new camp. Turenne countered by interposing his army between Montecuccoli and Strasbourg at Freistett, where Turenne constructed redoubts on either side of the river and put soldiers on boats in the river to intercept anything from Strasbourg. Turenne was still winning the chess game, but the lack of supplies was hurting his army just as it was damaging Montecuccoli's; Turenne's horses were down to eating leaves, and the troops suffered under the continual rain. Turenne resolved that when the weather turned better, he would cross the Rench and extend his foraging to the other side so as to hinder his enemy.

On 22 July, Turenne began a turning movement designed to pin the imperial army against the river and defeat it before it could cross over into Alsace. When imperials countered with attacks to drive off the French vanguard established at Gamshurst, fighting surged back and forth over the next day and night. This serious clash alerted Montecuccoli to the danger he faced, and on the night of 25–6 July he began to withdraw his army east toward the mountains. Turenne chased the retreating imperials and forced them to face him at Sasbach on 27 July. There, as the two armies readied for battle, Turenne and Saint-Hilaire, his artillery commander, reconnoitred an enemy battery established on the French right flank. Perhaps because the red cloak worn by Saint-Hilaire caught the attention of enemy gunners, they fired at the group of officers, and a cannonball tore off Saint-Hilaire's arm and smashed into Turenne's torso, killing him outright. The French tried to hide the death of their great commander for a time, but to little avail. When Montecuccoli, surprised that the battle had not started by mid-afternoon, learned of Turenne's death, he commented, 'Today died a man who did honor to mankind.'[54] De Lorge, the lieutenant-general of the day, took charge of the French forces, and although the armies fired back and forth no battle resulted.

Turenne's death compromised the French campaign. The French army fell back in good order on 29–30 July. Montecuccoli pressed the withdrawing French, and a very hard fight raged at the Schutter River. Vaubrun, commanding the French rear guard, died with a musket

---

54 Montecuccoli in Rousset, *Histoire de Louvois*, vol. ii, p. 161.

ball to the head, and fifteen of the sixteen captains of the Regiment of La Ferté fell with him. With Turenne gone, there was no doubt that the French would retire back to Alsace; only some cavalry forces remained on the right back of the Rhine in the Breisgau. Montecuccoli's army crossed over into Alsace at Strasbourg, which now allowed his passage. A shocked and saddened Louis ordered Condé to Alsace, where he arrived in mid-August. By then, the French situation had only worsened.

Along the Moselle, Créqui was routed at the Battle of Conzer-Brucke by Charles of Lorraine on 11 August. After the destruction of his army, Créqui rallied what troops he could and entered Trier, which Charles put under siege. Créqui conducted a heroic defence, but after three weeks, with the walls breached, his troops mutinied against him and demanded to capitulate on 6 September. Créqui held out to the last with a few faithful officers and men in the church until a lack of ammunition forced his surrender. Once Créqui was exchanged and returned to his army, individuals among the rebellious units were chosen by lot to be hanged for their offence.

In Alsace, the French clung to Saverne and Haguenau, neither of which was a particularly strong fortress, and the imperials now besieged Haguenau. Condé reviewed his troops and found that he commanded only 15,000 to 16,000 troops, with many battalions down to only 300 men and many squadrons down to 70 troopers.[55] Concerned that Charles could soon march south to join Montecuccoli, Condé wanted to relieve Haguenau and strengthen his hold on Alsace. When the French army approached, Montecuccoli fell back on Strasbourg. Condé established his army at Ensheim, until lack of forage compelled him to withdraw to Benfeld, and then when Montecuccoli moved toward Sélestat, Condé returned to the camp of Châtenoi, where he remained for the rest of the campaign. Montecuccoli laid siege to Saverne on 10 September, but gave up the siege against a very aggressive French garrison a few days later. Soon the imperials went into winter quarters, some withdrawing to the right bank of the Rhine and some occupying Wissembourg and Landau in the Palatinate. Perhaps simply the name of the Great Condé had been the greatest French advantage in Alsace in August and September. If so this was a fitting end to his career, for at the end of this campaign, Condé left the army to spend his final decade on his estate at Chantilly. Montecuccoli too would retire at the close of this campaign. The death of Charles IV of Lorraine on 17 August removed another venerable war horse

55 Ibid., p. 184.

from the field of battle. Charles IV was succeeded by his nephew, now Charles V, who was already a general serving Emperor Leopold I and would replace Montecuccoli as the supreme commander of imperial forces.

The campaign of 1675 in Roussillon was not particularly notable. The Spanish army there had been depleted by troops dispatched to fight in Sicily, and the French forces under Schomberg were too few in number, and too inept perhaps, to accomplish much. Schomberg besieged Bellegarde, which he had wanted to retake the year before. He opened the trenches there on 19 July and the governor surrendered the fortress the next day. Schomberg later led his army to the Cerdanya, which he laid under contribution. He eschewed ravaging the country, because he wanted to use it as a logistical base should he besiege Puigcerda, the mountain fortress that guarded the main road that crossed the Pyrenees into the Cerdanya. But not being commanded to undertake this siege, he put his army in winter quarters.

On and around Sicily the fighting grew into a major amphibious operation for the French during 1675. Spain held Sicily, united with the southern boot of Italy as the Kingdom of the Two Sicilies. Opposition to new taxes in Messina had led to riots in 1672, and in July 1674 the city broke out in full-scale rebellion, as crowds fired on Spanish troops and expelled the Spanish governor. When the rebels appealed to the French, a squadron of vessels bearing wheat arrived on 27 September. After the departure of this squadron in October, Spanish forces blockaded the rebel city, but the fact that Messina was a port town allowed it to be supported from the sea. While some believed that the French could conquer the entire island, Colbert insisted there was no money for such a grand venture, so Louis sent a modest force of five companies of infantry. They arrived on 1 January 1675 only to find that Spanish vessels blockaded the harbour, but the small fleet under Jean-Baptiste, bailiff of Valbelle, forced its way through. The French now had a military presence in Messina.

The commander of the small French military detachment, Villavoire, begged for more troops, and in response, Louis dispatched the duke of Vivonne, an experienced galley sailor and a lieutenant-general of the army, soon to be promoted to marshal. He commanded an expeditionary force of nine warships, 3,000 soldiers, and a number of vessels carrying grain. The fleet set sail from Toulon at the end of January and reached Messina on 11 February, where it confronted a Spanish fleet of twenty warships and sixteen galleys. As Vivonne's force battled the Spanish, Valbelle's six ships ventured out from the harbour of Messina and fell on the rear of the Spanish fleet. The Spanish, now caught in a crossfire, broke and withdrew to Naples, leaving Vivonne master of the waters around Messina. Louis dispatched additional galleys to aid the French fleet in June. Particularly in blockade operations, shallow waters, and calm seas, galleys retained considerable naval utility at this time. But if French power had grown, Spanish forces on the island had also been substantially reinforced by German regiments. When Vivonne received further troops from France in May, he attempted to surprise the Spanish headquarters at Milazzo in June, but without success. In August, however, the French succeeded in taking Augusta, on the coast between Syracuse and Catánia, and then moving inland to take Lentini. As the months went on, life in Messina became more difficult, and tensions between its inhabitants and the French rose. Rumours that a Dutch fleet under De Ruyter was on its way to aid the Spanish only made things worse.

THE THIRD PHASE OF THE WAR, 1676–78

The last three years of the war did not do much to alter the outcomes achieved by the end of 1675. Louis's aims seem to have become essentially defensive. Louis would never reestablish a French hold in the United Provinces, but he was able to acquire several more towns to rationalize his frontier with the Spanish Netherlands. William did what he could to counter the French, but was unable either to deny them the towns they attacked or to break through the Meuse barrier. Only two major field battles took place in the Netherlands during the last three years of the war, and the second of these actually took place after the peace treaty had already been signed. Luxembourg, who replaced Condé in Alsace, lost Philippsburg to the able Charles V of Lorraine in 1676, but Créqui, who took command there when Luxembourg went north in 1677, demonstrated considerable talent in protecting Alsace, winning signal victories in 1678. The armies in Roussillon and Catalonia did little, although Navailles took Puigcerda in the last months of the war. Perhaps the most interesting fighting in the last years of the war concerned the French expedition to Sicily. While the French won on land and at sea, they abandoned Messina to its fate before the general peace was concluded.

Faced with the opposition of a large coalition, Louis increased the number of his troops through the end of the war. While 150,000 were considered enough for his original plan, when the French faced a great coalition they marshalled nearly 280,000 men, at least on paper – a theoretical total which may have approached 250,000 in actuality.[56]

1676

Louis marshalled five armies to fight in 1676. The king would once again command the main field force of 50,000 in the Spanish Netherlands; he would have with him his brother, Créqui, the duke of Humières, Schomberg, la Feuillade, de Lorge, and, of course, the indispensable Vauban. Another army formed between the Sambre and Meuse rivers went to the hard-charging Rochefort, while the duke of Luxembourg led the French in Alsace. The army in Roussillon was commanded by Navailles, who replaced Schomberg. The last land force fought on Sicily under the command of Vivonne; although small, it was supported by the most powerful French naval squadrons committed to the war.

In the Spanish Netherlands, the year would witness only sieges, along with the constant, essential, but largely invisible small-scale actions associated with courses, convoys, foraging, and reconnaissance. Once again the French took to the field earlier than their foes, owing to Louvois's excellent magazine system. Humières razed chateaux in the area of Condé, fated to be the first French target of the year, but his actions also threatened Valenciennes and Bouchain. Créqui finally laid Condé under siege on 16 April, while Humières moved on to put the Waes county under contribution. The trenches were opened on the night of 21–2 April and the fortress surrendered three days later.

By the end of April the king joined his army. He detached his brother with Créqui and Vauban to take Bouchain, which they invested on 2 May. Louis, with the main force, covered the siege as enemy troops were assembled around Mons by the prince of Orange and the duke of Villahermosa, the Spanish commander. William now advanced against the French, and learning of this, the French army interposed itself between William and Bouchain by taking up position at Denain. On 10 May, Louis, the king of sieges, would have his

[56] AG, Bibliothèque du ministère de guerre, Tiroirs de Louis XIV, p. 110, 'Troupes que le Roy auvis sur pied le premier janvier 1678'. Quincy, *Histoire militaire*, vol. i, p. 373, identifies the withdrawal of England from the war as the event that triggered French army expansion in the Dutch War. For an analysis of French army growth see John A. Lynn, 'Recalculating French Army Growth During the *Grand siècle*, 1610–1715', *French Historical Studies* 18, no. 4 (Fall 1994), pp. 881–906 reprinted in Clifford Rogers, ed., *The Military Revolution Debate: Readings on the Military Transformation of Early Modern Europe* (Boulder, CO, 1995), pp. 117–47.

chance to reign as the king of battles. He proclaimed, '*Voilà*, a great day for me!'[57] The two armies formed lines of battle between the wood of St Amand and the Scheldt river close to Valenciennes. William, held back by his Spanish allies, entrenched and waited for the French to attack. All was ready if, indeed, there was to be a battle. But instead of impetuously leading his army into combat, Louis asked counsel of his generals. Louvois reminded Louis that the purpose of the army was to cover the siege of Bouchain, not to fight a battle; perhaps mindful of the fate of Turenne less than a year ago, Créqui, Schomberg, and la Feuillade concurred. Only Marshal de Lorge pressed for battle.[58] Louis accepted the majority verdict, 'As you have more experience than me, I cede, but with regret.'[59] In later years he would mourn this decision not to fight this 'Battle of Heurtebise', for he would never command in another battle. Louis simply covered the siege, and Bouchain surrendered the next day. Learning this, William sent a large force of 3,000 men, of whom 2,000 were mounted, to reinforce the garrison of Cambrai and drew off. This force raided across the Somme so effectively that eventually Louis had to detach a large body of cavalry to keep the garrison at bay.

Apparently satisfied with his take so far, Louis did not order another siege in the Netherlands until mid-July. After dispatching a sizeable force of eight battalions and twenty-five squadrons to Marshal Luxembourg in Alsace, Louis advanced his army to Ninove, close to Brussels, on 27 May, where the French stayed, living off the area, until 18 June, when they shifted down to Quiévrain between Valenciennes and Mons to live off the surrounding country, to the discomfort of both fortresses, still in enemy hands. Louis finally departed to return to court on 4 July, leaving Marshal Schomberg in command.

About this time, William resolved to besiege Maastricht. Realizing that this might be his course, the French under Calvo had brought all the forage in the area into the fortress. William's attempt to break the Meuse barrier would not distract the French from besieging Aire, one of the last two Spanish-held fortresses in Artois. Louis calculated correctly that the garrison of Maastricht could hold off an attack long enough for relief to come after Aire had fallen.

57 Quincy, *Histoire militaire*, vol. i, p. 477.
58 This account follows Rousset, *Histoire de Louvois*, vol. ii, pp. 221–2 and Corvisier, *Louvois*, pp. 198–9. Quincy tells the story very differently, not mentioning Louvois at all and having de Lorge argue for caution, with La Feuillade the only dissenter. Quincy, *Histoire militaire*, vol. i, pp. 478–9. Corvisier argues for his account by pointing out that it is corroborated by contemporaries: Saint-Simon, Primi-Visconti, and Pellisson.
59 Rousset, *Histoire de Louvois*, vol. ii, p. 222.

Humières marched with 15,000 men against Aire on 18 July, the same day William opened trenches at Maastricht. Schomberg's army covered Humières while Villahermosa stood off to observe. Aire surrendered on 31 July, freeing Schomberg to relieve Maastricht. Leaving Humières in French Flanders to guard against Villahermosa, Schomberg left the area around Aire on 6 August, and arrived at Tongres near Maastricht on 26 August. There he fired a battery of thirty-two cannon to announce to Calvo that help had arrived.

William had invested Maastricht on 7 July and brought 40,000 men to the siege. Once the lines of circumvallation were complete, William opened the trenches on 18 July. After initially aiming toward one of the gates, the siege trenches veered off to attack a bastion known as the Dauphin which changed hands back and forth during the first days of August. Calvo even used mines himself to repulse the enemy from the contested bastion. Accelerating his efforts when he heard that Aire had fallen, William took part of the chemin couvert on 12 August. Schomberg's signal of 26 August precipitated a final Dutch assault on the French works, but it was driven back. William called a council of war and decided to raise the siege. The last major act of the campaign came when William thought he could cut Schomberg's army off from France, but Schomberg outmanoeuvred the prince handily, and both armies went into winter quarters.

If the campaign of 1676 witnessed no major battles in the Netherlands, neither did it see any along the Rhine. Luxembourg assembled his troops around Sélestat in the spring, while Charles of Lorraine marshalled his troops in the Palatinate. Charles made Philippsburg the object of his campaign. Montecuccoli had already laid the groundwork for this siege the previous autumn by fortifying Lauterbourg on the left bank of the river and seizing other posts. After initial manoeuvres, the imperials closed around Philippsburg, where the prince of Baden conducted the siege while Charles commanded the covering army. Philippsburg sat on a difficult marshy site that made siege operations extremely complicated. The imperials only opened their trenches on 24–5 June. Although he carried out an active defence, the governor Dufay could not expect to hold out unless he was relieved, so on 3 July Luxembourg received orders to come to the aid of the fortress. He arrived at Amback, a league from the enemy camp, on 6 August, but decided not to attack the well-entrenched imperials. Dufay received word that he had carried out such a good defence that he could surrender when appropriate. After the enemy breached an outer work of the fortress and Dufay exhausted his ammunition, the French beat the chamade on 8

September. Meanwhile, Luxembourg had moved troops across the Rhine into the Breisgau to live at the enemy's expense. At the end of the campaign season Luxembourg put his troops into winter quarters in Alsace and Lorraine, which had been protected from enemy occupation again.

The campaign in Roussillon saw little accomplished. Navailles arrived to replace Schomberg in February. He assembled an army of 15,000 as best he could, including pulling men out of garrisons. A Spanish attempt to retake Bellegarde was frustrated, but Navailles's scheme to surprise a Spanish camp failed when *miquelets*, the Spanish local partisan and militia light infantry, reported their movements. At the beginning of July, the king drew 3,000 to 4,000 troops from this army to go to Sicily, hampering any plans Navailles might have had. He withdrew forces to Roussillon and satisfied himself with courses for the remainder of the campaign.

The Sicilian campaign provided a major test of French naval power in 1676, and the French passed admirably. At the end of 1675 a sizeable Dutch fleet under De Ruyter arrived in Sicilian waters around the Lipari Islands, blocking the northern approach to Messina. Abraham Duquesne, sailing from Toulon, encountered De Ruyter on 8 January near the island of Stromboli; the battle was a draw, as the French lost several fireships but were able to circumnavigate Sicily and reach Messina. Duquesne, with the French fleet of thirty vessels and seven fireships, put out to sea from Messina on 19 April, and De Ruyter sailed to meet him with twenty-nine vessels and nine galleys; the two fleets collided on 22 April at the Battle of Augusta. They blasted away at one another with particular fury, and in the torrent of shot, De Ruyter's legs were smashed. The French won the day, but Spanish galleys managed to tow some crippled Dutch ships to safety in Palermo, where on 29 April the great Dutch admiral died of his wounds.

Louis dispatched his galley fleet to Sicily, so when Vivonne led a naval expedition a month later, his fleet counted twenty-eight vessels and twenty-five galleys. On 2 June Vivonne attacked the combined Dutch and Spanish fleet of twenty-nine vessels and nine galleys anchored off Palermo. To escape enemy fire, many of the allied vessels cut their anchor cables and drifted into the coast. French fireships set a number of these vessels ablaze, and the fire spread to the city. Vivonne's victory broke Spanish naval power for the rest of the war, and the Dutch withdrew from Sicilian waters.

The state of the French expedition grew worse in spite of its victories. Lacking adequate state funds to care for his men, Marshal Vivonne borrowed funds on his own credit and handed them over to the *intendant* to feed his army.[60] Despite the fact that he was starved of resources and lacked an artillery train, after his victory at Palermo and with the Spanish hold around Messina weakened, Vivonne undertook a series of operations through 1676 and 1677 that increased the French control on the eastern coast of Sicily. Expanded holdings on the island only imposed greater responsibilities on the French. War did not feed war on Sicily, but simply demanded that the French feed the people under their sway, a fact Louvois never quite grasped. At the strongest, Vivonne only commanded 6,000 to 7,000 French troops, which was not enough to conquer the entire island. When all is said and done, the French court regarded the Sicilian expedition as little more than a way to tie down Spanish forces so as to limit what they could do in Catalonia and Roussillon. When the prospect arose that the English and their fleet might enter the war against France in 1678, the French withdrew from Messina in mid-March of that year. As a parting act of concern, the fleet offered to board any Messinians who believed they would suffer retributions from the returning Spaniards, and 500 prominent families embarked for France. The great amphibious venture, and the only sustained naval victory of Louis's reign, was over.

1677

In the main theatre of the war, the Spanish Netherlands, the war of sieges continued through 1677, as the French consolidated their hold. This expressed the conservative conceptions of Louis's primary strategic advisers, Louvois and Vauban. The targets for French action followed from the gains of the previous year. On the Scheldt, the French had taken Bouchain and Condé, now they would add Valenciennes and Cambrai. After seizing Aire in 1676, the French would complete the conquest of Spanish garrisons in Artois by attacking St Omer. The sole battle in the Netherlands that year, Cassel, was a by-product of the siege of Cambrai. Likewise, just as William III had tried to break the Meuse barrier at Maastricht the previous year, he would attack Charleroi with similar disappointment in 1677.

---

60 In late May alone, he advanced 30,000 livres to the *intendant*. Rousset, *Histoire de Louvois*, vol. ii, p. 429.

The Wars of Louis XIV

The campaign began particularly early in 1677. Humières took to the field in February and feinted against Mons to mislead the Spanish, while Luxembourg invested Valenciennes on 28 February. Humières then linked up with Luxembourg, and on 4 March Louis arrived before Valenciennes. With the full menu of lines of circumvallation and assault trenches, made a particular chore by the ice and snow of winter, the French finally took Valenciennes on 17 March. Louis maintained the momentum by marching to Cambrai, where he personally commanded the siege; his troops invested that fortress on 22 March. At the same time he detached part of his army under the command of his brother Philippe to take St Omer.

With the assistance of 6,000 peasant pioneers, the French dug lines of circumvallation at Cambrai, and on the night of 28–9 March they opened the assault trenches. Within a week the governor surrendered the town and retired with his troops to the citadel. At this point Louis sent some of his troops to Philippe, because the king would need fewer men to attack the citadel. As will be seen, these troops would be particularly welcome to Philippe. At St Omer, Philippe's army opened the assault trenches on the night of 3–4 April, and after considerable artillery preparation launched the first attack on 6–7 April. However, Philippe had to turn to meet a new threat.

While Valenciennes still lay under siege, William had rallied an army at Dendermonde, between Ghent and Antwerp. When the French went on to their next targets, William marched to the relief of St Omer. Leaving some of his army in the siege lines, Philippe left St Omer to confront William. On 10 April the two armies drew up face to face at Cassel; the nine battalions detached from Louis's forces arrived that night, at which point both armies numbered about 30,000 men.[61] In the battle that followed next day, the French right under Humières drove their foes back in retreat, while the French left, under Luxembourg, broke a Dutch attack. William's defeated army might well have been destroyed had not the French paused to take prisoners and pillage William's baggage train. The French lost 1,200 killed and 2,000 wounded, while William's army lost 7,000 to 8,000 dead and wounded in addition to 2,500 captured.[62] Returning to St Omer, Philippe's victorious army finally took the city on 22 April. The citadel at Cambrai had surrendered to Louis a few days before, on 17 April. Louis restored his new conquests to a defensible state, and

61 Bodart, *Kriegs-Lexikon*, p. 101.
62 Rousset, *Histoire de Louvois*, vol. ii, p. 300. Bodart, *Kriegs-Lexikon*, p. 101, gives the casualties as 4,400 dead and wounded for the French and a total of 11,000 for William's army.

after reviewing his troops at the end of May, he and his court, who had accompanied him, returned to France. Louis left Luxembourg in command of the army in the Netherlands with strict instructions to stay on the defensive. With little happening during the summer, William put his troops in rest quarters (*quartiers de rafraichissement*), but when William saw the French follow suit, he reassembled his army and marched on Charleroi, arriving before the fortress on 6 August. Learning of this, Louis dispatched Louvois to the Netherlands and ordered Luxembourg to take the field. Soon the French mustered an army of 40,000 that crossed to the right bank of the Sambre to deny William's army forage from the Sambre and Meuse, while Humières hampered supply from Brussels. This response forced William to raise the siege on 14 August. The only remaining notable action in the Netherlands during 1677 occurred when Humières took St Ghislain in December.

During the winter of 1676–77, because the imperials possessed Philippsburg and enjoyed an alliance with Strasbourg, the French could not protect Alsace effectively and adopted the Vosges rather than the Rhine as their strategic barrier. Forced into Lorraine, Créqui assembled his army around Nancy. After crossing into Alsace in mid-April, Charles left some troops there under the prince of Saxe-Eisenach and marched north to the Moselle. Créqui left Nancy to pursue the imperials in mid-May. For the next few months Charles and Créqui manoeuvred against one another, at times facing off but not risking a battle. By adroit moves, Créqui kept Charles from joining William at Charleroi, thus helping to guarantee the failure of that siege. Charles suffered as he retreated south to Trier. At the same time Créqui led his better-maintained army back to Alsace, where his return forced Saxe-Eisenach to withdraw via Strasbourg on 7–8 September. Créqui burned to take up the offensive and attack Freiburg and Offenburg across the Rhine. He soon crossed to the right bank of the Rhine on 21 September, where he surprised and shattered Saxe-Eisenach's force. But when Charles arrived, Créqui returned to Alsace with Charles following. There they fought a cavalry action at Kockersberg, between Strasbourg and Saverne, on 7 October. The French got much the better in this clash, in which the young Villars distinguished himself.[63] As both armies went into winter quarters, Créqui saw his chance to take Freiburg, and catching Charles

---

63 See Claude Louis Hector Villars, *Mémoires du maréchal de Villars*, ed. marquis de Vogüé (5 vols; Paris, 1884–95), vol. i, pp. 43–5.

off guard, he invested the town on 9 November. The governor capitulated a week later. This allowed Créqui to winter some of his troops in the Breisgau, just as Charles was quartering troops in Alsace. With the majority of his forces, Créqui then returned to Alsace to quarter the rest of his army on the left bank of the Rhine.

In Roussillon the campaign of 1677 started later and it would end sooner. The slowness of the Spanish to take to the field allowed Navailles to forage their country, and in early May he crossed the mountains with his small army of 8,000 men to live at Spanish expense. A more numerous army of 11,000 men under the count of Monterey moved against the French and caught up to them at Espolla in early July. The French were in the process of withdrawing across the Pyrenees when the Spanish attacked on 4 July. During this six-hour fight, the Spanish suffered some 5,000 casualties, an enormous loss considering their modest forces. Although victorious that day, Navailles continued on his path back to France. The front was quiet for the rest of the year.

In the West Indies, the count d'Estrées, who had taken Cayenne the previous year, launched an expedition against Tobago in February 1677. Although d'Estrées failed to take the island, he destroyed the Dutch squadron there in battle on 3 March, ending naval confrontations in the West Indies for the rest of the war. This victory battered the French as well, so Louis dispatched another squadron from Brest to Tobago that autumn. D'Estrées arrived at the island next on 7 December and quickly seized its fort.

1678

The final year of the war witnessed some of the toughest fighting of the conflict, even though peace negotiations were well under way. Louis, who wanted to induce the Dutch to accept his peace terms, launched a venture intended to rivet their attention – the taking of Ghent. The struggle along the Rhine continued, as Créqui duelled against Charles of Lorraine, a contest that resulted in major fighting. Down along the Pyrenees the waning months of war brought the most important siege of the contest at Puigcerda. Finally, the French and Dutch signed a peace treaty on 10 August, but in one of the cruelest of ironies Dutch and Spanish forces confronted Luxembourg at the bloody Battle of St Denis four days after the ink was dry.

Louis did an effective job of misleading his enemies about his plan to besiege Ghent at the start of the 1678 campaign. By taking Ghent, Louis hoped to secure peace before Parliamentary opposition could force Charles II into the war against France. Louis later boasted of his clever deceits. In order to add fanfare to movements meant to make the enemy believe that the French would attack either Luxembourg or strike into Germany, he dragged along the ladies of the court to Metz, including his pregnant mistress the marquise of Montespan, who was both his evening star and the star of his court. After Louis's army marched north and left Luxembourg behind, French forces invested Ypres, Namur, and Mons, creating new uncertainty. Villahermosa was so confused that he withdrew men from Ghent in order to reinforce Ypres.

Finally French forces converged on Ghent, which they invested on 1 March. The governor, Pardo, did what he could to hamper the attackers by inundating the country around the fortress, but his remaining garrison of only about 500 infantry was small. By 4 March, when Louis arrived, the French marshalled eighty-four squadrons and sixty-seven battalions around their prey. This attacking army opened the assault trenches on the night of 5–6 March under the direction of Vauban. After the outer works were taken on the night of 8–9 March, the town capitulated the next day and the castle two days later. Careful misdirection resulted in a quick victory.

With the fall of Ghent, the army marched to Ypres and invested that fortress on 15 March. After the French opened trenches threatening the citadel side of Ypres on 18 March – and the Spanish moved troops and guns to this flank – the French opened other trenches approaching the city side as a diversion. The garrison did not hold out for long, as the governor beat the chamade on 25 March, and the garrison departed the next day. After the fall of Ypres, Louis once again sent troops from Flanders to reinforce Créqui in Alsace and Lorraine. Louis toured his new conquests and then rejoined the queen and the ladies at Lille; on 7 April he left the front for the comforts of St Germain, undoubtedly to the relief of the court. Luxembourg took command of the army in the north.

Louis returned to his northern frontier in mid-May, but he had not come to lead a new campaign but to proclaim his desire for peace. Louis's ambassadors had already presented his conditions to the Dutch on 15 April, hopefully while the shock of Ghent and Ypres was still sharp. His appearance now at the front advertised his resolve for peace, because he ordered his address to the States General to be printed, promised to undertake no more sieges in Flanders through

June, and commanded Luxembourg to remain inactive near Brussels. The king returned to St Germain in June. Louis prepared for the peace to come. Knowing what towns he intended to give up, he directed commanders at Oudenarde and Charleroi to degrade, damage, or destroy the fortresses' defences. In late June, Louis ordered Luxembourg to send reinforcements to Marshal Schomberg on the Meuse, leave forty squadrons to blockade Mons, and pull back the remainder of his army to French borders. William, on the contrary, continued to manoeuvre to relieve the pressure on Mons, and Louis finally authorized Luxembourg to fight. Louvois wrote to the marshal, using a medical analogy, 'The king awaits news that you have fought, and that the blood letting will be great enough to eliminate the humours opposed to peace in the body of the Dutch Republic.'[64] A peace treaty between the French and the Dutch would be signed on 10 August, but it did not end the fighting immediately. In what remains something of a mystery, the word apparently did not reach the armies in time to avert William from attacking the French in the Battle of St Denis to the west of Mons on 14 August.[65] Fighting was very hot that day; the Allies lost as many as 4,000 dead without counting wounded and captured, and French losses were on the same level.[66] That night, news of the peace treaty arrived in both camps.

Along the Rhine, Créqui received orders for 1678 that strictly circumscribed his activity. He was not to antagonize the Germans by moves against Strasbourg or the Swiss by endangering the forest cities. He was just 'to keep things on the same footing as last year, that is to conserve the king's fortresses and troops . . . without exposing himself to the risk of a general action'.[67] The Germans were slow to take the field; only in mid-May did Charles assemble his army near Offenburg. Créqui formed up at Sélestat, then moved to Breisach and Freiburg. Charles demonstrated in different directions, but Créqui recognized that the real target was Freiburg. Charles probed for a weak point in the French lines covering Freiburg, but lack of supplies and forage forced him back to Offenburg. Now reinforced with troops

---

64 AG, A¹616, 25 July 1678, Louvois to Luxembourg, in Rousset, *Histoire de Louvois*, vol. ii, pp. 510–11.
65 Some French insisted that he knew of the treaty; see Quincy, *Histoire militaire*, vol. i, p. 591, for an example.
66 Ibid., p. 594.
67 AG, A¹534, 9, 13, 18 April 1678, Louvois to Créqui in Rousset, *Histoire de Louvois*, vol. ii, pp. 540–1.

from Flanders, Créqui rushed south to Rheinfeld on the Swiss border. Charles pursued with his main army and detached a flying column of 5,000 men under Starhemberg, who reached the town in time to oppose Créqui's troops at the Battle of Rheinfeld on 6 July. As the French swept forward, the fortress commander closed the gates of the town to save it, but this trapped Starhemberg's men between the French and the walls, where they were eliminated.

Further successes did not wait long. Créqui's victory at Rheinfeld broke down Louis's and Louvois's resistance to a venture against Offenburg, so Créqui marched north rapidly and surprised that imperial base. On 23 July at Ortenbach, he encountered the imperial troops left to protect Offenburg, and behind them stood Charles with the imperial cavalry just returned from their dash south. The main body of Charles's army was still on the road, but units were arriving with each hour. French impetuosity won the day, but Créqui did not rout the imperials, who eventually formed a new line with troops back from their long march. Créqui next closed the imperial gate into Alsace by cutting the bridge at Strasbourg/Kehl. When the magistrates refused to turn over Kehl and its bridge, he opened trenches on the night of 25–6 July and took the fortress two days later with an assault by the grenadiers of the army. After razing the fortifications and destroying the eastern section of the bridge, Créqui marched to Altenheim and crossed the Rhine via a pontoon bridge on 8 August. He then turned on Strasbourg, where, on 11 August, he took Fort Péage guarding the western end of the bridge. With Fort Péage in his hands he could destroy the rest of the bridge.

Denied Strasbourg's bridge, Charles marched to Philippsburg to cross the Rhine and descend into Alsace, but he was blocked by Créqui on the Lauter. Suffering from lack of supplies owing to the usual administrative shortcomings of the Germans, Charles's run-down army, now reduced to half its initial strength, finally took to winter quarters in October. The emperor would agree to peace before a new campaign could begin.

The French army in Roussillon grew with the return of troops withdrawn from Sicily in March, and this freed Marshal Navailles to undertake the siege of Puigcerda, a project the French had considered for some time. Sending some detachments into eastern Catalonia, Navailles brought most of his troops west toward Puigcerda, which his vanguard invested on 29 April. The fortress governor was so confident that he had danced away the previous night celebrating the marriage of one of his officers. Well he might feel secure, because the mountains provided a fine defence for Puigcerda, surrounding the fortifications like natural outer works. After opening trenches on 30 April, the French unsuccessfully attacked the chemin couvert on 3 May. The French artillery only arrived two days later, thanks to the efforts of Swiss soldiers who manhandled the guns up mountain roads when mules refused. Soon the guns breached the wall, but the garrison refused to capitulate. The count of Monterey made a couple of attempts to relieve the fortress, but pulled back when resisted by French troops who guarded the approaches. Only after his defences were in ruins from cannon shot and mine blast did the Spanish capitulate on 28 May. Louis had no intentions of keeping Puigcerda, so Louvois ordered Navailles to disarm it and destroy all fortifications. This was the last major act of the war in the Pyrenees, for negotiations were soon to bring peace.

After a false start at Cologne, serious negotiations finally began in Nijmegen during the summer of 1676. In the spring of the previous year, the warring parties had reached a consensus to meet there, but the wheels of diplomacy turned very slowly, as dust and blood collected. Louis's war aims moderated after 1675. As the campaigns of 1676 and 1677 demonstrate, the king had become more concerned with consolidating and defending what he held than with adding new territories. Louis made more dramatic gains in 1678, but without the intention of keeping them; even as he took Ghent he announced that he would return it to Spain with the peace. By early 1678 it seemed that England might enter the war against France momentarily, and this spurred on French negotiators. Even though a small English expeditionary force landed at Ostend to help the Allies, Louis reached a bargain with Charles II in May to assure English neutrality. The States General, pleased with the moderate demands that the French had put forward in April, voted on 22 June to make a separate peace with France. After some further delays, including French demands that Sweden recover its losses suffered at the hands of Brandenburg, the French and Dutch signed the Treaty of Nijmegen on 10 August. Once the French had broken the alliance by a separate peace with the Dutch, the other belligerents came into line. A Franco-Spanish treaty followed on 17 September, and peace followed with the emperor on 6 February 1679.

Louis gained a great deal by the Treaty of Nijmegen. From Spain he took Franche-Comté and a number of valuable cities, including Valenciennes, Cambrai, Aire, St Omer, Ypres, Condé, Bouchain. The campaigns of 1676–78 had not been for nothing. Louis gave up other fortresses that he had seized during the war for logistical or strategic reasons and some he had held before, such as Oudenarde. The exchange of cities extended and rationalized French domains. In addition, although the treaty provided for the restoration of Lorraine to Duke Charles, it did so on such conditions that he refused, and the French retained possession of that important duchy. Along the Rhine, while the French lost the right to garrison Philippsburg, they gained Freiburg, preserving a bridge across the Rhine. The Dutch received back all their territory, and the French also rescinded the 'fighting tariff' of 1667 and even privileged some Dutch trade. At the end of the conflict, putting aside for a moment the terrible human costs of the war and its huge financial burdens, the French and the Dutch had both come out ahead. Spain ultimately paid for their victories.

CONCLUSION

The War of Devolution and the Dutch War were both wars for *gloire*, political actions intended to establish the king's personal reputation and prowess. To that extent, their rationale was relatively frivolous to the modern mind. But if they were about glory, they were also about moderate territorial gain – not about limitless conquest or European domination – at least in the long run. The French king did not pursue substantial territorial gain through bloody conquest in any other area than the Netherlands. Along the Rhine he committed forces solely to defend his new territories of Alsace and Lorraine, both secured before a shot was fired in the Dutch War. Louis did grab Franche-Comté, already surrounded by French territory on three sides, but that plum had been ripe for the picking for some time. Conquered once in the War of Devolution, it fell to him again in 1674, through fighting that was little more than perfunctory. Along the Pyrenees the French and Spanish went through the motions with little intent other than to make the war difficult for the other side and to preserve the existing border. Concerning Sicily, Louis consistently resisted urgings to conquer all of the island; the fighting there was nothing more than a diversion.

Only in the Netherlands was Louis bent on conquest, but how much and from whom? In his original conception the war was designed to push the Dutch aside so that Louis could deal with the Spanish Netherlands as he chose. Louis's arrogance, fed by French successes in the first months of the war, subverted his original intentions into exaggerated demands that would have reduced the United Provinces to a marginal state. It is worth noting that the noted diplomatic historian John Rule believes that Louis's demands upon the Dutch were simply bargaining chips to be exchanged for lands in the Spanish Netherlands.[68] No one can say what the fate of the Spanish Netherlands would have been had the Dutch agreed to Louis's proposals; perhaps he would have claimed it all. From a purely French perspective, Louis would never again demand as much as he did in the summer of 1672. But if he set his sights too high in June, he lowered them again before long. He soon realized that he could not eradicate Dutch power, and that the Dutch would never allow him a free hand in the Netherlands. Louis responded by moderating his expectations as early as 1673 and then reshaping them into a search for defensible frontiers by 1676. Acting in accord with the cautious advice of Louvois and Vauban, Louis held off William III while consolidating and rationalizing his frontiers. If he ever strove to dominate Europe, it was neither his first nor final goal, simply an arrogant, and passing, fancy.

From a purely military standpoint, the Dutch War cautions against too easy a stereotype of seventeenth-century warfare, because styles of campaigning varied considerably from front to front. Siege warfare dominated in the Netherlands. The seven years of the Dutch War witnessed only three major battles in the Netherlands, at Seneffe, Cassel, and St Denis, and the last two were associated with sieges or blockades. In addition, manoeuvre was restricted in the Netherlands; there were no great chases as occurred south of the Meuse. The abundance of strong fortifications in the Netherlands would seem to account for both the prevalence of positional warfare and the limited mobility. In addition, since the goal of the war in the Spanish Netherlands was securing and protecting terrain that parties hoped to retain after the peace, the fighting centred on fairly fixed lines. The fact that Louis formed his notions of war almost exclusively in the Netherlands where he attended numerous sieges but never witnessed a battle gave him a special idea of warfare, not incorrect but certainly limited.

In contrast, campaigning between the Meuse and the Moselle, and particularly along the Rhine, brought a good number of battles and few sieges. Interestingly, few open field fights were by-products of positional warfare. Great manoeuvres were the stock in trade of the French under Turenne and Créqui, who fought in very similar styles. Montecuccoli and the two Charleses were similarly prone to rapid and constant movement. The modest size of contending forces, the rarity of strong fortress towns, and the need to change venues

---

68 John Rule, letter of 26 January 1998.

to guarantee forage and supply all encouraged attempts to achieve results by manoeuvre. Also, since the permanent conquest was not the ultimate goal here, the pressures to defend fixed lines were less.

The Mediterranean fronts were different as well. The forces contending along the Pyrenees were quite small, and on the whole they fought only along a restricted and static front. In lieu of full-scale armies devoting their energies to numerous sieges, frequent battles, or dramatic manoeuvres, war along the Pyrenees often came down to raids and the ravages of partisan warfare. Of course partisan warfare was common on all fronts, but it was a question of degree. Local militia/light infantry know as *miquelets* fought on both sides. Small forces, rugged terrain, sparse population, limited supply, and restricted roads gave war along the Pyrenees its own character. The style of operations in Sicily was absolutely unique. The island geography, the presence of substantial naval forces, and the lack of ground forces made sea battles critical and amphibious operations productive.

It is fair to say that Louis's strategic principles developed during the Dutch War. While the invasion of the United Provinces failed in the first two years of the war, French forces won sufficient victories and secured enough territory in the next five years to give Louis the glory he desired. He was now proclaimed as the Sun King. From conquest, he turned to security; one needs only to examine the last three campaigns to realize this. But if an emphasis on security seems more reasonable, and even more humane, than a lust for glory, the need to secure defensible frontiers demanded certain key additions to French territory. Most notably, the fact that Strasbourg had provided the imperials with easy passage into Alsace marked that city for absorption. Louis could reasonably insist that he could no longer tolerate an independent Strasbourg that could compromise Alsace in the future. By this logic, the coming Reunions were a necessary extension of the Dutch War.

5 VIOLENCE AND STATE POLICY: REUNIONS, MEDITERRANEAN EXPEDITIONS, AND INTERNAL STRUGGLES

If it was not war in name, it was war in fact. The period between the signing of the Treaty of Nijmegen and the outbreak of the Nine Years War may not have witnessed the full mobilization of French military forces, but they were hardly years of peace. Military violence undergirded Louis's policy during the 1680s.

Louis and his advisers regarded the Dutch War as a success, even though the French had abandoned their initial goals after 1675. In fact, to Louis, it seemed that the peace treaty had not rewarded French victory sufficiently, despite the gain of an entire province, Franche-Comté, and several cities in the Spanish Netherlands. Now, as at other key junctures, a sense of success was dangerous for Louis, for he failed to reap lasting advantage from a favourable twist of fate, but overplayed his hand when he felt he had some good cards. His overbearing demands after the French advance into the Dutch Netherlands in 1672 demonstrated this; so would his propensity to bully Europe in the 1680s.

Foretelling his shift toward a more heavy-handed policy, Louis removed the skilled and moderate Pomponne from the office of secretary of state for foreign affairs and replaced him with Charles Colbert, marquis of Croissy (1625–96), in November 1679. He blamed Pomponne for not having gained more at the peace table. Croissy, although a Colbert and thus a natural rival of Louvois, a Le Tellier, shared the war minister's bluntness and predilection for violence as a tool of state policy.[1] Croissy also harboured a lawyer's contentiousness and petty insistence on winning every small point, characteristics that would not serve him well as a diplomat. If Pomponne had moderated Louvois's tendency toward brutal means, Croissy reinforced them.

[1] See Andrew Lossky, *Louis XIV and the French Monarchy* (New Brunswick, NJ, 1994), pp. 170, 237, for this view of Croissy.

Louis, now acclaimed as Louis the Great because of victory in the Dutch War, was at the height of his powers, with little tendency to show restraint. Justified by success, he now resorted to military action to solidify and expand his frontiers, to chastise those who offended his grandeur, and to impose religious unity on France. Only in the form of the brief War of the Reunions do historians label this use of violence as warfare, but military action was the hallmark of Louis's policy. We must then expand the definition of war to include significant military combat even in the absence of a formal declaration of hostilities. This probing of the definition of war also requires an examination of the phenomenon of civil rebellion during Louis's regime. Looked at closely, the 1680s do not look like a period of confident peace, but like one of almost gratuitous violence in the name of state policy.

THE REUNIONS, 1679–84

For the five years following the Dutch War, Louis imposed his aggressive conception of a just peace along French borders as, in fact, war, because he went beyond diplomatic argument and appealed to armed violence. In a series of 'Reunions', the Sun King seized lands that he did not yet hold, absorbing them into his growing kingdom. These seizures combined legalism and defensive strategy with arrogance and aggression, in a way that defies easy categorization.

The treaties of Westphalia and Nijmegen provided the justification for the Reunions. Treaty language of the day was intentionally imprecise; for example, it commonly granted one party a particular town or district and 'its dependencies', leaving the parties involved to work out in detail what 'dependencies' were actually involved. The Treaty of Westphalia was notoriously vague, even self-contradictory, in this regard. Muddying the waters allowed conflicting parties to accept a treaty more easily because they were agreeing to their own interpretations of the text, so treaties might end a war without ending the dispute. However, this language also reflected the necessarily confused realities of frontiers at this time.

During the second half of the seventeenth century, the concept of state borders was in the process of evolution.[2] Earlier tradition and political practice conceived of the juridical (*limites*) and the military

---

2 On this evolution, see Peter Sahlins, 'Natural Frontiers Revisited: France's Boundaries since the Seventeenth Century', *American Historical Review* 95, no. 5 (December 1990), pp. 1423–51.

161

frontiers (*frontières*), across which opposing states faced, or 'fronted', each other, not as lines on the ground but as zones of overlapping rights, authorities, and positions. These zones were evolving into more modern, clearer lines on the map under Louis XIV. For Richelieu a proper frontier opened neighbouring territory to invasion or influence; thus he sought fortresses as gates (*portes*) to provide access for French armies. Such a conception of frontier required footholds on the right bank of the Rhine or across the Alps in Italy. Louis continued this policy, but it came to be overshadowed by the notion of a frontier as a barrier to an enemy, with fortresses less valuable in providing gates than in forming an impenetrable wall that protected and defined a border. Louis did not follow an articulated policy of achieving 'natural frontiers', as once argued by historians such as Albert Sorel, but in search of more defensible and better delineated frontiers, where natural barriers provided important demarcations. So, under Louis, the Pyrenees, the Alps, and the Rhine became effective natural frontiers for military and political reasons, although the new definition of France became conceptual as well, a sense of identity and space.[3] The Reunions increased Louis's domains, to be sure, but they represented more than territorial greed; they consolidated and framed a more defensible frontier.

Alsace was particularly afflicted by long-standing, treaty-bred confusion concerning the frontier zone. Although the Treaty of Westphalia awarded the Bourbons the remaining Habsburg claims in Alsace, it was unsure what those territorial claims were, and it was equally unsure whether or not Alsace as a whole left the Holy Roman Empire when parts of it passed to France. Many communities in Alsace regarded themselves as part of the Holy Roman Empire, not France, and so in the Dutch War they willingly aided Imperial troops and resisted Bourbon forces.

Louis, Croissy, and Louvois determined to resolve border disputes flowing from the treaties by creating special courts, or chambers, that would consider the king's claims. As a consequence of the Treaty

---

[3] Ibid., p. 1434. The Treaty of Ryswick would make the Rhine a clear border, and the Treaty of Utrecht would define the border between France and Savoy as 'the watershed of the Alps'. Sahlins pursues his argument as if the primary rationale behind French policy was essentially conceptual, when harsh military realities had a great deal to do with them. Adopting the Rhine from Philippsburg to Switzerland as a hard and fast border may have been important in defining 'identity' and 'an imagined national space' (p. 1425); however, it also had much to do with keeping out the Germans, whose invasions of the 1670s tormented Louis. The whole business can be read as further evidence of Louis's defensive mentality.

of Nijmegen, Spanish and French commissioners met in Courtrai to settle complicated issues concerning the border between France and the Spanish Low Countries. But while that commission was bilateral, Louis created new 'chambers of reunion' from his own royal law courts in Metz, Besançon, and Breisach, to deal respectively with Lorraine, Franche-Comté, and Alsace.[4] (While Lorraine at this point did not technically belong to France, Louis had integrated this province into his kingdom after occupying it in 1670 and would not relinquish it to its duke until 1697.)

The chamber at Besançon quickly declared the villages in the county of Montbéliard to be under French sovereignty. This disputed county just west of Belfort linked Franche-Comté with Alsace and would provide an enemy with a base to threaten both. Its incorporation made good strategic sense. The chamber at Breisach, not surprisingly, also demanded that towns and nobles in Alsace swear loyalty to Louis XIV without reference to the empire or the emperor. French forces stationed in Alsace intimidated the reluctant. Through this means, Colmar, Wissembourg, Haguenau, and other major towns finally pledged themselves to France, so by August 1680 Louis secured his hold on all of Alsace, with the exception of Strasbourg. The conditions set by the Treaty of Westphalia guaranteed the Protestant faith in that province.

But the gains made by the other chambers were modest compared with those registered by the chamber of reunion in Metz. Soon it laid claim to lands around the bishoprics of Metz, Toul, and Verdun. But then in July 1681 the Metz chamber determined that the county of Chiny in the Duchy of Luxembourg had once belonged to Metz, so French troops took it from the Spanish, who counted Luxembourg among their lands. After determining that Chiny held still other parts of Luxembourg as dependencies in the past, the French grasped them as well, until little of the duchy remained in Spanish hands besides the formidable fortress town of Luxembourg itself. Now that the French held the territory surrounding it, they blockaded the fortress, for Louis determined to take it in order to bolster his defensible frontier.

Meanwhile, on 30 September 1681 Louis's troops seized Strasbourg and its outpost on the right bank of the Rhine, Kehl. Imperial troops had exploited this bridge across the Rhine repeatedly during

---

4 The chambers of reunions in Metz and Besançon were composed of members of the local *parlements*, which were law courts. That in Brisach was made up of members of a lesser sovereign court in that city. Officially, the only true 'chamber of reunion' was in Metz, but the two other courts are generally referred to by this title as well.

the later stages of the Dutch War, and Louis and his advisers believed that Alsace would not be secure so long as Strasbourg remained an independent imperial city. Vauban asserted in 1678 that taking Strasbourg would be 'of the greatest consequence'.[5] Louvois went to great lengths to amass the food and materiel necessary for a siege, while disguising his actions. When all was ready, French troops glided into place with little fanfare, and the magistrates faced an ultimatum backed by overwhelming force. They wisely decided to capitulate to French demands on condition that Strasbourg retain many of its old rights and privileges, and the city fell without a shot.

European confusion was all the greater because on the very same day that his troops entered Strasbourg, French troops from Dauphiné took Casale in Italy as an additional bridgehead across the Alps. Casale stood on the banks of the Po River about forty miles due east of Turin. Casale did not end up in French hands through the process of the Reunions but via a deal struck between Louis and its master, the dissolute and impecunious duke of Mantua, who surrendered the fortress to Louis in exchange for an initial payment of about 1,000,000 livres and an annual subsidy of 60,000 livres. The double coup of Strasbourg and Casale stunned European statesmen.

With Strasbourg in Louis's hands, the French demanded that the city's old cathedral, which had become a Protestant church, be returned to Catholic worship. This could only have been seen as an insult by the locals. Louis arrived to receive the cheers, however reluctant, of his new subjects on 23 October and heard mass in the newly reconverted cathedral the next day.

The initial gains of the Reunions raised the ire of Louis's foes, but stopped short of open warfare; however, in the winter of 1681–82 cold war turned hot. In order to feed his starving garrison, the Spanish commander of Luxembourg sortied from the fortress, attacked blockading French troops, and brought in a convoy of food and supplies. Louis punished this challenge to the royal will by invading the Spanish Netherlands and devastating the lands around Courtrai. There, the Franco-Spanish commission continued its discussions, although Louis had already carried on largely without regard to these negotiations. One provision of the Treaty of Nijmegen awarded Louis either Charlemont or Dinant, a Gordian knot he cut simply by occupying both. The French incursion around Courtrai must have provided ample

---

5 Vauban 'Mémoire des places frontières de Flandres qu'il faudrait fortifier pour la sureté des pays de l'obéissance du Roy', November 1678, in Albert Rochas d'Aiglun, *Vauban, sa famille et ses écrits* (2 vols; Paris, 1910), vol. i, p. 191.

warning once again to the Spanish commissioners that Louis expected to get what he wanted. At the same time, Louis authorized Boufflers, in command of troops around Luxembourg, to bombard the city with mortar shells. This type of attack became a vogue for the French in the 1680s. Bombardment promised to intimidate a foe without risking the cost and casualties suffered in a full-scale siege. All one needed to do was approach close enough to bring this new weapon in range; there was no need to pay the cost of storming the fortress. Powder-filled mortar shells, or bombs, killed and destroyed by their explosive power and the shrapnel of their shell casings, but their greatest effect came in igniting fires which could gut buildings of an enemy town even though the attackers had never breached its walls. Despite Louvois's penchant for bombardment, not all authorities agreed on its value. Vauban, in particular, disapproved of it as causing destruction without real result, but he was a reasonable and humane soldier.

Now, however, the Ottoman invasion of Habsburg lands along the Danube broke the momentum of Louis's confrontation with Spain. With Turks beginning a campaign that would climax at the siege of Vienna in 1683, Louis decided that it would be impolitic for him, the Most Christian King, to continue an assault on another Christian power, an assault that could be seen as aiding the infidel. So Louis ordered a stop to the bombardment and in March 1682 he withdrew his troops from around Luxembourg, ending his stranglehold, and proposed that France and Spain submit their cases to the arbitration of the king of England. We cannot read Louis's mind at this time, but some have suggested that he hoped to become the protector of Germany should the Turks triumph over the Austrian Habsburgs, whom he probably believed to be the weaker party, because the Germans were still recovering from the Thirty Years War. With a Habsburg defeat, he alone would be strong enough to drive the Turks from Germany, which would then reward him by granting him virtual dominion over the empire, perhaps by even electing Louis or his progeny to be Holy Roman Emperor.[6]

While the case against Louis is compelling, it is not absolutely conclusive. True, Louis meddled in the Ottoman invasion. First, he assured the Turks that should they attack, French enmity with the emperor would keep him from sending aid to the Habsburgs. Second, Louis tried to keep the Polish king, Jan Sobieski, from coming to the

6 John B. Wolf, *Louis XIV* (New York, 1968), pp. 413–15, argues strongly that Louis worked to bring about this scenario.

aid of beleaguered Vienna. Third, he failed to send a French army to defend Vienna, even though Pope Innocent XI asked him to do so. None the less, distracting the Habsburgs by encouraging the Turks was an old French gambit dating back to François I at least, and it does not in itself prove Louis's lust for domination. It is to be noted that the success of this scenario depended not on French actions but on those of the Ottoman Turks, for if they had taken Vienna and continued to drive further into central Europe, Louis would have been obliged to intervene militarily, plot or no plot. However, as it turned out, French intervention was unnecessary, for an attack by combined German and Polish relief armies smashed the Turks before the walls of Vienna on 12 September 1683, and the Ottoman threat ebbed.

If it could be proven, a Bourbon plot of 1682–83 would be the best evidence that Louis did, indeed, aim at European hegemony. Still, at most, this was only a momentary digression from a very long course of pragmatic and moderate territorial acquisition. And none of Louis's actual military campaigns after 1675, including the acquisitions of the Reunions, justify in themselves European fears and historians' speculations that he intended to dominate the Continent.

As the Ottomans stalled before Vienna, Louis returned to the attack a few days before the Christian victory there. On 31 August 1683, his ambassador declared to the new governor of the Spanish Netherlands, the marquis of Grana, that since the Spanish king had rejected arbitration by the king of England and refused to satisfy French claims, the French would cross the border and subsist 35,000 troops at Spanish expense through the imposition of contributions amounting to 3,000,000 florins.[7] French troops renewed their blockade of Luxembourg as well. Grana appealed to the Dutch to live up to their treaty obligations, and they sent 8,000 troops to aid him, with the promise of more. On 12 October, Grana ordered that force be met with force, and Spanish raiding parties struck French villages and imposed their own contributions. Louis responded to what he regarded as this outrage by ordering Marshal Humières 'always to burn fifty houses or villages for every one which will have been burned on my lands'.[8] Such was the brutal arithmetic of escalation. On 26 October the Council of Spain declared war on France, beginning the War of the Reunions, which in several respects would prove to be Louis's most successful war. Oddly enough this is also Louis's 'forgotten war', in that most histories pass over it without mention.

[7] Camille Rousset, *Histoire de Louvois* (4 vols; Paris, 1862–64), vol. iii, p. 236.
[8] AG, A¹722, 24 October 1683.

Learning of the Spanish declaration, Louis appealed to the Dutch, saying that he would give up his claims on Alost, Ghent, and other places in the Spanish Netherlands if the Spanish would do one of the following: (1) concede to him the duchy and city of Luxembourg; (2) give him Dixmude and Courtrai as well as Beaumont, Bouvines, and Chimay in Flanders; (3) surrender to him Puigcerda, la Seu d'Urgell, Camprodon, and Castellfollit in Catalonia; (4) transfer Roses, Gerona, and Cap de Quiers with their dependencies in Catalonia to France; or (5) transfer Pamplona and Fuenterrabia with their dependencies in Navarre to his domain. The deadline for this deal was 31 December. Meanwhile, Louis ordered Humières to besiege Courtrai, where the marshal opened trenches on the night of 3–4 November. The city fell the next day, and the citadel capitulated on 6 November. From Courtrai, Humières advanced to Dixmude, which gave up without a fight on 10 November, because its garrison numbered only seventeen soldiers commanded by a single officer.

Even though the Dutch dispatched troops to support Grana, this war proved a most unequal struggle. The Spanish expected aid from the emperor and the Germans as well, but Leopold was engaged in the struggle with the Ottomans and could not afford to be diverted by a war in the Spanish Netherlands and along the Rhine. The War of the Reunions progressed on three fronts: the Pyrenees, the Spanish Netherlands west of the Meuse, and Luxembourg. Louis dispatched Marshal Bellefonds to the Pyrenees in March 1684, apparently to demonstrate that he could take the Spanish towns that he had proposed as fair compensation for his claims on Alost and Ghent. First Bellefonds drove a small force of regulars and militia up from St Jean-Pied-de-Port through the snow to Roncesvalles and Burguete in Spanish Navarre on the road to Pamplona. Then he immediately withdrew back to St Jean, which he left in late March to take command of forces marshalling in Roussillon to attack Catalonia. He advanced these forces to La Junquera on 1 May, fought his way across the Ter River on 12 May, and then briefly, and unsuccessfully, besieged Gerona.

After the seizure of Courtrai and Dixmude the War of the Reunions in Flanders and Hainault degenerated into sheer destruction. Each side imposed contributions on the other's villages, which suffered execution by burning if they refused to comply. Executions led to reprisals, as Louis and Louvois demonstrated regrettable brutality in this contest. When, in February 1684, Louvois ordered the count of Montal to burn twenty villages near Charleroi because the Spanish had burned two barns on the extremities of two French villages, the minister commanded the general to 'throw around some broadsides that say that this is in reprisal for the burning of the two barns'. Louvois charged Montal to leave not a single house standing in the twenty villages.[9] And then there were continued bombardments. French shells consumed Oudenarde from 23 to 26 March 1684, and its fate was not unique. In April, Louis took command of an army of 40,000 troops gathered around Condé and Valenciennes, but the sole purpose of this force was to keep the Spanish from shifting forces south to resist the siege of Luxembourg, the primary target of French operations that spring.

Assisted by Vauban and his engineers, the very able Marshal Créqui undertook the siege of that fortress. Earlier, between 22 and 26 December Créqui had advanced on Luxembourg, bombarded the fortress with 3,000–4,000 mortar shells, and then withdrew with great difficulty. This bombardment failed to convince the Spanish that they must agree to Louis's ultimatum, so in April another French army converged on Luxembourg. The French troops surrounded the city on 29 April and began digging lines of circumvallation. Once these were completed, the attacking troops opened their trenches during the night of 8–9 May. The garrison of 2,500 soldiers actively and resolutely defended their fortress, using every method at their disposal, including several sorties. No one was immune to danger; a cannonball even decapitated one of Créqui's valets. French grenadiers drawn from several regiments played a particularly valorous role in the siege. Finally, on 3 June the Spanish commander, Chimay, ordered his drummer to beat the chamade. The French accorded him and his garrison all the honours of war as they marched out with flags flying and drums beating a few days later. When Louis learned that Luxembourg had fallen, he left Valenciennes for Versailles, site of his new palace.

At this point Louis sought a general truce that would guarantee his gains even if he could not secure permanent Spanish and European agreement to his acquisitions. Louis promised to give back Courtrai and Dixmude, after he razed their fortifications, and abandon nearly all he had gained since August 1683 if the Spanish would accede to his possession of Luxembourg. Soon Louis split the alliance against him. By the end of June the Dutch agreed to try to convince the Spanish to accept the long truce, but should the Spanish refuse, the Dutch would then withdraw their troops. Now without hope of

---

9 Order to Montal, 18 February 1684, in Jacques Hardré, ed., *Letters of Louvois, University of North Carolina Studies in the Romance Languages and Literatures*, no. 10 (Chapel Hill, 1949), p. 343.

international rescue, the Spanish king accepted the truce, as did the emperor. The final agreements, signed at Ratisbon on 15 August 1684, allowed Louis to retain Strasbourg, Luxembourg, and other Reunions, while he returned Courtrai and Dixmude to Spain. This Truce of Ratisbon marked the high-water mark of Louis's territorial acquisitions at the end of his briefest and most successful war.

The Reunions mixed legal and reasonable claims with specious ones made not in the name of justice but in the name of strategic necessity. Chamlay, an important military counsel to the king, would write, '[The courts] found several good and incontestable titles, others very doubtful, and rather than keeping within just limits which would have secured the greatest advantages to the King, they pushed things too far ... so that ... [they] aroused great umbrage.'[10] Enmity that Louis created by overreaching would come back to haunt him, and soon. The seizures of Strasbourg and Luxembourg alarmed German princes, and, together with Louis's religious intolerance, would engender fear and resentment that William of Orange would mobilize in anti-French coalitions. William could himself be doubly outraged because Louis also seized William's traditional family lands of Orange, an enclave in France along the Rhône, in 1680. This had nothing to do with the legalities of the Reunions; it was simply an assault on a personal enemy of the French king. Throughout this period, Louis showed himself unnecessarily disdainful of European opinion and demonstrated just how far he had abandoned the more conciliatory diplomacy of Mazarin.

The necessity and legitimacy of the Reunions as a whole can be debated. For some historians, Lossky in particular, they were 'indiscriminate' and 'an abandonment of the sensible aim of seeking a defensible frontier'.[11] While they certainly displayed the arrogance that Louis was all too liable to display when things were going his way, they were not necessarily poorly conceived. Defensive logic, at least the logic of an impermeable defence, compelled Louis to consolidate what he believed was his rightful hold on Alsace, based on the treaties of Westphalia and Nijmegen. Taking the county of Montbéliard also made perfect sense, since it lay between Franche-Comté and Alsace.[12] Strasbourg had served as a gateway for German invasions into Alsace three times during the Dutch War; there was little wonder why Louis believed that he must take it.

---

10 Chamlay in Wolf, *Louis XIV*, p. 407.
11 Lossky, *Louis XIV*, p. 171.
12 Wolf, *Louis XIV*, p. 406.

The case of Luxembourg is less obvious, but, again, not unreasonable from a defensive point of view. In November 1678, even before the emperor had signed the peace treaty ending the Dutch War, Vauban wrote a memoir suggesting what enemy fortifications in the Spanish Netherlands should be taken at the start of any future war. Interestingly, his cautionary piece includes the names of fortresses later claimed during the period of the Reunions. Vauban rates Luxembourg very high on the list of fortresses that had to be seized, not because it opened up new territory for French conquest but because it was of great value to an enemy who intended to make war feed war by launching raids into Bourbon-held lands. The lay of rivers and roads exposed northern Lorraine to Luxembourg, 'which ruined twenty leagues of our country and would give us twenty other leagues if we took it'.[13] In a later memoir of 1694 recommending which fortresses Louis might reasonably sacrifice to gain peace in the Nine Years War, Vauban again stressed the importance of Luxembourg. There he advised that Louis could give up Luxembourg 'only on condition of a total demolition that would not leave one stone standing on another throughout the entire extent of the old and new fortifications; otherwise one must never give it back'.[14] Defensible frontiers in seventeenth-century Europe meant more than simply a neat line on a map.

Likewise, the addition of other objects of the Reunions along France's northeast border – Charlemont, Courtrai, and Dixmude – may seem to have confused a rational frontier along the border with the Spanish Netherlands, but the logic here, again, was militarily sound, not simply the product of indiscriminate greed. Vauban put these towns on his 1678 list of fortresses that should be taken at the first shot of a new war.[15] The interesting point here is that Louis repeatedly expressed his willingness to trade Courtrai and Dixmude (after their fortifications had been levelled) for Luxembourg.

With his triumph in the War of the Reunions, Louis now consolidated his northern and eastern frontiers with a spate of fortress renovation and construction. The budget for fortifications nearly

---

13 Vauban, 'Mémoire des places frontières de Flandres', in Rochas d'Aiglun, *Vauban*, vol. i, pp. 189–91.

14 Vauban, 'Places dont le Roi pourrait se défaire en faveur d'un traité de paix sans faire tort a l'état ni affaiblir sa frontière', memoir addressed to the king, January 1694, in Rochas d'Aiglun, *Vauban*, vol. i, p. 207. He also argues that the French needed Longwy as a fortress only because of the threat posed by Luxembourg. The 1694 memoir argues strongly for keeping Luxembourg.

15 Rochas d'Aiglun, *Vauban*, vol. i, pp. 189–91.

quadrupled; it had averaged 2,300,000 livres per annum from 1662 to 1668 but now increased to an average of 8,000,000 livres for 1682 to 1688.[16] And this says nothing of the money contributed by towns toward the building of their own works. Louis's strongest instincts drove him in the direction of territorial defence, and he invested in it heavily.

TERROR FROM THE SEA: NAVAL BOMBARDMENTS IN 1681–5

In addition to the fighting on land associated with the Reunions, the French dispatched their navy to punish foes along the shores of the Mediterranean. Again the mortar proved to be the preferred weapon for intimidation with comparatively low risk. This impersonal but deadly form of attack would be used to devastating effect in the appalling bombardment of Genoa in 1684, but it was first to be inflicted by French fleets on the Moorish corsairs of north Africa.

Muslim corsairs had preyed on French vessels in the Mediterranean for centuries, and during the personal reign of Louis XIV his navy periodically attacked their vessels and their bases. These attacks sought to intimidate the north African raiders so that they would spare French shipping, and, in addition, the navy liberated Christian, particularly French, slaves forced to man the corsairs' galleys. In 1664 Louis dispatched an ambitious but inadequate expedition to take Djidjelli on the Algerian coast and establish a French naval base; however, after initial success, the Turks were able to repel the foreign invaders.

The War of Devolution and the Dutch War absorbed France's naval energies for more than a decade, but the 1680s brought a series of French naval raids against north African targets. The first of these did not hit Africa directly, but struck at corsair vessels at Chios in the Aegean in 1681. There, the ageing French naval hero Duquesne blockaded corsairs from Algiers in port until they agreed to a peace settlement favourable to France. However, in October of that year, the dey of Algiers summoned the French counsel, Father Le Vacher, and announced that he would break the peace with France. The dey then dispatched a dozen armed vessels to prey on French commerce.

Louis sent Tourville and Hery to cruise the Algerian coast, while Duquesne marshalled a fleet for a punitive expedition. He sailed from Toulon on 12 July 1682 and headed for the Balearic Islands, where

---

16 Jean Roland de Mallet, *Comptes rendus de l'administration des finances du royaume de France* (London, 1789), pp. 352–7.

he rendezvoused with other elements of the fleet. From there the French struck out for the north African coast just west of Algiers, which they reached on 21 July. The assembled fleet consisted of eleven sailing vessels of war, fifteen galleys, two fireships, and five *galiotes à bombes*, or bomb ketches, which had sailed down from Brest to join Duquesne. These last ships would play the central role at Algiers, as the French employed bombardment at sea just as they were shelling their enemies on land.

Bomb ketches were new to the fleet, and at Algiers the French were still in the process of working out the best methods for their use. In order to hold their stations as platforms for the two mortars they usually mounted, the ketches had to be tethered between a heavy anchor dropped in the direction of the target and a larger vessel to seaward, which was anchored itself. Placing the anchors inshore was a dangerous business, because they must be dropped close enough to hold the ketches in mortar range, well within reach of enemy shore batteries. The fact that mortar ketches had to moor relatively close to shore where they were exposed to enemy fire made it advisable to operate at night. Thus, at Algiers, they were towed into position and moored to their lines under cover of darkness, and, after firing their deadly rounds, they left before the light of day. The character of their weapons and the natural swaying of decks, all complicated by firing at night, limited their accuracy, but mortars were terror weapons, not precision munitions. Still, bomb ketches required calm seas to perform their duty with any effect.

This bombardment did not go smoothly. At Algiers the weather did not cooperate, as high winds repeatedly delayed the start of the bombardment, which only began on the night of 5–6 August. Not until 13 August could they attack again, and once again the winds rose, giving the entire French fleet a very rough time indeed. The weather was not the only problem. Since the French were still experimenting with this new weapons system, mistakes were inevitable. At one point, the French found that they had moored the ketches too far from shore, making most of the bombs land in the water short of the town. To remedy this, the French took up the inshore anchors and moved them closer to the target. Some argued that the weather was so bad nothing more should be attempted, but Duquesne insisted that they try once more, which they did on 20–1 August, firing 114 bombs that night. They could not bombard the city again until the night of 4–5 September, which was to be their last attack. By then the mortars had caused considerable damage, including the destruction of half the grand mosque, where, according to Father Le Vacher, hundreds were buried in the wreckage. However, the dey of Algiers had not yet conceded to French demands when the fleet departed. It would return.

The second bombardment of Algiers came in June 1683. Then Duquesne led another fleet, which now included seven bomb ketches. After setting the anchors and waiting for calm seas, the French fleet advanced its ketches and fired on Algiers during the night of 26–7 June. Duquesne parleyed with the dey's representatives early in July, but although some slaves were liberated and hostages exchanged, negotiations broke down and the bombardment began again. By this point the bombardment continued around the clock, with three ketches firing during the day and four at night. Duquesne only withdrew from Algiers in mid-August after firing the fleet's entire supply of shells. However, while the main fleet departed, Duquesne left vessels to blockade Algiers in order to keep up the pressure on the corsairs. Finally, Algiers sued for peace on Duquesne's conditions, and an ambassador of the dey travelled to Paris to submit to Louis XIV in June 1684.

In 1685, d'Estrées led another naval expedition to Tripoli, another den of corsairs. The French dropped anchor off Tripoli on 19 June, and during the next few days, ketches fired over 500 shells, which reportedly killed 300, a cost in destruction and death that drove Tripoli to sue for terms on 25 June. Tripoli agreed to pay 600,000 livres indemnity and to liberate all Christian slaves held. After this victory at Tripoli, d'Estrées sailed for Tunis, where he quickly obliged the corsairs of that city to liberate their Christian slaves, accept French peace terms, and pay the costs of the French expedition.

As mentioned above, the most destructive naval bombardment of the 1680s was not inflicted on the infidel corsairs, however, but on the Christian Republic of Genoa. Genoa traditionally worked closely with Spain; during the Spanish heyday Genoese bankers had financed Spanish campaigns and the republic had supplied a necessary entrepôt for men and materiel bound for the Spanish Road. Along with this history of alliance with the Spanish came a hostility to the French. Not surprisingly, when the Spanish and French squared off against one another, Genoa gave modest support to the Spanish, allowing them to recruit mercenary troops on Genoese territory and build some galleys for the Spanish fleet despite French warnings that they should not. In the context of the times, these were not particularly hostile acts, but Louis took umbrage. His distaste for republics in general could only have fuelled the fire.

With the experience of Algiers under their belts, a shelling by naval mortars seemed the surest and safest means of punishment. The new secretary of state for the navy, Seignelay, shared Louvois's taste for bombardment as a terror weapon. A French fleet under the command of Duquesne assembled in Toulon during April 1684. In order to witness the pyrotechnics, Seignelay travelled to Toulon and boarded the fleet, which numbered fourteen sailing ships of war, twenty galleys, and ten bomb ketches. The Toulon contingent set sail on 5 May, rendezvoused with other elements a week later, and reached Genoa on 17 May. That day the anchors were set and the ketches took up their stations just outside the harbour.

Genoese senators sailed out to bargain with the French, who insisted that the Genoese formally admit their errors, assure the French of their good conduct in the future, and hand over galleys built for the Spanish. After the emissaries returned to the town, the Genoese replied by opening fire. French mortars began spewing their bombs, and within two hours fires could be seen in the city. The French paused in their bombardment between 22 and 25 May for repairs, and again, the two sides parleyed, but to no effect. Bombing resumed and continued until 28 May, when the French fleet retrieved the ketches' anchors and set sail for home the next day. Between 17 and 28 May the French showered 13,300 bombs on Genoa, destroying two-thirds of the city.

Fearing a land attack as well, the Genoese resolved to do anything to appease Louis's wrath, and the French prescribed an appropriate penance. The ageing Doge of Genoa, accompanied by four senators, travelled to the French court in May 1685 to deliver a humiliating public apology for Genoa's transgressions. After entertaining the Genoese delegation for some time, Louis sent them home with diamond-encrusted miniature portraits of himself. One can only imagine what the Doge and senators thought of their gifts.

RELIGIOUS REPRESSION AND WARFARE

Louis XIV committed the most regrettable actions of his reign in the name of the highest purpose: religion. Most of Louis's conduct in foreign affairs can be explained as rational, even though it was all too often twisted by bouts of arrogance, but his conduct toward his own Huguenot subjects and toward Protestants on his border was too extreme to be regarded as reasoned or reasonable. The Protestant community in France had demonstrated its loyalty to the Bourbon monarchy many times over since the end of its last rebellion in 1629. No longer did Huguenots pose a threat to political unity, but Louis was still affronted by religious diversity in his kingdom and wished to end it. He was convinced that Huguenots had so declined in fervour and in numbers that there was little reason to continue a tolerant policy that troubled his mind and his soul. His attempt to eradicate Protestantism in his lands involved more than military coercion, but it played a key role, and in 1686 he launched what can only be called a religious war of extermination in neighbouring Piedmont.

Intolerance grew in momentum from the beginning of Louis's personal reign and peaked in the 1680s. The anti-Protestant policies of Louis's regime actually predate his personal reign, because they grew naturally from enactments late in the ministry of Mazarin.[17] Already before the personal reign, a royal declaration pronounced in 1656 gave rise to commissions that closed Huguenot churches and other institutions. Repeatedly, councils of clergy demanded actions against the Huguenots, and they could remind him that they had contributed money to his war efforts. Between 1661 and 1678, twelve edicts were directed against the Huguenots. A decree of 1663 forbade Huguenots who had converted to Catholicism to recant their conversions; another in 1669 forbade Huguenots to exit France without gaining special permission. After the Dutch War the pace of pressure and persecution intensified, as no less than eighty-five hostile edicts appeared between 1679 and 1685.[18] In 1677 Louis established a fund that offered poor Huguenots who chose to convert a reward of 6–12 livres, and this action was simply one of the incentives meant to multiply conversions in the 1680s. Along with encouragement came punishment. An enactment of 1680 barred Huguenots from juridical or financial office; then mixed marriages were outlawed; and in 1682 Huguenots could no longer sell their landed property and leave France.[19]

Louis did not shrink from using force and intimidation to convert his subjects to Catholicism. Part of his conversion policy involved quartering soldiers on Huguenot households, a definably early modern type of military coercion. Because only a few towns and fortresses boasted sufficient barracks to house garrisons for passing troops, the standard manner of housing troops in town was to quarter them in civilian homes. The state was supposed to compensate

---

17 On policies followed between 1661 and 1685, see Élisabeth Labrousse, 'Calvinism in France, 1598–1685', in Menna Prestwich, ed., *International Calvinism* (Oxford, 1985).
18 Lossky, *Louis XIV*, p. 217.
19 Ibid., pp. 217–18.

householders for the expenses incurred, but even in the best of circumstances, the boarding of troops was usually an unwelcome imposition. If the troops were not closely supervised, things could get quite unpleasant, as when soldiers demanded more than they were entitled to or treated the house and its occupants roughly, including the abuse of wives, daughters, and serving girls. Exemption from quartering was a much prized personal privilege, enjoyed by nobles and other favoured groups. Quartering could be so burdensome that it could function as a seventeenth-century penalty for communities that had not paid their prescribed taxes. ·Officials billeted troops on recalcitrant towns without compensation. Then the offending locality would either pay in order to escape quartering or would suffer continued uncompensated quartering in lieu of paying taxes. Louis used quartering as coercion against Huguenots in a different way. On the one hand, he issued an ordinance in 1681 promising a two-year exemption from all quartering to Huguenots who converted to Catholicism. Then by stationing troops in a given area he could make its residents yearn for these exemptions. This was not war, to be sure, but it was the use of the king's troops actively to coerce his subjects, and if soldiers were not commanded to use violence, it was no surprise that they did.

The use of quartering to compel conversion has received the title 'dragonnades', because it made use of dragoons in particular, although they were not the only troops boarded with Protestants. The first dragonnades came in 1681, when a dragoon regiment was quartered with Huguenots in the province of Poitou. Marillac, the *intendant* in Poitou, pushed these actions to extremes, too much so even for Louvois, who had to rein him in. Soldiers engaged in such provocative violence that it drew protest from Protestant capitals of Europe, such as London. In response Louis pulled the cavalry out of Poitou in November of that year and dismissed the overzealous Marillac in February 1682. Huguenots enjoyed a respite for a time after the dragonnades of 1681, but religious persecution began to mount again before long.

The most notorious dragonnades came in 1685. That year, a large number of troops assembled in southwest France under the command of Boufflers as a precaution against continued troubles with Spain, still resentful after its humiliation in the War of the Reunions. At the end of July, when the threat seemed to have passed, Louvois ordered that the troops be used 'to diminish as much as possible the great number of Protestants' in the *généralités* of Bordeaux and Montauban by quartering his army on Huguenot households.[20] As soon as any household converted, it would be relieved of its burden. This order aimed at creating a majority Catholic population in each community, 'so that if, at a future day, His Majesty should wish no longer to permit the exercise of this religion in his realm, there would be no need to fear that the small number of remaining Huguenots could undertake anything'.[21] Here quartering troops was seen explicitly as a preemptive strike in what could very well turn into a full-scale religious war. The same instruction sent to Boufflers also went to the *intendants* of Languedoc and Dauphiné, so most of southern France was affected by the initial order.

The policy went through a number of modifications, and officials who were either too adamant or too lax received reprimands. In the autumn of 1685, Louis introduced the dragonnades to northern France, where Marillac, who had been so zealous several years before, enforced them in Normandy. The archbishop of Reims requested troops to lodge with Huguenots in Sedan, and received the Regiment de Champagne and 300 cavalry to accomplish this task.[22] But other local religious authorities, such as bishops Le Camus, soon to be a cardinal, and Percin, opposed the practice in the south.

Louis's strong-arm tactics seemed to be effective. Louvois claimed that in the month between 20 August and 17 September, 130,000 souls had converted in Bordeaux, Limoges, Montauban, and Poitiers. The results were even more impressive in Languedoc and Dauphiné, where Louvois predicted that only 5,000–6,000 Protestants would remain by the end of October.[23] Whole towns converted *en masse*. Louis was convinced that his policy was a great success and that it was all accomplished with very little unpleasantness; Louvois made sure that reports of the worst abuses never got to the king.

Convinced of the success of his conversion policies and in response to those who wished to go even further, Louis finally decided to ban the practice of the Protestant religion altogether. Therefore, on 22 October 1685, after nearly a century of official tolerance, Louis issued the Edict of Fontainebleau to revoke the Edict of Nantes. The new edict banned any Protestant religious gatherings and ordered all Protestant churches to be razed. Huguenot pastors who refused to convert had to leave France in two weeks, but those who converted would receive pensions. Huguenot parishioners would not be forced

---

20 AG, A¹747, 31 July 1685, Louvois to Boufflers, in Rousset, *Histoire de Louvois*, vol. iii, p. 465.
21 Louvois's instructions to Boufflers, 31 July 1685, in Lossky, *Louis XIV*, p. 221.
22 Rousset, *Histoire de Louvois*, vol. iii, p. 475.
23 Lossky, *Louis XIV*, p. 222.

to convert, but they could only pursue their religion individually, and children born to them after the edict would have to be baptized Catholic and brought up as such. And, crucially, Huguenots would not be allowed to emigrate from France; men caught fleeing would be condemned to serve on the galleys, and women would be sent to prison. Louis's fear of losing valuable Huguenot subjects was justified, and his Protestant neighbours were happy to welcome them. Immediately after the Edict of Fontainbleau appeared, the elector of Brandenburg issued his Edict of Potsdam, which invited Huguenot refugees to resettle in Brandenburg. As will be seen, Louis would do terrible things to stem the flight of his Protestant subjects. The Edict of Fontainebleau was to apply to all of France, save Alsace and Strasbourg, Louis's only Protestant city. The conditions set by the Treaty of Westphalia guaranteed the Protestant faith in that province.

The army and navy suffered from the new intolerance. An ordinance of 27 November 1685 forbade French regiments to include Protestant soldiers, although foreign regiments in French service could continue to practise their own religion. To encourage Protestant soldiers to convert to the Catholic faith, Louis offered bounties: two pistoles for an infantryman, four for a sergeant, three for a trooper.[24] Huguenot naval officers could receive 1,000 livres for converting.[25] None the less, the revocation hurt the French armed forces; Vauban estimated that 500 to 600 Huguenot officers and 10,000 to 12,000 of the best soldiers left their regiments, while 8,000 to 9,000 sailors joined enemy fleets.[26] Louis XIV himself proselytized when he tried to convince the veteran commander Marshal Schomberg to abjure his Protestant faith. However, the old soldier refused, so Louis allowed him to retire and leave France. Schomberg's retirement did not last long; he soon joined the army of the Protestant prince of Orange and died fighting against Louis. Among Louis's major commanders, only the old sea dog Abraham Duquesne was allowed to retain his Protestant faith and his rank, although his sons and nephews converted.

The flood of conversions in southern France created a new, large, and potentially dangerous class of Catholics, the *nouveaux convertis* or newly converted. Although happy to see his Huguenot subjects take the proper religious turn, Louis and many of his advisers doubted

---

[24] Philippe Contamine, ed., *Histoire militaire de la France*, vol. i (Paris, 1992), pp. 403–4.

[25] Geoffrey Symcox, *The Crisis of French Sea Power, 1688–1697: From the guerre d'escadre to the guerre de course* (The Hague, 1974), p. 30.

[26] Vauban, 'Mémoire pour le rappel des Huguenots', December 1689 in Rochas d'Aiglun, *Vauban*, vol. i, p. 466.

the sincerity of these conversions. This sentiment was shared by Mme de Maintenon, the woman he took as his morganatic wife after the death of the queen in 1683 and who was his confidante during the second half of his personal reign. They staked their long-term confidence on the fact that all the children would now be raised as Catholics, but in the meantime, their parents still posed the risk of religious war. The answer was to create forces designed to watch and intimidate the *nouveaux convertis*. Local militia forces in Languedoc, Montauban, and Dauphiné provided muscle.[27] Such forces, while recruited only among old Catholics, were paid for by the *nouveaux convertis*, who thus paid the salaries of their own jailers. Companies of this militia drilled once a week and held an annual review. The *intendant* of Languedoc reported that 'The general review of these regiments that the commander of the province has performed every year under the eyes of the *nouveaux convertis* has made them understand anything that they might try would only bring defeat and that we were in condition to repress them immediately.'[28] In fact, even with these precautions, the War of the Spanish Succession brought a revival of religious war in Languedoc among the *nouveaux convertis* of the Cévennes, but that is a topic for chapter 7.

While the forced conversion of Protestants resulted in armed surveillance within France during the 1680s, its consequences brought outright war to Alpine districts of Piedmont in Italy. In order to bar the flight of Huguenots in the south of France, Louis brutally attacked the Vaudois, a small Protestant community just across the French border in Piedmont. These Vaudois inhabited certain Alpine valleys just to the southwest of Turin. Of all the Protestant havens for Huguenots, Louis may have turned his wrath on the Vaudois simply because they were so vulnerable. His fortress of Pinerolo sat right at the edge of their lands, and he could exert considerable pressure on the local ruler, Victor Amadeus II, duke of Savoy (1675–1730), not yet twenty in 1685 and married to a French princess. The young duke had no real reason to persecute the Vaudois, who had been inoffensive and obedient, but Louis insisted they must be punished for welcoming Huguenot refugees.

Immediately after revoking the Edict of Nantes, Louis instructed his ambassador, the marquis of Arcy, to pressure the duke of Savoy

---

27 André Corvisier, *Armies and Societies in Europe, 1494–1789*, trans. Abigail T. Siddall (Bloomington, IN, 1979), p. 32.
28 Basville, *intendant* of Languedoc, memoir of 1697–98, in André Corvisier, *Les Français et l'armée sous Louis XIV* (Vincennes, 1975), p. 139.

to deny tolerance to his Protestant subjects as well. The duke responded that he preferred gentle methods, but Louis insisted that stronger tactics would be more effective, and should Victor Amadeus lack the means to compel his subjects, France could supply the troops. When the duke commanded that the Vaudois could not accept religious fugitives from France, Louis shot back 'if one does not effectively keep my subjects from crossing over into Savoy, I will order the governor of Pinerolo to apprehend them even in the lands of the duke'.[29] In early January 1686 the duke capitulated and informed Louis that he would convert his subjects by force if it came to that and would call on French troops if necessary. Within a month, Victor Amadeus issued a declaration very much like the Edict of Fontainebleau and sent troops to the Vaudois's valleys. Then on 16 February Arcy reported that the duke had requested French troops. Louis responded with an offer of five regiments of infantry and ten squadrons of cavalry to be led by Marshal Catinat, governor of Casale. Catinat first went to Turin to confer with the duke and then continued to Pinerolo. Swiss emissaries arrived early in April to try to mediate a settlement that would allow the Vaudois to emigrate to Protestant states, but they would not be able to win over the majority of Vaudois, who resolved to stay and fight. Victor Amadeus issued a final edict on 12 April granting an amnesty if the Vaudois would lay down their arms and go home; however, if they refused, military action would begin when the offer ran out on 20 April. The Swiss pleaded with the Vaudois once more, but to little avail.

Serious operations began on 21 April. French troops based on Pinerolo and Piedmontese troops based on Bricherásio advanced into the valleys. The total force amounted to 7,000–8,000 men, about evenly split between French and Piedmontese; the Vaudois were thought to have roughly half that number of fighting men. In regular combat the Vaudois, or Barbets as the French also called them, did not match up to the troops sent against them. An attempt by 500 Barbets to cut off the French from Pinerolo by attacking a detachment left at St Germain to guard the line of communication was a near thing, but a relief force arrived from Pinerolo, and the Vaudois suffered severe casualties. Barbets now abandoned their towns to advancing regulars, and in early May turned to guerrilla tactics. By this point the French and Piedmontese had collected about 6,000 Vaudois men, women, and children as prisoners.

29 Archives des Affaires Etrangères, Correspondance de Savoy, 81, 16 November 1685, king to Arcy, in Rousset, *Histoire de Louvois*, vol. iv, p. 6.

The Vaudois fought effectively as guerrillas, ambushing small groups of regulars, sniping at columns, and disappearing into the mountains. When this second phase of the fighting began during the first days of May, the French responded by breaking their forces into a number of small columns and pursuing the guerrillas. Vaudois caught with arms in their hands received no quarter and were strung up from the nearest tree. In little time, the Catholic forces rooted out all opposition. Catinat reported on 9 May, 'The country is completely desolated; there are no longer any people or livestock at all. The duke of Savoy has about 8,000 souls held prisoner. I hope that we will not leave this country, and that the race of Barbets will be entirely eliminated from it.'[30] Some tried to escape by crossing the Alps, but when they did they found French troops on the other side to push them back or turn them over to the duke of Savoy. The fighting ended by June, and Catinat returned to Casale.

Now began the saddest aspect of this campaign. The Piedmontese concentrated the Vaudois they held in prisons and camps, where the ill-clothed and ill-fed prisoners died of malnutrition and disease. The total count of detainees reached 10,000 to 12,000 at its highest, but death took a terrible toll. Of 900 held at Verrue, there were only 150 left by late October. Hearing of the death of the Vaudois, Louis callously wrote, 'I see that sicknesses delivers the duke of Savoy of some of the embarrassment caused by having to guard the rebels..., and I do not doubt at all that he easily consoles himself for the loss of such subjects who make room for better and more faithful ones.'[31] In December the duke turned over the 4,000–5,000 surviving Vaudois to representatives from Berne who asked to settle them elsewhere in Protestant Germany, mainly in Brandenburg. This would not be the last that would be heard of the Vaudois, because during the Nine Years War a band of them fought their way from Geneva to their old valleys, and Victor Amadeus signed a peace treaty with them.

THE LIMITED EXTENT OF TAX REVOLTS UNDER LOUIS XIV

At times, Louis seemed to be willing to take on most of Europe single-handed, but he would not have been able to face such odds had France been torn apart by internal discord as it had so often during

---

30 AG, A¹776, 9 May 1686, Louis to Louvois, in Rousset, *Histoire de Louvois*, vol. iv, p. 24.

31 Letter from the king to marquis of Arcy, 8 November 1686, in Rousset, *Histoire de Louvois*, vol. iv, p. 28.

the century before his personal reign. Louis instituted a regime of religious intolerance against his Huguenot minority, but this did not precipitate outright religious warfare in France until 1702, when the Cévennes turned hot. Perhaps it was the very benign calm of his Huguenot minority that tempted him to eliminate it. In any case, Louis only found religious turmoil within France when he created it himself. Of greater interest, important types of revolts that had shaken the first half of the seventeenth century either petered out early in the personal reign or never threatened Louis at all. The first of these genre of troubles was the tax revolt; the second was the aristocratic rebellion. If it is important to chronicle the wars that Louis fought, it is also of value to note the conflicts he avoided, thus freeing himself to focus strategy on other matters.

Considering the prevalence of tax revolts during the long war with Spain, 1635–59, it is not surprising that a string of domestic rebellions troubled France early in Louis's personal reign. What is remarkable is the fact that these revolts were relatively minor and died out before the 1680s. None of these rebellions deserves the full title of civil war in the way that the wars of religion or the Fronde do, but Louis dispatched troops to suppress them, and so they fall within the context of this chapter on the use of military violence in state policy. The reaction to these rebellions reminds us that armies were and are two-edged swords, designed both to fight foreign enemies and to enforce internal order.

The first decade of Louis's personal reign brought a string of tax revolts, each of which was highly localized but which, at the same time, came as a result of broader, national policies. With the return of peace in 1659 and then the death of Mazarin, Louis and Colbert confronted the financial crisis of the state. Major financiers found themselves on trial before a Chamber of Justice, which annulled much of the debt owed them. Colbert tried to collect back taxes, regularize tax collection, and, in some cases, force areas to accept as permanent taxes levies that had been instituted as temporary wartime expedients. In an important sense, the tax revolts of the 1660s were consequences of the war with Spain.[32]

Colbert's policies immediately resulted in armed resistance. The area around Bordeaux would be the site of more than one revolt. There in December 1661, peasants who were resisting Colbert's efforts

---

[32] For brief accounts of rebellions, 1661–80, see Ernest Lavisse, *Louis XIV* (2 vols; Paris, 1978), vol. i, pp. 349–61, and Charles Tilly, *The Contentious French* (Cambridge, MA, 1986), pp. 147–53.

to collect back taxes seized the chateau of Bénauge and attacked a handful of troops to enforce the new policy of taxation.[33] A force of 700–800 troops easily defeated the rebels, who saw two of their leaders hanged and four others sent to the galleys as punishment. Anther tax revolt shook the Boulonnais during the summer of 1662; this Lustucru rebellion, as it was known, opposed the state's intention to convert certain extraordinary wartime levies into permanent taxes. The rebels may have numbered as many as 5,500 peasants. At the approach of royal soldiers, including men from the guards regiments, about 1,000 rebels barricaded themselves in a village, but they were driven from this village to the castle of Heudin, where they surrendered to the regulars. In all, 3,000 people were arrested and 1,200 tried; the state executed four rebels and sent 365 to serve in the galleys for life, a form of living death.

A pair of armed peasant revolts broke out across the Pyrenees in 1663 with aftershocks that continued for nearly a decade. In the western Pyrenees, the Audijos, named after their very capable aristocratic commander, fought a guerrilla war against tax collectors throughout the mid-1660s. Audijos, who had served a decade in the army, proved to be so successful both at resisting royal troops and at avoiding escape that Louis finally rewarded him with a regimental command during the Dutch War, and he died fighting for the king at Messina. In the eastern Pyrenees rebels know as the Angelets fought against the imposition of the salt tax, or *gabelle*, and this outbreak first took the form of guerrilla resistance that lasted for years. The breakdown of a compromise reached only in 1669 raised the intensity of the fighting. In 1670 royal troops relieved the town of Céret which the rebels had besieged. Only after two more years of struggle and negotiation did this rebellion cease.

While the Angelets were still fighting royal authorities, another revolt hit the Vivarais. This Roure rebellion, lead by Jean-Antoine du Roure, may have marshalled as many as 4,000 armed men, and during the spring and summer of 1670 they controlled much of the hilly country around Aubenas. Roure, like Audijos, was a noble with military experience who was sympathetic to rebels and willing

---

33 We need to know much more about the kind of 'troops' used to enforce tax policies. In the normal course of affairs, these could be units specially created to aid tax collectors, not soldiers from the regular army. The whole question of the relationship between the regular army and the enforcement of royal authority requires reexamination, as France at this time contained a variety of armed insitutions, from the army itself, to local militias and companies raised by and answering to provincial law courts.

to lead them. The trouble began when rumours of a new head tax prompted a crowd to assault the tax collector of Aubenas. This revolt also had strong social overtones, as the rebels attacked the homes of well-to-do nobles. By the end of July royal troops were on the move to repress the Roure rebellion and did so at a battle in which 180 rebels died and 80 were taken prisoner. The king's justice condemned rebels to death and sent 500–600 to the galleys. The Roure rebellion followed that curious seventeenth-century pattern in which the rebels expressed loyalty to the king while resisting his agents; their cry was 'Long live the king, and down with the revenue collectors!'

The next tax revolt was also the last large rebellion of this type to challenge Louis XIV. It also stood out from its immediate predecessors because it struck in the midst of a major war, unsettling French strategy. As the needs of the Dutch War pressured the monarchy's finances, Colbert raised old levies and instituted new ones, and in 1675 these sparked resistance in a number of western towns, including Le Mans, Poitiers, and Agen, with the main rebellion flaring up in Bordeaux and Brittany. Colbert's new impositions included a stamp tax that required the use of paper bearing a special royal stamp for legal documents. Resistance to the use of this stamped paper set Bordeaux alight, as crowds burned bundles of the hated sheets, and this stamped paper, or *papier timbré*, gave its name to the urban form of the rebellion that now rocked Brittany. Rebels chanted 'Long live the king, without the *gabelle*!' This Papier Timbré revolt hit Rennes, the traditional capital of the province, early in April, and the situation worsened. Finally on 19 April, the son of the absent governor of Rennes called out the town militia, but even before it assembled, he dispersed a menacing crowd with a mounted charge by only twenty or thirty nobles. Although disturbances broke out again on 25 April, these were easily quelled. When troubles next broke out in Nantes, Louis dispatched troops to the province. The governor of Brittany, the duke of Chaulnes, recognized that the clumsy use of force would just make the situation worse, and asked Louvois to scale back the number of troops he intended to dispatch, as 'only the fear of these troops has prolonged... the sedition'.[34]

Meanwhile, revolt spread to the countryside of Brittany, where it was known not as the Papier Timbré, but the Bonnets Rouges, or red caps. Peasants were as intent on attacking landlords as the city

34 The duke of Chaulnes to Louvois in Jean Lemoine, *La Révolte dite du Papier Timbré ou des Bonnets Rouges en Bretagne en 1675* (Paris, 1898), doc. LXV.

dwellers were on threatening tax collectors. The head of the Jesuits in Quimper estimated that the armed rebels totalled 18,000–20,000 men, a number which may have been exaggerated by his fears. However, the arrival of troops quelled the rebellion without a single military engagement. As the *Gazette de France* reported on 31 August, 'The seditions in lower Brittany have been entirely dissipated by the mere rumour of the march of the king's troops.'[35] Brittany would now pay a terrible price for rebellion. Understandably concerned with hostile amphibious expeditions, such as had struck in 1674, Louis worried that rebellion might invite further descents on his coasts. In fact, the French ambassador in Liège reported that in Cologne Louis's enemies 'place great hopes on the rebels in France'.[36] The answer was not only repression, but retribution. Louis quartered 10,000 troops in Brittany over the winter of 1675–76, and their brutal conduct was meant to set an example. Mme de Sévigné reported, 'See how the troops come for winter quarters; they go to live with the peasants where they steal and they ruin. . . . The other day they put a little baby on a spit.'[37]

Tax revolts, which had loomed so large in French history through much of the seventeenth century, essentially ended after 1675.[38] This would be an important war that never was. A major revolt would not break out in France again for nearly thirty years, so most of Louis's personal reign would be marked by internal peace, even though wars raged on the frontiers. Military force played its part in pacifying France, but much more was involved. The French, as never before, were coming to accept the authority of the monarchy and the need for strong central institutions, while Louis knew how to accommodate and compromise with traditional élites. Internal peace might have continued indefinitely were it not for Louis's misplaced zeal in matters of religion. Some have argued that the French standing army was really created to repress Louis's internal foes more than to fight his external enemies, but while the army did serve to maintain internal order in a handful of cases, the most consistent use of military force for repression and control under Louis XIV was *vis-à-vis* the Protestants and *nouveaux convertis*, and this was not a problem that brought the standing army into existence – after all, it was well established by 1685.

35 'Extraits de la Gazette de France' (31 August 1675) in ibid., doc. CLXIII.
36 Ambassor's letter in Lavisse, *Louis XIV*, vol. i, p. 358.
37 Mme de Sévigné letter in ibid., p. 359.
38 There were other quite minor tax revolts in Vitry-le-Croisé in Champagne in 1680 and in the Dauphiné in 1683.

PACIFYING THE NOBILITY

Noble rebellions had been a fixture of the first half of the seventeenth century. The Fronde in particular shook the Bourbon monarchy to its foundations, and while that civil war had many facets, it certainly constituted the most important aristocratic armed rebellion of the century. The defeat of the Fronde in 1653 need not have spelled an end to this form of resistance after it had been so prevalent under Louis XIII, Richelieu, and Mazarin; there was nothing inevitable about its demise. Louis pursued a set of clever and effective policies designed to pacify the nobility and make it an ally of the crown. He realized that the possibility of renewed civil war called for preemptive action, and he took it.

His efforts benefited greatly from French exhaustion with war and rebellion. Twenty-five years of extremely costly and destructive war made the French, including the nobility, ready to rest, recover, and regroup by 1659. They expected, and even more so they *needed*, Louis to be a great and powerful king. The Fronde, though a near thing, ended by discrediting those segments of the élites who had participated in it, including the legal magnates of the great crown courts and the princely grandees. They were hardly ready to take up the sword again immediately, and Louis established his authority and his largess soon enough to forestall a later rising.

Louis did not accomplish his goals through a policy of intimidation or repression toward the aristocratic élite. To be sure, there is no doubt that Louis insisted upon and achieved a level of authority over the central institutions of government unequalled by his predecessors. He arrested and imprisoned Nicolas Fouquet, the ambitious *surintendant des finances*, in 1661 primarily to advertise his resolve to rule and control. However, this does not mean that he seized all authority on all levels. For one thing, slow communications and the still meagre personnel and rudimentary systems devoted to enforcing central control set limits to the imposition of the royal will in the provinces, so an attempt to enforce royal ascendancy on every level would have been unworkable. But Louis would also have found such an effort undesirable, perhaps even unthinkable. In the past, scholarship has overestimated Louis's power throughout France, and a body of recent works has challenged this traditional view by announcing with revisionist enthusiasm that Louis never superseded all local authority and that, in fact, he caved in to his nobility and preserved an essentially feudal regime in the provinces. Both traditional and revisionist views join partial truth with exaggeration. Louis did insist upon and achieve monarchical authority over important central institutions and policies, particularly those concerned with foreign policy and war. He asserted his control over state finance with less success, because finance always required him to struggle against an unholy alliance of financiers, provincial estates, local élites, and so on. In the provinces, things worked better if Louis limited his assaults on local institutions to a modest level, consistent with necessity. And certainly, the safest way to deal with the nobility was to win them over with monetary gratuities, appointments, lands, and titles rather than to abuse them.

Louis employed two powerful incentives to tie the nobility to the monarchy: the court and the army. Always a master of style, Louis recognized that power had both a substance and a mystique, and he very skilfully separated the two. The substance of power, the actual authority and work of running the government, he retained for himself, as explained in chapter 2. By employing scions of recently ennobled houses or nobles of limited pretensions to head administrative departments he denied the highest, and most dangerous, nobility any hold on the central government. But Louis welcomed, and eventually required, the high nobility to attend him at court, where they might share in the reflected power and grandeur of the Sun King. He gave them the atmosphere and perquisites of power without sharing the ability to decide and command. There were material rewards as well, because Louis doled out pensions, gratuities, and posts to the élite, and to win these favours an individual ought to be at court. Louis rejected petitions by those who did not attend him, dismissing them as 'people I never see'. Instead of disputing real issues, the court nobles were reduced to scuffling over precedence in the hierarchical etiquette that governed court life. Louis's great palace, the chateau of Versailles, was the most memorable theatre of this stage drama, but it did not become the permanent home of the court until the 1680s. Still, long before the move to Versailles, Louis had established the principle that major nobles must be at court and that it was both ridiculous and a sign of disgrace to reside elsewhere.

Snaring the great nobles at court was a conscious and well-articulated policy, but the use of the army to provide patronage for the nobility was mainly a useful corollary of Louis's desire for a larger army. As the army expanded to wartime levels which rose to 400,000 men, at least on paper, the number of officers soared as well, for such a force required an officer corps of over 20,000.[39]

---

[39] Victor Belhomme, *L'Armée française en 1690* (Paris, 1895), pp. 104, 119, sets the figure at 23,000 officers; AG, MR 1701, #13, 'Estat contenant le nombre des

187

According to Vauban, 52,000 noble families resided in France by 1707; therefore, the officer corps included representatives of a large percentage of noble households. There is no question that young nobles found these posts very desirable. They clamoured for such openings and welcomed war because it provided more slots for them. Louis XIV described with pride how in 1667, when word that there would be war in Flanders hit the court, captains begged him to be allowed to add recruits or even to raise entire companies, bearing the costs themselves.[40] Throughout his reign, Louis levied new regiments at the expense of young and well-heeled colonels, and there always seemed to be enough willing candidates; in 1702, seventy-two applicants pestered Louis for eighteen new regiments.[41]

The rush to serve resulted from the perceived value of commissions in the eyes of the nobility. On the one hand, Louis understood that masculine aristocratic values pressured men to prove their valour in combat. In such an environment, military service became a rite of passage and an obligation. On the other hand, military service helped to legitimate individual nobles and entire aristocratic families. Holding a commission, particularly as colonel or captain, could increase a well-placed noble's clientage and, thus, his influence. Families might seek to increase their prestige through military service. For example, the Lacgers, a Huguenot robe clan, rose through legal and judicial service, but the last *parlementaire* in the family died in 1688, and the family abandoned the bench. By then the men of the Lacgers had turned to land-owning and the army. The first to enter the army held a commission in the 1660s, and by the Revolution, fourteen scions of the family had followed the colours, primarily in the infantry Regiment of Auvergne.[42] The Lacgers demonstrated their loyalty to the crown, despite their Protestant origins, by taking up the sword.

Although, by giving them war, Louis harnessed élite values to state policy, it would be putting the cart before the horse to argue that Louis forged a large army precisely to create patronage for the nobility and so bind it to him. His army was a tool of war, not a

---

officiers, des soldats, des cavaliers, et des dragons dont les regimens etoient sur pied en 1710', puts it at 21,000.

40 Louis XIV, *Mémoires de Louis XIV pour l'instruction du dauphin*, ed. Charles Dreyss (2 vols; Paris, 1860), vol. ii, pp. 116, 229.

41 Georges Girard, *Le Service militaire en France à la fin du règne de Louis XIV: Rocolage et milice, 1701–1715* (Paris, 1915), p. 15.

42 The story of the Lacger family is told in Raymond A. Mentzer, Jr, *Blood and Belief: Family Survival and Confessional Identity among the Provincial Huguenot Nobility* (West Lafayette, IN, 1994).

social device. However, the by-product of military expansion was a rich source of patronage which tied the nobility to the monarchy with sentiments of gratitude and obligation. Patronage also focused the nobility on competing for royal bounty rather than on resisting royal authority. A willingness to leave the power and prestige of the nobility alone on the local level, combined with largess at court and in the army, allowed Louis to form a sufficient consensus with the nobles that he could avoid aristocratic revolts that could have undermined his power and policy. It is true that he also showed a willingness to put down civil disturbances, but none of these involved the nobility, and, in fact, local nobles rallied to the government cause in case after case. So actual repression of noble unrest was hardly a factor after 1661. Instead of confronting the nobility with armed force, Louis stressed conciliation and reward. In this policy of consensus, the court, the palace at Versailles itself, and military command can be seen as powerful instruments and, in an odd sense, as weapons of war that won a struggle that was never fought.

The finesse Louis displayed in his dealings with his nobles was an exception to the unfortunate *modus vivendi* of the 1680s, when he revealed his tendency toward ill-considered violence at its worst and set the stage for his next contest against a European alliance, the Nine Years War. The Reunions, even though some may have been legitimate, were too brash and brutal. And French conduct in the War of Reunions sank to regrettable levels, in which fire and mortar shells became the messengers of Bourbon policy. The attacks on north African corsairs may not have given rise to European fears, but the bombardment of Genoa certainly did. And when Louis turned against his own Huguenot minority he alarmed European Protestants. The vicious war against the Vaudois justified fears that his Catholic policies might be directed against his Protestant neighbours.

The challenge to Louis's triumph took form even as he seemed omnipotent. While prisoners from the Vaudois still languished in camps and prisons, representatives of Sweden, Spain, the emperor, and south German princes met in Augsburg to form a defensive league in July 1686. In the words of the diarist Dangeau, this League of Augsburg 'seems to be directed uniquely against France'.[43] The league might not have immediately threatened Louis, as long as the

---

43 Dangeau in Wolf, *Louis XIV*, p. 429.

majority of its forces were, in fact, still fighting the Turks, but it marked a growing, and coalescing, resistance to the great monarch. Its creation boded ill. In the name of erecting defensible frontiers and ensuring internal unity, Louis's heavy-handed methods virtually guaranteed the coming catastrophe.

6 THE GREAT MISCALCULATION: THE NINE YEARS WAR

French excesses of the 1680s culminated in a great miscalculation, the Nine Years War. It is not that Louis wished to avoid violence, for violence had become a favourite and successful tool of state policy. Rather, he expected a short conflict in the pattern of the War of Reunions, when French forces had brushed aside far weaker foes and gained quick capitulation to his demands. For Louis the Nine Years War was always a struggle to reinforce French security, not a war of conquest. However, Europe understandably read his actions as further expression of what seemed his limitless lust for territory and power. Thus, instead of simply overawing a meagre coalition of German states, Louis soon faced the Grand Alliance determined to thwart the Sun King. In the resulting clash, Louis imposed great suffering on the coalition, exemplified by the devastation of the Palatinate, but France too suffered from the oppressive costs of a long war, made all the worse by famine and financial crisis. Viewed battle by battle, the Nine Years War was an impressive French victory, at least on land, but eventually Louis was willing to make substantial concessions to secure a treaty. Even the massive resources of France were drained by this war of attrition, and it was a humbled and chastened Louis who welcomed the return of peace in 1697.

Louis's fears, not his pride, best explain the onset of war in 1688. As he watched Habsburg successes multiply against the failing Ottoman Turks, he expected the emperor to turn on France at the next pause in the war along the Danube. Louis's apprehension was, indeed, justified, and Habsburg victory at Mohacs and the seizure of Buda in 1687 made this day of reckoning seem near. In response, Louis sought to guarantee his territorial gains of the Reunions. He hoped to force his German neighbours to turn the truce established by the Treaty of Ratisbon into a permanent settlement. An ultimatum that he issued in 1687 failed to achieve the hoped-for assurances when the emperor refused to concede them.

A disputed succession in Cologne also brought matters to a head. Cologne, one of those curious petty Rhineland states in which the temporal ruler, the elector, was also a Catholic archbishop, sheltered part of France's German frontier, not only because the electoral archbishop held the town of Cologne but because other key territories fell under his sway. The old archbishop, Max Henry, influenced by the French agent Cardinal William Egon von Fürstenberg, favoured French interests, but when Max Henry became ill the choice of his successor became immensely complex and contentious. Louis wanted Fürstenberg to succeed the old man, and diplomatic manoeuvrings were well under way when he died in June 1688. The emperor opposed Fürstenberg and favoured Joseph Clement, the brother of Max Emanuel, the elector of Bavaria.

As negotiations over the archbishopric of Cologne heated up in Rome, Habsburg success at the siege of Belgrade, while welcome in the rest of Catholic Europe, alarmed Versailles. Louis feared that the Turks were close to collapse, and when Belgrade fell, as it would any day, Louis expected an Ottoman capitulation that would free the emperor's armies to take action against France. (In fact, the war between Austria and the Turks continued until 1699.) Louis felt he must have a quick resolution of the situation along his German frontier, and war promised what threats and demands were unable to impose. On 24 September 1688 he published a manifesto, his 'Mémoire des raisons', demanding that the Treaty of Ratisbon be transformed into a permanent treaty and that Fürstenberg be appointed archbishop of Cologne. He gave the German princes and the Habsburg emperor three months to agree.

Another and far more important troubled succession played a key role in the autumn of 1688. James II had succeeded his brother on the English throne in 1685. James, who had openly converted to Catholicism and married a Catholic princess as his second wife, embarked on a heavy-handed programme to win religious rights for his fellow Catholics, which alienated Parliament. The birth of a son to the ageing James on 10 June 1688 guaranteed a Catholic succession, which before then seemed sure to pass to the Protestant daughters of his previous marriage. The prospect of a Catholic monarchy in perpetuity was intolerable, so prominent English figures invited William of Orange, married to James's eldest daughter Mary, to take the throne. This was revolution, but it had the support of the Protestant majority. At the end of September William accepted the invitation. Louis's envoy to The Hague declared to the States-General of the United Provinces that if William landed in England with troops,

Louis would consider that a *casus belli*. William sailed for England, and Louis interpreted this as a declaration of war. Although Louis was correct that the need to secure the English throne would dominate William's attention for some time, the Sun King miscalculated in believing, first, that William would not succeed in securing the crown, and, second, that his attempt would paralyse the Allies in Flanders.

In fact, French efforts along the Rhine backfired, because by committing his army there Louis freed William to intervene in England. He landed at Torbay in November and entered London in December, as James II fled to France. Louis's arch enemy, the Dutch stadholder, now held the crown as William III of England jointly with his wife, Mary. With William at the head of the English government as well as the Dutch, England would now stand against France in the coalition that formed in 1689.

ONSET OF A GREAT WAR, 1688-89

The day after Louis issued his manifesto, well before his enemies could have known its details, French forces crossed the Rhine. As the army marched into Germany, Louvois and Louis were confident that the matter would be settled by January 1689, but the war would only be picking up momentum at that point.

The devastation of the Palatinate

The campaign plan for the autumn of 1688 required the French to besiege Philippsburg and occupy Rhineland towns in order to compel the German states to accept French conditions. The seizure of Philippsburg was clearly intended to protect Alsace, which during the Dutch War had suffered several invasions, a spectre that haunted Louis, ever-resolved to protect his territory. The French already held Huningen, Breisach, Freiburg, Strasbourg, and Fort-Louis, so the taking of Philippsburg would effectively seal the Rhine. Should the Germans agree to French terms, Louis announced in his manifesto, he would return the site, after demolishing its fortifications. So Louis could claim he desired only German guarantees, rather than further territorial concessions. Of course, should the emperor choose to attack France as Louis feared, Louis would then have barred the last 'gate' into Alsace by taking Philippsburg.

A siege of Philippsburg presented peculiar difficulties as the fortress occupied marshy ground on the east bank of the Rhine. After crossing the river at Strasbourg, Montclar's cavalry arrived before Philippsburg on 27 September. These horsemen formed the vanguard of a besieging army that included twenty-nine battalions and forty-five squadrons, about 30,000 men, under the command of an experienced marshal, the duke of Duras, with the dauphin as its royal chief. The dauphin, Louis's only surviving son with his queen Marie Thérèse, was a man of modest talents at best. Vauban would direct the siege works. Inside, fortress governor Starhemberg, brother of the defender of Vienna, mustered a garrison of 2,000 infantry and 300 cavalry. Duras, marching with the main forces, got to Philippsburg on 1 October. After preparing lines of circumvallation, the French opened trenches against the Fort du Rhine, a fortified bridgehead on the west bank, during the night of 3–4 October. It fell on 5 October, and trenches were opened against the fortress itself on 7–8 October. The fortress finally surrendered on 30 October, and the garrison departed with full honours of war on 1 November. This siege cost the French 588 officers and men killed and 953 wounded.[1]

Louis's forces soon collected other towns. The dauphin's army turned against Mannheim, where it opened trenches on 8 November, and the garrison capitulated on the evening of 11 November. There, French success resulted not only from Vauban's skill but also from the fact that the rebellious German garrison had not been paid for seventeen months.[2] The dauphin then took Frankenthal, while other towns surrendered without resistance, including Neustadt, Oppenheim, Worms, Bingen, Alzey, Kreuznach, Bacharach, Kaiserlautern, Heidelberg, Pforzheim, Heilbronn, and Speyer; above all, the key fortress of Mainz accepted a French garrison. Louis would also have liked to take Koblenz, but its lord, the elector of Trier, stubbornly refused to surrender it. In response, Louis ordered that Lieutenant-General Boufflers bombard the city in November to burn its interior without the necessity of breaching its walls. Vauban opposed the bombardment, but to no effect, and with terrible success it gutted the city.[3]

[1] Charles Sévin, marquis de Quincy, *Histoire militaire de Louis le Grand roi de France* (7 vols; Paris, 1726), vol. ii, pp. 137–8.
[2] Camille Rousset, *Histoire de Louvois* (4 vols; Paris, 1862–64), vol. iv, p. 144.
[3] 'What will be the good of it?... Would it not be better to husband our bombs than to waste them in useless expeditions which produce nothing...?' AG, A¹832, 2 November 1688, Vauban to Louvois, in ibid., p. 142. Louvois seemed to enjoy the prospect, as he praised Boufflers: 'The king has seen with pleasure that after having thoroughly burned [*bien brûlé*] Koblenz and done all the harm possible to the palace of the Elector, you should return to Mainz.' AG, A¹812, 14 November 1688, Louvois to Boufflers, in ibid., p. 143.

Louis XIV now mastered the Rhine south of Mainz to the Swiss border, and had good reason to believe that the campaign was over. However, instead of agreeing to his demands, the Germans resisted. Major German princes, including the elector of Brandenburg and the duke of Hanover, met in late October at Magdeburg to fashion an alliance against Louis XIV. Soon Louis faced the forces of Brandenburg, Hanover, Hesse-Kassel, Saxony, and Bavaria, in addition to those of the Habsburg Emperor, Leopold I, and on 26 November the Dutch entered the war as well. The Imperial Diet declared war on 24 January. Already in December, German cavalry opposed the French in the field. In addition, *schnapphahns* emerged from the local peasantry again to snipe at the French.

If the German princes were not willing to accede to his manifesto, then Louis resolved to punish them for resistance and, perhaps, to intimidate them into submission. However, most certainly he meant to make it as hard as possible for them to attack France by, as it were, clearing a firebreak to the north and east of the French fortress line that ran from Breisach to Strasbourg to Philippsburg to Landau. Under the influence of Louvois and Chamlay, Louis resolved upon a scorched-earth policy to make it impossible for a hostile enemy to maintain itself on local resources. History records the resultant destruction as the infamous 'devastation of the Palatinate', although not only the Palatinate suffered.[4]

The first discussions of destroying individual towns had only to do with the nasty business of collecting contributions from the Germans or with the attempt to deny the enemy the protection of town walls. In a notable letter of 27 October Chamlay suggested to Louvois that the French demolish the fortifications of a number of towns situated between the Rhine below Philippsburg and the French main fortress line from Landau to Saarlouis to Montroyal.[5] This was not, however, a matter of destroying everything within entire towns, but only of tearing down their defences; in fact, as Chamlay stipulated, French troops could be put in the towns for winter quarters while or after the walls were rendered useless. Meanwhile Louvois ordered General Montclair to drive east to the Neckar and

---

4 On the devastation of the Palatinate, John A. Lynn, 'A Brutal Necessity? The Devastation of the Palatinate, 1688–1689', in Mark Grimsley and Cliford Rogers, eds, *Civilians in the Path of War* (forthcoming). The paragraphs on the devastation here are borrowed from that chapter. The classic account is Kurt von Raumer, *Die Zerstörung der Pfalz von 1689* (Munich, 1930).

5 AG, A¹826, 27 October 1688, Chamlay to Louvois, in Rousset, *Histoire de Louvois*, vol. iv, p. 160.

pillage Stuttgart, Esslingen, and Tübingen, and to occupy Heilbronn, while tearing down its walls.[6] At the same time, everything was to be done to extract the most money out of the frightened state of Württemberg.

However, in the 27 October letter, Chamlay suggested more odious actions: 'I would dare to propose to you something that perhaps will not be to your taste, that is the day after we take Mannheim, I would put the city to the sword and plow it under.'[7] On 15 November the news of Mannheim's surrender reached Versailles, and two days later Louvois echoed Chamlay's severe proposal in an order to the military *intendant* La Grange: 'I see the king is rather disposed to entirely raze the city and citadel of Mannheim, and, in this case, to utterly destroy the houses, in such a manner that no stone stands on another.'[8] Here the intention was not simply to squeeze what one could out of a conquered people.

As Louis, his advisers, and his generals realized that this would not be a brief and decisive parade of French glory, but rather a bitterly contested and probably long war, their methods turned savage. While French troops recoiled from the advancing Germans, Louvois wrote to Montclair on 18 December: 'His Majesty recommends to you to completely ruin [*faire bien ruiner*] all the places that you leave along the lower and upper Neckar so that the enemy, finding no forage or food whatever, will not try to approach there.'[9] Already by 20 December, Louvois had marked upon a fateful map all the cities, towns, villages, and châteaux intended for destruction. It is worth noting that the king agreed to the list of the doomed, only sparing certain religious buildings.[10]

During late December and on into January 1689, a string of letters demanded a faster pace of destruction, and the frenzy of destruction peaked from March through the first days of June. Under the direction of Tessé, a subordinate of Montclair, retreating French troops forced out the inhabitants and put Heidelberg to the torch on 2 March. However, townsmen who possibly had been warned of French intentions and made advance preparations returned to put out the fires once the French had departed, so that instead of over 400 houses destroyed, the fire only claimed about 30 to 35.

6 AG, A¹871, 19, 20, 29 November and 6 December 1688, Louvois to Montclair, in ibid., p. 164.
7 AG, A¹826, 27 October 1688, Chamlay to Louvois, in ibid., p. 163.
8 AG, A¹871, 17 December 1688, Louvois to la Grange, in ibid., p. 164.
9 AG, A¹871, 18 December 1688, Louvois to Montclair, in ibid., p. 165.
10 AG, A¹871, #175ff, cited in John B. Wolf, *Louis XIV* (New York, 1968), 452.

Mannheim would not be so fortunate; it suffered the worst of this devil's work. On 13 January, truly an unlucky thirteenth for the people of Mannheim, Louvois condemned that city to destruction in an order to Montclair. 'The king wants that the inhabitants of Mannheim be warned to withdraw to Alsace, and that all the buildings of the city be razed, without leaving any structure standing.'[11] However, only in March did the French put Mannheim to the torch. On 4 March Montclair told the magistrates that the French intended to tear down the dwellings in the town, and he had the gall to suggest that the townspeople demolish their own homes 'to avoid disorder', but they refused.[12] Louvois wanted the inhabitants to evacuate the town and withdraw to Alsace. The people of Mannheim were ordered to take their belongings and leave, but so little time was allowed – in some cases no more than four days – that they were permitted to put their belongings in churches for ten to twelve days until transport could be arranged.[13] The actual burning began on 8 March and proceeded on the following days.[14] Fire promised to do the job well, according to Montclair: 'since the town is almost all built of wood, it will soon be consumed'.[15] Soldier work crews tore down walls and filled in ditches, and in addition, peasants were rounded up and used as forced labour for this and other destructions. Later, when the town had been evacuated and the destruction completed, Louvois ordered Montclair to kill any residents who tried to return to their homes.[16] In the words of Chamlay, Mannheim had been levelled, 'like a field'.[17]

The fate of Mannheim awaited other unfortunate towns. On 12 May Duras wrote of the necessity to burn Speyer and Worms, but he was apparently tortured by the prospect, because he confided in Louvois on 21 May: 'The pain of having to destroy cities as considerable as Worms and Speyer leads me to put before His Majesty the bad effect that such a desolation would have on his reputation and his *gloire* in the world.'[18] However, Louvois was not to be moved by

11 Letter in Rousset, *Histoire de Louvois*, vol. iv, p. 166.
12 AG, A¹875, 4 March 1689, La Grange to Louvois.
13 On these details see AG, A¹875, 6 March 1689, La Grange to Louvois.
14 Raumer, *Die Zerstörung der Pfalz*, p. 145.
15 AG, A¹875, 6 March 1689, Montclair to Louvois, from Mannheim.
16 AG, A¹872, 16 May 1689, Louvois to Montclair, in Rousset, *Histoire de Louvois*, vol. iv, pp. 168–9.
17 AG, A¹876, 21 May 1689, Chamlay to Louvois, in ibid., p. 178.
18 AG, A¹876, 12 May 1689, Duras to Louvois, in ibid., p. 177; and 21 May 1689, Duras to Louvois, in Joël Cornette, *Le Roi de guerre: Essai sur la souveraineté dans la France du Grande Siècle* (Paris, 1993), p. 325, from Henri Griffet, *Recueil de*

197

such sentiment, and the same day Chamlay set out a plan for the destruction of these two cities and Oppenheim.[19] The inhabitants were to be given six days to remove their furniture and other goods, and they would be encouraged to resettle in Alsace, Lorraine, and Burgundy, where they would be exempt from all taxes for ten years. Then on 31 May, fire consumed Oppenheim and Worms, although it is to be noted that the fortifications of both towns had already been razed, that is, breaches torn in the walls and ditches filled in, and only the residences stood to be fired. Flames consumed Speyer the next day, 1 June, and Bingen on 4 June. Duras reported that amidst the smoking ruins of Worms not a single habitation remained standing.[20]

All in all, the French destroyed over a score of substantial towns, and to this toll must be added the numerous villages reduced to ashes, for as fires gutted the great towns they also charred the surrounding countryside. Tessé reported that while the French destroyed Mannheim they also burned all villages around it to a distance of four French leagues, or ten miles.[21] The French resolve to destroy everything in their paths spelled the end for hovels as well as fine houses, as French war parties collected tribute and burned their way across the countryside.

While Louis and Louvois instructed soldiers to carry out their work in a disciplined manner, the line between purposeful destruction and outright pillage blurred. It proved nearly impossible to command a soldier to burn down a house but not to steal any of its contents or abuse its occupants. In addition, much of the work was done by isolated patrols operating far from the eyes of senior commanders. The conduct of such raiders must have varied depending on the rapaciousness of the particular men involved, and undoubtedly some cared little for official directives or common decency. To make matters worse, soldiers were not always in control of themselves, but literally grew drunk with pillage, as soldiers consumed the wine from doomed cellars. Soldiers committed awful excesses, and brutality bred reprisal, as Germans murdered Frenchmen. Obviously such acts simply drove the French to commit further obscenities.

lettres pour servir à l'histoire militaire du règne de Louis XIV (8 vols; 1760–64), vol. vi, p. 17.

19 AG, A¹876, 12 May 1689, Duras to Louvois, in Rousset, *Histoire de Louvois*, vol. iv, pp. 177–8.

20 AG, A¹882, 31 May 1689, 10 p.m., Duras to Louvois, from Odernheim, in Ronald Thomas Ferguson, 'Blood and Fire: Contribution Policy of the French Armies in Germany (1668–1715)', Ph.D. dissertation, University of Minnesota, 1970, p. 116.

21 AGH, A¹875, 9 March 1689, Tessé to Louvois, from Mannheim.

The campaign season brought a close to the devastation of the Palatinate, Baden, and Württemberg as German and Dutch forces advanced against the French and forced them back toward their fortress line. Military concerns in the Rhineland shifted to the siege of Mainz that summer, as large German forces took back much of what the French army had seized since the previous September.

The savage character of the devastation of the Palatinate stood out at the time, even though seventeenth-century Europe witnessed the horrors of war on a grand scale. Perhaps revulsion with the suffering inflicted by the Thirty Years War engendered a hope that the brutality would end, or at least diminish, and thus the devastation of the Palatinate shocked all the more. Yet this destruction was not the first time since the Treaty of Westphalia that war brought the horror of systematic destruction upon a civilian population. The Dutch War saw the French lay waste to parts of the Dutch Netherlands in 1672–74. Then in 1674 Turenne devastated the lands between the Main and the Neckar in order to impede any German advance against Alsace, and in 1677 the French wreaked havoc on the Meuse country, again to create a logistic obstacle against their enemies. Neither would the devastation of the Palatinate be the last such action during the wars of Louis XIV; for example, the armies of Marlborough and Eugene of Savoy would ravage Bavaria in 1704. But it was not these other instances of brutal destruction but the devastation of the Palatinate that burned itself into the European conscience. And there is reason to believe that memories of the Palatinate were one of the influences that inspired Europeans to try to make the conduct of war more restrained and humane in the eighteenth century.

1689

Faced with a war that he had neither desired nor expected, Louis mustered additional new levies for the campaign of 1689. This included summoning the first battalions of the new royal provincial militia in November 1688. Because his enemies had multiplied, so must his regiments. French forces engaged along four fronts during 1689. Marshal Duras continued to lead an army in the Rhineland; Marshal Humières commanded in Flanders; Marshal Noailles led forces arrayed against Catalonia; and Louis dispatched ships and troops to support James II. Louis would fight beyond his borders in Flanders, and on the other fronts of this war, not in the name of conquest, but in order to make war feed war and to keep the enemy from exploiting French territory. Throughout this war, Louis also feared an internal enemy, his Huguenot subjects, whom he had forced to convert to Catholicism. He had reason to be wary: in 1689 emissaries and pastors from Amsterdam and London circulated in Huguenot areas.[22] In response, Louis augmented local militias and charged them with surveillance over the *nouveaux convertis* and even called upon the *ban* to watch over these restive subjects.

In this war as in the last, Louis would make his major military commitment in Flanders, as French generally termed the Spanish-held portions of Flanders and Hainault, as well as Brabant. And as before, the fact that fortresses lay so thick on the ground there would shape campaigns, leading to an emphasis on sieges. However, 1689 produced nothing beyond a stand-off in Flanders, as both sides marshalled forces and planned for a long war. On 14 May, Humières assembled his army for the new campaign near Boussières on the Sambre, where he marshalled twenty-four battalions and seventy-five squadrons. At the same time, the prince of Waldeck commanded the enemy army near Tirlemont. Through an uneventful summer, both armies manoeuvred cautiously, as troops occupied themselves with the usual forages, essential in sustaining a field army, and engaged in a few skirmishes.

This war and the next witnessed considerable use of entrenched lines to control territory, hem in enemy raiders, and hamper the march of armies. Louis quickly ordered his troops to reestablish and extend lines that dated back to the Dutch War. In October 1689, Humières employed 5,000 pioneers digging and repairing such defensive positions with 1,200 troops to cover them.

Before Humières went into winter quarters he detached four battalions of Gardes françaises to march to the Rhineland, where the French faced their greatest challenge of 1689. Louis, caught off-guard by German resistance, could not match the number of troops opposed to him there in 1689, so he resolved to keep the wolf from his door by razing enemy lands and by charging Duras's battalions to hold the hostile armies at arm's length.

Louis had wished to detach the elector of Bavaria from the hostile alliance but had failed, so he dispatched Feuquières with a sizeable body of raiders to traverse Württemberg, cross the Danube, and put part of Bavaria under contribution. This course of 500 miles through Germany saw him briefly take Würzburg, Nuremberg, Ulm,

---

22 Geoffrey Symcox, *The Crisis of French Sea Power, 1688–1697: From the guerre d'escadre to the guerre de course* (The Hague, 1974), p. 81.

Augsburg, and Pforzheim, as he netted 500,000 livres in contributions for the king.

The main enemy army under Charles, the duke of Lorraine, assembled near Koblenz at the end of May. It numbered 40,000 men, but with other forces converging on the Rhineland, Louis would soon face armies totalling 150,000 troops there.[23] A war council at Frankfurt decided to besiege Mainz, taken by the French the previous autumn. German troops had already begun to assemble on the Main near Mainz in mid-May, and by the end of that month, their cavalry on the right bank of the Rhine cut Mainz's communications east. Meanwhile, another army of 21,000 commanded by the elector of Bavaria advanced on Fort-Louis, but French resistance there forestalled a siege.

Hard-fought and long, the actual siege of Mainz lasted from July into September. The main German army, now grown to 60,000 men under Charles, only arrived around Mainz on 17 July, and they opened trenches on the night of 22–3 July. Huxelles in command of the French garrison of about 8,000 soldiers conducted an active defence. As was often the case in siege warfare, the attackers usually carried out their assaults after dark. The prevalence of night-fighting in sieges, the most common form of combat at this time, meant that it played a major role in seventeenth-century warfare. Conditions at the siege of Mainz took on the character of World War I trench warfare, with its subterranean combat, vicious struggles at close quarters, and bombardment with explosive shells. After the enemy had breached the walls in early September, and after several nights of particularly hard fighting, the defenders capitulated on 8 September, and Huxelles marched out on 11 September with 6,000 able-bodied men and walking wounded. French casualties were 200 officers and 2,000 enlisted men killed or wounded. The French had lost Mainz, but they had occupied Charles's army for the entire summer at a relatively small cost; even Huxelles's forces came out largely intact.

Other French actions were relatively secondary. Marshal Duras lacked enough troops to break the siege of Mainz; therefore, he penetrated Württemberg to levy contributions instead. He both succeeded in aiding French war finances and in hindering the siege, by disrupting enemy supply. Other French actions were small in scope. Boufflers with forty-six squadrons of cavalry and 2,400 foot seized the small fortress of Cochem on the Moselle. He summoned the garrison to surrender immediately, stating that he would not accept a capitulation

23 Quincy, *Histoire militaire*, vol. ii, p. 172.

later, but they refused. In the bitter fighting that ensued, the garrison lost 1,300 men, a harsh penalty for disregarding Boufflers's summons. The French lost only 215 officers and men, killed or wounded. Earlier in the summer, the Allies carried out operations further north on the Rhine. At Kaiserwerth, Fürstenberg had established a garrison under French command, but the elector of Brandenburg besieged this fortress in June. There, the elector, under the guidance of the famed Dutch engineer Menno van Coehoorn, opened the trenches on 24 June. The garrison capitulated two days later and marched out on 28 June, following the road to Luxembourg. Once Kaiserwerth fell, the elector of Brandenburg led his army of 28,000 men against Bonn. Because he had to detach troops to aid Charles, the elector lacked sufficient forces to undertake a regular siege, so he simply blockaded the city. But when Charles marched up with most of the army that had besieged Mainz, Bonn capitulated on 10 October, having enduring a blockade and siege of several months.

After the fall of Mainz, the French braced for a further German advance, but Charles went into winter quarters. The French followed suit, wintering their men in Lorraine and Alsace. The French lost much more than they gained that year along the Rhine, but at least Louis's lands were not compromised.

Along the Catalan border, combat in 1689 centred on the small stronghold of Camprodon in the Spanish Pyrenees. The duke of Noailles reviewed his modest French army at le Boulou in Roussillon on 16 May and that evening detached a force of 3,700 men to invest Camprodon. The rest of the army followed, suffering through a snow storm in the Pyrenees. Reaching Camprodon, they opened trenches on 19 May, and the garrison of 500 capitulated on 22 May, marching out the next day. Noailles left a French garrison there and withdrew to Roussillon.

After resting his army, Noailles moved forward to camp at La Junquera on 14 June. At this time a Spanish army of 10,000 men under the command of Villahermosa assembled with the intention of attacking him, so he withdrew again, returning to Boulou on 29 June.

Villahermosa's army, now increased to about 20,000, advanced against Camprodon to retake it. In response, Noailles reassembled his troops and left Ille on 17 August, marched to Villefranche-de-Conflent, and turned south into the mountains. The arrival of Noailles near Camprodon lifted the Spanish siege in the sense that the Spanish broke their ring around the fortress and regrouped into a camp that faced off against Noailles's camp. The opponents bombarded one another during this stalemate. Finally, Noailles withdrew his garrison from Camprodon on the night of 25–6 August, and the French then returned to Roussillon. With this withdrawal, both armies entered winter quarters.

During the first phase of the Nine Years War, French troops assisted James II in his vain efforts to retake the English throne by Irish campaigns. In March 1689 James II took ship for Ireland to rally Catholic support there. Louis aided James both because the Sun King believed fervently in the Stuart's God-ordained right to the English throne, and because a war in Ireland would divert William and his army away from Flanders. These mixed motives would continue to inspire Louis's support of his brother king.

A French fleet of twenty-four third- and fourth-rate vessels and two frigates and transports under the command of Château-Renault departed Brest on 6 May to ferry over weapons and supplies for James; this led to the major naval confrontation of the year. Admiral Herbert, soon to be known as Lord Torrington, cruised off the Irish coast to intercept any French squadron. Because the presence of the English made offloading at Kinsale impossible, Château-Renault anchored his fleet in Bantry Bay on 10 May. On the morning of 11 May, Herbert's squadron of nineteen ships of the line came into view. Château-Renault, enjoying the weather gauge, drove Herbert from Bantry Bay into the open sea, where Herbert bore off. The four-hour battle gave the French a limited tactical victory, for while little damage was done to either fleet, Château-Renault had protected the transports, allowing them to unload. His fleet returned to Brest on 18 May. The French and English had already crossed swords, although Louis did not declare war against William's England until 23 June.

The summer months did not bring another major sea fight, although the French battle fleet was united at Brest. To bring French forces together, Tourville sailed his squadron of twenty rated vessels and four frigates from Toulon in June, arriving in Brest the next month. The assembled fleet of sixty-two rated vessels and twenty-nine fireships left Brest on 15 August with Seingelay on board bearing orders to give battle. However, the French were unable to close with the enemy fleet, and after a few weeks of cruising, Tourville brought the fleet back to Brest, where it disarmed, with the exception of a winter guard of twenty vessels.

Bound to France with naval cords, James II's adventure in Ireland proceeded. For this expedition to Ireland, James received the service of three French frigates charged with cruising off the Irish coast and transporting troops and supplies for James. They performed fine service, even defeating a small English squadron on 20 July. Louis also committed 8,000 of his troops, under the count of Lauzun. Thanks to French aid, James mustered an army of 30,000 Irish, but they were ill supplied and ill disciplined. With this force he besieged the Protestant town of Londonderry, but was forced to raise the siege in July and withdraw to Dinmikilling. William dispatched Schomberg, Louis's erstwhile Protestant marshal, to command his army in Ireland, which grew to 40,000.

The coming of the Nine Years War marked the end of an era for France. The first half of Louis's personal reign, full of splendour and success, ended chronologically and spiritually as Louis's army crossed the Rhine to besiege Philippsburg. After years of construction, Louis had moved his court to Versailles in the early 1680s. The great hall of mirrors and the salons on either side celebrated his *gloire* in the Dutch War with huge battle paintings and reliefs. In 1695 Saint-Simon regarded these paintings as so provocative that they 'have not played a little part in irritating all of Europe and causing it once again to league against the person of the king and his kingdom'.[24] The grandeur of the hall of mirrors was completed by massive silver tables and candelabras, but the Nine Years War quickly dulled this brilliance. In 1689 Louis sent to the mint these opulent silver furnishings, along with silver dishware, to be melted down and transformed into coin to pay for the mounting costs of a great war. The second half of his personal reign would be more about survival than celebration.

THE CRUX OF THE FIGHTING, 1690–92

The next three years of the war brought the full weight of the contending foes against one another. On the Continent, the French won a string of successes, while at sea Louis's fleet both enjoyed victory and suffered defeat. Despite Bourbon support for James II in Ireland, William III triumphed in the British Isles. The close alliance between the Maritime Powers, their animosity to Louis, and their relative invulnerability to French invasion ensured that the war would not soon be over. England was sheltered by the Channel and its increasingly powerful fleet, while even if the Dutch could be approached on

---

[24] Saint-Simon in Cornette, *Le Roi de guerre*, p. 239. Someone would practically have to lie on his or her back to study them.

land, Louis's frustration in 1672–74 demonstrated that the unique circumstances of the Dutch Netherlands made it virtually impossible for Louis to conquer them. The land-based foes of France duelled with Louis within the confines of a band of territory along the French borders; there would be no far-reaching campaigns on the Continent. The pace and goals of the land war, 1690–92, although not its expense, would be surprisingly limited.

1690

Augmented French forces engaged enemies who literally surrounded Louis's kingdom on land and sea. In December 1689 Louis again ordered the raising of new regiments to buttress French armies in the field. In 1690 the primary army fought in Flanders under the excellent Marshal Luxembourg, who retained this command until his early death in 1695.[25] He was to be supported if need be by an army on the Moselle under Boufflers. The dauphin held largely honorific command of the French army in the Rhineland, as Marshal de Lorge actually led the army. There he opposed the elector of Bavaria, who succeeded to allied command with the death of Charles of Lorraine. Catinat led an army in Dauphiné, faced off against the duke of Savoy, while Noailles again commanded forces deployed on the border of Catalonia.

Luxembourg's army in Flanders for 1690 included thirty-four battalions and ninety-four squadrons as it assembled around St Amand in mid-May. After a review on 15 May, the army moved camp to Leuze-en-Hainault. From there elements of the army conducted a major forage in the direction of Ghent on 18 May, an act that would be part of the regular rhythm of the army's existence.[26] On 21 May the army set up camp at Harelbeke, where the artillery joined it. A few days later Luxembourg moved the army to Deinze within three leagues of Ghent, sending foraging parties right up to the gates of the town.

The Allies were surprised by the rapidity with which the French entered the campaign. Prince Waldeck commanded the main army, as William laboured to secure his throne and defeat James II in Ireland.

25 On Luxembourg, see Pierre marquis de Ségur, *Le maréchal de Luxembourg et le prince d'orange, 1668–1678* (Paris, 1902).
26 It is worth noting that throughout the historical narrative of these campaigns by Quincy, an officer who had led troops in this era, he consistently regards major foraging expeditions as important enough to be worth mention.

Waldeck had hoped to be able to delay his campaign until the elector of Brandenburg was on the Moselle to tie down Boufflers, but Luxembourg forced the campaign early, allowing Boufflers to move north between the Sambre and Meuse to support Luxembourg. Waldeck left his assembly point at Tienen and advanced to Wavre, where he dispersed his troops to live off the forage and grain of the country. His army reassembled and advanced to Genappe on 8 June.[27]

Waldeck's moves forced Luxembourg to split his forces. In mid-June, he detached several battalions under Marshal Humières to observe the Spanish forces, reinforced by Hanoverian troops, while the main French army left Deinze on 17 June and marched south below Mons and crossed the Sambre at Jeumont on 23 June. Meanwhile, Boufflers detached part of his command under Rubantel to rendezvous with Luxembourg's army, which continued its march, camping at Boussu on 27 June.

As Luxembourg manoeuvred south of Mons and Charleroi, Waldeck shifted his camp forward to a position between Nivelles and Pieton on 28 June. He had not expected Luxembourg to reach the Sambre between Charleroi and Namur before 30 June, but he was mistaken.

On the evening of 28 June Luxembourg personally led a large detachment that set out from Gerpinnes on a forced march with bridging pontoons to establish a river crossing at Ham, just east of Jemeppe on the Sambre. There, Luxembourg's troops had to take a chateau on the other bank at Froidment. The fortified position, held by about 100 men, had been garrisoned precisely to hinder a crossing at this point. While troops swam the river and used a boat they found, Luxembourg moved up the pontoons, and once they were in place, several artillery pieces rolled across and forced the surrender of the chateau. At the same time, French dragoons, stripped of all their clothing, swam the Sambre with their swords in their teeth to seize another enemy redoubt that the enemy had abandoned on the approach of the French battalions.

The army followed the victorious troops who had established the bridgehead, and on the morning of 30 June the last of Luxembourg's troops crossed the Sambre. All the heavy baggage remained on the south bank near Ham. On that day, Waldeck decamped and swung his army toward the French bridgehead in an attempt to shelter the country north of the Sambre and Meuse from French contributions. On flat land just to the east of Fleurus, French and Dutch cavalry,

---

27 Quincy refers to these towns as Thienhem, Waverhem, and Jenap.

sent to reconnoitre the French position, crossed swords in a dramatic, but inconclusive, clash. At the end of the day, the French cavalry withdrew to Velaine, where the rest of the army joined it and set up camp only a mile and a half from the enemy. That night Luxembourg interrogated prisoners to learn about the enemy position and forces. The next morning his own troops, who expected to withdraw across the river, received ball and powder instead and marched toward Fleurus.

Just to the west of Fleurus, Waldeck's allied army of 38,000 troops set up for battle in the two customary lines stretching from the village of Heppignies on the right past the chateau of St Amant on the left. The front of the allied position was covered by the Orme stream and its elevated banks that made a frontal assault all but impossible, so Luxembourg opted to attack the enemy's flanks. That day Luxembourg commanded about 35,000 troops who marched from Velaine in five columns; the two on the French right comprised the first line, the centre column the artillery, and the two on the left the second line.[28]

Taking a considerable risk, Luxembourg audaciously divided his forces and sent them against both flanks of Waldeck's army. For this to succeed, he had to divert Waldeck's attention and hide his movements. The columns of the first line split off to form a battle line from near Heppignies to Fleurus with some troops up toward St Amant, forming an elbow. The two right columns of Luxembourg veered off to the north, passing the Orme on bridges thrown across by the French. The lay of the land, embellished with hedges and wheat fields, and a screen of French cavalry kept the enemy from viewing the path of Luxembourg's right. Forty cannon meant to support the advance were set up in several batteries near the chateau of St Amant. Another thirty guns took position from the chateau to Fleurus. The columns of troops continued their march through a marsh that at first seemed impassable and then up the hills that overlooked the left of the enemy line. Had Waldeck realized that Luxembourg had split his army in two, he might have overwhelmed the isolated French left before the right came into position, but he did not. Once the French troops had reached their positions enveloping both of Waldeck's flanks before he could respond, Luxembourg had essentially guaranteed himself a victory.

28 The numbers of troops at Fleurus is a matter of debate. Quincy fails to give a number for Luxembourg, but credits Waldeck with 9,200 cavalry, 1,400 dragoons, and 27,200 infantry for a total of 37,800 men. Quincy, *Histoire militaire*, vol. ii, p. 252. Corvisier sets the numbers at 35,000 for Luxembourg and 50,000 Allies. Philippe Contamine, ed., *Histoire militaire de la France*, vol. i (Paris, 1992), p. 425.

The Wars of Louis XIV

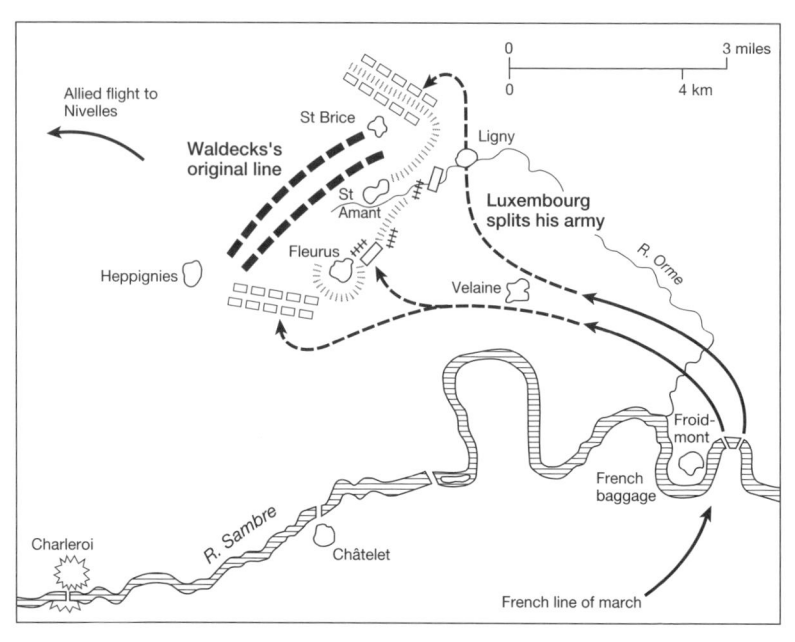

Map 6.1 Battle of Fleurus, 1 July 1690
Adapted from: Charles Sévin, marquis de Quincy, *Histoire militaire de Louis le Grand roi de France* (7 vols; Paris, 1726)

When the French right had taken position, the French artillery opened fire about 10 a.m., striking allied infantry with great effect. Gournay commanded the French left, while Luxembourg stood on the other flank. Gournay opened the attack on the left by charging with his cavalry but was killed in the effort. His death put the attack in disorder, and the horsemen retired to regroup near Fleurus. A charge at the same time on the French right met with more success, driving enemy cavalry back. On the heels of this second cavalry assault Luxembourg's infantry advanced. Troops from the French left and right attacked the enemy line, and, taken in both flanks, the enemy line broke. Some of the survivors, both infantry and cavalry, regrouped on an elevation near Fleurus, where they struggled to resist the French, but were overwhelmed. Meanwhile, Waldeck was able to create a new line with his remaining troops further back, though pressed by French cavalry. Flushed with their initial success, French infantry came up after some delay, reformed in line, and shattered this final allied position. Waldeck's troops now streamed toward Nivelles as best they could. The heaviest of the fighting that

The Great Miscalculation

day had lasted from 11:30 a.m. to 2 p.m. Luxembourg crushed Waldeck's army, which suffered 6,000 dead, 5,000 wounded, and 8,000 prisoners, a casualty rate mounting to 50 per cent of his forces. The cost had not been light for the French with 3,000 dead and the same number wounded.[29]

But if the tactical plan of Fleurus and its overwhelming victory were truly Napoleonic, the operational result was typically seventeenth-century. The enemy army retired on Brussels, while Luxembourg did not pursue. There the Allies rebuilt the force by drawing from fortress garrisons and replacing them with troops cut up in the battle. Spanish troops under Gastañaga joined the main army, and Tilly arrived on 22 July with troops from Liège and Brandenburg. On 2 August the elector of Brandenburg and his army joined Waldeck to form a combined allied army totalling 55,000 men, considerably more than it had mustered at Fleurus a month before. Now at full strength, the army marched to Genappe on 5 August and then proceeded to Nivelles on 7 August.

During this period, Luxembourg did not press the foe. Louvois might have ordered Luxembourg to besiege Namur or Charleroi immediately; the minister wanted to do so, and at first Louis concurred, but then immediately reversed himself. Worries about his son's forces in Germany and concern about the imminent arrival of Brandenburg's army moved him to caution, and he ordered Luxembourg to detach troops to buttress Boufflers's army and forgo a siege. At least one biographer interprets this as Louis losing his nerve.[30] But while the enemy was impotent for a month, Luxembourg achieved the kind of victory that so mattered in a war of attrition: he put much of the land east of Brussels under contribution.

The remainder of the campaign was relatively uneventful. As the enemy army grew, so did that of Luxembourg, who also took troops from garrisons. Boufflers joined his forces to those of Luxembourg for a time, but in late August shifted back to the area between the Sambre and Meuse rivers. Long lines of entrenchments between fortresses were proving their worth in this war, and Waldeck tried to force the French lines near Ypres with a flying column of 1,500 cavalry and an additional 1,500 infantry riding on the croups of the horses. Quick action on the part of Montbrun cut off and threw back this column. While the French and the Allies engaged in minor thrust

---

[29] Quincy, *Histoire militaire*, vol. ii, pp. 259, 266, and Gaston Bodart, *Militärhistorisches Kriegs-Lexikon (1618–1905)* (Vienna and Leipzig, 1908), p. 112.
[30] See Wolf, *Louis XIV*, pp. 458–9. See also Rousset, *Histoire de Louvois*, vol. iv, pp. 416–19.

209

and parry, fighting and foraging in Flanders, Louis's general Tessé led a raid by 2,000 cavalry into Jülich to put the country under contribution, amassing 1,200,000 livres on this course.[31] In October both armies went into winter quarters, Luxembourg being certain to station most of his army on enemy territory; most of the Dutch quartered in and around Maastricht; the Hanoverians returned home; while many from Brandenburg and Luneberg found quarters in fortresses of the Spanish Netherlands.

In the Rhineland during the winter of 1689–90, French troops put the electorate of Cologne under contribution and dispatched courses into other Rhineland electorates. When the campaign season arrived in Germany, the dauphin once again took command of the army of the Rhine, as he had in the previous years, but now actual command devolved on Marshal de Lorge. This army, as it assembled in late May not far from Mainz, contained thirty-six battalions and ninety-seven squadrons. By 8 June the army had settled down in Vachenheim, where it would remain for two weeks.

The Allies formed three bodies of troops to operate against the French in the Rhineland. The elector of Bavaria led the largest of these, which included not only Bavarian units but troops from Saxony and smaller German states. The second, commanded by the elector of Brandenburg, would, as has been shown, march north to join Waldeck. General Dunenvald headed the third with imperial troops and men from Hesse-Kassel and Franconia. These allied forces began to move about 1 June; however, this campaign season produced no major engagements or sieges. When in mid-August the dauphin heard that the Germans would cross the Rhine, he decided to take his forces, then numbering 40,000, across that river at Fort-Louis to allow his army to live off enemy resources. A bloody battle seemed imminent in September, but the clash failed to materialize. The uneventful manoeuvres came to an end when the dauphin left his army to return to Fontainebleau at the end of September, and shortly thereafter the armies went into quarters. This campaign season produced none of the rapid marches typical of Turenne and Créqui and none of the destructive fury of 1688 and 1689.

While things stalled along the Rhine, war raged in Italy, where Louis found a new enemy in Victor Amadeus II, duke of Savoy. His territories split into several distinct areas, notably Nice, Savoy, and Piedmont. Nice enjoyed a Mediterranean coast where the maritime Alps meet

31 Quincy, *Histoire militaire*, vol. ii, p. 273.

the sea. Mountainous Savoy to the north occupied the Alps bordering on the French province of Dauphiné. Sparsely populated difficult country, it blocked passes from France to Piedmont. Piedmont linked the mountains to the Po valley and contained the capital city of Turin. By previous treaty, the French held two fortresses in Italy, and one of them, Pinerolo, lay only about twenty miles to the southwest of Turin in Piedmont. The other, Casale, half-way between Turin and Milan, was purchased by Louis in 1681, as described in the previous chapter. French possession of these two fortresses flies in the face of modern notions of political borders, but they were regarded as useful gates into the Italian plain and as leverage over Piedmont. They gave Louis a military presence in Italy even at the start of the conflict with the duke of Savoy.

During this war and the next, Victor Amadeus II concluded alliances and broke them to suit his needs, and this earned him a reputation as duplicitous. However, it is reasonable to point out that no one was in quite as vulnerable a position as he was, caught between Bourbon lands to his west and Habsburg possessions to his east and with a major French fortress not far from his capital. When war came to Italy, it was bound to be fought back and forth across his domains, and he manoeuvred as best he could to take advantage of his unenviable situation.

War against the duke derived a particularly bitter and vicious aspect from the fact that the Vaudois reenter the story now as they were reconciled with their erstwhile ruler, Victor Amadeus, and took up arms to regain their valleys. Little quarter was asked or given when they fought the French.

The French began the year still dealing with Victor Amadeus, for he had yet to declare himself against Louis. The French general in command, Catinat, represented the rare case of a general who did not hail from one of the great military families of France. While it is sometimes said that he was a commoner, it is closer to describe him as the son of a family from the new legal and administrative nobility. In any case, compared with his fellow-generals, he had but a modest birth. Still, he demonstrated real ability in the field, and considerable brutality when he carried out Louis's aggression against the Vaudois. At first Louis demanded guarantees, including the citadel of Turin to show the duke's good faith, but outright hostilities began in June. On 2 June French residents in Turin were arrested and remaining Vaudois held in confinement were released. As soon as this news reached Louis, he ordered Boufflers and Huxelles to send troops to Dauphiné, and Saint-Ruth was detailed to lead them. Before Saint-Ruth arrived,

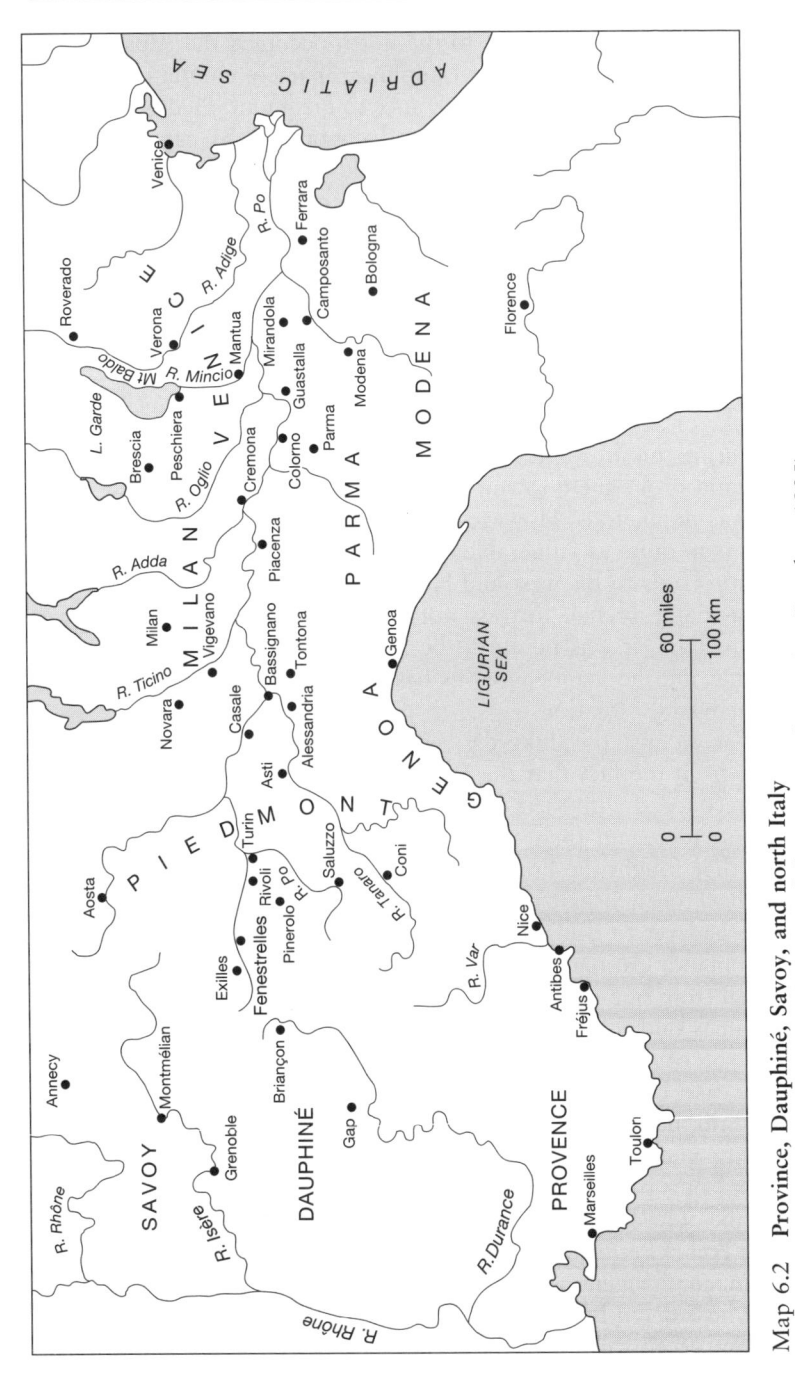

Map 6.2 Province, Dauphiné, Savoy, and north Italy
Adapted from: M. S. Anderson, *The War of the Austrian Succession* (London, 1995)

The Great Miscalculation

the marquis of Larré exercised command over the force of 10,000 militia and four companies of cavalry that he was able to assemble. Catinat led a small army of only 12,000 troops, but they would account themselves very well. He began by assessing contributions and sending out forage parties. French war parties taxed the town of Carmagnola 50,000 livres and even demanded 1,200,000 livres from Turin. Catinat sent grain and animals taken in courses to Pinerolo. Victor Amadeus received Spanish reinforcements, who marched over from the Spanish possession of Milan, while he was promised 4,000 German troops under Prince Eugene of Savoy. This highly gifted general was the son of Eugene Maurice, count of Soissons and prince of Savoy-Carignan. Eugene grew up around the French court, but when he petitioned Louis for a position in the royal army, the king refused him. In response, Eugene developed an intense dislike of Louis and offered his sword to the emperor in 1683; thus, Louis's haughtiness created a major nemesis of his regime.

The summer witnessed hard marching and bitter fighting. With an army too small to besiege the fortress of Turin, Catinat tried to command as much of Victor Amadeus's territory as possible and to support French forces at his expense. Meanwhile the marquis of Larré advanced into Savoy and put Chambéry and other towns under contribution. Catinat detached Feuquières to tax or burn enemy strongholds, but Feuquières with 1,200 had a very tough fight at Luserna and was forced to abandon the town, suffering 600 casualties in his retreat. Believing that Feuquières was lost and anxious to catch the French while they were weak, Victor Amadeus left Villafranca, where he had been securely encamped for some time, with the intention of attacking and surrounding Catinat. Catinat, who was under orders to fight the duke of Savoy, left his camp at Cavour and marched south to take Saluzzo. It is worth noting that while other French forces did not employ regiments of the royal provincial militia with their main battle forces, Catinat was so strapped for manpower that he included six militia regiments with his army. When Victor Amadeus moved to stop Catinat, the result was the Battle of Staffarde, fought near Saluzzo on 18 August. Marshes and hedges impeded movement on the battlefield and sheltered the enemy line, but Catinat's troops broke Victor Amadeus's army, killing or wounding 2,800, capturing 1,200 prisoners, and seizing eleven of their twelve cannon. French killed and wounded totalled about 1,000.[32] Saluzzo immediately fell

---

[32] Bodart, *Kriegs-Lexikon*, p. 113 on casualties; Quincy, *Histoire militaire*, vol. ii, pp. 301–2.

to the French. Meanwhile, Saint-Ruth seized all of Savoy, with the exception of Montmélian.

Catinat followed up his victory at Staffarde by placing more of Victor Amadeus's towns under contribution, burning Cerisoles, Autrive, and other places where the duke had ordered the inhabitants not to pay contributions to the French. The duke holed up in Turin during these actions. In the last act of the campaign, Catinat besieged Susa on one major route to Savoy. Victor Amadeus made some effort to stop Catinat's advance to Susa, but the French general outmanoeuvred the duke. The French opened trenches before Susa on 11 November, which capitulated two days later. After this, Catinat sent his army into winter quarters in Savoy, Dauphiné, and Provence. Even though Louis committed few troops to the Italian campaign in 1690, his army had won notable success.

Noailles in Roussillon also commanded a small army of 11,000–12,000 troops, including 800 of the native light infantry of the Pyrenees and Catalonia, known as *miquelets*. Because France and Spain both held mountainous districts that spawned the *miquelets*, both sides fielded them. Having such a small army condemned Noailles to a defensive campaign against Spanish forces under the command of Villahermosa. After some tentative moves into Catalonia, as Noailles tried to live at the expense of the Catalans, he retired back to Roussillon. Villahermosa with only 12,000–13,000 troops could not be much more adventurous, and the two armies spent most of the summer simply observing one another.

Combat at sea earned the French navy glory in 1690, even if it reaped little strategic value from its victory. In general, the French were quicker off the mark than were their enemies in 1690. On 17 March a squadron ferried 6,000 French troops over to Ireland, and brought back 6,000 Irish recruits for French service; they arrived back in Brest on 1 May. By the end of March orders arrived to arm eighty-two rated vessels in Brest and Rochefort.

After a false start on 11 June, Tourville sailed from Brest on 23 June. His combined fleet numbered seventy-seven ships of the line and twenty-three fireships. As was the fashion, Tourville divided his fleet into three squadrons marked by white and blue, white, and blue pennants respectively. Tourville aboard the *Soleil Royal* personally commanded the centre or white squadron. The allied fleet he now sought had only fifty-seven English and Dutch ships of the line. The furore over French privateering led the English to commit too many

The Great Miscalculation

ships to commerce protection, thus thinning the battle fleet. On 2 July Tourville came up with the allied fleet off the Isle of Wight, and for several days the two fleets sailed west up the Channel, shadowing one another. Admiral Torrington wanted to retire from the superior French fleet because he believed that the very existence of a 'fleet in being' would be of too great a strategic importance to risk battle against unfavourable odds, but on 9 July he received a direct order from Queen Mary to fight the French. The next day, off Beachy Head near Eastbourne, Torrington marshalled his fleet in line of battle. Enjoying the weather gauge, he advanced toward the French, who formed line with Château-Renault and his blue squadron in the French van. The allied van, composed mainly of Dutch vessels, became entangled with the French van, which cut across the path of the Dutch. In heavy fighting, the Dutch took a terrible pounding before more of Torrington's ships came up to support them. Overmatched, Torrington ended the battle about noon by taking advantage of the tide. His fleet dropped anchor as the current carried the French fleet out of cannon range.

From a purely tactical point of view, Tourville had won the greatest French naval victory of the seventeenth century; however, the results were disappointing. The allied fleet lost only six ships as a result of the battle, and only one Dutch vessel sank during the fighting. Tourville now mastered the English Channel, but he did not make much of it. His failure to pursue Torrington with vigour infuriated Seignelay. Tourville anchored off Le Havre to refit and land his sick. This gave the English squadrons time to rally to the main fleet, while dockyards turned out new vessels. By the end of August the Allies had ninety sail cruising the Channel and French control was a thing of the past. Tourville might have better exploited his victory by sailing into the Irish Sea to cut off William, but this apparently did not occur to Tourville, Seignelay, or Louis.

Far more important than Beachy Head was a battle that never occurred in the Irish Sea. For as Tourville was clearing Brest, Sir Clowdesley Shovell escorted William III and a sizeable army to Ireland. Louis intended to station a strong squadron off the Irish coast, and to that effect dispatched Forant from Brest in early July with eight frigates to join three already in Ireland. But they arrived too late to contest the passage of William's forces, and this effectively doomed James II. As Tyrconnell, James's chief lieutenant in Ireland wrote on 26 June, 'The want of a squadron of French men of warr in St George's Channel has been our ruine, for had wee had that since the beginning of May, the prince of Orange had been

215

confounded without striking a stroke.'[33] The Irish Sea, and not the English Channel, should have been the true lynchpin of French naval strategy for 1690.

Tourville's victory at Beachy Head in no way forestalled William's triumph at the Boyne on 11 July.[34] William's army of 35,000 English and Dutch troops were marching south on Dublin from their landfall to the north, when 23,000 Irish and French troops under James II contested their crossing of the Boyne River. The superior cavalry of the English decided the brief battle with relatively few casualties; William's army lost only about 500 men. A few days after Forant made landfall at Kinsale, the defeated James arrived and commandeered four of Forant's frigates to sail for France. Forant went on with his remaining ships to Limerick, there to evacuate French troops under Lauzun. In October of this year, John Churchill, then the earl of Marlborough, made a superb debut as an army commander by taking Cork and Kinsale for William III. But he soon fell out of favour with the new monarch, and Marlborough would have to wait another decade to demonstrate his greatness in the next war.

1691

The struggle for Ireland continued into 1691, but William III felt secure enough on his new throne to return to the war on the Continent. He made a triumphal entry into The Hague on 5 February and consulted there with the electors of Brandenburg and Bavaria, the landgrave of Hesse-Kassel, the duke of Brunswick, and the Spanish governor of the Netherlands, Gastañaga. With William's urging they agreed to field forces totalling 220,000 that campaign season.[35] After this he retired to his country home in mid-March, but news that Louis was besieging Mons soon disturbed his rest.

The great goal of the 1691 campaign in fortress-rich Flanders was the siege of a major stronghold, Mons. The plan dictated making a major effort there and then redistributing troops to hold the line in Flanders and on the Rhine. Louvois engineered the tremendous

---

33 Tyrconnell to Maria-Beatrice in Symcox, *Crisis of French Sea Power*, p. 97.
34 The date of this battle is given as 11 July by some and 12 July by others. In fact 11 July is more correct as it was fought on 1 July on the old Julian calendar, and to update it to the modern Gregorian calander requires adding only ten days. After 1 January 1700, dates had to be changed by eleven days, thus creating the confusion.
35 Stephen Baxter, *William III and the Defense of European Liberty, 1650–1702* (New York, 1966), p. 293.

preparations for this siege. When the French had considered taking Mons in 1684, they decided not to because of insufficient forage in the area. To prepare for this operation Louvois ordered his *intendants* nearly a year before to purchase 900,000 rations of hay in as much secrecy as possible to hide Louis's intentions.[36] Louvois also stockpiled 220,000 red-skinned Dutch cheeses in the citadel of Tournai for the besieging army.[37] The attackers also required a total of 360,000 rations per day from stores in Namur, Philippeville, Dinant, and Givet, with the ovens established at Judoigne.[38]

Once again, Louis joined his army in the Spanish Netherlands, as he had in the previous war. He, his brother Philippe, the dauphin, and other great lords of court left for the front on 17 March, arriving at Mons four days later. Boufflers had already invested Mons on 15 March, and thousands of pioneers laboured on the lines of circumvallation, which Louis visited immediately after he arrived. The great king would make his presence known and felt at Mons. His publicists emphasized his bravery; one well-known engraving shows him in the siege lines observing an attack, and next to him lies a dead soldier labelled, 'soldier killed by a cannon shot behind the king'.[39] To be sure, this reports a true incident that occurred on 27 March, but the function was to foster a myth of the brave warrior-king.

The firing and fighting that compelled Mons to surrender rated as some of the most intense of Louis's wars. The forces committed to the siege were also unprecedented to that point: the king's besieging army of 46,000 surrounded Mons, while Luxembourg commanded an army of observation of equal size. The garrison numbered 6,000, and the Allies formed an army of 38,000 under William to relieve the fortress.[40] The French opened the trenches on the night of 24–5 March. Two batteries of 12 mortars each bombarded the city, setting much of it alight on the side targeted for the French assault. Barbarity was punctuated with gallantry, as on the morning of 26 March the musicians of the Régiment du Roi played a serenade for the women of the town, some of whom mounted the ramparts to listen. The guns fell silent on both sides for the concert. Back to their grimmer work,

---

36 AG, A¹1043, 13 May 1790, Louvois to Bagnols and Chauvelin in Rousset, *Histoire de Louvois*, vol. iv, p. 459.

37 Christopher Duffy, *The Fortress in the Age of Vauban and Frederick the Great, 1660–1789, Siege Warfare*, vol. ii (London, 1985), p. 29.

38 Victor Belhomme, *L'Armée française en 1690* (Paris, 1895), pp. 192–3.

39 This print is reproduced as plate 93 in Contamine, *Histoire militaire*, between pp. 466 and 467.

40 Bodart, *Kriegs-Lexikon*, p. 137; Pierre Lazard, *Vauban, 1633–1707* (Paris, 1934), pp. 225–6; and André Corvisier, *Louvois* (Paris, 1983), p. 468.

by 30 March the French had fired 7,000 cannonballs and 3,000 mortar shells at Mons. The usual process of destructive artillery fire and deadly trench fighting led to the inevitable result, and at 5 p.m. on 8 April the besieged beat the chamade. Conditions were settled, and the 4,500 remaining men of the garrison marched out on 10 April.

This siege had begun and ended well before the normal commencement of the campaign season, so now both sides began to prepare for the rest of the year's bloody work. Louis left for Versailles on 12 April, and, after distributing his troops to various garrisons, William returned to The Hague. Many French troops who had participated in the siege now marched off to the Moselle, the Rhine, and to buttress coastal defences. Those destined to remain with the army of Flanders went back into garrison quarters until better weather allowed them to return to the field. As would be the rule during this war, Louis created five armies for 1691: Flanders, the Moselle, the Rhine, Piedmont, and Roussillon. In addition he stationed troops to guard against a descent on Atlantic and Channel coasts. Multiple threats required multiple armies.

The largest army took station in Flanders; command of these 49 battalions and 140 squadrons went to Marshal Luxembourg again. He had clearly shown himself to be Louis's finest living marshal. Luxembourg assembled his force between Menin and Courtrai in mid-May. He took Halle at the end of the month and razed its fortifications. Luxembourg continued its march toward Brussels until the French and allied armies faced off against one another at Anderlecht, but the marshal decided not to fight since the ground favoured the enemy. William arrived at Anderlecht on 2 June to take command of the army of 63 battalions and 180 squadrons, totalling 56,000 troops. He also could rely on a force under Flemming with 14,000 Brandenburg troops. Gastañaga busied himself raising an army of 17,000 in Brussels.

Meanwhile, Boufflers and his force designated for the Moselle bombarded Liège, which had accepted a garrison from the prince of Orange, even though the Liègeois had declared neutrality. Boufflers arrived before the city on 1 June with an army of 15,000–16,000 men. His mortars caused great damage at the loss of only 22 men for the French; in a real sense, bombardment had become a low-cost alternative to the siege.

By early July, the French caught wind that William intended to besiege Dinant. As William marked time at Gembloux, waiting for the siege artillery to come up the Meuse from Maastricht, Luxembourg camped at Soignies. There he received reinforcements from Boufflers and Villars. After a review on 13 July he crossed the Sambre on a pontoon bridge, reaching Silenrieux on 21 July and passed Philippeville the next day. Luxembourg encamped at Florennes as William crossed the Sambre and established his army at Gerpinnes. Luxembourg's manoeuvre blocked William from besieging Dinant. Meanwhile, Boufflers sent forty squadrons of cavalry to forage around Dinant with the express purpose of consuming all the available fodder to make it difficult for the enemy to maintain himself there. Next, Luxembourg attempted to frustrate William, but their manoeuvres resulted in little action. By 7 September Luxembourg had returned to camp at Soignes. His goal at this point was to consume as many local resources as possible. He camped near Ninove and then shifted south to Lessines. On 17 September William's army decamped and headed for Leuze. At this point William left the army and Waldeck assumed command. Near Leuze Luxembourg caught up with the allied forces on 19 September and won an engagement when the van of his army attacked the rear guard of Waldeck's retreating force. Cavalry dominated in this action, which cost the French 700 casualties and the Allies 1,900.[41] Soon Luxembourg, Boufflers, and their allied opponents went into winter quarters, having achieved little since the siege of Mons. At least Luxembourg frustrated any plan William might have had for a victory to offset the loss of Mons.

In Germany the French assembled their forces in June around Neustadt. They had time to bring down units from the Netherlands, because the German armies habitually assembled late. De Lorge sparred with the German force of some 40,000 men in what became a war of detachments, with smaller bodies of troops detailed to raid or perform one task or another. Sickness forced changes of command upon the Germans as first the elector of Saxony fell ill followed by Caprara. In mid-September both armies returned to winter quarters. The marquis of Quincy, a general of Louis XIV turned historian, praised de Lorge's campaign thus: 'Marshal de Lorge found the means to feed [*vivre*] the army of the king on the enemies' country during the entire campaign, to take from them large contributions and to subsist at their expense.'[42] In his experienced eyes subsistence was victory in a war of attrition.

In contrast to the sterile manoeuvring along the Rhine, the campaign against Victor Amadeus in 1691 was very active. In Piedmont, both sides reinforced their armies in 1691. Schomberg even raised three

41 Bodart, *Kriegs-Lexikon*, p. 115.
42 Quincy, *Histoire militaire*, vol. ii, p. 408.

regiments of refugee French Huguenots to fight against Louis's troops in Italy. With these and the presence of the Vaudois, there remained a tone of religious war on the Italian front. Catinat began the fighting with an attack on Nice. He set out with troops from Provence in late February. A detachment under Vins invested Nice, while Catinat with the rest of the army took the neighbouring port of Villefranche, which gave him a place to land siege supplies. He arrived there on 13 March, and that town surrendered after firing a single shot. His troops closed in around Nice by 24 March. With inadequate defences, the town fell quickly, but the citadel held out. The French opened trenches on the night of 29–30 March, and the garrison beat the chamade on 2 April, using twelve drummers when the first lone one could not be heard over the din. This success cost Catinat only 100 men.

In Piedmont, Feuquières, who had abandoned Luserna the previous year, marched out of Pinerolo to attack the Vaudois and refugee French Huguenots there on 18 April. Encountering little resistance, he entered the town, killed many there, and sacked and burned much of it.

Catinat marched to Susa in the spring with the intention of taking Avigliana, which covered Turin, and relieving Casale. He left Susa on 27 May and took Avigliana two days later, destroying the fortifications of the town and its chateau. Catinat then crossed the Po at Carigano and approached Carmagnola, arriving around the town on 6 June. The garrison capitulated in only three days. A later attack on Cuneo by Feuquières led to a serious setback and the loss of 700 to 800 troops. In August 13,000 German troops who had fought against the Ottomans arrived to reinforce Victor Amadeus, who now had 45,000 soldiers split into three bodies. On 26 September the Allies crossed the Po and besieged Carmagnola. Catinat lacked the forces to relieve the fortress, which surrendered on 8 October.

While Catinat sparred with the far larger forces of Victor Amadeus, Hoguette commanding French troops in Savoy crossed the little St Bernard Pass in mid-June and carried out a campaign arching from Aosta to Ivrea. After seizing livestock and assessing contributions, Hoguette headed back while blowing up the bridges behind him. Because the French already held Susa and Hoguette's raid made the other major route into Savoy virtually impassable, Victor Amadeus would not be able to send support to Montmélian, his last remaining stronghold in Savoy. Hoguette now invested Montmélian, and the town fell on 5 August, although the citadel held out. After waiting to receive reinforcements, Hoguette undertook a siege of the citadel which resisted resolutely, but finally capitulated on 22 December.

The success of 1691 was such that Louis tried to win over Victor Amadeus to a peace settlement, by which he would receive everything back, save Nice, Villefranche, Montmélian, and Susa, but the duke refused.

The duke of Noailles departed Versailles on 16 April to return to his command in Roussillon. With his small army of only fourteen battalions and eight squadrons with some *miquelets* – a force of little over 10,000 men – Noailles besieged and took la Seu d'Urgell in late May. After this victory, Noailles established camp at Bellver to observe the Spanish, who were forming under Medina-Sidonia, while a French detachment under Chaseron advanced toward Barcelona with the goal of consuming enemy forage. Noailles also hoped to send courses as far as Aragon. When Medina-Sidonia began to march toward Bellver, Noailles fortified Bellver and added Roussillon militia and some garrison troops to his army. It was a characteristic of the usually troop-starved operations in Roussillon and Catalonia that militia were raised and employed. Medina-Sidonia came up to Bellver on 15 August, but, deterred by Noailles's preparations, turned west to besiege Prats-de-Mollo, where Noailles marched after him and foiled Spanish plans. After this, both armies ended the uneventful campaign by going into winter quarters.

The navy in 1691 received several strategic chores, as was typical of French maritime strategy. The defence of French coasts, so vital to Louis, would fall to both the navy and the army. Tourville, with the main fleet from Brest, put to sea in what has become known as his '*campagne du large*'. War dragged on in Ireland with half-hearted French support, but even while the effort flagged, it continued to divert troops and funds from Continental battlefields. In the Mediterranean, the fleet would support the army and embarrass the Spanish.

Regulars and militia, including the *milice gardes-côtes*, or coastguard militia, watched and waited on the coasts. General officers received commands in lower and upper Normandy, Brittany, and Aunis country to attend to their defences. Generals also were appointed in provinces populated by the *nouveaux convertis*. Louis feared an allied landing would mobilize this population to fight a Protestant crusade against him. The fleet was also intended to forestall a descent on French coasts.

Louis feared that the English might do exactly what he was doing in Ireland – support political and religious dissidents who opposed the crown in an effort to weaken an enemy from within. In June Louis dispatched a large convoy of forty ships escorted by twelve war vessels under the command of the marquis of Nesmond. This convoy carried food and munitions, including 16,000 fusils and muskets, nineteen cannon, and shoes and clothing for 20,000 men. Leaving on 5 June the convoy arrived at Limerick on the 18th. Before returning to Brest, Nesmond left four frigates on station off Ireland. However, the aid did not forestall defeat. On 10 June Ginkel in command of William's forces assembled his army, which took Balimorre on 19 June and Athlone on 10 July. Saint-Ruth, now in command of James's army, approached Athlone and determined to fight a battle to the death, destroying the bridges behind his own army to make it fight in place at Kilconnell. The battle on 22 July destroyed his army, and Saint-Ruth himself perished, the victim of a cannonball. James's remaining strongholds in Ireland fell in rapid succession until Limerick was the key position left in Catholic hands. Ginkel invested this port town on 1 September. Louis intended to send Sourdis with a relief force, but it never sailed. Limerick capitulated on 13 October; part of the agreement allowed the surviving French soldiers, and Irish who chose to, to sail to France. As a consequence, about 14,000 Irish troops landed at Brest, and James reviewed them at Vannes.[43] The Irish diversion was over.

In 1691 Tourville sailed on his *campagne du large*. This year, the French again concentrated their fleet in the Atlantic, although war with Spain and Savoy made them conscious of the need for a Mediterranean presence as well. Tourville was ordered to cruise the mouth of the Channel west of Brest. His primary purpose was to guard against an enemy descent on the French coasts. His orders read, 'His Majesty's principal intention is to guarantee his coasts from assaults by the enemy.'[44] In addition, Tourville was to prey on allied shipping if possible, particularly the rich Smyrna convoy coming up from the Mediterranean in June. This campaign does not mark the switch from *guerre d'escadre* to *guerre de course*, however, because, after all, Tourville was still commanding a full fleet, *escadre*, and because its primary purpose was not commerce raiding. Tourville sailed from Brest on 25 June with 73 vessels rated from 52 to 106 guns. He manoeuvred for nearly two months in a masterful game of naval chess, as he zigzagged off the mouth of the Channel to avoid superior allied numbers. While he missed the Smyrna convoy, Tourville drew

---

43 Ibid., p. 472.
44 Instruction of 26 May 1691 in Symcox, *Crisis of French Sea Power*, p. 112.

the enemy battle fleet out into the Atlantic in a futile chase, and this forestalled threatened allied landings on the French coast.

Based on Toulon, d'Estrées employed his fleet against land targets. In March he supported Catinat's siege of Nice by delivering essential siege artillery and supplies at Villefranche. In July his fleet of twelve vessels of war, twenty-five galleys, and three bomb ketches bombarded Barcelona, igniting the city with 800 bombs on 10 and 11 July. Then on 22 July he anchored at Alicante, where he came in quite close to his target and hit it with hundreds of mortar shells before a Spanish fleet arrived on 29 July and forced him to withdraw. Alicante suffered 2,000,000 livres of damage in this attack.

1692

For 1692, Louis framed essentially defensive operational plans for Germany and Piedmont but devoted troops and resources to more vigorous prosecution of the war in Flanders and Catalonia. The five land armies of 1691 would again take to the field under the command of the same generals who led them before. To these, Louis added another army in Flanders destined to besiege Namur, and sponsored a force assembled for an invasion of England.

Louis, attended by individuals from the court, including ladies once again, left Versailles for Flanders on 10 May and joined his army at Givry on the 17th. The women of the court travelled on to Mons, where the king joined them two days later. On 20 May he reviewed his army of 40 battalions and 90 squadrons and then crossed to the north bank of the Haine to review Luxembourg's host of 66 battalions and 205 squadrons. The ladies dressed appropriately for the occasion, as Amazons.

The target of these formidable forces was Namur at the juncture of the Sambre and Meuse Rivers. To cover the siege, Luxembourg marched up to Villers-Perwin and Marbais, while Louis marched to Namur via Fleurus. French cavalry invested Namur during the night of 25–6 May, and the army arrived the next day. This siege would be a particularly notable siege of Louis's reign. First, the absolute masters of contemporary siege warfare, Vauban and Menno van Coehoorn, directed the besiegers and the besieged respectively. Second, the topography of Namur and its surroundings made the siege particularly challenging. Namur lay at the juncture of the Sambre with the Meuse, therefore any besieging army would be trisected by these major rivers, adding to the problems of united action. As can be seen in the view

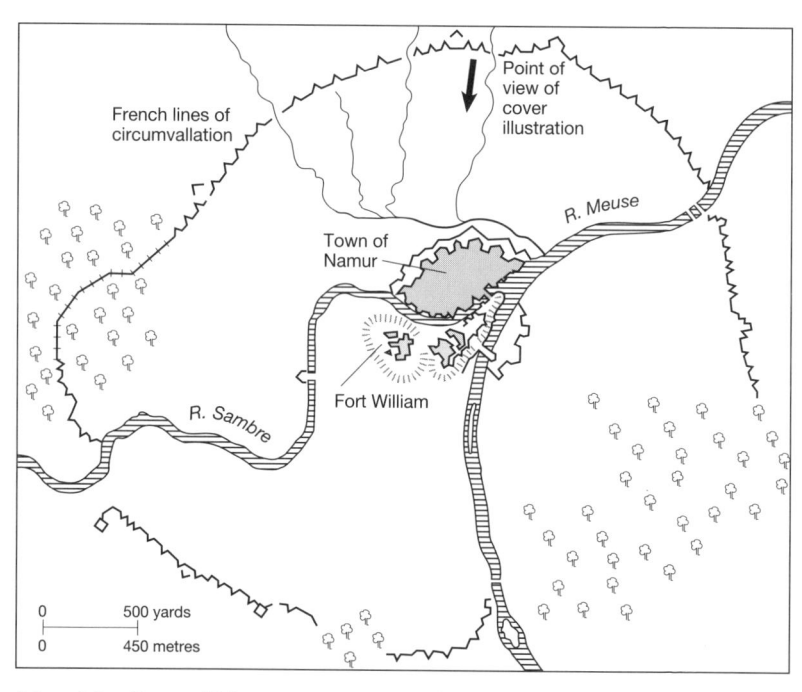

Map 6.3 Siege of Namur, 25 May–1 July 1692
Adapted from: Charles Sévin, marquis de Quincy, *Histoire militaire de Louis le Grand roi de France* (7 vols; Paris, 1726)

of the siege presented on the cover of this volume, the actual town of Namur sat on flat, low land, on the north bank of the Sambre.[45] It is dominated by heights on all sides, and the French would quickly occupy those to the north. While the town boasted strong fortifications, it would not be the most difficult target. The greater challenge was the complex of fortifications constituting the citadel that occupied an impressive mount on the south bank of the Sambre pinched between the confluence of the two rivers. There a series of forts beginning at river level and rising to the crest provided a textbook in mutually supporting works. The key to the position was Fort William, situated a bit to the west of the other main strongpoints.

This would be a siege in the grand style. Louis's entourage during the siege even included Racine, dramatist and poet but now present as royal historiographer, who was taken aback by the sights

---

[45] *Louis XIV devant Namur*, by Martin Jean-Baptiste le Vieux (1659–1735), painted in 1694.

of war. The forces assembled outstripped even those that took Mons. The arrival of Boufflers's army boosted the besieging army to 60,000 men with 151 guns; Luxembourg's army of observation also had about 60,000 men. The garrison of Namur totalled 6,000 men under the duke of Barbançon. William and the elector of Bavaria assembled a relief army at Anderlecht on the outskirts of Brussels, but it would be unable to save Namur.

Louis took the town fortifications with little delay. Vauban knew them well for he had reconnoitred Namur's walls the previous year, when he and a few associates brazenly circumambulated the entire town within musket range of the walls. 'Sometimes', he reported, 'we staged a little horseplay, and ran after each other. Sometimes we lay down as if we were tired – that was when we drew up our plans.'[46] Guided by Vauban's plans, the French constructed lines of circumvallation and then opened trenches for three lines of advance on the night of 29–30 May. The town capitulated on 5 June, at which time it was agreed there would be a truce until daybreak on 7 June. During this time the allied garrison crossed over to the citadel complex and the French entered the town. In addition, it was agreed that the Allies would not fire on the town if the French did not attack from that direction.

Meanwhile, William's army slipped southwest closer to Namur, from a position between Louvain and Bierbeck to one around Orp and Jauche. Luxembourg responded by taking the army of observation from Gembloux to Longchamps. William hoped to force a battle with Luxembourg on the Méhaigne, but the rain-swollen river made a crossing impossible.

Then began the extremely bitter and costly fighting for the citadel. The first task was to take an outlying redoubt, La Cachotte, which covered the approaches to Fort William. The trench was opened on 8 June and a major assault came on 12 June. Seven battalions charged the works, and the king's Musketeers also took part on foot. This was a very hard fight, and Vauban was so worried that his soldiers would pursue the enemy into deadly crossfire that he stationed five drummers near him to sound the recall at his command. With the fall of La Cachotte, Vauban turned to seizing Fort William. This became almost a personal duel, because Coehoorn directed the defence of Fort William himself. The fort was well sited, just over the crest of the rise, so attackers could not see it until they were just upon it.

---

46 Vauban in John A. Lynn, 'Vauban', *MHQ, The Quarterly Journal of Military History* 1, no. 2 (Winter 1989), p. 57.

Moreover, the crest masked the walls from artillery fire. French sappers approached it from two directions while rain turned their work into misery as they burrowed through the blue clay.

Coehoorn conducted a determined and active defence, and, in a gesture worthy of one of Racine's tragedies, ordered his own grave dug to demonstrate his resolve. He nearly filled it, for he was wounded in the head by a shell that killed his valet. When the final assault came on 22 June he conducted the defence as well as he could, but the two-pronged attack was more than his garrison could parry. When Coehoorn left Fort William with the garrison the next day, Vauban pressed forward to meet his worthy adversary and consoled him that 'he had the honour of being attacked by the greatest king in the world'. To which, Coehoorn replied that his real consolation lay in the fact that he had made Vauban move his siege batteries seven times.[47]

Once Fort William fell, the other works did not hold out long. The nearly two hundred men who had garrisoned Fort William were lost to the defence after they capitulated, for their terms ordered that they march to Ghent. The final capitulation came on 30 June, with the garrison leaving on 1 July. Luxembourg's army of observation fired salvos to celebrate the victory. It was a costly gain, since the besieging army lost 7,000 dead and wounded to the enemy's 4,000. With the siege brought to a successful conclusion, Louis and his entourage left Namur on 2 July and reached Versailles two weeks later, much, one would surmise, to the relief of the ladies. Louis's army split up at this point, and William too divided his forces.

Luxembourg waited while Namur was put into a state of defence, and after the enemy decamped on 8 July so did he to continue the campaign, following William toward Nivelles. Louis, worried that William planned to retake Namur, ordered Luxembourg 'to march with speed and approach him... and fight him'.[48] On 1 August, William shifted to Halle and Luxembourg set up between Herne and Steenkerque. William too sought battle, and wanted to engage Luxembourg in terrain unsuitable to the superior French cavalry. Thus, on 3 August he attacked over wooded broken ground near Steenkerque. The attack surprised the French, and things went well for the Allies at first. But as the fighting wore on, more French troops came up and stalled William's advance. At the end of the day, the Allies retired from the field in good order. Casualties appear to have

---

47 Report by Coehoorn's son in ibid.
48 Louis in Wolf, *Louis XIV*, p. 471.

been about 7,000 killed and wounded for the French and perhaps as many as 10,000 for the Allies.[49] Both sides could claim a win: the French because they repulsed the assault, held the ground, and possibly forestalled an attack on Namur; and the Allies because they bloodied the noses of the French and perhaps kept them from moving against Liège that year. After the battle, the two armies continued to jostle one another for the rest of the summer, but nothing of note occurred before they went into winter quarters.

Boufflers's campaign was relatively uneventful after Namur. He bombarded Charleroi and attended to various French posts around the Sambre. In a surprise move that winter, after a clever feint on Huy, Boufflers took Furnes; his forces invested it on 28 December, and the garrison capitulated on 6 January. This loss also forced the enemy to abandon Dixmude, which Boufflers entered on 10 January.

In 1692, German forces outnumbered de Lorges's army, so he had to maintain an essentially defensive posture. However, just as Boufflers carried off a winter surprise in the Netherlands, so did Tallard in Germany. Crossing the Rhine at Philippsburg with cavalry and dragoons, he conducted a course up to Heilbronn and placed the country under contributions. Melac also descended upon the country around Mannheim in February and executed villages which had not paid contributions. As soon as his army assembled, de Lorge ravaged the country on the west bank of the Rhine up to Mainz in order to make it difficult for the enemy to subsist there. Enemy forces crossed at Mainz and drove him back. De Lorge devoted the rest of the campaign season to thrusts and parries designed to impose contributions on German lands and to keep the enemy out of French territory. In August he received reinforcements from Flanders and later crossed the Rhine to levy renewed exactions on Württemberg. In October de Lorge relieved the siege of Hebernbourg on the east bank of the Rhine. Shortly thereafter the army went into winter quarters.

In Italy Catinat suffered from the same numerical disadvantage as did de Lorge. Catinat's army of 15,000–16,000 men would have to confront three enemy forces that totalled nearly 50,000 troops. He responded to allied moves while successfully guarding both Susa and Pinerolo. The ambitious allied campaign plan, hammered out by

---

49 Quincy, *Histoire militaire*, vol. ii, p. 537. Bodart, *Kriegs-Lexikon*, p. 117, gives the casualties as 7,000 killed and wounded for the French and 6,600 killed and wounded and 1,400 prisoners for the Allies. Baxter, *William III*, p. 304, says 3,000 killed and wounded for both sides.

a war council in July, charged an army of 15,000 men under Palfi to observe Catinat, while two forces of 19,500 and 7,500 invaded Dauphiné via mountain trails shown to them by the Vaudois. Victor Amadeus invested Embrun on 5 August, and the commander capitulated ten days later. The garrison of 2,800 men, under parole not to fight against the Allies for six weeks, took the road to Pinerolo on 19 August. Savoy marched on to Gap on 20 August and found it abandoned and burned. Finally, after receiving reinforcements, Catinat, with the further assistance of local peasantry, was able to prevent further conquests by blocking the roads to Grenoble. The duke remained until mid-September and then abandoned Dauphiné. When he departed from Embrun on 16 September, he left the country so ruined no one could winter there; seventy villages and chateaux were pillaged and burned. On the march out, the duke left a garrison in the valley of Barcelonnette in order to preserve an entry into Dauphiné.

True to form, Louis, incensed by the allied incursion, dispatched Vauban to see what could be done about improving the fortifications in the province. Vauban arrived in October and inspected Grenoble. He then had to inform the king that nothing could be done to improve fortifications before the next campaign season because construction would be impossible during the winter.

Even though Louis had intended that Noailles would have enough troops to plot a more aggressive course in 1692, the attack on Dauphiné required that Noailles give up troops to be sent to bolster Catinat's forces. This transfer of battalions from one front to another, a hallmark of the wars of Louis XIV, condemned Noailles to a more passive campaign. Medina-Sidonia began the campaign by marching his army of 16,000 to 17,000 troops against Roussillon. He fortified the pass at le Perthus and descended to Moureillas in Roussillon, but then Noailles's army, which had assembled at le Boulou, advanced against the Spanish. By closing in around them and making it difficult for them to forage, Noailles forced Medina-Sidonia to withdraw. Noailles then advanced into Catalonia at La Junquera. The Spanish entrenched at Figueres. At this point, orders arrived commanding Noailles to send troops to Catinat, so Noailles was compelled to withdraw. For the rest of the campaign Noailles and Medina-Sidonia simply faced off against one another.

The navy was expected to carry out great things in 1692, but the plans went awry. In still one more effort to support James II, Louis readied a force of about 8,000 French regulars and fifteen battalions of Irish under Marshal Bellefonds. They expected to launch a cross-Channel invasion of England as Tourville's fleet from Brest nullified the main allied naval forces. In order to even the odds with the larger allied armada, d'Estrées would bring up sixteen rated vessels from Toulon to join Tourville.

The problems the French encountered in trying to mount this venture read like a list of the basic structural flaws of French naval institutions. At Brest it took too long to arm the ships and muster the sailors, so when Tourville sailed from Brest on 12 May, some of his ships were still not ready and could only join him later. With the port of Toulon 1,500 sailing miles from Brest, difficulties and delays in uniting the fleet were very likely to occur, and they did. D'Estrées did not depart the Îles d'Hyères until 2 April, and headwinds impeded his progress so that his voyage to Brittany took two months, and he arrived too late to take part in the battle. Tourville received a series of changing orders, but the last that reached him assumed that Tourville would be leading seventy rated vessels, including d'Estrées's squadron, and that the Allies would be slow in gathering their fleet; therefore, Tourville would be strong enough to take on the Allies in battle. To force the action, the king commanded Tourville to find and fight the enemy as soon as possible. These orders ended with a fateful diktat: 'The contents of this Instruction are my will, which I desire to be carried out without any alteration.'[50] In fact, when Pontchartrain learned that the allied fleet would be quite large and that d'Estrées was still *en route*, he sent new orders allowing greater flexibility. But these, drafted on 20 May, took a week to arrive on the coast, Paris being so far from French naval ports, and they never got to Tourville in time.

The coming battle would be a very uneven struggle, although the French handled themselves very well in the actual fighting. By 25 May Tourville was off Plymouth, where reinforcements brought the size of his fleet to forty-four rated vessels. On the morning of 29 May he sighted the allied fleet off the Norman coast near Point de Barfleur. That day admirals Edward Russell and George Rooke commanded ninety-nine rated vessels which outgunned the French 8,980 cannon to 3,142.[51] Many of the French, including Louis and Pontchartrain,

50 'Instruction pour M. le comte de Tourville', 12 May 1692 in Symcox, *Crisis of French Sea Power*, p. 120.
51 Ibid., p. 122; Daniel Dessert, *La Royale: Vaisseaux et marins du Roi-Soleil* (Paris, 1996), p. 264. Other historians supply different numbers. Jean Meyer in Contamine, *Histoire militaire*, p. 524, credits the French with 45 ships and 3,240 guns and the Allies with 88 ships and 88 vessels and 6,750 cannon; and gives the date of the

believed that a number of English commanders were secretly devoted to James II, and so would desert William when put to the test. This was not to happen; in fact, Russell administered a loyalty oath to his captains before the battle.

Believing his orders gave him no option, and afraid that retreat would demoralize his fleet, Tourville bore down on the superior allied fleet. Tourville again sailed aboard the *Soleil Royal* leading the white squadron. Winds were light, and Tourville held the windward gauge. The French kept a tight formation and actually outgunned their foes at the point where the French collided with the allied line that morning. During the battle Tourville's van anchored at one time, blocking the enemy fleet from doubling back on the French. However, as the fierce cannonade continued, the Allies eventually enveloped the French ships. Before Tourville was entirely surrounded, a fog came up in the late afternoon, and he took advantage of it to disengage his fleet.[52] Although his ships suffered a terrible pounding, none had gone down during the day-long battle, although the Allies lost two.

However, the retreat would be costly. As it fled west that night, the French fleet lost formation and scattered. The faster ships rounded Cape La Hogue at the tip of the Cherbourg peninsula and escaped to St Malo, but the slower vessels were caught in the changing tide and had to seek some protection at anchor. The allied fleet split into three squadrons to pursue or corner the French. The lack of good ports on the Channel cost the French dearly in this case, because the large French war vessels could not find adequate shelter in French harbours. Tourville had transferred his flag from the *Soleil Royal*, slowed by bulk and battle damage. Along with two other damaged ships, it anchored off Cherbourg, where, after beating off several assaults by a squadron of seventeen allied vessels, the French crews burned their vessels on 1 June. Tourville, now aboard the *Ambitieux*, led another twelve vessels to shelter in an anchorage at La Hogue. There he hoped to take advantage of the guns of Fort La Hogue and redoubts that held the shore line, but these did not provide enough fire power to keep the allied fleet at bay. As the enemy cornered them, it was decided to beach the vessels and defend them with longboats from allied efforts to burn them. However, the Allies put 200 longboats in the water, overwhelmed the French, and burned all the vessels on

---

battle as 28 May. Quincy gives the French fleet as 44 of the line, and the Allies as 81 vessels with 5,846 cannon. Quincy, *Histoire militaire*, vol. ii, p. 579.

52 Symcox, *Crisis of French Sea Power*, p. 123. Quincy gives the time of the mist as 8.30 p.m.

2–3 June. The only consolation was that the French were able to save the crews. English historians give this Channel fight a single name, La Hogue; however, French historians are prone to separate the initial honourable sea battle from the later disastrous actions on the shore, labelling the first as Barfleur and only the second as La Hogue.

In any case, Barfleur–La Hogue cost the French fifteen ships, undermined French naval morale for the rest of the year, and, by giving the Allies dominance in the Channel, doomed the descent on England. The Irish troops marched off to the Rhineland, and the French regiments joined the army of Flanders or were devoted to shore defence in Normandy, Brittany, and around La Rochelle. The defeat shook the French to be sure, but it did not spell the end for *guerre d'escadre*.

Now masters of the Channel, the Allies planned their own raid on the French coast. Four regiments of French refugees were said to be waiting in Ireland under the duke of Leinster with arms for an additional 30,000 men. This invasion force was to land and raise the *nouveaux convertis* against Louis.[53] Other English regiments waited at Portsmouth. Russell returned to pick up troops, and sailed to St Malo with the intention of seizing it. He arrived off the port in mid-July, but decided that he would be unable to take it and departed. The troops gathered for invasion were sent to Flanders instead. Just as the French had wasted their naval dominance in 1690, the Allies got little offensive value out of their mastery in 1692 beyond foiling the attempt at a Jacobite landing.

During 1688 and 1689, Louis launched the war he had wanted to fight, and then saw it grow uncontrollably into something far beyond his intentions and his resources. The war hit full stride after 1690, and by 1692 one of the great questions of the wider conflict had been resolved by the triumph of William III, who had secured the English throne and defeated James II's attempts to regain it.

As the war took on a stubborn existence of its own, Louis and his foes were already beginning to seek an end to the conflict. Emissaries from France and other states made the first small steps toward a negotiated settlement. Importantly, the cast of characters around Louis was changing again. Louvois died on 16 July 1691, and while he may have been a talented military administrator, he was also prone to push brutal policies. Within two weeks of his passing, Louis recalled Pomponne back to the *Conseil d'en haut*, where the presence

---

53 Quincy, *Histoire militaire*, vol. ii, p. 590.

of this supple and intelligent diplomat reduced the influence of the hard secretary of state for foreign affairs, Colbert de Croissy.[54] This would bode well for diplomatic initiatives, which were not long in coming. As early as 1690 the Swedes offered to mediate, and after the fall of Mons the next year they renewed their offer. In 1691 Louis attempted to unglue the Grand Alliance through diplomatic means. In August he asked Cardinal Janson-Forbin to contact Cardinal Salazar in Rome in order to explore the possibility of contracting a peace between France and the Catholic states ranged against Louis. When this led to nothing, he also made overtures to Madrid in the hope of accommodating Spain.

In 1692–93 Pomponne pursued contacts with parties who might join in bringing the war to an end. One of these contacts was none less than Emperor Leopold I, and secret talks with him continued until 1696. Louis's most inflexible condition was his insistence on the right of James II to be recognized as king of England, and this plea registered with Leopold, who did not find it easy to conscience James's overthrow. From 1692 Louis even negotiated with the Turks, still at war with the emperor, in an effort to distract and outflank the Allies. William too was thinking enough about a peace settlement in 1692 to confide the fact that he wanted a general peace soon to Anthonie Heinsius, the grand pensionary of Holland. It was typical of this era that contending parties pursued both military operations and diplomatic initiatives at the same time. Even when things went well for him in 1693, Louis continued earnestly to seek a negotiated settlement rather than carry on the war: 'The success of my arms upon which the benediction of God continues to rain, has not erased from my heart the desire that I have to make a good peace.'[55]

WAR AND FAMINE, 1693–95

War thundered on during 1693–95 in the face of frustrating indecision and economic crisis. Louis learned the hard but eternal lesson that it is far easier to start a war than to end one. By 1693 he fervently wished for peace, but not at any price, a formula that

---

[54] Andrew Lossky, *Louis XIV and the French Monarchy* (New Brunswick, NJ, 1994), p. 247. John Rule believes that Croissy's importance did not diminish; Rule also feels that there we lack hard evidence that Pomponne opened up contacts with other international players. Rule letter of 26 January 1998.

[55] Letter from Louis dated 14 October 1693, in Wolf, *Louis XIV*, p. 475, from *Madame de Maintenon, Correspondance*, ed. M. Langlois (5 vols; Paris, 1933–39), vol. iv, no. 814.

paradoxically always seems to lead to paying a very high price in the long run. The gods of war demanded greater sacrifice, so Louis raised even more troops, and the army reached an official size of over 400,000 men. Louis also rewarded the commanders of this expanded force; in 1693 marshal's batons went to the notable fleet and army commanders Tourville, Boufflers, Catinat, and Noailles, as well as to Choiseul, Villeroi, and Joyeuse.

1693

In 1693 Louis tightened his hold on Flanders. Already, he had loaded the fortresses with such potent garrisons that he could create an army of 80,000 men in a day. And in preparation for still one more major siege he amassed supplies, but this initial effort against Liège would come to naught. As in 1692 there were to be two armies of Flanders, the first led by the king and the second commanded by Marshal Luxembourg. Forces directly under the king included 50 battalions and 109 squadrons, while those with Luxembourg boasted 78 battalions and 152 squadrons. Marshal Boufflers commanded a supporting Army of the Meuse with 51 battalions and 112 squadrons. Louis left Versailles on 18 May with an entourage of major court personages including twenty-seven ladies.[56] He arrived at le Quesnoy on 25 May but was detained there by illness for a week, and only reviewed his troops on 3 June. This delay gave the Allies time to respond. William had joined his army on 22 May, and when Louis and Luxembourg moved west, the main allied army was poised just north of Brussels while Liège prepared for a siege. By 7 June Louis's army had reached Gembloux and Luxembourg camped near Nivelles. At this point Louis abandoned his plans for an assault on Liège, an attack doomed by the king's illness and a late start. Just as his plans for the armies of Flanders came up short, he learned of de Lorge's success against Heidelberg and decided to reinforce the army of the Rhine with about half the forces mustered in his army at Gembloux. The dauphin led this considerable force south on 12 June. With his court, Louis left Namur the next day for the trip back to Versailles. According to Saint-Simon, Marshal Luxembourg literally fell on his knees to beg Louis to stay with the army and to continue the attack.[57] Louis would never take the field with his army again; he was now aged

---

[56] Louis de Rouvroy, duc de Saint-Simon, *Mémoires*, ed. A. de Boislisle (42 vols; Paris, 1879–1930), vol. i, p. 228n.
[57] Ibid., p. 231.

fifty-four, the same age as was the Great Condé when he retired from war, and time had taken its toll on the grand monarch.

Buttressed by other troops from the king's army, Luxembourg's forces swelled to 99 battalions and 221 squadrons, but lack of supplies kept him from undertaking any great ventures for several weeks. He detached troops for courses and foraged the country, until he received sufficient supply to undertake serious operations again in July. Then he moved against Huy, which he invested on 19 July. William sent his baggage to Diest and marched to lift the siege, but his army had gone no further than Tongeren when he learned that the citadel had capitulated on 23 July.

William now detached the duke of Württemberg with eleven regiments of infantry and a similar number of cavalry, perhaps as many as 15,000 men, to attack French entrenched lines near Ypres. The duke arrived at the lines on 18 July, attacking them in three places, and then hit them near Tournai on 23 July. Württemberg brought with him pioneers to fill in the entrenchments, and once he had breached the lines, he sent a detachment to put areas of Artois under contribution.

Luxembourg realized that by sending off such a large body of troops to Flanders and by reinforcing the Liège garrison, William had weakened his army, and the French marshal resolved to force the allied army into a battle. William's army numbered 50,000 to Luxembourg's 80,000. William intended to return to the vicinity of the abbey of Parck near Louvain after the fall of Huy. With the goal of pulling William toward him, Luxembourg feigned a siege of Liège by sending cavalry to reconnoitre the area. Then, he dispatched Marshal Joyeuse with a sizeable force supposedly to aid French forces against the duke of Württemberg, but in fact to mislead the Allies. William encamped near the Geete River just south of Zoutleeuw, and Luxembourg marched the rest of his army northwest to confront him. After picking up Joyeuse's diversionary troops on the way, Luxembourg's army caught William off guard by arriving in front of the allied camp on 28 July.

Battle broke out the following morning. William established his troops in a strong entrenched position; his left rear sheltered behind a marsh, the centre paralleled a ravine that would protect it, while the rest of the position stood on high ground. Two villages, Neerwinden and Landen, anchored the entrenchments on either flank, and Luxembourg concentrated his attack on them. His artillery concentrated on enemy guns, because the troops were largely hidden from view. Counterattack followed attack, as Neerwinden changed hands repeatedly. The Allies put up a good fight, so good that some French commanders counselled withdrawal, but Luxembourg persisted. A final assault led by the brigade of the Gardes françaises and the Gardes suisses took Neerwinden and its entrenchments about noon. Now French troops enveloped William's right and compelled him to retreat back to Louvain, where he had already sent his baggage. That day William lost 12,000 killed and wounded in addition to 2,000 missing and prisoners, and left the great majority of his cannon and sixty standards on the field. Luxembourg earned the title of the 'Tapissier de Notre Dame' because of all the captured battle flags he sent to be hung there. But Luxembourg had not purchased victory cheaply; 7,000–8,000 of Louis's troops lay dead or wounded.

Neerwinden won Louis limited benefit. William recalled Württemberg, and when he rejoined the army at Ellingen, the allied field army had regained the strength it had on the day of battle. Victory had not led to the peace table; instead, William continued to shadow the movement of Luxembourg, who now took the opportunity to besiege Charleroi at the king's strong insistence. Vauban had pleaded for a French attack on that fortress for some time, since it served as a safe harbour for raiding parties who ravaged French territory and attacked convoys: 'This single fortress...obliges us to maintain guards at eighteen or twenty small fortresses.... It causes the ruin of a territory equivalent to a good province...and obliges the king... to maintain in his fortresses 15,000 or 16,000 more men who will be lost annually in convoys and escorts.'[58] Luxembourg detached units from his own army, and these, combined with troops pulled out from the garrison of Namur, produced forces of sufficient size to besiege the fortress, while Luxembourg covered the siege with his main army. On 12 September the pioneers began the lines of circumvallation, and the French opened the attack trenches on the night of 15–16 September. This would be a formal siege, undertaken according to Vauban's methodical techniques. When younger officers there wanted to employ the more aggressive methods associated with Coehoorn, Vauban chided them with the words, 'Let us burn gunpowder and spill less blood.'[59] The siege progressed relentlessly until the French were ready to explode mines to blow breaches in the enemy wall on

---

58 Letter of 29 June 1693, from Vauban to Le Peletier, in Albert Rochas d'Aiglun, *Vauban, sa famille et ses écrits* (2 vols; Paris, 1910), vol. ii, p. 390.
59 Vauban in Lazard, *Vauban*, p. 25. Commenting on Coehoorn's storming of Namur in 1695, Vauban dismissed it 'as one of the most utterly foolish acts that has ever been committed in the attack of a fortress'. Vauban in Reginald Blomfield, *Sebastien le Prestre de Vauban, 1633–1707* (New York, 1971), p. 137.

10 October, when the garrison capitulated. The fighting had been very harsh, and of the 4,500 men who had originally made up the garrison, only 1,200 marched out of the fortress. The fall of Charleroi completed a band of fortresses that provided Louis with a new and impressive forward line of defence: Mons, Charleroi, Namur, and Huy.

After the fall of Charleroi, French and allied troops entered winter quarters.

Marshal de Lorge joined his army along the Rhine in early May. As before, the troops assembled near Neustadt, but unlike the previous few years, they immediately undertook a siege, attacking Heidelberg. After crossing the Rhine at Philippsburg on 16–17 May, de Lorge separated his forces. The largest corps marched to observe the army of the prince of Baden forming around Heilbronn, while the smaller corps moved north to invest Heidelberg. De Lorge put the army of observation under Marshal Choiseul and joined the forces surrounding Heidelberg. The French opened the trenches on 21 May, and the garrison capitulated the next day. As mentioned above, this victory inspired Louis to detach a large force under the dauphin to reinforce de Lorge on 12 June. Boufflers brought units of his army to increase this corps to twenty-seven battalions and forty-five squadrons which arrived at Speyer on 15 July.

De Lorge now hoped to bring Baden to battle. The marshal left Heidelberg on 30 May to engage his foe, but Baden withdrew across the Neckar into a strong position. With the allied army out of reach, de Lorge raided Württemberg, placed it under contribution, and then imposed exactions on the Palatinate as well. De Lorge seemed to be trying to draw Baden out of his position safe behind the Neckar. Once the dauphin arrived, he crossed the Rhine near Philippsburg on 16 July and worked in conjunction with de Lorge. Finally the two forces merged at Melingen, forming an army of about 45,000 men now under the nominal command of the dauphin. They marched toward Besigheim, an advance which brought Baden out to approach the French. Baden established a very strong entrenched camp on the east bank of the Neckar, just south of and covering Heilbronn. The dauphin's army came within sight of the enemy lines on 31 July. The two armies glared at each other from their respective camps but did little. The prince of Baden sent his apologies to the dauphin that he could not deliver his respects in person. After a vicious storm on 10 August blew down all the tents in the French camp and caused considerable confusion as most of the horses escaped, the dauphin withdrew his army back across the Neckar two days later.

The campaign now sputtered to its conclusion. After remaining between the Enz and the Neckar until 24 August, the dauphin shifted his camp to Leonberg, where the forage was better. At that camp, representatives of the duke of Württemberg arrived to contract for contributions of 1,200,000 livres, with an additional 300,000 livres to be paid each year thereafter. Württemberg provided hostages, including two of the duke's councillors to guarantee payment. At the end of the month, Boufflers and 15,000 men took the road back to Flanders. On 3 September the dauphin left his troops and returned to Versailles. De Lorge and Baden continued to manoeuvre against one another and then dispersed their troops in winter quarters.

Because of the investments in troops that Louis made in Flanders, Germany, and Catalonia, the king did not expect much from Catinat in 1693. The 50,000 allied troops available to defend Piedmont against him far exceeded Catinat's resources. Therefore, it would be enough if he simply frustrated the plans of Victor Amadeus, but the marshal and his army would accomplish much more than that.

Catinat assembled his forces for the next campaign between Susa and Pinerolo, while Victor Amadeus formed his at Carignano. From there the duke marched against the French fortress of Casale to assist in taking the supporting strongpoint of St George, which fell on 4 July. After the capitulation, the duke ordered the construction of two other small forts which, with St George, would allow an effective blockade of Casale. Then he returned to Turin and reviewed his troops at Avigliana on 22 July in preparation for the next stage of the campaign. During the action around Casale, Catinat fought into the valley of Barcelonnette to drive out Victor Amadeus's troops. By late June the French under Larré had advanced as far as Larche and Meyronnes and soon controlled the entire valley. With this access now blocked, the duke thought of opening a route to Savoy through Susa and then to Briançon, but Catinat strengthened the garrisons of Barcelonnette and Briançon and then returned to Fenestrelle, south of Susa.

Victor Amadeus now committed his troops to a siege of Pinerolo. Catinat decided to leave that fortress to its own resources, because it was prepared to resist a siege and because Catinat refused to risk his still feeble army in an attack on the duke's main force. Victor Amadeus began his siege by attacking the small fortified position of St Brette on high ground near the main fortress. His troops opened trenches there on 30 July, and the garrison abandoned the strongpoint, blowing it up, on 14 August. Next the duke bombarded Pinerolo itself, firing 4,000 shells against the fortress from 20 August to 1 October.

At this point Catinat, who had now received reinforcements from Catalonia and Provence, marched south against him on 27 September. A few days into the march, *gendarmerie*, heavy armoured cavalry, dispatched from the army in Germany caught up with Catinat. Larré also marched with troops from Savoy to rendezvous with Catinat, giving the marshal a total of about 40,000 men. Learning that Catinat was *en route*, the duke of Savoy lifted the siege and withdrew his army of 36,000 back toward Turin.[60] Catinat intercepted the duke's army at Marsaglia, mid-way between Pinerolo and Turin.

At the Battle of Marsaglia, which took place on 4 October, the two opponents each tried to envelop the other. Catinat led a charge of his right; his troops surged forward in very good order, as the infantry did not fire but came on with the bayonet only. In the collision, the French bent the enemy left back. At the same time the enemy right attacked the French left, but there, at the critical moment, the *gendarmerie* charged and broke the advancing allied troops. This decided the day, and after four and a half hours of fighting, the allied troops fled up the road to Turin. French casualties had been about 3,000, while Victor Amadeus lost 9,000 to 10,000 killed and wounded along with another 2,000 prisoners, total casualties amounting to one-third of his army. The siege of Casale was a further casualty of the battle, for enemy forces began to withdraw there on 6 October. This allowed the French to reoccupy fort St George and resupply Casale. Catinat extended contributions throughout nearly all Piedmont, being so bold as to do so right outside the duke's camp. Victor Amadeus became so desperate that he called up his *ban* to protect against French courses.

In November both armies went into quarters. Catinat would have liked to maintain his forces in Piedmont, but decided it would be difficult, since he did not hold Cuneo, which controlled the road south. Therefore, after stocking supplies for Pinerolo and Susa, Catinat led his forces back to Dauphiné.

French arms also gained considerable success in Catalonia during 1693. The campaign began with a combined army and navy operation against Rosas some thirty miles south of Perpignan. Marshal Noailles formed his army at Boulou and reached Rosas, by way of Prats-de-Mollo, on 29 May. D'Estrées had arrived with a squadron from Toulon two days before. Since Rosas lay on the coast, the French had to blockade it by sea as well as surround it on land. Noailles opened

---

[60] Size figures from Bodart, *Kriegs-Lexikon*, p. 119.

the trenches on the night of 1–2 June, and the governor, whose arm had been broken by a shell blast, surrendered Rosas on the afternoon of 9 June. The garrison marched out the next day. However, the nearby fort of La Trinité was not included in the capitulation, so the French began operations against it on 11 June, and it fell two days later. After the surrender, d'Estrées weighed anchor on 16–17 June and sailed to rendezvous with Tourville off Cape St Vincent.

After his victory at Rosas, Noailles had to assume the defensive, because he received orders to dispatch five battalions of his army as reinforcements for Catinat. They were ferried to Nice via galleys. Therefore, after providing for the security of Rosas, Noailles withdrew into Roussillon. Medina-Sidonia made preparations for a Spanish siege of Bellver, but he gave up the effort after the preliminary moves, and both armies returned to winter quarters.

Support for Noailles's siege of Rosas followed the familiar French pattern of harnessing naval resources to army goals, but the navy also undertook a valuable maritime campaign. Louis made great efforts to repair the losses of 1692, so that in 1693 he sent out the largest battle fleet that he ever ordered to leave port. After the ships were armed, on 15 May vessels from the Rochefort joined those prepared in Brest, and the combined force sailed from Brest on 26 May under Tourville's command. Again divided into three divisions, the total number of ships stood at 71 rated vessels and 3 fireships. Louis wanted this fleet to leave port early because he feared an allied attack on his coast, and he wanted his vessels at sea to forestall his foes. D'Estrées left Toulon with 28 ships of the line, to be joined by 35 galleys, off Rosas and then sailed to join Tourville off Cape St Vincent. As an additional task, Louis ordered Tourville to ambush the Smyrna convoy, a massive assembly of 400 commercial vessels travelling under escort from allied ports and the north to the Mediterranean. In his orders, the king wrote, 'If you can capture that convoy you will render me as great a service as if you had won a battle.'[61] After arriving on station, Tourville took his fleet inshore near Lagos to clean the bottoms of his slower vessels and to air out his ships. While at anchor on 26 June, his picket ships darted into the bay, firing their guns to announce that they had sighted the Smyrna convoy coming in three columns. Tourville sailed that evening, and the next day his fleet encircled and overwhelmed the 20 escort vessels under Rooke's command. Gabaret, who led the rear division of Tourville's fleet, failed to close the trap

---

61 Louis in Symcox, *Crisis of French Sea Power*, p. 134.

and allowed the escort to escape, so at this Battle of Lagos, the Allies lost only two Dutch vessels, sacrificed by their captains to cover the escort's retreat. A long pursuit ensued over the next days, during which time the French fell upon the merchant fleet and destroyed 92 ships, a loss to the enemy that amounted to as much as 30,000,000 livres.[62] Some have labelled this operation as marking the onset of *guerre de course*, but while it indeed resulted in the destruction of enemy shipping, more was involved. The fact that Tourville was at sea had as much or more to do with fears of allied landings as it did with attacking commerce.[63] Also there seems to have been some idea that after destroying the escort, and thus evening the odds between the allied and French fleets, Tourville could return to the Channel to give battle, although this did not happen.

During the pursuit, which Tourville pressed as far as Málaga, he was joined by d'Estrées to form a fleet of eighty-eight vessels. Tourville sailed on to Catalonia and conferred with Noailles, who discussed the use of naval forces in a possible siege of Palamos, a siege that Louis at first endorsed. However, the need to ship reinforcements to Catinat killed that plan, and Tourville sailed with the majority of the fleet for Brest in mid-September.

In another response to the fear of an enemy invasion by sea, Louis dispatched his brother, a creditable soldier, to command in Brittany. He arrived at Vitry on 2 June. The troops he collected were confined to camp in order to prevent pillage and disorder; he probably did not want any replay of the excesses troops committed in Brittany during and after the Papier Timbré/Bonnets Rouges troubles during the last war. Philippe inspected fortifications and at one point called up the *ban* and local militia.

No invasion came in 1693, but the autumn witnessed an enemy bombardment of the privateering port of St Malo. On 26 November an enemy fleet of twenty-five vessels came into view off the port and began to shell the town the next day. The bomb ketches lobbed about 150 shells during the following few days. The English then exploded an infernal machine on the shore. This was a ship packed with gunpowder and loaded with scraps of iron and so forth to form a giant destructive shell. Fortunately for St Malo, the infernal machine grounded on a rock some fifty yards out before reaching the town walls, so when it went off it did little damage to the defensive installations of the port, although it damaged hundreds of roofs in the town.

[62] Dessert, *La Royale*, p. 256.
[63] On this key point, see Symcox, *Crisis of French Sea Power*, pp. 133–9.

1694

Although they did not prove sufficient to force the Allies to the peace table, a substantial list of victories crowned French military efforts in 1693: Heidelberg, Rosas, Lagos, Huy, Neerwinden, Charleroi, Marsaglia. But the year also witnessed a crushing human catastrophe: famine. From the summer of 1693 through the summer of 1694, France suffered one of its worst famines on record. The harvest failed in 1693, setting in motion the mechanisms of misery. Lack of crops brought starvation; starvation led to disease and death. France lost at least a tenth of its population within a matter of only a few months. Food shortage also precipitated general economic crisis, for this was still a pre-industrial economy driven by its agricultural sector.

War and famine rode together, true horsemen of the Apocalypse. War increased the impact of famine by disrupting the economy in general and by making it extremely difficult to bring in supply by sea. Moreover, mass buying of grains for the army raised prices and left less for the civilian community. And at the same time that war amplified famine, economic crisis reshaped French strategy, because decreasing tax revenues forced Louis and his military advisers to curb original campaign plans and redraft them to fit the dictates of fiscal shortfalls.

The campaign of 1694 in Flanders would, in fact, be remarkably uneventful. Louis stood on the defensive there and saved the state the considerable monetary cost of a major siege. Although he announced that he would return to his armies in 1694, Louis remained at court and sent the dauphin to command the main army in Flanders with Marshal Luxembourg. This force of 98 battalions and 190 squadrons could also expect support from Boufflers commanding an army of 20,000 men on the Meuse meant to link or aid armies in Flanders and on the Rhine. Luxembourg left to join his army around Mons on 27 May, and the dauphin departed court on the last day of the month. While this was a late start to the campaign season when measured by the standards established by Louvois, in a famine year problems of securing food and forage can only have slowed assembly. In fact, the army remained largely in quarters still waiting for sufficient forage in the fields before beginning the campaign. William did not join his troops until 11 June. Luxembourg launched his army at this point, crossing the Sambre and then marching into Gembloux on 15 June. Throughout the summer William and Luxembourg marched and countermarched without any major clashes, although this does not mean that troops were inactive. Armies changed camps to shadow their foes and to ensure new supplies of fodder. The usual war of posts continued on as always, as war parties launched their brutal courses. For three months Luxembourg manoeuvred to protect the French system of entrenched lines and to parry William's thrusts towards Courtrai and Ypres. Finally, on 18 September the dauphin left the army to journey back to Versailles and officers were authorized to go on leave.

However, the Allies gained some success that autumn in Flanders. The day after the dauphin's departure, William injected 2,000 men into Dixmude, where the French had failed to put a garrison. After preparing to attack Furnes but then reconsidering, William finally left his army on 18 October. Further to the east, the Allies retook Huy from the French. Brandenburg troops joined by allied soldiers drawn from lines around Liège invested Huy on 17 September. Trenches opened on the night of 18–19 September, and the governor capitulated on 27 September when his garrison had been reduced to only 350 able-bodied men. The besieging forces had fired 25,000 cannonballs and 700–800 mortar shells to do the job.[64]

Marshal de Lorge conducted a modest campaign along the Rhine in 1694. His army of 45 battalions and 133 squadrons assembled in late May, and crossed the Rhine at Philippsburg on 8 June. The marshal wanted to send men north of the Neckar, but he learned that the country was so ruined that he could not subsist his cavalry there, so he returned to the left bank of the Rhine. Such marches and manoeuvres continued throughout the summer with undramatic results, similar to the conduct of the war in Flanders. A German threat to Alsace and the French response in September seemed likely to result in battle, but Baden withdrew back across the Rhine. The campaign petered out in October.

In Italy as well, 1694 was a relatively quiet year. Louis decided to push the war in Catalonia, so Marshal Catinat was forced to mark time with only fifty battalions of infantry and little cavalry. Still reeling from the defeat he suffered at the end of the previous campaign, Victor Amadeus thought mainly of protecting as much of Piedmont as he could from French contributions and courses. August brought renewed allied actions against Casale. Fort St George came under attack on 24 August and once more capitulated four days

[64] Quincy, *Histoire militaire*, vol. iii, p. 29.

later. After this, the duke advanced his troops into the Susa valley for most of September, but all that this accomplished was to leave the Piedmont plain vulnerable to exploitation by Catinat. By the time the troops returned to winter quarters, Catinat could be satisfied that he had held Savoy, kept the duke from accomplishing anything of note in Piedmont, and subsisted French forces on enemy territory.

The most eventful campaign of 1694 took place in Catalonia, as the Sun King had intended. Marshal Noailles boasted an army of 20,000 infantry and 6,000 horse, modest forces by the standards of Flanders but substantial for operations along the Pyrenees. He assembled at Boulou and decamped to march into Catalonia on 17 May. Tourville at Toulon and Château-Renault were to assist his operations on the Spanish coast, and by 24 May Tourville arrived with a squadron of nine rated vessels in the Gulf of Rosas and consulted with Noailles. The army continued to advance, passing the Fluvià River on 26 May and arrived the next morning on the Ter River, where the Spanish army of about 20,000 troops waited under the command of the viceroy of Catalonia, the duke of Escalona. The Spanish entrenched behind the river that served them as a moat, but Noailles's troops forded the river under fire. The worst fighting occurred in the town of Verges that anchored the left of the Spanish line. By 11 a.m. the battle was over and the Spanish were in retreat. They suffered heavy casualties: 3,500 killed and wounded plus an additional 2,200 prisoners, who were transported by ship to Collioure and then to Languedoc. The French lost far less with 1,300 casualties.[65]

After this victory, Noailles moved with great speed to besiege Palamos in a joint operation with the navy. An advanced detachment invested the town during the night of 29–30 May, and the main forces arrived on the 31st. Tourville landed the heavy siege artillery and took up station off Palamos. Sappers opened the trenches on the night of 1–2 June. When the assault trenches reached the glacis and with no relief in sight, the governor asked for an honourable capitulation on 10 June, which would have allowed his garrison of nearly 3,000 men to depart. Noailles refused the offer, because, as man-starved as were the opposing armies, 3,000 troops would have substantially increased Spanish field forces. Instead, the garrison became prisoners of war.

With Palamos in French hands, Noailles advanced to Gerona, which his troops invested on 17 June. Gerona sat astride the Ter

[65] Ibid., p. 59 states French losses as only 300, but Bodard, *Kriegs-Lexikon*, p. 119, puts the number at 1,300.

River in a valley dominated by high ground to the north where the Spanish had constructed several forts. These forts constituted the key to taking the city, since it would be difficult to defend if the high ground were lost. The garrison totalled 5,000 foot and 600 cavalry. Since the high ground was little better than barren rock, the French had to construct barriers above ground level rather than dig trenches below it. For this purpose the French brought in earth and fascines, that is, bundles of sticks, from the surrounding country. But although the French faced all these difficulties, the garrison capitulated on 29 June after the French had only lost sixty soldiers in the siege. As a reward for his victories and in anticipation of controlling much of Catalonia, Louis appointed Noailles viceroy of Catalonia, a dignity he assumed on 9 July.

The French advance had yet to run its full course, for Noailles drew closer to Barcelona. He seized Ostalric on the road to Barcelona and dispatched a column to Granollers, where the main Spanish army was camped, but it withdrew into the city upon seeing the French. Noailles moved toward the sea at Blanes in September. Troops from Gerona foiled a Spanish attempt to retake Ostalric. Noailles would have gone on to besiege Barcelona in the autumn, but the appearance of a strong allied fleet in the Mediterranean made this impossible, so his troops solidified their holdings and went into quarters.

French success in Catalonia brought forth an impressive allied naval response. The king of Spain threatened that if the English and Dutch did not come to his aid he would consider a separate peace with Louis, so William III dispatched a fleet under Lord Russell to the Mediterranean. This expedition became the most successful use of allied naval power yet during the war.

The French planned to make their major naval commitment for 1694 in the south and leave only a few vessels to cover the French Atlantic coast; they would be faced with challenges on both fronts. By February naval workers were busy arming forty major vessels at Brest and other Atlantic ports, while another twenty-five were made ready at Toulon. On 7 May Château-Renault sailed from Brest with thirty-five northern vessels, and a week later they passed through the Straits of Gibraltar to join Tourville, who came out from Toulon. Meanwhile the combined Dutch and English fleet arrived off Brest too late to intercept Château-Renault, but it destroyed twenty-five of fifty-five merchant ships in a convoy found just outside the harbour mouth. After this, Russell returned to Torbay, where allied naval strength now numbered over ninety vessels of from forty-six to one hundred guns each. This fleet now split in two on 23 May, and Russell took about fifty vessels with him to enter the Mediterranean and left the rest with Barclay to carry out an amphibious assault on Brest.

This attack in June realized Louis's fears of allied invasion and justified the measures he took to defend against it. Concerned about such a possibility, Louis bestowed the command of Brest upon the defensive master, Vauban, in May. On 1 May Louis wrote to his great engineer that the Allies would try to land 6,000 to 7,000 troops at Brest to become masters of the port and burn the many ships at anchor there. When this letter reached Vauban, he was already at St Malo inspecting the fortifications to improve them following the previous year's raid. To resist the allied expedition, Louis gave Vauban the 1,300 naval personnel in the port, plus he dispatched seven infantry battalions and two mounted regiments. In addition, about 3,000 local nobles joined the defensive force.[66] Vauban found Brest protected by fortifications mounting 265 cannon and 17 mortars, and he ordered additions and new construction to raise the armament to 468 cannon and 36 mortars. With naval warehouses right at hand, he had no trouble finding the hardware. Vauban would have little time to make ready, for on the evening of 17 June the enemy fleet of warships and transports entered Camaret Bay just outside the harbour at Brest. A successful landing there would give the Allies control of the southern shore of the harbour mouth.

Vauban had prepared well, and the Allies met disaster. With the enemy in view, Vauban summoned French galleys to come around into the bay to deal with enemy landing craft. By the time the enemy attempted a landing the next morning, Vauban had put eight companies of regulars from La Marine, plus some militia men, in entrenchments covering the landing spots. His shore batteries exchanged fire for two hours with the enemy ships before the Allies tried to land an initial force under the personal leadership of General Talmach. Many of their small boats did not make it to shore, but some 600–700 men reached dry land. After cutting the enemy down with a withering fire, French troops charged out of their entrenchments, driving the landing parties back or forcing them to surrender. A Dutch frigate of thirty guns ran aground and was taken with its crew by the French. In a letter to the king written that evening Vauban announced that the Allies had been repulsed with considerable loss. The failed landing cost them almost 600 prisoners and 400 dead, among them General

---

66 Louis to Vauban, 1 May 1694, in Rochas d'Aiglun, *Vauban*, vol. ii, pp. 411–12.

Talmach, at a cost of only forty to fifty French casualties.[67] The Allies did not attempt a second landing but sailed off.

A series of allied bombardments followed their failure at Brest. After the allied fleet returned to Rye for a time, it appeared again off Dieppe on 22 July and bombarded that port throughout the day. Another attempt to employ an infernal machine failed, because the French blocked the harbour entrance with sunken ships loaded with stones. The bombardment continued after nightfall with more than a thousand shells, which caused fire and a great deal of damage. From there the enemy fleet sailed to Le Havre, which it bombarded on 25–6 July. Citizens and soldiers organized parties to extinguish fires before they spread in order to avoid the fate of Dieppe. The fleet recommenced the bombardment on 31 July. The Allies also wished to attempt a landing, but troops had arrived by then. A similar expedition, now led by Shovell, sailed against Dunkirk, where the fleet arrived on 21 September, but Vauban's fortifications at the port kept the Allies at arm's distance. There another infernal machine blew to little effect. From Dunkirk Shovell sailed to Calais and bombarded that privateer port during the night of 27–8 September.

The allied ships that sailed to the Mediterranean produced much more strategic benefit for the Allies. Russell's fleet rendezvoused with Spanish vessels off Cadiz, and together formed an armada of forty-eight rated vessels and some ninety other sail that anchored off Barcelona on 9 August. The approach of this force induced Tourville to sail back to Toulon and forestalled any French siege of Barcelona that year. In fact, by keeping its ships in Spanish waters at Cadiz, rather than returning to their home ports – a decision protested strongly by Russell – the allied fleet preserved Barcelona from attack through 1695 as well. And by shielding Barcelona, the allied fleet kept Spain in the war for two more years.

Louis continued to send out diplomatic feelers to moderate or end the war. In 1694 he secured a treaty of neutrality to suspend conflict in the western Pyrenees. His envoys also attempted to subvert the position of William III by negotiating with the patrician party in the United Provinces. Louis dispatched a series of agents with authority to speak in the king's name. However, these efforts came to nothing,

---

67 Vauban to Louis, 17 June 1694, in ibid., pp. 414–15. The numbers given here are from Quincy, *Histoire militaire*, vol. iii, p. 80. Vauban stated that the French took 1,198 prisoners and that there were at least 500 enemy killed or drowned, but this was a first report shortly after the heat of action. The French forces lost only 40–50 men killed and wounded.

because Heinsius stood by William. As it turned out, the deadlock would be broken not in Flanders, but in Italy.

1695

The French war effort entered a new phase in 1695. On 5 January Marshal Luxembourg died at age sixty-seven. At the time of his death, Luxembourg stood out as Louis's most brilliant commander. Although there were others of solid talent – marshals Catinat and Boufflers, for example – the Sun King would not find another military star until Villars emerged from the pack in the War of the Spanish Succession. All this being said, the bulk of the land fighting in the Spanish Netherlands was already passed by the opening of the campaign season in 1695, and a masterful defence of Namur by Boufflers would occupy William's army for most of the summer. A more fundamental transition occurred in the naval war, as for budgetary and strategic reasons the French abandoned *guerre d'escadre* in the Channel and the Atlantic and turned exclusively to *guerre de course*.

Louis chose Marshal François de Neufville, duke of Villeroi, to replace Luxembourg in Flanders for the next campaign. A man of less audacity and far less talent than his predecessor, he also commanded fewer troops than his adversaries in 1695. Villeroi's army of 73 battalions and 153 squadrons would be seconded by a 'flying camp' of 10,000 men under Montal stationed on the Flemish coast between Dunkirk and Furnes and by Marshal Boufflers with forces destined once again for the Meuse.

The first act of the campaign fell to Boufflers in April, when Louis ordered him to construct new fortified lines between the Lys at Courtrai and the Scheldt at Avelghem, a distance of about ten miles. This would be an elaborate affair, for entrenched lines at the time were not simple slit trenches. The ditches were to be eight feet deep and eight feet wide with earthen parapets rising behind them a full nine feet tall and six feet wide in front of the firing step. The lines incorporated angles on the pattern of fortress bastions. Such a massive project called for a great deal of labour, so Boufflers summoned 20,000 pioneers, to be covered by 20,000 troops during the project. With so many workers the project went fast, requiring only the week 6–13 April.[68] During the project, the duke of Bavaria came out of Brussels and assembled an army of 24,000 troops at Ninove, but

---

68 Detailed description of lines in Quincy, *Histoire militaire*, vol. iii, p. 101.

upon reconnoitring the lines and Boufflers's preparations, he withdrew. The construction of new lines emphasized Louis's profoundly defensive intentions for the army in Flanders that year. When Villeroi proposed more offensive action in June, Louis replied that the safest plan was simply to hold the lines. 'If in holding the lines, one loses a great many troops, one can hope that the enemy will lose considerably more. . . . One must defend my country foot by foot.'[69] Villeroi objected to this operational strait-jacket, but Louis restated his insistence and praised him for 'having work done on the entrenchments to prevent the enemy from penetrating my land'.[70]

The main French forces assembled in early June. On the 6th Villeroi ordered his troops to Leuze, while Boufflers's troops formed in the region of Charleroi. At the same time, William joined his army composed of 70 battalions and 80 squadrons assembled between Thielt and Deinze. The Allies boasted their own small mobile file force, or *camp volant* (flying camp), of 20 battalions and 10 squadrons. In addition a second main army under the elector of Bavaria totalled 36 battalions and 150 squadrons, assembling between Brussels and Dendermonde.

The adversaries in Flanders began an armed *pas de deux*, as Villeroi left Leuze on 8 June to camp on the west flank of the lines at Avelgem, and then he went to inspect the new lines from the Scheldt to the Lys and then on to Ypres. William in turn left his position and set up at Roeselare closer to the French lines and came to within one league of the entrenchments. The elector of Bavaria brought his army up to the lines as well, but these feints came to nothing. The duke of Württemberg marched on the fortress at Kenoque, where there was some hard fighting on 19–20 June, but the Allies drew off.

While all this was going on, Brandenburg marched on Namur, and William's army at Roeselare decamped on 30 June to lay siege to the fortress. They completed the investment on 1 July, but not before Boufflers was able to bring in troops to increase the garrison to about 13,000 men. The fortress was well supplied with ammunition and enough provisions for six months if need be. The main enemy forces arrived on 3 July, and Coehoorn soon took charge of the siege, playing the opposite role to that he performed so well in 1692. Boufflers demonstrated that one could essentially win a campaign by losing a fortress, provided that you pinned down and exhausted the

---

[69] AG, A¹1309, #81, 23 June 1695, letter from Louis to Villeroi, in Wolf, *Louis XIV*, p. 481.
[70] AG, A¹1309, #131, 27 June 1695 letter from Louis to Villeroi.

attackers in the process. He conducted a classic active defence, launching attacks by the garrison against the enemy's siege works, contesting every advance as best he could. Because William's besieging forces totalled about 80,000, Villeroi opted not to take them on directly but to harass their foraging parties and attack their convoys. In mid-July he bombarded Brussels, as a reprisal and as a diversion. The reprisal came not only for the siege of Namur but also for the bombarding of French coastal towns. Villeroi presented an ultimatum from Louis to the prince of Bergues in Brussels that the French would forgo the bombardment of his city if the Allies would cease shelling French ports, but no agreement was forthcoming within the time limit set. Therefore, from the night of 13–14 August until 16 August, the French fired more than 3,000 mortar shells and 1,200 red-hot cannonballs against Brussels, causing tremendous damage. This brutal action, however, diverted neither William's attention nor his troops.

The siege continued. On 4 August the town of Namur capitulated, and the French garrison was allowed to cross the river into the citadel complex south of the Sambre, as had the allied garrison three years before. The lines edged forward on the hills. After regrouping at Soignies and receiving some reinforcements, Villeroi marched toward Namur. Seeing this, William left the elector of Bavaria in command around Namur and led an army out of the siege lines to a position near Gembloux. Villeroi reached Perwez on 30 August, and on the next day, accompanied by major officers and a large cavalry escort, he reconnoitred William's new entrenched camp. Judging it too strong a position, Villeroi decided not to attack. This sealed the fate of Boufflers and his garrison. Boufflers had held on against repeated onslaughts, but the garrison could not continue to persevere if no relief army promised to break the siege. The same day that Villeroi chose not to fight a battle with William, Coehoorn directed a simultaneous general assault on all the remaining French positions at Namur. The French endured this attack, but it was clear they could not last much longer. On 1 September the French agreed to capitulate on 5 September if no relief army arrived. It did not, and the remaining troops of the garrison marched out on 5 September. The campaign did not go on long after the fall of Namur, as the armies went into quarters at the end of the month.

The siege of Namur was the key military event of the year, and it served French purposes well. Of course, William took Namur, which gave him back the line of the Meuse from Namur to Maastricht. This was the strong river barrier that had mattered so much to the French back in the Dutch War. But on the other side of the ledger, the siege immobilized the main allied forces during the summer and cost them a great deal. And if the French garrison lost 8,000 dead and wounded, William suffered 18,000 to 20,000 casualties. Moreover, the siege entailed a huge monetary expense, and to this must be added the destruction caused by the bombardment of Brussels. Louis was pleased enough with his army's tenacity to award a dukedom to Boufflers.

The campaign along the Rhine was relatively uneventful in 1695, because the Allies mounted their primary effort in the Low Countries. Marshal de Lorge mustered an army of 46 battalions and 135 squadrons. On 7 June this army crossed the Rhine and established a camp at Bretten, as the opposing army under the landgrave of Bayreuth formed around Heilbronn. Baden brought his imperial troops to join this force near Eppingen. At first de Lorge enjoyed a clear superiority over his foes, but he had strict orders from Louis not to risk anything and to stay encamped. With more German reinforcements, Baden would outnumber de Lorge, but he too remained cautious and simply entrenched his camp in June. During the last week of that month, de Lorge developed a fever and passed command of the army to Marshal Joyeuse. When Baden broke camp and moved toward the French on 5 July, Joyeuse marched to Waldorf near Heidelberg. A further German advance forced him back around the ruins of Mannheim and then back across the Rhine on the night of 22–23 July. At this point, Joyeuse detached troops to march to Flanders, further weakening his army. Now he also called the local militia of Alsace to arms and commanded that two or three men per village go off to man redoubts along the Rhine, for he feared German courses into that province. Joyeuse's army consumed all the forage along the west bank of the Rhine and then camped near Frankenthal. De Lorge returned to the army on 4 September, and not too long after that the troops went into quarters. This unenergetic campaign had one advantage for the French – de Lorge and Joyeuse kept their forces outside Louis's domains and thus lived at the enemy's expense as much as possible.

The campaign in Piedmont that year concerned the siege of Casale, which was something of a put-up job, because negotiations between Louis and Victor Amadeus were making headway. Louis wisely regarded Victor Amadeus as the weak link among the Allies and hoped to break the allied chain there. For two years, representatives of Louis and Victor Amadeus had conducted a series of negotiations worthy of comic opera – the participants, including the French General Tessé, disguised themselves as peasants and postmen to avoid discovery.

The duke had come to fear increased Habsburg influence in Italy more than he feared the French, and he welcomed *rapprochement* if Louis were to disengage his troops from the fortresses that gripped Turin between them, Casale and Pinerolo. A formal peace treaty would not come for another year, but in 1695 the negotiators agreed that the French would surrender Casale after minimum resistance, on condition that it would be demolished and handed back to Mantua. After blockading it during the winter, a considerable allied force of 18,000 troops, which included Germans, Spanish, and the duke's men, gathered around it in late June. Meanwhile, Catinat held on to western Piedmont with Pinerolo and Susa, while he blocked the paths to Dauphiné and Provence. Trenches opened against Casale on 27 June, and the governor asked to capitulate on 9 July. Terms of surrender detailed that the fortifications would be destroyed and that Louis would share the expense of demolition with the enemy. After the work was completed the French garrison left on 18 September. Fighting between Victor Amadeus and Louis effectively came to an end with the demolition of Casale.

Catalonia also saw only limited action in 1695. The interests of the king of Spain had suffered in the previous campaign, so he made great efforts to strengthen his position. He hired Italian mercenary regiments and brought in Lombards, Neopolitans, and Germans. He also enjoyed support at sea from the continued presence of Russell's allied fleet that forestalled a siege of Barcelona. To gain more energetic leadership, Carlos II appointed Gastañada from the Low Countries to become governor-general of Catalonia. The first shots were fired when Spanish forces tried to take both Ostalric and Castelfollit, near Camprodon, in the spring, but relief reached both posts and preserved them for the French. The Spanish pressured Castelfollit again in the summer, but still another relief force got through to it on 8 July. Meanwhile, Marshal Noailles became so ill that the king replaced him with Louis-Joseph, the duke of Vendôme, who would prove himself to be one of Louis's finest generals. Gastañaga then assembled his main forces near Barcelona and took the field; at the approach of this army, Vendôme abandoned Ostalric, destroyed his advance posts, and retreated to a position near Gerona. A combined action by Gastañaga and Russell surrounded Palamos by land and sea in mid-August, but when Russell heard a false rumour, planted by Vendôme, that Tourville would soon leave Toulon, the allied fleet sailed off to confront the French. Without the fleet the siege collapsed. At this point the French destroyed both Palamos and Castelfollit as untenable and retired to Gerona. The only accomplishment of the Spanish that year had been taking Ostalric, while the French were again able to maintain their army in Catalonia for the entire year.

French naval strategy underwent a basic transformation in 1695, as *guerre de course* replaced *guerre d'escadre*. The crop failure of 1693–94 and the subsequent fiscal crisis precipitated this change. As discussed at length in chapter 3, France could not maintain the largest army in Europe while at the same time investing heavily in the fleet. As such the Allies outstripped the French in shipbuilding and arming to enjoy an increasing numerical advantage. Reevaluations of French fleet operations came to what was in all probability an inevitable decision that the fleet must be cut back. Vauban recommended such action in his 'Mémoire concernant la caprerie', and it is hard not to believe that his own success in 1694 against Barclay's landings at Camaret convinced him that land defences should be sufficient to guarantee the security of the Atlantic coast and that a large battle fleet was an expensive and unnecessary luxury. After 1694 there were no major fleet operations in the Atlantic for the rest of the war, although the bulk of the remaining French ships of the line would again concentrate in Brest in 1696. Thanks to new regulations forged in 1694, the French navy leased a number of its vessels to privateers in the last years of the war, and the most notable accomplishments at sea were those of its commerce raiders.

With the aid of supplies shipped from England in April, Russell reprovisioned his fleet at Cadiz and sailed for the Mediterranean on 10 May with fifty-four rated vessels, ten bomb ketches, and eleven fireships. Fearing an allied attack, Tourville did everything he could to strengthen the defences of Toulon. As Russell's superior fleet sailed near Toulon in June, Tourville stayed in port. At the end of the summer, Russell returned to England, although he left a squadron in Cadiz, which then received reinforcements under the command of Rooke. The combined fleet did not top thirty ships of the line, and the advantage of numbers in the Mediterranean switched back to the French.

Without a major Atlantic fleet at sea, the French relied on land forces for defence. Marshal d'Estrées bore responsibility for the Aunis country and La Rochelle, and Marshal Choiseul led forces on most of the Breton coast, while Vauban commanded twenty-two battalions of naval troops detailed to defend Brest and its surroundings. The Allies continued their attacks on French shore installations in 1695. They appeared off St Malo on 14 July and bombarded the town the next day, and then eighteen vessels with six bomb ketches appeared off Granville to bombard that port on 17 July. After this attack the allied fleet regrouped off Guernsey and then sailed to Gravelines, arriving there on 27 July. From there the Allies sailed to bombard Dunkirk, shelling it on 11 August, and after this Calais came under attack by the ketches on 27–8 August.

Between 1693 and 1695, the French war effort became a casualty of an even more fundamental fact of life: agricultural crisis. In 1693 Louis was winning, but in 1695 he was merely enduring. Louis, and Europe for that matter, was ready for peace, or at least ready for the war to end.

THE WAR WINDS DOWN, 1696–97

Even as the state tottered on the brink of bankruptcy, Louis commanded another supreme effort for 1696, augmenting his army once again. Not only would there be campaigns in Flanders, the Rhineland, Piedmont, and Catalonia, but James II would prepare another stillborn invasion of England employing French troops and ships.

Nevertheless, while military operations continued, the momentum towards a negotiated peace grew month by month. The first break in the coalition widened in 1696, as Victor Amadeus neared solidifying an alliance with his foe, Louis. By the spring of 1696 Louis was also talking with the Dutch again and making progress; then the news broke that the duke of Savoy had reached an agreement with Louis. This began a rush to conclude a settlement. The sense of urgency only increased with a growing certainty among European statesmen that King Carlos II of Spain would soon die, and that consequently the ongoing war was keeping them from dealing with far more important matters. Louis and William III shared an interest in a speedy settlement now that the throne of Spain was clearly up for auction.

Louis also gained leverage from the fact that he could shift troops away from Italy in 1696, although the full effect of these reinforcements would not be felt until 1697. By that point the warring parties were gathered around the peace table drafting a final settlement, the Treaty of Ryswick.

1696

In Flanders, the year proved to be uneventful, although sizeable forces faced off there. The Army of Flanders, once again under the command of Villeroi, included 84 battalions and 104 squadrons, supported by another 85 battalions and 96 squadrons in Boufflers's Army of the Meuse – a combined force of some 125,000 men[71] – to which should be added four flying camps under Montal, la Mothe, Harcourt, and Guiscard. French forces began assembling early, with many of the troops moving by 10 May. Villeroi's troops encamped between Courtrai and the Scheldt on 17 May, and then moved north to Deinze to live off the country. Bouffler's force assembled around Mons and marched to Fleurus on 19 May to exhaust the resources of the area and make it difficult for the enemy to subsist. To oppose Louis's armies, William III mustered a main army of 80 battalions and 100 squadrons, totalling 60,000 men, who assembled around Ghent, while the elector of Bavaria commanded another army of 39,360 men forming around Tirlemont.[72] The movements of the French and their enemies throughout late May and June had more to do with foraging than with fighting. In late June, the landgrave of Hesse arrived with an army of 22,000 men in Flanders, but his arrival did not bring on any major action. Boufflers covered Mons, Charleroi, and Dinant from enemy attack, while Villeroi held the enemy in check around Ghent. The face-off continued until October, when French and allied forces went into winter quarters.

The campaign along the Rhine in 1696 saw a great deal of marching back and forth but little heavy action. De Lorges could not command that year, for reasons of health, so Marshal Choiseul led the French. This force of 36 battalions and 106 squadrons – roughly 36,000 troops – formed around Philippsburg, where Choiseul arrived on 14 May. Combined German forces totalled about 70,000, but the departure of the landgrave of Hesse for Flanders left only about 48,000 under Louis of Baden to fight Choiseul. Choiseul conducted that year's campaign primarily with the goal of keeping Baden from doing any harm while the French lived off the enemy's country. In mid-August Hesse's forces left Flanders to march back to the Rhineland, so Baden became more aggressive in early September. From 10 September Baden and Choiseul occupied high ground on either side of

---

71 French estimates based on battalion and squadron figures from John A. Lynn, *Giant of the Grand Siècle: The French Army, 1610–1715* (New York, 1997), chapters 2 and 14.

72 Quincy, *Histoire militaire*, vol. iii, p. 210. A very interesting calculation on the army showing that 36 battalions were in English pay, and 44 in Dutch pay, while 79 squadrons were paid by the English and 21 by the Dutch. Quincy figures battalions were 600 men and 120 men per squadron.

Neustadt, but did not engage in battle. Meanwhile, fearing for the security of Alsace, Choiseul dispatched troops and called upon armed peasants to counter any enemy crossing of the Rhine. In mid-October both armies went into winter quarters.

The war in Italy underwent a dramatic change, as Victor Amadeus joined with Louis in 1696. Spies in the service of William and the emperor informed them that something was afoot. In order to guard the secrecy of the talks, the duke left Turin on the pretext of a religious retreat in February. In late June, both parties agreed to final terms that required the French to relinquish Pinerolo at the end of the war. These were formalized as the Peace of Turin, 29 August. With negotiations in full swing, military action remained limited. Catinat crossed the Alps back into Piedmont at the head of an army of 35,000 men in June. For obvious reasons, Catinat kept his forces at a distance from the duke's troops. A two months' truce published on 12 July formally ended hostilities between the French and Piedmontese. During the truce period Catinat and Victor Amadeus prepared to combine forces in an assault on the territory of Milan. On 18 September the duke invested Valenza. This siege progressed according to plan but was never completed, for on 7 October the duke and the Allies agreed to the convention of Vigevano, which stipulated a suspension of arms in Italy for the rest of the war.

In Catalonia the French did not undertake any major operations in 1696, even though they were no longer hampered by the presence of an allied fleet, which left Cadiz to return north in the spring. Vendôme, with twenty-eight battalions and thirty-three squadrons, commanded about 20,000 troops against a Spanish army of roughly the same size. Using Gerona as a base, he attacked Ostalric in July and then retired with his main forces to Banyolas. After minor actions, both armies broke up for winter quarters in late September.

The most adventurous French action of 1696 was to have been a landing in England designed to precipitate a rising that would put James II back on the throne. Like all his ventures, this too ended in failure. Louis invested the support of the French navy, an army of 12,000 veteran royal troops, and 100,000 gold Louis with the promise of much more money.[73] As always, James expected strong loyalist support on his arrival. The timing seemed propitious. One allied fleet

---

[73] Quincy, ibid., p. 202, says 16,000 troops, Symcox, *Crisis of French Sea Power*, p. 165, says 12,000.

was still at Cadiz, and the army was committed to Flanders, so William had few troops in England. Louis ordered a large fleet armed for the year, with some fifty vessels to be made ready at Toulon. The duke of Berwick went ahead to prepare the way. However, William, well informed by his spies, made preparations to resist. News came to William of a planned assassination to take place in late February, and when he informed Parliament of the plot he received enthusiastic promises of support. William ordered the arrest of James's supporters and commanded Catholics over the age of sixteen to leave London. Twenty battalions were to be shifted back to England, and Russell put to sea with forty-eight rated vessels and frigates from Spithead on 8 March. Meanwhile James's plot was coming apart at the seams. His supporters would not rise until the French landed, but Louis would not send French forces until the Jacobites had already taken up arms. James arrived at Calais in March and stayed until the beginning of the campaign season, but his invasion fleet never sailed. Troops assembled for it served in Flanders instead.

The invasion fiasco had caused Louis to bring his fleet north, which would eventually have important strategic consequences. The armament of ships at Toulon took longer than expected because of delays in the arrival of essential ships' stores. In fact, it was realized that the Mediterranean fleet could not arrive in time to support the invasion, because Château-Renault did not sail with his forty-seven ships of the line until the end of March. When he arrived in mid-May, the French had a naval presence once again at Brest, although the fleet did little but ride at anchor. Yet if they accomplished nothing else, the threatened invasion and the transfer of the bulk of French naval forces from Toulon to Brest drew the allied fleet away from the Mediterranean. Because Rooke sailed from Cadiz early in 1696 to resist the landings, French plans in Catalonia could be much more aggressive in 1697 without fear of intervention by a hostile fleet.

So while major fleet action had been contemplated early in 1696, the reality devolved to continued *guerre de course*. Already by the start of that year, the Allies had lost over 4,000 merchant ships.[74] Nesmond sailed with a privateer squadron in 1696, Château-Renault led a squadron of twelve vessels from Brest in a vain attempt to seize Spanish treasure ships, and Jean Bart commanded a squadron of seven of the king's rated vessels. Bart evaded a blockade of twenty enemy vessels before Dunkirk and raided into the North Sea, where he riveted allied attention and caused considerable damage, again

---

[74] Quincy, *Histoire militaire*, vol. iii, p. 201.

driving up the cost of this seemingly endless war. As always, single privateers slipped out to sea and attacked allied shipping.

Once again, the defence of French coasts fell mainly to forces on land, although many of these were composed of the unoccupied officers and crews of French war vessels. D'Estrées now commanded in Brittany, as Vauban returned to the frontier. Tourville commanded on the coasts of Aunis, and Joyeuse was responsible for Normandy. The Allies bombarded Calais again in May, firing 350 shells at the town. The Allies assembled a fleet of ninety ships of the line that summer, and d'Estrées feared another descent on Brest. That marshal stiffened the defences again with cannon and thousands of troops. He formed eleven regiments with men from Château-Renault's vessels. The enemy fleet appeared off the coast on 2 August, and a great number anchored off Brest. Fifty vessels sailed on to the Île de Ré, where they bombarded St Martin de Ré with over 2,000 shells and then attacked Sables d'Olonne with similar fury. Allied troops landed on the undefended island of Groua, but an attempt against Belle Île on 18 August was unsuccessful. The enemy fleet finally weighed anchor for Torbay on 20 August.

1697

While serious fighting continued in 1697, the contending sides were negotiating an end to the war. Some discussions had taken place as early as 1693, but the Treaty of Turin greatly accelerated the momentum for a general peace settlement. The contending parties agreed at the end of the year to meet at Ryswick, close to The Hague. The French negotiators arrived in mid-March. As the joint conference bogged down because of the conflicting positions among the Allies, William III dispatched his confidant, Bentinck, to open negotiations in secret with Marshal Boufflers in July. Louis welcomed the chance to forge a separate peace with William, and they soon resolved the sticking points. The terms of their agreement were ratified at Ryswick on 20 September, although Spain and the emperor took a few weeks to agree to the treaty. This meant that despite the fact that peace negotiations provided the backdrop for serious fighting in 1697, armies still took to the field for a full campaign season. In fact, the last year of the war won Louis a final series of successes in Flanders and Catalonia.

Louis committed three armies to Flanders, under Villeroi, Catinat, and Boufflers. Villeroi commanded 80 battalions and 107 squadrons as an army of observation for Catinat's smaller force of 50 battalions and 50 squadrons intended to occupy siege lines.[75] Boufflers, again along the Meuse, had 79 battalions and 107 squadrons. These three main forces totalled over 190,000 troops on paper.[76] This large French troop concentration outnumbered the Allies, who committed most of their units in a single main army of 96 battalions and 206 squadrons led by William and the elector of Bavaria.

After Villeroi and Catinat assembled around Tournai, the French invested Ath on 15 May; this would be the main target of the year's campaign. The artillery train of 72 cannon and several mortars left Douai the next day. Catinat's 40,000 men actually conducted the siege under the guidance of Vauban. Beginning on 16 May and completing their work on 22 May, peasant pioneers dug the lines of circumvallation in less than a week and were sent home.[77] The evening of their departure, the trenches were opened against the fortress. Ath was defended by a garrison of 3,840 men led by the governor, the count of Roeux, who sent his wife to Brussels under safe conduct from the French. Villeroi took station at Ostiches to cover the siege to the north, while Boufflers supported the siege by marching his army to Binche. William III arrived with his forces after the siege had begun, and once the elector of Bavaria united his army with William's, the combined allied force numbered 100,000 men centred on St Kwintens-Lennik, between Ath and Brussels.

The siege progressed methodically, but rapidly. Vauban drafted a written plan for the siege, dated 20 May. Here he dispensed with the third parallel given the layout of the fortifications, which he knew well because he had designed them two decades before. This was not his only innovation, because he also used a new style of cannon fire, *tir à ricochet*, which lobbed cannonballs just over the ramparts to bowl over men sheltering behind them.[78] On 5 June twenty companies of grenadiers prepared to assault the breaches that Vauban's batteries had battered in the enemy walls, but at 2 p.m. the governor beat the chamade and capitulated. The governor and his garrison marched out on the morning of 7 June. Immediately after the garrison departed,

---

75 Quincy, ibid., p. 295, says 50 battalions and 50 squadrons equalled 40,000 men. My own calculations state that the full strength of such a force would have been 43,750 and the discounted strength 35,600.

76 Quincy, ibid., p. 300, estimates the actual size of the forces at 120,000.

77 Ibid., p. 296. This interesting detail demonstrates that amateur pioneers were not the sappers, who should be skilled professional soldiers.

78 Lynn, *Giant of the Grand Siècle*, p. 570. Duffy, *The Fortress in the Age of Vauban*, pp. 30–1.

a force of 6,000 worked to raze the siege lines, fill in the trenches, and repair the breaches. Vauban boasted proudly that the siege of Ath was conducted 'with so much art and method, that it cost the king no more than one hundred men'.[79] After the completion of the siege, Villeroi made some moves to cut the allied forces off from Holland, but William avoided this by reaching Brussels, which he rendered essentially invulnerable. By late July, when negotiations between Louis and William were in full swing, the French armies settled down with Villeroi and Boufflers near Ninove and Catinat in lines around Courtrai.

In the Rhineland, the campaign followed the pattern it had developed in the preceding years. There was little serious action, as the French did their best to stymie German moves and, at the same time, live off enemy country. Choiseul fought at a numerical disadvantage against Louis of Baden's combined forces of 56,000 men, most of whom assembled around Eppingen in late May. The passion for defensive lines thrived on the Rhine just as it did in Flanders, and twenty battalions under Chamilly, based at Worms, constructed a new line from Durkheim to the Rhine at the start of the campaign. Choiseul busied himself parrying the moves of Baden's army during the summer. Following one particularly rapid march in which French troops covered seventy-five miles in three days, crossing the Rhine in the process, Choiseul's army and that of Baden stood only about a league apart on 12 July. Still, nothing came of this, except that Choiseul had blocked the road to Strasbourg. After some time, Choiseul recrossed the Rhine. In early September, Baden besieged the small fortress of Ebernberg on the Nahe near Bingen on the left bank of the Rhine. He invested it on 8 September, and it capitulated on 27 September; the next day the garrison of a mere 352 men marched out. Choiseul seemed content to keep his army in fortified lines. After the fall of Ebernberg, news of the peace arrived and the two armies drew back from one another.

The Catalan front witnessed a major triumph of French arms in 1697, when Vendôme besieged and took Barcelona. This siege had been delayed in the past by the presence of an allied fleet, but William was anxious for peace now, and had no desire to assist the recalcitrant Spanish in prolonging the war. The French had made considerable preparations in Perpignan, as Vendôme assembled an army of forty-two

79 Vauban, *Abrégé des services*, in Lazard, *Vauban*, p. 273.

battalions and fifty-five squadrons, or approximately 32,000 actual troops, the largest French force committed to this front to date. Against this, the Spanish could rally about 20,000 troops. When the French approached Barcelona in early June, the Spanish committed 12,500 regulars to garrison the city, aided by about 4,000 militia and perhaps another 3,000 from the crews of ships and galleys, while the remainder of Spanish forces withdrew behind the town. A considerable fleet of thirty galleys from Marseilles and a squadron of nine ships of the line sailed from Toulon under d'Estrées to join Vendôme and close Barcelona to seaward.

Learning that the galleys had reached Palamos, Vendôme ordered his troops to close in around the city on 4 June, and the siege began. Two days later, d'Estrées arrived with a convoy of 150 ships carrying food, siege supplies, 60 cannon, and 24 mortars. French troops invested Barcelona on 12 June, although it proved impossible to cut off the fortress from all communication and supplies because the Spanish controlled the adjoining hills on the coast just west of the fortress. Sappers opened trenches on the night of 15–16 June, as bomb ketches hurled shells into the town, starting a fire in a grain magazine which burned for seven or eight hours. The garrison under command of the prince of Darmstadt and the fortress governor, the count of Corsana, fought to delay and resist the French in a defence that was anything but passive. This would not be a short siege; in fact, it continued for two months.

When he heard that the viceroy in command of forces encamped near St Feliu intended to act in concert with Darmstadt in an assault on the French lines, Vendôme resolved to attack the Spanish outside Barcelona. The enemies in the hills could maintain contact with the town by using roads on the shore. Driving them back could break Barcelona's last contacts. On 14 July Vendôme and his lieutenant, Usson, attacked the Spanish positions with about 7,000 troops and caught their foes entirely off guard. The French pillaged enemy headquarters at St Feliu, even seizing the viceroy's gold. In the joint attack the enemy lost as many as 3,000 men to the French casualities of only 80 men *hors de combat*.

The ring of fire tightened around Barcelona. Mines blew up sections of the wall on 14 July and again on 22 July. The defenders exploded a mine themselves to destroy a bastion the French had taken, although this may have only succeeded in damaging walls still defended by allied troops. When the French were prepared to blow another mine and launch an assault with sixteen battalions, the marquis of Barbesières summoned the Spanish to surrender. The defenders asked for a day, and then for another, but when they requested a third, Vendôme granted them only twelve hours; serious negotiations began, and the garrison capitulated on 10 August. The garrison marched out the next day, and this front saw no major action again before the peace. Such a vigorously contested siege cost both sides heavily; French casualties amounted to about 9,000, and the Spanish lost 12,000, killed, wounded, and captured. The siege over, on 16 August d'Estrées left to return to port.

Beyond the squadron action of d'Estrées the fleet did little in 1697. *Guerre de course* reigned at sea, as privateers continued to raid allied commerce. Louis once again relied on land forces to defend his northern coasts. However, this last year of the war brought one of the most extraordinary privateering ventures. Through an agreement with the king, the baron of Pointis, a naval officer turned privateer, was able to assemble a fleet of seven ships of the line, three frigates, one bomb ketch, a flute, and a corvette. With this privately financed squadron he carried out a long-laid plan to attack the Spanish colonial port of Cartagena, in present-day Colombia. The ships sailed from Brest on 9 January, an early date chosen to put Pointis's squadron in position to attack Cartagena before the treasure fleet had departed. After picking up additional soldiers in the West Indies, Pointis arrived before the town in April and laid siege to it. Cartagena capitulated on 2 May. The haul from Cartagena was immense, amounting to 10,000,000 livres. Pointis reembarked his troops on 1 June and escaped a pursuing English fleet by sailing north all the way to Newfoundland before crossing the Atlantic back to Brest, where he arrived on 29 August.

The Cartagena raid was the single most noteworthy event of the war in the New World. The extension of the Nine Years War in North America, known among the English colonies as King William's War, was not a major affair if judged by European standards.[80] The British colonists mobilized militia and allied Native American tribes, including the Iroquois, to fight the French, who mixed some regulars with

---

80 John B. Wolf calls the Nine Years War 'the first world war', and certainly military actions took place in North America, South America, the Caribbean, and South Asia as well as in Europe. However, the struggles outside Europe involved so few people and assets, and were of such minor consequence, as to be mere skirmishes when viewed alongside the war in Europe. A far better case for the first global conflict can be made for the War of the Austrian Succession or the Seven Years War. These wars witnessed much more serious conflict in North America, and the contenders were also fully engaged in India.

their militia and native allies, notably the Algonquins and Abenakis. At the start of the war, Louis XIV ordered Frontenac to return to Quebec as governor in order to energize French efforts. The most ambitious operations occurred in 1690, when the French raided Schenectady, and English colonists seized Port Royal, but failed in attempts to take both Montreal and Quebec. Throughout the war, raids ravaged settlements and Native American villages on both sides. In some localities, the war had severe, although temporary, demographic effects, but when viewed as a whole, the losses among European settlers were light. Casualties among them in New England and New York during the entire conflict amounted to only about 650 dead, either in fighting or in captivity; this number reached about 300 for the French. Losses to Native Americans were certainly greater. This war made life on the American frontier hard and dangerous, but it did not exert any appreciable influence on events in Europe.

The Nine Years War also touched South Asia. The success of the French trading settlement at Pondicherry on the Coromandel Coast of India raised the ire of the Dutch, and after the war began in Europe, they launched an expedition against their commercial rivals. In late August 1693 a Dutch fleet including nineteen ships of the line and bearing 1,500 European troops appeared off Pondicherry and overwhelmed the small garrison there under François Martin, who surrendered on 6 September. The Nine Years War was also coincident with a humiliating defeat of the English East India Company by the Mughals, 1686–90, first in Bengal and then at Bombay; however, this was not really a part of the European struggle.

Representatives of France, the Dutch Republic, England, and Spain agreed to the Treaty of Ryswick on 20 September. The emperor at first resisted the Treaty, but finally signed it as well on 30 October, ending a war that had brought death, suffering, and economic hardship to Europe for nearly a decade. By the terms of the treaty, Louis returned Luxembourg and other fruits of the Reunions, but kept Strasbourg. Lorraine returned to its duke, although the French retained the right to march troops through Lorraine, as long as they paid for food, and so on, that they received. Breisach became German again, as Louis was forced to give up the right bank of the Rhine altogether; therefore, Ryswick set the ultimate Rhine boundary of France, an important aspect of the treaty.[81] With Breisach in German

---

81 See Peter Sahlins, 'Natural Frontiers Revisited: France's Boundaries since the Seventeenth Century', *American Historical Review* 95, no. 5 (December 1990), p. 1434, on this point. Sahlins claims that because of this new, better-defined Rhine frontier,

hands, a French Neuf Brisach soon rose from the marsh on the left bank of the Rhine to guard that passage. Louis agreed to recognize William III as king of England and to give James II no aid in trying to regain the throne. Colonial prizes taken during the war were returned to their original European owners, so the French regained both Port Royal and Pondicherry. Beyond this, the French also achieved *de jure* recognition of their ownership of half of the island of Hispaniola. In subsidiary agreements, the French restored the moderate tariffs of 1664 on Dutch goods and the Dutch were to garrison a line of fortresses in the Spanish Netherlands, the famous barrier fortresses, to provide an added measure of security for their border.

Did the treaty amount to victory or defeat for Louis? Vauban saw it as humiliating. While the French navy had lost at La Hogue, the army had gone from victory to victory, never losing a major battle in the field and taking several major fortresses at the cost of only a few held by the French. It could be argued that France won the war but lost the peace. Perhaps, but peace was victory to Louis by 1697, and most of what he had fought for he had retained.[82] If Louis came out poorer at Ryswick, it was not so much that he had lost lands key to France, but that the emperor was gaining in power because of his victories over the Turks, who would soon concede Transylvania and Hungary. Louis may not have been defeated, but the comparative strength of France had suffered in the new balance of European power.

CONCLUSION: THE NINE YEARS WAR AS ARCHETYPE

Each of the wars of Louis XIV was unique, to be sure, but if one conflict could be proposed as the archetype of the Sun King at arms, it would be the Nine Years War. Not only did it see the French navy reach its apogee, the army attain its greatest size, and Louis's generals win an impressive chain of victories, but this war also exemplified the fundamental purpose, pattern, and parameters of warfare during his

---

'by the Treaty of Ryswick, France's capacity to intervene in Germany was also disabled'. French campaigns in the Rhineland during the War of the Spanish Succession certainly undermine this last assertion. The Rhine frontier was pretty permeable, particularly when the French held Strasbourg.

82 Wolf, *Louis XIV*, pp. 487–8 sees the Treaty of Ryswick as a defeat, but Lossky, *Louis XIV*, p. 255, views it as a victory: '[W]ith the exception of these Lorraine provisions, Louis obtained at the Rijswijk settlement the terms he had sought to impose in his ultimatum of September 24, 1688.'

personal reign. Louis did not undertake the war to rewrite the map of Europe, or even of France. In fact, the point of the initial attack in 1688 was to compel his German neighbours to ratify as permanent the Truce of Ratisbon, which recognized the territorial *fait accompli* after the Reunions. But Louis and his advisers miscalculated, and a war meant to be brief, concentrated on a single front, and fought against only a few opponents, grew into a general European conflict, spread across multiple fronts, and fought against a great coalition.

Once the nature of the war changed, Louis pursued no new plan to bring it to a rapid decision through battle. He may have dreamed of quick, decisive strokes, but his more fundamental understanding of war grew out of long conflicts of attrition. When easy victory proved to be a chimera, he seems very quickly, and almost comfortably, to have accepted that he was once more involved in a long war in which he must outlast, rather than destroy, his foes.

Military operations were not decisive in character, nor does it seem that they were supposed to be. Louis expanded his army to unprecedented size, and expense, but he never concentrated his troops in such a way as to drive even a single opponent from the war by military means alone. No thrust was ever so directed at the heart of an opponent as to bring him down with a single lunge of the sword. His armies never exploited initial victories by hounding enemy forces until they were eliminated. Maintaining an operational momentum seemed to mean little. When Louis's armies in Flanders conducted successful sieges early in a campaign season, they then dispersed to reinforce other fronts. The only exploitation of a victory in Flanders was the siege of Charleroi, which followed the battlefield triumph at Neerwinden, but then by a full six weeks. Only in Catalonia did French armies put together a string of victories in quick succession, at the Ter, Palamos, and Gerona in 1694, but even these were secondary affairs which alone could never have driven Spain out of the war. From a modern perspective, the most surprising thing about the war is how rare battles and sieges actually were. It was not uncommon for an entire campaign season to pass on a front without any large-scale combat. Many campaigns, particularly in secondary theatres, seemed to have had survival as their only goal – the purpose of the campaign was to fight one more campaign. In fact, the only decisive military action during the entire war came in Ireland, where William crushed the forces of James II, but that was a struggle meant to change the very foundations of legitimacy and power in the British Isles; it was conflict without compromise, and Louis's Continental wars never were.

The prosecution of the war went hand in hand with diplomatic initiatives. Indecisive military operations did not end the conflict, but it almost seems that they were not intended to. Fighting provided a foundation and a prelude for diplomatic negotiations; it did not dictate a solution. And with sheer attrition playing such a role, the record of battlefield victory or defeat was, in the end, less compelling than the need to conclude a peace to end the expense of war. It is entirely fitting that one of the reasons that the Nine Years War ended as quickly as it did once the major parties began to talk in earnest was the sense that a more important diplomatic matter would soon be on the table. Concern for the Spanish succession transformed the Nine Years War from a costly impasse into an unwanted distraction.

7 THE FINAL CONTEST: THE WAR OF THE SPANISH SUCCESSION

The Treaty of Ryswick chastened the ageing monarch, who interpreted the disappointment and suffering that the Nine Years War had inflicted on him, his state, and his people as an act of divine will, as caution or even condemnation. In addition, Louis was no longer a young man driven by the need to establish his glory through warfare, and could be more confident in his frontiers, having buttressed them through numerous annexations. Thus, he now worked to find a peaceful way to distribute the lands of Carlos II, as that Spanish king came to the end of his life. However, fate overcame the best efforts of princes and diplomats when Carlos II died leaving all this domain to Philippe of Anjou, the grandson of the Sun King. Unfortunately, and perhaps unavoidably, war overcame Europe again over this matter of the Spanish succession. Already weakened by the huge costs of the Nine Years War, France could ill afford another great war so soon after the conclusion of the last. French arms, virtually invincible for so long, were anything but in the new conflict, and the duke of Marlborough and prince Eugene of Savoy gained years of victories over Louis's less talented commanders. Still, France did not collapse, any more than had its foes in the Nine Years War, when Louis's armies had seemed so dominant. Instead, France suffered and survived until Marshal Villars led French armies to victory during the last years of the war. It would be foolish to call the War of the Spanish Succession a triumph for Louis, but neither did it end in defeat, for he finally won the Spanish throne for his grandson, retained the territorial gains he had gained in earlier wars, and reasserted French military prowess.

THE ONSET OF AN UNWANTED WAR, 1698–1701

After Ryswick, Louis's primary concern, and that of other European leaders, was the Spanish succession. Carlos II had already lived longer than anyone had expected he would, but European statesmen now believed that the end was fairly near, and they knew he would die childless. Hopeful pretenders for the soon-to-be-vacant throne had powerful backers. The dynastic marriage game dealt several contenders strong hands, with the progeny of Louis XIV and Leopold I holding the best cards. The dauphin had the strongest trump to play, because both his mother, Marie Thérèse, and his grandmother were Spanish princesses; in fact, both were eldest daughters, and Spanish practice allowed daughters to inherit the throne in the absence of sons. Louis had earlier made claims to Spanish lands in the name of his wife; now he could in the name of his son. But Louis was not the only ruler who wanted his descendants to rule Spain; Leopold I, the Habsburg Holy Roman Emperor, was also the grandson of King Philip III of Spain. Leopold defended the claim of his son, Archduke Charles. Luckily another youth, Joseph Ferdinand, electoral prince of Bavaria, also stood in line and might serve as a reasonable compromise candidate to avert a clash between France and Austria.

The great powers fashioned partition treaties in the hopes of averting a European war over the Spanish inheritance. An early attempt to solve this problem in 1668 resulted in Austrian acquiescence to French claims, but the much stronger position Leopold I gained in the late 1680s led him to be more assertive. He signed a treaty with the Dutch and English in 1689 that would have passed on all of the Spanish inheritance to Archduke Charles, but French strength rendered this an untenable position. A more balanced partition treaty which came in 1698, a time when Louis wanted to avoid another armed struggle at all costs, gave Spain itself, the Spanish Netherlands, and the extensive overseas colonial holdings of Spain to Joseph Ferdinand. Archduke Charles would receive Milan, while the dauphin would gain Naples, Sicily, and fortresses in Tuscany. Of course, if and when the dauphin ascended to the throne, these territories would become part of the royal domain. The untimely death of Joseph Ferdinand in 1699 scuttled the treaty, however, and Louis scrambled to draft a new one with the English and Dutch in March 1700. With Louis's assent, this treaty would have awarded the lion's share to Charles; he would garner everything earmarked for Joseph Ferdinand in the previous treaty. The dauphin would receive his previous portion plus Milan. William III was hesitant to hand France such a dominant position in Italy, so a clause of the treaty pledged the dauphin to try to exchange his Italian gains for Lorraine or territory of the duke of Savoy. However, Leopold refused to take part in negotiations, because he adamantly insisted that the entire inheritance must now go to Archduke Charles.

In any case, the elaborate plans erected by the great powers fell like a house of cards from the whiff of Carlos II's dying breath on 1 November 1700. Carlos II's greatest concern was to keep his lands intact, and so he contrived to avoid their partition by willing them to Louis's grandson, Philippe of Anjou. The Spanish court had brought up Philippe's name because he was not immediately in line for the French throne – his father, the dauphin, and his elder brother, the duke of Burgundy, stood between Philippe and the crown – so granting him the Spanish inheritance would not unite France and Spain. Still, bequeathing Philippe the entire inheritance would enlist Louis and the power of France to guarantee the settlement. Thus, a Spanish courier arrived from Madrid to offer the entire inheritance to Philippe, and, if Philippe refused, to extend the offer to his younger brother, the duke of Berry. However, if both French princes refused to accept the whole of Spanish domains, the messenger was instructed to continue on to Vienna where he would offer them all to Archduke Charles. The courier would not have to take the road to Vienna, for the dauphin and the duke of Burgundy set aside their claims in favour of Philippe, making him the legitimate Bourbon candidate, and Louis accepted the will. The old monarch formally received his grandson no longer as Philippe of Anjou but as Philip V of Spain.

Throughout this manoeuvring, Louis's goals remained essentially dynastic, that is, securing lands for his son, and later his grandson, not himself. True, the partition treaties of 1698 and 1700 would have added territory to France, but only when the dauphin succeeded Louis. Moreover, by accepting the will of Carlos II, Louis forwent any territorial addition to France, then or in the future. In fact, Louis would later insist that accepting the will was a principled and selfless act because it meant abandoning a partition treaty that would have eventually added important domains to France.

Louis probably had little reasonable choice but to accept the will of Carlos II, even though this act would make war with the Habsburgs almost unavoidable. If he had abided by the partition treaty of 1700, which the Austrian Habsburg emperor refused to sign in any case, he would have faced a Habsburg succession and occupation in Spain. Louis would have had to fight Leopold just to gain the scraps that the treaty allowed Philip, and he would have had to attack the combined forces of Spain and the Empire to get them. And who is to say that England and the Dutch would have aided him in enforcing the treaty. By accepting the will, he would still have to fight Leopold I, but he could fight a defensive war on Spanish territory, with French and Spanish forces allied against the emperor. The trick was to convince the Maritime Powers that Louis really had no choice and that his goal was purely dynastic. But Louis now misplayed his cards.[1] After recognizing his grandson as king of Spain, Louis issued letters patent declaring that Philip retained his right to succeed to the French throne. This was not an attempt on Louis's part to unite the crowns of France and Spain as his enemies feared. In fact Carlos's will stipulated that the new Spanish king must reside in Madrid, and this alone made it impossible for one Bourbon to rule both countries. Louis's decision expressed his belief that God established the principles of succession and that His choice must be honoured. Certainly, in 1700 the chance of Philip inheriting the French throne seemed far more theoretical than real. The English and Dutch probably could have lived with retaining Philip as a possible, albeit remote, claimant to the French crown, but Louis's next move enraged William III. The Sun King insisted on sending French troops to take over the Dutch-held barrier forts in the Spanish Netherlands. The Dutch had reached an agreement with Carlos II in 1698 to station Dutch troops in ten fortresses within the Spanish Netherlands as a way of guaranteeing the security of the burgher republic. But with Carlos now gone, Louis ordered his troops to surround these posts in order to pressure the Dutch to recognize Philip as king, and after they soon did, Louis allowed the garrisons to march back to Dutch soil, but French troops occupied the fortresses.[2] Louis assured Europe the French garrisons would withdraw as soon as Philip raised the troops to man the fortresses with Spanish forces. From William's perspective, losing this protective belt overturned the work of twenty years. Louis further alienated the English by having Philip V grant French merchants the coveted *asiento*, the right to supply slaves to the Spanish colonies, and thus denying it to English merchants. And a final insult came when Louis acclaimed James II's son as the legitimate king of England when the father died in September 1701. But here again, Louis's firm belief

---

1 Experts disagree whether Louis's conduct at this point was arrogant or reasonable and whether or not war was inevitable. Steven Baxter, *William III and the Defense of European Liberty, 1650–1702* (New York, 1966), insists that Louis's actions made war inevitable, while Mark A. Thomson, 'Louis XIV and the Origins of the War of the Spanish Succession', in Ragnhild Hatton and J. S. Bromley, eds, *William III and Louis XIV* (Toronto, 1968), argues that war was not inevitable and that Louis acted in a basically reasonable fashion. Another point of view argues that war was inevitable but for structural reasons that Louis could not change: William Roosen, 'The Origins of the War of the Spanish Succession', in Jeremy Black, ed., *The Origins of War in Early Modern Europe* (Edinburgh, 1987).

2 It can be argued that if Louis regarded war as inevitable, this was a very reasonable move.

in divinely sanctioned laws of succession bound his hands. Although Torcy advised him to at least not make the recognition public, Louis felt he must. A case might be made for each of these decisions in isolation, but taken as a group they appeared overbearing. Louis seemed to have gone from penitent to arrogant with his acceptance of the Spanish will.[3]

Rival alliances formed quickly. Obviously France and Spain were bound together, but Louis was also able to secure Bavaria as an ally in March 1701 and Savoy the next month. Therefore these enemies of the last war now circulated in the Sun King's orbit. Portugal would at first embrace a French and Spanish alliance in the spring of 1701. Louis also gained another ally, the Hungarian rebel Ferenc Rákóczi, in an attempt to divert Habsburg forces to the east. While preparing to fight, Rákóczi was arrested but later escaped to take up arms against the Habsburgs in 1703. In opposition to Louis and Philip, Emperor Leopold I secured a Prussian promise of aid by permitting Elector Frederick of Brandenburg to style himself King Frederick I *in*, and later *of*, Prussia in November 1700. On 7 September 1701 England, the United Provinces, and the emperor signed the second treaty of the Grand Alliance and other German states rallied to it over the succeeding months. Finally on 15 May 1702 England, the United Provinces, and Habsburg Austria declared war on France.

Actual fighting broke out in Italy a year before this declaration. French cavalry advanced quickly through a friendly Savoy and Piedmont to secure Milan, a Spanish holding. At the same time infantry landed at Mediterranean ports and advanced through Genoese territory to Milan. With reinforcements and local forces, Marshal Catinat and Marshal Tessé commanded a total of about 30,000 troops. Against this, Prince Eugene of Savoy marched south with an imperial army of roughly the same size. Eugene outmanoeuvred Catinat and struck Tessé at Carpi, driving him back on 9 July 1701. Louis then ordered Marshal Villeroi, a favourite of the king but a general of limited skill, to take command in Italy. Villeroi advanced against Eugene, who had seized Chiari, and there in a bloody fight that lasted several hours, Eugene repulsed Villeroi, who withdrew back across the Oglio River. These imperial victories allowed Eugene to occupy most of Mantuan territory. The bizarre final act of the campaign came after the armies

---

[3] As J. B. Wolf, *Louis XIV* (New York, 1968), p. 513, commented, after seeking peace diligently, and even meekly, after 1697, Louis once again acted like the Sun King, and paid a terrible price. Paul Sonnino, 'The Origins of Louis XIV's Wars,' in Black, *The Origins of War*, p. 129, sees these acts of 1700 and 1701 as the king 'casting off his penitential robes and reverting to his old self'.

went into winter quarters, when Eugene tried to seize Cremona by a *coup de main* on 1 February 1702. This brazen attack resulted in the capture of Marshal Villeroi, although French troops drove the imperials from the town. A poem soon circulated about this odd feat:

> French give thanks to Bellona[4]
> Your joy is without equal,
> For you have saved Cremona
> But you have lost your gen'ral.[5]

The War of the Spanish Succession had begun inauspiciously for Louis, and worse was to come.

CONTENDING FORCES AND GENERALS

As the belligerents formed into rival alliances, they expanded their forces to meet the challenge of war. In 1701 Louis multiplied his regular forces by issuing commissions to create 100 new infantry regiments. He expanded the cavalry by adding more men to existing companies and raising 120 entirely new companies of cavalry and 7 regiments of dragoons. In addition, he revived the royal provincial militia, calling for a levy of 33,000 in 1701, and before long many of these conscripts marched off to Italy to make good French losses there. At first Louis could not have realized the full extent of the threat he would face, but over several years his army grew to meet it. However, it seems unlikely that it attained the numerical peak it had reached during the Nine Years War, because depleted French resources could not produce and sustain as many men.[6] Still, by 1707 the army hit a paper figure of 373,000 men, which probably stayed at about that level until war's end. In real terms, this theoretical size should be discounted to something more like 255,000 actual troops. To this should be added Spanish troops and, for the early years of the war, Bavarian and Savoyard contingents. Against this, the first commitment of the Grand Alliance saw England pledge 40,000 troops for field duty in 1702, the United Provinces 60,000, and the emperor 90,000, to which could be added the smaller forces furnished by lesser German princes.[7]

---

4 In mythology, the sister of Mars, and thus the goddess of war.
5 In Wolf, *Louis XIV*, p. 519.
6 This runs counter to the usual judgement that Louis mustered his largest army for the War of the Spanish Succession, but see John A. Lynn, *Giant of the Grand Siècle: The French Army, 1610–1715* (New York, 1997), chap. 2 on the size of the French army 1610–1715.
7 David Chandler, *Marlborough as Military Commander* (London, 1973), pp. 56–7.

Numbers alone would not dictate the course of the war; generalship would weigh heavy in the balance as well. Here Louis's army was too often at a disadvantage, for it faced one of history's most brilliant commanders, John Churchill, duke of Marlborough. At the start of his career during the Dutch War, Marlborough served Louis XIV in an English regiment. He commanded troops effectively in Ireland early in the Nine Years War for his new monarch, William III. Marlborough's capture of Cork and Kinsale in October 1690 marked him as man of great merit, but he was falsely suspected of plotting against William III in 1692 and imprisoned in the Tower of London for some weeks. He would not again achieve royal favour until William III began to prepare his forces for renewed war against France. William's untimely death in March 1702 further strengthened Marlborough's position, because he was already close to Queen Anne (1702–14), who succeeded William. Marlborough's talented but temperamental wife, Sarah, had been a confidante and favourite of Anne since the early 1680s. To a large extent, Marlborough's leverage depended on Sarah commanding the ear of the queen. Also, his position in England depended on finesse in domestic politics, so he could not simply concentrate on the war. Winters found him mounting a political tightrope to preserve his command. His fall from that perch was prepared by two political blows in 1710: Sarah lost favour with the queen, and a Tory ministry replaced Marlborough's Whig friends.

Despite his proven brilliance, the battle-hungry Marlborough would not achieve the victory over France that he longed for. He blamed this on the complicated command situation with which he was saddled. Queen Anne made him captain-general of English forces. The Dutch, now led politically by Anthonie Heinsius, conferred command of their field forces on Marlborough as well, but only in consultation with Dutch field deputies and generals. Marlborough's correspondence is full of sound and fury as to how he wanted to fight decisive engagements but was held in check by the conservative foot-dragging of the Dutch; however, there is good reason to suspect this as a self-serving analysis.[8] The duke belittled the contribution of his allies to the war effort, and later British historians who take Marlborough at face value without due reference to Dutch histories

---

8 I am borrowing this approach from Jamel Ostwald, 'Decisive Battle in Early Modern Europe: The Strange Case of the Duke of Marlborough and Ramillies, 1706', a paper delivered at the 1998 annual meeting of the Society for Military History, 24 April 1998.

of the war continue to underestimate the Dutch.[9] In fact, they supplied the majority of the allied troops in the Spanish Netherlands, either their own regiments or forces subsidized by them. The much maligned Dutch field deputies also assured allied logistics, without which the army would not have survived. And the quality of Dutch forces, particularly their infantry, was very high indeed.

Many admirers claim that Marlborough transformed the art of war, or at least fought outside the constraints of his day.[10] Some insist that he brought battle back into fashion and rejected siege warfare. But no single general, even one of Marlborough's brilliance, could negate the nature of warfare in the *ancien régime*. Marlborough may have praised the power of battle, but he fought only five great field battles in the decade he held command, 1702–11, while at the same time he besieged and took over thirty enemy fortresses. Without doubt, Marlborough was more likely to manoeuvre than his adversaries and not inclined to shelter behind entrenched lines like the French and his own allies, but while he was better at maintaining the operational tempo at critical times, he qualifies more as a great practitioner who tested the limits of a military system, rather than as a reformer who radically redefined them. The iron constraints of warfare during his day, and not the Dutch, denied Marlborough the decisive campaigns he craved.

In any case, Marlborough benefited from an excellent working partnership with another great commander, Prince Eugene of Savoy, who commanded the emperor's troops. Eugene worked extremely well with Marlborough in several shared victories and, therefore, somewhat lessened Marlborough's problems as a coalition general.

French generalship did not rise to the level of Marlborough, but it eventually proved capable enough to outlast him. And, to be sure, because French strategy need only be defensive, the more difficult task of conquering territory and dictating terms fell to the Allies. To his advantage, Louis's directing presence gave French command a greater unity and saved his commanders from the disputes and lack of coordination inherent in coalition warfare. Such autocratic central

---

9 Readers who want a Dutch perspective, and who read the language, should refer to J. W. Wijn, *Het Staatsche Leger: Het Tijdperk van de Spaanse Successioorlog, 1702–1715* (8 vols; The Hague, 1959–64).
10 See, for example, David Chandler, who portrays Marlborough as a true Napoleon. 'From first to last he was the proponent of the major battle as the sole means to break an enemy's military power and thus his will to resist.' Chandler, *Marlborough as a Military Commander*, p. 63.

direction spared his generals the need to glance over their shoulders to monitor politics on the home front as did Marlborough; however, the fact that Louis kept his generals on a short leash discouraged dramatic action. Moreover, all too often, Louis erred in his choice of generals, at least until well into the war. Inferior marshals such as Marsin and Villeroi undermined French campaigns, and Louis cannot escape blame for having ridden some of the wrong horses for too long. Still, even if Turenne and Luxembourg were only memories, the army was not without its share of fine generals – Berwick, Vendôme, and, above all, Villars – but it would take time and defeat to weed out incompetence. Early in the war when French generalship did not seem up to the task, military administration also seems to have declined under the charge of Chamillart, who succeeded the son of Louvois, the marquis of Barbezieux, in January 1701. However, the more capable Daniel Voysin replaced Chamillart in 1709, a time when Louis also elevated his best general, Villars, to command in the crucial Flanders front.

It should be noted that a good deal of the credit for ultimate French success goes to the excellence of French diplomacy under the direction of the marquis of Torcy, secretary of state for foreign affairs, an office he shared in 1696 and held exclusively from mid-1699 through the rest of Louis's reign. But all of this is the tale to be told in this chapter.

THE END OF INVINCIBILITY, 1702–5

The first years of the war shook confidence in French military preeminence. Fighting that had already begun in Italy spread north to the Rhine and the Low Countries and eventually spread to Spain and even Hungary. At Blenheim, Marlborough and Eugene inflicted the first great battlefield defeat on French land forces in over half a century. Initial French setbacks disappointed and discouraged Louis, but they did not bring despair. Success and survival on one front balanced against defeat on another, so if the aura of invincibility had been lost, the picture was not unremittingly black.

1702

In 1702, the war was still gaining momentum as the adversaries defined themselves. England, the United Provinces, and Leopold I only declared war on France in mid-May, and the empire as a whole did not officially enter the fray until the autumn.

During opening moves of the first northern campaign, the French lost a handful of fortresses on the Rhine and east of the Meuse, but established a firm defensive line in 'Flanders', that is, the Spanish Low Countries west of the Meuse. The French had fought here as invaders before; now they came as champions of the legitimate sovereign. Before the main armies formed for that year's campaign, the Grand Alliance moved against Kaiserwerth. This fortress belonging to Cologne, a French ally, capitulated to an English and Dutch force on 15 June after a hard-fought siege of two months. On the whole, the summer months that followed were devoted to manoeuvres on both sides that led to scant results. Louis awarded his army in Flanders to his grandson, the duke of Burgundy, under the watchful tutelage of Marshal Boufflers. With the forces at hand during the first full campaign of the war, Boufflers could not protect all the French and Spanish positions along his front. Marlborough found his initial intentions frustrated by Dutch resistance, but at the end of August the allies besieged Venlo, down the Meuse from Roermond. Its French garrison surrendered the poorly fortified town on 25 September. Next Roermond fell on 7 October. These were outposts at the limit of French defences, and Burgundy and Boufflers made little attempt to hold them.

But now the Allies marched on Liège, and Boufflers had committed so many troops to garrison duty in the Netherlands that he could not bar the allied advance but simply detailed more troops to T'Serclaes, the commander at Liège. Marlborough's forces drove south to Liège and arrrived on 13 October; the town capitulated the next day. The citadel held out longer, however, and obliged the Dutch engineer Coehoorn to direct a formal siege that compelled it to surrender on 23 October. A week later the Fort de Chartreuse, another part of the defences at Liège, capitulated. The year had gone well for Marlborough, but France's loss of Liège, while serious, did not necessarily compromise the primary defences of the Spanish Netherlands.

From the start of the conflict and throughout its course, the French would rely very heavily on a series of entrenched lines designed to stop enemy raiders and to make the advance of allied armies difficult. The first set of lines, known as the lines of Brabant, began at the Channel, covered Antwerp, and then ran roughly southwest to the Meuse, exploiting rivers as barriers and crossing open country with ditches and parapets. Elaborate lines suited Louis's defensive purposes in the War of the Spanish Succession, but the Allies dug them as well, particularly along the Rhine. If Marlborough's taste for daring marches and dramatic action typified this war, so did a penchant for entrenchments rivalling those of 1914–18. Yet Louis's lines differed from World War I trenches, not only in architecture, but in the fact that Louis never commanded enough troops to hold the lines along their entire length. Garrisoned with men and artillery, the lines posed formidable obstacles even to large enemy armies, but without troops in them, the lines were little more than inconveniences for main forces. More than once Marlborough would prove apt at surprise marches designed to cross French lines.

Along the Rhine in 1702, German troops under Louis of Baden closed in on Landau. A French army commanded by Marshal Catinat moved north from Strasbourg to break the siege if possible, but Baden blocked them at Wissembourg. Baden's troops surrounded Landau from the spring, and the actual siege lasted through most of the summer; the garrison capitulated on 9 September. Landau's resistance essentially forestalled any other offensive schemes. And while the siege occupied Baden, Max Emanuel, the elector of Bavaria, captured Ulm on the Danube by a *coup de main* on 8 September. Soon after this success, Catinat dispatched Villars with troops to support the elector. When Catinat sent Villars still more reinforcements, the latter commanded most of the army, some 17,000 men, and with these troops Villars defeated 14,000 imperials under Baden at the Battle of Friedelingen on 14 October. This victory in the Black Forest opened the path between Elector Max Emanuel on the Danube and the French on the Rhine. Thus Villars gained the advantage in the first of several successful campaigns that he conducted in Germany during the war.

In Italy Vendôme assumed command after the startling, and embarrassing, capture of Villeroi at Cremona. Louis seemed determined to hold on to Italy and committed considerable reinforcements to this front. Fighting resumed east of Milan, around Mantua. This was Spanish territory, and the new king Philip V arrived with more reinforcements from Naples to take personal command. Vendôme and Philip pushed Eugene back across the Mincio River, saved Mantua, and, in July, took Reggio and Modena. Eugene saw his foothold in Italy diminished and finally threatened altogether. In a desperate but necessary action, he attacked the French at Luzzara on 15 August. The tough fighting there inflicted 4,000 casualties on the French, while costing Eugene 2,000, but at the end of the day Eugene withdrew from the field of battle. His attempt to break through the French position had failed, but the damage was so great that Vendôme did not risk another battle that year, so Eugene was able to hold on south of the Alps. Still, by the end of the campaign the French had regained most of what they had lost to Eugene the year before. Just as along the Rhine, the French in Italy got the best of their foes.

Louis dispatched a small army to Spain to shore up Philip's forces there, but there would be little campaigning in Spain during the first few years of the war. The major action of 1702 came with an Anglo-Dutch amphibious assault on Cadiz. In July Admiral Rooke sailed with a formidable armada of fifty warships and transports carrying 14,000 troops commanded by Ormonde. They anchored off the port on 23 August and disembarked a few days later up the coast and marched against Rota. The allied land force spent the next month in a futile advance on Cadiz, then reembarked and sailed off at the end of September.

On the voyage back toward the English Channel, Rooke, who had never favoured the Cadiz expedition, learned of a target that suited him better, the Spanish silver fleet. Escorted by a small French fleet under Château-Renault, it had left Havana in July and anchored in Vigo Bay on 23 September. Rooke arrived off the bay with his fleet on 22 October. The next day, after taking the forts guarding the bay's entrance and cutting a boom across the water, the Anglo-Dutch force overwhelmed the French and Spanish fleet at anchor in the bay. Château-Renault lost all thirteen of his war vessels, most of which were burned by their crews, making Vigo Bay a major naval disaster for the French. Although Rooke sailed back to England with a rich haul of £14,000 of silver, the Spanish had unloaded the great majority of the silver before the battle. Even with the loss to the English and Dutch, this turned out to be the largest amount of silver ever pocketed by the Spanish treasury in a single year, and much of it went to support the war effort. By demonstrating Anglo-Dutch power in the Atlantic, victory at Vigo Bay helped to convince the Portuguese king, Pedro II, to change sides, and on 16 May 1703 he joined the Grand Alliance.

Beyond the regular military and naval campaigns, 1702 realized one of Louis's abiding fears – a Protestant revolt within his kingdom. This revolt of the Camisards, named after the white shirts the rebels wore, took place in the southern province of Languedoc in the plain around Nîmes and in the rugged hills of the Cévennes further inland. The root cause of the Camisard revolt was religious persecution, but pressures that taxation put on the suffering community also contributed to the rising. Shortly after the revocation of the Edict of Nantes forced conversions among the overwhelmingly Protestant people of this area, prophets appeared among the *nouveaux convertis*. The epidemic of prophets, usually youths, spread, and they seemed to have become omnipresent by 1702. This kind of religious fervour troubled the provincial *intendant*, Lamoignon de Bâville, and he ordered harsh methods to control the dangerous 'fanaticism'. These included threats of imprisonment and even death to the parents of the young prophets. Bâville's severity mirrored that of the local Catholic clergy. One of Bâville's administrative agents, and a clergyman as well, the abbé Chayla, had made several arrests and detained these prisoners in his residence. On 23 July 1702 a Protestant mob stormed the house to free the unfortunates held there and stabbed Chayla to death as he tried to escape.

The revolt set off that day would last in its most intense form for two years, and sputter on until late in the war. From the outset, the revolt turned extremely brutal. The military commander of the area, the duke of Broglie, scattered small garrisons across the countryside in an attempt to quell these troubles, but violence between the outposts and the population escalated.

Unlike the case in so many other risings, no nobles stepped forward to take leadership of the revolt, instead the Camisards found their commanders among the more humble people who made up the bands. The most notable chief was Jean Cavalier, only twenty at the start of the troubles. Cavalier led forces in the plains, while another successful rebel leader, Rolland, stalked the hill country of the Cévennes.

Royal authorities fought the rebels with local militia forces and regulars. The first serious battle between rebels and royal forces took place on 11 September and resulted in a draw. Cavalier routed a force of 350 men from the garrison at Mas Rouge on 23 December, handing the king's troops their first loss. Less than a month later, Broglie himself met defeat at the head of a small force of dragoons. Particularly vicious fighting followed in February with murders and massacres on both sides. Things became so bad that the bishop of Nîmes complained, 'The churches are closed, the priests are fugitives, the exercise of the Catholic religion [is] abolished in the country and fear is spread throughout.'[11]

Foreign powers encouraged the Camisards but did little effective to support the revolt. Months before Chayla's murder, Broglie complained to Chamillart, 'The n*ouveaux convertis* are in continual

---

11 Esprit Flechier, *Oeuvres complètes*, vol. ii (2 vols; n.p., 1856), col. 1139. I have been much informed on the subject of the rebellion in the Cévennes by the work of my graduate student, Roy McCullough, from whom I have borrowed citations.

communication with the [Protestant] refugees in Holland, England [and] Geneva.'[12] Louis would later charge that the English, the Dutch, the duke of Savoy, Victor Amadeus II, and even the emperor were aiding the rebels, and, in fact, all save the emperor were involved. In May 1703 Queen Anne resolved to offer to supply arms and money to the Camisards as long as English officers accompanied the aid.[13] In July Cavalier and Rolland talked with David Flotard about an invasion from Savoy and Dauphiné. Flotard served as the personal agent of the English envoy to Victor Amadeus, Richard Hill, who masterminded the affair, supplying money to the Camisards. Later in the autumn, Victor Amadeus also played with the idea of sending forces, but neither this nor other plans ever bore fruit.

The greater the threat posed by the rebels, the more adamantly Louis desired to end this dangerous eruption. In February 1703, Marshal Montrevel replaced Broglie, much to the chagrin of Bâville, who was Broglie's brother-in-law. Bâville's bitter pen has branded Montrevel with charges of incompetence and failure, but Montrevel broke the back of the insurgency by resorting to harsh action over the next year. In April he disarmed all of Nîmes. When other military measures came up short, in September Montrevel ordered systematic devastation and thus the '*dépeuplement*' of the Cévennes, a task that continued into November.

1703

On the whole, 1703 went well for Louis. In addition to progress against the Camisards, the French held their own in Flanders, although Marlborough continued to challenge and chip away at Spanish and French defences. Louis's armies and that of his ally, the elector of Bavaria, achieved notable successes along the Rhine and the Danube. In Italy the balance remained much as it had the year before; Vendôme drove north to Trent, but failed in linking up with the Bavarians moving south in the Tyrol. Spain remained quiet in 1703. The most portentous ill omens of the year came with the desertion of first Portugal and then Victor Amadeus from their alliances with France. But the full implications of the turnabouts were as yet unclear.

---

12 Joseph Vaisette, *L'Histoire générale de Languedoc*, vol. xiv (Toulouse, 1876), col. 1550–1.
13 Letter from Heinsius to Marlborough, 8 May 1703, in B. van T'Hoff, ed., *The Correspondence, 1701–1711, of John Churchill and Anthonie Heinsius* (The Hague, 1951), p. 65.

The French would confound the main allied plan in the Spanish Netherlands in 1703, even while losing Huy. Louis confided his forces in Flanders to Marshal Villeroi from the spring of 1703 until Marlborough defeated that ill-fated commander at Ramillies in 1706. Villeroi had remained under arrest by the Austrians for six months after his capture at Cremona, but he had been released and now stood at the head of the major French army with the capable Boufflers serving under him.

Marlborough's plan for that year, what he described as the 'Grand Design', prescribed an attack on Antwerp. This was not intended to win the war in a single campaign, but simply to wreck the first line of defence established by the French in the Spanish Netherlands and take one of its two major cities. The Grand Alliance began the campaign early when forces under Marlborough and the ranking Dutch commander and engineer Coehoorn besieged Bonn, the residence of France's ally the archbishop of Cologne. Invested on 24 April, the fortress capitulated on 15 May. The Allies now held the lands of the archbishop, who had already sought refuge in France in the autumn of 1702. Immediately after the fall of Bonn, Marlborough returned to Maastricht to outline the coming campaign. He proposed sieges of Ostend and Huy to draw the French away from the vital centre at Antwerp, but the Dutch vetoed this plan. Instead, Marlborough feinted toward Huy, drawing French attention there while the Dutch general Obdam led a subsidiary army to break the French defensive line near Stekene some sixteen miles west of Antwerp in the region the French called the Pays de Waes. Obdam overwhelmed French opposition led by La Mothe at Stekene on 27 June, but allied forces did not exploit their victory. Meanwhile, Boufflers rushed troops to the threatened sector; on one single day, 29 June, this corps marched over thirty miles – a feat worthy of Napoleon. Boufflers, now at the head of 19,000 French and Spanish troops, attacked Obdam's Anglo-Dutch army of 15,000 early the next day at Eeckeren. In hard fighting, Obdam lost nearly a quarter of his force in a defeat that ended his career. Boufflers reported to Louis: 'Yesterday, Sire, a very tough and dogged combat took place between the army of Your Majesty in Brabant and that of the enemy commanded by Obdam, in which Your Majesty's army carried off all the advantage and all the marks of victory.'[14] The Allies quickly retreated and the French restored their lines.

---

14 Letter from Boufflers to Louis XIV, 1 July 1703, in François Eugène de Vault and J. J. G. Pelet, eds, *Mémoires militaires relatifs à la succession d'Espagne sous Louis XIV* (11 vols; Paris, 1836–42), vol. iii, p. 64.

The Final Contest

After Eeckeren, Villeroi and Marlborough sparred around Antwerp for some time, but the Dutch commander Coehoorn finally vetoed the project in August. Then Marlborough committed himself to siege warfare. His first target was Huy, one of his original goals for the campaign. Louis believed that the presence of Villeroi's army would forestall any such siege, but he erred. Anglo-Dutch forces invested Huy on 15 August, and the garrison abandoned the town and moved into the castle, the oldest fortification at Huy, on 18 August. Under intense bombardment, this castle did not hold out for long. After cannon battered a large breach in the wall and the beleaguered garrison fought off two attacks, it capitulated on 26 August. The campaign ended with an allied siege of Limbourg, as Marlborough's main forces encamped around St Truiden. Invested on 10 September, the garrison surrendered on 29 September and was taken as prisoners of war. Despite the gain of Huy and Limbourg, this had been a frustrating year for Marlborough. His grand scheme had led to little, and while he was ready to engage Villeroi in battle, his Dutch colleagues would not accept such a bloody course of action.

Louis heard good news from Germany in 1703. There his most talented general, Marshal Villars, conducted an effective campaign that brought his army to the Danube, linked up with that of the elector of Bavaria, and won substantial victories. Just as the winter was loosening its grip, Villars took Kehl on the Rhine just opposite Strasbourg. Seizure of Kehl, which capitulated on 9 March, guaranteed Villars a secure bridgehead across the Rhine – a bridgehead he would need immediately, because he received orders to aid Max Emanuel, elector of Bavaria, who was contesting control of the Danube by a series of sieges. Max Emanuel's first notable target was Neuburg, which he took in early February. Marlborough wrote in late February, 'I wish wee could hear any good newse from the Uper Rhyne, but our letters from Vienna gives us but a very mallincolly prospect.'[15] After the fall of Neuburg, the elector with a modest force of 12,000 defeated a small imperial army of 10,000 at Siegharding on 11 March. Next he moved on Ratisbon, site of the imperial diet, or assembly. Arriving there on 6 April, he received the town's capitulation in a matter of days. The elector now possessed several strong points along the Danube from Ulm to Ratisbon.

[15] Letter from Marlborough to Heinsius, 27 February 1703, in T'Hoff, *Correspondence*, p. 55.

Villars sought a route to join Max Emanuel. His opponent on the Rhine, Louis of Baden, trusted in an entrenched line running about ten miles from the wooded hills just east of Bühl to the Rhine at Stollhofen. These lines of Stollhofen were already formidable and would become even more so over the next few years. He probed the lines near Bühl in mid-April but found them too strong, and Baden was understandably unwilling to come out of them. While Villars was so occupied, Marshal Camille, count of Tallard, brought troops to Strasbourg and then moved on Stollhofen, but again the lines were too tough to crack. Villars finally gave up on the lines, and, leaving Tallard in command of the Army of the Rhine, began to cross the Black Forest to reach the Danube. He reached Hornberg on 1 May, and his advanced units contacted the Bavarians on 9 May around Reutlingen.

Sending Villars into Germany did not simply offer strategic possibilities; it promised financial benefits as well. Louis instructed Villars to draw contributions from Germany in 1703 so as to 'husband as much as you can my finances which are too burdened by the immense expenses which I am obliged to bear'.[16] Villars's 1703 campaign provides the best-documented example of a field army that relied heavily on contributions to support it in the field. The acting *intendant*, Baudouin, reported to the war ministry that the treasurer of Villars's army brought with him only 450,000 livres and that, since his arrival, another 350,000 livres came in letters of exchange; to this sum, contributions added 460,000 livres, while hostages promised another 128,000 livres. According to these figures, cash impositions made by the army accounted for 42 per cent of the army's funds. This was at a time when Villars estimated the rock-bottom cost of pay and bread for his army at 531,000 livres per month. Knowing this, Louis only promised Villars 300,000 livres per month,

16 AG, A¹1676, #41, 27 April 1703, Louis to Villars in Ronald Thomas Ferguson, 'Blood and Fire: Contribution Policy of the French Armies in Germany (1668–1715)', Ph.D. dissertation, University of Minnesota, 1970, pp. 11, 180, and 190. For other appeals to raise money via contributions in 1703, see AG, A¹1675, #85, 24 February 1703, Louis to Villars in ibid., p. 190, 'You know . . . the immense expenses with which I am burdened, I hope that by your efforts they shall be considerably lightened for this winter, that you shall find [a] way to maintain my cavalry at the expense of the enemy, and draw from him enough money in contributions to be used to pay part of my troops'; AG, A¹1675, #166, 27 March 1703, Chamillart to Villars in ibid., p. 192, in which Chamillart reminded Villars that the enterprise in Germany would hardly cost the king anything as soon as Villars entered Germany; and AG, A¹1676, #106, Chamillart to Villars in ibid., p. 11fn, 'With regard to contributions you know, as I, the necessity there is to levy them as far away as possible . . . that . . . shall considerably relieve the finances of the King for the payment of the army. . . .'

urging Villars to 'act in such a way that this sum and that which you will raise in contributions will ... meet the needs of my army'.[17] Such details remind the twentieth-century reader that the need to make war feed war was never far from the mind of the early modern strategist.

When meeting Max Emanuel in a warm and emotional encounter, Villars surprised the elector with a daring and probably overly ambitious plan to march directly on Vienna in two bodies while wreaking destruction as they advanced. Vienna, Villars argued, would be hard put to face an attack by the large combined forces of France and Bavaria; in fact, this would be even more of a problem than he realized, because Rákóczi had finally succeeded in launching his rebellion in Hungary that year.

At first Max Emanuel complied, but he soon scuttled Villars's scheme. To Villars's dismay, just as the plan was being set in motion, Versailles ordered Villars to serve under the orders of the elector, and the elector decided against the manoeuvre on Vienna when his forces received a rebuff at Amberg. Villars fumed. At this point he also embarrassed himself by insisting that his young wife join him on campaign; the wags insisted that it was because he feared her amours at Versailles. Louis highly disapproved of this action. In opposition to Villars, Max Emanuel resolved on a campaign in the Tyrol and called for Vendôme to drive north to meet him. The elector advanced, but Vendôme did not act quickly to join him, as will be seen, and the elector began to withdraw from the Tyrol on 19 July. In the meantime, Villars simply held the Danube from Ulm to Donauwörth. Allowed this respite, imperial forces rallied and began to march on the Danube.

Back along the Rhine, Tallard and the duke of Burgundy, who held official command of the army, gained successes over the distracted German forces. With 24,000 troops, Burgundy and Tallard besieged Breisach from mid-August to 7 September. The surrender of Breisach after such a short defence so infuriated the emperor that he ordered the commander beheaded. After this victory, Tallard crossed the Rhine, advanced north, and invested Landau on 12–14 October.

---

17 AG, A^{1}1676, #183, 20 August 1703, letter from Baudouin; AG, A^{1}1675, #143, 22 March 1703, 'Dépense pour un mois de trente jours', memoir by Villars; AG, A^{1}1676, #41, Louis to Villars, 27 April 1703, the text actually says 30,000 livres, but by checking surrounding correspondence, it is clear that this was a copyist's mistake and that 300,000 was the correct figure; Ferguson, 'Blood and Fire,' p. 180, gives the figure as 30,000. For another case, see the following documents from the Archives Nationales concerning French troops in Italy, 1701–4: G^{7}1775, #54; G^{7}1775, #322; G^{7}1776, #466.

While the siege progressed, Tallard heard that the prince of Hesse-Kassel was advancing with an army of 22,000 troops. With only about 18,000, Tallard came out of the siege lines and defeated the prince at the Battle of Speyer on 15 November. Having lost as many as 8,000 men, Hesse-Kassel withdrew, and Landau fell to the French two days later.

Through all of this, Baden had brought an army from the Rhine to the Danube to redress the balance, and other forces closed in. Max Emanuel, now out of the Tyrol, joined with Villars on 1 August. After an acrimonious week without agreement, the elector ordered Villars to march with him on Augsburg, but by the time they arrived, Baden had already slipped past and manned the defences so stoutly that an attack was out of the question. Heated words flew between Villars and Max Emanuel, and finally Villars asked to be relieved. Before this could happen, however, Villars learned that an enemy army under the imperialist general Count Styrum had begun to march on Donauwörth. Villars summoned Max Emanuel to join forces with him and fall on Styrum. On 20 September the foes fought on the banks of the Danube at Höchstädt, where Max Emanuel and Villars in command of 23,000 troops inflicted a severe defeat on Styrum, who commanded 18,000 that day. The battle was a particularly confused and bloody affair, with the total number of dead and wounded mounting to as many as 12,000.[18] Villars wanted to exploit the victory by pursing Styrum, but the elector commanded a renewed attack on Augsburg. However, Baden remained too firmly entrenched to be pried out of Augsburg, and this final disappointment led to a last exchange of insults between Villars and Max Emanuel. It should be noted that hostility between Villars and the elector arose not simply over military operations but over money as well, because Max Emanuel, hard-put for funds, claimed the right to skim off two-thirds of the take from contributions as his price. With such rancour between the two, Louis XIV felt compelled to replace Villars with the more compliant Ferdinand, count of Marsin, while Villars returned to Versailles in disgrace. After his departure, Augsburg finally fell to the elector in December after a short siege. Marsin then set up his headquarters in the city.

The Italian campaign of 1703 brought little significant military action, although Vendôme's operations there were supposed to be tied closely

---

[18] Claude C. Sturgill, *Marshal Villars and the War of the Spanish Succession* (Lexington, KY, 1965), p. 49.

to Franco-Bavarian manoeuvres in Germany. After some fighting around Bonanella and Bersello during February, March, and April, the campaign season began in mid-May. Vendôme split his field forces into two armies, one under his personal command and the other under Vaudémont. They totalled about 40,000 men, against which the Allies could muster only about 23,000 troops.[19] Eugene had returned to Vienna to preside over the Imperial War Council, so Starhemberg exercised command over imperial forces in Italy. When requested by Max Emanuel to march north to link up with Bavarian forces driving south in the Tyrol, Vendôme complied but only after delaying several weeks before even acknowledging the elector's request. Vendôme reached Trent late in August, but this was too late to aid the Bavarian thrust. After bombarding the town on 5–6 September in response to Trent's refusal to pay contributions, Vendôme withdrew south to deal with a looming crisis in Lombardy.

While Vendôme's troops were off on what turned out to be a futile campaign, Victor Amadeus negotiated with the Grand Alliance to change sides. Learning of this defection, Vendôme surrounded, disarmed, and took prisoner most of the Savoyard troops in Lombardy on 29 September. The duke immediately closed the gates of Turin to the French and concluded a formal treaty with the Allies on 8 November. With Starhemberg's aid, the duke fought as best he could to hold off the French the following winter, but Franco-Spanish forces began a systematic conquest of Piedmont and Savoy that steadily progressed over the next two years, leaving the embattled duke isolated at Turin.

In Spain, Philip V arrived from Italy to enter Madrid in January 1703. He immediately threw himself into war preparations, including raising more troops. Fortunately for him, he would have time to carry out this labour, as 1703 was another quiet year in Spain.[20] Far to the east, the Habsburg candidate for the Spanish throne, Archduke Charles, was crowned King Carlos III in Vienna on 12 September 1703 and left within days to travel first to England and then sail for Portugal, where he arrived on 4 March 1704. This ensured that 1704 would be far from quiet.

---

19 French forces as battalions and squadrons from Charles Sévin, marquis de Quincy, *Histoire militaire de Louis le Grand roi de France* (7 vols; Paris, 1726), vol. iv, pp. 148–51, then multiplied by discounted sizes of 420 men per battalion and 130 men per squadron. Imperial forces from ibid., vol. vi, pp. 156–7.

20 Ibid., vol. iv, pp. 218–19, has Berwick arriving in Spain with twenty-one battalions and nineteen squadrons in early 1703, but Henry Kamen, *The War of Succession in Spain, 1700–15* (Bloomington, IN, 1969), p. 11, says first French troops entered Spain in February 1704.

1704

The war's course shifted sharply in 1704. Thanks to Marlborough's genius, the fighting along the Danube went from near disaster for the Grand Alliance to absolute triumph at Blenheim on 13 August. To be sure, with Marlborough in Germany, the situation stagnated in Flanders, but the Grand Alliance made progress against Philip V in Spain. An Anglo-Dutch force seized Gibraltar and then frustrated a French effort to recapture it at the naval Battle of Velez-Málaga. Still, Louis could take some small comfort from victories in Italy against Victor Amadeus and by an end to the worst troubles in the Cévennes. At Blenheim Louis's armies lost a major land battle, thus ending French confidence in their invincibility, and Bavaria was effectively knocked out of the war. Yet if hindsight tells us that 1704 ushered in a string of allied victories and French defeats, Louis could view the year at the time as simply an awful anomaly.

The Blenheim campaign

The Blenheim campaign dominated 1704; it also provides one of the greatest examples of marching and fighting before Napoleon. Were he to have fought only this campaign, the duke of Marlborough would still rate as one of the most outstanding generals of early modern history. Still, Marlborough did not break the mould of contemporary warfare so much as he displayed its full potentials and abiding limitations.

Concern for the fate of Vienna and the need to ensure the continuing involvement of the emperor in the Grand Alliance explain the great efforts of 1704. Although the French had not taken Vienna and driven the emperor from the coalition in 1703, they meant to bring more troops into the theatre and try again. Pressed by the French and Bavarians to the west and the Hungarian rebellion to the east, Austria faced the very real possibility of being forced out of the war. Frustration in Flanders had originally convinced Marlborough to make his primary effort along the Moselle in 1704, but repeated appeals by the emperor's ambassador, beginning in the autumn of 1703, convinced Marlborough and Queen Anne of the absolute necessity of sending aid to the Danube. Marlborough resolved to march into Germany, forestall a French and Bavarian advance on Vienna, and possibly force Bavaria out of the war as well. In April Marlborough drafted his design, and from the start he resolved to mislead the Dutch, whom he regarded as the primary obstacle to his bold gambit.[21] To

---

21 He first put this plan on paper on 29 April: 'My intentions are to march all the English to Koblenz, and to declare here that I intend to command on the Moselle. But

deceive his Dutch allies he pretended simply to move his English troops to the Moselle, a plan approved by The Hague, but there he slipped the leash and rushed to link up with Austrian forces in southern Germany. Marlborough's march was a monument to mobility. He left Bedburg, about eighteen miles west of Cologne, with about 20,000 English troops near the Meuse on 19 May and reached Launsheim on 22 June; thus, in five weeks he covered a distance of roughly 250 miles, an exceptionally impressive distance for the time, in such a fashion that the troops arrived in fighting trim. Captain Robert Parker, who took part in the march, explained:

> We frequently marched three, sometimes four days, successively, and halted a day. We generally began our march about three in the morning, proceeded about four leagues, or four and a half each day, and reached our ground about nine. As we marched through the countries of our Allies, commissaries were appointed to furnish us with all manner of necessaries for man and horse; these were brought to the ground before we arrived, and the soldiers had nothing to do, but pitch their tents, boil their kettles, and lie down to rest. Surely never was such a march carried on with more order and regularity, and with less fatigue both to man and horse.[22]

The daily rate of march was not unprecedented nor even particularly fast, since it averaged less than 7.5 miles per day, figuring in the days of rest, or, as Parker testifies above, reaching 13 miles on the days the army was in motion. Certainly Marlborough did not outmarch Turenne, Créqui, or even Boufflers. What stands out is the total distance covered, the ability to sustain the march for so long, and the fine condition of the troops when they arrived. At the base of this triumph of mobility lay excellent logistic arrangements. So thorough was he that he even arranged to have shoes stockpiled for his troops at Frankfurt and distributed to his foot-sore soldiers. Marlborough did not rely on a Napoleonic style of foraging to live off the country, but employed a form of the *étapes* system common to armies of the period, in which local authorities supplied food at predetermined

---

when I come there to write to the [Dutch] States that I think it absolutely necessary, for the saving of the Empire, to march with the troops under my command and to join those in Germany....' George M. Trevelyan, *England Under Queen Anne: Blenheim* (London, 1930), p. 344.

22 Parker in David Chandler, ed., *Robert Parker and Comte de Mérode-Westerloo: The Marlborough Wars* (Hamden, CT, 1968), p. 31.

stops along the course of a march.[23] The golden key to Marlborough's success was the cash that he brought with him in his strongboxes, a luxury extremely rare or even impossible for other armies of the period. With such treasure he could pay for the foodstuffs on the road, a practice that guaranteed supplies would continue to be supplied.

As he advanced, Marlborough kept the French guessing until after he crossed the Neckar. The march to the Moselle suggested that he would attack up that river; thus, while Villeroi with 30,000 French troops drawn from Flanders shadowed Marlborough's advance, the French marshal thought not of intercepting the column but of guarding the Moselle. Even the Dutch did not learn the Moselle was not Marlborough's true object until after he had reached it. Then at Koblenz Marlborough crossed the Rhine and continued south. He ordered pontoon bridges thrown across the Rhine near Philippsburg to mislead the French that he intended to attack Alsace. This forced Villeroi, who continued to follow Marlborough's advance, Coingies who protected the northern flank of Alsace with 10,000 troops, and Marshal Tallard, who commanded 36,000 men near Lauterbourg, to stay on the left bank of the Rhine.

As Marlborough marched south his army grew to 40,000 troops with the addition of Hanoverian, Prussian, Hessian, and Danish contingents. This force rendezvoused at Launsheim with the 40,000 men commanded by Louis of Baden and then continued on to the Danube, where 10,000 men under Styrum observed Ulm. Well down the river, the Austrians also had some 20,000 troops covering Vienna. Eugene stayed behind on the Rhine with 28,000 in the lines of Stollhofen to keep Tallard and Villeroi from joining Marsin and the elector. Marlborough hoped to enjoy an advantage along the Danube, because the French and Bavarian troops massed there did not equal his numbers. In mid-May, Tallard had brought another 10,000 recruits to reinforce Marsin and the elector of Bavaria, but Marsin's army now totalled only 35,000 men, to which must be added Bavarian units.

Lacking siege artillery, Marlborough could not crack the very tough nut of Ulm; besides, he could not afford to become bogged down in a formal siege. Therefore, he skirted this fortress and Lauingen to pounce instead on Donauwörth, where he could secure a bridge across the Danube. Donauwörth lacked modern permanent fortifications, but its garrison of 10,000 French and Bavarians under d'Arco

---

23 On the *étapes* system see John A. Lynn, 'How War Fed War: The Tax of Violence and Contributions During the *Grand Siècle*', *Journal of Modern History* 65, no. 2 (June 1993), and *Giant of the Grand Siècle*, pp. 132–40.

had done their best to improve its medieval walls and to create a large entrenched camp on the adjoining Schellenberg Heights. To the surprise of the garrison, the allied army reached Donauwörth on the afternoon of 2 July. Marlborough convinced the normally cautious and staid Louis of Baden to agree to an immediate assault, for again Marlborough reasoned that he lacked both the guns and the time to engage in a more formal attack. He chose to attack the entrenched camp rather than the town. Shortly after 6 p.m., Marlborough's troops stormed the camp at some distance from the town, and in order to repel this assault, d'Arco drew troops from the section of the entrenchments where they joined the old town walls. This was now where Baden charged and broke through the allied defences, cutting d'Arco off from Donauwörth. By 8.30 p.m. the garrison had been routed, and the survivors fled across the Danube to safety as best they could. The allied army lost about 5,000 killed and wounded, a heavy price to pay, but Marlborough had spilled blood to save time. D'Arco lost fully half his forces in the crushing defeat.

Marlborough did not gain the full fruits he might have expected from the Battle of Donauwörth, because he was unable to impose terms on the elector of Bavaria. The French and Bavarian army concentrated behind strong defences at Augsburg and defied the Allies. In response, Marlborough and Baden ravaged Bavaria with a ruthlessness that rivalled the devastation of the Palatinate in 1689. The elector came close to succumbing to this pressure but he learned that a large French army under Tallard was marching to his relief. With strengthened resolve, Max Emanuel held out; however, he dispersed many of his forces to protect his personal estates, a move that wasted troops he would later need.

As Marshal Marsin and the elector waited at Augsburg, Tallard and Eugene headed east from the Rhine. After his own long march from Flanders, Villeroi reached Landau on 9 June and conferred with Tallard immediately after his arrival. They drafted a plan to overwhelm Eugene, still holed up behind the lines of Stollhofen, but Louis XIV vetoed the scheme and instead ordered Tallard to march off to join the elector and Marsin, while Villeroi remained on the Rhine. When the orders arrived, Tallard headed for Strasbourg on 28 June. Tallard's army crossed there on 1 July and remained at Kehl on 2–3 July, before moving south toward Freiburg, reaching Emmendigen on 7 July. There 2,500 peasant carts joined the army to carry its foodstuffs. The route of march then passed through Hornberg and to Villingen, where Tallard delayed for six days to besiege the small fortress but abandoned the effort and took to the road again on 22

July, covering the eighty-five miles to Dulmunling near Ulm in seven days – a rate of march exceeding Marlborough's. Villeroi's speed is even more surprising because, unlike Marlborough, he had to cart his supplies with him. What delayed Villeroi most was not his slow progress on the roads, but his decision to try to take Villingen.[24] Still, the French suffered much more on their march than had the English under Marlborough; the hard-put French forces seem to have lost as much as a third of their strength on the road owing to straggling, desertion, and attacks by the local German peasants. As Mérode-Westerloo reported, 'The enraged peasantry eventually killed several thousand of our men before the army was clear of the Black Forest.'[25]

Tallard's troops continued on to Augsburg, which they reached on 3 August, and with their arrival the French and Bavarian armies assembled there mounted a combined field force of 60,000 men. After a bit of rest, this army struck camp on 6 August and marched towards Lauingen, where it crossed the Danube on 10 August.

Meanwhile, Eugene responded to Tallard's departure from the Rhine by hurrying to the Danube with a cavalry-heavy army of eighteen battalions and sixty-two squadrons, after leaving thirty battalions and twenty-eight squadrons in the lines of Stollhofen to hold off Villeroi. On 7 August Marlborough, Louis of Baden, and the newly arrived Eugene met and decided that Baden should lead a force of 15,000 men to besiege Ingolstadt, while Marlborough and Eugene faced off against the Franco-Bavarian field army.

Eugene, whose troops had set up around Höchstädt, fell back from there on 10 August and rushed off a message to Marlborough, who concentrated his army on Donauwörth to counter the Franco-Bavarian advance. Marlborough and Eugene linked up on 11 August. The next day Tallard camped behind the Nebel River near the village of Blenheim. Tallard's French troops rested their right flank on the

---

24 Much is said of how rapidly Marlborough moved and how slowly Tallard marched. Chandler, *Marlborough as Military Commander*, p. 136, writes: 'Tallard's progress was almost pitifully slow.' On the march from Kehl to Villingen, a span of 75 miles covered in 13 days, Tallard averaged only about 6 miles per day, when days off are counted. This was slower, but not greatly slower, than Marlborough's average of 7.5 miles per day counted in the same way. Villeroi's last week on the march equalled Marlbrough's most rapid pace for the entire week. Had Villeroi not stopped to besiege Villingen, he would have marched 160 miles in 20 days, or 8 miles per day overall, a rate in excess of Marlborough's average. This simply shows that Marlborough's march was not that out of character for an early modern army.

25 Mérode-Westerloo in Chandler, *Robert Parker and Comte de Mérode-Westerloo*, p. 160.

Danube near Blenheim and their left on Oberglau. Farther to the left, the combined forces of Marsin and the elector held from Oberglau to Lutzingen. Against this position, Marlborough and Eugene, both of whom had moved their camps forward to Münster on 12 August, advanced early in the following morning.

Franco-Bavarian forces did not expect battle that morning, nor were they well placed to receive it. Even as opposing battalions marched into position, the French continued to believe that this was only a demonstration, but when allied intentions became obvious, they hurriedly assembled. Cannon fire signalled foragers to return; troops rushed into battle formation without striking their tents. Behind the Nebel, troops of Marshal Marsin and the elector of Bavaria quickly formed up as one body, while to its right, Tallard's men hastily stood to as a separate force. Thus, the French and Bavarian soldiers on the field deployed and fought essentially as two armies rather than as one. Moreover, the centre of the Franco-Bavarian line where the two forces met was held by unsupported cavalry. Tallard apparently relied upon the marshy banks of the Nebel to hobble any allied advance between Oberglau and Blenheim, but the ground, though difficult, was hardly impenetrable.

Marlborough and Eugene launched their combined forces of 56,000 men toward the French and Bavarians at about 12:30 p.m. Recognizing Oberglau and Blenheim as keys to his foes' line, Marlborough attacked them to draw his opponents' attention. The French overreacted and concentrated too many troops in the towns, particularly in Blenheim. Although the commander there, Clérambault, beat back the initial English assault, he called for Tallard's entire infantry reserve, so by 2 p.m. the French had crammed twenty-seven battalions and twelve dismounted squadrons in and around Blenheim. Tallard, off consulting with Marsin on the left, was not there to overrule Clérambault. This blunder wasted troops – most of the men in Blenheim could not even bring their flintlocks to bear against the enemy – and denuded the centre still more. While Blenheim swallowed up a disproportionate number of troops, Oberglau too witnessed hard fighting but held. Even further to the left, Marsin and the elector enjoyed a numerical advantage and blunted Eugene's attack.

This battle established Marlborough's classic tactic of threatening the flanks of a foe and then smashing through a weakened centre. As the fighting raged around Blenheim and Oberglau, he massed a considerable force of eighty-one fresh squadrons and nineteen battalions in the open ground between the towns, where the French could oppose

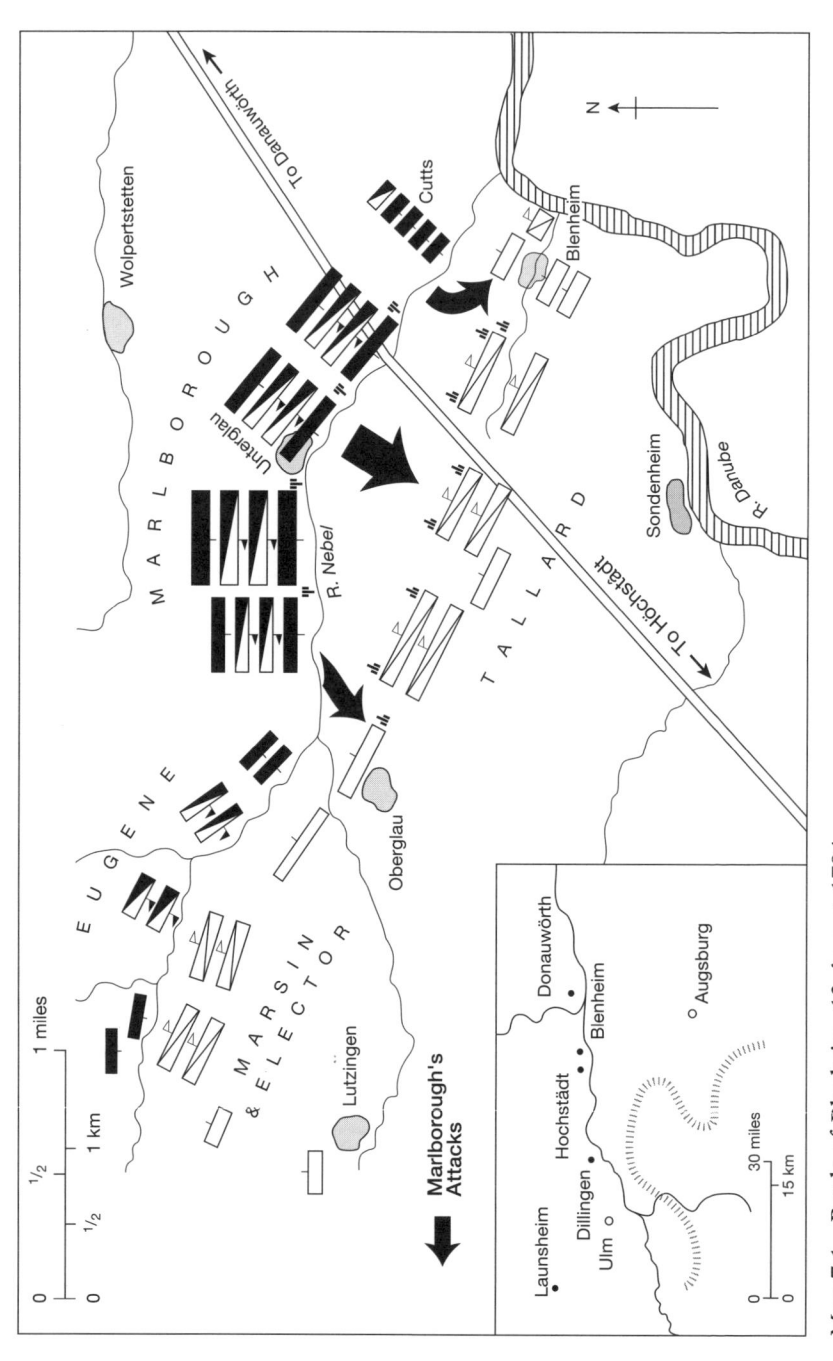

Map 7.1 Battle of Blenheim, 13 August 1704
Adapted from: J. F. C. Fuller, *A Military History of the Western World*, vol. ii (New York, 1955)

him with only sixty-four tired squadrons and nine battalions of recruits. Tallard had little else to commit, and Marsin and the elector failed to send him any aid. Initial French charges bought a bit to time, but a final allied offensive at about 5:30 carried all before it. Losses mounted quickly, and even Tallard fell into enemy hands as he tried to make his way to Blenheim. Seeing the centre collapse, Marsin and the elector thought only of withdrawal. By 6 p.m. the mass of French troops bottled up in Blenheim were entirely surrounded, but they still might have fought their way out. Unfortunately, Clérambault had deserted his men and drowned in the Danube, so the French lacked effective leadership. British Lieutenant-General the Earl of Orkney then bluffed and blasted French battalions into surrender one by one. The total number of Franco-Bavarian troops captured that day reached 14,000, and the Allies also seized a hefty toll of sixty French and Bavarian cannon as trophies. On the battlefield, as many as 20,000 French and Bavarians lay dead or wounded. The Allies suffered heavily with 13,000 casualties, but such a large butcher's bill purchased an overwhelming victory.

Blenheim led to immediate and great consequences. Defeated French and Bavarian troops streamed back to Ulm, where they rested for some days and then continued to withdraw toward the Rhine. Left isolated, Ulm finally fell in September. Villeroi advanced toward Villingen to aid the retreating forces. The remnants of the once considerable armies of Tallard and Marsin made their way to the Rhine, losing another 7,000 men along the way to desertion, and crossed that river during the last days of August and the first of September. Wrote one survivor, 'We travel with little bread, having burned a good part of our baggage. We are finally [returning to Strasbourg] with the debris of three armies.... If we erred, it was to have risked this battle at a time when French arms were glorious on all sides.'[26] For this unfortunate, a reputation had perished with the dead. Imperial forces occupied Bavaria quickly, and on 7 November the elector's wife signed the Treaty of Ilbersheim ending hostilities and allowing the occupation of Bavaria by imperial forces. Blenheim not only knocked Bavaria out of the war but allowed the Habsburgs to absorb it and its resources for the rest of the conflict.

The victorious Allies marched through Württemberg for the Rhine as the battered French withdrew. The imperials undertook a siege of Landau, where the armies under Louis of Baden and Prince Eugene

---

26 Letter from baron de Montigny-Languet, 25 August 1704, in Vault and Pelet, *Mémoires militaires*, vol. v, p. 588.

invested the fortress on 9 September. The French garrison under Laubanie conducted an active and resolute defence that occupied the best efforts of the imperials for eleven weeks, until, after the wall had been breached, Laubanie capitulated on 23 November. Villeroi did not attempt to break the siege, but camped along the Moder River, where he employed 12,000 peasant pioneers plus forty men drawn from each battalion to construct an entrenched defensive line to bar an allied advance deep into Alsace. Marlborough left his imperial colleagues at Landau and returned to the Moselle, where on 26 October he surprised and seized Trier, which the French had abandoned. Next Trarbach was invested on 3 November and fell on 20 December. But by then Marlborough had left his army, and the campaign season was well over.

French failure along the Danube stands as an even greater lost opportunity when one considers the potential of the concurrent Rákóczi rebellion in Hungary to divert Habsburg troops from Vienna. Ferenc Rákóczi returned to Hungary in May 1703 and raised his fellow countrymen, soon 'liberating' two-thirds of his homeland. In July 1704 he was elected prince of Transylvania. If Rákóczi was not immediately threatening Vienna, his insurrection tied down the emperor's forces and, therefore, opened up the prospect of victory through a two-front war against the Habsburgs. Blenheim eliminated this possibility, and Rákóczi reconciled himself to a long conflict. His forces soon suffered two setbacks in the autumn and winter, at Pata and Tymau, and he continued to lose in the field. In hopes of diverting as many imperial troops as possible to the east, Louis sent Rákóczi financial aid until the rebellion sputtered out in 1711.

Blenheim altered the course of the war, which in the main had favoured the French until then. Bavaria and Cologne were now out of the war and exploited by the Allies, while the king of Portugal and the duke of Savoy had previously joined the Grand Alliance. Thus, France and Spain now stood alone against a powerful coalition led by great military commanders. However, the oft-repeated claim that Blenheim turned back a Napoleon-like bid by Louis XIV to dominate Europe is unjustified, for Louis never harboured such a goal. The campaign in Bavaria was designed to knock the emperor out of the war and gain a favourable peace settlement, not to annex huge chunks of Germany. Considering that the war continued for another decade, claims that Blenheim ranks as a great decisive battle also ring hollow, unless substantially qualified. It could be stated that Blenheim was decisive for Bavaria and that it ended the French presence along the Danube, but that is all.

Other fronts in 1704
Flanders, usually the major theatre in Louis's wars, played only a tertiary role in the campaign of 1704. Marlborough would march from the Spanish Netherlands in mid-May, and Villeroi shadowed him south. This effectively short-circuited any major fighting in Flanders, as the Dutch were unlikely to undertake anything dramatic. Henrik van Nassau, lord of Ouwerkerk, in command of an allied army of the 50,000 troops still in Flanders, threatened the defensive lines held by the Spanish commander Bedmar near Mierdorp in early July, but was parried. He later bridged the Méhaigne and marched south to the Meuse. Crossing that river, some allied forces occupied Dinant, which had lost its fortifications by the Treaty of Ryswick, and imposed contributions on the country between the Sambre and Meuse. Then Ouwerkerk bombarded Namur on 26–8 July with over 3,000 shells, but he failed in his goal to burn the magazines in that fortress town. He then withdrew his troops from Dinant and the surrounding area, recrossed the Meuse and withdrew to St Truiden. His army outnumbered, Bedmar requested and received French reinforcements to forestall any other enemy adventures, and the campaign wound down with little more activity.

In Italy, the French under Vendôme fared well as the fighting along the Danube drew Imperial attentions and forces away from the Po Valley. Vendôme campaigned between Milan and Turin, first taking Vercelli, which he invested on 5 June and took on 20 July. Elsewhere in June, Lieutenant General, the duke of la Feuillade captured Susa. After Vercelli, Vendôme struck east, taking Ivrea on 30 September and then engaging in the long siege of Verrua on the Po, a fortress he invested on 14 October. There he would have liked to have drawn Victor Amadeus out to fight in the open field, but the duke remained behind the walls of Turin. Verrua held out through the winter, falling only on 9 April 1704. The ring was closing on the treacherous duke.

The war truly came to the Iberian Peninsula in 1704 with the arrival of Archduke Charles at Lisbon in March. The next month one of the best French generals, the duke of Berwick, arrived in Madrid to command the small French army that Louis sent to Spain. In one of the ironies of history, Berwick was nephew to Marlborough, as the former was the natural son of Marlborough's sister and James II of England. A Franco-Spanish army of 26,000 troops under Berwick and Philip V scored victories on the border with Portugal. Salvatierra fell on 8 May, Pena Garcia on 11 May, Castelo Branca on 23 May, and Portalegre on 8 June. But after this string of successes, hot weather forced a pause. The need to suspend operations during the heat of the summer typified campaigning in the Iberian Peninsula throughout the War of the Spanish Succession. Philip returned to Madrid, entering the city on 16 July, and his army went into what were called at the time 'refreshment quarters' to wait out the unbearable summer temperatures.

Warfare in Spain now shifted to waters off the Iberian coast. An Anglo-Dutch fleet of forty-nine vessels under Admiral Rooke sailed from Lisbon in May and headed for Italy, but diverted to attack Barcelona. There they were frustrated by the Spanish governor and sailed back to Portugal. Reinforced by additional vessels under Admiral Sir Cloudesley Shovell, Rooke sailed again for the Mediterranean and learned that a French fleet under the Admiral of France, the count of Toulouse, had sallied out of Toulon. Allied commanders finally decided to attack Gibraltar in order to gain a Mediterranean base from which to engage Toulouse. Rooke's Anglo-Dutch fleet reached the bay of Gibraltar on 1 August. Gibraltar then lacked the importance and aura it claimed later, and the Spanish had garrisoned it very lightly. On the evening of 3 August that meagre force capitulated, and three days later Anglo-Dutch troops from the fleet occupied the rock as its inhabitants departed. Gibraltar, of course, remains in British hands to this day.

This seizure of Gibraltar precipitated the only full-scale battle at sea between rival fleets during the entire war. The count of Toulouse with the Toulon squadron was joined by more vessels from Brest to form an impressive total of fifty ships of the line, nine frigates, nine fireships, and twenty-four galleys, a fleet bristling with 3,522 guns and manned by 24,275 sailors. Off Málaga, this armada approached Rooke's fleet of fifty-three of the line, six frigates, and seven fireships – 3,614 guns and 22,545 men – on the morning of 24 August. The French formed an unusual crescent line while the Anglo-Dutch fleet adopted the straight line-ahead in light winds. From 10:30 a.m. until 4:30 p.m. the opposing fleets battered away at each other in earnest. Both sides suffered heavily, with the Anglo-Dutch losing about 3,000 dead and the French about 1,600 dead and wounded.[27] The fleets separated during the night. An ammunition shortage in the allied

---

27 These figures come from Daniel Dessert, *La Royale: Vaisseaux et Marins du Roi-Soleil* (Paris, 1996), p. 234. Casualty estimates vary considerably from author to author.

fleet caused by the fact that many of its ships had expended much of their ball and powder in the attack on Gibraltar might have given the French considerable advantage had they opted to renew the battle the next day, but Toulouse agreed with the majority in a hastily convened council of war and decided against further combat. A more aggressive commander might have won an impressive triumph for Louis. In fact, while tactically indecisive, the Battle of Velez-Málaga resulted in an important strategic victory for the Allies, because the French abandoned their effort to retake Gibraltar and bore off for Toulon. After the failure of naval action, Franco-Spanish land forces began an unsuccessful siege of Gibraltar in October.

The return of campaigning weather brought a new French commander to Spain. When the court at Madrid ordered Berwick to march his army to Andalucia after the fall of Gibraltar, he refused to comply out of fear that allied forces mustered on the Portuguese border would attack. This act of disobedience, and conscience, cost him his command, and Marshal Froullai, count of Tessé, arrived from France to replace him. Tessé went south as ordered in February 1705 to try to speed the siege of Gibraltar, but these efforts failed, and the French gave up the siege at the end of the following April.

In Languedoc, the revolt of the Camisards wound down, a fact that, along with successes in Italy and Spain, gave Louis some modest consolation for the disaster along the Danube. Marshals Montrevel and Villars ended the worst of the Camisard revolt in 1704 through a combination of stick and carrot. The first action of the year went well for the rebels when on 15 March Cavalier defeated a strong royal force, including a sizeable element from the Regiment de la Marine, the finest regiment in Languedoc. However, success was short-lived, for on 16 April 1704, Montrevel destroyed Cavalier's force, killing 400 of the 1,000 in the band, at the Battle of Nagés, which turned out to be the critical clash of the revolt. Then on 19 April another 200 rebels perished fighting around Euzet, where the French found and seized a major rebel supply cache.

Unfortunately for Montrevel, his replacement was on the way before he fought at Nagés. Louis judged the situation serious enough to require the attentions of one of his best commanders, so on 29 March Chamillart ordered Marshal Villars to go to the Cévennes. After the fury of Montrevel, Villars adopted a conciliatory policy which brought quick rewards against a foe already badly shaken. Villars set out his approach to the king: 'I will endeavour to end the misfortunes by kindness, as severe measures appear to me not only useless, but totally contrary.'[28] The king concurred. Villars offered an amnesty to those who would quickly surrender, while threatening the sword against those who fought on. Less than a month following Villars's arrival, Cavalier asked to discuss terms and soon surrendered. The young rebel leader did not achieve all his goals, but he did win limited freedom of conscience and peace for the Protestant population. Not all followed Cavalier's lead, and Rolland opted to continue a guerrilla war which dragged on at a low level for years to come. However, on 1 October 1704 Villars could proclaim to Louis that Languedoc was pacified. Early in 1705 Villars left to resume command on the front along the Moselle, and Marshal Berwick took over in Languedoc, but there was very little left for him to accomplish.

1705

After the shocks of 1704, the next year brought a respite for the French, a respite that made Blenheim seem like a temporary deviation from a positive course. Most importantly, Marlborough was unable to carry over the momentum of victory. He began the campaign season on the Moselle, where he hoped to advance along that river and the Sarre; however, the skilful Villars now opposed him. Villars requested permission to attack the allied army, but Versailles refused, and in the meantime he entrenched his forces at Sierck. Marlborough was frustrated by Villars's unwillingness to engage him, the strength of the French lines, and the tardy arrival of imperial troops meant to support him. When Marlborough received news that Villeroi in Flanders had taken Huy and that Liège was in danger, he disengaged from Villars in mid-June and marched north. All of Marlborough's remaining campaigns would be fought in Flanders. Upon his departure, the French transferred troops from Villars to Villeroi, and only imperials remained to oppose the French on the Moselle. Villars left some forces to guard the Moselle and marched to Sarre-Louis and then on to the Rhine. North of him, allied forces abandoned Trier at the approach of French units on 27 June.

In Flanders, the French won a degree of success at first, and eventually suffered the loss of part of their lines in Brabant, but the year brought no crucial action. Villeroi began the campaign by taking Huy, which he invested on 27 May, and with the fortress's defences

---

28 Villars in André Ducasse, *La Guerre des camisards: La Resistance huguenote sous Louis XIV* (Paris, 1946), p. 160.

in ruins, the garrison capitulated on 10 June. The elector of Bavaria, who now commanded troops in Flanders, attacked Liège on 18 June; he quickly took the town, but the garrison held on to the citadel. Marlborough's march north compelled the elector to withdraw behind French defensive lines. After a brief siege, Ouwerkerk retook Huy on 12 July.

Marlborough now fastened on a plan to penetrate the French lines of Brabant, which ran about seventy miles from the Meuse just below Namur to Antwerp. His target would be the lines just south of Zoutleeuw along the Little Gheete. The lines here were formidable but not well garrisoned. As a diversion, Ouwerkerk would lead Dutch troops in a feint to the south where the lines themselves were less imposing, although better manned. The actual manoeuvre occurred on 17–18 July, and succeeded with few allied casualties. Villeroi hurriedly withdrew his troops towards Louvain, so in a matter of days the Allies held a large section of the lines from Aarschot to well south of Zoutleeuw, although that town remained in French hands.

Louvain, uncovered by the loss of this section of lines, now became a target of the allied advance. On 19 July an enemy herald approached the town and demanded that its citizens open the gates or pay contributions, but the magistrates refused. Marlborough now attempted to cross the Dyle, but Villeroi turned back the main thrust on 30 July. The Dutch, who were not as sanguine as Marlborough, restrained him as well.

The summer's campaigning was by no means over yet, however, and in mid-August Marlborough attempted to bring Villeroi to battle by a clever manoeuvre. When Marlborough advanced toward Brussels, Villeroi dispersed his forces to cover the possible targets of this move, but then Marlborough suddenly swung north toward Villeroi's camp on the Yssche River. Villeroi scrambled to prepare a defensive position. By noon on 18 August all was ready for battle, but the Dutch general balked and delayed the attack. The French used every minute to strengthen their lines. By late afternoon, it was clearly impossible to launch the attack that day, and a furious Marlborough gave up the attempt and withdrew. Villeroi claimed victory. Louis responded to his letter announcing the repulse: 'You ought not to doubt the joy that your letter of the 20th of this month has given me, and the satisfaction that I had in learning that the great stir caused by the march of Marlborough has finally ended in a shameful retreat.'[29]

---

[29] Letter from Louis XIV to Villeroi, 24 August 1705, in Vault and Pelet, *Mémoires militaires*, vol. v, p. 607.

The rest of the campaign in Flanders produced adjustments to the belligerents' positions but nothing dramatic. After allied troops abandoned Aarschot, the elector of Bavaria reoccupied and strengthened this post on the lines of Brabant, and the French also retook Diest in late October. At the same time, allied forces under General Dedem invested Zoutleeuw on 12 September, and it fell on 5 October. Crews razed the French lines from Zoutleeuw to the Méhaigne, creating a permanent gap in French defences almost twenty miles long. After these final moves, the contending armies entered winter quarters.

As Marlborough fought along the lines of Brabant, a separate force of 10,000–12,000 allied troops under General Spar campaigned to the west of Antwerp. Crossing the canal between Ghent and Bruges in early August, Spar struck into the Waes country. The elector detached troops to drive Spar back, and he withdrew across the canal after assessing contributions and seizing hostages. Spar razed a section of French lines as he retreated.

In Germany, the death of Emperor Leopold I on 5 May did not forestall military operations; he was succeeded by his son, who ruled as Joseph I. Imperial forces would make headway along the Rhine by the end of this year, as the French army there was eventually weakened by detachments. Marsin began the campaign behind the lines of the Moder, which he had improved over the winter. In July he joined with Villars, who had come over from the Moselle after Marlborough took his troops north to Flanders. They formed a joint force of 60 battalions and 100 squadrons which marched on Wissembourg and then attacked the imperial camp at Lauterbourg. However, news of Marlborough's success against the lines of Brabant decided Versailles to order Marsin to Flanders. After destroying the walls of Wissembourg so that they would be of no use to the foe, he marched north in late July. At the same time, Villars detached other troops to Italy. This left French forces along the Rhine much reduced.

Villars marched south to cross the Rhine at Strasbourg to subsist his army on enemy territory in early August. Louis of Baden crossed over to the left bank of the Rhine at Lauterbourg on 19 August, forcing Villars to return to Alsace two days later. Villars moved to Pfaffenhoffen to block Baden's route south. However, he was not able to keep the imperials from besieging Hagenau, which they invested on 28 September. Most of the French garrison broke out on 5–6 October after the imperials had refused it terms. Villars and Baden continued sparring into November, when forces went into quarters with the imperials still lodged in Alsace.

The Final Contest

In Italy the French army under Vendôme continued to solidify its hold. Even the much-praised Prince Eugene could not stem the tide of French success. Mirandola fell to the French on 10 May, before Eugene could relieve it. Meanwhile la Feuillade took the towns of Villefranche and Nice on 1 April. The citadel of Nice held out and concluded a six months' truce with the French. After the fall of Mirandola, Vendôme marched east, where Eugene's army defended a line along the Chiese, the Mincio, and Lake Garda. Once he received reinforcements, Vendôme mustered a field army of 22,000 troops, and, leaving Grand-Prieur to face off against Eugene, he turned west to attack Chivasso near Turin. He surrounded Chivasso in mid-June. On 26 July Vendôme left troops in the siege lines and came out to join with Grand-Prieur against Eugene. On the night of 29–30 July Victor Amadeus abandoned Chivasso and Castegnato and fell back on Turin. La Feuillade remained close to Turin to observe the duke. In September, la Feuillade conducted tentative siege operations against Turin and bombarded the city, but gave up the effort because of the approaching winter.

Meanwhile, Eugene had been reinforced and was marching west, crossing the Oglio. On 16 August Vendôme confronted with Eugene at Cassano on the Adda River west of Milan. In a four-hour battle, Vendôme, leading 22,000 troops, defeated the formidable prince, who commanded 24,000 that day. After his victory, Vendôme did not pursue Eugene, who retreated to Treviglio, but slipped south to Rivolta, which he considered a healthier campsite. In October Eugene left his camp at Treviglio and marched to take Cremona, but failing there he withdrew to Crema. Finally he withdrew again to Chiari and then Lonato, and Vendôme camped from Desenzano to Carpenédolo. In January the armies went into quarters. While Vendôme marched from success to success, Berwick arrived on 31 October to take command in Nice, where the citadel continued to resist the French. The citadel finally fell to his troops on 4 January 1706.

In Spain, allied forces based on Portugal advanced into Estremadura while on the Mediterranean an allied expedition took the Catalan capital of Barcelona in 1705. The long and unsuccessful Franco-Spanish siege of Gibraltar gave the Allies sufficient time to reorganize and prepare for the next campaign. On 2 May, Das Minas, the new allied supreme commander on this front, led an army of 8,000 to the gates of Salvatierra, which surrendered without a fight thanks to treachery of the fortress governor. Valencia de Alcántara fell to another allied army led by the earl of Galway after a brief siege on

9 May. Next Albuquerque fell to Galway, with its garrison marching out by the breach in its walls on 22 May. By this time Marshal Tessé had formed his army and was marching to Estremadura, crossing the Tagus on 17 May with the intention of covering Badajoz. The Allies also headed for Badajoz, which they intended to besiege. However, the timely arrival of Tessé forestalled a siege in the early summer, and soon the armies went into quarters to escape the hot weather. When campaigning began in the autumn again, Galway laid siege to Badajoz in October. Tessé again brought up his army to save the city and drove the Allies back into Portugal.

Allied triumph would not come in Estremadura but in Catalonia and Valencia that year. The Catalans had long disliked the French, who periodically invaded their province, and in addition, Catalans harboured suspicions toward a Bourbon monarchy that they feared would limit Catalan independence in the name of a more centralized state. They were ripe for rebellion against Philip V. An Anglo-Dutch fleet commanded by Shovell sailed from Lisbon on 24 July with the intention of taking Barcelona in the name of Archduke Charles, or Carlos III of Spain, as he styled himself. In order to carry out this amphibious operation the ships carried a small army led by the earl of Peterborough. This force picked up more troops at Gibraltar and on 10 August anchored at Altea. This port town came over to Carlos III, giving the Allies its first foothold in Valencia. At Altea, the Allies landed a rebel Spanish force under Juan Bautista Basset y Ramos, who proceeded to raise much of Valencia against Philip V. The siege of Barcelona began on 22 August, when the fleet of fifty war vessels anchored off the Catalan capital, cutting it off to seaward. The fleet disembarked an allied land force of some 7,000 troops, who then received the aid of 3,000 local *miquelets*. Barcelona capitulated on 9 October. On 16 December Basset entered the city of Valencia, and two coastal provinces seem to have slipped away from Philip V.

The first five years of warfare since 1701 had not led to the quick peace that Louis would have desired. He had lost his German allies, Victor Amadeus had turned against him, and in addition, parts of Spain were in rebellion against his grandson. Still, the French were hardly defeated, as they still held the key areas of the Spanish Netherlands and the Po Valley, and most of Spain embraced Philip V. Blenheim had been a severe shock, but it had not cracked the French armour, only forced Louis XIV to withdraw his armies from the Danube. For the Sun King, the worst was yet to come.

YEARS OF UNDENIABLE DISASTER, 1706–8

The next period of the war transformed French defeat from a survivable anomaly to an oppressive reality. Two key battles, Ramillies and Turin, radically reversed French fortunes in 1706 by driving Franco-Spanish forces from most of the Spanish Netherlands and all of the Po Valley. Allied troops even occupied Madrid that year. Louis gained a respite in 1707, as his armies won victories along the Rhine and in Spain, while defeating the allied attempt to take Toulon. However, 1708 brought a further collapse in the Spanish Netherlands, and the year ended with one of the great cities of France, Lille, falling into allied hands. By this point Louis was ready to accept peace on almost any terms – almost.

1706

In purely military terms, 1706 stands out as this war's *annus horribilis* for the Bourbons. Marlborough's triumph at Ramillies and Eugene's at Turin imposed the greatest loss of territory and resources Louis would suffer. The duke of Marlborough won his most outstanding, and most profitable, victory in May. The fact that the Battle of Ramillies came so early in the campaign season would allow the duke to spend the summer exploiting it to an unusual degree. The Battle of Turin had nearly as profound an effect.

For once Marlborough, who protested how hungry for battle he was, benefited from French intentions. Louis XIV wanted peace because, coming on the heels of the exhausting Nine Years War, the War of the Spanish Succession was already exceeding his means. He now believed that a display of offensive force would work to his advantage in that close match of warfare and diplomacy that defined this era: 'I see nothing that can better convince them to reach an accommodation that has become necessary than to make them see that I have sufficient forces to attack them everywhere.'[30] Over the winter the French raised new recruits and beefed up their forces. Not believing that Blenheim was a portent of the future and emboldened by what he saw as some success in 1705, Louis instructed Villeroi at Louvain with an army of 60,000 to come out from behind its works and recapture Zoutleeuw at the start of the campaign. Marsin would move north to Metz and reinforce Villeroi if necessary. As ordered, the ill-fated Villeroi left his entrenchments and advanced toward

---

30 Letter from Louis XIV to Villeroi, 6 May 1706, in ibid., vol. vi, p. 18.

Tirlemont on 22 May. Aware that Marsin would come to Flanders, Marlborough wanted to engage Villeroi before Marsin arrived. To this end, Marlborough assembled an army of about 60,000 troops near Maastricht, marched past Zoutleeuw, and advanced over the ruins of the lines of Brabant. Soon he clashed with Villeroi near the village of Ramillies on 23 May.

As at Blenheim, the French did not expect to fight that day and they adopted a defensive position that presented Marlborough with the opportunity to defeat his foe in detail. Villeroi's army, which included the remnants of the Bavarian army under the elector, formed in two lines on an arc running from the Autre Église and Offus to Taviers and Franquenée on the Méhaigne, with the village of Ramillies at its centre. This disposition, concave in relation to the allied army, stretched the available Franco-Bavarian forces too far, over three miles, and gave Marlborough the opportunity to form a more compact line within the curve of Villeroi's forces. This aided Marlborough in transferring forces along his line once the fighting began. Also, Marlborough recognized that the critical plain between Ramillies and Taviers was too broad to be dominated simply by holding those two towns. In addition, he enjoyed a numerical superiority in artillery, with a hundred cannon and twenty howitzers, and he concentrated thirty 24-pounders to batter Ramillies.

The cannonade began at 11 a.m. and continued until 2 p.m. As it lifted, Marlborough attacked the flanks of Villeroi's line.[31] Dutch guards took Franquenée and Taviers by 3:15 p.m., and a considerable body of French and Bavarian infantry and dragoons were committed to a counterattack, but this met with disaster, as the dismounted dragoons were ridden down by allied cavalry. While battle raged on the French right, Orkney led twelve English battalions in an assault on the extreme left of the French line. By 3:30 it was clear that this attack would not succeed, but it riveted Villeroi's attention to this flank. Another advance threatened the French centre at Ramillies, where Schulenberg led his troops against that village. The struggle there grew into a massive cavalry engagement just south of Ramillies, where at first the French got the better of the fighting and exposed Schulenberg's left. Now Marlborough skilfully disengaged mounted troops from his right and sent thirty-eight squadrons to reinforce his centre. The lay of the land was such that the French could not

---

31 These French details are from Quincy, *Histoire militaire*, vol. v, p. 6; other accounts put the cannonade at 1 p.m.

The Final Contest

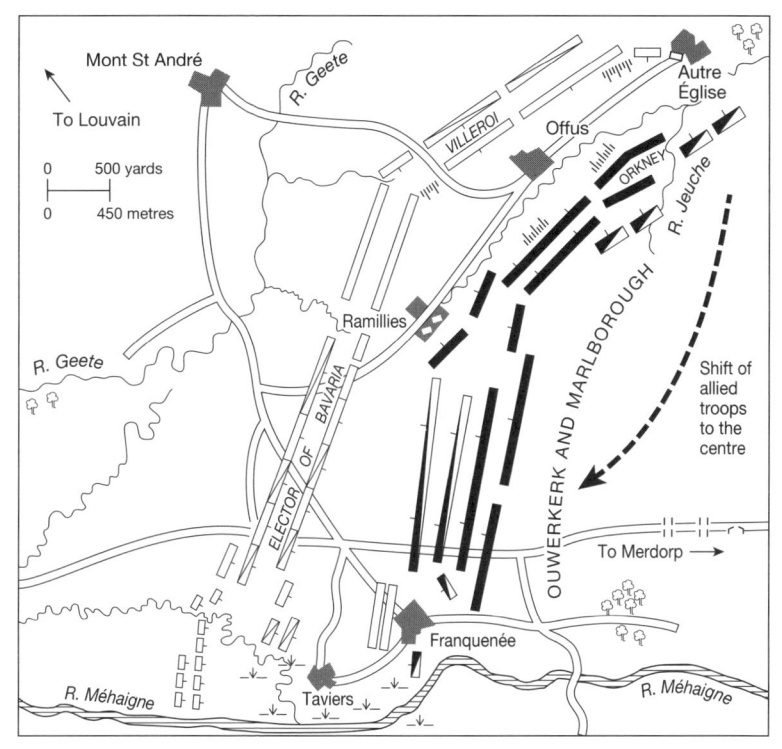

Map 7.2 Battle of Ramillies, 23 May 1706
Adapted from: David Chandler, *Marlborough as a Military Commander* (London, 1973)

clearly see this redeployment. With these fresh horsemen, Marlborough renewed the cavalry action on the plain south of Ramillies. He personally led two charges and at one point was thrown from his horse. As he remounted, a major assisting him fell victim to a cannonball that had passed between Marlborough's legs. As 25,000 cavalry thundered on the plain, the Allies enjoying a five to three advantage which won the contest there, but that success alone did not give them the battle.

The fighting subsided between 5 and 6 p.m., during which time Marlborough pulled down infantry forces from his right to further reinforce the critical attack on the French centre. Cleverly, he ordered these battalions to leave their flags in place back on the right so as to give the French the impression that the troops were still there. General

305

Gassion, who realized that troops were being pulled from the allied right to reinforce the centre, warned Villeroi, 'If you do not alter your order of battle you are lost.'[32] However, Villeroi failed to heed this advice. At 6 p.m. Marlborough ordered a renewed attack that broke the French centre, which streamed back. Victorious allied troops now rolled up the French line from Ramillies to Offus, where Villeroi tried to form a new line at right-angles to his original disposition in hopes of blocking the allied advance, but this gave way as well.

Soon the French retreat became a rout. The élite Regiment du Roi, retiring from Ramillies back to where it had left its haversacks, suffered when its men dispersed to gather up their belongings and were attacked by allied cavalry. Other regiments withdrawing through the camp they had occupied the previous evening could not maintain order among the tents, ropes, and paraphernalia of the encampment. As one participant reported, 'We had not got forty yards on our retreat when the words *sauve qui peut* went through the great part, if not the whole army, and put all to confusion. Then might be seen whole brigades running in disorder.'[33] Marlborough pressed the pursuit; by midnight he had ridden twelve miles to Meldert. In the bloody terms of that era, victory had been fairly cheap. The allied army lost about 1,100 killed and 2,600 wounded as it inflicted 13,000 casualties on the French, Bavarians, and Spanish.

Marlborough realized the great opportunity created by his victory at Ramillies: 'We have now the whole summer before us, and with the blessing of God, I shall make the best use of it.'[34] The greatest contrast between Marlborough and the other generals of his age was his resolution and capacity to increase the tempo of operations and relentlessly maintain his momentum. In no other campaign is this ability as clear as in his Flanders campaign of 1706. As he confided to his wife, 'I hope I shall do more in this campaign than was done in the last ten years' war in this country.'[35] For two weeks after Ramillies, allied forces took a string of towns: Louvain (25 May), Brussels (26 May), Malines (26 May), Lierre (26 May), Ghent (30 May), Alost (30 May), Damme (2 June), Oudenarde (3 June), Bruges (3 June), and Antwerp (6 June). As one English observer

---

32 Voltaire, *The Age of Louis XIV*, trans. Martyn P. Pollack (London, 1926), p. 210.
33 Peter Drake in George M. Trevelyan, *England under Queen Anne: Ramillies* (London, 1932), p. 115. *Sauve qui peut* means 'every man for himself'.
34 Letter from Marlborough to Goldolphin, 27 May 1706, in W. C. Coxe, ed., *Memoirs of John, Duke of Marlborough* (3 vols; London, 1905), vol. i, p. 424.
35 Letter from Marlborough to Sarah, 31 May 1706, in ibid., p. 426.

commented, 'Towns that we thought would have endured a long siege are yielding without a stroke.'[36]

However, the rapid fall of these towns did not demonstrate that victory in battle could eliminate the need for siege warfare.[37] The towns which fell were, in fact, not well fortified, and they depended for their security more on the presence of a strong army than on their walls. Villeroi had warned Louis in 1704 that 'all of Brabant remains open to the enemies... [it] does not have a single fortress which could delay an army for twelve hours without the protection of our army.'[38] This meant that after the initial gains, Marlborough confronted tougher nuts to crack, and he had to return to the laborious pattern of siege warfare. When, on 4 June, allied forces summoned Dendermonde to capitulate, the garrison refused, and the town would not finally fall to Marlborough until September. Thus, after two weeks of making impressive gains, Marlborough had to wait another two weeks for his siege train: '[W]e can advance no farther til we have our cannon.'[39] During the pause, he visited The Hague, as there was little else to do.

The French responded, but they could not regain their balance for some time. At first, Villeroi dispersed troops to strengthen garrisons, but these garrisons had to be withdrawn to reconstitute a field army. Villeroi gave up the line of the Dyle, then the Scheldt. As he fell back, French reinforcements marched toward Flanders. Marshal Marsin continued his advance with twenty-two battalions and twenty-two squadrons and arrived in the Spanish Netherlands only days after the disaster at Ramillies. Louis ordered Villars to send up an additional twenty battalions and six squadrons from his army along the Rhine, and soon after they left Villars, another ten battalions and twenty squadrons followed. So as before, the French transferred troops from one front to another, as one army became the reserve for its neighbour. When Louis XIV learned of the disaster, he recalled Vendôme from Italy, where things had been going so well, in order to transfer command in Flanders to that more able marshal. However, it would take weeks for command to change hands; Vendôme travelled first to

---

36 Col. Blackader in C. T. Atkinson, *Marlborough and the Rise of the British Army*, 2nd edn (London, 1924), p. 298, in Chandler, *Marlborough as Military Commander*, p. 179.

37 The argument and material in the following paragraph relies on Ostwald, 'Decisive Battle in Early Modern Europe'.

38 Vault and Pelet, *Mémoires militaires*, vol. iv, p. 12.

39 Henry Snyder, ed., *The Marlborough–Godolphin Correspondence* (3 vols; Oxford, 1975), vol. i, p. 566, #579.

Versailles, and then left to take over in Flanders on 1 August. After returning to court, the mediocre Villeroi would never again receive a major command. He bemoaned, 'I cannot foresee a happy day in my life save only that of my death.'[40]

The French continued to lose ground after Vendôme arrived, but not at such a fast pace. Marlborough took Menin in a siege that lasted from 9 to 18 August. Marlborough next conducted a formal siege of Dendermonde from 27 August until its capitulation on 5 September. Ouwerkerk invested Ath on 16 September and took the fortress on 2 October, capping the impressive allied gains in Flanders that year. Marlborough's drive had slowed, to be sure, but it was still very impressive. He denied the French most of the Spanish Netherlands west of the Meuse and north of the Sambre by the end of the campaign season. This was an unsurpassed operational triumph for Marlborough, but once again it was not decisive; these gains did not defeat France. Louis's armies and their Bavarian and Spanish allies now dug on a new defensive line studded with Ypres–Lille–Tournai–Condé–Mons–Charleroi–Namur.

Along the Rhine, Louis's finest marshal, Villars, returned to command French forces assembled there. However, the fact that his army would be tapped for troops to shore up the French position in Flanders limited what he could accomplish. Louis of Baden still held the lines of the Moder in the spring of 1706, and the Germans also occupied Hagenau and Drusenheim, and, thus, blockaded Fort-Louis, still in French hands. French war plans called for Villars to drive Baden out of his lines, and to that purpose Villars assembled his army at the end of April. At this point Marsin was still with Villars. On 1 May both Marsin and Villars led forces against the lines, and Baden withdrew around Drusenheim on the Rhine. Striking so early in the year, Villars had caught Baden off guard. Marsin now marched off to the Moselle, and Villars invested Haguenau and Drusenheim. After isolating these two enemy garrisons, Villars dispatched troops to open the road to Fort-Louis. The imperial troops before him retired to Lauterbourg, and Haguenau fell on 12 May. With the lines of the Moder and the fortresses in French hands, Villars marched north to Speyer. From there he levied contributions in the Palatinate. Meanwhile, the French began to build a defensive line along the Lauter River to bar the door to Alsace. As this first phase of the campaign came to a successful conclusion, news arrived of Ramillies,

---

40 Villeroi in Chandler, *Marlborough as Military Commander*, p. 179.

and Villars detached troops in mid-June to reinforce the French in Flanders.
With a weakened army, Villars still gained some advantages during the summer. Louis wanted him to besiege Landau, but he lacked the necessary forces. None the less, Villars took an island in the Rhine that flanked the formidable lines of Stollenhofen. Next year Villars would assault those lines; however, this year it was enough to hold Baden at bay.

The campaign also began with promise in Italy, though it brought disaster by the autumn. In mid-April, 41,000 French and Spanish troops under Vendôme defeated a force of 19,000 imperials and Prussians under Reventlau at the Battle of Calcinato near Montichiari in the Brecia. This battle inflicted 6,000 casualties on the shattered allied army. Vendôme pursued the defeated enemy north; during their retreat Prince Eugene joined them and continued the march toward the Trentino. Vendôme attacked and took Salo on Lake Garda. Eugene regrouped and assembled an army near Castelbardo, as German reinforcements arrived in June and July.

Back at Turin, the French began the siege intended to complete their conquest of Piedmont but which brought anything but triumph. The actual conduct of the siege fell to the duke of la Feuillade; this thirty-three-year-old lieutenant-general had succeeded to his father's title when the old marshal died in 1691. General la Feuillade owed his rapid advance in part to marrying the plain daughter of the minister of war, Chamillart. La Feuillade closed in around Turin again as he had the year before, and began digging lines of circumvallation on 14 May, although the lines did not entirely surround the city. The actual siege of the citadel on the northwest quarter of Turin began during the first days of June. This siege dragged on for three months without achieving its objective. Vauban, who volunteered for the siege but was refused as being too old to go on campaign, offered advice on how to conduct the operation, but la Feuillade and Vendôme rejected his counsel. The old master of siege warfare became so vocal in his disapproval of the techniques used there that Chamillart wrote to his son-in-law: 'Vauban announces to his friends and the world at large that he is willing to have his throat cut if you ever succeed in taking Turin by keeping up the attack on the point you have chosen.'[41] Turin

---

41 Chamillart to la Feuillade, 6 July 1706, in Christopher Duffy, *The Fortress in the Age of Vauban and Frederick the Great, 1660–1789, Siege Warfare*, vol. ii (London, 1985), p. 54.

was a particularly tough target; its modern fortifications even included a system of masonry countermine galleries designed to frustrate underground works. In addition, the large garrison of 14,700 imperial and Piedmontese troops under Lieutentant-General Wirich Daun mounted a very active defence.

As the siege progressed, armies coalesced that would meet in battle later that autumn. Victor Amadeus escaped the city with modest forces in mid-June. To the east Eugene's army grew, and Vendôme pulled back to the Adige, then the Mincio. Summoned by Louis, Vendôme departed for Versailles on 15 July, leaving command of the Italian theatre to Louis's nephew, the duke of Orléans, with Marshal Marsin serving as his adviser. Eugene outmanoeuvred Orléans, attacking Carpi and then marching for Parma and continuing to Stradella by the third week of August. This left Orléans behind and to the north, and he took much of his army and rushed west. Eugene pressed on to Turin and united with the forces of Victor Amadeus on 29 August, while Orléans linked up with la Feuillade. On 7 September Eugene and Victor Amadeus, with about 30,000 troops, attacked the French from the west. La Feuillade and Orléans boasted about 41,000 men, but they had to face in both directions, for Daun managed to mount an attack on the French camp during the battle. The long siege of the citadel had already tired and depleted the French, and now, paradoxically, they were themselves besieged, with the enemy assaulting them from both sides. Orléans and la Feuillade suffered a crushing defeat, losing 3,800 dead and wounded along with an additional 6,000 taken prisoner, a total casualty list amounting to nearly a quarter of the available troops. Among the dead was Marshal Marsin. After the battle, the beaten French retired to Pinerolo. Far to the east French and Spanish troops won the Battle of Castiglione near Brescia on 9 September, but this smaller contest could not undo the harm of Turin. Italian towns fell to the allies after Turin just as had Flemish towns after Ramillies. Novara capitulated on 21 September; soon other fortresses, including Pavia, Alessandria, and Casale, were in allied hands. The Battle of Turin proved to be an even more influential victory than Ramillies, for the Convention of Milan signed on 13 March 1707 essentially handed over all of the Po Valley to the Allies. French garrisons in Lombardy and Mantua were free to return to France with their baggage; prisoners were to be set free. Louis had lost northern Italy, but at least he had rescued some valuable troops.

Bad tidings also came from Spain. Having lost Barcelona in 1705, Philip V resolved to retake it early in 1706, and to this end he joined the Franco-Spanish force that Marshal Tessé had assembled at Caspe in Aragon. They advanced on the Catalan city, which they reached on 3 April, and Tessé besieged Barcelona with a combined army of 24,000 troops aided by a French fleet from Toulon under Toulouse. However, the arrival of an allied fleet off Barcelona on 7 May forced the French ships to sail back to Toulon and doomed the Franco-Spanish effort. Tessé abandoned his camp and withdrew on the night of 11–12 May. He crossed into Roussillon with an army diminished to only 15,000 troops.

The investment of so much in the siege of Barcelona left Franco-Spanish forces weak elsewhere, particularly on the Portuguese front, and from that base the allied generals Das Minas and Galway advanced with little opposition against the Spanish capital of Madrid. Lacking troops, Marshal Berwick, who had once again assumed command in Estremadura, could do little more than observe the enemy. Das Minas took Ciudad Rodrigo on 26 May and Salamanca on 7 June. Philip fled Madrid on 25 June, and the Allies entered two days later, but it boded ill for them when crowds supposed to shout '*Viva Carlos III!*' cried '*Viva Filippo V!*' instead. The Allies continued their juggernaut by taking Saragossa on 29 June, a conquest that now gave them the four largest cities in Spain.

However, the majority of the Spanish people remained loyal to Philip, and the Allies could not maintain their armies so deep within the peninsula and so far from the sea. Reinforcements reached Berwick, so he grew stronger as the Allies' condition became more strained. In the early autumn the Allies had to abandon Madrid, and Philip V reentered his capital on 4 October. Instead of retracing their steps back to Portugal, Das Minas and Galway withdrew into Valencia in order to reestablish a safe line of communication to the sea. Archduke Charles made Valencia city his new capital. With the Allies in retreat, Berwick recaptured strongholds in Castile and Murcia. Philip suffered a severe setback in 1706, but he recovered.

1707

Louis XIV made some peace overtures in the autumn of 1706 but these led to nothing. As he confided to his grandson, 'Negotiations are not happy when not seconded by the events of war.'[42] After gaining such stunning success in 1706, the Allies rejected any compromise

---

42 Louis in Wolf, *Louis XIV*, p. 556.

and insisted on 'no peace without Spain', meaning that Archduke Charles must receive the entire Spanish inheritance. Louis, while anxious for peace, was not yet reduced to extremes. The French hoped to incite the Swedish king, Charles XII, to attack the emperor, but failed. In any case, 1707 would reward the French with important battlefield successes and salved some of the sting left from Ramillies and Turin.

Instead of extending the momentum of victory, Marlborough endured frustration in 1707. The great allied project for the year was to be an invasion of Provence and an attack on Toulon, but with so much devoted to this venture, less remained for an effort in Flanders. Marlborough wanted to campaign on the Moselle, but the Dutch vetoed his plan. And with the French busily entrenching new lines across the Low Countries, Marlborough admitted, 'And as they work to build lines and take other precautions, I want to state . . . that my hopes are not great for this front.'[43] Combined French, Spanish, and Bavarian forces totalled 123 battalions and 187 squadrons in Flanders. This outnumbered Marlborough's 99 battalions and 187 squadrons, and he would be called upon to detach troops to bolster allied ventures elsewhere as news of French victories arrived. Marshal Vendôme repeatedly requested permission from Versailles to besiege Huy, but Louis refused. Reconciled to a defensive posture, Vendôme and the elector of Bavaria needed only to distract and parry the Allies, which they did even as Louis drained off troops from Flanders to reinforce his armies in the south. Summer brought neither battle nor siege in the Low Countries. The English god of battles, Marlborough, could not dictate to fate that year.

Meanwhile, along the Rhine, Villars scored a notable triumph by breaking the enemy lines of Stollhofen, penetrating German lands, and imposing contributions. Villars's campaign would be as much financial as military, for in this war of attrition where survival was a kind of victory, resource mobilization could be everything. Louis had lost much of Flanders and its wealth, but Germany promised a rich harvest. Already in dire financial straits, Chamillart, serving both as secretary of state for war and as controller-general of finance, begged Villars's assistance. 'Remember . . . that Germany is full of abundance and that I am in great distress, since for a long time it has not been possible to support at the cost of the kingdom an expense as great as

---

43 Letter from Marlborough to the Duke of Savoy, 27 December 1706, in George Murray, ed., *The Letters and Dispatches of John Churchill* (5 vols; London, 1845), vol. iii, pp. 268–9.

that which the King is obliged to bear.'[44] A month later, the same minister appealed again: 'Take me out of the sad situation in which I find myself concerning providing funds for the armies; contributions can, it seems to me, spare the King the expense. . . . You can easily draw all the money you will need from that.'[45] According to Louis, the levying of contributions ranked as the 'principal and sole object' of Villars's army in 1707, in contradiction to Napoleonic principles.[46] So much for Napoleonic analyses of this campaign and of this war. Such evidence makes it clear that the goals of destroying the enemy's main forces or capturing his capital were hardly relevant.

The formidable lines of Stollhofen, originally built in 1703 and improved since then, stretched about nine miles from Stollhofen on the Rhine to Bühl and then on to the mountains just east of Bühl. The lines involved not only impressive defensive works but extensive inundations carried out by Dutch engineers. Louis of Baden was so confident in this defensive position that he built a fine house behind them in Rastatt. In May 1707, an army of about 20,000 troops under command of the margraf of Bayreuth defended the lines.

Against this indomitable barrier, Villars deployed 30,000 troops in a masterful plan of misdirection. He intended to threaten crossings of the Rhine on the right flank of the lines, first at the island of Dalhunden, between Drusenheim and Fort-Louis, and second, a little way down river at the island of Marquisat. These attacks, involving only four and nine battalions respectively, were only feints. At the same time, the marquis de Vivans would attempt a major crossing with twenty battalions and forty-five squadrons near Lauterbourg. With the remaining troops, Villars would advance on Bühl to hit the left flank of the lines. To deceive his enemies by giving them the impression that nothing was afoot, he scheduled a ball for the ladies of Strasbourg on the night of 19–20 May. The storm would break soon on the unsuspecting Bayreuth.

The attack began on the afternoon of 22 May and continued on the next day. At 6 p.m. the first day, with great sound and fury,

---

[44] AG, A¹2027, #98, 28 May 1707, Chamillart to Villars in Ferguson, 'Blood and Fire', p. 10.
[45] AG, A¹2027, #105, 2 June 1707, Chamillart to Villars in ibid., pp. 10–11fn. For other appeals to raise money via contributions in 1707, see A¹2027, #97, 28 May 1707, in ibid., p. 14fn, 'subsist my army at the expense of enemy country . . . aid my finances whose state you know and the need they have of aid', and AG, A¹2027, #137, 13 June 1707, Chamillart to Villars in ibid., p. 11, 'I shall receive with gratitude several million if you are in a position to send it from Germany as Prince Eugene did from the Milanais to the Emperor.'
[46] AG, A¹2027, #160, 23 June 1707, Louis to Villars in ibid., p. 240.

French troops attacked at Dalhunden and Marquisat, while Villars, who had assembled troops at Offenburg, advanced to Sasbach to observe the lines at Bühl. Meanwhile, to the north, Vivans mustered his command and during the evening and night crossed one arm of the Rhine to the island of Neuburg, where his troops dug in and brought over artillery pieces to bombard Germans on the far bank of the river. At daybreak on 23 May he sent battalions across the other arm of the Rhine to the east bank. French guns on Dalhunden and Marquisat bombarded the western end of the lines of Stollhofen as if Villars intended to cross there as well. Villars, in fact, prepared to assault the lines at Bühl and approached them to reconnoitre the enemy position that morning, but fog obscured the position. When the fog lifted, Villars realized that Bayreuth had abandoned the lines! With French troops to his front and right flank and a powerful force crossing the Rhine to his north, Beyreuth regarded the lines as too compromised to be defended, and he ordered his men to withdraw to the east, abandoning his artillery where it stood. Villars had taken the impregnable lines without casualties.

Not only did Villars win an impressive victory at no cost, but he now exploited it to support his army. He moved into Baden's fine house; and French detachments fanned out to demand contributions. One even rode as far as Ulm. Bayreuth, fearing that Villars intended to invade Bavaria once more, fell back and left Villars unhampered throughout June. Württemberg agreed to pay contributions of 2,200,000 livres, Dourlach 220,000 livres, and Baden 330,000 livres. Bayreuth and his army finally advanced towards the Rhine in July. Villars held fast to the lines of Stollhofen, but carted his booty and hostages back to the left bank of the river and put more troops under Vivans in the lines of the Lauter. The French continued to manoeuvre against the Germans on both banks of the Rhine for the remainder of the summer and into the autumn. French troops now held the lines of Stollhofen against their erstwhile defenders.

In Italy the allied parade of victory continued during the spring of 1707. Eugene entered Milan on 16 April. In May a small army of 10,000 men under General Daun marched south to conquer Naples for Archduke Charles and succeeded in doing so that summer with relatively little fighting. The centrepiece of the campaign along the Mediterranean was to be an invasion of Provence urged by the English. Designed to seize Toulon and humble the proud Sun King, such a campaign also promised to draw troops from Spain and cripple the Franco-Spanish efforts there. The main allied army, which numbered

35,000 under Eugene and Victor Amadeus, now marched south via Cuneo to Nice and then over to Toulon. This effort would require support from an Anglo-Dutch fleet, which arrived off the Italian coast in mid-June. Eugene left Turin on 1 July and his forces reached Limone-Piemonte on 3 July.

As the threat grew, Marshal Tessé, in command of French and Spanish troops, consolidated his forces and blocked the entry routes to Savoy, Dauphiné, and Provence as best he could, and reinforced the garrison of Toulon. However, he lacked the strength to bar Eugene's advance. Louis dispatched more of his troops to the front; as early as 18 June Vendôme sent four battalions south, and as the campaign progressed, more troops received marching orders. On 1 August Louis commanded that another thirteen battalions and six squadrons from Flanders go to join Tessé's army. With reinforcements, Tessé commanded enough troops in Provence to forestall any resurgence of the Cévennes rebellion in neighbouring Languedoc.

The allied advance continued: Eugene reached Sospel on 7 July, Nice on 10 July, and Cannes on 16 July. Marshal Tessé arrived at Toulon on 24 July, and put 6,000 pioneers to work building a large entrenched camp to hold the reinforced garrison of 9,000 troops under Goësbriand. After this, the marshal went to Aix and Marseilles to organize defences. Eugene and the duke of Savoy began formal siege operations around Toulon on 28 July. In fact, the Allies had already scored a signal naval victory simply by attacking Toulon. Unable to sally the warships berthed in Toulon because of the strong Anglo-Dutch fleet off shore, the French feared that these ships would be burned by the bombardment that was sure to come. Therefore, they sank fifteen ships of the line in the harbour to protect them from fire, with the intention of raising the ships after the siege. However, these ships were not raised, and their loss constituted a naval disaster on the scale of La Hogue, if measured simply by the number of vessels destroyed.

The siege progressed slowly. Although the Allies gained advantages, French counterattacks frustrated the besieging force. While reinforcements steadily increased Tessé's forces, the allied army suffered from hunger, disease, and desertion. Eugene, never enthusiastic about the campaign, only came to doubt its wisdom more, and finally the Allies withdrew on 21–2 August. Eugene went on to take Susa in October, but it hardly compensated for Toulon. True enough, the siege had cost the French fleet a number of warships and perhaps slowed French progress in Spain by drawing reinforcements to Provence, but it had also absorbed the primary allied energies and resources that year.

315

Versailles might well feel justified in considering the siege of Toulon a major allied defeat.

The campaign in Provence did not forestall the French from winning a critical battle in Spain during 1707. Marshal the duke of Noailles led French forces in Roussillon that year, while Marshal Berwick assumed command of Franco-Spanish forces in Valencia, where he faced Galway. Galway's troops had wintered in Portugal and were shipped back to Valencia for the campaign, landing there in early March. Galway assembled his forces around Xátiva at the end of March, and Berwick mustered his army at Chinchilla in mid-April. Within days, Berwick advanced toward the coast to relieve an allied siege of Villena, and Galway turned to fight him. At the resulting Battle of Almanza on 25 April, Berwick's army of 21,000 enjoyed a numerical advantage over Galway, who only had 16,000 on the field. Galway accepted the odds in an attempt to defeat the Franco-Spanish army before it received reinforcements from the duke of Orléans. Fought on the plain before Almanza, this battle was largely decided by cavalry action in only about two hours. After hard fighting, French mounted troops broke the right wing of Galway's army. Berwick's Spanish cavalry attacked Galway's left without success until the victorious French horsemen joined the Spaniards in charging and smashing it. At this point the centre gave way. Galway lost 4,000 killed and wounded and 3,000 prisoners – casualties of nearly 50 per cent. Orléans arrived the day after the victory, and he and Berwick pursued the defeated Allies. Valencia city fell to the Franco-Spanish army on 8 May, while Xátiva capitulated in June. Orléans turned north and took Saragossa in Aragon on 26 May. The Catalan town of Lerida fell on 14 October and its citadel capitulated a month later. Defeat at Almansa cost the Allies the province of Valencia and other strongholds, and by consolidating Philip's hold on most of Spain, Almansa ranks as the single most important battle fought in Spain during the war.

Elsewhere in Spain, Philip gained along the Portuguese border after the summer heat had passed. There the marquis of Bay attacked Ciudad Rodrigo with a force of only about 9,000 troops. He invested the allied-held strongpoint on 18 September and took the town on 4 October.

1708

Things had gone well for the French in 1707, giving Louis some reason for revived optimism, but 1708 would lead to a new crisis for the Bourbon cause. During this year the focus shifted back to Flanders, where Marlborough won at Oudenarde and took the great fortress of Lille. In Germany, Savoy, and Spain little of note occurred. Louis rotated his generals for 1708. Berwick left Spain in January and took command of forces on the Rhine, where he would serve with the elector of Bavaria. Villars, who had been so successful in Germany, was moved down to Dauphiné to forestall any invasion. Berwick's departure from Spain left the duke of Orléans in charge of Franco-Spanish forces there. Vendôme, who still enjoyed a good reputation, retained command in Flanders 'under' the duke of Burgundy, son of the dauphin. The shuffling of generals leaves the impression that Louis was still searching for the right combination.[47]

During the winter months, in what would become the familiar pattern, the diplomats worked while the soldiers rested, and Louis once again approached the Allies to discuss peace terms. However, his emissary Mesnager once again encountered a stone wall at The Hague in January. The terms offered by the Allies demanded the removal of Philip V from the Spanish throne, as well as the cession of Ypres, Menin, Condé, and Maubeuge. Louis, who understandably regarded 1707 as a successful year, rejected such demands as entirely out of keeping with the flow of the war on the battlefield.

Early in 1708 Louis supported a descent by James Stuart, the Old Pretender, upon the British Isles.[48] During the Nine Years War, efforts to secure the French coast against sea-borne enemy attacks and French amphibious ventures directed toward Ireland and England had consumed a great deal of energy and treasure. In contrast, during the War of the Spanish Succession the major theatre for amphibious operations was the Iberian Peninsula. However, in 1708 Louis mounted a naval expedition to land the Stuart claimant for the British throne in Scotland. At Dunkirk the French assembled a fleet of eight ships of the line, twenty-four frigates, and transport vessels under the Chevalier de Forbin. The fleet carried twelve battalions of infantry and 13,000

---

[47] There was also the issue that if Burgundy was to take command in Flanders, the Duke of Bavaria should not collide with his authority, so he would have to be sent elsewhere. But the decision to put him on the Rhine meant Villars had to be elsewhere, since the two did not get along. Tessé was dropped from major command in the shuffle, even though he could claim victory at Toulon. It should be noted that at this point Louis did have his three best generals up front – Villars, Berwick, and Vendôme. But Bavaria did come back to Flanders in September.

[48] On this expedition, see John S. Gibson, *Playing the Scottish Card: The Franco-Jacobite Invasion of 1708* (Edinburgh, 1988).

fusils, 10,000 saddles and bridles, and a similar number of pistols for rebels who were expected to rise in support of the Stuart pretender. On 16 March the troops embarked, and the whole sailed a few days later, escaping the British naval forces attempting to blockade Dunkirk. On 25 March the French fleet reached the Firth of Forth, but the approach of the British fleet under Byng drove the French off before they could land the troops. The invasion fleet sailed north and attempted to put in at Inverness, but this too came to naught, and the ships sailed back to Dunkirk. Had the landings succeeded they would have, at the very least, diverted British troops from Flanders. In 1709 the French would again consider supporting an expedition to Scotland, but this scheme was shelved in January 1710 for lack of support and finances.[49]

The armies that would oppose each other in Flanders assembled once again during May. The Franco-Spanish field army of 139 battalions and 204 squadrons under Vendôme and the duke of Burgundy formed along a line from Marchiennes to Namur, and the allied force of 113 battalions and 180 squadrons commanded by Marlborough marshalled close to Brussels. The French commanders planned to capitalize on their advantage, but disputed their first move: Vendôme wanted to besiege Huy, but Burgundy insisted on an advance against Brussels. The twenty-six-year-old prince won out, but Marlborough parried his advance, finally taking up station near Louvain during the first days of June. The French settled into camp at Raine-l'Alleud.

After a month of inactivity, Vendôme engineered a successful example of deception and finesse that caught Marlborough flat-footed and won back Ghent and Bruges. On 4 July he dispatched two detachments to take Ghent and to seize bridges on the Dendre River. To cover these operations, that evening Burgundy marched west with the main army across the Senne River as if he were withdrawing to Tournai. Meanwhile, reaching Ghent on the morning of 5 July, the French detachment under Grimaldi sent ahead a few infantry and cavalry who, pretending to be deserters, begged entry and secured one of the gates without firing a shot. Grimaldi entered and established a pro-French government before noon. At the same time the count of la Mothe with troops from Menin marched on Bruges, which he summoned to surrender. Hearing that Ghent had already

---

[49] John C. Rule, 'France and the Preliminaries to the Gertruydenberg Conference, September 1709 to March 1710', in Ragnhild Hatton and M. S. Anderson, eds, *Studies in Diplomatic History* (London, 1970), pp. 100–2.

The Final Contest

fallen, the magistrates asked to send a rider to learn the truth. Confirming that the French were in Ghent, authorities in Bruges capitulated as well. In fact, the two towns were ripe for the picking. Marlborough blamed the Dutch: 'the [Dutch] have used this country so ill that I no ways doubt but all the towns will play us the same trick as Ghent had done'.[50] With their army safely over the Dendre and the bridges broken behind them, Vendôme and Burgundy had reason to feel secure and now debated where to station their army; they chose a safe course and planned to establish a camp near Ghent across the Scheldt. The first round had gone to the French, but the fight was not over.

As the French advanced west, a column came up to Oudenarde, the last important allied fortress on the Scheldt; however, allied reinforcements arrived in the nick of time to hold this crucial bridgehead, which would soon witness another of Marlborough's victories. Before Vendôme could establish a new camp, Marlborough carried off a forced march that at one point covered fifty miles in sixty hours. Preparing eight days' bread and trimming transport to a minimum, Marlborough rushed to reach Lessines and cross the Dendre before the French could cut him off. Learning of the march, Vendôme tried to get to Lessines before Marlborough, but, failing, he veered toward Gavere with its bridge over the Scheldt. Marlborough's old ally, Prince Eugene, was also on the move. He originally formed his army on the Moselle but now marched north, reaching Maastricht on 7 July and finally rendezvousing with Marlborough three days later. On the evening of 10 July, Marlborough's army camped on the west bank of the Dendre near Lessines, while Vendôme and Burgundy bedded down on the east bank of the Scheldt near Gavere. The troops could not know they were to fight a great battle the next afternoon.

Unlike Blenheim or Ramillies, the Battle of Oudenarde was a meeting engagement, or an encounter battle; that is, the armies were not fully deployed before the fighting began but came onto the field unit by unit during the combat. Vendôme and Burgundy could not agree on a course of action on 11 July, for the latter wished to avoid combat. In contrast, Marlborough moved decisively to impose battle on his foes, with his trusted lieutenant Cadogan in the lead. By noon allied forces were crossing the Scheldt at Oudenarde. The French also moved to the right bank via Gavere. The first clash between the two armies came about 1 p.m., when allied horsemen encountered French

---

50 Marlborough in Linda Frey and Marshal Frey, eds, *The Treaties of the War of the Spanish Succession* (Westport, CT, 1995), p. 325.

cavalry, who had no idea Marlborough's army was so close. When he learned the Allies were across the river and marching toward him, a surprised Vendôme commented, 'If they are there, the devil must have carried them, such marching is impossible.'[51] The allied army of some 80,000, still crossing at Oudenarde and on pontoon bridges thrown across the Scheldt, now collided with Vendôme's 85,000 coming down from Gavere.

As is so often the case in a meeting engagement, the battle was a confused affair, but by bringing his forces up faster, Marlborough held the advantage at one point after another. At about 3 p.m., Cadogan's troops pushed forward against French cavalry at Heurne. As the French concentrated on the battlefield, Vendôme led the French right, while Burgundy took command of the left. Vendôme made headway, but his appeals to Burgundy to attack the right flank of the allied army went unheeded. The lay of the land and the fact that both armies had advanced at such a pace that their cannon were left behind rendered this primarily an infantry battle. Because Burgundy's wing was largely ineffectual, Vendôme, fighting alongside his men, bore the major weight of the battle, and by the evening his line had been hammered into a horseshoe threatened at each flank. When it seemed as if the Allies would cut off all escape for Vendôme's men, the oncoming darkness and rain allowed most of his men to pull out of the trap. Franco-Spanish casualties were high: French sources admit to 7,000 killed or captured, while the Allies claimed to have inflicted as many as 15,000 casualties, a number increased by another 5,000 deserters. There seems good reason to split the difference at a total loss of about 14,000–15,000. Marlborough and Eugene suffered 3,000 killed and wounded in the bitter combat.[52]

The consequences of Oudenarde were not as dramatic as the aftermath of Ramillies, but they were none the less substantial. The main French army withdrew to Ghent, so it did not immediately surrender its reconquests in Spanish Flanders, but these would be impossible to hold by the end of the year. Marlborough shifted south and encamped near Wervik, as his units attacked and then razed the French defensive lines near Ypres.

In the allied debate over how best to take advantage of victory, Marlborough advocated a bold advance along the coast to bypass the main French fortresses, but the Dutch, and even Eugene, found this

---

51 Vendôme in Winston Churchill, *Marlborough, His Life and Times* (4 vols; London, 1933–38), vol. iii, p. 408.
52 See Quincy, *Histoire militaire*, vol. v, p. 501, and the discussion in Chandler, *Marlborough as Military Commander*, pp. 221–2.

plan too risky. Instead they resolved upon a siege of the great fortress city of Lille, the capture of which would breach the first fortress line of Vauban's *pré carré* and bring the Allies literally to the front door of France. Lille would not be taken easily. The French were regrouping. Days before the battle, Marshal Berwick received orders to march north with troops from the Rhine, and he took up station in southern Flanders near Douai upon his arrival in mid-July. He reinforced several threatened garrisons, and then, recognizing that Lille was the likely target, Berwick marshalled 14,000 troops under the ageing Boufflers to defend the city. Boufflers further complicated the Allies' task by flooding the surrounding countryside.

After bringing supplies forward from Brussels in massive convoys, the Allies invested Lille on 14 August. The siege of Lille was not only to be long, but hungry, requiring great amounts of food, fodder, and ammunition. Eugene with 35,000 men besieged Lille, while Marlborough with 75,000 dealt with French efforts to relieve the city. Eugene opened trenches on 22–3 August. A week later the French concentrated both Berwick's troops and the army under Burgundy and Vendôme near Gerardsbergen on the Dender River. This impressive force of about 100,000 men moved towards Lille, and Marlborough expected a great battle northwest of the town, but the large French army did not attack, although it faced off against Marlborough's hastily prepared positions. Next the French tried to cut off allied forces by holding the line of the Scheldt and seizing every crossing. But Marlborough countered by shifting his lines of communication to Ostend. At Wyendael on 27 September the French attacked an ammunition convoy coming down from Ostend; in what became a battle between 20,000 French and 10,000 allied troops, the British forces frustrated the French.

The defenders as well as the attackers had to show ingenuity and effort to continue the fight. When Boufflers ran short of gunpowder in September he got a message out requesting supplies. In response, the chevalier of Luxembourg assembled a force of 2,000 cavalry, gave them each a 50-pound bag of gunpowder and ordered them to wear Dutch insignia in their hats and masquerade as allied cavalry to carry the powder through the lines to Lille. Most of the cavalry bluffed their way through, but then the ruse was discovered. During the chaos that followed and the race to get into Lille, a great many of the powder bags blew up, killing men and horses. In this incident, known as the *affaire des poudres*, some 160 French died, but those who survived delivered 40,000 pounds of powder to Boufflers. At Lille, the French smuggled some messages in and out via Madeleine

Caulier, a poor girl who worked at an inn near the city. Her brother served in the garrison, and she was allowed to cross the lines to visit him. Learning this, French officers asked her to carry messages. This she did and in return requested only that she be allowed to enlist in a dragoon regiment as a man. Her request granted, she fought well and died at the Battle of Denain.[53]

Although Boufflers conducted a very active defence, the town of Lille could not hold out for ever. The garrison attacked enemy sapping parties, contested the outer defences of the fortress, and augmented defensive works to the northeast of the town where the Allies concentrated their attack. Still, enemy artillery tore breaches in the town walls, and the Allies nullified Boufflers's efforts to plug the gaps with new defences. Finally, the attackers dug mines which could be set off soon. Thus, on 22 October Boufflers, considering further defence to be futile, offered to surrender the town, but not the citadel. As part of the agreement, three days later the French garrison withdrew into the Lille citadel, an impressive five-bastioned fortress on the west side of the town. There they would continue to bleed the Allies for another six weeks. Taking the town alone cost the Allies 12,000 killed and wounded; many more would fall before the siege was over.

While the last phase of the siege progressed, the elector of Bavaria, who had returned to Mons in September, conducted a desperate attack on Brussels to distract the Allies. He assembled an army of 14,000–15,000 troops drawn from garrisons and detachments and reached Brussels on 22 November, but, lacking sufficient forces for a siege, he simply bombarded the city. Marlborough responded by advancing towards Brussels, retaking the line of the Scheldt and its bridges, and forcing the elector to retreat lest he be cut off from his base at Mons. After this gambit failed, Boufflers beat the *chamade* on 8 December, and his garrison marched out two days later. The French had hoped that if Boufflers resisted long enough into the winter, the Allies might lift the siege, but the resolute garrison could not last that long.

The French hold on northern Flanders could not survive the loss of Lille. In an operation following the fall of that fortress, allied troops advanced on Ghent, which surrendered on 30 December, and the surrounding territory soon reverted to allied control. That winter at Versailles Louis rewarded Boufflers for resisting so long and thereby

---

53 Charles Armand Romain (pseud. for Armand Charmain), *Les Guerrières* (Paris, 1931), p. 104; Alfred Tranchant and Jules Ladimir, *Les Femmes militaires de la France* (Paris, 1866), p. 317.

The Final Contest

tying down Marlborough for the rest of the campaign, but the glory won by Boufflers could not change the fact that the French had been driven out of almost all of the Spanish Netherlands.

With so many troops concentrated on the fighting in the Spanish Netherlands, forces along the Rhine were depleted. Prince Eugene had meant to support actions on the Rhine from his position on the Moselle, but after some minor action in June, he went north to combine efforts with Marlborough. The elector of Bavaria had shifted some of his army to the Moselle, and on 6 July he received orders to detach Berwick with nearly all these troops, thirty-nine battalions and sixty-nine squadrons, to march to Flanders. Other troops on the Rhine were deployed north as well. The French were once again transferring units from one front to another as crisis overtook campaign plans. Bavaria returned to Alsace and sparred with the modest German forces remaining there under the elector of Hanover, later reinforced by General Mercy. This conflict resolved into sterile manoeuvres and foraging. Finally, on 9 September the elector of Bavaria left a subordinate in charge of his army, and travelled north to Mons, as noted above.

Franco-Spanish troops who stood in Dauphiné, in French-occupied Savoy, and on the French borders with Nice hoped simply to block any invasion of Louis's territory on that front. To deny the Allies, Marshal Villars commanded a small army of perhaps 35,000 men stretched along that mountainous frontier, and Victor Amadeus and the imperial general Daun marshalled an equal number of Piedmontese and German troops against him. During the winter and spring the French laboured to buttress their defences; Toulon's fortifications were repaired and expanded, while 5,000 workers constructed a defensive line along the Var River.

The duke of Savoy intended to storm into Savoy, still held by French troops. Allied forces advanced via Mount Cenis and the Little St Bernard into Savoy, while Villars concentrated his forces at Fort de Barraux near Montmélian. From Mount Cenis, the duke advanced along the Arc River toward Villars, but this was only a feint. The real attack materialized when troops detached by the duke on 29 July marched on Modane, crossed the La Rouë pass and descended on Oulx, Cesana, and Montgenèvre on the road to Briançon. Their goal was to cut the road from Grenoble to Briançon and eventually seize the latter town, but French forces blocked the passage of allied troops at Cervières. This compelled the duke to retrace his steps back up the road to Cesana. When he heard of this rebuff, Villars brought his army from Montmélian via the Galibier Pass to Briançon and on to Montgenèvre, which he reached on 10 August. From there Villars launched an attack on the enemy's main forces at Cesana and drove them back into Piedmont. All the Allies had to show for this campaign was the post of Fenestrelle, which they took while retiring toward Turin.

Three Franco-Spanish armies fought for Philip V in Spain during 1708. The first, under the duke of Orléans and the count of Bezons, assembled at Flix on the Ebro River; the second, under the duke of Noailles, campaigned in Catalonia; and the third, under the marquis of Bay, fought in Estremadura. Allied forces underwent a change of command as the imperial General Starhemberg assumed supreme command in Spain, and Stanhope replaced Galway as the chief of British troops in the peninsula.

The war grew very nasty in Spain. Napoleon would not be the first to encounter Spanish partisans, for the *miquelets* active during the wars of Louis XIV were the precursors of the guerrillas of the Napoleonic Wars. For example, when two companies of troops came out to forage from Lerida on 30 March, *miquelets* ambushed them. To punish the town of Granadella, south of Lerida, for the action of the *miquelets*, troops marched out of Lerida and pillaged Granadella.

In the most impressive gain made during this year of comparatively minor action, the duke of Orléans took Tortosa on the Ebro. The Allies had hoped to reinforce it, but troops arrived too late from Italy. Orléans invested the town on 12 June, and it capitulated on 11 July. The duke of Noailles facilitated the siege of Tortosa, by threatening Gerona in order to divert allied forces. Assembling at le Boulou in Roussillon, he marched into Catalonia via La Junquera and Figueres in May. After the fall of Tortosa, Orléans marched to Lerida and then shifted his camp to Balaguer in August, while Starhemberg encamped at Cervera, blocking the road to Barcelona. By this point it was too hot to campaign.

In late August Starhemberg detached Stanhope with British troops to participate in the attack on the island of Minorca. Once again the Allies gained their major success at sea. An amphibious force under Admiral Sir John Leake took the island in September, with Port Mahon falling on the 29th of that month. This would be Leake's second Mediterranean coup of the summer, for he had earlier secured Sardinia.

After the fall of Tortosa, the chevalier Asfeld had returned to the province of Valencia with some of the Franco-Spanish troops who had taken the town. Philip intended to secure the Valencian coast by taking Denia and Alicante. Asfeld arrived before Denia on 6 November, and it fell on 17 November. The town of Alicante, invested on 30 November, surrendered a few days later; however, the English troops who had defended the town withdrew into its chateau to continue their resistance, and the French blockaded them. Only on 18 April 1709 did the beleaguered English finally capitulate.

The autumn would bring another change in command, as the duke of Orléans became *persona non grata* at the Spanish court. He made the mistake of offending the French princess des Ursins, a counsellor to the young queen and an individual whom Louis regarded as an essential influence in the Spanish court. Orléans's sharp tongue cost him his command, and he returned to France to sit out the rest of the war.

Famine, negotiations, and Louis's appeal

Although Louis's armies held the line in the Rhineland and made limited gains in Spain during 1708, nothing could compensate for defeat at Oudenarde and the subsequent loss of nearly all of Flanders. After the catastrophic collapse of 1706, 1708 confirmed the vulnerability of Louis's military position. He could take no comfort from events in the east either, because on 3 August an imperial army of only 10,000 smashed a Hungarian host of 15,000 under Rákóczi at the Battle of Trencsén. Rákóczi's rebellion would never really recover from that defeat. Louis rightly feared that an end of this revolt would allow the emperor to transfer forces west.

Famine further sapped the vigour of the French war effort. A meagre harvest in 1708 made things bad enough, but during the winter of 1708–9, France experienced the worst natural disaster of Louis's reign. Horrendously cold weather struck western Europe in January 1709. Penetrating cold killed people, animals, trees, and vines. So deep was the freeze that it even destroyed the young winter wheat in the ground, causing a crop failure of biblical proportions. The suffering of 1709 even beggared that of 1694.

Recognizing Louis's weakness, and his desire for peace at nearly any price, the Allies adhered to particularly harsh conditions when negotiations began again during the interval between campaign seasons. The French envoy Pierre Rouillé travelled to The Hague in early March, but was appalled as the Allies steadily raised their demands. Things having reached an impasse, the French minister of foreign affairs, Torcy, arrived on 6 May to conduct the negotiations himself with the leading allied statesman: Heinsius, Prince Eugene, Marlborough, and Townsend, a Whig leader of Parliament. After three weeks Heinsius handed Torcy the allied terms, the 'Preliminary Articles'. Philip V was to turn over all his Spanish possessions to Archduke Charles, while Louis was to guarantee his grandson's actions by evacuating a long list of frontier fortresses. All the Allies offered in exchange for this sacrifice was a two-months' truce, and should Philip and Louis not comply fully with the treaty by then, the war would resume, but at that point Louis would be without the fortresses he had docilely abandoned to the Allies. The permanent settlement would include other serious losses for France itself, such as the cession of Strasbourg and the occupation of a number of fortresses by the Dutch as part of their 'barrier', including Furnes, Ypres, Lille, Douai, Tournai, Condé, and Maubeuge. To make matters worse, Louis had to commit French armed forces to drive Philip V from his throne if he failed to vacate it peacefully. On the face of it, these terms should have been entirely unacceptable to Louis; however, when Torcy arrived back at Versailles on 1 June, Louis declared his willingness to accept all terms except the demand he direct his armies to attack Philip in the eventuality of the latter's resistance. Although the Allies might have secured a great deal with only minor compromise at this point, they would not release Louis from the unacceptable condition that he unseat his own grandson, and negotiations collapsed. Louis fought on. None the less, at this point he withdrew many of his troops from Spain in 1709 in the hope that this might facilitate an acceptable agreement with the Allies.

Faced with unacceptable terms, Louis issued a public explanation of why he felt compelled to continue the costly war. Such a direct appeal to popular opinion in wartime was probably unprecedented in European experience; certainly it was unique for Louis. On the urging of Torcy, Louis dispatched two letters dated 12 June, one to the Archbishop of Paris and another to the provincial governors of France.[54]

> But although the tenderness for my peoples is no less strong than that I have for my own children ... and [although] I have made all Europe see that I desire to let them enjoy peace, I am persuaded that they would themselves refuse to receive it on

---

54 In fact, it is known that Torcy drafted the all-important letter to the provincial governors. Joseph Klaits, *Printed Propaganda Under Louis XIV* (Princeton, NJ, 1976), p. 214.

conditions so contrary to the justice and the honour of the French name. My intention is therefore that all those who for so many years have given me signs of their zeal by contributing their efforts, their goods, and their blood to undertake such a burdensome war should know that all that my enemies proposed to give in return for my offers... was a suspension of arms,... which... would procure for them advantages greater than what they could have expected from keeping their troops on campaign.[55]

This unprecedented letter received wide circulation within the kingdom; governors added cover letters and had it printed, and booksellers copied and sold it to enthusiastic buyers.[56]

Some notable historians have argued that this appeal precipitated a great patriotic explosion in support of the war, but this seems an exaggeration of what actually occurred.[57] Mme de Maintenon commented that, 'All good Frenchmen have felt... the harshness of the peace conditions that are to be rejected.'[58] However, on close examination, the much-quoted testimony reflects only the sentiment of the nobility. Louis's propaganda effort seems to have precipitated little sacrifice for the defence of the realm. The only widespread act of self-denial that caught the public attention was the élite's donation of silver and gold plate to be melted down in order to coin new money for the war effort. Chamillart reported to Villars, 'The people have not been less indignant than the soldiers at the conditions that the enemy wants to force the king to accept.... The majority of the lords of the country here have sent their plates and utensils to the mint and offered to the king all that he could take. His Majesty, to set the example, has sent there all his golden vessels, even the new ones.'[59] But this sacrifice was not as great as might at first be supposed. In

[55] Letter in Vault and Pelet, *Mémoires militaires*, vol. ix, pp. 299–300.
[56] Klaits, *Printed Propaganda*, pp. 217–18. The printer of the *Gazette de France* was one who printed and sold copies, as advertisements on the back of the *Gazette* for 6 and 13 July 1709 announced.
[57] For statements concerning the enthusiasm engendered by the king's appeal and the popular response witnessed by a 'flood' of volunteers, see André Corvisier, *Armies and Societies in Europe, 1494–1789*, trans. Abigail T. Siddall (Bloomington, IN, 1979), pp. 69, 133, 134; Chandler, *Marlborough as Military Commander*, p. 245; and even the popular historian Nancy Mitford, *The Sun King* (London, 1966), p. 225.
[58] Letter from Mme de Maintenon to the duke of Noailles, 30 June 1709, in Maintenon, *Lettres de madame de Maintenon*, vol. v (Amsterdam, 1756), pp. 123–4.
[59] Letter from Chamillart to Villars, 9 June 1709, in Vault and Pelet, *Mémoires militaires*, vol. ix, p. 302. See as well Claude Louis Hector Villars, *Mémoires du maréchal de Villars*, ed. marquis de Vogüé (5 vols; Paris, 1884–95), vol. iii, p. 49.

regards to the donation of silver vessels, Noailles commented in his memoirs, 'There remained few French, especially at court, who had the zeal and the courage of patriotism.'[60] The actual take, though considerable, was certainly not enough to float the war effort.

Those who claim that 1709 was a great patriotic war see the War of the Spanish Succession as the greatest mobilization of manpower under Louis XIV. But as already discussed, the army of 1709 was not the largest Louis raised, rather it was considerably smaller than that created to fight the Nine Years War. The belief that Louis's army was so large in 1709 is in part founded on the notion that it was swamped by enthusiastic volunteers. As evidence of this idea, some refer to the fact that many recruits offered to sign up for reduced bounties or even without bounties. But this fact is best explained not by patriotism but by the famine that drove men into the army to find a crust of bread, just as was the case in the famine of 1694.

At base, there is scant evidence to suggest that the crisis of 1709 brought a great war of patriotic defence. It remained a major clash between dynasties feuding over who would occupy the Spanish throne. As Fénelon commented in August 1710: 'Our great misfortune comes from the fact that to date the war has been only the affair of the king, who is ruined and discredited.'[61]

RESOLUTION AND SURVIVAL, 1709-11

The period 1709-1711 brought a change in the fortunes of war for Louis XIV. While the Allies continued to score important victories, the momentum of allied success slowed enough that the Bourbon cause did not collapse. By 1711, Louis had outlasted the will of the British Parliament to continue a costly Continental war, and the circumstances of that war had changed enough to make a Bourbon king of Spain a reasonable alternative for the Maritime Powers.

1709

After Louis announced his intentions to continue the war, the task ahead of his armies seemed insurmountable. Years of armed struggle had bankrupted the state, famine wore down the army just as it weakened the civilian population, and in Flanders – the most critical

---

60 Duc de Noailles, *Mémoires du duc de Noailles*, in Alexandre Petitôt and Louis Monmerqué, eds, *Collection des mémoires relatifs à l'histoire de France* vol. lxxii (Paris, 1828), p. 451.
61 Letter from Fénelon to the duke of Chevreuse, 4 August 1710, in Fénelon, *Lettre à Louis XIV* (Neuchâtel, 1961), p. 129.

front and that which most endangered Paris – the situation neared collapse. Marlborough appeared to be able to accomplish nearly anything that he attempted, and no French general had yet made him pull up short. The court lost faith in the able Vendôme after the fall of Lille; Mme de Maintenon wrote: 'M. de Vendôme will not go out [to the army] any more, at least not this year ... We have all been deceived by that man.'[62] Vendôme would not receive another command until the autumn of 1710. His disgrace left Louis with little choice; he now awarded the Flanders command to Villars, a marshal whose ability and rapport with his troops promised success. As Mme de Maintenon wrote in March 1709, 'We finally have a general who has faith in the soldier, in the fate of France, and in himself.'[63] In fact, Villars possessed an unmatched record in the war to date, but his headstrong personality had hampered his rise, particularly when he tangled with the elector of Bavaria. In addition to Villars in Flanders, the duke of Harcourt would lead the army on the Rhine; Berwick would defend Dauphiné and Savoy; and the count of Bezons and Noailles shared command over French troops in Spain until Louis ostentatiously pulled troops out of the peninsula to put pressure on Philip V and to improve the chance for fruitful negotiations with the Allies.

Villars's first concern on the Flanders front was to feed his army. When he arrived at Cambrai in mid-March he made a tour of cantonments to survey the army's needs and spirits. Driven by hunger, garrisons at le Quesnoy, Arras, Mons, St Omer, Tournai, Nassau, Valenciennes, and Cambrai mutinied that spring.[64] On 9 May Villars left the front, and went to court to plead the case of his starving army. He showed up at Chamillart's residence and bluntly confronted the war minister. He attended meetings of the king's council and spoke brusquely of his army's sorry condition. A shaken Louis replied, 'I put my confidence in God and in you.'[65] Villars protested that his army in 1709 required 1,200 sacks of flour each day, and asked where could he find so much in the midst of dearth.[66] Back at

---

62 Letter from Mme de Maintenon to Mme the princess des Ursins, 18 March 1709, in Wolf, *Louis XIV*, p. 557.
63 Letter of 4 March 1709, in Émile G. Léonard, *L'Armée et ses problèmes au XVIIIe siècle* (Paris, 1958), p. 83.
64 AG, A¹2149, 249–54, 256, 258, in Sturgill, *Marshal Villars*, p. 82.
65 Louis in François Ziegler, *Villars: Le centurion de Louis XIV* (Paris, 1996), p. 188.
66 Villars, *Mémoires*, vol. iii, p. 42.

the front, Villars wrote to the king, 'We can go some time without money, but without bread it is impossible.'[67] Lacking sufficient supplies, Villars did anything he could to feed his men. He sent his cavalry to commandeer foodstuffs in Picardy, Soissonnais, Normandy, and Champagne. No fan of *munitionnaires*, he broke into their warehouses and seized everything they contained. Villars got part of what he wanted, for in June Louis removed Chamillart as minister of war and replaced him with the more capable Voysin, but the problems were too great for any administrator to solve.

Marlborough and Eugene again worked together in Flanders during 1709, and their combined field army numbered about 100,000 troops. Also suffering from the effects of the winter, the Allies began campaigning late and adopted the conservative goal of besieging still one more Franco-Spanish fortress, Tournai. Faced with allied forces larger than he commanded, Villars planned to put strong garrisons in Ypres and Tournai and then devote his main strength to creating a new defensive line from the Lys to Douai. After feinting a possible attack on the French defensive lines, the Allies invested Tournai on 27 June. With its particularly strong fortifications and a garrison of 7,000 men under the marquis of Surville-Hautfois, Tournai would not fall quickly; in fact, Louis and his generals expected it to hold out for two or three months and possibly occupy the Allies for the rest of the campaign season. Marlborough opened trenches on the night of 7–8 July, while Eugene covered the siege. After a determined resistance, during which the French exploded a mine under one of the allied siege batteries, Surville surrendered the town on 28 July and, by terms of the capitulation, withdrew into the formidable citadel to continue fighting. By this point, Villars, who wanted to relieve the siege in some way, informed Louis that his army must fight or risk simply dissolving, but Louis continued to resist risking the army in battle. Villars dispatched troops to bolster French garrisons in what he believed to be menaced forts and continued work on new sections of the defensive lines, which now stretched nearly fifty miles from St Venant to Douai to Hellemmes and to the Scheldt. The Tournai citadel finally capitulated on 3 September, after another particularly tenacious defence, replete once again with extensive countermining.

From start to finish it had taken Marlborough and Eugene most of the summer to take Tournai, but they were not ready to end the campaign and planned one more major venture, a siege of Mons. Immediately after Surville's capitulation, the Allies marched towards

---

67 Letter of 1 June 1709 from Villars to Louis, in ibid., p. 47.

Mons. Villars was actually relieved by the allied decision, because he feared more for Ypres. Now he prepared for battle: 'The citadel of Tournai once gone, I do not hope long to avoid a fight.'[68] Louis panicked with the fall of Tournai, and in this excited state authorized Villars to do whatever he thought necessary: 'Should Mons follow the fate of Tournai, our case is undone; you are by every means in your power to relieve the garrison; the cost is not to be considered; the salvation of France is at stake.'[69] Villars's main army held lines between Denain and Douai; now he assembled all the forces, calling units out from defensive lines and garrisons. At this point, the sixty-five-year-old Marshal Boufflers, who had been too ill to campaign earlier in the summer, returned to the front eager to serve under Villars, although Boufflers was senior.

To confront the Allies, Villars shifted to Quiévrain on 7 September and encamped there. Villars wanted to approach Mons so the Allies could not invest it completely; however, he learned that the Allies had invested Mons on 6 September and that Marlborough was camped at Givry at some distance from Eugene's army. Some argue he should have attacked Marlborough on the morning of 9 September, while Eugene was still camped at Bossu, but this would have left Villars vulnerable to a flank attack from Eugene. Villars had reason to be cautious. His was the last army between the Allies and Paris, and like Jellicoe at Jutland, he was the only man who could lose the war in an afternoon. Instead, Villars slipped his army east to a position running from the site of present-day la Noire Boutaille to Aulnois. He anchored his left flank in the Sars Woods and the right flank in the la Lanières Woods. A stretch of open ground about a mile wide separated the two dense woods, and the village of Malplaquet rested in the centre of that gap.

While the allied army gathered for the coming battle, the French devoted the day of 10 September to constructing field fortifications to buttress their front. In particular they dug in along the edges of the woods on either side of the open ground and constructed redoubts in the centre. Villars brought to the field about 135 battalions and 260 squadrons with 80 cannon, a force that probably totalled 75,000

---

68 Letter of Villars to Voisin, 28 August 1709, in Maurice Sautai, *La Bataille de Malplaquet* (Paris, 1910), p. 35, in Chandler, *Marlborough as Military Commander*, p. 251.
69 Louis in Chandler, *Marlborough as Military Commander*, p. 251. Chandler cites this as Vault and Pelet, *Mémoires militaires*, vol. ix, p. 86, but as is the case from time to time, Chandler's citation is incorrect, and chasing his footnote does not produce the document he employs.

troops.[70] He gave Boufflers command of the right half of the army. On the extreme right Lieutenant-General Pierre of Montesquiou d'Artagnan with 46 battalions entrenched in the la Lanières Woods. De Guiche with 18 battalions, including the Gardes françaises and the Gardes suisses, held the centre in front of Malplaquet. More battalions occupied the ground from these positions to the left: 13 in redoubts in the left centre, 21 holding the edge of the Sars toward the enemy, and on the extreme left, Goësbriand dug in behind the Sars Woods with 17 battalions. Other battalions stood in support. Villars stationed his cavalry behind the infantry along the entire line. The open ground at the centre could be swept by defensive fire from three directions; should Marlborough engage in his favourite central attack, there would be a high price to pay.

With a combined force of 86,000 troops and 100 cannon, Marlborough and Eugene enjoyed the advantage of numbers at the bloody Battle of Malplaquet; they also held the initiative, because Villars's intentions were entirely defensive. Eugene on the right would begin the allied attack by sending Schulenburg and Lottum against the French left in the Sars Woods. An hour and a half later, the prince of Orange would assault the French right in the la Lanières Woods. It was expected that this would cause Villars to weaken his centre, as had been the French response in previous battles; then Orkney would lead a force of allied infantry against the redoubts in the centre, while Marlborough's cavalry would punch through. His artillery began to bombard the French lines about 8 a.m. on the morning of 11 September, and the infantry of the allied right ploughed forward into the French positions. The fighting there became intense and deadly, as the French rushed cannon forward to enfilade the advancing allied infantry. On the extreme right flank, General Withers led a force of infantry and cavalry wide of the French positions and penetrated the woods unopposed. The slaughter was even greater on the allied left, where the prince of Orange led thirty Dutch and Scottish battalions against Montesquiou d'Artagnan's position. In the first half hour the Dutch alone suffered 5,000 casualties to French musketry and the awful fire from a battery of twenty artillery pieces. After terrible bloodshed, Orange had to withdraw. The French were about to hurry them along with a bayonet charge when allied cavalry came up to make them think twice.

70 There is much debate on the size of Villars's army. This is discussed in detail in André Corvisier, *La Bataille de Malplaquet 1709* (Paris, 1997), pp. 74–5. His figures are used for allied strength as well.

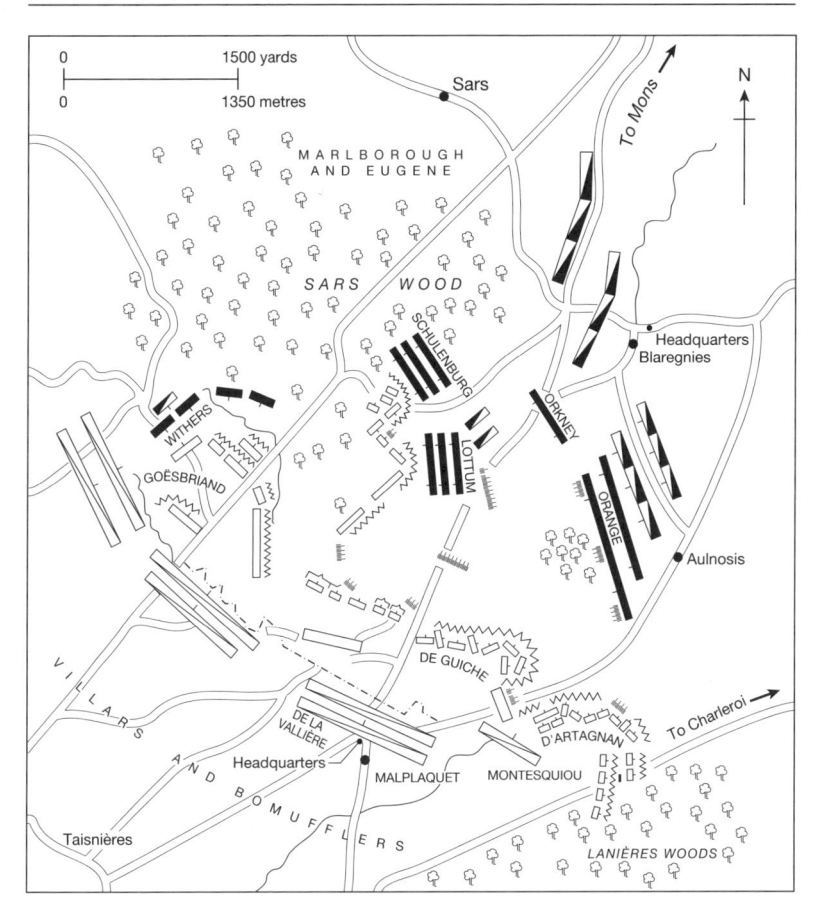

Map 7.3 Battle of Malplaquet, 11 September 1709
Adapted from: David Chandler, *Marlborough as a Military Commander* (London, 1973)

By 10 a.m. both of the allied flank attacks had stalled; reinforcements came forward to renew the effort of the allied right, and it made progress, but at great cost. As allied infantry drove the French through the wood, Villars became so concerned about Withers's advance that he summoned twelve battalions from his centre to reinforce his left. By 11:45 a.m. the French redoubts in the centre were denuded of infantry as Villars built up a force of fifty battalions to throw the Allies back from the Sars Woods. Seeing this, Marlborough sent Orkney to seize the redoubts and alerted his cavalry commanders to prepare for the climactic charge. Meanwhile, Villars personally led a charge to drive the Allies back as their forces came out of the woods on his left. Fire from one allied volley felled his horse, and a ball from the next volley shattered his knee. In great pain, Villars tried to retain command but had to be carried off the field, and the French counterattack on their left bogged down. The crisis had come by 1:30 p.m., as allied cavalry, perhaps 30,000 in all, formed up to break the French centre. Boufflers, now in command, forestalled their attack by personally leading the élite French household cavalry in a charge on the growing mass of allied horsemen. Charges and counter-charges tore across the plain, and allied numbers finally told. At this point both French flanks were also breaking contact with the enemy and falling back. The battle was virtually over by 3 p.m.

Defeated the French were, but this was not Blenheim or Ramillies, for they retired in good order, with flags waving, drums beating, and drawing off sixty-five of their cannon with them. The Allies were too exhausted and bloodied to pursue. Marlborough himself testified in a letter that day, 'The French have defended themselves better in this action then in any battle I have seen.'[71] Villars reported to the king, 'Your Majesty's troops have done marvels, although your army is in retreat, it will become clear that it has lost less men than the enemy.'[72] Villars was correct. The Allies sacrificed 21,000 killed and wounded, a quarter of their force, while the French suffered 11,000 killed and wounded, and only 500 were taken prisoner.[73] Marlborough's triumph proved to be a Pyrrhic victory. Malplaquet was the bloodiest battle fought during the wars of Louis XIV; the contemporary news bulletin, the *Gazette de France*, declared, 'In more than a century there had not been a single moment so bloody or so unremitting.'[74] Neither the British nor the Dutch government would allow Marlborough to bleed the army so again; Malplaquet was his last battle. Villars insisted to Louis, 'If God gives us the grace to lose another similar battle, your Majesty can count on his enemies being destroyed.'[75] It is true that Malplaquet did not save Mons,

[71] Letter from Marlborough to Heinsius, 11 September 1709, in T'Hoff, *Correspondence*, pp. 463–4.

[72] AG, A¹2152, #170, in Chandler, *Marlborough as Military Commander*, p. 266. It is often claimed that Malplaquet was the costliest battle until the bloodbaths of the Napoleonic Wars; however, at Kunersdorf in 1759, the Russians lost about 16,000 casualties, while Frederick the Great suffered 20,000.

[73] For an exhaustive presentation of the varying casualty figures claimed at Malplaquet, see the tables in Corvisier, *La Bataille de Malplaquet*, pp. 121–4.

[74] *Gazette de France*, no. 40, 5 October 1709, p. 281.

[75] Letter from Villars to Louis, AG, A¹2152, in Wolf, *Louis XIV*, p. 569.

which capitulated on 21 October, but it may have saved France. Malplaquet suited the French style in this war; they need not destroy the enemy, but only make it impossible for the enemy to destroy them, and it demonstrated that Blenheim and Ramillies were the past, not a prediction. Louis recognized the value of Villars's accomplishment and showered rewards on the marshal and his army.

Elsewhere in 1709, the French and their Spanish allies simply maintained the status quo, neither scoring a major victory nor suffering a major defeat. With Flanders the primary theatre, little of importance occurred along the Rhine in 1709. Marshal Harcourt began with thirty-eight battalions and sixty-seven squadrons, but early in the campaign he dispatched twenty-two squadrons to Flanders. His opponent, the elector of Hanover, mustered forty-three battalions and sixty-six squadrons in the allied field army, with an additional twenty-one battalions committed to garrison duty. The Germans had dug a new defensive position, the lines of Ettlingen north of the old lines of Stollhofen. In June French troops crossed over onto the right bank of the Rhine, and, later, Hanover crossed to the left bank and threatened the French lines on the Lauter, forcing Harcourt to put more troops in those lines. Imposing contributions and carrying out forages once again became a significant concern along the Rhine.

In Savoy and Dauphiné, allied forces led by Daun advanced as far as Annecy in 1709, but turned back at the end of the campaign season. French troops under Marshal Berwick, who replaced Villars on this front, guarded the routes through Savoy which could be employed to threaten Dauphiné. Major French forces remained at Briançon, where Berwick went to command. Daun marched into Savoy via the Mount Cenis Pass while Schulemburg came through the Little St Bernard. They continued their advance toward Montmélian as far as St Pierre d'Albigny in July, but Berwick held Montmélian with forces strong enough to block Daun. Daun then seized Annecy in August, but while this might have led to an allied invasion of Franche-Comté, the lack of imperial success on the Rhine ruled out this option. Eventually Daun decided to withdraw all his troops before the snow fell, and Savoy reverted once again to French control.

Spain also saw little substantial action. As already mentioned, the chateau of Alicante capitulated on 18 April. In late spring nearly half the main army that had been engaged in Valencia returned to France, leaving only twenty-nine battalions. To the west, after assembling his army of 16,000 troops at Badajoz, the marquis of Bay scored a success over a somewhat larger Portuguese and British army under Galway at the Battle of Campo Maior in Portugal on 7 May. In July and August Louis recalled more French troops serving in Spain as a concession to the Allies in hopes of stimulating peace talks. While Torcy maintained that Louis 'had withdrawn all his troops from Spain', there remains good reason to doubt this assertion.[76] The archives suggest that while Louis withdrew eleven more squadrons of cavalry and eleven or twelve battalions of infantry, significant French infantry remained. Still, on 2 September the French ambassador departed Madrid, and the public French pullout seemed complete. In fact, Louis was trying both to placate the Allies and to put pressure on Philip, but without leaving him entirely in the lurch.

1710

In hindsight, 1709 brought a change in the momentum of the war, but this view comes from knowing that Villars would provide fine military leadership just at a time when the ground was beginning to shift under Marlborough's feet. During the winter and spring of 1710 this was not clear. The implications of Malplaquet had yet to emerge; in fact, Marlborough incorrectly confided to Heinsius that, thanks to the victory at Malplaquet, 'you may have what peace you please.'[77] There is no question that Louis was still in a lamentable situation early in 1710: his finances were in shambles, he continued to lose ground in Flanders, the famine continued, and, to make it worse, Villars had still not recovered from his wounds and might not be available to lead the army. But while Louis was willing to accept harsh terms to gain peace, the Allies believed that he really was even more desperate than he was.

Preliminary contacts between the Dutch and the French in the last months of 1709 led to the holding of a peace conference at Gertruydenberg in the United Provinces from March through July 1710. Instead of moderating their position from the Preliminary Articles, the Allies made even stronger demands regarding what Louis had to do to remove Philip V from his throne. They insisted that if Philip refused to step down willingly, French forces would have to drive him from Spain without the assistance of the Allies. In other words, Louis had to declare war on his own grandson while the Allies simply watched from a safe distance. All the Allies conceded

---

[76] Torcy in Rule, 'France and the Preliminaries to the Gertruydenberg Conference,' p. 111.
[77] Letter from Marlborough to Heinsius, 11 September 1709, T'Hoff, *Correspondence*, p. 464.

The Final Contest

was that Philip could retain Sicily. Louis could not agree to such terms. But the battered monarch so desired peace that, while he could not conscience sending French troops to depose Philip, he was willing to offer a subsidy of 500,000 livres for allied troops to do the job. Still, the Allies rejected Louis's proposal. To undermine the position of the allied negotiators with their own people, a disgusted Louis ordered his envoys to give the text of his concessions to the Amsterdam newspapers in mid-June. As nothing came of negotiations, armies took the field again in 1710.

By this point Louis's armies were no longer deployed predominantly in the Spanish Netherlands but rather now they fought in French Flanders, Hainault, and Artois. Villars, so crippled by his knee wound that he had to be strapped in the saddle, returned to the Army of Flanders in May with Marshal Berwick at his side. Knowing the supply difficulties suffered by the French, Marlborough and Eugene had already taken the field before the French could do likewise. As Villars complained, 'Lacking magazines, we can only assemble our armies when the countryside can feed the horses.'[78] The Allies mustered an army of 60,000 men who had wintered in Flanders, and marched for Douai at a time when the French only had a small field army to oppose them. Beginning a siege that would last two months, Marlborough invested Douai between 22 and 25 April. He would later claim that he was hampered again by Dutch conservatism, but, in any case, his campaign for 1710 focused on the capture of Douai, Béthune, St Venant, and Aire. These fortresses stood in the second line of Vauban's *pré carré*, so by taking them, Marlborough would tear a fifty-mile-wide hole in the vaunted *frontier de fer*.

Louis was willing to fight for Douai, and would, if necessary, risk the outcome of the war on another great battle. He urged Villars to relieve the fortress and speculated on the results of a battle: 'Their army would have small chances to retreat if you should succeed in defeating them while they still await some troops that have not yet come up.'[79] Villars marched to the relief of Douai on 25 May, but after reconnoitring the allied lines, he thought better of attacking Marlborough and Eugene there. They were well dug in, and Villars believed himself to be outnumbered, since, as he said, his battalions

---

78 Villars, 15 March 1710, in Vault and Pelet, *Mémoires militaires*, vol. x, p. 241.
79 Letter from Louis to Villars, A. A. E. Holland, 228, in Wolf, *Louis XIV*, p. 572. Sturgill, *Marshal Villars*, p. 103, argues the very opposite – that Villars was told not to risk anything. Wolf and his evidence are more compelling here.

337

had sunk to a size of only 300 men, less than half their paper strength.[80] With an effective attack on allied forces impossible, Villars simply observed the siege, and Louis dispatched Berwick to Dauphiné. After the capitulation of Douai on 25 June, Villars withdrew his army to Arras, while reinforcing the garrisons of Ypres, Béthune, St Venant, and Arras. He may well have seen Arras as the key to the defence of France at this point. Villars defended it not only by committing more men to its garrison, but also by stripping the area of forage necessary to a besieging army and by constructing new defensive lines that incorporated the city's defences.

However, Béthune was the next allied target, and an army of 30,000 troops under Schulenberg invested it on 15 July. The French garrison of 4,000 men held out until 28 August. As that siege neared an end, Torcy wrote to Villars pleading for some kind of military success: 'It is impossible to bring our enemies to reason as long as they believe France to be at the last extremity.'[81] The French had to demonstrate their capacity to continue the war. But Villars's task was, at base, easier than Marlborough's: Villars must avoid being destroyed and keep his army between Marlborough and Paris – and buy time. After Béthune fell, the Allies took St Venant, a minor fortress with only earthen walls, in a siege that lasted from 6 to 29 September. At this point, Villars left the front. Tired and in pain, he received permission from the king to retire to take the waters at Bourbonne, and Marshal Harcourt took over his command on 25 September. After Villars's departure, Marlborough and Eugene added one more trophy, as their forces took Aire, an important link in the chain of the *pré carré*. Invested on 12 September, Aire held out for two months, finally capitulating on 8 November. The sieges of St Venant and Aire overlapped. It was unusual for one army to undertake two sieges at the same time, but St Venant was so weak that it required only a small besieging force, and the two fortresses were only seven miles apart, allowing one army of observation to guard both operations.

The campaign of 1710 brought no noteworthy operations either on the Rhine or on the Italian front. Again, with the major concentration on the Flanders front, the French made only modest efforts elsewhere. Marshal Harcourt, seconded by Marshal Bezons, led Louis's army on the Rhine. With Eugene fighting alongside Marlborough, Grosfeld

---

80 Villars makes this estimate in his *Mémoires*, vol. iii, p. 80.
81 Torcy to Villars in Ziegler, *Villars*, p. 217.

The Final Contest

received command of imperial forces on the Rhine. During the campaign, Grosfeld thought of little but holding the lines of Ettlingen and reinforcing the garrison of Landau. Harcourt deployed most of his forces in the lines of Wissembourg on the Lauter, while his cavalry raided across the Rhine. Forced by illness to leave, Harcourt turned over command to Bezons on 25 June, and at the same time Bezons detached more troops to march to Flanders. Bezons also stayed close to his entrenched lines even when he ventured out of them to respond to German manoeuvres.

In Savoy, Marshal Berwick took command after leaving Villars. Daun tried to penetrate the French defences by advancing on Barcelonnette, but could not continue. When Berwick was reinforced to sixty battalions and thirty-six squadrons during the summer, he held a line protecting Dauphiné and Provence, from St Jean de Maurienne through the Galibier Pass, to Briançon to Guillestre and then along the Var. With the conclusion of this campaign, the Allies had not made any gains of substance on this front for three years.

The most dramatic campaign of 1710 took place in Spain, where things went from crisis to triumph as the outcome of the war in that theatre was essentially decided. Philip V began the campaign weakened, because his grandfather had withdrawn much French support in an effort to promote peace talks. And so long as the discussions continued at Gertruydenberg, Louis kept his distance. Philip did what he could to increase his army, which he knew, must fight without the full support of France.

Bereft of French generals, Philip awarded the command of his main army in Aragon to Villadarias, and this army soon took some rude shocks at the hands of the allied supreme commander, Starhemberg. Philip, in the spirit of the Bourbon house, joined his soldiers in the field. After facing off against each other near Lerida, Villadarias and Starhemberg clashed at the Battle of Almenara on 27 July. There Starhemberg with 24,000 troops defeated Villadarias with 22,000 men. Villadarias and Philip quickly withdrew to Lerida, and Philip replaced Villardarias with the marquis of Bay. From Lerida, the royal army pulled back to Saragossa, where Starhemberg caught up with them and defeated the Spanish in a second and even more bloody battle on 20 August. The vanquished Spaniards fled back on the road to Madrid. With this victory, the Allies reasserted their control over Aragon. Soon they were advancing on Madrid, reaching Calatayud on 4 September. As Starhemberg approached, Philip V left Madrid on 9 September and fled to Valladolid. Starhemberg's troops also occupied Toledo.

Allied forces entered Madrid on 21 September, and Archduke Charles arrived at the capital a week later. But the tide had already turned against the Allies. With the collapse of the Gertruydenberg Conference, Louis could now support Philip, so once again French reinforcements marched south. Vendôme and Noailles met with Philip V at Valladolid on 17 September. It was agreed that all the major commanders would return to familiar venues. Bay went back to Estremadura; Noailles took command in Catalonia; and Vendôme took charge of the main Franco-Spanish army. Vendôme, a man rather similar in energy and earthy qualities to Villars, took a central position at Talavera de la Reina in mid-October with 25,000 troops. Starhemberg had hoped to be joined in Madrid by an army advancing from Portugal, but it was still marking time at Elvas, and Vendôme blocked the road from Portugal to Madrid. Starhemberg did not want to winter in Castile, for not only had Vendôme cut the route to Portugal, but Madrid had risen for Philip, and guerrilla bands were making it difficult for Starhemberg to maintain himself there. Therefore, he abandoned the city in late November, as the Allies also left Toledo. Philip V returned on 3 December, never to be driven out again.

Starhemberg's retreat became a nightmare. As his army withdrew, Vendôme pressed forward via forced marches and overtook the rear guard, composed of Stanhope's British troops, at Brihuega on 8 December. By the next morning, Franco-Spanish troops had surrounded the British, trapped within the weak walls of the town. French cannon breached the walls, and Vendôme demanded Stanhope's surrender, which was tendered about 9 p.m. Those among the 4,000-man British contingent who did not fall during the fight were now taken prisoner, including Stanhope. At the first approach of Vendôme's forces, Stanhope had sent an appeal to Starhemberg, who wheeled about to aid him. On 10 December, Starhemberg with 14,000 of his men stood at Villa Viciosa, where Vendôme with 25,000 attacked. Both armies fought hard, and although Vendôme paid a high price of 4,000 casualties, he was unable to drive Starhemberg from his position and, in fact, pulled back from the field himself as night fell. For this reason, the Allies claimed Villa Viciosa as a victory. But such a 'victory' was hollow, for Starhemberg had lost even more men than had Vendôme, and the next day he began a precipitous retreat. Unable to bring his artillery and baggage with him for lack of draught and pack animals, Starhemberg spiked his guns, left his supplies, and rushed back to Catalonia as rapidly as he could. As Philip reported to Louis, 'The debris of the enemy army retired in much haste . . . licking their wounds.'[82] The battles of Brihuega and Villa Viciosa beat down the allied threat to Castile and Aragon for good. Torcy commented upon learning the news from Spain, 'No matter what, never has a victory been more complete, and this day will change the face of affairs in Spain and at the same time those of Europe.'[83]

After Vendôme made a strategic victory out of a tactical impasse, Noailles advanced into Catalonia, where he laid siege to Gerona on 15 December. Gerona fell on 25 January, opening the way for a further advance toward Barcelona. By this time, Vendôme had advanced to Cervera, and the allied hold on Spain had been reduced to the triangle of Tarragona, Igualada, and Barcelona, from which the Allies would not extend their control until they were finally compelled to vacate Spain altogether in the last year of the war.

1711

Such sweeping victory in Spain made it all the more unlikely that Philip V would entertain any suggestions that he vacate the throne or that Louis would ever conscience removing him. Louis had gained a far stronger hand by the end of 1710. In fact, the difference in Louis's position from the Conference of Gertruydensberg to his negotiations with the English in 1711 constituted a true revolution. Survival in Flanders coupled with success in Spain had brought about this change, which all the battlefield brilliance of Marlborough proved unable to avert.

The onset of negotiations in 1710 did not have to wait until the armies returned to winter quarters. In March, noted Tories made contact with François Gaultier, a Catholic priest living in London. Gaultier carried on a clandestine correspondence with Torcy during the war and now served as the conduit between the French and English. In August, Queen Anne, who had never been comfortable with Marlborough's Whig friends, replaced the Whig cabinet with Tories. The Tories had less interest in the war on the Continent than they had in trade and colonial expansion, and to them the Dutch were more commercial rivals than military allies. Torcy and Gaultier recognized the possibilities this change of ministry presented and pursued further contacts with the Tories. The bellicose duke of Marlborough's influence was eroded not only by the replacement of his Whig allies with Tory foes but by the row between Queen Anne and his wife Sarah in April, which led to her falling from favour.

[82] Philippe in Wolf, *Louis XIV*, p. 576.
[83] Torcy, *Mémoires*, in ibid., p. 577.

Louis, upset with the Dutch concerning their conduct at Gertruydenberg, was determined not to negotiate through them any longer, and the opening with the British served his purposes. In December, a letter arrived from England announcing to Torcy that the British would not demand the throne of Spain for Archduke Charles, 'provided France and Spain will give us good security for our commerce'.[84] Next month Gaultier journeyed to Versailles to confer with Torcy. In January Louis wrote, 'The happy events that have occurred in Spain since last month should deprive the enemies of hope . . . to become master of the country. . . . The affairs of the king, my grandson, are now in better shape than they have been since the beginning of the war.'[85]

In the spring, Louis's bargaining position improved still more. On 17 April smallpox took the life of Emperor Joseph I at the age of thirty-two, and since he died without fathering a male heir, his brother Archduke Charles succeeded Joseph as Emperor Charles VI. Because the Allies, particularly the Maritime Powers, could not be expected to show much enthusiasm for making Charles VI a king of Spain as well, Philip V looked like a more and more reasonable alternative.

On the other side of the balance, the Allies could take some heart from the demise of the Rákóczi rebellion. On 1 May Rákóczi's lieutenants signed the Peace of Szatmár, which effectively ended the revolt, although Rákóczi personally did not accept the treaty. This Habsburg success freed troops to redeploy to the west, but it was too late for this alone to revivify the alliance.

Negotiations continued through 1711, but by late September Louis's emissaries and Tory representatives of Queen Anne had reached a tentative agreement, finalized as the London Preliminaries, signed on 8 October. These provided that Louis would recognize Anne and the Protestant succession in Britain as legitimate, that the thrones of France and Spain should never be united, that the Dutch and Germans would receive fortress barriers to protect their lands (although not at the sacrifice of French territory), and that the fortifications of the privateer port of Dunkirk would be razed. These Preliminaries would become the basis for negotiations at Utrecht in 1712.

The improving possibilities for peace affected the Flanders campaign in 1711. Neither Louis nor the British government was willing to take strong action or pay a great price to win the war there. Versailles

---

84 Letter in ibid., p. 576.
85 Louis in ibid., pp. 578–9.

muzzled Villars, who testifies in his memoirs how anxious he was for battle. The king instructed him on 26 April, 'I do not believe it to be apropos for you to seek to fight the enemies... the present conjuncture does not require that we risk any considerable action.'[86] Marlborough and Eugene took the field in late April and threatened Arras; Villars moved up to challenge Douai. When they faced off across the Sensée River on 1 May, instead of preparing for battle, the outposts began to fraternize, and in the next few days Villars and James, the Old Pretender, openly rode to the lines where British troops spoke with their 'king'. Eugene, Marlborough, Villars, and James exchanged pleasant notes. During June, the court ordered Villars to dispatch troops from his army to go to the Rhine. In mid-June Villars received more instructions, 'by which His Majesty forbid me to give battle, trusting in the divisions among the enemy powers that diminished their forces, and the orders were to confine myself to defending the lines that I occupied'.[87] Villars would later complain that this campaign was particularly cruel in limiting his chance to fight.[88]

In the manner typical of this war, the French laboured to build a new, and even more formidable, defensive line. Villars had christened these works the 'Ne Plus Ultra Lines', thus announcing that Marlborough would go no further. These lines, intended not simply to block enemy raiding parties but to hold Marlborough's main forces, ran from the coast at Montreuil by Arras, Cambrai, Valenciennes, and le Quesnoy to the Sambre, where they connected with the older barrier along that river to Namur. The French now maintained a system of defensive lines running some 200 miles across northern France and into the Spanish Netherlands. The French also manned strings of outposts further east to protect against enemy courses. These ran along the Semoy River and tried to cover a span from the mouth of the Semoy to the Sambre, particularly the gap between the Somme and Oise that seems to have been something of a highway for raiders. Further measures were taken along the Aisne, which demonstrates just how far enemy parties could penetrate. Allied victories in 1709 and 1710 had intensified the partisan war in northern France even as the general situation of the Bourbon cause improved.

Marlborough achieved his most impressive feat of 1711 when he crossed the Ne Plus Ultra Lines without losing a man to enemy fire.

---
86 AG, A¹2303, in ibid., p. 581.
87 Villars, *Mémoires*, vol. iii, p. 111. Letter in Vault and Pelet, *Mémoires militaires*, vol. x, p. 402.
88 Villars, *Mémoires*, vol. iii, p. 128.

This involved a clever ploy to convince Villars to weaken his own lines at Arleux. On 6 July allied troops took Arleux and fortified it, an action calculated to draw Villars's attention. French troops then retook Arleux and, to deny its use to the Allies, demolished the works and abandoned the position; this left the post weaker than at the start. Next, Marlborough, alone now since the departure of Eugene in June, set up camp close to the Ne Plus Ultra Lines at Villiers, twenty-five miles west of Arleux, and Villars responded by establishing his position nearby on the other side of the works. On 4 August Marlborough conducted a very obvious reconnaissance of the lines in front of his camp, but his real intention lay elsewhere. That afternoon some of his troops used the cover of Vimy ridge to head east with his artillery, and when night fell, Marlborough followed with the rest of his army as the campfires still burned to convince the French that his troops remained in place. Meanwhile, troops under Hompesche and Cadogan advanced the much shorter distance from Douai to Arleux, found it and the lines deserted, and crossed quickly. The next morning Marlborough arrived with the main body. Learning of Marlborough's manoeuvre some hours after it began, Villars pressed on through the night as well, but he arrived too late and discovered Marlborough strongly positioned. Villars could not attack, but he, in turn, dug in so well that Marlborough chose not to force a battle. After all, neither was really authorized to risk a bloodbath.

After crossing the lines, Marlbrough left Villars unmolested and shifted ten miles east to besiege Bouchain. This would not be an easy siege, both because of the quality of the fortress and because of problems posed by the river and inundations. Allied troops under Baron Fagel moved around it by 11 August. Marlborough's army encamped at Avesnes-le-Sec, and Villars refrained from attacking him there. With two breaches blasted through the fortress walls, the commander of Bouchain surrendered unconditionally on 12 September, and the garrison marched out two days later. Parker with Marlborough's army claimed that this siege was crucial, 'for Bouchain is a fortress . . . which opens a passage into the Kingdom of France'.[89] Truth to tell, after the fall of Bouchain the road to Paris was still obstructed with obstacles; Arras, Cambrai, le Quesnoy, and Landrecies, all still in French hands, would have blocked or flanked any allied advance. These constituted the last line, but Marlborough would have had to devote another campaign to crossing it, and Marlborough, for all his successes, had run out of time.

---

[89] Parker in Chandler, *Robert Parker and Comte de Mérode-Westerloo*, p. 106.

The Final Contest

With his political position undermined, Marlborough had become vulnerable, and with an agreement already hammered out between the British and the French, he was now expendable. In January 1712, while visiting England, he learned that Anne had removed him from command.

The campaign on the Rhine in 1711 amounted to little more than a stand-off. With the death of Joseph, the empire had to choose a new emperor, and this election, though essentially *pro forma*, would absorb energy and concern. Villars argued that the French should use military force to interfere with the procedure, and Prince Eugene seemed intent on keeping the front quiet. The German army assembled in May around Ettlingen and Mühlberg and stayed close to or in the lines of Ettlingen. Initially the French army counted only thirty-six battalions and thirty-six squadrons, at first under Marshal Bezons and later under Marshal Harcourt, who arrived on 27 May. The main force occupied the lines of Wissembourg on the Lauter, while cavalry ranged over the right bank of the Rhine to forage and raid. In July, reinforcements arrived from the Army of Flanders to increase Harcourt's force. Eugene, now in command of the imperial army, also benefited from reinforcements. After Charles was formally elected the new emperor, Eugene came out of the lines of Ettlingen on 27 August, crossed the Rhine, and camped at Speyer. He reconnoitred the French lines but opted not to attack. The uneventful confrontation between Harcourt and Eugene continued to sputter for the rest of the campaign season without result.

The Italian front received more attention and resources from the Allies, but to little profit. The duke of Savoy complained that the imperials had done little in 1710. His withdrawal from the Nine Years War had caused the Grand Alliance to implode, and the Allies wanted to avoid giving him an excuse in 1711, so London and Vienna promised him more troops. To oppose the larger allied army, the French once again dispatched Marshal Berwick to command the sixty-five battalions in Dauphiné and Savoy. The Allies marched into Savoy by two common routes, Schulemberg advancing via the Val d'Aosta and the Little St Bernard Pass, while the main force under Daun and Victor Amadeus formed up at Susa and crossed the Mount Cenis Pass on 8 July. This larger force advanced along the Arc River to St Jean de Maurienne and on to the Isère. The duke of Savoy left troops back in Piedmont with orders to attack Briançon if the French left it unguarded.

345

Berwick, who had been at Guillestre, rushed to meet the attack, marshalling his main body at Montmélian, where they would block the enemy advance. The allied forces converged on that town and also sent detachments to occupy Annecy, Faverges, and Chambéry. By 28 July the Allies had reached Les Marches and occupied a line from there to St Pierre d'Albigny. Berwick concentrated his outnumbered troops at Barraux. This allied penetration alarmed the French beyond the mountains, and militia from Bresse, the Lyonnais, and Provence took station to guard their regions. The Allies debated whether or not to attack Berwick's camp, but Victor Amadeus opposed the plan. Instead, on 5 September he ordered troops to return back up the road to St Jean de Maurienne and descend by the Galibier Pass to the road to Briançon and take that town, but Berwick moved fast enough to block them. It became harder and harder for the Allies to sustain themselves in Savoy; eventually, they had to pack all their food and supplies by mule from Piedmont, and rains made the roads difficult. This convinced the Allies they could not winter in Savoy, so in mid-September they withdrew over the mountains back into Piedmont, with Berwick in pursuit. All the Allies' efforts had been wasted, for they ended the campaign back where they started.

The Franco-Spanish forces simply consolidated their position during 1711. In February a Spanish army under Valdecañas advanced from Lerida. After its allied defenders abandoned Balaguer, Valdecañas attacked and took Calaf. Meanwhile, Starhemberg, who now commanded an army of 21,000 infantry and 5,000 cavalry, plus *miquelets*, worked to improve the defences of Taragona and Barcelona. Across Spain, the Portuguese sent an army under Villaviede to invade Estremadura in the spring. Bay, with an army of 16,000 troops, marched to block Villaviede at Albuera on 27 May, but after they faced off, Bay retired to Badajoz and left the road free for Villaviede to continue. But the resourceful Bay then raided into Portugal as far as Elvas, and this caused the Portuguese government to recall Villaviede back to Portugal.

When the campaign began again in the late summer, Starhemberg took up a position at Igulalada to cover Taragona and Barcelona. An allied attempt to retake Tortosa was foiled by the townspeople. Venasque fell to the Franco-Spanish army in mid-September, and then Vendôme detached 8,000 troops to besiege Cardona. They invested the town in mid-November but gave up the siege on 22 December. During the autumn, Noailles, now short of troops, simply held road from Gerona to Barcelona, as the Allies' grip on Spain loosened.

The privateering and colonial struggles

The War of the Spanish Succession was above all a Continental struggle, but it was not without its naval and colonial aspects. The only great fleet action of the war, the Battle of Velez-Málaga, came in 1704, but that does not mean the French were idle at sea. *Guerre de course* both delivered a harvest of prizes to French ports and severely wounded allied maritime trade. From 1702 to 1714 the French took 4,545 ships that were brought before prize courts. The full value of prizes seized may be as high as 149,000,000 livres. Fortunes were made at sea, however, only by the principal *armateurs* and the bankers who funded them. Most of these prizes, 3,618, were taken in the Eastern Atlantic, with only 692 seized in the Mediterranean. Others met their fates in colonial waters. Dunkirk far and away surpassed all other privateering ports, with 959 captures; Brest was next with 506, followed by Calais (461), St Malo (374), Toulon (208), and many lesser ports. Beyond prizes seized and brought to French prize courts, records report 2,118 ransoms of smaller vessels. With prize courts jammed, French privateers were authorized to accept ransoms to release coasters and fishing vessels at sea, eliminating the need to bring them into port. Dunkirk and Calais accounted for the vast majority of such ransoms. The high point of French privateering, as measured by the number of total number of prizes and ransoms reported, came from 1707 to 1711. Interestingly, by far the greatest of these annual totals, 831, came in 1711 just as the French were negotiating with the Tories for peace. With the well-known Tory concern for commerce, they could not but have been stimulated to reach a settlement by the mounting toll of French prizes. The numbers only tell part of the story, of course, for the harm done to allied commerce was not only in the value of goods and ships lost, but also in the shaken confidence and rising anxiety of the commercial community.[90]

In addition to the constant bleeding of allied maritime trade by prizes and ransoms, French *armateurs* and captains inflicted some more dramatic wounds with ventures of a grander sort. In 1702 and 1704 French squadrons extorted ransom from Fort Gambia on the African coast; Iberville demanded £42,000 and 1,400 slaves as the price for leaving the Caribbean island of Nevis, which he occupied in 1706 after the French had attacked St Kitts. Cassard attacked the

---

90 The figures in this paragraph come from J. S. Bromley, 'The French Privateering War, 1702–13', in H. E. Bell and R. L. Ollard, eds, *Historical Essays, 1600–1750, Presented to David Ogg* (New York, 1963), pp. 203–31.

Cape Verde Islands with a sizeable squadron of six rated vessels and two frigates, and then went on to Dutch holdings in the Caribbean and off the northern coast of South America in 1712–13. At Surinam, the Dutch governor paid a ransom of 1,000,000 livres beyond the booty the French took to get his unwelcomed guests to depart.

The greatest single maritime raid of the war was that carried out against Rio de Janeiro by the prince of privateers, René Duguay-Trouin. Du Clerc had tried to take Rio in 1710, but he was forced to surrender, and he and his men were badly treated by the Portuguese. Revenge was in order. On 3 June 1711, Duguay-Trouin sailed with seven ships of the line, six frigates, a bomb ketch, and three transports loaded with 2,400 troops. This squadron arrived off Rio on 11 September and the next day negotiated the narrow and difficult mouth of the harbour while harrassed by enemy gunfire. Under French attack, the Portuguese abandoned the town. After securing the enemy forts as well, the French demanded a ransom of 2,200,000 livres not to burn the town. The governor agreed to pay, and on 13 November Duguay-Trouin set sail for France with his treasure. He would pay a price on the voyage home, for in a storm off the Azores he lost two ships with 1,128 men and 600,000 livres of ransom money.

Aside from the periodic activities of privateers, fighting in the colonies was relatively small-scale, as it had been during the Nine Years War. In fact, colonial conflict was more restricted in the later conflict because fighting did not extend to the South Asian subcontinent, where the rival commercial settlements observed an uneasy truce. In the Americas, fighting engulfed the southern seas, but not for long. The British Royal Navy launched ill-fated amphibious expeditions against Spanish and French holdings in Florida and the Caribbean during the first years of the war. The governor of the Leeward Islands took French possessions on St Kitts in July 1702, but in 1703 he lost several hundred men in an unsuccessful siege of Guadeloupe. James Moore, governor of Carolina, mounted an expedition against the Spanish at St Augustine, Florida, in October 1702. His attack by land and sea broke against the stone walls of Fort San Marcos, although the English colonial force sacked and burned the town of St Augustine itself. When Spanish warships arrived on Christmas Day, Moore gave up his siege.

Further to the north, the War of the Spanish Succession, known by the British settlers as Queen Anne's War, witnessed several expeditions against French strongholds, but the impact upon the British colonies themselves was comparatively minor. New York essentially stayed out of this affair, to a large degree because the neutrality of the Iroquois, who also avoided this war, provided a buffer between that colony and the French. New England was not so lucky, suffering destructive frontier raids, the most notable of which struck Deerfield, Massachusetts, on the night of 28–9 February 1704. There 38 settlers died and 111 were led off into captivity. As in the previous war, the English colonists focused on Port Royal. Two expeditions attacked this valuable French port in June and August of 1707, but were repulsed by Auger de Subercase, the new governor. However, a third attack carried out by thirty-six vessels and over 3,000 regular and militia troops under the command of Francis Nicholson took Port Royal in October 1710. By that point Auger de Subercase had only 156 men in his garrison. Port Royal, rechristened Annapolis Royal, remained in English hands, and along with it, the peninsula of Acadia became British Nova Scotia.

The expedition to Port Royal was not the only investment of regulars and the Royal Navy that London made in the colonial phase of the war. The next year the British launched an unprecedentedly large two-pronged operation to take New France. A sea-borne force under Admiral Sir Hovenden Walker was to sail up the St Lawence to attack Quebec, while the victorious Nicholson led an army overland from Albany to strike Montreal. The invasion fleet of seventy-one vessels bearing 7,500 men sailed from Boston on 30 July, but foundered in the mouth of the St Lawrence, where bad weather and poor piloting resulted in the loss of eight transports with 900 British sailors, soldiers and accompanying women on 23 August. The fleet withdrew, some ships sailing directly to England while others made their way back to Boston. The land-based invasion of some 2,000 men got no further than Lake Champlain when it learned of the naval disaster and turned around.

For all its drama, Queen Anne's War cost relatively few casualties in North America, to a large degree because of the neutrality of New York and the Iroquois. The French and Spanish lost no more than 60 killed in action, while New England lost 200 dead, and forces from the Carolinas suffered 150 fatalities. The greatest European losses were among British troops who died in the ill-fated expeditions directed against Guadeloupe and Quebec. Native Americans suffered more, particularly in the South, owing not only to deaths in battle but to enslavement and forced removal. The gain of Annapolis Royal and Nova Scotia strengthened the British position, but the fact that the French continued to hold Île Royale – present-day Cape Breton Island – and soon built the fortress of Louisbourg on it cancelled much of the immediate benefit to the British.

WINNING A WAR LOST, 1712-14

The War of the Spanish Succession became a different war in 1712. The British effectively dropped out of the conflict; gone were their troops and ships, gone was their money, and gone was the military genius of Marlborough. It was to Louis's benefit that the war continued for two years after the British had essentially withdrawn, for it gave the French time to turn what looked like defeat into what could been seen as victory.

1712

In line with agreements formed by the French and the British, a peace conference convened at Utrecht on 29 January 1712. Louis sent the marquis of Huxelles, the abbé of Polignac, and Nicolas Mesnager as his plenipotentiaries. Queen Anne was represented by the Bishop of Bristol and the earl of Strafford; while Charles VI dispatched Sinzendorf, la Corzana, and Cronsbruch. A gaggle of Dutch representatives looked out for the interests of their several provinces. As is so often the case, the negotiations began with seemingly petty matters, such as determining how many horses and carriages each delegation could employ.

Besides the basic issues of the London Preliminaries, the parties involved brought other matters to the table. Louis was concerned to protect the interests of his ally, the elector of Bavaria. Louis wanted either the southern Netherlands or Sicily, and with it a royal title, as compensation for the elector, in addition to the restoration of Bavaria to Max Emanuel, but the latter would be all he received. The British protected the interests of Victor Amadeus, and their backing won him Sicily at the peace table, a gain he later exchanged for Sardinia, which was closer to home. Philip V pushed the interests of his own odd protégé, the strong-willed princess des Ursins, whose demands for some principality of her own in the Spanish Netherlands almost stymied the meetings at Utrecht.

Soon after the conference began, death confronted the participants with an unacceptable possibility. A paramount goal of the Allies was to guarantee that Philip V could never occupy the throne of France as well as that of Spain. When the dauphin succumbed to smallpox in 1711, grief had descended on the French royal family, but his passing had not threatened the diplomats' work, because there were still three healthy males between Philip and the French crown. However, the first months of 1712 swept away that biological buffer. Measles took the duke of Burgundy, who was Philip's elder brother and heir to the throne, in February. On 5 March the duke's oldest son died of the same disease, and, thus, the only person who stood between Philip V and the right to succeed the seventy-three-year-old Louis XIV was the remaining son of the duke of Burgundy, a two-year-old toddler, himself ill with measles. It seemed unlikely that he would survive, although he cheated death and took the throne three years later as Louis XV. The diplomatic roadblock caused by Philip's position in the line of succession would not be removed until late June, when Louis accepted a formula for Philip to renounce his claims to the French throne, which the Spanish monarch did first in Madrid on 8 July and then again as part of the treaty process on 5 November 1712.

The French and British discussed terms concurrently in Paris and London, then forwarded decisions to the negotiators at Utrecht. The French foreign minister Torcy played a key role in these talks, which progressed far enough that Queen Anne issued secret 'Restraining Orders' in May. These instructed the new British commander, James Butler, duke of Ormonde to 'avoid engaging in any siege, or hazarding a battle, till you have further orders from Her Majesty'.[91] In July Ormonde announced that the French and British had agreed to a suspension of arms, and British troops withdrew to wait out the rest of the war. A formal armistice halted the fighting between Louis and the British on 21 August.

The British had opted out of the war, but a great deal more haggling would precede the actual signing of peace treaties at Utrecht in April 1713. And while the talking continued, so did the fighting.

The Flanders front again dominated the campaign season, which began with grim expectations for the French. Some courtiers advised Louis to withdraw his court to the Loire, because the Allies might break through the now very thin defences in northeast France. Louis, however, refused and with tears in his eyes dispatched Villars to the front. After initial skirmishes in March and April the commanders marshalled their main armies in May. At this point Villars's army was seriously outnumbered. With the collapse of the Hungarian rebellion, the emperor sent 23,000 more troops to Flanders. The Allies now had 155 battalions and 272 squadrons plus 72 more battalions in garrisons. Against this force, Villars and his second in command, Montesquiou d'Artagnan, now promoted to marshal, mustered only 130 understrength battalions and 156 squadrons.

91 Restraining Orders in Frey and Frey, *The Treaties of the War of the Spanish Succession*, p. 378.

With Marlborough gone and imperial troops present in large numbers, Eugene became the allied commander in Flanders, and he resolved to breach the last fortress line guarding France. To his end, his first target was the fortress of le Quesnoy, which the Allies invested on 8 June. The garrison commander, Labadie, asked for terms on 3 July, but was refused as the allied general insisted that the garrison must surrender as prisoners of war. After taking up the fight again, Labadie agreed to surrender the next day. Eugene had now taken a major fortress, but the allied situation had already begun to erode. Ormonde received the Restraining Order in May, and while this was supposed to remain a secret, it became increasingly obvious that something was afoot. Then on 16 July Ormonde announced the suspension of arms and withdrew his twenty British battalions and five squadrons to Ghent and Bruges. The majority of the forces he had commanded were not British, but German units in British pay. They quickly changed their allegiance to the Dutch as their new paymasters.

Shaken by the British defection, but still enjoying a numerical advantage, Eugene next directed his forces against Landrecies, the last *pré carré* fortress between his army and Paris. His forces invested Landrecies on 17 July. This difficult operation required Eugene to ensure a supply line from magazines at Marchiennes to the forces surrounding Landrecies. To protect this route, Eugene ordered built a double line of entrenchments across the plain that separated Marchiennes from Denain. This served as a conduit for convoys which crossed the Scheldt at Denain, and from there sheltered behind the La Selle River to Landrecies.

Eugene suspected that Villars would still be reluctant to engage in a major battle, but he figured wrong. That marshal had concentrated the Franco-Spanish army along the Scheldt south of Cambrai and took the initiative. As Ormonde informed his allies of the suspension of arms, Villars announced it to his troops and, thus, demonstrated that there was reason for optimism. At a war council on 18 July Villars resolved to attack Eugene, and the next day his forces crossed the Scheldt and marched as far as Haucourt. The chevalier of Quincy reported that 'Joy was spread across the faces of the soldiers and officers alike; there was a unanimous presentiment that we were marching to certain victory.'[92] On 20 July Villars's army reached the left bank of the La Selle and camped along it. This was a direct threat

---

[92] Chevalier de Quincy in Ziegler, *Villars*, p. 237.

to the forces around Landrecies, and allied attention focused there. On 21 July Villars considered striking across the Sambre and reconnoitred the area, and on 22–3 July his forces camped between the Selle and the Sambre, with his headquarters at Maxingheim. All this effort to probe the lines around Landrecies from the west and south convinced the enemy that an attack could come there, and forces continued to build around the fortress. But the strength of the position at Landrecies convinced Villars that he must strike at Denain, a course of action that he and his generals had discussed for some days.

The decision taken, Villars resolved to mislead his foes into believing he would attack: 'All the measures that could be taken to persuade them that we wanted to attack the lines of circumvallation around Landrecies were employed; all the little and great ruses to fool the enemy, and even my own army, were used.'[93] And then to the surprise of all, as night fell on 23 July, Villars struck out for Denain to cover the distance of nearly twenty miles by next morning. At 8 a.m. his troops began crossing the Scheldt on pontoon bridges upstream from Denain. After this they straddled the enemy's defensive lines and came down north of Denain. Albermarle commanded about 10,000 Dutch troops who defended an entrenched camp that abutted the fortress. An alarmed Eugene promised Albermarle reinforcements, but it would take time for them to march to his relief. Meanwhile the French garrison of Valenciennes was on the road to attack the allied right at Denain.

The storm struck at 1 p.m., when 30,000 French troops bore down on the Dutch entrenchments. French infantry, grenadiers in the lead, advanced line after line in the confined space without firing as they suffered repeated salvoes of canister from enemy artillery. Hundreds of men fell to this murderous fire, but the French battalions maintained their momentum and their good order. Then enemy musketry ate into their ranks, but the French reached the ditch in front of the camp, clawed up the other side, and rolled into the enemy positions. The Dutch fell back; Albermarle tried to regroup, but panic gripped his troops, as Eugene viewed the unwelcome spectacle from high ground near the battlefield. Fifteen battalions of allied reinforcements tried to cross the river in support of the Dutch, but the garrison of Valenciennes under the prince of Tingry barred their way. In such circumstances, victory did not take long. In fact, once Villars had put his superior forces across the Scheldt before the enemy could respond in kind, the battle was virtually a foregone conclusion. But if victory

---

93 Villars, *Mémoires*, vol. iii, p. 153.

was sure, it was not cheap. Villars lost 2,100 killed and wounded, most in the initial assault on the enemy entrenchments. The French attack inflicted about 6,500 casualties on the Allies, destroying the Dutch units that held the camp.

When the news reached Paris, Louis ordered a Te Deum sung and the sixty allied battle flags captured at Denain displayed. He could celebrate victory. Saint-Simon commented, 'There was an overflowing of joy at Fontainebleau, about which the King was so flattered that he thanked his courtiers for the first time in his life.'[94]

Villars exploited his victory. Quickly he invested Marchiennes, which fell on 30 July with a rich harvest of supplies and equipment, including 100 cannon. The Allies lost 7,000–9,000 men taken prisoner at Marchiennes. With Denain and Marchiennes in French hands, Eugene abandoned the siege of Landrecies; the artillery began to pull out on 29 July, and the rest of the army broke camp on 2 August. Villars next attacked Douai. His troops invested the fortress on 31 July, and the fortress capitulated on 8 September. Showing a hearty resolution to maintain such a favourable operational momentum, Villars's army next besieged le Quesnoy (8 September–4 October) and then completed the campaign by taking Bouchain (1–19 October). He had restored the *pré carré*. This effectively ended the war in Flanders.

With the major effort in the northeast, the campaign along the Rhine had little drama. Marshal Harcourt had been chosen to command but was too ill, so Marshal Bezons replaced him. He arrived with his army at the end of May in Strasbourg and ordered his infantry to form in the lines of Lauterbourg. Troops were on the way up from Dauphiné to reinforce him. His opponent, the duke of Württemberg, stayed close to the lines of Ettlingen at first, and then crossed the Rhine at Philippsburg on 25 June. By mid-campaign, Württemberg had seventy-four battalions and thirty-eight squadrons, while the French, once again under the command of the recovered Harcourt, counted only forty battalions and fifty-seven squadrons based on the lines of Lauterbourg. Württemberg resolved to break these lines at Wissembourg in mid-September, but after doing little more than bombarding the lines he withdrew his army across the Rhine on 22 September. The French, in turn, sent cavalry to raid on the right bank of the Rhine, after which both sides went into winter quarters.

---

94 Saint-Simon quoted in Joël Cornette, *Le Roi de guerre: Essai sur la souveraineté dans la France du Grande Siècle* (Paris, 1993), p. 43.

The Final Contest

The war on the Italian front also marked time in 1712. The duke of Savoy quarrelled with the imperials during the winter, a dispute that the Dutch mediated. Imperials successfully besieged the Spanish fortress of Porto-Ercole on the Tuscan border from late March to early May. In the Alps, snows made manoeuvre difficult, and Marshal Berwick, who was back in command, did not move until early June. He had twenty-seven battalions and twenty-six squadrons garrisoned in Savoy and Dauphiné, with his main army of thirty-five battalions and three squadrons camped at Oulx, on the road between Briançon and Susa, in mid-July. All these forces totalled 30,000–35,000 troops, if both battalions and squadrons are estimated to be understrength. Against this, Daun led an imperial army of 23,300 men, and Victor Amadeus commanded 22,860 troops. The Allies assembled slowly around Susa in August. The two armies did little more than face off during the rest of the summer, Berwick bottling up the allied genie by never giving their armies a chance to descend into Savoy. When Berwick finally withdrew from the camp at Oulx early in September, he detached twenty battalions and ten squadrons to join French forces in Catalonia. Then the armies on both sides retired into winter quarters.

Actually, the war came to a standstill in Spain as well during 1712. The main armies of both Spain and the Allies squared off on the Portuguese border in Estremadura, where Bay again commanded for Philip V; however, there was little notable action on that front. The commander of the Franco-Spanish army in Catalonia, Marshal Vendôme, returned to Spain in January, and left Madrid to join his troops on 1 March. After spending time in Tortosa and Valencia planning the next campaign, he fell ill with an intestinal ailment and died at age fifty-eight in June. Command devolved upon T'Serclaes in Catalonia and to Valdecañas in Aragon. On the other side, Starhemberg was reduced to 17,500 troops to start the campaign, and he remained inactive until the autumn. With Philip's initial renunciation of the French crown, negotiations went quickly, and on 19 August France, Spain, and Great Britain agreed to a suspension of arms, which Philip published in Madrid on 4 September. Philip raised the blockade of Gibraltar and gave British ships free entry into Spanish ports. The British broke up the regiments in their pay serving in Portugal and began to withdraw troops from Catalonia. During the autumn campaign in Estremadura, Bay besieged Campo Maior in October, but he gave up the effort before taking the town. On 7 November, another suspension of arms was agreed to between France, Spain, and Portugal which ended the fighting on that front.

355

There was more action in Catalonia during the autumn, as Starhemberg, now deprived of all but his Catalan allies, tried to take Rosas and Gerona. He blockaded Rosas in July, but the French attacked his supplies, making his task nearly impossible, and he gave up the effort. General Wentzel had also blockaded Gerona over the summer, but a hastily assembled French army under Berwick advanced from Perpignan in December and relieved the siege.

1713

The complicated and frustrating peace negotiations produced formal peace treaties on 11 and 12 April 1713, reconciling all the major parties with the exception of the Austrian Habsburgs. The British came off well. Not only did they win the *asiento* from Spain, but Louis ceded his colonies of Acadia, Hudson Bay, and Newfoundland to them. (He did, however, retain French fishing rights off Newfoundland.) Louis also recognized Anne as the rightful queen of England and denied support to the Old Pretender. France fared well too. Louis surrendered no significant French territory on the Continent; in fact, at Utrecht he gained the valley of Barcelonnette and legitimized his seizure of Orange on the Rhône, and next year at Rastatt he would add Landau to his domains. To be sure, he returned Savoy and Nice to Victor Amadeus, but he had only occupied these and never claimed them. Interestingly, the treaty made the first clear use of 'natural frontiers' as a delineation of the French border when it defined the line between France and Savoy as the 'watershed of the Alps'.[95] And as the French withdrew in the south, the Allies pulled out of northern France. Above all the House of Bourbon gained a throne, with Philip V recognized as the rightful king of Spain by all signatories.

However, there were still aggrieved parties after Utrecht, and they ensured that the war would drag on. The emperor had not received his due; in fact, Charles VI would style himself king of Spain until 1725. In addition, the Catalans, who had sided with Charles, had not made peace with Philip. Suspensions of arms followed by the Treaty of Utrecht had brought peace to the Spanish Netherlands and Italy, while imperial forces also withdrew from Spain. Thus, the only remaining hot front where the French could confront the imperials openly remained the Rhine frontier. There, Villars took command and

---

[95] Peter Sahlins, 'Natural Frontiers Revisited: France's Boundaries since the Seventeenth Century', *American Historical Review* 95, no. 5 (December 1990), p. 1434.

matched his skills against Prince Eugene, who had pressed the emperor for one more campaign. Eugene believed that Louis's advanced age, the fact that he had a sickly three-year-old as his heir, and the ill-health of Anne all presented possibilities. However, it was to be another military triumph for Villars.

The French, too confident of peace, made few preparations for a new campaign, but when it was clear that the fighting would continue, Louis ordered a large army to concentrate on the Rhine. Imperial forces also marshalled and could benefit from the fact that they no longer needed to maintain troops in Italy and Flanders. Villars reached Strasbourg at the end of May to take command of the main French forces, while another, smaller, French army formed on the Sarre and the Moselle. On 3 June Villars appeared at Fort-Louis, making every effort to convince Eugene that he wanted to turn the flank of the lines of Ettlingen. But the lines were not his goal; instead, on 11 June he invested Landau and opened trenches on 24–5 June. On 18 August mines blew two large breaches in the walls. The imperial commander of Landau had hoped that Eugene would try to raise the siege, but when he realized this hope to be false, he beat the chamade on 19 August and capitulated the next day.

Eugene expected that Villars would be satisfied with taking Landau and then subjecting the Palatinate to pillage and contributions, but Villars was more ambitious than that and chose to attack Freiburg in September. He opened trenches there on the night of 30 September–1 October. Eugene approached, but realized he could not stop the siege and retired to the lines of Ettlingen. The town of Freiburg capitulated and Villars entered on 31 October and demanded one million livres from the inhabitants to spare their town from pillage. He then insisted that the imperial commander, Harch, surrender the forts that surrounded the city or the French would force the women, children, and valets of the imperial army, who had been left in the town, out on the esplanade between the town and the main fort, where they would perish from gunfire and privation. Harch capitulated everything on 16 November.

Ten days after his success at Freiburg, Villars was at Rastatt to negotiate a final treaty with Eugene face to face. Although they led opposing armies, the two generals-turned-diplomats were old friends, and both desired peace. Eugene, realizing how much the French wanted an end to war, stated that, 'in spite of the military superiority of our enemies and the defection of our allies, the conditions of peace will be more advantageous and more glorious than those we would have obtained at Utrecht'.[96] The French wanted to retain Landau, receive adequate compensation for Freiburg, and gain full compensation for the elector of Bavaria. In the Treaty of Rastatt, signed on 7 March 1714, France did receive Landau, but surrendered Freiburg and other positions on the right bank of the Rhine. The electors of Bavaria and Cologne regained their lands and dignities, but the French recognized the electoral status of Hanover for the first time. Most importantly, by the Treaty of Rastatt, Louis allowed Charles to take the rich Spanish Netherlands. Lesser allies were left in the cold. Charles abandoned the Catalans, and no provision was made for their safety. Louis, in turn, relinquished his support of Rákóczi's claims in Hungary, although the rebel was allowed to carouse in Paris during the peace conference. The Treaty of Rastatt sealed the matter between France and the emperor, but left undone a final settlement between France and the Empire as a whole, which came out of a peace conference at Baden and was registered in the Treaty of Baden on 7 September 1714. In fact, its provisions were virtually identical with those in the Treaty of Rastatt.

All the peace-making left only the matter of Catalonia to be resolved. In accord with the treaty of neutrality signed on 14 March 1713, imperial troops left Barcelona that year. The wife of Charles VI sailed from that port on an English ship on 29 March 1713 followed by the soldiers who embarked on English convoys from May through August. But even stripped of their allies, the Catalan rebels refused to surrender Barcelona. At this point Philip V asked for French aid once more, but received no help immediately. However, the return of Spanish troops from the Low Countries and the Rhine encouraged Philip to undertake a siege of the Catalan capital, and his army began to close around it. In early 1714, Louis could once again devote forces to Spain, and Marshal Berwick reappeared at the court in Madrid. Louis committed sixty-eight French battalions to be joined by thirty-nine Spanish and Walloon battalions, while the French navy took to the Mediterranean. A bombardment of Barcelona began in March, and a close siege, directed by Berwick, began in early July. Because the Catalans had no hope of help, the only future for Barcelona was suffering, so it capitulated on 12 September. The war was over. In June 1715 a small Franco-Spanish expedition retook Minorca with virtually no fighting.

---

[96] Eugene in Frey and Frey, *The Treaties of the War of the Spanish Succession*, p. 374.

DEFEAT OR VICTORY?

Had the War of the Spanish Succession been a defeat or a victory for France and its king? The British, who, in the words of noted diplomatic historian Andrew Lossky, 'virtually dictated' the peace, walked off with a few colonial concessions in North America, the *asiento*, and guarantees that Queen Anne would be recognized on her throne and that Philip would never assume that of his grandfather. But France retained its *ante-bellum* borders with only minor alterations, and a Bourbon wore the Spanish crown. The final terms were particularly favourable in comparison with those that the Allies tried to make Louis accept in 1709 and 1710. Then, the Allies had demanded 'no peace without Spain', but this was certainly peace without Spain. Louis could count the war a victory in dynastic terms, which from his perspective was the essence of the war in the first place, and France escaped a new Habsburg encirclement. Moreover, Louis added some minor pieces of territory and retained his earlier conquests. Of course, these calculations do not weight the costs in gold and blood. The issues at stake hardly seem worth the lives it cost all sides; estimates of battle deaths alone climb as high as 1,251,000, and this does not consider later losses from wounds, deaths from disease, and the sufferings of millions of abused and starving victims whose only fault was to live in the path of contending armies.[97] Measured by such moral standards, how could either side claim victory?

The last great war of Louis XIV had come to an end. The old monarch did not long survive his final conflict, for he died on 1 September 1715. As he lay dying, Louis XIV is reported to have confided to the frightened boy of five who would succeed him on the throne of France, 'I loved war too much.'[98] This was a counsel of perfection for the young boy, of course. However, later ages must ask, did the old monarch fight because he loved war, or because he saw it as an acceptable means towards his ends? The answer is that in his early wars, even if he did not love war *per se*, he lusted after *gloire* that only war could win him. Yet he did not embark on the Nine Years War because he loved war, but because he had become addicted to violent solutions and too confident of success. And in his

---

[97] Jack Levy, *War in the Modern Great Power System, 1495–1975* (Lexington, KY, 1983), p. 90.

[98] Louis in Wolf, *Louis XIV*, p. 618. Whether he actually said these words is a matter of debate. There is more than one version of his final admonition. Saint-Simon put them down as 'Do not imitate me in the taste that I have had for buildings, nor in that which I have had for war. . .'. Louis, duc de Saint-Simon, *Mémoires*, ed. Gonzague Truc, vol. iv (Paris, 1953), p. 932.

last war, perhaps the most costly of them all, he seems to have had little choice. The interests of his Bourbon dynasty were clear, and he failed not in making the wrong decision but in executing a reasonable one in such a clumsy fashion that he created a European-wide war that he did not want. In the end, he had become a victim of his offensive arrogance, not of his love of war.

8 THE WARS OF LOUIS XIV IN THE CONTEXT OF THE HISTORY OF WAR

As Louis succumbed to death, the concerned courtiers gathered at Versailles could not foresee how the future would regard the era that they witnessed die with the old king. How could they have known that much of what they praised as glorious, modern observers would condemn as vainglorious, or that war, which seemed the very essence of history, would attract so little interest among historians today? Whatever the present has made of the past, there is little doubt that Louis, particularly the young Louis, viewed warmaking as a primary and defining aspect of kingship. Therefore, to understand his reign we must put his wars in perspective by considering their impact and their character.

During the reign of Louis, France enjoyed a preeminent position in the European state system. For fifty years, French armies had been strong enough to stand against coalitions of all the other great powers. But the treaties of Utrecht, Rastatt, and Baden marked a watershed in international relations. No longer could France maintain its former dominance. This reality reflected not only the relative decline of France, but the increased power of other European states. As no other state could supplant France, an uneasy balance of power followed, and by mid-century Prussia and Russia joined Great Britain, Austria, and France as competing great powers.

Although Louis added to the territory of France, this could not offset the costs of war. Along the border of what was the Spanish Netherlands before 1714, he gained the city of Lille and several other substantial towns with their surrounding areas, thus moving the French border north. He also joined Franche-Comté to his domains and retained Strasbourg in Alsace. Unlike Napoleon's far more dramatic conquests, Louis's remained within the limits and tolerances of the international system, and, therefore, he was able to make them permanent. In contrast, Napoleon eventually lost more than he won, and France was smaller in 1815 than it had been when he seized power in 1799. However, Louis's substantial additions to his domain did not make France immediately stronger, because the price had been too high. Louis left the state close to bankruptcy with a staggering debt of 2.5 billion livres.[1]

Whatever their impact on international history, Louis's wars also existed as military phenomena, and so in a volume such as this they should also be put in perspective *vis-à-vis* the history of war. The conflicts fought by Louis XIV exemplified, first, a shift toward moderation in warfare after 1648 and, second, the prevalence of wars of attrition during this era. Of course, any attempt to generalize about the wars of Louis XIV must recognize that each of his major conflicts was unique in cause, conduct, and course; the chapters presented in this volume demonstrate the important differences between them. However, these struggles also shared certain common characteristics, for example the primary importance of Flanders, the multi-front nature of strategy, and the strong emphasis on contributions. Many observers have argued that among these shared traits was a less extreme prosecution of armed struggle, resulting in what historians commonly refer to as 'limited war'. An additional key characteristic of these contests was their long, indecisive, and costly nature, a pattern of conflict that will be introduced here under the rubric 'war-as-process'. The remainder of these concluding remarks address limited war and war-as-process.

LIMITED WAR

Generations of military historians have claimed that an age of limited warfare lay between the Thirty Years War and the Wars of the French Revolution, and no historian put more emphasis on this notion than did John U. Nef in his classic *War and Human Progress*. 'For Western Europe as a whole, years of war were still the rule, years of peace the exception. Yet there was more or less continuous moderation in the fierceness of the fighting.'[2] The contention is that after a period of warfare typified by irrational, primarily religious, motivations and fought with little constraint against enemy soldiers and unfortunate civilians alike, war became more rational in its goals and more humane in its conduct. As religion ceased to be a primary motivation, war became more a question of dynastic politics, and regimes fought not to destroy one another but simply for limited territorial or economic

---

1 Ernest Labrousse, Pierre Léon, Pierre Goubert, Jean Bouvier, Charles Carrière, and Paul Harsin, *Histoire économique et sociale de la France*, vol. ii (Paris, 1970), p. 277.
2 John U. Nef, *War and Human Progress* (Cambridge, MA, 1950), p. 155. The period he is discussing is 1640–1740 in a chapter entitled, 'Less Blood and More Money'.

gain. At the same time, better military administration relieved the pressures that drove soldiers to prey on towns and villages just to survive, and laws of war regulated the conduct of armies toward civilians. Of course, there were exceptions to the rule, and from time to time armies committed terrible excesses, but in the main, wars became more reasonable in their goals and conduct.

From its earliest formulations, this concept has been attacked. In the European context, critics point to the assault on Prussia during the Seven Years War, 1756–63, as one designed to eliminate Prussia as a major power, not simply to defeat it. And certainly Frederick the Great had to respond by mobilizing his state as completely as he could to fight off the Austrians and the Russians. In addition, warfare along the southern frontier of Habsburg lands retained its religious dimension and victimized civilians on both sides.

There is also good reason to challenge the notion that the wars of Louis XIV were limited even in the context of French military history, even though knowledgeable historians continue to insist on the moderation of warfare under Louis XIV. The historian Jean Meyer goes so far as to talk about a transformation from *guerre totale* during the Thirty Years War and the war with Spain to *guerre contrôlée* during the wars of Louis XIV.[3] For Meyer and also for André Corvisier, when Louis XIV seized the reins of government in 1661, he ushered in an era of limited warfare that stretched until the French Revolution again redefined warfare at the close of the eighteenth century. This characterization of warfare under the great Louis cannot be accepted without comment and qualification.

It is worth noting, for example, that religion did not disappear as an issue for France and its enemies. Certainly, confessional issues declined as a *casus belli* in western European states after 1648, but when Louis revoked the Edict of Nantes in 1685, he resurrected the issue. After forcibly converting his Huguenot population, Louis feared their resentment, and even created a militia in Languedoc to watch over the *nouveaux convertis*. His 1686 campaign against the Protestant Vaudois ranks as the most rapacious and reprehensible of his reign. During the Nine Years War, one of his greatest anxieties was that the Allies would descend on his coast with troops and arms to support the erstwhile Protestant community. And while he worried that the Allies would play the religious card by fomenting a Huguenot rising against him, he tried to use Catholic sympathies in Ireland against William III.

---

3 Jean Meyer, ' "De la guerre" au XVIIe siècle', *XVII siècle* 37 (1985), p. 278.

Table 8.1 France at war, 1495–1815[a]

Period	Total years	War years	Interstate war years	Internal war years
1495–1559	65	50 (76.9%)	48 (73.8%)	3 (4.6%)
1560–1610	51	33 (64.7%)	17 (33.3%)	28 (54.9%)
1611–60	50	41 (82.0%)	30 (60.0%)	21 (42.0%)
1661–1715	55	36 (65.5%)	36 (65.5%)	6 (10.9%)
1716–88	73	31 (42.5%)	31 (42.5%)	0 (0%)
1789–1815	27	23 (85.2%)	23 (85.2%)	4 (14.8%)

[a] In this table, if a war consumed any part of a given year, it is counted as a war year; thus, the Nine Years War, 1688–97, is calculated here as involving ten years.

French wars changed in intensity, to be sure, but not in some simple sense of moving from 'total war' to 'controlled war'. In order to judge the transformation in warfare during the reign of the Sun King, the periods that preceded and followed it need to be included in the picture; this means considering certain parameters of war from 1495 to 1815, an era that can be subdivided into six different periods of conflict from the French perspective. Parameters deserving of note include the number of years in which wars took place, the extent to which France had to fight its interstate wars on its own territory, and the degree of internal or civil conflict that afflicted the state.

Table 8.1 presents the six periods of warfare, 1495–1815, and the percentages of war years and the percentage of internal or civil war years in each. A cursory examination suggests that, measured by the number of calendar years in which interstate war occurred, the period of Louis's personal reign, 1661–1715, had more in common with the eras that preceded it than it did with the remaining years of the *ancien régime*, but more needs to be said.

During the Italian Wars, 1495–1559, the Valois kings undertook wars against foreign enemies during three-quarters of the years involved, and while the years after 1542 witnessed several incursions into French territory, the lion's share of the wars were fought outside France in Italy. In addition, the Valois were bothered by little internal rebellion. The era 1560–1610 encompassed the French Wars of Religion; while interstate conflicts were significant, internal and civil war dominated, as over half the calendar years involved such conflicts, and virtually all French warfare was visited upon French territory itself, with the attendant political, economic, and human costs. The major fighting in the first half of the *grand siècle* shared some important similarities with the Wars of Religion. First, internal conflict still played a very great role, since 42 per cent of the years witnessed some form of internal war. Second, even during the great interstate conflict with the Empire and Spain, a great many of the campaigns took place on French soil. This internal mayhem climaxed in the years of the Fronde, which combined interstate and civil war in a deadly mixture.

In comparison to the periods 1560–1610 and 1611–60, the wars of Louis XIV were less disastrous. First, while Louis engaged in long interstate conflicts, these wars were primarily fought across French frontiers or right at the borders. Certainly some invasions did occur, particularly those that Alsace suffered during the Dutch War and the one Provence endured during the War of the Spanish Succession, but the enemy never penetrated far and never threatened the heart of France. Second, the forces of the French king, which had behaved so rapaciously toward his own subjects during the long struggle with Spain, now showed much greater discipline when on French soil. Third and last, little internal rebellion threatened Louis; the most obvious cases came in Bordeaux and Brittany, 1675, and in the Cévennes, 1702–4, but they struck only the peripheries of France, and the first involved little fighting. Jean Meyer concludes, 'This war, however, was no longer, after 1660, total war: it was war harnessed [*aménagée*], rendered supportable for states, for participants, and populations.'[4] But he goes too far. Calculating the extent, intensity, and expense of interstate war changes the picture. Louis spent 65.5 per cent of the years after 1661 at war, and late in his reign, 1688–1715, only a few years did not know armed struggles. Moreover, his wars were great conflicts, mobilizing huge armies for long periods of time. These characteristics make his wars look much less limited, since they resembled those that preceded them more than those that followed.

After one considers the martial character of Louis XIV's reign, the period 1716–88 looks quite peaceful. The French engaged in interstate wars on the more modest scale of 42.5 per cent of the calendar years. And if two quite minor wars – the first with Spain, 1718–20, and the second the War of the Polish Succession, 1733–38 – are excluded, then the percentage falls to 31.5, less than half that under Louis XIV. In addition, Bourbon dedication to warfare in Europe seemed less than complete, and French borders were never seriously threatened. Certainly the French suffered humiliation during the Seven Years War, initially at the hands of the Prussians in

---

4 Ibid., p. 286.

Germany and then at the hands of the British across the seas in North America and India. However, after 1757, the French failed to mobilize on the scale that they had under Louis XIV. With France never fundamentally at risk, and with the periods between major wars long enough to allow the state and people to recover, war never matched the intensity of the years before 1715. This era truly deserves the title of an age of limited war, since for the French, armed conflict did not really come to them; they literally had to journey from home to find it. André Corvisier even suggests that the lessened intensity of warfare, at least as viewed from the perspective of Paris, fostered the optimism of the Enlightenment.[5] That limited quality stands out all the more because it was followed by the Revolutionary and Napoleonic Wars, which afflicted France with desperate and sometimes glorious conflict continuously from 1792 to 1815, with only two pauses: the first, for a year after the Treaty of Amiens, 1802, and the second following Napoleon's abdication in 1814. Then the issues at stake were fundamental, from survival of the new republic to Napoleonic hegemony over Europe. Enemies invaded French territory at the start of the Revolutionary and at the end of the Napoleonic eras, toppling the French government on two occasions. The armed turmoil of the Revolution spawned one of the most costly civil wars of French history in the Vendée, as well as bringing armed revolt to Lyons, Bordeaux, and Toulon. The period 1789–1815 truly deserves Meyer's categorization as 'total war'.

Seen in this perspective, the reign of Louis XIV witnessed a transformation in the intensity of warfare, at least for France, but not of the kind usually described. Warfare of the period 1610–60 shared much in common with the century that preceded it in terms of the many years afflicted with war, the rapacious character of the conflicts, the prevalence of campaigns within French borders, and the propensity to major civil war. The period 1661–1715 saw diminished violence within the borders of France because better-paid and better-disciplined soldiers did not prey on Louis's own subjects, because the success of French arms meant that wars were fought primarily outside his realm, and because France was largely spared internal rebellions. Yet the percentage of years consumed by interstate wars remained relatively the same – 60.0 per cent for 1611–60 and 65.5 per cent for 1661–1715 – and the burdens of the latter wars were very great indeed. In the next era, 1716–88, the proportion of years

---

5 André Corvisier, 'Guerre et mentalités au XVIIe siècle', *XVII siècle* 37 (1985), p. 231.

spent in interstate warfare declined sharply to only 42.5 per cent or less, and the remote sites of those wars, plus the absence of any significant internal rebellion, made it seem a very benign age. In fact, then, it is reasonable to see the *grand siècle* as part of a movement toward more moderate levels of warfare, from the great internal troubles and terrors of the second half of the sixteenth century, through the very difficult years of the first half of the seventeenth century, followed by the period 1661–1715 with its decreased internal conflict but continued major interstate wars, finally to the internal tranquillity and lessened levels of interstate war of the era after the great king's death. The half-century between 1661 and 1715 did not bring 'controlled war', but it constituted an important step in that direction.

WAR-AS-PROCESS

The conduct of war during the reign of Louis XIV, in fact from the early seventeenth century up to 1789, was guided by different assumptions and followed different military practices than those that typified warfare during the Napoleonic epoch. Modern commentary on warfare is still founded in that Napoleonic style of warfare in which campaigns must strive to impose a settlement upon the enemy by destroying his main forces, capturing his capital, or in some way striking at his 'centre of gravity'. To the extent that a commander or planner does not do this, he has failed, or, even worse, he is blind to the immutable nature of war and thus is incapable of success. In this dramatic model, war should be resolved by a decisive confrontation, by an event. In fact, war itself is best conceived of as an event, that is, a crisis to be confronted and conquered quickly, preferably in one battle or a single campaign. Combat so decides the issue that the diplomats have only to recognize and legitimize the *fait accompli* established by force of arms. This modern paradigm of war-as-event contrasts sharply with the pattern of warfare under Louis XIV, a form that can be encompassed in the paradigm of war-as-process. Several characteristics define war-as-process: the indecisive character of battle and siege, the slow tempo of operations, the strong resolve to make war feed war, the powerful influence of attrition, and the considerable emphasis given to ongoing diplomatic negotiations. Such conflicts were not brief but dragged on, or, in the words of one commentator, 'We see the majority of wars eternalize themselves.'[6]

6 Julien Brossé in *Mémoires du marechal de Turenne*, ed. Paul Marichal, vol. ii (Paris, 1909), pp. xxvii–xxviii.

The indecisive character of battle and siege

Battles did not settle the fate of wars under Louis XIV. True, one could argue that some battles decided certain strategic gambits or ended conflicts on particular fronts, as did the battles of Blenheim and Turin, but single defeats never imposed a general peace. After all, the War of the Spanish Succession droned on for a decade after Blenheim and eight years after Turin. Military institutions and practices militated against truly decisive battles. Moreover, it is not simply that in early modern European war-as-process battles were indecisive; the outcomes of individual military engagements or even entire campaigns were often virtually inconsequential to the outcome of a war. So, in the Nine Years War, Louis XIV won the battles but did not win the war, and in the War of the Spanish Succession, Marlborough's invincibility did not guarantee the Allies a 'peace with Spain'.

The character of armies and the nature of campaigning during the wars of Louis XIV limited the decisive potential of battles. At the start of each of his three major wars, Louis hoped that he could defeat an isolated enemy in little time, but then became mired in a situation that forced him to mobilize much greater forces than he had originally intended. The state commission army could only be expanded slowly; it lacked the convenience of earlier 'off the shelf' mercenary bands or the later efficient conscription of Napoleon's *grande armée*. Beyond this, the tenets of the battle culture of forbearance demanded that troops be mechanically drilled and thoroughly trained in a lengthy process. As a consequence of military institutions and practices, then, Louis consumed a very long time in fleshing out his existing regiments and creating new ones; meanwhile, his foes used this time to form great alliances that increased the threat to France. Louis inevitably ended up with a much larger and more diverse challenge than he had originally anticipated. Unable to dispose quickly of his original adversary on a single front, he faced an assortment of enemies on several fronts. The Dutch War expanded beyond the United Provinces to encompass the Moselle basin, much of the Rhineland, the eastern Pyrenees, and Sicily. The Nine Years War spread from the Palatinate to the Netherlands, Italy, and Roussillon/Catalonia. And the War of the Spanish Succession was fought from Portugal to Bavaria, and from the Channel to the Mediterranean, to say nothing of colonial ventures.

The need to defend multiple fronts kept Louis from marshalling the full military might of his kingdom on any single one of them. This made it unlikely that he would have the forces needed to destroy an opponent by offensive operations in any particular theatre. While multiple fronts hobbled Louis's offensive capacity, they also shored up the defence, because the armies stationed on different fronts could function as reserves for each other. That is, a French army in a more secure situation could send reinforcements to bolster one that had fared badly. In fact, one of the common characteristics of the wars of Louis XIV was the continual shifting of forces from one front to another. Here the fact that fortresses could buy time by delaying an enemy worked into a grander pattern, because fortresses stalled enemy forces until help could arrive.

The seasonal nature of war on land and at sea also limited the impact of individual battles and even entire campaigns. With bad weather forcing armies into winter quarters and fleets back into port, defeated armies and navies enjoyed an annual hiatus to rebuild and regroup. Victorious forces worked under a deadline to take advantage of their success before the winter. In this system, battlefield victories in the spring promised the greatest rewards, because they allowed the most time for exploitation. This is what made Marlborough's triumph at Ramillies on 23 May 1706 so valuable, although his run of easy conquests lasted for only two weeks after the battle. In any case, spring victories in land battles between main contending armies were few and far between,[7] and only three – the Battle of the Ter, the Battle of Ramillies, and the Battle of Almanza – were fought in circumstances that multiplied and extended the impact of victory.

The fact is that battles were rare during the wars of Louis XIV. Because they promised only limited rewards, were so costly, and were so unpredictable, the battle culture of forbearance discouraged major clashes in the open field. For example, the eleven years of fighting between Louis and the Allies in Flanders, 1702–12, witnessed only four full-scale battles. Even battle-hungry generals such as Marlborough and Turenne, the most belligerent of all, spent most of their energies in manoeuvres or sieges.

Sieges provided the most common form of combat during this era, particularly in the fortress-rich areas of Flanders and northern

---

[7] Six notable battles were fought by French armies in April or May during the Wars of Louis XIV:

11 April 1677	Battle of Mont Cassel
27 May 1694	Battle of the Ter
19 April 1706	Battle of Calcinato
23 May 1706	Battle of Ramillies
25 April 1707	Battle of Almanza
22–3 May 1707	Battle of the Lines of Stollhofen

Italy. At least sieges rewarded an investment in blood and gold with measurable, predictable, and stable gains. In addition, in the context of wars of attrition, the capture of fortresses usually brought with it control over resource areas that supported the war effort. However, even sieges did not promise decisive results. The War of the Spanish Succession demonstrates that in campaigns that revolved around sieges, there always seemed to be one more fortress that had to be taken. And even the series of successes won by Marlborough year after year did not finally break through the fortified barriers erected by Louis XIV, although Marlborough seemed on the brink of doing so in 1711. The presence of nearby fortresses limited the impact of victories both in battle or in siege. They provided shelter and immediate reinforcements for the defeated and presented obstacles to the progress of the victorious.

Slow operational tempo and limited momentum

Both a product and a cause of the indecisive nature of combat, the operational tempo of war-as-process generally moved at a snail's pace. Clausewitz employed the analogy of trying to walk in water to demonstrate the difficulty of doing even simple things in war, but operations during the wars of Louis XIV often moved as if the participants were waist-deep in molasses. Of course there were bursts of rapid marching, such as Turenne's and Créqui's periodic exploits on the Rhine and Marlborough's descent to the Danube in 1704. However, in general, things moved slowly and did not go too far, and the reasons for this are not hard to find.

Part of the answer can be found in logistics. Dependence on field ovens and convoys to supply bread and the need to pause continually to gather fodder for horses slowed rates of advance. In the interest of convenience, armies spent large periods of time in camp, simply facing off against one another. Another part of the answer can be found in the confining influence of fortress barriers and entrenched lines, particularly in that most important theatre of operations, Flanders. The scarcity of modern fortifications in Spain and the consequently greater movement there, for example in 1706 and 1710, demonstrates this point. And another part of the answer may lie in pessimism concerning what could be gained by forcing the matter in the field, although this is the most difficult influence to measure. To the extent that this was true, the record of indecisive battles discouraged commanders and princes from seeking costly action; thus, indecisive fighting bred lethargy, which avoided decisive action.

The Wars of Louis XIV in Context

Operational tempo seemed particularly laggard after major victories, when maintaining the momentum of victory would seem to have promised the greatest rewards. An outstanding example of opportunity lost followed Luxembourg's crushing defeat of Waldeck at Fleurus in 1690. The greatest change that Marlborough brought to the conduct of operations during the War of the Spanish Succession was not in revolutionizing the role of battle, for he too fought few of them, but in increasing the operational tempo and maintaining momentum. Of course his most impressive example here came in 1706. Villars also approximated this tempo in 1712. However, the greater rule throughout the wars of Louis XIV remained the inability to keep the ball rolling after scoring a notable success. Here, the contrast with Napoleonic war-as-event is particularly striking.

The inability to muster the resources necessary to maintain operational momentum factored into strategic calculations under Louis XIV. Major sieges, for example, required massive amounts of war materiel, so much that Louis could not authorize multiple sieges. The winning of a single great fortress in one theatre of operations, such as in Flanders in 1691 and 1692, expended Louis's resources and satisfied his ambitions for the year. So expensive were sieges and battles that raiding became a very attractive form of military operation. Louis also had to juggle resources, including manpower, from one front to another in order to hold multiple enemies at bay. This meant that success on one front often did not lead to pressing the advantage there, but instead it justified taking troops from that theatre in order to reinforce another front.

Such practices, while frustrating to modern notions of operations, may have meshed well with the more limited strategic goals of Louis. In the main, after 1675 he adopted an essentially defensive posture, for which it was enough simply to hold resource areas and keep his foes from violating his frontiers. The only major deviation from this rule was the attempt to operate deep in Germany during 1703 and 1704, but even this can be seen as an attempt to aid his Bavarian ally. A lively operational tempo was simply not necessary, and perhaps not even possible for Louis XIV's armies in most circumstances.

Need for war to feed war

The necessity to make war feed war contributed to the indecisive character and slow tempo of military operations. Rather than concentrating on a Clausewitzian goal of eliminating the main forces of the enemy or in some other way rendering a foe powerless, armies tended to fight in order to secure resources. To an important degree, forces were expected to support themselves in the field, and planners who conceived of warfare as long and costly looked to the fighting itself as a way of sparing the royal treasury some of the burdens of war.

The need to garner resources on campaign influenced or determined military action. Luxembourg's course of action after Fleurus is illuminating in this regard, for after winning a battlefield triumph of truly Napoleonic proportions, the French marshal simply subjected the surrounding area to contributions instead of hounding his beaten foe into the ground. This pattern was repeated frequently, as commanders exploited victory for its logistic rather than its strategic benefits. Whole campaigns were crafted with resources in mind. Louis and Chamillart conceived of Villars's campaigns of 1703 and 1707 largely in terms of seizing German resources to keep French armies in the field.

Of course, other armies at other times benefited from funds, food, and fodder taken in the field, but under Louis XIV this aspect of war was not a short-term convenience but a defining characteristic. The term 'living off the country' employed by historians as a descriptive category, most notably by Martin van Creveld, can muddy the waters rather than clarifying military practice.[8] Napoleon's troops 'lived off the country' in the sense that they foraged for food while on the march, a practice that accelerated their pace. Louis's forces 'lived off the country' in the sense that they levied contributions intended to support the war, but this need slowed the momentum of campaigns. Napoleon may have milked defeated, conquered, and allied territories for resources after a war was concluded – consider his exploitation of Italy – but Louis expected enemy resources to maintain ongoing operations. Napoleon's rape of European wealth did not shape campaigns; it was a reward for rapid success. On the contrary, for Louis the mobilization of enemy resources was a principle guiding the conduct of operations in a effort to outlast his foes in long wars of attrition.

War of attrition

Lacking quick decision on the battlefield, the wars of Louis XIV plodded on. By nature, long struggles put tremendous strain on the

---

8 See John A. Lynn, 'The History of Logistics and *Supplying War*', in John A. Lynn, ed., *Feeding Mars: Logistics in Western Warfare from the Middle Ages to the Present* (Boulder, CO, 1993).

state's financial and other resources, and their conservation or exhaustion became critical factors in the conflict.

The dynamics of Louis's wars made them extremely expensive, particularly for France. As coalitions formed against the Sun King, they created an imbalance that Louis attempted to overcome by assembling the largest land forces Europe had ever seen since the Roman Empire. Maintaining such a gargantuan army sent costs soaring. But ultimately Louis could not mobilize enough manpower and weaponry to overmatch his combined foes, and the relative equality of forces between the Sun King and the alliances that opposed him prohibited either side from turning the war decisively to its advantage. This resulted in stalemate or at least slowed the military resolution of the conflict to such a crawl that the ability to continue the war collapsed before a clear victory could be won by either side.

The critical necessity for early modern war-as-process was not so much manpower or materiel as it was money. Financial concerns shaped military operations, and wars of attrition bankrupted states. Contemporaries recognized this clearly. A much-quoted passage from Guibert's *Essai général de tactique* is usually read as predicting the rise of patriotism during the Revolutionary and Napoleonic eras, but it is better read as appealing for war on the cheap and as condemning the way in which money determined campaigns:

> But imagine that there arose in Europe a people who joined to austere virtues and a national militia a fixed plan of aggrandizement that did not lose view of this system, who, knowing how to make war at little cost and to subsist from its victories, was not reduced to putting aside its arms because of financial calculations. One would see such a people subjugate its neighbours and overturn our feeble constitutions like a north wind bends frail reeds.[9]

Guibert wrote this in 1772, during the reign of Louis XV, but he aptly expressed the frustration of strategy.

Role of ongoing diplomacy

Because Louis's major struggles became long wars of attrition, resolving the issues at stake and drafting an acceptable peace involved the interplay of three factors: battlefield success, financial exhaustion,

---

9 Jacques Guibert, *Écrits militaires, 1772–1790* (Paris, 1977), p. 57.

and diplomatic finesse. With military action so indecisive and the attrition of state resources such a critical factor, diplomacy was not simply the handmaiden of martial victory, as it was in Napoleonic war-as-event. So, even as a succession of victories might seem to push in one direction, diplomacy might move in another, as the weight of attrition became insupportable. Thus, Louis's generals won the battles of the Nine Years War, but he urgently needed to end that conflict which had emptied his coffers and overstrained his resources. Likewise, despite Marlborough's triumphs, Louis outlasted the British commitment to the War of the Spanish Succession by 1711, and the Tories agreed to terms far more generous to France than the Allies had offered Louis before. Skill in diplomacy could not replace skill in war, but the former was essential to final success.

Not only did diplomacy possess considerable leverage at the end of armed conflicts, but negotiations also began rather early in wars and proceeded for years while the fighting dragged on.[10] Hugo Grotius in *De jure belli ac pacis* argued for ongoing negotiations to accompany warfare, and war-as-process adopted this counsel, at least after the initial few years of action. Diplomatic manoeuvres to end the Nine Years War, for example, started as early as 1691, and Louis began overtures for a negotiated peace in the War of the Spanish Succession even before the disastrous campaigns of 1706.

The power and wealth of Bourbon France made it a hegemon, and gave French diplomacy a critical task – that of splitting the coalitions ranged against Louis. Defining Louis's France as a hegemon does not mean that it dictated to Europe, but that it was strong enough to take on all of western Europe in an armed conflict, and that only a coalition of the other great powers could match it. In contrast, a balance of power situation exists in an international system composed of several states diverse enough in strength that no one dominates and that rival coalitions form between them to block and balance each other. The coalitions engaged in mid-eighteenth-century warfare typify balance of power, but the international system of Louis XIV was something quite different. France was the first such hegemon Europe had seen; even mighty Spain did not fight single-handed against all of western Europe.

While Louis suffered by having to fight so many enemies on several fronts, he enjoyed certain advantages as well. First, he always held the central position, and thus could employ interior lines. This

---

10 Ragnhild Hatton makes the same point in her inaugural lecture *War and Peace, 1680–1720* (London, 1969).

meant that France escaped the fate of sixteenth-century Spain, which ultimately lacked the resources to fight a great war at long range in the Netherlands, Germany, and northeast France. Second, Louis did not have to bargain with allies in forming military policy; he clearly directed strategy. Third, he might gain great advantage by detaching a single foe from a coalition ranged against him. Only a large alliance could successfully oppose Louis, and the bonds between allies were weak joints that diplomacy might unglue. Detaching one significant member of a coalition could so alter the military balance that other participants had to scramble to reach accommodation. So in the Nine Years War splitting off Savoy from the Grand Alliance brought peace, and in the War of the Spanish Succession, dealing directly with Great Britain undercut Habsburg Austria.

In this international system, diplomacy existed in symbiosis with military action. Thus, even though this volume concentrates on military history, and the narrative keys on operations in the field at sea, such an emphasis should not obscure the close relationship between war and diplomacy. For Napoleonic war-as-event, diplomacy was little more than mop-up operation, a way of registering a *fait accompli*; such was not the case in Ludovician war-as-process. Napoleon dictated; Louis negotiated.

Conscious policy or a product of circumstance?

Even if war-as-process defined international armed struggle in the era of Louis XIV, the question remains: did Louis consciously accept and apply this style of conflict, or was it simply imposed upon him by reality? In other words, was war-as-process influenced by conception or just by circumstance? There is no question that Louis tried repeatedly to avoid the spectre of a long contest. In no case did he set out upon a course of action expecting that it would result in a war of attrition. However, his three great conflicts all became such, and perhaps the most interesting aspect of Louis's prosecution of these wars is just how easily he made the transition from his original desire to engage in a short contest to his ultimate recognition he was trapped in a long struggle. It is worth noting, for example, that after the failure of initial French operations in the Dutch War and the Nine Years War, Louis made no second plan for a quick decision, but settled into strategy of outlasting his enemies. This suggests that Louis's resignation to a long and costly war was far more fundamental to his understanding of international armed conflict than was his intention to fight a short one.

This seems consistent with his own personal history. Louis grew up during France's seemingly interminable struggle with Spain, 1635–59. A young monarch who lived the first twenty-one years of his life while his country was continually at war might well see long struggles as nearly inevitable, even if undesirable, though that monarch did his best to avoid them. Certainly, there is no discounting the influence of factors beyond any individual's control. The very fact that Marlborough laboured so hard to escape the boundaries of war-as-process but ultimately failed speaks for the heavy and controlling hand of circumstance. However, Louis's reactions justify the conclusion that, while circumstance went a long way to impose war-as-process, it was also a pattern that Louis expected, accepted, and followed.

To the extent that the paradigm of war-as-process outlined here accurately describes the wars of Louis XIV, his struggles fall outside the competing paradigm of war-as-event as pursued in the West for the last two centuries. Of course, in real-world experience the two models are not so simple to separate; things overlap, and the contrasts are only clear in conceptual terms. And while Napoleonic war-as-event has continued to dominate thought about war in the West, war-as-process has survived in the non-Western sphere. The struggle in Vietnam, at least during its American phase, conformed to four of the characteristics of war-as-process, differing in that war did not feed war and in the fact that the struggle was more a civil war than it was a confrontation of states.[11] There is no question that a full understanding of the history of warfare must comprehend war-as-process in addition to war-as-event. This adds extra weight to the argument that the wars of Louis XIV deserve more attention than they have received from historians. Perhaps this volume can awaken an interest in these conflicts and help dissipate the fog of ignorance that surrounds them.

---

11 See John A. Lynn, 'War of Annihilation, War of Attrition, and War of Legitimacy: A Neo-Clausewitzian Approach to Twentieth-Century Conflicts', *Marine Corps Gazette* 80, no. 10 (October 1996), pp. 64–71.

CHRONOLOGY

A NOTE ON CALENDARS

The traditional Julian calendar had deviated significantly from the actual equinoxes by the early modern period; in fact, during the sixteenth century it was ten days behind astronomical events. Therefore, Pope Gregory XIII reformed the calendar in 1582, giving us the Gregorian calendar, but this reform was adopted by different countries at different times. He eliminated ten days, making 11 March into 21 March. France adopted the new calendar in December 1582, but England did so only in 1752 (by which point eleven days had to be cut). Orthodox countries kept the Julian calendar until the twentieth century. Because the French were already on the Gregorian calendar under Louis XIV, all the dates are given here in the Gregorian form. This leads to some confusion; for example, the Protestant Irish celebrate the Battle of the Boyne on 12 July because in the reform of 1752 they added eleven days, but the fact is that in the seventeenth century one would have added only ten, so the true date at the time was 11 July on the Gregorian calendar.

1589–1610	Reign of Henri IV
15 August 1598	Edict of Nantes
1610–43	Reign of Louis XIII
1618–48	The Thirty Years War in Germany
1624–42	Cardinal Richelieu first minister of France
1635	French entry into the Thirty Years War
5 September 1638	Birth of Louis
1642–61	Cardinal Mazarin first minister of France
16 May 1643	Death of Louis XIII, Louis XIV comes to the throne
1648–53	Revolt of the Fronde
7 November 1659	Treaty of the Pyrenees
9 March 1661	Mazarin dies, personal reign of Louis XIV begins

WAR OF DEVOLUTION, 1667–68

24 May 1667	Invasion of Spanish Low Countries
8 July–28 August 1667	Siege of Lille
19 January 1668	Partition Treaty concerning the inheritance of Carlos II concluded by Louis and Leopold I
23 January 1668	Triple Alliance formed between the Dutch Republic, England, and Sweden
February 1668	Invasion of Franche-Comté by Condé
2 May 1668	Treaty of Aix-la-Chapelle
22 May 1670	Treaty of Dover between Louis and Charles II

DUTCH WAR, 1672–78

17 March 1672	War began between England and the Dutch
6 April 1672	Louis declares war on the Dutch
7 June 1672	Battle of Sole Bay
6–30 June 1673	Siege of Maastricht
21 August 1673	Battle of the Texel
19 February 1674	Treaty of Westminster ending war between England and the Dutch Republic
16 June 1674	Battle of Sinzheim
July 1674	Revolt of Messina on Sicily
11 August 1674	Battle of Seneffe
4 October 1674	Battle of Ensheim
1 January 1675	French fleet arrives at Messina and fights its way in
5 January 1675	Battle of Turkheim
April–August 1675	Papier Timbré and Bonnets Rouge revolts in Brittany
27 July 1675	Death of Turenne
11 August 1675	Battle of Cronzer-Brucke
8 January 1676	Battle of Stromboli
22 April 1676	Battle of Augusta, De Ruyter dies of wounds a week later
10 May 1676	'Battle of Heurtebise' not fought by Louis

Chronology

2 June 1676	Battle of Palermo
23 June–11 Sept. 1676	Siege of Philippsburg
7 July–29 August 1676	Siege of Maastricht
28 Feb.–17 March 1677	Siege of Valenciennes
3 March 1677	Battle of Tobago
11 April 1677	Battle of Mont Cassel
17 April 1677	Seizure of Cambrai
15–26 March 1678	Siege of Ypres
6 July 1678	Battle of Rheinfeld
10 August 1678	Treaty of Nijmegen between France and the Dutch Republic
14 August 1678	Battle of St Denis
17 September 1678	Treaty of Nijmegen between France and Spain
6 February 1678	Treaty of Nijmegen between France and Austria
1679–84	The Reunions
1681	Dragonnades against Huguenots in Poitou
5 August–5 Sept. 1681	Bombardment of Algiers by French fleet under Duquesne
July 1681–March 1682	First blockade of Luxembourg
30 September 1681	French seizure of Strasbourg
26 June–17 Aug. 1683	Bombardment of Algiers by French fleet under Duquesne
17 July–12 Sept. 1683	Siege of Vienna

WAR OF THE REUNIONS, 1683–84

31 August 1683	French declared they would send troops into the Spanish Netherlands
26 October 1683	Spanish declares war on France
29 April–3 June 1684	Siege of Luxembourg
17–28 May 1684	Bombardment of Genoa
15 August 1684	Truce of Ratisbon
19–25 June 1685	Bombardment of Tripoli
July 1685	Dragonnades against Huguenots begin anew
22 October 1685	Edict of Fontainebleau revokes Edict of Nantes

379

Chronology

April–June 1686	Campaign against the Vaudois
July 1686	Creation of the League of Augsburg in Germany

NINE YEARS WAR, 1688–97

24 September 1688	Louis's 'Mémoire des raisons'
27 Sept.–30 Oct. 1688	Siege of Philippsburg
5 November 1688	William lands in England to seize the crown
8–11 November 1688	Siege of Mannheim
26 November 1688	Dutch Republic enters war against France
December 1688–June 1689	Devastation of the Palatinate
March 1689	James II sails to Ireland
11 May 1689	Battle of Bantry Bay
17 July–8 Sept. 1689	Siege of Mainz
16 Sept.–10 Oct. 1689	Siege of Bonn
8–9 February 1690	Attack on Schenectady, New York
9–30 May 1690	Expedition against Port Royal
1 July 1690	Battle of Fleurus
10 July 1690	Battle of Beachy Head (or Bézeviers)
11 July 1690	Battle of the Boyne
18 August 1690	Battle of Staffarde
October 1690	Amphibious operation against Quebec
15 March–10 April 1691	Siege of Mons
24 March–2 April 1691	Siege of Nice
25 June 1691	Tourville sails from Brest on his *campagne du large*
16 July 1691	Death of Louvois
July 1691	Bombardment of Barcelona
1 Sept.–13 Oct. 1691	Siege of Limerick
19 September 1691	Combat at Leuze
29 May–3 June 1692	Battle of La Hogue (or Barfleur–La Hogue)
25 May–1 July 1692	Siege of Namur
3 August 1692	Battle of Steenkerque
21–2 May 1693	Siege of Heidelberg
1–13 June 1693	Siege of Rosas
27 June 1693	Battle of Lagos
19–23 July 1693	Siege of Huy
29 July 1693	Battle of Neerwinden

Chronology

Summer 1693–94	Famine in Europe
10 Sept.–10 Oct. 1693	Siege of Charleroi
4 October 1693	Battle of Marsaglia
27–30 November 1693	Bombardment of St Malo
27 May 1694	Battle of the Ter
29 May–10 June 1694	Siege of Palamos
18 June 1694	Fight at Camaret near Brest
17 June–29 June 1694	Siege of Gerona
9 August 1694	Allied fleet arrives at Barcelona
17–27 September 1694	Siege of Huy
25 June–9 July 1695	Siege of Casale
1 July–6 Sept. 1695	Siege of Namur
15 July 1695	Bombardment of St Malo
17 July 1685	Bombardment of Granville
13–16 August 1695	Bombardment of Brussels
29 August 1696	Treaty of Turin between France and duke of Savoy
2 May 1697	Capitulation of Cartagena
15 May–5 June 1697	Siege of Ath
12 June–10 August 1697	Siege of Barcelona
8–27 September 1697	Siege of Ebernberg
20 September 1697	Treaty of Ryswick between France, Dutch Republic, England, and Spain
30 October 1697	Emperor signs Treaty of Ryswick
11 October 1698	Partition Treaty between France, emperor, Dutch Republic, and England
6 February 1699	Death of Bavarian electoral prince Joseph Ferdinand
25 March 1700	Partition Treaty between France, England, and Dutch Republic
1 November 1700	Death of Carlos II

WAR OF THE SPANISH SUCCESSION, 1701–14

9 July 1701	Battle of Carpi
1 September 1701	Battle of Chiari
7 September 1701	Treaty of the Second Grand Alliance between England, the United Provinces, and Austria
1 February 1702	Battle of Cremona

381

Chronology

19 March 1702	Death of William III
18 April–15 June 1702	Siege of Kaiserwerth
15 May 1702	England, the United Provinces, and Austria declare war against France
18 June–9 Sept. 1702	Siege of Landau
24 July 1702	Camisard uprising begins in France
15 August 1702	Battle of Luzzara
August–Sept. 1702	English attempt to take Cadiz
25 September 1702	Capitulation of Venlo
7 October 1702	Capitulation of Roermond
14 October 1702	Battle of Friedelingen
13–23 October 1702	Siege of Liège
23 October 1702	Battle of Vigo Bay
9 March 1703	Capitulation of Kehl
11 March 1703	Battle of Siegharding
6 May 1703	Rákóczi manifesto
24 April–15 May 1703	Siege of Bonn
16 May 1703	Portugal joins the Grand Alliance
16 June 1703	Rákóczi enters Hungary
15–26 August 1703	Siege of Huy
15 August–6 Sept. 1703	Siege of Breisach
20 September 1703	Battle of Höchstädt
10–29 September 1703	Siege of Limbourg
3 October 1703	Duke of Savoy declares war on France
15 November 1703	Battle of Speyer
12 October–17 Nov. 1703	Siege of Landau
2 July 1704	Battle of Donauwörth
3 August 1704	Capitulation of Gibraltar
13 August 1704	Battle of Blenheim
24 August 1704	Battle of Velez-Málaga
1 October 1704	Villars proclaims pacification of Camisards
8 October 1704	Battle of Pata
7 November 1704	Treaty of Ilbersheim
26 December 1704	Battle of Tymau
5 May 1705	Death of Leopold I
16 August 1705	Battle of Cassano
22 August–9 Oct. 1705	Siege of Barcelona
4–17 October 1705	Siege of Badajoz
4 January 1706	Capitulation of the citadel of Nice
19 April 1706	Battle of Calcinato
23 May 1706	Battle of Ramillies

Chronology

26 May 1706	Capitulation of Brussels
30 May 1706	Capitulation of Ghent
6 June 1706	Capitulation of Antwerp
27 June 1706	Allies enter Madrid
9–18 August 1706	Siege of Menin
27 August–5 Sept. 1706	Siege of Dendermonde
7 September 1706	Battle of Turin
4 October 1706	Philip V returns to Madrid
13 March 1707	Convention of Milan neutralizes Italy
25 April 1707	Battle of Almanza
22–3 May 1707	Villars crosses the Lines of Stollhofen
28 July–22 August 1707	Siege of Toulon
September 1707	Allies take Minorca
March 1708	Failed Jacobite expedition to Scotland
11 July 1708	Battle of Oudenarde
3 August 1708	Battle of Trencsén
14 August–8 Dec. 1708	Siege of Lille
1709	Famine strikes Europe
18 April 1709	Capitulation of the fort of Alicante
27 June–3 Sept. 1709	Siege of Tournai
11 September 1709	Battle of Malplaquet
9 March–20 July 1710	Gertruydenberg Conference
27 July 1710	Battle of Almenara
20 August 1710	Battle of Saragossa
21 September 1710	Allies occupy Madrid again
3 December 1710	Philip V reenters Madrid
9 December 1710	Battle of Brihuega
10 December 1710	Battle of Villa Viciosa
17 April 1711	Death of Joseph I
1 May 1711	Peace of Szatmár
4–5 August 1711	Marlborough crosses Ne Plus Ultra Lines
11 August–12 Sept. 1711	Siege of Bouchain
11 Sept.–13 Nov. 1711	Duguay-Trouin attacks and occupies Rio de Janeiro
8 October 1711	London Preliminaries signed
29 January 1712	Opening of Utrecht Congress
May 1712	Queen Anne issues 'Restraining Orders'
24 July 1712	Battle of Denain
30 July 1712	Capitulation of Marchiennes
31 July–8 Sept. 1712	Siege of Douai

383

Chronology

21 August 1712	Suspension of arms between France, Great Britain, and Spain in Spain
8 Sept.–4 Oct. 1712	Siege of le Quesnoy
7 November 1712	Suspension of arms between France and Portugal
14 March 1713	Suspension of arms between France and Savoy
11–12 April	Treaties of Utrecht
11 June–19 Aug. 1713	Siege of Landau
29 Sept.–16 Nov. 1713	Siege of Freiburg
7 March 1714	Treaty of Rastatt
7 July–12 Sept. 1714	Siege of Barcelona
27 September 1714	Treaty of Baden
14–30 June 1715	Franco-Spanish expedition takes Minorca
1 September 1715	Death of Louis XIV

GLOSSARY

armateurs	entrepreneurs who outfitted ships for privateering voyages
army of observation	army intended to protect forces engaged in besieging a fortress; such armies would generally be larger than the army actually occupying the siege lines
asiento	the lucrative monopoly granted by the Spanish government to supply slaves to the Spanish colonies in the New World
baggage (train)	an army's supplies and equipment carted to the field; this would often include the baggage of the officers and the army's funds – a tempting target for the enemy
ban, arrière ban	the traditional levies of regional nobility called out in accord with their feudal obligations
bomb ketch	a small vessel rigged to fire mortars from its deck
camp volant	a 'flying camp', a significant detachment of fast-moving troops, often cavalry, intended to raid and harass the enemy or act as a quick-manoeuvre force
chamade	the drum signal announcing one party's willingness to parley, usually to discuss its own surrender
chemin couvert	the 'covered way', a walkway immediately behind the parapet and firing step of fortress works sheltered from enemy fire
commissaires	'commissioners', administrative officers with a variety of functions and usually serving under the supervision of higher administrative officers, such as *intendants*

Glossary

contributions	payments to a hostile army made to protect a town, city, or area from pillage or destruction by that army; a form of war tax; an area made subject to demands for contributions was 'put under contributions'
course	a raid, usually to garner wealth or supplies from an area, to demand contributions, or to punish those who refused to pay them
fireship	a naval vessel meant to be set alight and sailed into an enemy fleet with the intention of setting the foe's vessels on fire
flute	a type of naval supply ship sailing with the fleet
fournisseurs	suppliers; entrepreneurs who provided necessary material to the navy or the army
frigate	a smaller war vessel carrying fewer cannon than the rated vessels
guerre de course	'war of raids', naval commerce raiding, as opposed to naval warfare concentrating on the enemy fleet
guerre d'escadre	'war of squadrons', naval warfare concentrating on the enemy fleet, as opposed to commerce raiding
intendants	major administrators in the French governmental system; they might have their main duties in districts called *généralités*, or certain *intendants d'armée* accompanied armies on campaign to handle administrative and financial details
invest	to surround, as when besieging forces began by 'investing' an enemy fortress before digging siege lines
lines of circumvallation	outward-facing entrenchments encircling a besieged fortress, dug by a besieging army to protect itself from attack by forces trying to break the siege from the outside
lines of contravallation	inward-facing entrenchments ringing a besieged fortress, dug by the attackers to protect themselves from sorties by the entrapped garrison
livres	the French 'pound', a unit of money, divided into 20 sols or sous; in reasonable times a loaf of bread cost about one sol

Glossary

miquelets	Spanish irregular infantry, usually mountain fighters of the Pyrenees; both regular and militia *miquelets* fought for and against the French in Roussillon and Catalonia
munitionnaires	entrepreneurs supplying the army; usually this term is applied to those supplying foodstuffs
nouveaux convertis	Huguenots who had recently converted to Catholicism, particularly in response to the pressure applied by Louis in the 1680s
pioneers	peasant labourers commandeered to do physical labour for an army, usually digging entrenchments, a necessary source of labour for sieges
pré carré	'duelling field' formed by a double line of fortresses developed by Vauban to defend the northeast frontier of France
rated vessels	used here to speak of first to fifth rate vessels, which carried from 100 to about 40 cannon, as distinguished from other smaller vessels
relief army	army trying to relieve a siege by defeating the besieging army
schnapphahns	literally German for 'highwaymen', but they would be called guerrillas in today's vocabulary; peasantry who rose to resist the French along the Rhine
ship of the line	ship carrying enough guns and of large enough size to stand in the line of battle at sea, first through fourth or fifth rate vessels

BIBLIOGRAPHICAL ESSAY

This brief historiographical discussion will speak to the reader in a decidedly French accent, as has this entire volume. Yet despite its emphasis on France, this essay will also try to present the reader with English-language volumes when possible. Library shelves sag under the weight of the great number of books on the personality and reign of the Sun King. Two works which are particularly good and particularly relevant to the study of war and diplomacy during this era are John B. Wolf, *Louis XIV* (New York, 1968) and Andrew Lossky, *Louis XIV and the French Monarchy* (New Brunswick, NJ, 1994). Wolf's treatment is older to be sure, but it is also broader; Lossky bills his work as a 'political biography'. There is much to be gained from reading the essays in John C. Rule, ed., *Louis XIV and the Craft of Kingship* (Columbus, OH, 1969). Joël Cornette offers an excellent and intriguing cultural perspective in his *Le Roi de guerre: Essai sur la souveraineté dans la France du Grande Siècle* (Paris, 1993). Louis's memoirs deserve attention, although, sad to say, they only cover the early years of his reign. See *Mémoires de Louis XIV pour l'instruction du dauphin*, ed. Charles Dreyss (2 vols; Paris, 1860) and the erudite English translation, *Mémoires for the Instruction of the Dauphin*, ed. and trans. Paul Sonnino (New York and London, 1970). Henri Griffet, *Recueil de lettres pour servir à l'histoire militaire du règne de Louis XIV* (8 vols; 1760–64), provides a useful collection of documents on the reign but it is not easy to find.

Interest in the topic of 'war and society' has stimulated the production of a good selection of broadly conceived works on military aspects of early modern European history. An early such work is G. N. Clark, *War and Society in the Seventeenth Century* (Cambridge, 1958), and the last two decades have brought a flood of others. See André Corvisier, *Armies and Societies in Europe, 1494–1789*, trans. Abigail T. Siddall (Bloomington, IN, 1979); John Childs, *Armies and Warfare in Europe, 1648–1789* (Manchester, 1982); M. S. Anderson,

War and Society in Europe of the Old Regime, 1618–1789 (New York, 1988); Frank Tallett, *War and Society in Early Modern Europe* (London, 1992); and Jeremy Black, *European Warfare, 1660–1815* (New Haven, CT, 1994). In my opinion, the best of the more recent volumes is that by Frank Tallett.

Works discussing military institutions must necessarily come to grips with the subject of the 'Military Revolution', a useful but somewhat umbrella term that hopes to include both military developments and their 'revolutionary' effects on government, society, and European colonial expansion. The historiographical tempest started to boil in this teapot when Michael Roberts delivered an inaugural lecture in 1954, later published as *The Military Revolution, 1560–1660* (Belfast, 1956). This piece and a selection of other essays on the subject have been conveniently packaged in Cliff Rogers, ed., *The Military Revolution Debate: Readings on the Military Transformation of Early Modern Europe* (Boulder, CO, 1995). The most extensive, and ambitious, book-length treatment is the now classic Geoffrey Parker, *The Military Revolution: Military Innovation and the Rise of the West, 1500–1800* (Cambridge, 1988). Jeremy Black and others have followed suit with volumes that include 'Military Revolution' in the title. For an evolutionary alternative to this thesis, see John A. Lynn, 'The Evolution of Army Style in the Modern West, 800–2000', *International History Review* 18, no. 3 (August 1996), pp. 505–45.

Two specialized but very valuable contributions to the general literature on early modern armies are Myron P. Gutmann, *War and Rural Life in the Early Modern Low Countries* (Princeton, NJ, 1980), which argues that the impact of war on local populations was not so great as previously believed, and Fritz Redlich, *The German Military Enterprizer and his Workforce, 13th to 17th Centuries, Vierteljahrschrift für Sozial- und Wirtschaftsgeschichte*, Beiheft XLVII (2 vols; Wiesbaden, 1964), which discusses the very important phenomenon of the military officer as entrepreneur.

Several authors focus on the contemporary art of war. These include two works on tactics and operations in the field: David Chandler, *The Art of Warfare in the Age of Marlborough* (New York, 1976) and the more recent Brent Nosworthy, *The Anatomy of Victory: Battle Tactics, 1689–1763* (New York, 1990). The prolific and expert Christopher Duffy has, among very many other fine works, produced a wonderful trilogy on fortifications and siege warfare: *Fire and Stone: The Science of Fortress Warfare, 1660–1860* (Newton Abbot, 1975); *Siege Warfare: The Fortress in Early Modern History, 1494–1660* (London, 1979); and *The Fortress in the Age of Vauban and Frederick the Great, 1660–1789, Siege Warfare*, vol. ii (London, 1985). The best work on the absolutely vital subject of logistics remains G. Perjés, 'Army Provisioning, Logistics and Strategy in the Second Half of the 17th Century', *Acta Historica Academiae Scientiarum Hungaricae* 16, no. 1–2 (1970), pp. 1–52. Care should be used when employing the better known Martin van Creveld, *Supplying War: Logistics from Wallenstein to Patton* (Cambridge, 1977). See my 'The History of Logistics and *Supplying War*', in John A. Lynn, ed., *Feeding Mars: Logistics in Western Warfare from the Middle Ages to the Present* (Boulder, CO, 1993).

Until recently, the French army of the seventeenth century had not received a general, integrated treatment in the historical literature, but hopefully my *Giant of the Grand Siècle: The French Army, 1610–1815* (New York, 1997) has accomplished that task, at least in a preliminary form. Steven Ross, *French Military History, 1660–1799: A Guide to the Literature* (New York, 1984) provides a reasonable bibliography for the period. That seminal work by the grand old man of French military history, André Corvisier, *L'Armée française de la fin du XVIIe siècle au ministère du Choiseul: Le Soldat* (2 vols; Paris, 1964), contains important material on the French army under Louis. A valuable, although all too brief, treatment of military and naval institutions has appeared in volume one of the four-volume series under the general editorship of Corvisier: Philippe Contamine, ed., *Histoire militaire de la France*, vol. i (Paris, 1992). On institutional matters see as well the classic works by Camille Rousset and Louis André listed below under military biography. Albert Babeau, *La Vie militaire sous l'ancien régime* (2 vols; Paris, 1890) contains lively anecdotes but is also prone to error, according to the erudite David Parrott. More specialized French studies worthy of mention include Victor Belhomme, *L'Armée française en 1690* (Paris, 1895), Victor Belhomme, *Histoire de l'infanterie en France* (5 vols; Paris, 1893–1902), Louis Susane, *Histoire de la cavalerie française* (3 vols; Paris, 1874), and the excellent scholarly study Georges Girard, *Le Service militaire en France à la fin du règne de Louis XIV: Rocolage et milice, 1701–1715* (Paris, 1915).

The British army boasts fewer detailed studies, except, of course, for the many works extolling the accomplishments of Marlborough. Two works deserving of mention are John Childs, *The Army of Charles II* (London, 1976) and R. E. Scouller, *The Armies of Queen Anne* (Oxford, 1966).

For obvious reasons, navies are more likely to catch British attention and less likely to be thoroughly examined by the French. The recent and quite excellent Jan Glete, *Navies and Nations: Warships and State Building in Europe and America, 1500–1860* (2 vols; Stockholm, 1993) presents surprisingly rich detail on early modern navies. See also J. S. Bromley, *Corsairs and Navies, 1660–1760* (London, 1987). A *summa* of French naval history under the Sun King has just appeared, Daniel Dessert, *La Royale: Vaisseaux et marins du Roi-Soleil* (Paris, 1996). On the critical decision to abandon fleet warfare, consult the superb Geoffrey Symcox, *The Crisis of French Sea Power 1688–1697: From the* guerre d'escadre *to the* guerre de course (The Hague, 1974). Specialist studies of note include Paul W. Bamford, *Forests and French Sea Power, 1660–1789* (Toronto, 1956), Eugene L. Asher, *Resistance to the Maritime Classes: The Survival of Feudalism in the France of Colbert* (Berkeley, 1960), and Paul M. Bamford, *Fighting Ships and Prisons: The Mediterranean Galleys of France in the Age of Louis XIV* (Minneapolis, 1973). Concerning the English, later British, navy, one could begin with the classic William Laird Clowes, ed., *The Royal Navy: A History From the Earliest Times to the Present* (7 vols; London, 1897–1903, reprinted New York, 1966). More intensive examinations of the Royal Navy include the following: Herbert Richmond, *The Navy as an Instrument of Policy, 1558–1727* (Cambridge, 1953); Frank Fox, *Great Ships: The Battlefleet of Charles II* (London, 1980); John Ehrman, *The Navy in the War of William III, 1689–1697* (Cambridge, 1953); and J. H. Owen, *The War at Sea under Queen Anne* (Cambridge, 1938).

The pages of this volume have centred on strategic and operational history and regarded institutional matters as mere background. A history that took war and the state as its primary subject would have to confront the vital question of war finance. For a short treatment of this subject see P. G. M. Dickson and John Sperling, 'War Finance, 1689–1714', in *New Cambridge Modern History*, vol. 4 (Cambridge, 1970). Key works on the French side of this question include Daniel Dessert, *Argent, pouvoir et société au Grand Siècle* (Paris, 1984) and Françoise Bayard, *Le Monde des financiers au XVIIe siècle* (Paris, 1988), in addition to the classic studies of Colbert, such as C. W. Cole, *Colbert and a Century of French Mercantilism* (2 vols; New York, 1939). On British war finance, see John Brewer, *The Sinews of Power: War, Money and the English State, 1688–1783* (London, 1989).

The wonderfully rich and immensely valuable Charles Sévin, marquis de Quincy, *Histoire militaire de Louis le Grand roi de France* (7 vols; Paris, 1726) still provides the foundation for any study of the wars of Louis XIV from a French perspective. For useful detail on actions, battles, and sieges, see Gaston Bodart, *Militär-historisches Kriegs-Lexikon (1618–1905)* (Vienna and Leipzig, 1908). Use this work, but use it with care. A more modern, and extremely useful, military reference is R. Ernest Dupuy and Trevor N. Dupuy, *The Encyclopedia of Military History* (New York, latest edition 1993). John Child presents more detail on the Nine Years War from a British point of view in *The Nine Years War and the British Army 1688–1697: The Operations in the Low Countries* (Manchester, 1991). The classic work on the devastation of the Palatinate remains Kurt von Raumer, *Die Zerstörung der Pfalz von 1689* (Munich, 1930).

The most studied conflict of Louis's reign is the War of the Spanish Succession. (See the section below on military biography.) In Linda Frey and Marshal Frey, eds, *The Treaties of the War of the Spanish Succession* (Westport, CT, 1995), the editors offer a useful work much broader in its contents than the title implies. Scholars can benefit greatly by employing the valuable source material collected in François Eugène de Vault and J. J. G. Pelet, eds, *Mémoires militaires relatifs à la succession d'Espagne sous Louis XIV* (11 vols; Paris, 1836–42). The much-overlooked Dutch receive their due in J. W. Wijn, *Het Staatsche Leger: Het Tijdperk van de Spaanse Successioorlog, 1702–1715* (8 vols; The Hague, 1959–64). Henry Kamen throws light on another dark corner of the war in *The War of Succession in Spain, 1700–15* (Bloomington, IN, 1969).

Biography has always been a popular way of approaching military history, and treatment of the wars of Louis XIV is no exception. The French have even approached the history of military administration through this genre. See the ageing but still essential studies by Rousset and André: Camille Rousset, *Histoire de Louvois* (4 vols; Paris, 1862–64); Louis André, *Michel Le Tellier et l'organisation de l'armée monarchique* (Paris, 1906); and Louis André, *Michel Le Tellier et Louvois* (Paris, 1942). Corvisier has recently offered a good study that parallels Rousset: André Corvisier, *Louvois* (Paris, 1983).

Louis's great field commanders have repeatedly been the focus of biographies. Jean Bérenger has recently provided a fine portrait of the victorious Turenne in *Turenne* (Paris, 1987). A good English-language biography of Condé exists: Eveline Godley, *The Great Condé: A Life of Louis II de Bourbon, Prince of Condé* (London, 1915). For Marshal Luxembourg's story, one must resort to French. Early in this century, Ségur penned volumes on this excellent, but little-known, commander: Pierre Marquis de Ségur, *Le Maréchal de Luxembourg et le prince d'orange, 1668–1678* (Paris, 1903) and *Le Tapissier de Notre-Dame: Les Dernières années du maréchal de Luxembourg, 1678–1795* (Paris,

1903). The great engineer Vauban has been the subject of many volumes, most recently Anne Blanchard, *Vauban* (Paris, 1996). There is also an older, but still good, English-language biography: Reginald Blomfield, *Sébastien le Prestre de Vauban, 1633–1707* (New York, 1971). An excellent collection of Vauban's papers appear in Albert Rochas d'Aiglun, *Vauban, sa famille et ses écrits* (2 vols; Paris, 1910). Vauban's methodical approach to siege warfare can be studied first hand in Sébastien le Prestre de Vauban, *A Manual of Siegecraft and Fortification*, trans. G. A. Rothrock (Ann Arbor, ml, 1968). The most successful French general of the War of the Spanish Succession receives well-earned praise in François Ziegler, *Villars: Le Centurion de Louis XIV* (Paris, 1996) and the older, and much thinner, biography by Claude C. Sturgill, *Marshal Villars and the War of the Spanish Succession* (Lexington, KY, 1965). Villars has also left the most extensive memoirs of any of the great seventeenth-century French commanders: Claude Louis Hector Villars, *Mémoires du maréchal de Villars*, ed. marquis de Vogüé (5 vols; Paris, 1884–95).

The attention lavished on John Churchill, the duke of Marlborough, surpasses that garnered by any French general. See, in particular, the biography by his descendant, Winston Churchill, *Marlborough, His Life and Times* (4 vols; London, 1933–38). The serious student also has at his or her disposal a fine selection of published memoirs and papers: W. C. Coxe, ed., *Memoirs of John, Duke of Marlborough* (3 vols; London, 1905); George Murray, ed., *The Letters and Dispatches of John Churchill* (5 vols; London, 1845); B. van T'Hoff, ed., *The Correspondence, 1701–1711, of John Churchill and Anthonie Heinsius* (The Hague, 1951); and Henry Snyder, ed., *The Marlborough–Godolphin Correspondence* (3 vols; Oxford, 1975).

On that other military spectre who haunted Louis's later years, Prince Eugene, see Derek McKay, *Prince Eugene of Savoy* (London, 1977). To study the prince's campaigns in detail requires facing the difficulties of the German language in *Feldzüge des Prinzen Eugen von Savoyen* (13 vols; Vienna, 1876–86).

However, neither Marlborough nor Eugene ranks as Louis's greatest foe; without question, that was William of Orange. Stephen Baxter penned a fine, but very laudatory, biography in his *William III and the Defense of European Liberty, 1650–1702* (New York, 1966). William's successor at the helm of Dutch foreign policy receives a good treatment in Hebert H. Rowen, *John de Witt, Grand Pensionary of Holland, 1625–1672* (Princeton, NJ, 1978).

Lastly, the history of international relations *per se*, while not the primary focus of this volume, obviously serves as essential context.

Bibliographical Essay

Diplomatic history claims a full and varied historiography which I will only hint at here. Of course, several of the works already mentioned deal extensively with foreign affairs, for example the biographies of Louis XIV by Wolf and Lossky and those of William III and John de Witt. For an economical introduction to the subject, consult the articles by Livet, Lossky, and Zeller in the relevant volumes of the *New Cambridge Modern History*. Also see the works of Ragnhild Hatton, including her inaugural lecture *War and Peace, 1680–1720* (London, 1969). See her important collections: Ragnhild Hatton, ed., *Louis XIV and Europe* (Columbus, OH, 1976) and Ragnhild Hatton and J. S. Bromley, eds, *William III and Louis XIV* (Toronto, 1968). The later volume, a *festschrift* for Mark A. Thomson, contains important articles by Thomson that provide a foundation for the current view of Louis as a more moderate statesman. Other general treatments include Gaston Zeller, *L'Organisation défensive des frontières du nord et de l'est au XVIIe siècle* (Paris, 1928) and Georges Livet, *L'Équilibre européen de la fin du XVe à la fin du XVIIIe siècle* (Paris, 1976). A recent article merits attention as well: Peter Sahlins, 'Natural Frontiers Revisited: France's Boundaries since the Seventeenth Century', *American Historical Review* 95, no. 5 (December, 1990), pp. 1423–51. On the much-discussed Dutch War, in addition to the above, see Paul Sonnino, *Louis XIV and the Origins of the Dutch War* (Cambridge, 1988) and C. J. Ekberg, *The Failure of Louis XIV's Dutch War* (Chapel Hill, NC, 1979).

INDEX

Aarschot, 299, 300
Abenakis, 262
absolutism, absolute monarchy, 16, 17–19, 24–7, 28, 46
Academy of Sciences, 30
Acadia, 349, 356
Adige River, 310
admiral of France, 91–2
Aegean Sea, 171
affaire des poudres, 321
Africa
  see North Africa
Agen, 184
aggregate contract army, 48–9
Aire, 75, 146, 147, 149, 156, 337, 338
Aisne River, 343
Aix-la-Chapelle, Treaty of, 109, 111
Albany, New York, 349
Albermarle, Arnold van Keppel, earl of, 353
Albuquerque, 302
Alessandria, 310
Algiers, 172, 173, 174
Algonquins, 262
Alicante, 223, 325, 335
Aligny, count of, 120
Almanza, Battle of, 316, 369
Almenara, Battle of, 339
Alost, 108, 167, 306
Alps, 14, 162, 164, 181, 210, 211, 255, 355, 356

Alsace, 3, 14, 37, 39, 110, 118, 121, 122, 128, 129, 131, 132, 135, 140, 141, 142, 144, 145, 146, 148, 151, 152, 153, 155, 157, 159, 162, 163, 164, 169, 178, 192, 197, 198, 202, 242, 250, 255, 288, 294, 300, 308, 323, 361, 365
Altea, 302
Altenheim, 140, 155
Alzey, 194
Amback, 147
Amberg, 283
Ambitieux, 230
Amiens, Treaty of, 366
Amsterdam, 34, 116, 117, 200, 337
Andalucia, 297
Anderlecht, 218, 225
Angelets rebels, 183
Annapolis Royal, 349
Anne, queen of England, 272, 279, 286, 341, 342, 345, 350, 351, 356, 357, 359
Anne of Austria, 10, 13, 28
Annecy, 335, 346
Antwerp, 79, 150, 275, 280, 281, 299, 300, 306
Aosta, Val d'Aosta, 220, 345
Aragon, 311, 339, 341
Arc River, 323, 345
Archbishop of Paris, 326
Arco, d', 288
Arcy, marquis of, 179, 180

395

Index

aristocracy, 28, 30, 51–2, 90–1, 186–9
anoblis, 91
pacification of the aristocracy, nobles, 186–9
robe nobility, 51
sword nobility, 51
Arleux, 344
Armada, 88
armament, arming of ships
  see navy
armateurs, 101, 102, 347
Army of Flanders, 218, 231, 253, 337, 345
army, general 36, 47–82, 187
  officers, 49, 187–8
  pay, for troops, 55
  recruitment, 49
  size, field army size in battle, 68
  size, growth of total forces, 4, 50–1, 106, 111, 144, 233, 263, 271
  tactics, 58–71
  training, 49, 67, 68
Army of the Meuse, 233, 254
Army of the Rhine, 210, 233, 282
Aragon, 221, 316
Arnoul, Pierre, 85
arquebus, 59
Arras, 75, 329, 338, 343, 344
arrière ban and *ban*, 123, 132, 200, 238, 240, 245
Artagnan, Charles de Batz-Castelmore, count d', 120
artillery, artillery pieces, cannon
  artillery organization, weapons, and tactics on land, 58, 63–5
  artillery weapons and tactics at sea, 94–5
  cannon, 64
    number with land forces, 65
    numbers with armies and fleets, 95
  canon de nouvelle invention, 64

mortars, 63, 64, 65, 165, 171–4, 189, 218
Artois, 3, 146, 149, 234, 337
Asfeld, Lt. Gen. Claude-François, chevalier of, 325
asiento, 40, 269, 356, 359
Atlantic Ocean, 14, 35, 86, 123, 124, 218, 222, 244, 247, 252, 277
Ath, 77, 108, 112, 258, 259, 308
Athlone, 222
Aubenas, 183–4
Audijos rebellion, 183
Auger de Subercase, Daniel d', 349
Augsburg, 189, 201, 284, 289, 290
Augsburg, League of, 189
Augusta, 144
Augusta, Battle of, 148
Aulnois, 331
Aunis, 123, 221, 252, 257
Austria, 361, 363, 375
Autrive, 214
Avelghem, 247, 248
Avesnes-le-Sec, 344
Avigliana, 220, 237
Azores, 348

Bacharach, 194
Badajoz, 302, 335, 346
Baden, 199, 314
  see Louis of Baden
Baden, Treaty of, 358, 361
Balaguer, 324, 346
Balearic Islands, 171
Balimorre, 222
ban
  see arrière ban
banks, national, 26–7
  Bank of Amsterdam, 26
  Bank of England, 26
Bantry Bay, Battle of, 203
Banyolas, 255
Barbançon, duke of, 225
Barbesières, marquis of, 260

Index

Barbets
  see Vaudois
Barbezieux, marquis de, 20, 274
Barcelona, 97, 221, 223, 244, 246, 250, 251, 259–61, 296, 301, 302, 310–11, 324, 341, 346
Barcelonnette, 228, 237, 339, 356
Barclay, 245, 252
Barfleur, 229
Barfleur-La Hogue, Battle of
  see La Hogue, Battle of
Barraux, 323, 346
barrier fortresses, 263, 269, 326, 342
Bart, Jean, 92, 93, 102, 256
Basset y Ramos, Juan Batista, 302
Bastille, 124
bastion, 73, 74
battalion, battalion size, 60–1
battle, battle formations, 69
battle culture of forbearance, 66, 70–1, 81, 368, 369
Baudouin, *intendant*, 282
Bavaria, 12, 110, 121, 195, 199, 270, 286, 289, 293, 294, 314, 322, 358, 368, 371
Bavaria, elector of
  see Max Emanuel, elector of Bavaria
Bâville, Lamoignon de, 278–9
Bay, marquis of, 316, 324, 335, 339, 340, 355
bayonet, 58, 60
Bayonne, 123
Bayreuth, Christian Ernst, margraf of, 250, 313, 314
Beachy Head, Battle of, 83, 88, 95, 96, 215, 216
Beaumont, 167
Bedburg, 287
Bedmar, Isidro, marquis of, 295
Behr, J. H., 71
Belfort, 133, 163
Belgrade, 192
Bellefonds, Marshal, marquis de, 123, 229

Bellegarde, 135, 143, 148
Belle-Île, 257
Bellver, 221, 239
Benfeld, 142
Bengal, 262
Bentinck, William, earl of Portland, 257
Bergues, 108
Bergues, prince of, 249
Bernard of Saxe-Weimar, 48
Berne, 181
Berry, Charles de France, duke of, 40, 268
Bersello, 285
Berthelot, *munitionnaire*, 133
Berwick, Marshal James Fitzjames, duke of, 256, 274, 295, 297, 298, 301, 311, 316, 317, 321, 323, 329, 335, 337, 338, 339, 345–6, 355, 356, 358
Besançon, 124, 163
Besigheim, 236
Bethume, countess of, 106
Béthune, 337, 338
Beuningen, Coenraad van, 109
Bezons, Marshal, count of, 324, 329, 338, 339, 345, 354
Bierbeck, 225
Binche, 258
Bingen, 194, 198, 259
Black Forest, 276, 282, 290
Blanes, 244
Blenheim, Battle of, 274, 286, 290–4, map 292, 302, 303, 319, 334, 335, 368
Bluche, François, 2
Bohemia, 121
bomb ketch, 94, 172
bombardment, as a means of intimidation, 165, 171–4, 218
Bombay, 262
Bonanella, 285
Bonn, 121, 139, 202, 280

397

Index

Bonnets Rouges revolt, 136, 184–5, 240
  see Papier Timbré revolt
Bordeaux, 176, 177, 182–3, 184, 365, 366
borders, concept of, 161–2
Bossu, 331
Boston, 349
Bouchain, 145, 146, 149, 156, 344, 354
Boufflers, Marshal Louis-François, marquis de, 132, 165, 176, 177, 194, 201, 205, 206, 209, 211, 217, 218, 225, 227, 233, 236, 241, 247–50, 254, 257–9, 275, 280, 287, 321–3, 331–4
Boulonnais, 183
Bourbonne, 338
Bournonville, 128, 129, 131, 132, 133
Boussières, 200
Bouvines, 167
Boyne, Battle of, 216
Brabant, 33, 115, 140, 280, 307
Brandenburg, 110, 111, 117, 118, 156, 178, 181, 209, 210, 218, 242
Brandenburg, elector of, 34, 45, 122, 131, 132, 133, 178, 195, 202, 206, 209, 210, 216, 248
  see Frederick William
Braudel, Fernand, 4
bread, 54
Brecia, 309, 310
Breda, Treaty of, 108
Breisach, 37, 154, 163, 193, 195, 262, 283
Breisgau, 142, 148, 152
Brest, 36, 86, 88, 92, 93, 96, 100, 152, 203, 214, 215, 221, 222, 229, 239, 240, 244, 245–6, 252, 256, 257, 261, 296, 347

Bretten, 250
Briançon, 237, 323–4, 335, 339, 345, 346, 355
Bricherásio, 180
brigades, 69
Briheuga, Battle of, 340, 341
Bristol, bishop of, 350
Britain, 204, 264, 355, 361, 368, 375
Brittany, 90, 123, 184–5, 221, 229, 231, 240, 252, 257, 365
Broglie, duke de, 278–9
Bruges, 300, 306, 318–19, 352
Brunswick, duke of, 216
Brussels, 119, 137, 140, 146, 151, 154, 209, 218, 225, 233, 247, 248, 249, 250, 258, 259, 299, 306, 318, 321, 322
Buda, 191
Bühl, 282, 313, 314
Bullion, Claude de, 10
Burguete, 167
Burgundy, 8, 109, 198
Burgundy, Louis de France, duke of, 268, 275, 283, 317, 318–21, 350–1
Burick, 113, 114
Byng, Sir George, 318

Cadiz, 246, 252, 255, 256, 277
Cadogan, 319–20, 344
Calaf, 346
Calais, 246, 253, 256, 257, 347
Calatayud, 339
Calcinato, Battle of, 309
Caligny, Hue de, 78
Calvo, 146–7
Camaret Bay, landing at, 245, 252
Cambrai, 75, 146, 149, 150, 156, 329, 343, 344, 352
Camisards, 277–9, 297–8
  see Cévennes
campagne du large, 221, 222
Campo Maior, Battle of, 336, 355

398

Index

Camprodon, 167, 202, 203, 251
Cannes, 315
cannon
  see artillery
Cap de Quiers, 167
Cape Breton Island, 349
Cape St Vincent, 239
Cape Verde Islands, 348
Caprara, Enea, 128, 219
Cardona, 346
Caribbean Sea, 347–8
Carignano, 220, 237
Carlos I, of Spain, 7
Carlos II, of Spain, 21, 32, 38, 39, 40, 42, 45, 105–6, 111, 244, 251, 253, 266, 268–9
Carlos III, of Spain, 285, 302, 311
Carmagnola, 213, 220
Carolinas, 348
Carpenédolo, 301
Carpi, 310
Carpi, Battle of, 270
Cartagena, 103, 261
Casale, 164, 180, 181, 211, 220, 237, 238, 242, 250, 251, 310
Caspe, 311
Cassano, Battle of, 301
Cassard, naval commander, 347
Cassel, Battle of, 149, 150, 158
Castelbardo, 309
Castellfollit, 167, 251
Castelo Branca, 296
Castiglione, Battle of, 310
Castile, 311, 340–1
Catalonia, 14, 122, 135, 136, 144, 149, 155, 167, 199, 202, 205, 214, 221, 237, 238, 240, 242, 243, 244, 251, 253, 255, 257, 259, 264, 302, 324, 340, 341, 355, 356, 358, 368
  see Spanish front
Catánia, 144
Cateau, 137

Catéchisme royal, 52
Catholic League, 9, 10
Catinat, Marshal Nicolas de, 27, 66, 180, 181, 205, 211, 213, 214, 220, 223, 227–8, 233, 237–8, 239, 242–3, 247, 251, 255, 257–9, 270, 276
Caulier, Madeleine, 322
Cavalier, Jean, 278–9, 297, 298
cavalry, 58, 62–3, 68, 69, 129
Cavour, 213
Cayenne, 152
Cenis, Mount Pass, 323, 335, 345
Cerdanya, 136, 143
Céret, 183
Cerisoles, 214
Cervera, 324, 341
Cervières, 324
Cesana, 323–4
Cévennes, 15, 179, 182, 277–9, 286, 315, 365
  see Camisards
chamade, defined, 108
Chamber of Justice, 182
chambers of reunion, 163
Chambéry, 213, 346
Chamillart, Michel de, 99, 101, 274, 278, 297, 309, 312, 327, 329, 330, 372
Chamilly, Marshal Nicolas, count of, 22, 123, 126, 127, 259
Chamlay, marquis de, 20, 23, 24, 169, 195, 196, 197, 198
Champagne, 110, 330
Chantilly, 142
Charlemont, 137, 138, 164, 170
Charleroi, 108, 112, 113, 118, 124, 138, 149, 150, 154, 167, 206, 209, 227, 235–6, 241, 248, 254, 264, 308
Charles, Archduke, 35, 39, 40, 121, 267–8, 285, 295, 302, 311, 312, 314, 326, 340, 342
  see Charles VI

399

Index

Charles II, king of England, 109–10, 117, 153, 156
Charles, IV, duke of Lorraine, 110, 111, 121, 127, 128, 138, 142, 143, 158
Charles, V, duke of Lorraine, 143, 144, 147, 152, 154, 155, 157, 158, 201, 202, 205
Charles V, Holy Roman Emperor, 7, 48
Charles VI, Holy Roman Emperor, 342, 350, 356, 357, 358
Charles XII, 312
Charleville, 75, 138
Chaseron, French commander, 221
Château-Renault, 203, 215, 243, 244, 256, 257, 277
Châtenoi, 142
Chaulnes, duke of, 184
Chayla, abbé, 278
chemin couvert, covered way, 73, 74, 77
Cherbourg, 230
Chiari, 301
Chiari, Battle of, 270
Chiese River, 301
Chimay, 167
Chimay, Spanish commander, 168
Chinchilla, 316
Chiny, 163
Chios, 171
Chivasso, 301
Choiseul, 233, 236, 252, 254, 259
Churchill, John, duke of Marlborough, 1, 46, 71, 132, 199, 216, 266, 272–4, 275, 279–81, 286–94, 295, 298, 300, 303–8, 312, 317, 318–23, 326, 329, 330–4, 336, 337–8, 341, 343–5, 350, 352, 368, 369, 370, 371, 374, 376
Churchill, Sarah, 272, 341
citadel
    see positional warfare

Ciudad Rodrigo, 311, 316
Clausewitz, Karl von, 37, 370, 371
Clérambault, 291–3
Clerville, Louis-Nicolas Chevalier de, 108
Cleves, 113, 115
client, clientage, 188
    see patronage
Cochem, 201
Coehoorn, Menno van, 202, 223–6, 235, 248, 249, 275, 280, 281
Coingies, French commander, 288
Colbert, Jean-Baptiste, 14, 20, 25, 26, 29, 35, 83, 84, 86, 87, 88, 89, 91, 112, 143, 182, 184
Colbert family, 21, 83, 160
Collioure, 135, 243
Colmar, 133, 134, 163
Cologne, 113, 156, 185, 192, 210, 275, 287, 294, 358
Cologne, archbishop of, 41, 280
Columbia, 261
commissaire généraux des fortifications, 72
company size
    infantry, 60–1
    cavalry, 62–3
Condé, 145, 149, 156, 168, 308, 317, 326
Condé (the Great Condé)
    see Louis II, prince of Condé
Conseil d'en haut, 20, 21, 22, 33, 231
conseils de construction, 88
contributions, 57, 58, 70, 80, 127, 130, 136, 143, 166, 167, 195, 200, 201, 206, 209, 210, 213, 214, 219, 220, 227, 234, 236, 237, 238, 282, 284, 285, 295, 299, 300, 308, 313, 314, 335, 357, 362, 372
controller-general of finance, 19, 20, 25

Index

Conzer-Brucke, Battle of, 142
Cork, 216, 272
Cornette, Joël, 29, 66
Coromandel Coast, 262
Corsana, count of, 260
Corvisier, André, 363, 366
Coulumb, 88
course, raid, defined, 70
court, royal, as a form of compensation to aristocracy, 187
Courtrai, 163, 164, 167, 168, 169, 170, 218, 242, 247, 254, 259
Crema, 301
Cremona, 271, 276, 280, 301
Créqui, Marshal François-Joseph, marquis de, 133, 137, 138, 139, 142, 144, 145, 146, 151, 152, 153, 154, 155, 158, 168, 210, 287, 370
Crève-Coeur, 115
Croissy, Charles Colbert, marquis of, 160, 162, 232
Cronsbruch, 350
cuirassiers, 62
Cuneo, 220, 238, 315

Dalhunden, 313, 314
Damme, 306
Dangeau, marquis de, 189
Danube River, 165, 191, 200, 276, 297
  campaigns along during the War of the Spanish Succession, 279, 281-4, 286, 288-94, 302, 370
Darmstadt, prince of, 260
Das Minas, marquis of, 301, 311
Daun, General Philipp Wirich, Graf, 310, 314, 323, 335, 339, 345, 355
dauphin
  see Louis, grand dauphin of France

Dauphiné, 164, 177, 178, 205, 211, 214, 228, 238, 251, 279, 315, 317, 323, 329, 335, 338, 339, 345, 354, 355
Dedem, General, 300
Deerfield, Massachusetts, 349
Deinze, 205, 206, 248, 254
Deittweiler, 132
De jure belli ac pacis, 374
Denain, 145, 331, 352
Denain, Battle of, 322, 353-4
Dendermonde, 150, 248, 308
Dendre River, 318-19, 321
Denia, 325
Dent, Julian, 25
De Ruyter, Michiel, 115, 123, 144, 148
Descombes, 22
Desenzano, 301
Dessert, Daniel, 87, 92
Deventer, 115
De Witt, John, 31fn, 110, 114
dey of Algiers, 171, 173
Dieppe, 35, 124, 246
Diest, 79, 140, 234, 300
Diet, Imperial, 122, 195
Dinant, 75, 136, 137, 138, 139, 164, 217, 218, 219, 254, 295
Dinmikilling, 204
Dixmude, 167, 168, 169, 170, 227, 242
Djidjelli, 171
Doge of Genoa, 174
Dole, 124
Donauwörth, 283
Donauwörth, Battle of, 288-9, 290
Dorsten, 112
Douai, 65, 75, 108, 258, 321, 326, 330, 331, 337, 338, 343, 344, 354
Dourlach, 314
Dover, Treaty of, 109-10
dragonnades, 175-7

401

dragoons, 62, 176
drill, 28, 66–7, 368
Drusenheim, 308, 313
Dublin, 216
Du Clerc, 348
duel, dueling, 52
Dufay, governor, 131, 147
Duguay-Trouin, Réné, 92, 93, 102, 348
Dulmunling, 290
Dunenvald, General, 210
Dunes, Battle of the, 11
Dunkirk, 35, 36, 75, 86, 93, 96, 102, 246, 247, 253, 256, 317–18, 342, 347
Duquesnes, Abraham, 92, 171, 172, 173, 174
Duras, duke of, 194, 197, 198, 199, 200, 201
Durkheim, 259
Dutch, Dutch Netherlands
see United Provinces
Dutch Revolt, 8
Dutch War, 6, 14, 15, 22, 23, 25, 34, 35, 36, 38, 44, 45, 46, 49, 58, 62, 63, 68, 78, 81, 86, 92, 105, 109–59, 160, 161, 162, 163, 170, 171, 175, 183, 193, 199, 200, 204, 272, 365, 368, 375
Dyle River, 299, 307

Eastbourne, 215
East India Company, British, 102, 262
Ebernberg, 259
Ebro River, 324
écoles de construction, 88
Eeckeren, Battle of, 280–1
Eighty Years War, 8
Ellingen, 235
Elne, 136
Elvas, 340, 346
Embrun, 228
Emmendigen, 289

emperor
see Holy Roman Emperor
Enghien, duke of (future Great Condé)
see Louis II, prince of Condé
Enghien, duke of (son of Great Condé), 124, 139
England, English, 8, 35, 45, 84, 96, 97, 103, 106, 109, 113, 122, 149, 156, 165, 166, 193, 214, 229, 231, 244, 252, 253, 255–6, 262–3, 267, 270, 271, 274, 275, 285, 317
English Channel, 86, 96, 113, 123, 204, 215, 216, 218, 222, 229, 230, 231, 240, 247, 275, 368
Ensheim, Battle of, 65, 69, 131–2, 142
Entendu, 90
Entreprenant, 35
Enz River, 237
Epernon, Jean-Louis de Nogaret, duke d' (d. 1642), 48
Eppingen, 250, 259
Escalona, duke of, 243
Espolla, 152
Essai général de tactique, 373
Esslingen, 196
estates, provincial, 24
Estates General, 18
Estrades, Lt. Gen., 118
Estrées, Marshal Jean, count d', 92, 115, 152, 173, 223, 229, 238, 239, 240, 252, 256, 260–1
Estremadura, 301–2, 311, 324, 340, 346, 355
étapes system, 287–8
Eugene Maurice, count of Soissons, 213
Eugene of Savoy, Prince, 1, 46, 199, 213, 266, 270–1, 273, 274, 276–7, 285, 288–94, 301, 309–10, 314, 315,

402

Index

319–21, 323, 326, 330–2, 337–8, 343, 344, 352–4
Euzet, 297
execution, of villages for contributions, 57, 70

Fagel, François Nicolaas, baron, 344
famine of 1693–94, 24, 99, 191, 241, 325, 328
famine of 1709, 24, 325, 328, 336
Fariaux, allied commander, 119
Faverges, 346
Fénelon, François de Salignac de la Mothe, 328
Fenestrelle, 237, 324
Ferdinand I, Holy Roman Emperor, 7
Feuquières, Antoine de Pas, marquis de, 200, 213, 220
Figueres, 228, 324
finance, state, 24–7
fireship, 93
Firth of Forth, 318
Flanders, 3, 8, 33, 35, 41, 115, 120, 125, 153, 155, 167, 188, 193, 199, 200, 203, 205, 210, 216, 218, 223, 227, 233, 234, 237, 247, 253, 254, 257, 259, 264, 275, 279, 286, 298, 312, 315, 317, 328, 336, 337, 341, 342, 351, 352, 357, 362, 369, 370, 371
see Spanish Low Countries, Spanish Netherlands
fleet in being, 98, 215
Flemming, allied commander, 216
Fleurus, 206, 223, 254
Fleurus, Battle of, 96, 207–9, map 208, 371, 372
flintlocks, flintlock mechanisms, 58, 59–60
Flix, 324
Florennes, 219

Florida, 348
Flotard, David, 279
Fluvià River, 243
fodder, 54, 55, 80
Fontainebleau, 210, 354
Fontainebleau, Edict of, 177–8, 180
food, 54, 55
Forant, 215, 216
Forbin, chevalier de, 317
foreign regiments within French army, 49, 178
see mercenaries
Fort de Chartreuse, 275
Fort Gambia, 347
Fort Péage, 155
Fort du Rhine, 194
Fort la Trinité, 239
Fort-Louis, 193, 201, 210, 308, 313, 357
Fort St George, 237, 238, 242
Fort San Marcos, 348
Fort William, 224, 225, 226
fortification, fortress, fortified lines
see positional warfare
Fouquet, Nicolas, 20, 186
Fourille, Lt. Gen., 118
fournisseur, 85
Franche-Comté, 3, 8, 35, 108, 109, 124, 156, 157, 160, 163, 169, 361
François I, 48, 166
Franconia, 121, 210
Frankenthal, 194, 250
Frankfurt, 131, 201, 287
Franquenée, 304
Frederick I, of Prussia, 270
Frederick II, the Great, of Prussia, 363
Frederick William, the Great Elector, 110, 111, 140
Freiburg, 151, 154, 157, 193, 289, 357, 358
Freistett, 141
French Revolution, 51, 188, 363
Friedelingen, Battle of, 276

403

Index

Froidment, 206
Fronde, Frondeurs, 11, 13, 18, 23, 128, 186, 365
Frontenac, count of, 262
Fuenterrabia, 167
Furnes, 227, 242, 247, 326
Fürstenberg, Cardinal William Egon von, 192, 202
fusil, 59–60, 61

Gabaret, Jean, 239
gabelle, 183
Galiber Pass, 324, 339, 346
galley, 83, 86, 91, 144, 171
Galway, Henri Massue, earl of, 301–2, 311, 316, 324, 336
Gamshurst, 141
Gap, 228
Garda, Lake, 301, 309
Gardes françaises, Gardes suisses *see* regiments
Gardes marines, 91
Gassion, General, 306
Gastañaga, 209, 216, 251
Gaston d'Orléans, 9
Gaultier, François, 341–2
Gavere, 319–20
Gazette de France, 185, 334
Geete River, 234
Gelderland, 115
Gembloux, 218, 225, 233, 241, 249
Genappe, 206, 209
Geneva, 181
Genoa, bombardment of, 65, 103, 171, 173–4, 189, 270
Gerardsbergen, 321
Germany, Germanies, Germans, 7, 11, 12, 35, 36, 37, 39, 68, 110, 117, 121, 129, 153, 167, 193, 199, 219, 238, 251, 254, 375
 see Rhine, campaigns along; Danube, campaigns along
Germersheim, 128

Gerona, 167, 243, 244, 251, 252, 255, 264, 324, 341, 346, 356
Gerpinnes, 206, 219
Gertruydenberg, conference of, 336, 339, 340, 341–2
Ghent, 150, 152, 153, 156, 167, 205, 226, 254, 300, 306, 318–20, 322, 352
Gibraltar, 244, 286, 296, 297, 302, 355
Ginkel, allied commander, 222
Givet, 138, 217
Givry, 223, 331
glacis, 73, 74
 see positional warfare
Glete, Jan, 84
gloire, glory, 23, 27–32, 33, 34, 35, 38, 41, 42, 44, 52, 58, 105, 157, 197, 204, 266, 359
Goësbriand, General 332
Gournay, General, 208
governor, fortress, defined 48, 108
Grana, marquis of, 166, 167
Granadella, 324
Grand Alliance, 45, 191, 232, 270, 271, 275, 277, 280, 285, 286, 294, 345, 375
Grand-Prieur, General, 301
Granollers, 244
Granville, 253
Grave, 123, 124, 125, 126
Gravelines, 75, 253
Gray, 124
Great Elector
 see Frederick William
Grenoble, 228, 323
Grimaldi, 318
Groningen, 115
Grosfeld, 338–9
Grotius, Hugo, 374
Groua, 257
Guadeloupe, 348, 349
Guernsey, 253
guerre de cabinet, 23, 71

404

Index

guerre de course, 36, 83, 85, 99–102, 103, 104, 222, 240, 247, 252, 256, 261, 347
guerre d'escadre, 36, 83, 85, 91, 93–8, 99, 100, 103, 104, 222, 231, 247, 252
Guibert, Jacques, 373
Guiche, General de, 332
Guillestre, 339, 346
Guiscard, French commander, 254
Guise, dukes of, 48
Gustavus Adolphus, 10

Habsburgs, 7, 8, 9, 10, 12, 33, 36, 191, 192, 211, 251
Habsburgs, Austrian, 165, 166
Hagenau, 132, 133, 142, 163, 300, 308
Hainault, 3, 33, 35, 125, 167, 200, 337
Haine River, 223
Halle, 218, 226
Ham, 206
Hanover, Hanoverian, 195, 206, 210, 288, 358
Hanover, duke of, elector of, 195, 323, 335
Harch, imperial commander, 357
Harcourt, duke of, 254, 329, 335, 338–9, 345, 352, 354
Harelbeke, 205
Harfleur, 124
Havana, 277
Hebernbourg, 227
Heidelberg, 129, 194, 196, 233, 236, 241, 250
Heilbronn, 194, 196, 227, 236, 250
Heinsius, Anthonie, 232, 246, 272, 326, 336
Hellemmes, 330
Henri III, 9
Henri IV, Henri of Navarre, 8, 9, 83
Henry VIII, 48
Heppignies, 207

Herbert, see Torrington
Herne, 226
Hery, French naval commander, 171
Hesse-Kassel, 195, 210, 288
Hesse-Kassel, landgrave of, 216, 254, 284
Heudin, 183
Heurne, 320
Heurtebise, Battle of, 146
Hill, Richard, 279
Hispaniola, 263
Höchstädt, 290
Höchstädt, Battle of, 284
Hoester, 118
Hoguette, General, 220
Holland, 117, 118
Holy Roman Emperor (Leopold I), 10, 34, 36, 45, 124, 128, 140, 156, 165, 167, 189, 193, 195, 213, 255, 257, 262, 271, 283, 286
Holy Roman Emperor (Joseph I), 312
Holy Roman Empire, 7, 162
Holy Spirit, Order of, 111
Hompesche, Reinhard Vincent, Freiherr von, 344
Hornberg, 282, 289
hospitals, military, 55
hostages, 70, 127
Hoste, Paul, 94
Hudson Bay, 356
Huguenots, 15, 42, 163, 164, 174–9, 182, 185, 188, 189, 200, 220, 298, 363
Humières, duke of, 145, 146, 150, 151, 166, 167, 199, 200, 206
Hungary, 263, 274, 283, 286, 294, 358
Huningen, 193
hussars, 62
Huxelles, Marshal marquis de, 201, 211

405

Index

Huy, 136, 137, 138, 139, 227, 234, 236, 241, 242, 280, 281, 298, 299, 312, 318

Iberville, Pierre le Moyne, Sieur d', 347
Igualada, 341, 346
Ilbersheim, Treaty of, 293
Île de Ré, 257
Île Royale, 349
Îles d'Hyères, 229
Ille, 202
India, 262, 366
infantry, 58–62, 69
Influence of Sea Power upon History, 1660–1783, 102
Ingolstadt, 290
Innocent XI, 166
inspectors, inspectors-general, 67, 88
intendant, provincial and army, 11, 53, 85
Invalides, Hôtel des Invalides, 55–6
Inverness, 318
Ireland, 103, 231, 264, 317, 363
  operations in during the Nine Years War, 203–4, 205, 214, 215, 221–2, 228–9
Irish Sea, 215, 216
Irish soldiers in French service, 214, 222, 231
Iroquois, 261, 349
Isère River, 345
Issel River, 114
Italian front, including Dauphiné, Savoy, and Provence
  campaigns there during the Nine Years War, 211–14, 219–21, 223, 227–8, 237–8, 242–3, 250–1, 255, 368
  campaigns there during the War of the Spanish Succession, 270–1, 276–7, 284–5, 295, 300, 301, 309–10, 314–16, 323–4, 335, 338–9, 345–6, 355
Italian Wars, 365
Italy, 35, 162, 179, 247, 274, 307, 357, 370, 372
Ivrea, 220, 295

Jacquier, François, 133
Jalons, camp of, 48
James II, 40, 42, 192, 193, 199, 203–4, 205, 215, 216, 222, 228, 229, 231, 232, 253, 255–6, 263, 264, 269, 295
James Stuart, the Old Pretender, 317, 343, 356
Janson-Forbin, cardinal, 232
Jauche, 225
Jellicoe, John, 331
Jemeppe, 206
Joseph I, 300, 342, 345
Joseph Ferdinand, prince of Bavaria, 39, 40, 267
Joyeuse, duke de, 233, 234, 250, 257
Judoigne, 217
Jülich, 210
Jutland, 331

Kaiserlautern, 194
Kaiserwerth, 112, 113, 202, 275
Kehl, 140, 155, 163, 281, 289
Kenoque, 248
Kilconnell, 222
King William's War, 261
Kinsale, 203, 216, 272
Knights of Malta, 91
Koblenz, 118, 194, 201, 288
Kockersberg, 151
Kreuznach, 194

Labadie, French commander, 352
La Cachotte, 225
Lacger, 188
La Corzana, conde de la, 350

La Feuillade, François d'Aubusson, duke de (d. 1691), 118, 145, 146
La Feuillade, Louis d'Aubusson, duke de, 295, 301, 309–10
Lagos, Battle of, 239–40, 241
La Grange, *intendant*, 196
La Hogue, Battle of, 88, 96, 99, 229–31, 263, 315
La Junquera, 167, 202, 228, 324
Lake Champlain, 349
La Lanières Woods, 331, 332
La Mothe, count of, 254, 280, 318
Landau, 129, 131, 142, 195, 276, 283, 284, 289, 293–4, 309, 339, 356, 357, 358
Landen, 234
Landrecies, 75, 344, 352, 353, 354
Landsknechts, 48
Langeron, Joseph Andrault, count of, 88
Languedoc, 177, 179, 243, 277, 297–8, 315
Larche, 237
La Rochelle, 9, 231, 252
La Rouë pass, 323
Larré, marquis of, 213, 237, 238
La Selle River, 352
La Seu d'Urgell, 167, 221
La Tremblade, 90
Laubanie, French commander, 294
Lauingen, 288, 290
Launsheim, 288
Lauter River, 155, 308
Lauterbourg, 147, 288, 300, 308, 313, 354
Lauzun, count of, 204, 216
La Vallière, duchess of, 106
Law, John, 27
League of the Rhine, 13, 110
Leake, Sir John, 324
Le Boulou, 202, 228, 238, 243, 324
Le Camus, bishop, 177
Leeward Islands, 348

Le Havre, 85, 215, 246
Leiden, 117
Leinster, duke of, 231
Le Mans, 184
Lentini, 144
Leonberg, 237
Leopold I, Holy Roman Emperor, 13, 32, 36, 38, 39, 45, 110, 111, 117, 167, 195, 232, 267–8, 270, 274, 300
Le Perthus, 228
Le Quesnoy, 233, 329, 343, 344, 352, 354
Lerida, 316, 324, 339, 346
Les Marches, 346
Lessines, 219
Le Tellier family, 21, 160
Le Tellier, Michel, 21, 22, 29, 33, 111, 112
Leuze, 205, 248
Leuze, Battle of, 219
Le Vacher, Father, 171, 172
Liège, 112, 113, 136–7, 185, 209, 218, 227, 233, 234, 242, 275, 298, 299
Liège, Bishopric of, 34, 113
Lierre, 306
Lille, 75, 76, 108, 109, 153, 308, 317, 321–2, 326, 329, 361
Limbourg, 137, 139–40, 281
Limerick, 216, 222
limited war, 362–7
Limoges, 177
Limone-Piemonte, 315
lines, entrenched lines
  see positional warfare
Lionne, Hugues de, 21, 115
Lipari Islands, 148
Lisbon, 295, 296, 302
Lisola, François de, 43, 136
Little Gheete, 299
Livet, Georges, 41
Loire River, 351
Lombardy, 285, 310
Lonato, 301

Index

London, 176, 200, 351
Londonderry, 204
London Preliminaries, 342, 350
Longchamps, 225
Lorge, Marshal de, 118, 119, 123, 141, 145, 146, 205, 210, 219, 227, 233, 236, 237, 242, 250, 254
Lorraine, 3, 35, 110, 129, 131, 133, 148, 151, 153, 157, 163, 170, 198, 202, 262, 267
Lossky, Andrew, 2, 13, 32, 42, 169, 359
Lottum, Philipp Karl, Graf, 332
Louis, grand dauphin of France, 40, 194, 205, 210, 217, 233, 236–7, 241, 267–8, 317, 350
Louis of Baden, 147, 236, 237, 242, 250, 254, 259, 276, 282, 288, 290, 293, 300, 308, 313, 314
Louis II, prince of Condé (the Great Condé), 10, 11, 22, 23, 34, 68, 70, 109, 113, 114, 117, 118, 120, 124, 125, 126, 127, 128, 129, 132, 133, 137, 138, 139, 140, 142, 144, 234
Louis XIII, 6, 9, 48, 51, 186
Louis XIV, *passim*
and absolutism, *see* absolutism
elements of his strategy, 17–46, 156, 371
preference for siege warfare, 71
religious policy, 161, 169, 174–81
Louis XV, 373
Louisbourg, 349
Louvain, 139, 225, 234, 235, 299, 303, 306, 318
Louvois, marquis de, 21, 22, 23, 29, 33, 35, 36, 37, 41, 49, 50, 55, 58, 65, 75, 100, 111–12, 118, 119, 126, 127, 130, 133, 137, 145, 146, 149, 150, 154, 155, 156, 158, 160, 162, 164, 167, 168, 174, 176, 177, 184, 193, 195, 196, 197, 209, 216, 217, 231, 241, 274
Low Countries, 8, 35
Lully, Jean-Baptiste, 30
Luneberg, 210
Luserna, 213, 220
Lusticru rebellion, 183
Lützen, Battle of, 10
Lutzingen, 291
Luxembourg, 37, 38, 42, 153, 163, 164, 165, 166, 167, 168, 169, 170, 262
Luxembourg, chevalier of, 321
Luxembourg, duke de, Marshal, 22, 65, 68, 95, 113, 114, 117, 120, 122, 144, 145, 146, 147, 148, 150, 151, 152, 153, 154, 202, 205, 205–10, 217, 218, 219, 223, 225, 226, 233–5, 241–2, 247, 274, 371, 372
Luzzara, Battle of, 276
Lyons, 366
Lys River, 247, 248, 330

Maaseik, 113, 119, 123
Maastricht, 76, 113, 115, 119–20, 123, 124, 127, 136, 137, 146, 147, 149, 210, 218, 249, 280, 304
Madrid, 232, 268, 285, 296, 303, 311, 336, 339, 340, 351, 355, 358
magazines, 55, 71, 112, 113, 145
Magdeburg, 195
Mahan, Alfred Thayer, 96, 102–3, 104
Main River, 129, 201
Maintenon, Mme, marquise de, 179, 327, 329

Index

Mainz, 131, 194, 195, 199, 201, 210, 227
Málaga, 240, 296
Malines, 306
Malplaquet, Battle of, 65, 69, 331–5, map 333, 336
Mannheim, 194, 196, 197, 227, 250
Mantua, 251, 276, 310
Mantua, duke of, 164
Marbais, 223
Marchiennes, 318, 352, 354
Marie de Medici, 9
Marie Thérèse, 12, 33, 105–6, 194, 267
Marillac, *intendant*, 176, 177
Maritime Powers, 45, 204, 269, 328, 342
Mark, 118
Marlborough, duke of
  see Churchill, John, duke of Marlborough
Marquisat, 313, 314
Marsaglia, Battle of, 238, 241
Marseilles, 35, 85, 86, 260
Marsin, Ferdinand, count of, 274, 288–93, 300, 303, 307, 308, 310
Martin, François, 262
Martinet, Jean, 67
Martinique, 123
Mary, queen of England, 192, 193, 215
Mas Rouge, 278
matchlocks, matchlock mechanisms, 58–9
Maubeuge, 75, 317, 326
Maureillas, 135
Maurice, Prince of Nassau, 117
Mazarin, Cardinal, 6, 10, 12, 15, 16, 28, 30, 31, 33, 45, 84, 182, 186
  strategic legacy of, 12–13, 169
Max Emanuel, elector of Bavaria, 41, 200, 201, 205, 210, 216,
225, 247, 248, 249, 254, 258, 276, 279, 281–4, 285, 288, 289, 291–3, 299, 300, 312, 317, 323, 329, 350, 358
Max Henry, archbishop of Cologne, 192
Maxingheim, 353
Medina-Sidonia, 221, 228, 239
Mediterranean Sea, 14, 35, 36, 83, 86, 100, 103, 122, 124, 135, 159, 171–4, 210, 221, 222, 244, 245, 246, 252, 256, 270, 296, 301, 314, 358, 368
Medway, 109
Méhaigne River, 138, 225, 295, 300
Meldert, 306
Melingen, 236
'Mémoire concernant la caprerie', 100, 252
'Mémoire des raisons,' 192
Menin, 218, 308, 317, 318
mercenaries, 47, 48
  see foreign regiments in French service
Mercy, General, 323
Mérode-Westerloo, 290
Mesnager, Nicolas, 317, 350
Messina, 122, 135, 143–4, 148, 149, 183
Metz, 138, 153, 163, 303
Meuse River, 43, 72, 78, 79, 113, 118, 119, 123, 129, 136, 137, 139, 140, 145, 149, 151, 154, 158, 206, 209, 218, 223, 241, 247, 249, 258, 275, 287, 295, 299
Meyer, Jean, 363, 365, 366
Meyronnes, 237
Mézières, 112
Mierdorp, 295
Mignet, François, 32
Milan, 40, 211, 213, 255, 267, 270, 276, 295, 314

409

Index

Milan, Convention of, 310
Milazzo, 144
military administration, 52–6
militia, *milice*, 123, 179, 184, 200, 213, 221, 240, 245, 250, 260, 261, 262, 278, 346
   of Languedoc, 135, 179, 363
   royal provincial militia, 49, 199, 213, 271
Mincio River, 276, 301, 310
ministers of state, 20
Minorca, 324, 358
miquelets, 148, 159, 214, 221, 302, 324, 346
Mirandola, 301
Modane, 323
Modena, 276
Moder River, 294
Mohacs, Battle of, 191
Molsheim, 131
Monmouth, Lt. Gen., 118
Monpensier, duchess of, 106
Mons, 54, 65, 76, 145, 146, 150, 153, 154, 206, 216–18, 223, 225, 232, 236, 241, 254, 308, 322, 323, 329, 330–1, 334
Monsieur
   see Philippe I, duke of Orléans
Montal, count de, 119, 167, 168, 247, 254
Montauban, 176, 177, 178
Montbéliard, 163, 169
Montbrun, French commander, 209
Montclair, 195, 196, 197
Montclar, 194
Montecuccoli, Raimondo, 61, 118, 120, 140, 141, 142, 143, 147, 158
Monterey, count of, 115, 120, 152, 156
Montespan, marquise of, 92, 106, 153
Montesquiou d'Artagnan, Pierre of, 332, 351

Montesquieu, baron de la Brède et de, 28
Montgenèvre, 323–4
Montichiari, 309
Montmélian, 214, 220, 221, 323–4, 335, 346
Montreal, 262, 349
Montreuil, 343
Montrevel, marquis de, 279, 297
Montroyal, 195
Moore, James, 348
mortars
   see artillery
Moselle River, 14, 139, 158, 201, 205, 206, 218, 286, 287, 288, 298, 299, 300, 308, 312, 357, 368
   campaigns along during the Dutch War, 119, 129
motivation, of common soldiers, 51
   of officers, 51
Moureillas, 228
Mughals, 262
Mühlberg, 345
Muiden, 117
Mulhouse, 133
munitionnaires, 53, 85, 330
Münster, 113, 291
Münster, bishop of, 106
Münster, Treaty of, 111
Murcia, 311
musket, 58–9, 61
Musketeers, 225
mutiny, mutinies, 48, 142, 329

Naarden, 122
Nagés, Battle of, 297
Nahe River, 259
Namur, 79, 137, 138, 153, 206, 209, 217, 223–6, map 224, 227, 235, 236, 247, 248–9, 295, 299, 308, 318, 343
Nancy, 121, 133, 151
Nantes, 184
Nantes, bishop of, 56

Index

Nantes, Edict of, 9, 177, 179, 277, 363
Naples, 40, 267, 276, 314
Napoleon I, 2, 81, 280, 286, 367, 368, 371, 372, 373, 375, 376
Nassau, 329
Native Americans, 261–2
Navailles, duke of, 124, 144, 145, 148, 152, 155
Navarre, 167
naval campaigns
  during the Dutch War, 123–4, 152
  during the Nine Years War, 214–16, 221–3, 228–31, 239–40, 244–6, 252–3, 261
  during the 1680s, 171–4, 221–3
  during the War of the Spanish Succession, 277, 296–7, 315, 324, 347–9
navy, 36, 82–104, 263
  armament, arming, 87
  crews, 89–90
  desertion, deserting, 90
  impressment, of sailors, 89
  naval administration, 83–7
  numbers in defining naval power, 96–9
  officers, 90–3
  ports, 86–7
  rates, of ships, 88–9, 97–8
  sailing ships, vessels, 87–9
  see guerre d'escadre, guerre de course
Nebel River, 290, 291
Neckar River, 129, 130, 195, 196, 236, 237, 242, 288
Neerwinden, Battle of, 65, 68, 95, 234–5, 241, 264
Nef, John U., 362
Negrelli, 138, 139
Nelson, Horatio, Lord, 88, 96, 104
Nesmond, marquis de, 102, 222, 256

Neuburg, 281, 314
Neuf Brisach, 263
Neustadt, 129, 194, 219, 236, 255
Nevis Island, 347
New England, 349
Newfoundland, 356
New France, 349
New York, 349
Nice, 210, 220, 221, 223, 239, 301, 315, 356
Nicholson, Francis, 349
Nijmegen, 115
Nijmegen, Treaty of, 35, 37, 156, 160, 161, 163, 164, 169
Nîmes, 277, 279
Nîmes, bishop of, 278
Nine Years War, 6, 14, 39, 44, 45, 46, 49, 50, 53, 58, 61, 62, 63, 68, 78, 82, 89, 92, 93, 97, 99, 102, 160, 170, 181, 189, 191–265, 266, 271, 272, 303, 317, 328, 345, 348, 359, 363, 368, 374, 375
Ninove, 146, 219, 247, 259
Nivelles, 206, 208, 209, 226, 233
Noailles, duke de, 199, 202, 203, 205, 214, 221, 228, 233, 238, 239, 240, 243–4, 251, 316, 324, 328, 329, 340, 341, 346
noble, nobles, nobility
  see aristocracy
Nogaret, Captain, 50
Noire Boutaille, 331
Nördlingen, Battle of, 10
Normandy, 123, 177, 221, 229, 231, 330
North Africa, 171–3, 189
North America, 261, 359, 366
North Sea, 102, 256
Notre Dame, 126
nouveaux convertis, 178–9, 185, 200, 221, 231, 363
Novara, 310

Index

Nu-Pieds, 11
Nuremberg, 200

Obdam, Jacob van Wassenaer, lord of, 280
Oberglau, 291
Offenburg, 140, 141, 151, 154, 155, 314
Offus, 306
Oglio River, 270, 301
Oise River, 343
Oppenheim, 194, 198
Orange, 169, 356
Orange, prince of, 332
Order of the Holy Spirit, 111
ordre de tableau, 50
Orkney, earl of, 293, 304, 332-3
Orléans, duke of
 see Philippe I and Philippe II
Orme River, 207
Ormonde, James Butler, duke of, 277, 351, 352
Orp, 225
Orsoy, 113, 114
Ortenbach, 155
Ostalric, 244, 251, 252, 255
Ostend, 156, 280, 321
Ostiches, 258
Ottenheim, 140
Ottomans, Ottoman Empire, 7, 36, 38, 165-6, 167, 171, 190, 191, 192, 220, 232
Oudenarde, 108, 109, 126, 127, 154, 157, 168, 306, 317
Oudenarde, Battle of, 319-20, 325
Oulx, 323, 355
Ouwerkerk, Henrik van Nassau, lord of, 295, 299, 308
Overijssel, 115

Palais Royal, 28
Palamos, 240, 243, 251, 260, 264
Palatinate, 128, 142, 147, 308, 357, 368
Palatinate, devastation of in 1674, 56, 129-31, 289
Palatinate, devastation of in 1688-89, 3, 39, 42, 56, 131, 191, 193-9
Palatine, elector, 128, 130
Palermo, Battle of, 148-9
Palfi, allied commander, 228
Pamplona, 167
papier timbré, 184
Papier Timbré revolt, 136, 184-5, 240
 see Bonnet Rouges revolt
Parck, 234
Pardo, governor, 153
Paris, 14, 73, 75, 110, 124, 126, 173, 229, 329, 331, 338, 351, 354
Paris, Archbishop of, 326
Parker, Captain Robert, 287, 344
parlements, 18
Parliament, 26, 109, 117, 153, 192, 256, 326, 328
Parma, 310
partisan warfare, 69-70, 159
Pata, Battle of, 294
patriotism, 51
patronage, patron/client relationships, 51, 188, 189
Pavia, 310
Pedro II, 277
Pena Garcia, 296
Percin, bishop, 177
Perpignan, 259, 356
Perwez, 249
Peterborough, earl of, 302
petit guerre
 see partisan warfare
Pfaffenhoffen, 300
Pforzheim, 194, 201
Phélypeaux family
 see Pontchartrain family
Philip II, of Spain, 7
Philip III, of Spain, 267
Philip IV, of Spain, 12, 33

Index

Philip V, of Spain, 41, 268–9, 276, 285, 286, 302, 310, 311, 317, 323, 326, 329, 336–7, 339–40, 341, 342, 350–1, 355, 356, 358, 359
Philippe of Anjou, 32, 40, 41, 42, 266, 268
  see Philip V
Philippe I, duke of Orléans (Monsieur), (d. 16), 106, 111, 118, 150, 217, 240
Philippe II, duke of Orléans (d. 1723), 310, 316, 317, 324–5
Philippeville, 217, 219
Philippsburg, 37, 39, 128, 129, 130, 131, 140, 144, 147, 151, 155, 157, 193, 194, 195, 204, 227, 236, 242, 254, 288, 354
Picardy, 330
Piedmont, 175, 210, 211, 218, 219, 220, 237, 238, 242–3, 250, 253, 270, 285, 309, 324, 345, 346
Pieton, 206
pike, 58, 59, 61
pillage, 48, 52, 56, 121, 198, 228, 240, 324, 357
Pinelli, allied commander, 138
Pinerolo, 179, 180, 211, 213, 220, 227, 228, 237, 238, 251, 255, 310
pioneers, peasant labours, 76, 78, 200, 217, 234, 235, 247, 258, 315
Plymouth, 229
Pointis, baron of, 102, 261
Poitiers, 177, 184
Poitou, 124, 176
Poland, 110
Pomponne, Simon Arnauld, marquis de, 115, 160, 231, 232
Pondicherry, 262, 263
Pontchartrain, Jérôme Phélypeaux, count de, 85
Pontchartrain, Louis Phélypeaux, count de, 85, 229
Pontchartrain family, 83
Po River, Valley, 41, 164, 211, 220, 295, 303, 310
Portalegre, 296
Port Mahon, 324
Port Royal, 262, 263, 349
Porto-Ercole, 355
Portsmouth, 231
Portugal, 270, 279, 285, 294, 301, 302, 316, 336, 340, 346, 355, 368
positional warfare – fortifications, fortresses, siege warfare
  artillery fortress, 73, 74
  citadel, 72, 137
  functions of fortresses and fortified lines, 37, 57, 63, 64, 71–82, 158, 162, 170–1, 259
  investment, defined, 75–6
  lines, 71, 78–9, 200, 209, 242, 247, 248, 275, 370
  lines of Brabant, 79, 275, 298, 299–300, 304
  lines of Cambrin, 107
  lines of Ettlingen, 335, 339, 345, 354, 357
  lines of the Lauter, 314, 335, 339, 345
  lines of Lauterbourg, 354
  lines of the Moder, 300, 308
  Ne Plus Ultra Lines, 79, 343–4
  lines of Stollhofen, 282, 288, 290, 309, 312–14, 335
  lines of Wissembourg, 339, 345, 354
  parallels, 76, 120
  pré carré, 75, 321, 337, 338, 354
  sieges, in general, 3, 63
  sieges, practice of siege warfare, 77–8
Potsdam, Edict of, 178

413

Prats-de-Mollo, 221, 238
pré carré
   see positional warfare
'Preliminary Articles,' 326, 336
Primi Visconti, 111
princes' wars, 9
private armies, 8, 48
privateer, 83, 91, 93, 99, 214, 240, 246, 252, 256–7, 261, 342, 347
   see *guerre de course*
prizes, prize courts, 99, 100, 101–2
   see *guerre de course*
prospect theory, 43–4
Protestants, Protestantism in France
   see Huguenots
Provence, 15, 90, 214, 220, 238, 251, 312, 314, 315, 339, 365
Prussia, 288, 361, 363, 365
Puigcerda, 143, 144, 152, 155, 156, 167
Puységur, Jacques-François de Chastenet, marquis de (d. 1743), 62
Pyrenees, 8, 14, 135, 143, 152, 156, 157, 159, 167, 183, 202, 214, 243, 368
Pyrenees, Treaty of the, 7, 11, 12, 14, 33, 105, 106, 136, 152

quartering of troops, 175–6
   see *dragonnades*
Quebec, 262, 349
Queen Anne's War, 348, 349
Quiévrain, 146, 331
Quimper, 185
Quincy, chevalier of, 352
Quincy, marquis of, x, 123, 219

Rabenhaut, General, 125
Racine, 224, 226
raids, raiders
   see course
Raine-l'Alleud, 318

Rákóczi, Ferenc, 270, 283, 294, 325, 342, 358
Ramilles, Battle of, 280, 303, 304–6, map 305, 308, 319, 334, 335, 369
Rastatt, 313
Rastatt, Treaty of, 356, 357–8, 361
Ratisbon, 281
Ratisbon, Truce of, 38, 169, 191, 192, 264
rebellions
   see revolts and rebellions in France
Reggio, 276
regiments, 60, 63
regiments of the French infantry, by name
   Auvergne, 188
   Champagne, 177
   du Roi, infantry, 67, 139, 217, 306
   Gardes françaises, 108, 200, 235, 332
   Gardes suisses, 235, 332
   la Ferté, 142
   la Marine, 245, 297
   Nonan, 58
   Orléans, 108
   Picardie, 108
Reims, archbishop of, 177
Rench River, 141
Rennes, 184
'Restraining Orders,' 351, 352
Retz, Cardinal de, 30
Reunions, 37, 159, 161–71, 189, 191, 262, 264
   Chambers of Reunions, 37
   see War of the Reunions
Reutlingen, 282
Reventlau, Christian, count, 309
revolts and rebellions in France, 161, 181–5
   see Bonnets Rouges, Camisards, Cévennes, Papier Timbré
Revolutionary and Napoleonic Wars, 366

Index

Rheinberg, 113, 114
Rheinfeld, Battle of, 155
Rhine River, 14, 36, 39, 43, 68,
  113, 114, 157, 158, 162,
  163, 167, 253, 262, 263,
  370
  campaigns along the Rhine
  during the Dutch War,
  117–18, 119, 120, 122, 125,
  127–35, 136, 140–3, 147–8,
  151–2, 154–5, 368
  campaigns along the Rhine
  during the Nine Years War,
  193–9, 200–2, 204, 205,
  210, 216, 218, 219, 223,
  227, 231, 236–7, 241, 242,
  250, 254–5, 259
  campaigns along the Rhine
  during the War of the
  Spanish Succession, 274,
  275, 276, 279, 282–4, 288,
  298, 300, 307, 308–9,
  312–14, 321, 323, 335,
  338–9, 343, 345, 354,
  356–7
Rhône River, 169, 356
Richelieu, Armand du Pléssis,
  Cardinal, 6, 9, 10, 13, 15,
  26, 84, 162, 186
Rigaud, Hyacinthe, 1
Rio de Janiero, 93, 102, 348
robe nobility
  see aristocracy
Roberts, Michael, 67
Rochefort, 85, 86, 88, 137, 138,
  139, 214
Rochefort, marquis de, 117, 118,
  121, 129, 145, 239
Rocroi, 75
Rocroi, Battle of, 10
Roermond, 139, 140
Roeselare, 248
Roeux, count of, 258
Rolland, 278–9
Rome, 192

Roncesvalles, 167
Rooke, George, 229, 239, 252,
  256, 277, 296
Rosas, 167, 238, 239, 241, 356
Rosas, Gulf of, 243
Rota, 277
roturiers, 91
Rouillé, Pierre, 325
Roure, Jean-Antoine du, 183
Roure rebellion, 183–4
Rousillon, 14, 122, 135–6, 143,
  144, 145, 148, 149, 152,
  155, 167, 202, 203, 214,
  218, 221, 228, 239, 311,
  316, 324, 368
Rousset, Camille, 112
Royal Louis, 88
Rule, John, 158
Russell, Lord Edward, 229, 230,
  231, 244–6, 251, 252, 256
Russia, 361, 363
Rye, 246
Ryswick, Treaty of, 253, 257, 262,
  263, 266, 295

Saarlouis, 195
Sables d'Olonne, 257
St Amand, 146, 205
St Amant, 207
St Augustine, 348
St Bernard Pass, little, 220, 323,
  335, 345
St Brette, 237
Saint-Clar, 125
St Denis, Battle of, 152, 154, 158
St Feliu, 260
St George's Channel, 215
Saint-Germain, 135–6
St Germain (France), 137, 140,
  153, 154
St Germain (Italy), 180
St Ghislain, 151
Saint-Hilaire, General, 69, 141
St Jean de Maurienne, 339, 345, 346
St Jean-Pied-de-Port, 167

415

Index

St Kitts, 347, 348
St Kwintens-Lennick, 258
St Lawrence River, 349
St Malo, 36, 93, 101, 102, 231, 240, 245, 252, 347
St Martin de Ré, 257
St Omer, 75, 149, 150, 156, 329
St Pierre d'Albigny, 335, 346
Saint-Ruth, 211, 214, 222
Saint-Rémy, Surirey de, 65, 78, 95
Saint-Simon, duke de, 72, 111, 204, 233, 354
St Trond, 140
St Truiden, 281, 295
St Venant, 330, 337, 338
Salamanca, 311
Salazar, Cardinal, 232
Salins, 124
Salle de guerre, 114
Salo, 309
Saluzzo, 213
Salvatierra, 295, 301
Sambre River, 113, 137, 145, 151, 200, 206, 209, 218, 219, 223, 224, 227, 241, 249, 295, 343, 353
sappers, 76
Saragossa, 311, 316, 339
Sardinia, 324, 350
Sarre-Louis, 298
Sarre River, 298, 357
Sars Woods, 331, 332
Sasbach, 141, 314
Saverne, 128, 132, 133, 142, 151
Savoy, 45, 210, 211, 213, 214, 222, 237, 243, 279, 285, 315, 317, 323, 329, 335, 345–6, 356, 375
Savoy, duke of, 40, 41, 181, 205
  see Victor Amadeus II
Saxe-Eisenach, prince of, 151
Saxony, 110, 195, 210, 219
Scheldt River, 146, 247, 248, 254, 307, 319–20, 321, 322, 330, 352

Schellenberg Heights, 289
Schenectady, 262
schnapphahns, 130, 195
Schomberg, Friedrich Hermann, duke von, 135, 145, 146, 147, 148, 154, 178, 204, 219
Schulenberg, 304, 332, 335, 338, 345
Schutter River, 140, 141
secretaries of state, 19, 20, 22
secretary of state for foreign affairs, 19, 20, 21
secretary of state for the navy, 19, 85
secretary of state for the royal household, 19
secretary of state for war, 19, 20, 21, 22, 52, 85
Sedan, 113, 177
Seigneley, marquis de, 85, 92, 174, 215
Sélestat, 133, 140, 142, 147, 154
Selle River, 353
Semoy River, 343
Seneffe, Battle of, 68, 81, 125, 138, 140, 158
Senne River, 318
Sensée River, 343
Servien, Abel, 53
Seven Years War, 363, 365
Sévigné, Mme. de, 30, 126, 185
Shovell, Admiral Clowdesley, 96, 215, 246, 296, 302
Sicily, 40, 103, 124, 135–6, 143, 143–4, 145, 148–9, 155, 157, 159, 267, 337, 350, 368
Sicilies, Kingdom of the Two, 143
siege, siege warfare
  see positional warfare
Siegharding, 281
Sierck, 298
Silenrieux, 219
silver vessels and furnishings, 204, 327

416

Index

Sinzendorf, Philipp Ludwig, graf von, 350
Sinzheim, Battle of, 128, 129
Smyrna convoy, 222
Sobieski, Jan, 165
Soignies, 218, 219, 249
Soissonnais, 330
Sole Bay, Battle of, 115
Soleil Royal, 88, 214, 230
Somme River, 146, 343
Sonnino, Paul, 38
Sorel, Albert, 32, 162
Sospel, 315
Sourdis, Jacques d'Escoubleau, chevalier de, 222
South Asia, 262, 348
Spain, 7, 8, 9, 10, 11, 12, 13, 16, 29, 33, 34, 35, 36, 40, 45, 106, 117, 121, 122, 143, 156, 157, 165, 173, 251, 257, 262-3, 264, 267-8, 274, 315, 316, 341, 355, 370, 375
Spanish front, including Rousillon
 campaigns there during the Dutch War, 135-6, 143, 148, 152, 155-6
 campaigns there during the Nine Years War, 214, 221, 222, 223, 228, 238-9, 243-4, 251-2, 255, 259-61
 campaigns there during the War of the Reunions, 167
 campaigns there during the War of the Spanish Succession, 277, 285, 295-7, 301, 310-11, 317, 324-5, 335-6, 339-41, 346, 355-6, 358
Spanish Low Countries, Spanish Netherlands, 14, 33, 34, 35, 38, 40, 55, 56, 68, 72, 75, 78, 79, 80, 105, 109, 117, 158, 160, 163, 165, 170, 268-9, 273, 295, 350, 358, 361
 campaigns in during the Dutch War, 124-7, 136-40, 144, 145-7, 149-51, 153-4
 campaigns in during the Nine Years War, 202-3, 205-10, 216-19, 223-7, 233-6, 241-2, 247-50, 253-4, 257-9
 campaigns in during the War of Devolution, 106-8, 122
 campaigns in during the War of the Reunions, 166-8
 campaigns in during the War of the Spanish Succession, 274-6, 280-1, 295, 298-300, 303-8, 312, 318-23, 329-35, 337-8, 342-5
Spanish Road, 8, 10, 173
Spar, General, 300
Speyer, 194, 197, 198, 236, 308
Speyer, Battle of, 284
Spithead, 256
squadron, 61-3
stadholder, 34, 114
Staffarde, Battle of, 213-14
stamp tax
 see papier timbré
Stanhope, 324, 340
Starhemberg, General, 155, 194, 285, 324, 339, 340, 346, 355, 356
state commission army, 47-52, 56, 58, 79, 81, 368
States General, Dutch, 156, 192
Steenkerque, Battle of, 226-7
Stekene, 280
Stomboli, Battle of, 148
Stradella, 310
Strafford, earl of, 350
Strasbourg, 37, 42, 131, 135, 140, 141, 142, 151, 154, 155, 159, 163-4, 169, 178, 193, 194, 195, 259, 262, 276, 281, 282, 289, 293, 300, 313, 326, 354, 357, 361

417

Index

Stuttgart, 196
Styrum, count, 284, 288
Sublet de Noyers, François, 53
Surinam, 348
Surville-Hautfois, marquis of, 330
Susa, 214, 220, 221, 227, 237, 243, 251, 295, 315, 345, 355
Sweden, Swedes, 109, 140, 156, 189, 232
Swiss pikemen, 48
Swiss soldiers in French service, 124, 156
  see regiments of the French infantry, Gardes suisses
Swiss, Swiss Confederation, Switzerland, 8, 11, 154, 180
sword nobility
  see aristocracy
Symcox, Geoffrey, 97
Syracuse, 144
Szatmár, Peace of, 342

Tagus River, 302
Talavera de la Reina, 340
Tallard, Camille, count of, 227, 282, 283, 284, 288–93, 289
Talmach, General, 245–6
Tarragona, 341
Taviers, 138, 394
Ter, Battle of, 243
Ter River, 167, 264, 369
Tessé, Froullai, count of, 196, 198, 210, 250, 270, 297, 302, 311, 315
The Hague, 117, 192, 216, 257, 287, 307, 317, 325
Thielt, 248
Thirty Years War, 7, 9, 10, 11, 12, 36, 110, 113, 128, 165, 199, 363
Tienen, 206
Tilly, Claude Frederic T'Serclaes, count of, 209
Tingry, prince of, 353
tir à ricochet, 258

Tirlemont, 140, 200, 254, 304
Tobago, 152
Toledo, 339, 340
Tolhuis, 114
Tongeren, 234
Tongres, 119, 120, 140, 147
Torbay, 193, 244, 257
Torcy, Jean-Baptiste Colbert, marquis de, 40, 270, 274, 326, 338, 341, 342, 351
Torrington, Lord, 203, 215
Tortosa, 324–5, 346, 355
Toul, 163
Toulon, 15, 85, 86, 88, 96, 136, 143, 171, 174, 223, 229, 238, 243, 244, 246, 251, 252, 256, 260, 296, 297, 303, 311, 312, 314, 315, 323, 347, 366
Toulouse, count of, 92, 296, 297, 311
Tournai, 65, 75, 108, 109, 137, 217, 234, 258, 318, 326, 329, 330, 331
Tourville, Anne-Hilarion de Constentin de, 89, 90, 91, 92, 95, 96, 99, 103, 171, 203, 214, 215, 221, 222, 229–30, 233, 239, 240, 243, 244, 246, 251, 252, 257, 308
Townsend, 326
Trafalgar, 88
Transylvania, 263, 294
Trarbach, 294
Trencsén, Battle of, 325
Trent, 279, 285
Trentino, 309
Treviglio, 301
Trier, 118, 121, 139, 142, 151, 294, 298
Trier, elector of, 194
Triple Alliance, 33, 109, 110
Tripoli, 173
Tromp, Cornelis, 123

418

T'Serclaes, Albert Octave, prince of, 275, 355
Tübingen, 196
Tunis, 173
Turenne, Henri de la Tour d'Auvergne, viscount, 11, 20, 22, 23, 33, 34, 49, 65, 68, 70, 106, 108, 109, 113, 115, 117–18, 119, 121, 123, 124, 127–35, 140–1, 146, 158, 210, 274, 287, 369, 370
Turin, 164, 179, 180, 211, 213, 214, 220, 237, 238, 255, 285, 295, 301, 309–10, 312, 315, 324
Turin, Battle of, 303, 310, 368
Turin, Treaty of, 255, 257
Turkheim, Battle of, 133–5
Turks *see* Ottomans
Tuscany, 267, 355
Tymau, Battle of, 294
Tyrconnell, 215
Tyrol, 283, 285

Ulm, 200, 276, 281, 283, 288, 290, 293, 314
uniforms, 55
United Provinces, 7, 8, 11, 34, 38, 45, 56, 83, 84, 97, 100, 106, 108, 109–12, 121, 122, 124, 144, 153, 154, 157, 158, 159, 160, 166, 167, 168, 192, 195, 199, 205, 214, 215, 244, 246, 253, 262–3, 267, 270, 271, 273, 274, 275, 286, 288, 336, 368, 375
campaigns in during the Dutch War, 113–17, 120, 122, 125
Urloffen, 141
Ursins, princess des, 325, 350
Usson, 260
Utrecht, 115, 118, 120, 342, 351
Utrecht, Treaty of, 350–1, 355, 356, 358, 361

Vachenheim, 210
Valbelle, Jean-Baptiste, bailiff of, 143, 144
Valdecañas, 346, 355
Valencia, 302, 316, 325, 335, 355
Valencia de Alcántara, 301, 311, 316
Valenciennes, 65, 75, 145, 146, 150, 156, 168, 329, 343, 353
Valenza, 255
Valois kings of France, 7, 48, 364
Valladolid, 339, 340
Van Creveld, Martin, 372
Vannes, 222
Var River, 323, 339
Vassem, Treaty of, 118
Vaubrun, French commander, 128, 141
Vauban, Sébastien le Prestre de, 22, 24, 29, 31, 35, 36, 37, 41, 58, 64, 65, 72, 73, 75, 76, 77, 78, 100, 101, 108, 109, 120, 126, 145, 149, 153, 158, 164, 165, 168, 170, 178, 188, 194, 223–6, 228, 235, 245, 246, 252, 257, 258, 259, 263, 309, 321, 337
Vaudémont, Charles-Henri de Lorraine, prince of, 285
Vaudois, 179–81, 189, 211, 220, 228, 363
Velaine, 207
Velez-Málaga, Battle of, 95, 286, 296–7, 347
Venasque, 346
Vendée, 366
Vendôme, Louis-Joseph, duke de, 251, 255, 259–61, 274, 276, 279, 284–5, 295, 301, 307, 308, 309, 312, 315, 317, 318–21, 329–41, 340, 355
Venlo, 275

419

Index

Verdun, 163
Verges, 243
Vermandois, duke of, 92
Verrua, 181, 295
Versailles, 50, 114, 118, 168, 187, 189, 192, 196, 204, 218, 221, 223, 226, 233, 237, 242, 283, 284, 298, 300, 308, 310, 312, 316, 322, 326, 342, 361
Vervins, Treaty of, 9
Vesoul, 124
vice-admiral of Levant, 92
vice-admiral of the Ponant, 92
Victor Amadeus II, duke of Savoy, 179–81, 210, 211, 213, 214, 219, 220, 221, 228, 237–8, 242–3, 250, 251, 253, 255, 267, 279, 285, 286, 294, 295, 301, 302, 310, 315, 323–4, 345–6, 350, 355, 356
Vienna, 36, 165–6, 194, 268, 281, 282, 285, 286, 288, 294
Vietnam, 376
Vigevano, convention of, 255
Vigo Bay, Battle of, 277
Villadarias, 339
Villafranca, 213
Villahermosa, 145, 147, 153, 202, 214
Villars, Marshal Claude Louis Hector, duke de, 15, 22, 57, 65, 79, 80, 125, 151, 218, 247, 266, 274, 276, 281–4, 297–8, 300, 307, 308–9, 312–14, 317, 323–4, 327, 329–35, 336, 337–8, 339, 343–4, 345, 351–4, 356–8, 372
Villa Viciosa, Battle of, 340, 341
Villaviede, 346
Villavoire, 143
Villefranche, 220, 221, 223, 301
Villefranche-de-Conflent, 202
Villena, 316
Villeroi, François de Neufville, duke of, 54, 233, 247–9, 254, 257–9, 270–1, 274, 276, 280–1, 288–90, 294, 295, 303–8
Villers-Perwin, 223
Villiers, 344
Villingen, 289, 290, 293
Vimy Ridge, 344
Vins, 220
Visé, 139
Vitry, 240
Vivans, marquis of, 313, 314
Vivarais, 183
Vivonne, Louis-Victor de Rochechouart, duke de, 136, 143, 144, 145, 148–9
Voltaire, 125
Vosges, 133, 151
Voysin, Daniel, count de, 274, 330
Waal River, 114
Waes, Pays de, 145, 280, 300
Waldeck, 117, 200, 205, 205–10, 219, 371
Waldorf, 250
Walker, Sir Hovenden, 349
Wallenstein, Albrecht von, 56
Wantzenau, 131
war-as-event, 367, 371, 374, 375, 376
war-as-process, 2, 3, 45, 46, 82, 362, 367–76
War of Devolution, 6, 13, 25, 33, 44, 46, 62, 105–8, 111, 112, 157, 171
war feeding war, 2, 56–8, 367, 371–2
War of the Grand Alliance
see Nine Years War
War of the League of Augsburg
see Nine Years War
War of the Polish Succession, 365
Wars of Religion, French, 8, 48, 364–5

Index

War of the Reunions, 6, 38, 161, 166–9, 176, 191
war with Spain (1635–59), 48, 52, 68, 182, 363, 376
War of the Spanish Succession, 1, 6, 15, 41, 44, 45, 46, 49, 53, 58, 61, 62, 63, 68, 71, 72, 78, 79, 84, 93, 106, 179, 247, 266–360, 365, 368, 370, 371, 374, 375
Wavre, 206
Wentzel, General, 356
Wervik, 320
Wesel, 113, 114
Weser River, 118
West Indies, 152, 261
Westminster, Treaty of, 122
Westphalia, 113, 118, 169
Westphalia, Treaty of, 11, 14, 161, 162, 163, 178, 199
Wick, 119
Wight, Isle of, 215
William III, of Orange, 34, 39, 40, 45, 68, 81, 114, 115, 117, 118, 119, 120, 121, 125, 126, 127, 137, 139, 140, 144, 145, 146, 147, 149, 150, 151, 154, 158, 169, 178, 192, 193, 203, 204, 205, 215, 216, 217, 218, 219, 222, 225, 226, 230, 231, 233, 234, 235, 241–2, 244, 246, 247, 248–50, 253, 254, 255, 256, 257, 258, 259, 263, 264, 267, 269, 272, 363
Willstätt, 140
winter quarters, wintering, 54, 67, 80
Wissembourg, 131, 142, 163, 276, 300
Withers, General, 332–3
Wolf, John B., 2
World War I, 79, 201, 275
Worms, 194, 197, 198, 259
Württemberg, 196, 199, 200, 201, 227, 234, 235, 236, 237, 248, 293, 314, 354
Würzburg, 200
Wyendael, 321

Xátiva, 316

Ypres, 75, 108, 153, 156, 209, 234, 242, 248, 308, 317, 320, 326, 330, 331
Yssche River, 299

Zeller, Gaston, 32
Zoutleeuw, 234, 299, 300, 303, 304

421